THE ENGLISH AND AUSTRALIAN COOKERY BOOK.

COOKERY

FOR THE MANY, AS WELL AS FOR THE "UPPER TEN THOUSAND."

BY

AN AUSTRALIAN ARISTOLOGIST.

Published by Ropesend Creek Press, Goulburn

First published by:
Sampson Low, Son, and Marston, London, 1864

ISBN: 978-1-925907-13-1

This edition © Ropesend Creek Press, 2024, all rights reserved. No part of this publication may be reproduced, stored in a retrieval system or transmitted, in any form or by any means, electronic, mechanical, photocopying, recording or otherwise without prior permission from the publisher.

LONDON: SAMPSON LOW, SON, & MARSTON, 14, LUDGATE HILL.

THE ENGLISH AND AUSTRALIAN COOKERY BOOK.

COOKERY

FOR THE MANY, AS WELL AS FOR THE "UPPER TEN THOUSAND."

BY

AN AUSTRALIAN ARISTOLOGIST.

"A little dinner, not more than the Muses, with all the guests clever, and some pretty, offers human life and human nature under very favourable circumstances."
DISRAELI, IN "CONINGSBY."

LONDON:
SAMPSON LOW, SON, AND MARSTON,
14, LUDGATE HILL.
1864.

[THE RIGHT OF TRANSLATION IS RESERVED.]

LONDON:
PETTER AND GALPIN, BELLE SAUVAGE PRINTING WORKS,
LUDGATE HILL, E.C.

DEDICATION.

> "Soon, Australasia, may thy inmost plains—
> A new Arcadia—teem with simple swains;
> Soon a Lycoris' scorn again inspire
> A Gallus' song to moan his hopeless fire;
> And while he murmurs forth his plaintive tale,
> The list'ning breezes waft it down the vale.
> What though no am'rous shepherd 'midst thy dells
> E'er charm'd responsive Echo from her cells!
> What though nor liquid flute, nor shriller reed,
> E'er shot their wild notes o'er thy silent mead!
> Thy blue-eyed daughters, with the flaxen hair,
> And taper ankle, do they bloom less fair
> Than those of Europe? Do thy primal groves
> Ne'er warble forth their feather'd inmates' loves?"

—*Extract from "Australasia," a poem, written for the Chancellor's Medal, at the Cambridge Commencement, 1823, by William Charles Wentworth, an Australian.**

* Mr. William Charles Wentworth is the first Australian who has done the State service, and they know it; and, as a consequence, his compatriots owe him a debt of gratitude, which they have partially repaid.

> "Patriots have toil'd, and in their country's cause
> Bled nobly; and their deeds, as they deserve,
> Receive proud recompense."

Against the autocracy of Downing Street he carried the Preferable Heir Act, which saved the colony from universal insolvency, and is the law to this day. He wrung from unwilling power "the liberty of the press," and his influence established the *first* Australian university. As a tribute to his public worth, his statue has been raised in the hall of the latter seat of learning. Graven at Rome, by a cunning hand, public subscription has imported the sculpture that "gives bond in stone." It was opened to the public under the patronage of the Governor, and inaugurated by a fellow-countryman—Mr. Martin—whose eloquent address on the occasion deserves a niche in the temple of Fame. Australia naturally thought that ere this some mark of the Royal favour would have encircled the brow of her favourite son. No! the bureaucracy of the Colonial Office have passed by the leading name, and awarded the *accolade* to some far, far inferior in every possible attribute to the respected gentleman to whom I have thus cursorily alluded, and who is, I believe, distantly connected with the British peerage; but that is hardly any recommendation with the Australian democracy.

> "Honour and shame from no condition rise:
> Act well your part—there all the honour lies."

I know little of Mr. Wentworth, except as a public man, and perhaps he may not thank me for thus sounding "the trumpet of his praise;" that I disregard, when I consider I am performing a public duty to my country. Mr. Wentworth has lately resigned the office of President of the Council, and left Australia for England, rumour states, being dissatisfied with the working of our free constitution, which doubtless requires a more Conservative balance.

DEDICATION.

"Beautiful land! Farewell! When toil and strife,
And all the sighs, and all the sins of life
Shall come about me; when the light of truth
Shall scatter the bright mists that dazzled youth,
And memory muse in sadness on the past,
And mourn for pleasures far too sweet to last!
How often shall I long for some green spot,
Where, not remembering, and remembered not,
With no false verse to deck my living bust,
With no fond tear to vex my mouldering dust,
This busy brain may find its grassy shrine,
And sleep untroubled in a shade like thine!"

—*Extract from "Australasia," a poem, which obtained the Chancellor's Medal, at the Cambridge Commencement, 1823, by the late Winthorp Mackworth Praed, of Trinity College.*

TO

HIS FAIR COUNTRYWOMEN OF THE "BEAUTIFUL LAND,"

THE "BLUE-EYED DAUGHTERS WITH THE FLAXEN HAIR,"

THE LADIES OF "THE SUNNY SOUTH,"

THIS BOOK,

OF THE COOKERY OF THE DAY, IS RESPECTFULLY INSCRIBED,

BY THEIR FAITHFUL SERVANT,

THE AUTHOR.

INTRODUCTORY PREFACE.

Mere parsimony is not economy. Expense, and great expense, may be an essential article in true economy. Economy is a distributive virtue, and consists, not in saving, but selection. Parsimony requires no providence, no sagacity, no powers of combination, no comparison, no judgment. Mere instinct, and that not an instinct of the noblest kind, may produce this false economy in perfection.—*Edmund Burke.*

Hospitality is enjoined by the precepts of Holy Writ, and is carried out by the most civilised and the most savage nations of the earth. What can be more simple and beautiful than the African mother's reception of Park?—

> "The winds roared, and the rain fell;
> The poor white man, faint and weary,
> Came and sat under our tree.
> *Chorus.* He has no mother to bring him milk,
> No wife to grind his corn."

In later days, who has not been delighted with the attention of the uncivilised natives to the explorers—Burke, Wills, and King—and the manner in which these wild children of Australia provided the seed of the Nardoo plant for their sustenance?

A writer of repute (Dugald Stewart) has said, that cookery and the fine arts are analogous. I cannot discover the resemblance; but I do contend that there is affinity between hospitality and cookery, for the former would be unavailable without the aid of the latter. I offer no excuse, therefore, for the publication of this small matter-of-fact work on the cookery of the present day, for it will be found practically useful to persons in every situation in life—to the English housewife, and to her prototype in the Colonies.

The following pages will show the British and Colonial mode of rendering the various articles that God has been pleased to give us for our use, nutritious and wholesome, as well as palatable to our tastes. It is a truism, well known, that meat properly cooked is more easily digested.

INTRODUCTORY PREFACE.

Liebig informs us, "That among all the arts known to man, there is none which enjoys a juster appreciation, and the products of which are more universally admired, than that which is concerned in the preparation of food;" and Byron truly writes—

> "Albeit all human history attests,
> That happiness for man—the hungry sinner—
> Since Eve ate apples, much depends on dinner."

My book will combine the advantages of Mrs. Acton's work with the *crême de la crême* of the cheapest of Soyer's productions. I will not be so ungallant as to affirm that a female cannot write a book on cookery, like the great moralist. Boswell tells us, in his very remarkable work, that the Doctor said to Miss Seward—

> "Women can spin very well, but they cannot make a good book on cookery. I could write a better book of cookery than has ever yet been written. It should be a book on philosophical principles."

The sex have been belied by Johnson, for Mrs. Acton's work is excellent of its kind. It is only faulty in being so elaborate, so that it is not within the compass of persons of moderate means; and that is one of the reasons that has induced me to enter the culinary field on this occasion.

I would respectfully take this opportunity of drawing the attention of the fair sex to the extreme desirability of their looking to the *cuisine* of their several establishments. The wisest of men has told us of the properties of a good wife:—

> "She looketh well to the ways of her household, and eateth not the bread of idleness. Her children arise up, and call her blessed; her husband also, and he praiseth her."
> —*Proverbs* xxxi. 27, 28.

With the many such a request is unnecessary; but with others, let me remind them of the obligation which Milton has enjoined of them—

> "Nothing lovelier can be found
> In woman, than to study household good."

I am certain that I should be thanked for this recommendation by many husbands. Meat badly prepared is wasted. True economy consists in having our comestibles the best of their kind, which consideration a talented Australian authoress has so well pointed out in her letter to me on the making of bread, which appears in this volume.

In the middle walks of life, it is the peculiar duty of the mistress to see to the arrangements of the table. Nothing can be more satisfactory to her helpmate, or tend to carry into practical results the words of the song, "Be it ever so homely, there is no place like home." While the slattern who will not trouble herself with this necessary office, I think,

INTRODUCTORY PREFACE.

should be treated like the wife of the Arab, whom Eastern writers say is discarded, and another one taken on, if the first cannot make good bread. In these days of divorces, I would commend this hint to the especial attention of Sir James P. Wylde, with a hope that he will consider the propriety of making a precedent on the point, which would do a power of good.

There should be no anfractuosity in a dinner, to borrow a word from the great lexicographer; it should pass off "right slick well." With John Bull, 'tis the dinner that unlocks the heart, and nothing can be done in commerce, religion, politics, and philanthropy without the assistance of some entertainment, from the Royal *recherché* banquets of the Queen, the more bountiful Lord Mayors' feasts, the English Ministerial and whitebait dinners, the Governors' and Cabinet feeds at the Antipodes, to the every-day parties in social life, where more generally prevails

"The feast of reason, and the flow of soul."

In the "Incidents of Travel," by Stephens, how delighted he was, when a long way up the Nile, to receive an invitation to dinner from an English family! He writes:—

Few things tend to give a better opinion of a man, of his intelligence, his piety and morals than by receiving from him an invitation to dinner.'

Perhaps the author on this occasion goes a little too far; but I give the extract to show the effect of a kindly-intended invite, and how it is appreciated, even in the desert.

A premier of Tasmania once obtained far more political support from his *dinners* than the *measures* of his government. On one occasion, a Member of the Assembly was returned, and, as a matter of course, was expected to join the Opposition, to which he belonged. Mr. —— invited him to a *recherché* refection. He voted with his Amphitryon ever afterwards, on the gastronomical rule—that you ought never to oppose a man after you have put your legs under his well-spread mahogany, at least for a given number of days, leaving it open to renew the obligation by a *refresher*.

I would remind the good housewife (for I address no other) that one dish properly cooked is worth a dozen badly done: good cookery is the cheapest in the end. The smaller the dinner, the better chance of its being well served; besides, a large party has no semblance of sociality. To use a Chinese metaphor, the guests merely assemble to make face.

In an interesting *brochure*, under the modest designation of "Hints for the Table," the compiler cites a descriptive account of the facetious Foote, showing that large parties are often failures:—

"As to splendour, as far as it went, I admit there was a very fine sideboard of plate; and if a man could have swallowed a silversmith's shop, there was enough to have satisfied him; but as to the rest, the mutton was white, the veal was red, the fish was kept too long, and the venison not long enough. To sum up all, everything was cold except the ice, and everything sour except the vinegar."

On another subject well worthy of reflection, Bulwer, no mean observer of fashionable life, informs us, with much truth, that if a man gives a dinner beyond his means, even the guests ridicule his presumption, and laugh at his fare.

I would enjoin the urgency of punctuality in household affairs, as a golden rule, and an essential attribute that must never be lost sight of. Nothing tends to annoy and even vex "the hungry sinner," so much as waiting for his meals. At the time, the exact hour, let the words be announced that our immortal Bard has put into the mouth of Anne, in the first act of the "Merry Wives of Windsor:"—

"The dinner is on the table."

Ude informs us that "Cookery is the soul of festivity, at all times, and in all ages;" and yet how many neglect this daily requirement, for not only the dinner requires attention; but the etceteras want looking after, as well as the dishes. A slight table adjunct may make or mar the most luxurious repast. An every-day incident of this kind is thus given in "Coningsby:"—

"Lord Monmouth's dinners in Paris were celebrated; it was generally agreed that they had no equals, yet there were others who had as skilful cooks—others who, for such a purpose, were equally profuse in their expenditure. What, then, was the secret spell of his success?—the simplest in the world: His Lordship's plates were always hot."

To the lovers of gastronomy, hot plates are a positive necessary to a dinner. A local story, well authenticated, is told of an epicure, dining at an hotel in Tasmania. The *garçon* handed a plate so hot that the fingers of the recipient were burnt. With great coolness the *gourmet* put his hand, still smarting from the effects of the caloric, into his pocket and handed the boy a crown, saying, "Such an unusual circumstance deserved a recompense." An ill-bred booby, placed in this dilemma, would not have appreciated the luxury, but would have "uttered curses, not loud but deep."

A dinner given by Baron Rothschild, in France, is thus described:—

"No burnished gold reflected the glaring sunset, no brilliant silver dazzled the eyes; porcelain, beyond the price of precious metals by its beauty and fragility, every piece a picture, consorted with the general character of sumptuous simplicity which rejoiced over the whole; again, every meat presented its own natural aroma, every vegetable its own shade of verdure."

It was Lady Morgan who drew this vivid "pen and ink sketch;" and

INTRODUCTORY PREFACE.

the presiding genius who officiated at the temple dedicated to Lucullus was the celebrated Carême, the *artiste* that the late autocrat of Russia propitiated, by the presentation of a diamond ring, as a tribute to his superior worth in his vocation. This elegant banquet took place in Paris— the city of all others in which it is said that the men excel in dressing dinners, and the women in dressing themselves; but I much fear that the fragility of the elegant crockery would prevent the desideratum of warm plates. Let the reader contrast the account of the dinner given by the Parisian millionaire with that of the Australian Wool King. An exquisite of the Lord Dundreary mould, from the mother country, was invited to dine with a colonist, who was not aware that, " to order a dinner well was a matter of invention and combination. It involves novelty, simplicity, and taste; whereas in the generality of dinners there is no character but that of dull routine, according to the season;" so writes Mr. Walker, in the "Original." The guest was subsequently asked what he had for dinner; the languid response was, "There was mutthon at th' twop of the twable, mutthon at ther botham of ther twable, and th' west of ther swheep in twandles." I am desirous of some reform in the *cuisine* of some of my countrymen's establishments, and I am vain enough to believe that I shall effect that object by this publication.

In getting up a work of this kind, my readings on the subject have necessarily been extensive, and I have met with odd ideas propounded. None more surprised me than an article in the *Quarterly Review* (No. CIV.—1. On the ultimate composition of alimentary substances; 2. Domestic cookery; 3. Code Gourmand), in which the critic describes a mode of making bread from sawdust; and the statement is made that Professor Autereith found that fifteen pounds of birchwood, three pounds of wheat leaven, two pounds of wheat flour, and eight measures of new milk yielded thirty-six pounds of good bread. I would rather put faith in Liebig, who writes, in his new "Letters on Chemistry,"—

"The proposals which have hitherto been made to use substitutes for flour, and thus diminish the price of bread in times of scarcity, prove how much the rational principles of hygiene are disregarded, and how unknown the laws of nutrition are still."

I think this sawdust bread would be found to afford as much sustenance as the recipe of one of England's dukes during the Irish famine. His Grace advised the preparation of a soup maigre, to be composed of a *small* quantity of curry powder, with a *large* quantity of water. The *Quarterly* proceeds to inform its readers that skin is jelly, and has

INTRODUCTORY PREFACE.

the property of albumen — the nutritive qualities of blanc-mange; adding that the lamented Sir John Franklin and his companions, on the shores of the Polar Sea, were compelled to make a repast of their old shoes. I have read of a French dancing master, who was cast away on a desolate island, and who lived without water for six months by merely sucking his pumps. In a marginal note the first story is out-Heroded, as we are further informed, on the authority of the late Dr. Marcet, that the stomach can digest harder substances than mere skin, for the fact is stated of a sailor swallowing several clasp-knives, which were not quite digested ten years afterwards, when he died. There may be some feasibility in these statements, as the poet tells us "that truth is stranger than fiction." Now, I do not profess to give the *modus operandi* of preparing for food saw-dust, old shoes, clasp-knives, or even a Utopian recipe which appears in some works—roasting a pound of butter. While on this subject, I may express a desire that none of my readers may be placed in the unfortunate situation of Sir John Franklin, to be obliged to have recourse to leather, and I would counsel no one to try the digestibility of clasp-knives, as the stomach of the mammalian species is not comparable with that of the ostrich.

The original matter to be found in any work of this kind must, *ex necessitate*, be trifling. I only lay claim to, and put forth "this little volume" (to borrow a term from Lever, elsewhere quoted) as an industrious, and, I trust it will be found, a judicious, compialtion.

I desire to return my thanks for the assistance I have had from amateurs and professionals. I am also bound to acknowledge, with every consideration, the grateful aid I have received from different authors who have preceded me. It must be seen that my object is a laudable one—to promote sociality and good-will, by enjoining hospitality; and, as an aid to the latter virtue, to show how the good things of this life may be rendered fit for the table.

> "Well-ordered home, man's best delight to make;
> And by submissive wisdom, modest skill,
> With every gentle care—eluding art—
> To raise the virtues, animate the bliss,
> And sweeten all the toils of human life."

While I do this, I am bound to impress on every one the propriety of moderation in enjoyment, or else we need the aid of the physician, whom Voltaire describes as "an unfortunate gentleman, who is every day requested to perform a miracle—viz., reconcile health with intemperance."

I have bestowed some trouble and research on this work, and I shall reap an ample reward if it obtains as much favour in the mother country

INTRODUCTORY PREFACE.

as, I think, it will receive in the colonies. To the latter I say, in the cant words of the times, "Advance, Australia!" for the progress of the offspring tends to the prestige of the parent. When Napoleon I. was asked by a learned lady who was the greatest female, he rejoined, "The mother who had borne the greatest number of children." By a parity of reasoning, Great Britain will be found to occupy the most prominent position in the world; and long, long may she do so, although there are croakers to be found who care little for the colonies, whom Haliburton has so ably exposed:—

"Them who say colonies are no good, are either fools or knaves. If they be fools, they aint worth answerin'; and if they are knaves, send them to the treadmill till they learn to speak the truth."

England without colonies means England with a redundant population—England with more mouths than she can feed; without an outlet for individual enterprise and individual restlessness; without constant vent for her industry and its fruits. It means Glasgow, Manchester, Leeds, Sheffield, and Birmingham, with a chronic paralysis of trade, and periodical stagnations of work. It means hunger, famine, exasperation, and sedition. It means tumult, threats, armed gatherings, revolt against authority, and persecution by authority. Who shall gauge the exact value of these evils, and their antidote in pounds, shillings, and pence? . . . . On the whole, then, what should we gain by the emancipation of our colonies from the gentlest and easiest sway ever exercised? We should save some millions a year in the army and navy estimates; we should save some millions a year which we now spend on colonial defences, by sea and by land. That would be our gain. But what should we lose? The friendship and devotion of millions of fellow-subjects in every sea, proud to be citizens of this great empire, and to feel that its highest prizes are open to them and their children; the friendship and alliance of great nations now in their first germ; and, let us not forget to add, markets which now annually consume *thirty million pounds' worth of our goods*. But we should lose something more valuable and indispensable—the esteem and honour of all nations, who have looked upon us as the great colonisers of modern days—as the people who have founded an empire no less firm and compact than that of ancient Rome; no less brilliant and heroic than those scattered but ephemeral communities which bore to alien shores and barbarous tribes the meteoric light of Grecian genius and art.—"*Quarterly Review*," on our *Colonial System, in July* number, 1863.

Of the dependencies of England, she has every reason to be proud of her Australian possessions; and most justly so, as they consume her manufactures more than any other. They employ her mercantile marine they absorb her redundant population, and they yield her valuable imports, as well as golden treasures taken from the bowels of the earth.

Our exports to the Australian Colonies amounted in each of the years 1858 and 1859 to £12,000,000. Estimating the population at 1,200,000, this would give precisely £10 per head of population.—"*The American Union*," by Spence.

By the Trade and Navigation Reports laid before Parliament in the year 1862, by command of Her Majesty, it appears that the import and export trade between the Australian Colonies and the United Kingdom, amounted to £23,000,000 in 1861; while the aggregate import and export trade of those Colonies with all parts of the world is stated, in the Introduction to the New South Wales Catalogue, at the International Exhibition, to have exceeded £47,000,000 in the preceding year, 1860.—*Thorry's* "*New South Wales and Victoria*."

The importance of the trade of these Colonies (Australia) was very great to England. The exports of British and Irish produce to foreign countries fell off between

INTRODUCTORY PREFACE.

1860 and 1862 from £92,000,000 to £82,000,000; while the exports to British possessions only fell off from £43,000,000 to £42,000,000; and to the Australian Colonies, the exports had increased from £9,000,000 to £11,000,000. To come still nearer, the exports to New Zealand and New South Wales had increased from £3,000,000 in 1860, to £4,750,000 in 1862.—*Sir S. Northcote. Debate in the House of Commons on the Panama Route, July 17th*, 1863.

I do not covet new territories upon the Continent: ships, colonies, and commerce are what I wish to possess.—*Napoleon I. to the Austrian officers after the victory at Ulm*, 1805. Thiers' "*Consulate and Empire.*"

I trust, therefore, it may not be inopportune, even in such a work as this, that I may be allowed to apostrophise my country, in the elegant language of Scott—

> "Breathes there a man with soul so dead,
> Who never to himself has said,
> This is my own—my native land!"

E. A.

BELLERIVE, TASMANIA,
  1864.

CONTENTS.

	PAGE
INTRODUCTION TO THE PORT ARTHUR HISTORIC SITES EDITION	vii
DEDICATION	xiii
INTRODUCTORY PREFACE	xv
INDEX	xxvii
GLOSSARY	xli
I.—SOUPS	1
II.—BROTHS	6
III.—ROASTING	9
IV.—BOILING	13
V.—BAKING	16
VI.—FRYING	17
VII.—BROILING	18
VIII.—MADE DISHES	19
IX.—SAUCES	29
X.—GRAVIES	34
XI.—THE COOK	36
XII.—CONDIMENTS	38
XIII.—SAVOURY PIES AND PUDDINGS	43
XIV.—POULTRY	45
XV.—PUDDINGS AND PIES	50
XVI.—PASTRY	59
XVII.—BASTINGS AND DREDGINGS	62
XVIII.—MACARONI AND VERMICELLI	63
XIX.—PICKLES	64
XX.—SALADS	65
XXI.—OYSTERS	67
XXII.—WATER	69
XXIII.—SAUSAGES	71
XXIV.—BREAD AND BREAKFAST CAKES	72
XXV.—DESSERT	80
XXVI.—GAME	81

CONTENTS.

	PAGE
XXVII.—CARVING	91
XXVIII.—FISH	92
XXIX.—FORCEMEAT AND STUFFING	100
XXX.—CIDER AND PERRY	102
XXXI.—GINGER	103
XXXII.—CONFECTIONERY	104
XXXIII.—FONDU	111
XXXIV.—DINNER ACCORDING TO COUNT D'ORSAY	112
XXXV.—APPERT'S MODE OF PRESERVING FRUIT OR VEGETABLES	113
XXXVI.—VEGETABLES	114
XXXVII.—TOASTED CHEESE	119
XXXVIII.—JONES'S PATENT FLOUR	119
XXXIX.—MILK	121
XL.—CHUTNEY	123
XLI.—TOAST	123
XLII.—A DINNER FROM THE "ORIGINAL"	124
XLIII.—THE HUNDRED GUINEA DISH TO PRINCE ALBERT	125
XLIV.—SPORTSMAN'S FOOD	127
XLV.—DINNER PARTY PRECEDENCE	128
XLVI.—SUPPERS AND LUNCHEONS	129
XLVII.—HOME-MADE WINES AND CORDIALS	130
XLVIII.—TABLE CLOTHS AND NAPKINS	134
XLIX.—TEA	135
L.—DINNER CEREMONIAL	138
LI.—SOY	140
LII.—BREAKFAST	140
LIII.—ICE	142
LIV.—PRESERVES AND CONSERVES	144
LV.—PRESIDENCY AT DINNER	146
LVI.—CAKES	147
LVII.—APPLES	155
LVIII.—BISCUITS	156
LIX.—OLD TUSSER'S GOOD AND BAD HUSWIFERY	159
LX.—DRESS AND MANNERS AT A DINNER PARTY	160
LXI.—BEER	162
LXII.—EGGS AND OMELETTES	168
LXIII.—MAGICAL DRINKS	171
LXIV.—WINES—FOREIGN AND COLONIAL	171
LXV.—NUTRITION	179

CONTENTS.

	PAGE
LXVI.—LIQUEURS	180
LXVII.—COFFEE	182
LXVIII.—STOVES	184
LXIX.—WHY ANIMALS TO BE EATEN MUST BE KILLED	185
LXX.—DINNERS A LA RUSSE	186
LXXI.—GERMAN SOUR-KROUT	187
LXXII.—STRASBOURG PIES	189
LXXIII.—HERRING AND ANCHOVY PASTE	189
LXXIV.—ORANGE-FLOWER WATER	190
LXXV.—VEGETABLE ESSENCES AND TINCTURES	190
LXXVI.—HAMS, BACON, AND SALT MEAT	191
LXXVII.—KETCHUP	196
LXXVIII.—VINEGAR	198
LXXIX.—THE DINNER HOUR	200
LXXX.—ELIZABETHAN LIVING	201
LXXXI.—DIGESTION	202
LXXXII.—CONVIVIAL MAXIMS	203
LXXXIII.—YEAST	204
LXXXIV.—SOYER'S BACHELOR'S DINNER	207
LXXXV.—CHOCOLATE	209
LXXXVI.—CURRY POWDER	209
LXXXVII.—BITTERS	210
LXXXVIII.—COPPER SAUCEPANS	211
LXXXIX.—COOKERY FOR THE DESTITUTE	211
XC.—DINNER PARTIES IN THE SIXTEENTH AND SEVENTEENTH CENTURIES	214
XCI.—MOSSES	215
XCII.—SOYER'S MINCEMEAT	216
XCIII.—LEMON-JUICE	216
XCIV.—AL FRESCO PARTIES	217
XCV.—BRITISH FISH	218
XCVI.—SOUTH AUSTRALIAN DITTO	219
XCVII.—TASMANIAN DITTO	220
XCVIII.—NEW ZEALAND DITTO	226
XCIX.—VICTORIAN DITTO	228
C.—NEW SOUTH WALES DITTO	231
CI.—SMOKING	233
CII.—SERVANTS	236
CIII.—PYROLIGNEOUS ACID	238

CONTENTS.

	PAGE
CIV.—Scraps and Sayings	239
CV.—Aiguillettes	242
CVI.—Preserved Meats	243
CVII.—Laver	245
CVIII.—Butter	246
CIX.—Hebrew Refection	248
CX.—Domestic Hints	259
CXI.—Clubs	262
CXII.—Edible Food	264
CXIII.—Drinks	267
CXIV.—The Last Dinner	284
CXV.—Conclusion	286
Index to Authors and Books, &c., Quoted	289

INDEX.

Abingdon Pudding, 51
Absinthe, 182
Acidulated Drops, 108
Aiguillettes, 242
Aitch Bone, 15
A la Mode Beef, 25, 252
Aleberry, 283
Ale, Devilled, 279
  ,, Mulled, 269
  ,, Posset, 268
  ,, to Make, 163
Al Fresco Parties, 217
Allspice, 38
Alma Pudding, 57
Almond Biscuits, 158
  ,, Pudding Recipe, 255
  ,, Puffs, 57
  ,, Sponge Cake, 149
Almondigos Soup, 249
American Dried Apples, 156
  ,, Puffets, 78
Amnastich, 252
Anchovies, 92
Ancient Sauces, 34
Anglica, 41
Animals Killed, 185
Appert's Preserving Fruit, 113
  ,, Preserving Vegetables, 113
Appleade, 270
Apple and Onion Compound, 64
  ,, Bread, 78
  ,, Jelly, 106
  ,, Pudding, 54
  ,, Sauce, 30
  ,, Trifle, 106
Apples à la Cremona, 155
  ,, American Dried, 156
  ,, Baked, 155
  ,, Compote of, 145
  ,, Dried, 155
  ,, to Preserve, 145
Apricot Drink, 277

Apricot Tart or Pudding, 53
Ariston—Aristology, 201
Arrack, 279
Arrowroot, 41
  ,, Blanc-mange, 106
  ,, Pudding, 55
Ash Cake, 79
Asparagus, 116
  ,, à la Français, 117
Athol Brose, 269
Avenzoar, 41
Aunt Nelly's Pudding, 57

Baba, 61
Bachelor's Pudding, 58
Bacon, 26
Badminton, 275
Baked Lemon Pudding, 58
Bakewell Pudding, 56
Baking, 16
Bang, 269
Barberries, 40
Barberry Tart, 58
Barley Bannocks, 78
  ,, Sugar, 107
  ,, ,, Drops, 107
Basil, 39
Bastings, 62, 63
Bath Buns, 149
Batter, Fowl in, 46
  ,, Pudding, 56
Bay, 41
Beans, 116
Béchamel Sauce, 32
Beef, à la Mode, 25, 252
  ,, and Beans, 252
  ,, Brighton Hunting, 195
  ,, Broth, 7
  ,, Dutch, 194
  ,, en Miroton, 20
  ,, en Roulade, 23
  ,, Flank of, 9

A

INDEX.

Beef Gravy, 34
" Hams, 194
" Hashed, 26
" Hung, 193
" Olives, 24
" Roast, 9
" Round of, 14
" Round of, to Cure, 196
" Salt, of Victoria, 194
" Smoked, 251
" Spiced, 253
Beef-steaks, 17
" Pudding, 44
Beef, Stewed, 28
" Tea, 5
" to Hash, 252
Beer, 162
" Berlin, 166
" Lager, 165
" Potato, 166
" Spruce, 276
" Sugar, 164
" to Make, 163
Beet-root, 40
Belvidere Cakes, 74
Biscuit Drops, 157
Biscuits, 156
" à la Française, 157
" Almond, 158
" Brighton, 157
" Captain's, 156
" Carraway, 156
" Crisp, 156
" Devilled, 157
" Hard, 156
" Invalid, 158
" Lemon, 157
" Norfolk, 158
" Oatmeal, 157
" Savoy, 157
" Soda, 158
" Sponge, 158
" Sweet, 157
" to Keep, 158
" Wexford, 157
Bishop, 279
Bitters, 210
Black Cock, 88
" Puddings, 192
" Swan, 90
Blanc-mange, 105
" Arrowroot, 106
Blonde Sauce, 33
Blow my Skull, 280
Boblink, American, 87
Boiled Calf's Head, 15

Boiled Cod, 96
" Cow-heel, 15
" Custard, 56
" Flounders, 98
" Mutton, 14
" Oysters, 67
" Round Beef, 14
" Turbot, 95
" Turkey, 47
Bola d'Amor, 254
" Plain, 258
" Toliedo, 255
Bonne Bouche, 33
Borage, 40
Bordeaux Cake, 151
Bouillon aux Herbes, 8
Braised Turkey, 45
Brandy, 282
" Orange, 276
" Smash, 279
Brazilian Stew, 28
Bread and Butter Pudding, 56
" Apple, 78
" Barley, 78
" Brown, 73
" Cakes, 72
" Cottage, 74
" Crumbs, Fried, 18
" French, 73
" Italian, 77
" Matso Diet, 259
" Persian, 73
" Pulled, 77
" Sauce, 31
" Sippets, 18
" to Make, 72
" Unfermented, 73, 78
" White, 77
Breakfast, 140
" Cake, 259
" Rolls, 77
Bream, Broiled, 92
Brine, Empress of Russia's, 193
Brighton Biscuits, 157
" Hunting Beef, 195
Brioches, 61
Brisbane Fish, 233
British Fish, 218
Broiled Bream, 92
" Chops and Steaks, 18
" Oysters, 68
Broiling, 18
Broth (à la minute), 8
" Barley, 7
" Beef, 7
" Bouillon, 8

INDEX.

Broth, Calf's Foot, **8**
,, Chicken, 8
,, Mutton, 7
,, Plum, 59
,, Scotch Barley, 7
,, Sheep's Head, 6
,, Spartan, 8
,, Veal, 7
Brown and Polson's Soufflé Pudding, 52
Brown Bread, 73
,, Gravy, 5, 34
Bubble and Squeak, 18
Buns, Bath, 149
,, Comfit, 150
,, Cross, 150
,, Plain, 150
,, Plum, 150
,, Scotch, 151
,, Seed, 150
Burnt Butter, 30
Butter, 246
,, Cakes, 258
,, Clarified, 30
,, Crust, 60
,, Melted, 29
,, Oiled, 30
Buttered Toddy, 268
Buttermilk Cakes, 76

Cabbage, 117
Cake, Almond Sponge, 149
,, Ash, 79
,, Bordeaux, 151
,, Breakfast, 259
,, Bride, 147
,, Chantilly, 152
,, Christmas Yule, 154
,, Common Seed, 148
,, Currant, 152
,, Easter, 152
,, Ginger, 149, 152
,, Handsome Tipsy, 152
,, Jenny Lind, 152
,, Johnny, 79
,, Plain Sponge, 148
,, Pone, 79
,, Pound, 148
,, Rice, 152
,, Rich, 148
,, Scotch, 154
,, Siesta, 257
,, Twelfth, 147
,, Victoria, 148
,, Wedding, 147
,, without Butter, 259

Cakes, Banbury, 149
,, Belvidere, 74
,, Butter, 258
,, Buttermilk, 76
,, Cobbett's Yeast, 207
,, Corn, 77
,, Derby, 151
,, Hanover, 154
,, Marlborough, 153
,, Matso, 258
,, Mrs. Hill's, 151
,, Northumbrian, 77
,, Oat, 75
,, Passover, 148
,, Portugal, 151
,, Queen, 148
,, Ratafia, 149
,, Rice, 74
,, Rock, 152
,, Rout, 151
,, Scotch Fancy, 151
,, Shrewsbury, 148
,, Soda, 76
,, Superior, 77
,, Yorkshire, 77
Caledonian Cream, 108
Calf's Foot Broth, 8
,, Head Boiled, 15
,, Head Hashed, 24
Calves' Feet Jelly, 106
Cambridge Drink, 276
Camp Ketchup, 197
Canards à la Braise, 46
Canvas-back Ducks, 86
Capers, 40
Capillaire, 278
Captain's Biscuits, 156
Caramel, 104
Cardinal, 279
Carrageen Moss, 215
Carraway Biscuits, 156
Carving, 50, 91
Cassia, 38
Caviare, 95
Cayenne, 38
Celery, 40
Ceylon Moss, 215
Champagne, Pink, 131
,, White, 132
Charlotte, Russian, 108
Cheesecakes, 55
Cheese, Toasted, 119
Chejados, 256
Cherry Bounce, 132
,, Wine, 131
Chervil, 40

A 2

INDEX.

Chicken Broth, 8
  ,, Pudding, 253
Chili Vinegar, 199
Chocolate, 209
Chorissa, 251
  ,, Omelette, 254
Chouder, New England, 92
Christmas Yule Cake, 154
Chutney, 42
  ,, English, 123
  ,, Indian, 123
Cider, 102
Cinnamon, 38
Cisterns of Venice, 70
Citron, 42
Claret Cup, 281
Clarified Butter, 30
Clary, 39
Clouted Cream, 109
Cloves, 38
Clubs, 262
Coburg Pudding, 58
Cock a Leekie, 4
Cocktail, 278
Cod, Boiled, 96
Coffee, 182
Cold Meat, 28
College Puddings, 55
Colonial Damper, 79
  ,, Jam, 144
Comfit Buns, 150
Comfits, 108
Compotes, 145
Condiments, 38
Confectionery, 104
Conger Soup, 93
Conserves, 144
Constantinople Rouge Roquelocum, 107
Convivial Maxims, 203
Cookery, Cheap, 213
  ,, for the Destitute, 211
  ,, Turkish, 188
Cook, the, 36
Cool Tankard, 277
Copper Saucepans, 211
Cordials, 130, 132
Corn Cakes, 77
Corstorphine Cream, 109
Côtelettes à la Soubise, 28
Cottage Bread, 74
  ,, Soup, 5
Cow-heel, Boiled, 15
Cracknels, American, 158
Crambambull, 279
Crayfish, 95

Crayfish, Salad, 66
Cream, Caledonian, 108
  ,, Corstorphine, 109
  ,, Devonshire, 109
  ,, French, 105
  ,, German, 107
  ,, Ice, 109
  ,, Italian, 105
  ,, Lemon, 105
  ,, Snow, 105
  ,, Spanish, 110
  ,, Swiss, 110
Crème à l'Eau, 108
Crimping Salmon, 94
Croquettes de Veau, 29
Cross Buns, 150
Crowdie, 8
Crumpets, 75
Crust, 60
  ,, Short, 60
  ,, Suet, 60
Cucumber Ketchup, 197
  ,, Salad, 66
Cuits, Milk, 78
Currant Cake, 152
  ,, Dumplings, 54
  ,, Jelly, 108
  ,, Red, Jelly, 144
Curry, 25
Curry-powder, 42, 209
Custard, Baked, 56
  ,, Boiled, 56
Custards, 105
  ,, Vanilla, 105
Cutlets à la Maintenon, 17
  ,, Prussian, 26
  ,, Salmon, 95
Cyprus Wine, 133

Damper, Colonial, 79
Damsons, to Keep, 145
Derby Cakes, 151
Descaides, 253
Dessert, 80
Devil, Unexceptionable, 27
Devilled Ale, 279
  ,, Biscuits, 157
Devonshire Clouted Cream, 109
  ,, Junket, 109
  ,, Squab Pie, 44
Digestion, 202
Dindon aux Legumes, 48
Dinner, 245
  ,, a Bachelor's, 207
  ,, according to D'Orsay, 112
  ,, Ceremonial, 138

XXV

INDEX.

Dinner from the "Original," 124
,, Hour, 200
,, Parties in the Sixteenth and Seventeenth Centuries, 214
,, Party, Dress and Manners at a, 160
,, Party Precedence, 128
,, Presidency at, 146
,, Sportsman's, 127
,, the Last, 284
,, the Philosophers at, 200
,, à la Russe, 186
Dog in a Blanket, 58
Dog's Nose, 271
Domestic Hints, 259
Dredgings, 62
Dress and Manners at a Dinner Party, 160
Dried Apples, 155
Drink Divine, 276
,, Tamarind, 275
,, Magical, 171
,, Superb, 276
Drinks, 267
,, at Washington, 274
,, Spanish, 275
Drops, Acidulated, 108
,, Barley Sugar, 107
Duck, Stewed, 46
,, Stuffing, 101
,, Wild, 88
,, Canvas-back, 86
,, Roast, 48
Dumplings, 56
,, Currant, 54
,, Light, 54
,, Sussex, 59
Dutch Beef, 194
,, Sauce, 33

Easter Cake, 152
Eating, 202
,, Classical, 242
,, Different Modes of, 197
Edible Food, 264
Eels, 98
Egg Balls, 101
,, Sauce, 249
,, Wine, 280
Egg-snow Trifle, 63
Eggs, 168
,, à l'Ardennaise, 169
,, au Miroir, 169
,, Boiled, 169
,, Bran's, 170

Eggs Dressed with Oil, 169
,, for Salad, 169
,, Fried, 169
,, Native, 170
,, Poached, 169
,, to Keep, 170
Elder Wine, 131
Elderberry Wine, 131
Elecampane, 38
Elizabethan Living, 201
Emeu, Roast, 84
Empress of Russia's Brine, 193
English Chutney, 123
Escobeche, 250
Eve's, Mother, Pudding, 53
Everton Toffy, 107

Fennel, 40
Fish at Brisbane, 233
,, British, 218
,, Fat to Fry, 100
,, Fried in Oil, 250
,, to Fry, 96
,, Gravies, 96
,, Maigre, 97
,, Muddy Taste, 96
,, of New South Wales, 231
,, New Zealand, 226
,, Salt, 97
,, Sauce, 249
,, Scalloped, 251
,, Small, Fried, 97
,, Soup, 5, 99, 250
,, South Australian, 219
,, Stewed White, 249
,, Tasmanian, 220
,, Twice-laid, 97
,, to Pot, 92
,, to Stew, 96
,, Victorian, 228
Flank of Beef, 9
Flattery at Meals, 248
Flau, 62
Flounders, Boiled, 98
Flour, Jones's Patent, 119
Flummery, Spanish, 111
Fondu, 111
Food, Edible, 264
Forcemeat, 100
,, Balls, 101
,, Plain, 100
,, Veal, 101
Fowl à la Marengo, 49
,, Cold, 48
,, in Batter, 46
,, Roasted, 48

INDEX.

Fowl, Stewed, 49, 253
  ,, with Oysters, 46
French Bread, 73
  ,, Cream, 105
  ,, hung Beef, 193
  ,, Ragoût of Mutton, 21
  ,, Salad, 66
  ,, Sausages, 72
  ,, Shalot Sauce, 33
  ,, Vol-au-vent, 44
Fricassee de Poulet, 29
Fricondelle, 252
Fried Bread Crumbs, 18
  ,, ,, Sippets, 18
  ,, Meat Sauce, 31
  ,, Oysters, 68
  ,, Parsley, 18
Fritters, 53
  ,, Haman's, 256
  ,, Passover, 257
Fruit Charlotte, 258
  ,, Pies, 57
  ,, Preserving, 113
Frying, 17

Galette, 154
Game, 81
  ,, Hashed, 48
  ,, Pie, 43
  ,, Salmis of, 90
  ,, Tainted, 90
Garlic, 39
  ,, Gravy, 35
Garnishes, 63
Gateaux d'Epice, 152
Geneva, 282
German Cream, 107
Gherkins, 40
Giblet Gravy, 35
Giblets, Stewed, 26, 254
Gin, 282
  ,, Punch, 277
  ,, Sling, 274
Ginger, 38, 103
  ,, and Lemon Cakes, 149
  ,, Beer, 270, 271
  ,, Cake, 152
  ,, Preserved, 145
  ,, Wine, 132
Gingerbread Nuts, 150
  ,, Orange, 150
Girambing, 271
Glasgow Punch, 267
Goose, Cold, 48
  ,, Roast, 48, 49

Goose, Stuffing, 101
Gooseberries, to Keep, 145
  ,, Whole, to Preserve, 146
Gooseberry Fool, 110
  ,, Sauce, 30
  ,, Trifle, 110
Grace, Apemantus', 201
Grape Wine, 131
  ,, ,, Common, 133
Gravies, 34
  ,, Fish, 96
Gravy, Beef, 34
  ,, Brown, 5, 34
  ,, Garlic, 35
  ,, Giblet, 35
  ,, Roast Meats, 35
  ,, Savoury, 34
  ,, Shalot, 35
  ,, Soup, 4
  ,, to Clarify, 35
  ,, Veal, 34
  ,, without Meat, 35
Green Peas, 116
  ,, ,, Purée, 117
  ,, Stick, 256
Ground Rice Pudding, 55
Grouse, 88
Guinea Fowl, 88

Haggis, 24
Half-pay Pudding, 58
Ham, best way to Cook, 195
  ,, Mutton, 193
  ,, to Dress, 195
Hams, 192
  ,, Beef, 194
  ,, Cooking, 193
Haman's Fritters, 256
Handsome Tipsy Cake, 152
Hanover Cakes, 154
Hare, 89
  ,, Jugged, 85
  ,, Stuffing, 101
Haricot Mutton, 24
Hashed Beef, 26
  ,, Game, 48
  ,, Kangaroo, 85
Hashed Poultry, 48
  ,, Venison, 85
Heart, Ox, 12
Hebrew Refection, 248
Herring and Anchovy Paste, 189
Herrings, 95
Hippocras, 270

INDEX.

Hodge Podge, 20
Horseradish, 40
" Salad, 66
Hot Purl, 280
Hundred Guinea Dish, 125
Huswifery, Tusser's, 159
Hydromel, 280

Ice, 142
" Cream, 109
" Vanilla, 108
Icing for Cakes, 109
Impanada, 251
Imperial Pop, 270
Indian Chutney, 123
" Pudding, 58
Invalid Biscuits, 158
Irish Stew, 27
Italian Bread, 77
" Cream, 105
" Macaroons, 149

Jam, Colonial, 144
" Raspberry, 144
Jaune-mange, 107
Jelly, Apple, 106
" Calves' Feet, 106
" Currant and Raspberry, 108
" Posset, 268
" Red Currant, 144
Jenny Lind Cake, 152
Jersey Wonders, 153
Jingle, 280
John Collins, 279
Johnny Cake, 79
Jones's Patent Flour, 52, 119
Juditha, 258
Jugged Hare, 85
" Kangaroo, 85

Kangaroo Ham, 195
" Hashed, 85
" Jugged, 85
" Pan Jam, 86
" Pasty, 82
" Roast, 83
" Slippery Bob, 86
" Steamer, 82, 83, 84
" Stuffing, 101
" to Cook, 82
Kelly's Sauce, 31
Ketchup, Camp, 197
" Cucumber, 197
" Marine, 197
" Mushroom, 196

Kid, Roast, 12
King Cup, 269
Kinsmil Meat, 251
Kitchener's, Dr., Barley Broth, 7
" Sauce Superlative, 32
Knuckle of Veal, 22
Kugel and Cornmean, 250

Lager Beer, 165
Lait Sucré, 270
Lamb à la Poulette, 26
" Leg of, 26
" Roast, 12
Lamb's Head, 26
" Wool, 277
Lamplich, 257
Lampreys, 93
Laver, 245
Lemonade, 269
" au Lait, 277
Lemon, 42
" and Orange Wine, 132
" Biscuits, 157
" Cream, 105
" Juice, 216
" Pudding, Baked, 58
" Sponge, 107
Lime-juice, 42
Liqueurs, 180
Lobster Salad, 66
Lobsters, 97
" to Stew, 99
Loin of Mutton, 20
Loving Cup, 281
Luction, a, 255
Luncheons, 129

Macaroni, 63
" Pudding, 56
Macaroons, Italian, 149
Mace, 38
Macédoine of Vegetables, 118
Macrotes, 256
Made Dishes, 19
Magnum-bonum Plums, 55
Maids of Honour, 153
Maigre Fish, 97
Manchets, 79
Maria Louisa's Consomme, 4
Marinaded Oysters, 68
Marine Ketchup, 197
Marjoram, 39
Marlboro' Pudding, 59
Marlborough Cakes, 153
Marrow Bones, 27
" Pudding, 54

INDEX.

Martinique Noyeau, 181
Matso Cakes, 258
  „ Diet Bread, 259
  „ Soup, 249
Matsos, Fried, 258
Maxims, Convivial, 203
Mead, 273
Meat Cecils, 24
  „ Pie, Danger of, 45
  „ Salads, 66
  „ Sanders, 24
Meats, Preserved, 243
Melena Pie, 254
Melted Butter, 29
Meringues, 106
Milk, 121
  „ Coagulated, 122
  „ Cuits, 78
  „ Punch, 269
Minced Veal, 23
Mincemeat à la Soyer, 216
Mint Julep, 273
  „ Sauce, 30
Mississippi Punch, 275
Mock Turtle Soup, 3
Monastic Living, 216
Moost Aye, 55
Moss, Carrageen, 215
  „ Ceylon, 215
Mosses, 215
Morils, 40
Mother Eve's Pudding, 53
Mountain Dew, 270
Muffins, 75
Mug, 267
Mulligatawny Soup, 6
Mushroom Ketchup, 196
Mushrooms, 40
Mustard, 38
Mutton, best Age for, 10
  „ Birds, 85
  „ Boiled Leg of, 14
  „ Broth, 7
  „ Hams, 193
  „ Haricot, 24
  „ Loin, Stuffed, 20
  „ Ragoût of, 21
  „ Roast, 10
  „ Roast Leg of, 13
  „ Salt, 195
  „ Sausages, 71
  „ Simple Dish of, 27
  „ Stewed with Celery, 252

Naleskikes, 52
Napkins, 134
Nasturtiums, 40
Nectar, Common, 275
  „ Supreme, 275
  „ Welsh, 275
Negus, 267
Nesselrode Pudding, 57
New South Wales Fish, 231
  „ Zealand Fish, 226
  „ „ War, 227
Norfolk Biscuits, 158
Northumbrian Cakes, 77
Nottingham Pudding, 56
Nougat, 107
Noyeau, 132
Nutmeg, 38
Nutrition, 179

Oat Cakes, 75
Oatmeal Biscuits, 157
Oiled Butter, 30
Oil Twist, 258
Olive, 41
Olives, Beef, 24
  „ Veal, 22
Omelette, 53
  „ aux Confitures, 170
  „ aux Fines Herbes, 168
  „ Chorissa, 254
  „ Soufflé, 170
  „ Sweet, 168
Omelettes aux Huîtres, 69
Onion Salad, 66
  „ Sauce, 30
Onions, 39
Orangeade, 271
Orange, 41
  „ Brandy, 276
  „ Flowers, 41
  „ Flower Water, 190
  „ Gingerbread, 150
Orgeat, 272
Ortolans, 86
Ovens, Portable, 185
Ox Cheek, 26
  „ Heart, 12
  „ Tail Soup, 1
  „ Tails, Stewed, 26
  „ Tongue, Roasted, 10
Oxford Night Cap, 268
  „ Sausages, 72
Oyster Patties, 68
  „ Sauce, 68
  „ Soup, 5
Oysters, 67
  „ Artificial Breeding, 229
  „ Boiled, 67

INDEX.

Oysters, Broiled, 68
,, Fried, 68
,, Marinaded, 68
,, Roasted, 68
,, Scalloped, 68
,, Stewed, 68

Palestine Soup, 248
Pan Jam, 86
Pancakes, 52
,, Pink, 53
Paon Revêtu, 87
Parmentier's Salad Vinegar, 67
Parsley, 39
,, Fried, 18
Partridges, 88
Passover Cakes, 148
,, Pudding, 257
,, Fritters, 257
Paste, Puff, 59
,, Ude's, 60
Pastry, 52, 59
,, Mrs. ——'s, 61
Pasty, Kangarao, 82
Paté de Foie Gras, 189
Patties, Oyster, 68
Peaches, Suèdoise, 110
Peacock, 87
Pease Pudding, 44
Peas, Green, 116
,, Purée of, 117
,, Stewed with Oil, 254
Pea Soup, 3
Pears, to Preserve, 145
Pennyroyal, 39
Perry, 102
Persian Bread, 73
Peterborough Soup, 7
Petits Puits d'Amour, 52
Pheasants, 88
Physiology of Tea Drinking, 136
Picnics, 217
Picnic, Tasmanian, 225
Pickle, Mild, 192
Pickles, 64
,, Apple and Onions, 64
Pie, Cup in a, 57
,, Devonshire Squab, 44
,, Game, 43
,, Rump-steak, 43
,, Salmon, 251
,, Sea, 43
Pies, Apple, 54
,, and Puddings, 43
,, Fruit, 57
,, Raised, 43

Pigeon Compote, 46
Pigeons, Stewed, 50
,, Wild, 89
Pikelets, 153
Pineapple Rum, 271
Pink Champagne, 131
,, Pancakes, 53
Plum Broth, 59
,, Buns, 150
,, Pudding, 50
,, ,, Sauce, 51
Plums, Magnum-Bonum, 55
Poached Eggs, 169
Poivrade Sauce, 33
Polish Pancakes, 52
Pone Cake, 79
Poor Clergyman's Pudding, 59
,, Man's Sauce, 32
Pope, 279
Pork, Portuguese Roast, 11
Portable Ovens, 185
Porter, 164
Portugal Cakes, 151
Portuguese Roast Pork, 11
Potage Maigre, 3
Pot au Feu, 1
Potato, How to Choose it, 115
,, Beer, 166
,, Rolls, 75
,, Shavings, 253
,, Yeast, 205
Potatoes, 114
,, Cooking, 116
Poulard à la Montmorency, 49
Poulet à Moi, 47
Poultry, 45
,, Hashed, 48
Pound Cake, 148
Prawn Curry, 25
Prenesas, 255
Preserved Meats, 243
Preserves, 144
Prussian Cutlets, 26
Pudding, Abingdon, 51
,, Alma, 57
,, Almond, 255
,, Apple, 54
,, Apricot, 53
,, Arrowroot, 53
,, Aunt Nelly's, 57
,, Bachelor's, 58
,, Baked Lemon, 58
,, Baked Rice, 55
,, Bakewell, 56
,, Batter, 56
,, Beef-steak, 44

INDEX.

Pudding, Bread and Butter, 56
„ Chicken, 253
„ Coburg, 58
„ Ground Rice, 55
„ Half-Pay, 58
„ Indian, 58
„ Macaroni, 56
„ Marlboro', 59
„ Marrow, 54
„ Mother Eve's, 53
„ Moost Aye, 55
„ Nesselrode, 57
„ Nottingham, 56
„ Passover, 257
„ Pease, 44
„ Poor Clergyman's, 59
„ Rowley Poley, 58
„ Save-all, 55
„ Soufflé, 52
„ Spring, 56
„ Suet, 56
„ Vermicelli, 56
„ Yorkshire, 44
Puddings, 43
„ and Pies, 50
„ College, 55
Puff Paste, 59
Puffets, American, 78
Puffs, 61
„ Almond, 57
„ Spanish, 62
Pulled Bread, 77
Pumpkin Soup, 3
Punch, Gin, 277
„ Glasgow, 267
„ Milk, 269
„ Mississippi, 275
„ Oxford, 268
„ Regent's, 268
„ West India, 273
Purée of Green Peas, 117
Purées, 117
Purl, Hot, 280
Pyroligneous Acid, 238

Quails, 88
Queen Cakes, 148
Quinces, to Preserve, 145
Quin Sauce, 33

Rabbits, 89
Rachael, 255
Ragoût of Mutton, 21
Raised Pies, 43
Raisin Wine, 130
Raspberry Jam, 144

Raspberry, Vinegar, 277
Ratafia, 132
„ Cakes, 149
Red Grouse, 88
Rice, 15
„ Cake, 152
„ Cakes, 74
„ Pudding, 55
„ Sauce, 31
Rinoles, 28
Roast Beef, 9
„ Emeu, 84
„ Goose, 48
„ Goose à la François, 49
„ Haunch of Venison, 81
„ Kangaroo, 83
„ Kid, 12
„ Lamb, 12
„ Leg of Mutton, 13
„ Mutton, 10
„ Ox Tongue, 10
„ Pig, 11
„ Pork, 11
„ Sucking Pig, 11
„ Turkey, 47
„ Veal, 12
„ Venison, 81
„ Wombat, 85
Roasted Oysters, 68
Robert Sauce, 31
Rock Cakes, 152
Rolls, 74
„ Breakfast, 77
„ Potato, 75
Rouge Roquelocum, 107
Rout Cakes, 151
Roux, 33
Rowley Poley, 58
Rum, 282
„ Pineapple, 271
„ Shrub, 133, 272
Rump-steak Pie, 43
Rump-steaks, 25
Russian Charlotte, 108

Sack Posset, 272
Saffron, 41
Sage, 39
Sago, 42
„ Pudding, 55
Salad, Crayfish, 66
„ Cucumber, 66
„ French, 66
„ Horseradish, 66
„ Lobster, 66
„ Onion, 66

INDEX.

Salad, Spanish, 66
Salads, 65
" Meat, 66
Sally Lunns, 76
Salmis of Game, 90
Salmon, Crimping, 94
" Cutlets, 95
" in Tasmania, 224
" Ova, 225
" Pie, 251
Salsop, 42
Salt, 42
" Fish, 97
" Meat, 191
Salting, 192
Sangaree, 267
Sarsaparilla, 267
Sauces, 29
Sauce à la Rimolade, 32
" Apple, 30
" à la Tartare, 249
" au Maitre d'Hotel 32
" au Roi, 31
" Bèchamel, 32
" Blonde, 33
" Bread, 31
" Dutch Horseradish, 33
" Egg, 249
" Fish, 249
" for Fried Meat, 31
" for Plum Pudding, 51
" for Wild Ducks, 32
" French Shalot, 33
" Gooseberry, 30
" Kelly's, 31
" Mint, 30
" Onion, 30
" Oyster, 68
" Poivrade, 33
" Poor Man's, 32
" Quin, 33
" Rice, 31
" Robert, 31
" Sage and Onion, 30
" Shalot, 33
" Sharp, 31
" Steak, 32
" Superlative (Dr. Kitchener's), 32
" Tomato, 30
" Turtle, 33
" Universal, 33
" Wine, 31
" Wou-Wou, 31
Saucepans, Copper, 211
Sausage Rolls, 72

Sausages, 17, 71
" French, 72
" Mutton, 71
" Oxford, 72
" Veal, 71
" Worcester, 71
Save-all Pudding, 55
Saveloys, 71
Savoy Biscuits, 157
Savory, 39
Savoury Gravy, 34
" Sausages, 71
Scalloped Fish, 251
" Oysters, 68
Scones, 75
Scotch Barley Broth, 7
" Buns, 151
" Cake, 154
" Collops, 21
" Fancy Cakes, 151
" Haggis, 35
" Kail, 6
" Shortbread, 75
Scraps and Sayings, 239
Sea Pie, 43
Seasonings, 102
Seed Buns, 150
Servants, 236
Shalot Gravy, 24
Shandy Gaff, 279
Sharp Sauce, 31
Sheep's Head, 21
" " Broth, 6
" Trotters, 21
Sherbet, 267
Sherry Cobbler, 274
Shin of Beef Soup, 1
Shortbread, Scotch, 75
Short Crust, 60
Shoulder of Veal, 23
Shrewsbury Cakes, 148
Shuv'-in-the-Mouth, 280
Siesta Cake, 257
Sighs of Love, 182
Slippery Bob, 86
Smoked Beef, 251
Smoking, 233
Snipe, 88
Snow Cream, 105
" Trifle, 104
Soda Biscuits, 158
" Cakes, 76
" Water, 276
Sopa d'Oro, 255
Sorbet, 271
Soufflé de Pomme de Terre, 54

INDEX.

Soufflé Pudding, 52
Soup à la Mousquetaire, 4
,, Almondigos, 249
,, Chicken, 2
,, Cottage, 5
,, Conger, 93
,, Fish, 5, 99, 250
,, Golden, 255
,, Gravy, 4
,, in an Hour, 2
,, Julienne, 4
,, Kettle, the, 1
,, Maigre, 3
,, Matso, 249
,, Mock Turtle, 3
,, Mulligatawny, 6
,, Ox-tail, 1
,, Oyster, 5
,, Palestine, 248
,, Pea, 3
,, Pumpkin, 3
,, Shin of Beef, 1
,, Turtle, 2
Soups, 1
Sour-krout, 187, 251
South Australian Fish, 219
Soy, 42, 140
Spanish Beans, to Stew, 254
,, Cream, 110
,, Drinks, 275
,, Flummery, 110
,, Gaspacho, 20
,, Puffs, 62
,, Salad, 66
Spartan Broth, 8
Spiced Beef, 253
Spider, 278
Spinach, 116
Sponge Biscuits, 158
,, Cake, 148
,, Lemon, 107
Spring Pudding, 56
Spruce Beer, 276
Staffin, 257
Steak Sauce, 32
Steaks, Rump, 25
Stew, Brazilian, 28
,, **Irish**, 27
Stewed Beef, 28
,, Duck, 46
,, Fish, 96
,, Fowls, 49
,, Giblets, 26, 254
,, Knuckle of Veal, 22
,, Lobsters, 99
,, Ox Cheek, 26

Stewed Ox Tails, 26
,, Oysters, 68
,, Pigeons, 50
,, Rump Steaks, 25
,, Tripe, 28
Stock, 1
Stone Fence, 274
Stonewall, 274
Stoves, 184
Strasbourg Pies, 189
Stuffing, 100
,, Balls, 101
,, for Goose and Duck, 101
,, ,, Hare, 101
,, ,, Kangaroo, 101
,, ,, Veal, &c., 101
Sucking Pig, 11
Suédoise of Peaches, 110
Suet Crust, 60
,, Pudding, 56
Sugar, 41
,, Beer, 164
,, ,, without Yeast, 164
,, Plums, 108
Superior Cakes, 76
Suppers, 129
Supreme Nectar, 275
Sussex Dumplings, 59
Swan Black, 90
Sweet Omelette, 53, 168
Swiss Cream, 110
Syllabub, 110
Symposiacs, 217
Syrup d'Absinthe, 146
Syrups, 145

Table Arrangements (A.D. 1779), 239
,, Cloths, 134
Tamarind Drink, 275
Tapioca, 42
Tarragon, 39
Tart, Apricot, 53
,, Barberry, 58
,, de Moy, 256
Tarts, Fruit, 57
Tasmanette, 133
Tasmanian Fish, 220, 225
,, Picnic, 225
Tea, 135
,, Black, 137
,, Drinking, 136
Teal, 88
Tears of the Widow of Malabar, 181
Tewahdiddle, 280
Thickening, 33
Thyme, 39

INDEX.

Timmins's, Dinner at, 12
Toad in a Hole, 27
Toast, 123
Toasted Cheese, 119
Toddy, Buttered, 268
Toffy, Everton, 107
Tomato Sauce, 30
Tongue, Ox, Roasted, 10
Tourtes à la Crême, 61
Treacle Parkins, 155
Trifle, 106
,, Apple, 106
,, Egg-snow, 63
,, Gooseberry, 110
,, Snow, 104
Tripe, Stewed, 28
Truffled Turkey, 47
Truffles, 40
Trumpeter, 93
Turbot, to Boil, 95
Turkey, Boiled, 47
,, Braised, 45
,, Bustard, 89
,, Cold, 48
,, Roast, 47
,, Truffled, 47
Turkish Kebobs, 23
,, Pilau, 21
Turnips, 16
Turtle Forcemeat, 101
,, Sauce, 33
,, Soup, 2
Tusser's (Old) Good and Bad Huswifery, 159
Twelfth Cake, 147
Twice-laid, 97

Ude's Royal Paste, 60
Unfermented Bread, 73, 78

Vanilla, 41
,, Custards, 105
,, Ice, 108
Veal, Breast of, and Peas, 27
,, Broth, 7
,, Croquettes de Veau, 29
,, Cutlets, 17
,, en Roulade, 23
,, Gravy, 34
,, Forcemeat, 101
,, Fricandeau, 253
,, Fry, 17
,, Knuckle, 22
,, Minced, 23
,, Neck of, Braised, 23
,, Olives, 22

Veal, Rissoles, 17
,, Roast, 12
,, Sausages, 71
,, Shoulder of, 23
,, Sweet Bread, 242
Vegetable Essences, 190
,, Marrow, 116
Vegetables, 13, 114
,, Appert's Mode, 113
,, How to Preserve, 118
,, Macédoine of, 118
Venison, Hashed, 85
,, Haunch, 81
,, Pasty, 81
Verjuice, 41
Vermicelli, 63
,, Pudding, 56
Victoria Cake, 148
Victorian Fish, 228
Vinegar, 42, 198
,, Chili, 199
,, in Twenty-four Hours, 199
,, Parmentier's, 67
,, Raspberry, 277
,, Sugar, &c., 193, 199
Vol-au-vent, 44

Waflers, 256
Water, 69
,, Purifiers, 70
,, Rain, 70
Wattle Bird, 89
Welsh Nectar, 275
,, Rabbit, 119
Wexford Biscuits, 157
Whale Steaks, 94
Whig Cake, 154
Whisky, 282
Whitebait, 97
White Champagne, 132
Wild Ducks, 88
,, Sauce, 32
Wine, Cherry, 131
,, Cup, 278
,, Cyprus, 133
,, Egg, 280
,, Elder, 131
,, Elderberry, 131
,, Ginger, 132
,, Grape, 131
,, ,, Colonial, 133
,, Lemon, &c., 132
,, Raisin, 130
,, Raspberry, 131
,, ,, and Currant, 131
,, Sauce, 31

INDEX.

Wine, to Mull, 283]
Wines, 171
,, Ancient, 283
,, Colonial, 178
,, Home-made, 130
,, Victorian, 177
Wise Counsel, 18
Wombat, Roast, 85
Woodcock, 88
Worcester Sausages, 71
Wou-Wou Sauce, 31

Yeast, 204
,, Artificial, 206
,, Cakes, Cobbett's, 207
,, How to Make, 205
,, Patent, 206
,, Potato, 204
Yorkshire Cakes, 77
,, Pudding, 44

Zranzy, 19

GLOSSARY.

In the hands of an expert cook, alimentary substances are made almost to change their nature, their form, consistence, odour, savour, chemical composition, &c. Everything is so modified, that it is impossible for the most requisite sense of taste to recognise the substance which makes up the basis of certain dishes. The greatest utility of the kitchen consists in making the food agreeable to the senses, and rendering it easy of digestion.—*Majendie.*

We are not altogether an admirer of French cookery, yet we are bound to give our Continental friends credit for the goodness of some of their dishes, and the unexceptionably savoury qualities of others—so much so, that we have introduced a few into this work; and as reference is made in extracts from authors to terms which some of our readers may not well understand, we have thought it desirable to add the following explanation :—

Atelets.—Small silver skewers.
Assuttes.—Small plates of eatables handed round.
Bain Marie.—An open utensil to hold boiling water, to keep saucepans warm.
Béchamel.—A white sauce, named after a celebrated maître d'hôtel to Louis XIV.
Blanch.—To whiten articles for cookery.
Braise.—To stew with bacon and herbs.
Caramel.—Burnt sugar.
Compote.—A stew of meat, or fruit served in syrup.
Consommé.—Stock or gravy.
Entrées.—Small dishes with the first course.
Entremets.—Ditto, with second course.
En papillote.—In paper.
Escalops.—Collops.
Glacer.—To glaze.
Hors d'œuvres.—Small dishes served with the first course.
Maigre.—Soup without meat.
Menu.—Bill of fare.
Purée.—Meat or vegetables pulped.
Ragoût.—Stew or hash.

GLOSSARY.

Roux.—French thickening.
Rissoles.—Light paste.
Sauce Piquante.—Sharp sauce.
Salmi.—Ragoût of game.
Sauter.—To dress in a saucepan.
Soubise.—Sauce called after the Prince de Soubise, who was a man of true science, and had princely notions of expenditure.
Tamis.—A tammy cloth.
Timbale.—A pie mould.
Tourte.—A tart or fruit pie.
Vol-au-vent.—Crust of paste, filled with any kind of ragoût, fricassée, or fruit preserve.

CAMBACERES' DINNERS.—Among the most successful of the *parvenu* nobles under Napoleon was Cambacères, second Consul under the Republic, and Arch-Chancellor under the Emperor, who never suffered the cares of Government to distract his attention from "the great object of his life." On one occasion, for example, being detained in consultation with Napoleon beyond the appointed hour of dinner—it is said that the fate of the Duc d'Enghien was the topic under discussion—he was observed, when the hour became very late, to show symptoms of impatience and restlessness. He at last wrote a note, which he called a gentleman usher in waiting to carry. Napoleon, suspecting the contents, nodded to an aide-de-camp to intercept the dispatch. As he took it into his hands, Cambacères begged earnestly that he would not read a trifling note on familiar matters. Napoleon persisted, and found it to be a note to the cook, containing only the following words:—" *Gardez les entremets; les rôtis sont perdus.*" When Napoleon was in good humour at the results of a diplomatic conference, he was accustomed to take leave of the plenipotentiaries with, " Go and dine with Cambacères."—*The Art of Dining.*

ENGLISH AND AUSTRALIAN COOKERY.

"BETTER IS A DINNER OF HERBS WHERE LOVE IS, THAN A STALLED OX AND HATRED THEREWITH."—Prov. xv. 17.

I.—SOUPS.

"C'est la soupe qui fait le soldat."—*French Axiom.*

Shin of Beef Soup.—Take a shin of beef, of about six pounds; chop the bone in three pieces; put it into a soup-kettle to *simmer*, and cover it well with cold water. After about an hour, add two carrots, two turnips, a head of celery, a little allspice, cloves, savory, thyme, and parsley, and let it continue simmering for two or three hours; add pepper and salt. Some persons strain the soup, and throw away the meat; but we prefer the vegetables and soup served up thick; and the boulli and gristle in a separate dish, with a small quantity of parsley and butter over it.

Oxtail Soup.—Made in a similar way, and pieces of the tail, in joints, served up with the soup; and the vegetables and herbs taken out of the soup, before being served.

THE SOUP-KETTLE.—The first thing that struck me, on my arrival, as odd and singular in the streets of Constantinople, was an extraordinary, greasy-looking fellow, dressed in a leathern jacket, covered over with ornaments of tin. He was followed by two men, also fantastically dressed, supporting a pole on their shoulders, from which hung a large copper kettle. They walked through the main streets with an air of great authority, and all the people hastily got out of the way. This, I found on inquiry, was the soup-kettle of a corps of janissaries, and always held in high respect; indeed, so distinguishing a characteristic of this body is their soup, that their colonel is called *Tchorbadgé*, or distributor of soup. Their kettle, therefore, is, in fact, their standard; and whenever that is brought forward, it is the signal of some desperate enterprise. Their kettles were now solemnly displayed in the Etmeidan, inverted in the middle of the area; and in a short time twenty thousand men rallied round them.—*Walsh's "Constantinople."*

Pot au Feu, or Stock.—The best pieces of beef to make good stock of are the shin, the leg bone, and the neck. Put the meat, cut in pieces, in a digester, with a sufficient quantity of water. When the meat has been skimmed sufficiently, add carrots, parsnips, turnips, leeks, celery, and onion, which have been browned in a pan—the quantity of vegetables depending on the quantity of meat. Simmer for four or five hours; take out the meat, and strain the stock for use.

Soup in an Hour.—Chop two pounds of beef into pieces, add a carrot; turnip, an onion, some celery, all cut up, and put with the meat into a saucepan; season it with pepper and salt, and add a quantity of water. Let it boil an hour, and strain it through a tamis sieve. You can serve the meat with gravy, adding a few fine herbs, or parsley and butter, just as you please.

CHICKEN SOUP.—"Here, waiter, take this to the landlady, with my compliments, and say, if she has no objection, you'll draw the chickens through it again."

Turtle Soup.—The following is the simplest mode that we can recommend:—Hang up the turtle the night before it is to be dressed, cut off its head, or a weight may be placed on its back, to make it extend itself. When dead, cut the belly part clear off, sever the fins at the point, take away the white meat, and put it into water. Draw, cleanse, and wash the entrails; scald the fins, the head, and the belly shells; saw the shell about two inches deep all round, scald and cut it into pieces; put the head, shell, and fins in a pan, cover them with stock, add shalots, thyme, marjoram, and spice—chop the herbs. Stew it till tender, then take out the meat, and strain the liquor through a sieve. Cut the fins in three pieces, and take out all the brown—as the meat is called—from the bones, and cut it in square pieces. Melt some butter in a stewpan, and put the white meat to it; simmer it till nearly done, then take it out of the liquor, and cut it into slices of a medium size. Cover the bowels, lungs, heart, &c., with stock, and herbs and spices, and stew them till tender. The liver must be boiled by itself, being bitter, and not improving the colour of the other entrails, which should be kept as white as possible. The entrails being done, taken up, and cut in pieces, strain the liquor through a sieve. Melt a pound of butter in a stewpan large enough to hold all the meat; stir in half a pound of flour, put in the liquor, and stir the whole until well mixed. Make a number of forcemeat balls; put to the whole three pints of Madeira wine, a high seasoning of cayenne pepper, salt, and the juice of two lemons. The deep shell must be baked, whether filled or not, as the meat must be browned. The shell being thus filled, the remainder is to be served in tureens. In filling up the shells and tureens, a little fat should be put at the bottom, the lean in the centre, and eggs and forcemeat balls, with part of the entrails, on the top. Be cautious not to study a brown colour, the natural green being preferred by every connoisseur. If you warm turtle soup often, it loses its flavour. The fins of the turtle make a luxurious side dish. Turtle may be enjoyed in steaks, cutlets, or fins.

The usual allowance for a dinner in the City of London is six pounds, live weight, per head. The *New Monthly* advises the epicure, if he would enjoy turtle in perfection, to journey to the West Indies, where they are too plentiful to require the meretricious aid of stock or gravy. Turtle soup may be kept for a few weeks by being covered an inch thick with lard. The green fat is the gourmet's *regina voluptatis*, remember.

Mock Turtle Soup.—Line the bottom of a stewpan that will hold five pints with an ounce of lean bacon or ham, a pound and a half of lean gravy beef, a cow-heel, the inner rind of a carrot, a sprig of lemon-thyme, winter-savory, three times the quantity of parsley, a few green leaves of sweet basil, and two shalots; put in a large onion with four cloves stuck in it, eighteen corns of allspice, the same of black pepper; pour on these a quarter of a pint of cold water, cover the stewpan, and set it on a slow fire to boil gently for a quarter of an hour; then, for fear the meat should catch, take off the cover, and watch it; and when it has got a good brown colour, fill up the stewpan with boiling water, and let it simmer gently for two hours. If you wish to have the full benefit of the meat, only stew it till it is just tender, cut it into mouthfuls, and put it into the soup. To thicken it, pour to two or three table-spoonfuls of flour a ladleful of the gravy, and stir it quickly till it is well mixed; pour it back into the stewpan where the gravy is, and let it simmer gently for half an hour longer; skim it, and then strain it through a tamis into the stewpan. Cut the cow-heel into pieces about an inch square; squeeze through a sieve the juice of a lemon, a table-spoonful of mushroom ketchup, a tea-spoonful of salt, half a tea-spoonful of ground black pepper, a little nutmeg, and a glass of sherry or Madeira; let it simmer for five minutes. Forcemeat or egg balls may be added.

The above is Dr. Kitchener's celebrated recipe; but mock turtle is made infinitely superior from calf's-head.

Pea Soup.—To make pea soup, you must first soak the peas over night, say a pint; then put them on to simmer in two quarts of water, with some mutton bones, two heads of celery, a sprig of savory, and a little sweet marjoram, pepper, and salt; let it simmer for an hour. Add an onion, cut small; when nearly done, take out the mutton bones, and add a pound of bacon, cut into little pieces. Serve with toasted bread and powdered mint. Pea soup is invariably made first-rate on board ship.

Pumpkin Soup.—Take part of a pumpkin, pare off the skin and remove the seeds; cut it into small pieces, and place them in a stewpan on the fire, with some water. When the pumpkin is pulped, put in about half a quarter of a pound of butter, and a little salt. Boil a quart of milk, and mix it with the pumpkin pulp. Put some bread, cut in thin slices, in the tureen, and pour the soup hot over it.

Potage Maigre.—(*For Fast Days.*) A soup maigre can be made by using vegetables boiled tender enough to be rubbed through a tamis; add a piece of butter, and the yolks of three eggs well beaten. Add water to the soup before the eggs are put in.

Soup Maigre.—(*Another way.*) Melt a quarter of a pound of butter in a stewpan, shake it well, and throw in half a dozen sliced onions; shake the pan for a few minutes, then put in a few heads of celery, two handfuls of spinach, two cabbage lettuces, cut small, and some parsley; shake the pan well for five minutes, put in two quarts of water, some crusts of bread, a tea-spoonful of pepper, and a few blades of mace, also a handful of white beet leaves, cut small; let it simmer for an hour, and before serving, beat up and add the yolks of two eggs, and a table-spoonful of vinegar.

Living low occasionally is very preservative of health. Baglivi tells us that a large proportion of invalids in Italy invariably recover their strength during the period of Lent.

Cock a Leekie.—Boil four pounds of lean beef until the liquor is good. Take out the meat, and put into the soup a fowl cut into pieces, with half the quantity of leeks intended to be used. Let it simmer; and half an hour before serving, add the remainder of the leeks, and the seasoning of pepper and salt.

This was said to be a very favourite dish of James I., and was in great request by our Scotch friends at the last London Exhibition.

Gravy Soup.—Cut half a pound of ham, or the same quantity of lean bacon, into slices, and lay them at the bottom of a digester, with six pounds of lean beef, cut into pieces. Clean two onions, two turnips, and two carrots, and a head of celery, a few cloves, and a blade of mace. Cover the digester close, and set it over the fire; when the meat adheres to the bottom of the digester, turn it; and when there is a brown glaze on the meat, cover with hot water; and when coming to a boil, put in half a pint of cold water, take off the scum, then put in some more cold water, and again skim it; set it aside to simmer for full three hours. When done, strain it through a tamis, turn it into a pan; and, when cold, take off the fat. If thick, it must be clarified with the whites of two eggs.

This stock is the basis of all gravy soups, which are called by name of the vegetables that are put into them. Potatoes mashed, carrots, turnips, onions, asparagus, artichoke, green peas, celery, or a mixed vegetable soup; or you may add rice, barley (Scotch), maccaroni, or vermicelli. Onion soup is more agreeable to the stomach than any other.

"Palestine soup!" said the Rev. Dr. Opiman, dining with his friend Squire Gryll; "a curiously complicated misnomer! We have an excellent old vegetable, the artichoke, of which we eat the head; we have another, of subsequent introduction, of which we eat the root, and which we also call artichoke, because it resembles the first in flavour, although, *me judice*, a very inferior affair. This last is a species of the helianthus, or sunflower genus, of the *syngenesia fructianea* class of plants. It is, therefore, a girasol, or turn-to-the-sun. From this girasol we have made Jerusalem, and from the Jerusalem artichoke we make Palestine soup."—"*Gryll Grange*," *in Frazer.*

Soup Julienne.—Cut up small, carrots, turnips, and celery heads, onions, and leeks, and put them into a stewpan, with a little butter. Then add to them lettuces, sorrel, and celery, cut in pieces. To these vegetables put sufficient stock, and simmer until the vegetables are well done. Serve with or without bread.

Soup à la Mousquetaire.—Boil in a pint of stock a pint of green peas and a handful of sorrel; add a quart of water, and boil a few pounds of mutton in it, which, when done, glaze as a fricandeau, and serve together.

Maria Louisa's Consomme.—In about two quarts of water put two pounds of lean beef, cut in slices, a fowl divided, two large carrots, two onions, a bay leaf, and two cloves. Let it simmer for six hours; skim off the fat, and serve.

This was a favourite dish of the late Empress, and has been called after her. With George III. and George IV. a vermicelli soup, with a few green chervil leaves in it, was said to be a pet *potage*.

Beef Tea, or Brown Gravy.—When one pound of lean beef, free from fat, and separated from the bones, in the finely-chopped state in which it is used for sausages or mincemeat, is uniformly mixed with its own weight of cold water, then slowly heated to boiling, and the liquid, after boiling briskly for a minute or two, is strained through a sieve, from the coagulated albumen and the fibrin, which are then become hard and horny, we obtain an equal weight of the most aromatic soup, of such strength as can be had even by boiling for hours from a piece of flesh; also when mixed with salt, and other additions by which soup is usually seasoned, and tinged somewhat darker by means of roasted onions, or burnt sugar, it forms the very best soup that can be prepared from a piece of flesh.—*Liebig*.

The above eminent chemist states that beef tea, or essence of beef, might be made at a small cost in Australia, and advantageously imported into Europe. Salted beef could be as easily cured for the Royal Navy in Australia at a great saving.

Oyster Soup.—Put the liquor of a hundred oysters into a stewpan, with a quart of new milk, and the same quantity of water; season with pepper and salt, with a quarter of a pound of fresh butter and flour; let this boil for a short time, after which set it to cool; then beard the oysters, and add them to the liquid, and let them boil for two minutes. A little nutmeg and mace may be added.

The oyster soup we would recommend is with a less quantity of oysters, with no milk or butter, added to a tureen-full of weak stock or broth. The flavour and goodness of the oysters are then obtained, without so much oleaginous matter.

Soups made of game are generally very good sort of things. Kangaroo, hare, partridge, pheasant, and grouse soups are excellent, and the Scotch are first-rate hands in making the latter, for they stew down six or seven brace for a stock, and add beside a young grouse for each person at the table. Some persons prefer the game added to veal, beef, or mutton stock, with the necessary adjuncts in the shape of spice, pepper, salt, and a little port or claret wine.

Fish Soup.—Take a sufficient quantity of fish of the kind you have for the soup, cut into pieces, and put into a stewpan, with two quarts of veal, beef, or mutton broth; add a few slices of lean ham, two or three carrots, onions, and heads of celery, some sweet herbs, salt, and cayenne. Stew the fish until it will pass through a coarse sieve, then return it to the stewpan, with a piece of butter, and some flour to thicken; add two glassfuls of white wine, and a table-spoonful of garlic vinegar. This stock will, if re-boiled in cold weather, keep for a month.

Any kind of fish soup may be made in this way, as well as eel, crayfish, lobster, or prawn. The flat-head (Tasmania), when skinned and dressed as above, would satisfy the palate of the most fastidious, whether he be a gourmand or an epicure.

Cottage Soup.—Fill an earthen pot or saucepan with six quarts of water, add one pound of bacon, with a proportionate quantity of carrots, turnips, cabbages, leeks, and onions; season with pepper and salt, and simmer for five or six hours. This will make a savoury and economical repast for six or eight persons, with a modicum amount of the staff of life.

Mind invariably to eat plenty of bread with soup; it is not wholesome without. According to the defined rules of gastronomy, no dinner is perfect without soup—it is the *overture* to the performance; and after it has been taken it must be followed by a glass of wine, which, according to the proverb, deprives the doctor of his fee.

Mulligatawny Soup.—This is simply curry soup, made from fowl, as follows, and is a favourite in the East Indies. Fry a few onions of a brown colour, put a few slices of bacon into the stewpan, cut a fowl up in moderate pieces, and brown them; put in the fried onions, a little garlic, and about a quart and a half of stock, and simmer till the fowl is tender; skim carefully, and when the fowl is nearly done, rub two table-spoonfuls of curry to the soup, add salt and lemon pickle, or mango juice. Send up boiled rice with the mulligatawny, in a separate dish.

Mutton or rabbit may be used instead of fowl, but the latter is the proper ingredient. In warm climates, hot curries and mulligatawny soups are always dishes in request; the former a favourite with the matutinal meal.

HINTS FOR CARVING.—Never pour gravy over white meat, as the latter should retain its colour.
The shoulder of a rabbit is very delicate; and the brain is a tit-bit for a lady.
Of roasted fowl, the breast is the best part; in boiled fowl, the leg is preferable.
In helping roast pheasant or fowl, add some of the cresses with which it is garnished.
The most elegant mode of helping hare is in fillets, so as not to give a bone, which would be a breach of good manners.
The most delicate parts of a calf's head are—the bit under the ears, next the eyes, and the side next the cheek.
Never pour sauce over meat or vegetables, but on the side; and in helping at table, never use a knife where you can use a spoon.

II.—BROTHS.

Every individual, who is not perfectly imbecile and void of understanding, is an epicure in his way; the epicures in boiling potatoes are innumerable. The perfection of all enjoyments depends on the perfection of the faculties of the mind and body; the temperate man is the greatest epicure, and the only true voluptuary.—*Dr. Kitchener.*

Scotch Kail.—Take a cupful of pearl barley, and put it, with about three quarts of cold water, in a pot, and allow it to simmer. When it does so, put into the pot about two pounds of neck of mutton, and let it continue simmering for an hour, skimming occasionally. Then add two carrots, two turnips, and a few small onions, cut in pieces, with some pepper and salt; also a cabbage cut into pieces, or a similar quantity of greens. [Leeks are preferred to onions by our countrymen north of the Tweed.] Simmer another hour, and add a little more boiling water if necessary. The meat is served in a separate dish, and is garnished with carrots and turnips. The broth is served in a tureen.

This is said to be a universal dish among the middle class of Scotland, and very good it is, if properly made. It is called "kail" from the name of the greens that are employed in its composition.

Sheep's Head Broth.—Clean the head properly, and put it on to simmer, with a cupful of pearl barley; skim it carefully, and, when it has simmered an hour, add two carrots, two turnips, an onion cut into slices, and some parsley. Season with salt and pepper, and, when the head is sufficiently tender, serve. The head can be put on a separate dish, and parsley and butter poured over it, and garnished with parsley leaves or boiled beet.

Beef Broth.—Take part of a leg of beef, crack the bone in two or three places, and put it into half a gallon of water, let it simmer. Skim well, add a few blades of mace, a bunch of parsley, and a crust of bread. Let it simmer for two hours, and serve with toasted bread.

PETERBOROUGH SOUP.—Mr. Baron Bramwell lately tried the case of Wilkins *v.* Smith, in the Court of Exchequer, which was an action for libel, brought by the proprietor of the refreshment rooms at the Peterborough railway station against the *Daily Telegraph* newspaper. A special reporter from the paper accompanied the Prince of Wales on his journey to the North, and the train stopped at Peterborough station for refreshments. On the publication of the report of the journey the following day, the reporter said he trusted His Royal Highness had not tasted the "detestable juice of horsebeans, which is retailed to Her Majesty's lieges at that station at a shilling a plate." The defendant declined to apologise, and the jury gave a verdict for £25 damages—*Home News.*

Scotch Barley Broth.—Put a neck of mutton on the fire in a saucepan, with half a gallon of water, and three table-spoonfuls of Scotch barley, and let it simmer. After it has been on some time, add some turnips, and onions cut into dice. Skim well, and allow it to simmer about a couple of hours.

Veal Broth.—Put part of a knuckle of veal on the fire, and follow the same mode as the above. The meat can be used served up in a separate dish, with parsley and butter.

Mutton Broth.—Take two pounds of mutton, any part; put it into a stewpan, with sufficient cold water, a tea-spoonful of salt, a small quantity of pepper, a table-spoonful of the best grits, and an onion; let it simmer, and skim it often. Put into it three turnips and an onion, let it simmer for a couple of hours. It can be thickened with oatmeal, rice, or Scotch barley.

Dr. Kitchener's Barley Broth (Scotch).—Wash three-quarters of a pound of Scotch barley in a little cold water; put it into a soup-pot, or digester, with a shin or leg of beef of about eight pounds' weight, or the same weight of mutton, sawn in pieces; cover it well with cold water; set it on the fire; when it boils, skim it, and put in two onions; let it simmer for about a couple of hours; put in two heads of celery, and a large turnip cut into pieces. Let it simmer a short time longer, and take out the meat to serve separate with the broth. When the meat is taken out, season with pepper and salt, and a glass of port wine may be added or not. The meat must be done tender, not to rags; may be served with caper sauce or minced gherkins or walnuts.

The doctor calculated that the above dish of soup and meat would dine eight persons with an excellent savoury meat, at a cost of fivepence per head, exclusive of bread and vegetables.

BROTHS.

Crowdie.—This favourite Scotch broth is generally made from the liquor meat has been boiled in. Put half a pint of oatmeal into a porringer, with a little salt, and thicken the crowdie sufficiently with meal. This is a dish easily made, is nutritious, wholesome, and costs little.

Chicken Broth.—Put half a chicken, cut into pieces, into a stewpan, with about a quart of water. Let it simmer for an hour, skim well, add salt and a table-spoonful of rice; put it on the fire again for half an hour, and it will be found to be excellent broth.

Broth Bouillon.—(*Made in an hour.*) Take a pound of beef or veal, cut into dice, chop them, and put them into a stewpan, with an onion, a carrot, a bit of bacon, and a glass of water; just as it comes to the boil throw in another glass of water, add some salt, boil it a little longer, and add about a quart of boiling water; take it up, strain, and serve.

Broth.—(*A la minute.*) Boil a quart of water; put to it half a pint of the gravy from roast meat; add salt, and it will serve for all purposes.

Bouillon aux Herbes.—(*Strengthening.*) Take leaves of sorrel, leeks, lettuce, purslain, and chervil, about two handfuls of each; pick and wash them; add salt, some fresh butter; boil together in three pints of water till it is reduced to half; take it off and strain it. If you like you can add the yolks of two eggs, beaten with a spoonful of cream.

Calf's Foot Broth.—Simmer the foot in water, with a little lemon-peel, taking off the scum. Put it into a basin, and, when cold, take off the fat. When wanted, warm it up again with a little of the broth, adding butter, sugar, and nutmeg; add the yolk of an egg and serve. Shanks of mutton make excellent stock for any kind of gravy, and are good stewed of themselves; and they are cheap—a dozen may be purchased for a penny, enough, with seasoning and herbs, to make a quart of nutritious soup.

SPARTAN BROTH.—The black broth of Lacedæmon will long continue to excite the wonder of the philosopher and the disgust of the epicure. Julius Pollux says it was blood thickened in a certain way. Dr. Lester, in "Apicium," supposes it to have been hogs' blood; if so, this celebrated Spartan dish bore a resemblance to the black puddings of our day. The citizens of Sybaris having tasted it, declared it was no longer a matter of astonishment why the Spartans were so fearless of death, since every one in his senses would die, rather than exist on such miserable food.—*Athenæum.* When Dionysius, the tyrant, had tasted the black broth, he exclaimed against it as miserable stuff. The cook replied, "It was no wonder, for the sauce was wanting." "What sauce?" says Dionysius. The answer was, "Labour and exercise, hunger and thirst—these are the sauces we Lacedæmonians use, and they make the coarsest fare agreeable."—*Cicero.*

"A difference between crockeryware and plate,
As between English beef and Spartan broth,
And yet great heroes have been bred by both."

III.—ROASTING.

Antipholus of Syracuse: I'll make you amends next, to give you nothing for something. But say, sir, is it dinner time?
Dromio of Syracuse: No, sir; I think the meat wants that I have.
Antipholus: In good time, sir; what's that?
Dromio: Basting.
Antipholus: Well, sir, then 'twill be dry.
Dromio: If it be, sir, I pray you to eat none of it.
Antipholus: Your reason?
Dromio: Lest it make you choleric, and purchase me another dry basting.
Antipholus: Well, sir, learn to jest in good time: there is a time for all things.
Comedy of Errors.

Roast Beef.—King Charles II. is said to have honoured this joint with the accolade of knighthood, and hence the term of *Sir*-Loin.

> Our Second Charles, of fame facete,
> On loin of beef did dine;
> He held his sword, pleas'd, o'er the meat,
> "Arise, thou famed Sir-Loin."
> *Sir John Barleycorn's Ballad.*

There is no act in cookery so simple as roasting, and yet how few can do it properly! Over-done meat is equally unwholesome as that which is under-done. The art is to seize the *juste milieu*, and roast the beef without losing the gravy or scorching the outside. Ten pounds of the sirloin will take about two hours and a half, but it is impossible to indicate the time accurately. The joint must at first be put at a distance from the fire, which must be brisk and clear. As the meat warms, it must be brought nearer. During the time it is roasting it must be well basted; the fat must be paper-covered. When nearly done dredge it with flour, and, a few minutes before you take it up, sprinkle some salt on it. Put horseradish round the dish, and serve with its own gravy, quite devoid of fat, and you have in perfection "the roast beef of old England, oh!"

The flesh of the ox is wholesome and nutritious, and well adapted to persons of good appetite, or that labour or take exercise. For persons labouring under debility it is superior to all other animal food. If not over-done, and left full of gravy, it sits lightly on the stomach, and its fat is more digestible than veal. Dr. Paris tells us, with a warning, that experience, dearly bought, has taught us that headache, flatulency, hypochondriasis, and a thousand nameless ills, have arisen from the too prevailing fashion of loading our tables with that host of French *entremets* and *hors d'œuvres* which have so unfortunately usurped the roast beef of old England.

ROAST BEEF.—I was soon in great hunger and confusion, when I thought I smelled the agreeable savour of roast beef; but could not tell from which dish it arose, though I did not question but it lay disguised in one of them. Upon turning my head, I saw a noble sirloin of beef on the side table, smoking in the most delicious manner. I had recourse to it more than once, and could not see without some indignation that substantial English dish banished in so ignominious a manner to make way for French kickshaws.—*The Tatler*, 148.

Flank of Beef Roasted.—Take a flank of beef and roll up very tight, and roast until well done. Serve with gravy, and grate some horseradish over the top before coming on the table.

Care should be always taken that the meat should not be under-done, nor ought it to be *over-dressed*; for, although in this latter state it may contain more nutriment, yet it is less digestible, on account of the density of its texture.—*Spallanzani on Digestion.* Boiled, and roasted, and even putrid meat, is easier of digestion than that which is raw. —*Hunter on the Animal Economy.* A well-cooked piece of meat should be full of its own juice or natural gravy.—*Johnston's Chemistry of Common Life.*

Roast Ox Tongue.—Put before the fire in a cradle spit, and baste it well when being roasted. When done, stick cloves in the tongue, in the part uppermost in the dish. Make some gravy with port wine, rather thick, and add the juice of a lemon. Serve hot. This is a very good dish, and the cook must not forget to peel the outside skin off before putting the tongue down, as well as trim the root.

Roast Mutton.—Gently stir and blow the fire,
  Lay the mutton down to roast;
  Dress it quickly, I desire;
  In the dripping put a toast,
    That I hunger may remove;
  Mutton is the meat I love.

  On the dresser see it lie;
  Oh, the charming white and red!
    Firmer meat ne'er met the eye,
  On the sweetest grass it fed;
    Let the jack go quickly round,
  Let me have it nicely brown'd.

  On the table spread the cloth,
  Let the knives be sharp and clean;
    Pickles get, and salad both,
  Let them each be fresh and green.
    With small beer, good ale, and wine,
  Oh, ye gods! how I shall dine!
—Dean Swift.

All or any parts of the sheep are good roasted; the leg, the shoulder, the saddle or loin, or even the neck. Good mutton requires no sauce or condiment, but a good appetite. If the diner requires a zest to a leg, saddle of mutton, or shoulder, he may have sharp, onion, oyster, or celery sauce, and the thin flank is excellent cold for breakfast after being stuffed with sage and onion, rolled and browned by being roasted or put in a quick oven. A cook who understands her business can make an epicurean dish out of the head and fry; and even the feet, well cleansed and stewed, are excellent. The kidneys dressed plain, broiled, kibobbed, or they may be extravagantly stewed in champagne, *à la mode de Paris.* Broiled mutton bones are first-rate picking. If the mutton is kept, no meat is sweeter or more wholesome. So thought the late Duke of Devonshire; while George IV. preferred the neck roasted. The cook must always remember—

"*A feast must be without a fault;
And if 'tis not all right, 'tis naught.*"

Best Age for Mutton.—The sheep is in its best condition as food when about five years old—an age which it is almost never allowed to attain, unless when intended for the private use of the owner and not for market. It is then sapid, full-flavoured, and firm, without being tough; and the fat has become hard. At three years old, as commonly procured from the butcher, it is well tasted, but is by no means comparable to

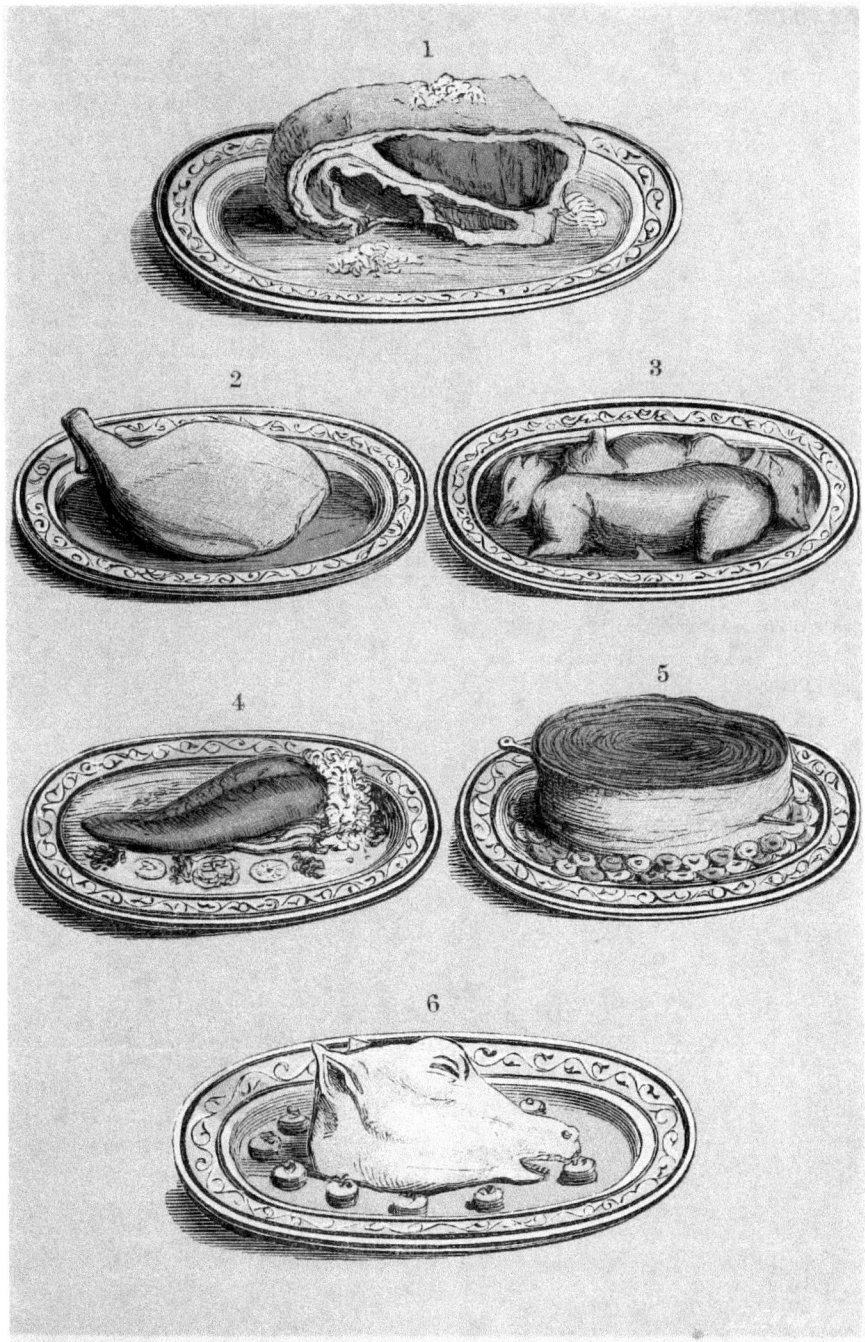

1. Roast Sirloin of Beef.
2. ,, Shoulder of Mutton.
3. ,, Sucking Pig.
4. Boiled Tongue.
5. ,, Round of Beef.
6. ,, Calf's Head.

that of five years. If younger than three years, it is deficient in flavour, and its flesh is pale. Meat which is half mutton and half lamb is very unpalatable food. M. Ude says — "Always choose mutton of a dark colour and marble-like appearance." — *The Yeoman.*

Portuguese Roast Pork.—Cut the skin of the loin across at the distance of half an inch; roast as usual. Cut two onions up small, and put them into the dripping-pan, with a pint of vinegar; baste well with this, and serve hot.

Roast Pork.—Every kind of pork must be well done. Under-done pork is unbearable. Should a joint appear in this state, on with the gridiron and prepare for a grill. A leg of pork to be well roasted requires full three hours; but this, again, all depends on the fire, and whether the fire radiates well from the screen. Pork must invariably be scored, and the leg must be stuffed with sage and onion, mixed fine, and bread crumbs, with pepper and salt. Rub a little salad oil on the skin to crisp the crackling, and do not put the meat too near the fire at first. Serve with apple sauce. The sparerib, the loin, the chine, and any other part of the pig, may be roasted.

At New Zealand, among the Maoris, the meat (pork) must be well done. "A Pakeha Maori," in his "History of the War of the North of New Zealand," against the chief, Heki (a most interesting little book), tells us that these people, like the Romans of old, and the Thugs of our day, believe in omens; and that it is a bad augury on any occasion when business of importance is on hand, or before a battle, if the food is served under-done.

Roast Sucking Pig.—This is a *bonne bouche* of the epicure, and must be very carefully roasted. Rub the skin all over with salad oil, and stuff the pig with onion, sage, and bread crumbs, mixed together with egg, some pepper and salt. Baste the pig well, as everything depends on this attention. The pettitoes, liver, and brains are generally made into gravy, and served up in a sauce tureen with the pig. Very good baked.

Sucking Pigs.—Roasted sucking pigs are a dish mentioned by Epicrates in his "Merchant:"—

"On this condition I will be the cook;
Nor shall all Sicily boast that even she
Produced so great an artist as to fish,
Nor Ellis either, where I've seen the flesh
Of dainty sucking pigs well brown'd before
A rapid fire."
The Deipnosophists.

Roast Pig.—Of all the delicacies in the whole *mundus edibilus*, I will maintain it to be the most delicate—*princeps obsoniorum*. I speak not of your grown porkers—those hobble-dehoys—but a young and tender suckling, under a moon old, guiltless as yet of the stye, with no original speck of the *amor immunditiæ*, the hereditary failing of the first parent, yet manifest; his voice as yet not broken, but something between a childish treble and a grumble, the mild forerunner or *preludium* of a grunt. He must be roasted. I am not ignorant that our ancestors ate them seethed or boiled; but what a sacrifice of the exterior tegument! There is no flavour comparable, I will contend, to that of the crisp, tawny, well-washed, not over-roasted, *crackling*, as it is well called. The very teeth are invited to the share of the pleasure at this banquet in overcoming the coy, brittle resistance, with the adhesive oleaginous—call it not fat! but an indefinable sweetness growing up to it—the tender blossoming of fat—fat cropped in the bud—taken in the shoot—in the first innocence—the cream and quintessence of the child-pig's yet pure food; the lean no lean, but a kind of animal manna—or, rather, fat and lean (if it must be so)—so blended and running into each other, that both together make but one ambrosial result, or common substance.—*Charles Lamb.*

Ox Heart.—This is an excellent dish if well basted and attended to. Stuff it in the centre with veal stuffing, and have a few stuffing balls in the dripping-pan. Put paper on the heart at first, and afterwards take away the paper, and flour it so as to put a froth on. Serve hot, with hot water plates and currant jelly. It is very excellent cut in slices and hashed, but be sure to mind the fluid is not too watery. Half a dozen sheeps' hearts are very nice indeed dressed in this way.

The art of roasting victuals to the precise degree is one of the most difficult in this world, and you may find half a thousand good cooks sooner than one perfect roaster.—*Almanach des Gourmands.*

Roast Lamb.—The fore-quarter is considered the prime part of lamb. It must be roasted before a clear fire, and basted from the time it is warmed until it is thoroughly done. It should never be placed so near the fire as to scorch the fat; serve with a little gravy made in the pan, and have mint sauce in a tureen, with a lemon cut ready for use. A salad is a favourite addition. The hind-quarter, or any other part, may be dressed in the same way. Lamb is good dressed in any mode, and an excellent dish cold in summer. It may be baked, or stewed, or hashed, or made into a pie.

Quarter of Lamb Roasted, with Bread Crumbs.—Lard the lamb on the thin side with small pieces of bacon, and sprinkle the other part with bread crumbs; when almost done take it from the fire, and sprinkle it a second time with crumbs of bread, seasoned with salt and parsley. Put the joint down to brown, and when done serve with sharp sauce.

Roast Kid.—This is very good eating. It is in great request on the Continent of Europe. Put a quarter down to roast, and let it be well browned; serve with gravy, slices of bacon, and some veal stuffing balls. It is more tender than lamb.

A LITTLE DINNER AT TIMMINS'S.—Of course it does not become the present author, who has partaken of the best entertainment which his friends could supply, to make fun of their (somewhat ostentatious, as it must be confessed) hospitality. If they gave a dinner beyond their means, it was no business of mine. I hate a man who goes and eats a friend's meat, and then blabs the secret of the mahogany. Such a man deserves never to be asked to dinner again; and though at the close of a London season that seems no great loss, and you sicken of a whitebait as you would of a whale, yet we must always remember that there's another season coming, and hold our tongues for the present. As for describing, then, the mere victuals on Timmins's table, that would be absurd. Everybody (I mean the genteel world, of course, of which I make no doubt the reader is a polite ornament)—everybody has everything in London. You see the same coats, the same dinners, the same cutlets, fish, and cucumbers, the same lumps of Wenham Lake ice, &c. The waiters, with white neckcloths, are as like each other everywhere as the peas which they hand round with the ducks of the second course. Can't we invent anything new?—*Thackeray.*

Roast Veal.—Veal requires great care and attention in the roast. It must be continually basted. The fillet will require stuffing and force-meat, and the time it will take depends on the fire and the size of the joint. A loin is the preferable part for a roast. The kidney must be papered, and fat served up hot on toast for the veal *gourmet.* The shoulder is excellent roasted, as well as the breast. The sweetbread is par-boiled before being roasted. Roast veal of every kind must have some good melted butter put over it, and it is indispensably necessary that it should be well browned, and accompanied with a little bacon or ham, either as a garnish or separate dish. A little lemon is an improvement.

Roast Leg of Mutton, with Garlic.—Being at Bordeaux, we one day gave a dinner, at the hotel at which we lodged, to a few English friends whom we had met there. Anxious to taste, and let our guests taste, a *gigot à l'ail* (a leg of mutton and garlic), a dish for which the Bordelais cooks are celebrated, we ordered one as part of the repast. When the roast was placed on the table at the second course, it appeared to us all to be a *gigot aux haricots* (a leg of mutton and kidney beans); but the meat was delicious, and the beans certainly superior to, and bearing a different flavour from, any *haricots* we had ever tasted before. Vexed, however, at what we considered an inattention to our orders, we summoned the landlord, and begged to know why, when we had ordered a *gigot à l'ail*, he had presumed to send up a *gigot aux haricots?* " I have shown no inattention," he replied, " and made no mistake. The dish of which you have just eaten, and which your guests seemed to have liked, was a *gigot à l'ail*, and what you have mistaken for beans is garlic."

" Is it possible!" we exclaimed. Again we tasted the garlic; its rankness was gone; but there was in it a delicious flavour for which we could not account. After apologising to our host, " If the question be not indiscreet, and the matter no secret, how can you impart this delicious flavour to garlic?" we asked.

" There is no secret in the case," he replied; " the process is very simple. The garlic is thrown into five boiling waters, with a little salt, and boiled five minutes in each. It is then drained, and put into the dripping-pan under the roasting mutton."

Since our return to England we have often had this dish dressed, and no guest of ours, until he was told of it, ever discovered that he had been feasting on garlic.—*Correspondent of " Domestic Economy."*

VEGETABLES.—We presume it is unnecessary to expatiate on such vegetable luxuries as broccoli, green peas, and asparagus, but it may be a useful piece of information to state that parsnips are excellent fried, and that beet-root, boiled well, sliced, and sent up hot, forms the best possible accompaniment to roast meat.—*Quarterly Review.*

IV.—BOILING:

The operation of dressing food in water in a state of ebullition, or nearly approximating to it. The practice of cooking animal food by boiling, although exceedingly simple, and often most convenient, is neither judicious nor economical when the broth or liquor in which it is dressed is to be rejected as waste; as in this way the most nutritious portion of the flesh of animals, consisting of soluble saline and other matter required for the formation of bone and the nutrition of the muscular fibres, &c., is to a great extent lost. This particularly applies to small pieces so dressed, and to those presenting a large surface to the action of the water in proportion to their weight. Large pieces of meat suffer less in proportion than small ones, for the same reason; but even with them the outside should be rejected, as it is both insipid and innutritious compared with the interior portion. To reduce the solvent and deteriorating action of the water to the lowest possible point, the articles to be boiled should not be put into the water until it is in a state of full ebullition, which should be maintained for five or six minutes afterwards, by which time the surface will have become, to a certain degree, hardened, and will then act as a shield to the inner parts. To induce tenderness, the subsequent portion of the operation should be carried on at a mere "*simmer*," the slighter the better. The practice of dressing meat by putting it into cold water, which is gradually raised to the boiling point, cannot be too much censured. A quarter of an hour per pound for dressing young meat, poultry, and small pieces, and twenty minutes per pound for old, tough, and large ones, are the usual times allowed by cooks for this purpose.—*Cooley's " Practical Receipts."*

We intend to give only a few recipes in boiling, for the mode is so well described by Cooley, that were we to write a dozen pages we could not improve the detail of cooking by this mode. Joints must invariably continuously *simmer*; if any meat is what is called *galloped*, it is rendered tough, the juices are absorbed, and it is indigestible. Cooks should be made to comprehend the difference between a boiling simmer and a boiling gallop.

Boiled Leg of Mutton.—This favourite dish is simply simmered until done, the scum is taken off occasionally, and the dish must be done, and not over-done; for, according to Johnston's " Chemistry of Common Life," meat well cooked should be full of its own natural gravy. It is quite impossible to give the exact time to boil a joint; it must, of course, depend upon its weight, and the boil. There are many chances against this very simple joint being served up in perfection; and, according to Charles Lamb, it must be accompanied with mashed turnips, which must be neither stringy nor bitter. If the latter, a little sugar put in the water will absorb that unpleasant taste; but we are vulgar enough to prefer a Swede to the white stone. Assuming that the turnips are good flavoured, and properly mashed, there are said to be *seven* chances against this simple dish being served in perfection, as between the cook and the eater:—

1st. The mutton must be *good*.
2nd. Must have been kept a *good* time.
3rd. Must be boiled by a *good* fire.
4th. By a *good* cook.
5th. Who must be in *good* temper.
6th. The mashed turnips must be *good*; and
7th. The eater must have a *good* appetite.

Round of Beef.—This is a noble dish at all times, supposing it is well and properly salted. Skewer it tightly, and as round and evenly as possible. Put more fat in the centre, if the meat is too lean. The pot must be roomy. Heat gradually, according to Cooley, and allow it to simmer until done. Take off the scum. When dished, see that the silver skewers hold the meat well together, and ladle a small quantity of the liquor over the meat. Garnish with sliced carrots. If to be eaten cold, let it remain in the water until it cools, and the meat will be more mellow.

FLESH VERSUS VEGETABLES.—At a meeting of the Dublin Royal Society, Mr. Houghton read a paper on "The Advantages of Vegetarianism." He contended that man is not a carnivorous animal, and that it is contrary to his nature to eat flesh, and brought forward many authorities in favour of his system, which was completely demolished by Colonel Walsh, Dr. Shaw, Dr. Jacob, and Mr. Ross, who has been fifteen years in the service of the Hudson's Bay Company, during which long period he had never tasted vegetables. In low latitudes, the latter asserted animal food was absolutely necessary, and he had himself repeatedly drank melted grease with great gusto.—*Newspaper Report of Proceedings of Dublin Royal Society.*

An Aitch or H Bone of Beef.—This is boiled like the round, and the slower it boils the better it will look, and the more tender it will be. Serve with carrots or parsnips.

This common dish has a variety of names. It is called edge bone, haunch-bone, hook-bone, each-bone, ridge-bone, watch-bone, and inche-bone.

Calf's Head Boiled.—Tie the head in a cloth, and boil for two hours in plenty of water. Tie the brains up in a separate cloth, with a little parsley and a leaf of sage; boil them one hour, chop them small, warm them up in a saucepan, with a little butter, pepper, and salt. Lay the tongue, which has been boiled at the same time, peeled, in the middle of a small dish; place the brains round it. Or mince the brains and put them into parsley and butter, and pour over the head, and serve with bacon, ham, or pickled pork in another dish. Lemon garnish.

Rice.—Rice is not often boiled properly, and there is nothing so easily done. The usual mode is to boil the grains until they are done, and then put the rice into a colander to drain. The Indian mode is to put the rice into water, and allow the grain to absorb all the moisture; at the same time, it must not burn. It must be served in curries quite dry, so that each grain will separate; if over-done, it becomes pappy. The best rice requires little washing and no soaking. The black fellows' recipe is: "Wash him well, water boil, throw in rice; boil short time, rice drink all water. When done, him dry, put in little cold water, so rice not stick."

Cow-heel, Boiled.—Let it be perfectly clean, and boil it well for five or six hours, together with five or six onions and a quart of milk. Add a little salt. Serve with parsley and butter, and a little ham, bacon, or corned pork.

There is nothing more wholesome than cow-heel; whether in the shape as above, or fried, potted, or made into soup, it is equally nutritious and agreeable.

Neck of mutton and caper sauce; leg of lamb, with spinach; knuckle of veal, with parsley and butter; beef boulli, with parsley and butter; hams, bacon, tongues, aitch-bone and brisket of beef; pickled pork and greens; rabbits and tripe, with cream sauce, or smothered in onions, are all well in their way, if properly boiled and served, not forgetting a boiled leg or hand of corned pork, with accompaniment of pease-pudding. Bacon, boiled along with rice, for a summer dish, is also by no means to be despised.

If a vessel containing water be placed over a steady fire, the water will grow continually hotter till it reaches the limit of boiling, after which the regular accessions of heat are wholly spent in converting it into steam. The water remains at the same pitch of temperature, however fiercely it boils; the only difference is, that with a strong fire it sooner comes to a boil, and more quickly boils away and is converted into steam.—*Buchanan's "Economy of Fuel."*

BOILING—NOTHING BUT BOILING.—Our seamen and marines are now fed exclusively upon beef and pork—that is, they can have boiled salt beef, boiled fresh beef, and boiled salt pork, but all must be boiled in the ship's coppers. From the date of a ship's commission to her paying off there is nothing but "boil." . . . The meat is weighed out and cut up into junks under proper supervision, and handed over to the ship's cook, who bundles it, according to old usage, into the ship's coppers, with a small quantity of vegetables, and boils the whole until reduced to a kind of soup, that would be uneatable were it not for the vegetables in it. The meat is, at the same time, transformed into a pulpy, stringy substance, which is no longer nutritious. Fresh beef soup, with a few shreds of vegetables, is a capital thing in its way; but if people on shore were compelled to live on it, with nothing for a change but boiled salt beef or boiled salt pork, the chances are that they would soon pray heartily for a change of diet.—*The London Times.*

TURNIPS.—Charles Lamb travelling once in company with a farmer, the latter took the author to be of the same occupation as himself, and asked him, "What he thought of turnips this year?" The writer of "Elia" replied, "That will entirely depend on the boiled legs of mutton."—*Anecdotes of Charles Lamb.*

V.—BAKING.

Come, sir, to dinner. Dromio! keep the gate.
Husband, I'll dine with you to-day.
Adriana, in the Comedy of Errors.

This is a much more easy mode of cookery than roasting, and the prejudice exists solely from the imperfect way it is done. In the American cooking stoves the difference cannot be discovered by the most fastidious epicure. There are many joints to which baking is peculiarly applicable, such as legs and loins of pork, legs and shoulders of mutton, veal, &c. A baked sucking pig will be found equal to a roasted one, if occasionally basted, which is the great secret of the domestic oven. Poultry dressed in this way are good. A hare baked, and basted with butter and milk, is first-rate food. A baked ham is far preferable to a boiled one, being of finer flavour, and more full of its natural juices. What nicer dinner can the housewife put on the table than a piece of beef or mutton, with baked potatoes under the meat, or a Yorkshire pudding, or even both? Such a dish ought to satisfy the appetite of the most particular *gourmet*, and so it would were he in the least hungry. In baking one matter must be borne in recollection: there must not be a variety of dishes in the oven at the same time, evolving their different flavours and odours; this is one of the causes of the failure of the bake. A story is told in the *Quarterly* how some connoisseurs were deceived in ordering a roast turbot for dinner at Friceurs', in 1836. They partook of the fish with great gusto, voted it excellent, and dined under the idea that they had made a grand discovery in gastronomy. One of the party, however, more inquisitive than the rest, wished for a "second edition" of the dish, and applied to the Frenchman for the secret mode of the roast, when the truth came out: " Why, sare, we no roast him at all; we put him in oven and bake him!" Baked fish and baked joints of meat are unexceptionable when, like everything else in cookery, it is properly done and well attended to. This mode was in full operation in days of yore, for we are informed in "Hamlet" that—

" —— the funeral *baked* meats
Did coldly furnish forth the marriage tables."

THE OVEN.—The Dutch oven combines the twofold advantage of roasting and baking, and is useful for small dishes or birds, or for warming cold meat; it is easily heated, and causes no increased fuel; and with an ordinary stove, either English or American, the oven is always ready to impart the necessary heat that the cook requires. Kitchener tells us with truth that baking is the cheapest and most convenient way of dressing a dinner in small families, and that the oven is the only kitchen a poor man has if he wishes to enjoy a joint of meat at home with his family.

VI.—FRYING.

Under an impoverished diet, the moral and intellectual capacity is deteriorated, as well as the bodily.—*Coombe.*

Veal Rissoles.—Mince and pound veal fine; grate into it some remains of cooked ham. Mix them together with Bechamel sauce; form into balls, and inclose each in pastry. Fry them of a nice brown.

NOT GENERALLY KNOWN.—I have learned by experience, that of all the fats that are used for frying, the pot-top, which is taken from the surface of the broth and stock-pot, is by far the best.—*L'Art de Cuisinier.*

Veal Cutlets, en Papillote.—Cover the cutlets on both sides with an egg, a forcemeat of bread crumbs, bacon, parsley, chives, and mushrooms, all chopped fine; add salt and pepper; over this seasoning lay thin slices of bacon; envelope the whole carefully in white paper, well buttered; let them fry gently over a slow fire, and serve them in the paper.

Veal Fry.—Cut the liver and heart into slices, and fry with bacon. Serve with sharp sauce.

Veal Cutlets (plain).—Put the cutlets in the frying-pan, with salt and pepper, parsley, shalots, chopped fine, and fry in the best dripping, over a quick fire. When the cutlets are done on one side, turn them, and brown them. After you have taken out the cutlets, pour all the fat out of the pan but a couple of spoonfuls, to which add half a pint of water, thickened with flower. Let this gravy brown, and pour over the cutlets. Garnish the dish with broiled ham, or bacon toasted.

This is one of the modes of eating veal, and the simplest cooked.

Cutlets à la Maintenon.—This has almost become an English dish. Cut veal cutlets, mutton, or lamb-chops, about half an inch thick, and flatten them; brush them over with the yolk of an egg; put over them crumbs of bread and sweet herbs, *quant. suff.*, and fold each cutlet in a separate piece of paper. Fry them until nearly done, when take them out of the pan, and put them on the gridiron to finish and dry. They are very delicate eating, if properly done. They are named after a celebrated mistress of Louis XIV.

Beef-steaks and Onions.—Have the steaks cut rather thinner than for broiling, put some clarified dripping into the pan, and fry the steaks until done. Then put in the onions, having been previously sliced, and fry them of a light brown. Serve with brown sauce.

Sausages, sweetbreads, lamb and mutton-chops, pork-chops, calf's liver and bacon, bacon and eggs, and cutlets *à la Marengo*, are all dressed in a similar way, as well as sheep's fry. Frying is nothing more nor less than boiling the several meats in fatty matter; a species of cookery by no means to be recommended, unless the cook attends to the propriety of excluding the unctuous adherence. If meat is fried, either in chops or steaks, the great art is to make a gravy with it, by pouring out of the pan all the fat but a couple of table-spoonfuls, and replacing it with flour and water, and allowing it to boil in the pan until of the proper consistence. If this is done, *secundem artem*, a meat fry is not so bad after all.

Bubble and Squeak.—Cold salt meat is slightly fried in a pan, and cold cabbage is warmed, after having been cut into pieces, and a little salt and pepper put on it. The fried cabbage is then dished up, and garnished with the beef. It is desirable that the boiled beef should be rather underdone, before it is again warmed through in the pan.

Bubble and squeak is said to be a favourite dish in Shropshire. The late George IV. partook of it in that county, and this homely dish was afterwards often seen on the table of Carlton House.

Fried Bread Crumbs.—Rub stale bread through a colander, put them in a pan, with two ounces of butter, place them over a moderate fire, and stir them with a wooden spoon, until they are slightly brown. Spread them on a sieve to drain.

Fried bread crumbs are served with game of any kind, and sometimes with roasted poultry.

Fried Parsley may be dressed in a similar way to bread crumbs, and is a garnish for chops, fish, &c.

Fried Bread Sippets.—Cut slices of stale bread thin, into any shape you wish, put in a pan, and fry of a delicate brown; take them out of the pan and drain them.

Fried bread sippets are an accompaniment to any made dishes, and they are also sent to the table with pease, and other soups.

WISE COUNSEL.—I beseech all persons who shall read this work, not to degrade themselves to a level with the brutes or the rabble, by gratifying their sloth, or by eating and drinking promiscuously whatever pleases their palates, or by indulging their appetites of every kind. But whether they understand physic or not, let them consult their reason, and observe what agrees, and what does not agree with them, that, like wise men, they may adhere to the use of such things as conduce to their health, and forbear everything which, by their own experience, they find do them hurt; and let them be assured that, by a diligent observation and practice of this rule, they may enjoy a good share of health, and seldom stand in need of physic or physicians.—*Galen's Treatise on Health.*

VII.—BROILING.

The wholesomest cookery is broiling, in which the portion of the meat is of no great thickness, and its fibre is cut across. The action of heat upon the divided fibre and the connecting tissue renders the texture more penetrable, and from the cut surface the melted fat easily exudes.—*Mayo.*

Broiled Chops and Steaks.—Cut the chops a little over half an inch thick, broil them over a clear fire until done, turning them with the beef-steak tongs—about three times—pollute them not with a fork; sprinkle pepper and salt over them in moderation. Serve hot. An oleaginous feeder would prefer butter being put over them when done, but a real judge will eat them *au naturel.* A great novelist suggests tomato sauce, but many prefer minced shalot. Beef-steaks are dressed on the gridiron in the same way, and cut about the same thickness. A chop or a steak properly cooked on the grill, over a clear fire, is a favourite dinner with Englishmen all over the world. Pork-chops are cooked in a like way, with a little salt, pepper, and sprinkling of dried mint thrown over them; as well as kidneys. Under-done cold meat, of every kind, is often broiled; also poultry, rabbits, and pigeons, and served with various sauces. The only art in broiling is to have a clear fire, and no smoke. Beef or mutton steaks, with shalots and tarragon, are recommended. The meat must be hurriedly done over the fire; no words more appropriate than—

———'twere well,
If 'twere done quickly;

for if allowed to remain a long time in this mode of cooking, the meat hardens, and wastes its juices and its nutritious qualities. Beef and mutton bones are dressed on the grill, and almost anything: a spatch-cock well done on the grill, with sharp sauce, is a meal for an emperor. Soyer suggests a double chop cut off a saddle of mutton; but the old-fashioned cut chop cannot be improved. Meats dressed *à la Maintenon*, in paper, are finished on the grill, to allow the fire to absorb the oleaginous matter adhering to the meat; as also are fish-cutlets *en papillote*. A connoisseur has stated to us, that if a beef-steak be soaked for a few minutes in pyroligneous acid, and afterwards broiled, such addition will add to the tenderness of the meat, as well as its flavour: we are of opinion that a good steak requires no such adventitious assistance. Dr. Paris, on "Diet," states, that by this operation the sudden browning or hardening of the surface prevents the evaporation of the juices of the meat, which impart a peculiar tenderness to it. It is the form selected, as the most eligible, by those who seek to invigorate themselves by the art of *training*.

SIMPLE FARE.—A hospitable gentleman, residing in Hobart Town, a few years since, was in the habit of inviting his friends to a steak dinner, the course only consisting of three dishes artistically cooked. There were the steaks stewed with onions, the steaks fried with sauce, and the steaks on the plain grill—with the addition of cut shalots, to those who liked the relish. The latter were brought in by relays—hot and hot—a steak at a time. They were cut not too thick nor too thin, and there were plenty of excellent vegetables; and the Amphitryon would only allow his guests "to run riot" on most superior claret of first growth. This simple repast could hardly be excelled, and it would certainly have satisfied the fastidious taste of the author of the "Original," or of any even more scrupulous feeder than Mr. Walker.

A TRAGEDIAN'S DISH.—Kean enjoyed a beef-steak at the Coal Hole, or a devil, or a grill, at one of the small taverns near the theatre; but the dress and ceremony, and good behaviour incident to "company," overset him altogether.—*Proctor's Life of Kean.*

VIII.—MADE DISHES.

Just so many strange dishes.—*Benedick, in "Much Ado about Nothing."*

ZRANZY.—Cut lean beef into thin slices, sprinkle them with salt, and beat them to flatten them. Make a forcemeat of boiled meat, sausage meat, parsley and lemon-peel chopped fine, three eggs, some bread crumbs soaked in milk and drained, and a little curdled milk. Spread some of this forcemeat on each slice of beef, roll it up and tie and put it into a stewpan, with a bay leaf, lemon-peel, onion stuck with cloves, peppercorns, ginger, *bouillon*, vinegar, and wine; cover it up and let it stew; when half done, add a *roux;* when quite done, strain the sauce, and serve with rolled slices untied.

This is a Polish dish; but the brave Poles having been robbed of their nationality, their *cuisine* has almost disappeared. The time was when they were the most hospitable and convivial of nations. Let us indulge the anticipation that, with the assistance of "Freedom's battle," they will recover their kingdom and cookery at the same time. We hope that astonishing institution, "the Secret Government of Warsaw," will order this dish on their anniversary from slavery.

Beef en Miroton.—Slice a few onions, fry them with a piece of butter and a little flour, until they are of a fine brown colour; add a little broth, a glass of white wine, and stew the whole until the onions are well done; then add boiled beef cut in small thin slices, called *miroton;* stew them until they are well flavoured with onion; flavour them with mustard or a dash of vinegar, and serve.

Hodge Podge.—This is a savoury kind of medley, made as follows:—Cut a pound of mutton, a pound of beef, and half a pound of lean pork into pieces, and put the meat into two quarts of water, and set it on the fire to simmer for an hour. Then add a good-sized carrot, two turnips, two onions cut in pieces, a shalot, and a few lettuces, and again simmer. Add again half a dozen potatoes cut up, and a pint of green peas, pepper and salt, and the squeeze of a lemon; simmer till done, and serve in a tureen.

It is said that this dish was used by the delegates of the different colonies lately assembled at Melbourne; and from the *talk* that occurred during meal-time, it oozed out, *first* at Sidney, where speculators operated largely, that increased duties were to be raised by the respective legislatures on certain articles, although a Tasmanian venal print "tried it on" to fix the matter of publicity on the agents of that colony. The name of the dish has no reference to the collective wisdom of the state papers agreed on by the conference.

It seemeth to me that this word (hotchpot) is in English a pudding, for in this pudding is not commonly put one thing alone, but one thing with other things together.—*Littleton,* sect. 267.

Hutspot, or hotspot, is an old Saxon word, and signifieth so much as Littleton here speaks.—*Coke upon Littleton,* 477.

Loin of Mutton Stuffed.—Take the skin off a loin of mutton with the flap on; bone it neatly; fill the inside of the loin, where the bones were removed, with veal stuffing; roll it up tight, skewer the flap, and bind it together; put the outside skin over it till nearly roasted, and then remove it that the mutton may brown. Serve with brown gravy, with a little port wine in it. A leg may be dressed in a similar way, or stuffed with sage and onions, or dressed as a *braise.*

Spanish Gaspacho.—Take two onions, some tomatoes, a handful of green pimento, a cucumber, a clove of garlic, parsley, and chervil; cut the whole into small pieces, and put them into a salad bowl. Add as much crumbed bread as will form double the quantity which the dish already contains; season with salt, pepper, oil, and vinegar, like a salad, and complete the *gaspacho* with a pint of water to make the *bouillon.* Gaspacho is eaten with a spoon; it is a kind of raw soup, and is a favourite dish with the Andalusians.

MADE DISHES.

Scotch Collops.—No cold meat will make this favourite dish in perfection. Cut beef in pieces of about half an inch square; flour them and fry until half done. Then remove the collops and put them in a stewpan with a small quantity of stock; add an onion cut up small, ketchup, pepper, and salt, with a dessert-spoonful of lemon acid. Let it simmer until done, and on no account must it be done too much. To give time to cook this dish in perfection, as some works have it, is simply ludicrous.

Turkish Pilau.—This dish, as made at Constantinople, is as follows:—According to the number of guests, take mutton, fowls, or pigeons, boil them until half done, then put the meat and broth into a basin. Cut the half-cooked meat into pieces, and put them into a pot, with some butter, and fry them of a light brown colour. The necessary quantity of rice, being well washed, it is then placed over the meat in the pot, and the broth is poured over the rice till it is covered to a full finger's depth; then cover the pot, and keep a clear fire under it, until the rice is done; when cover the top of the pot with a cloth folded, and melt some butter and pour in. Cover it again, and let it simmer; pepper and salt. It is served in dishes, with the meat arranged at the top. One dish may be of its natural colour, white; another made yellow with saffron; and a third red, with pomegranate juice.

Sheep's Trotters en Marinade.—Sheep's feet are generally thrown away in Australia, although they make an excellent dish stewed, and are delicate for jelly. For the present dish they must be well cleaned, and boiled in water. Steep them a day in vinegar and salt; drain them, and fry them with egg and bread crumbs, until of a good colour.

Sheep's Head and Fry.—This is one of the best dishes made; take the head, and, after being well cleaned, parboil it. Then egg and crumb it well, and put it before the fire to brown, or in an oven. Mince the liver, the heart and tongue, and add to it a small quantity of stock, or good gravy; add pepper and salt, with the squeeze of a lemon, a little ketchup, and let it simmer. Fry the brains in thick batter. Put the mince in the dish, the head in the centre, and round the dish the brain fritters. The ingredients of this dish are generally thrown away in Australia; but let this conjoint mince, fritters, and browned head be once tried, and it will be discarded no longer. Lamb's head is of course more tender. The sheep and lamb's fry are very good, fried with bacon, and a little gravy served with them, or brown sauce.

French Ragout of Mutton.—Put in a saucepan a quarter of a pound of dripping; when hot, cut into small pieces a dozen turnips, put them into the dripping, and brown. Take them out, and put into the fat a quarter of a pound of flour; stir it until brown. Cut up three pounds of mutton into small pieces, and put in the saucepan, and add sufficient water to cover the meat. When the mutton is nearly done, add the turnips, season with a tea-spoonful of salt, one of pepper, and one of brown sugar, and a little garlic. A ragout of veal or lamb may be done in a similar way.

To Stew a Knuckle of Veal.—

  Take a knuckle of veal—
You may buy it, or steal;
In a few pieces cut it,
In a stewing-pan put it;
Salt, pepper, and mace
  Must season this knuckle;
Then what's joined to a place,[1]
  With other herbs muckle;
That which kill'd King Will,[2]
And what never stands still;[3]
Some sprigs[4] of that bed
Where children are bred.
Which much you will mend, if
Both spinach and endive,
And lettuce and beet,
With marigold meet.
Put no water at all,
For it maketh things small,
Which, lest it shall happen,
A close cover clap on.
Put this pot of Wood's metal[5]
In a boiling hot kettle;
And there let it be,
  Mark the doctrine I teach,
About, let me see,
  Thrice as long as you preach.[6]
So skimming the fat off,
Say grace with your hat off;
Oh, then with what rapture
  Will it fill Dean and Chapter!—GAY.

[1] Salary. [2] Sorrell. [3] Thyme. [4] Parsley. [5] Metal saucepan of the day. [6] Four hours.

Veal Olives.—Cut them not too thick, and rub over them some egg yolk, strew on the bread-crumbs, mixed with chopped parsley, lemon-peel grated, pepper, salt, and nutmeg. Lay on each piece a thin slice of bacon, roll them tightly, skewer them, rub the outside with egg rolled in bread-crumbs, and put them in a Dutch oven to do. Pour the following sauce into the dish:—Take a pint of good gravy, thicken it with flour, add ketchup, pickled mushrooms; boil this up a few minutes. Forcemeat balls may be added.

AN ITALIAN DINNER.—The dinner was a specimen of simple Italian fare, and, as such, I shall record it for the benefit of the curious in such matters. It commenced with a tureen full of *tagliarini;* a paste composed of flour and eggs, rolled out exceedingly thin and cut into shreds—on the lightness and evenness of which the talent of the cook is displayed—boiled in broth and seasoned with Parmesan cheese. Slices of Bologna sausage, and fresh green figs—for which, the General informed us, the neighbourhood was famous—were next handed round; and then appeared the *lesso,* a large piece of boiled beef, from which the broth had been made, with the accompaniment of tomata sauce. After this came a large dish of fried fish, and the *arrosto*—roast veal or roast chickens, or something of the kind—which, with a *dolce*, or sweet, completed the repast. Several sorts of wine, the produce of last year's vintage, were produced by Signor Bonaventura. The dessert consisted of oranges, peaches, grapes, figs, and a melon—considering how far the autumn was advanced—was wonderful for even Italy, and bore witness to the mildness of the temperature.—"*Three Days in an Italian Home.*" *Chambers's Journal.*

Shoulder of Veal à la Bourgeoise.—Bone the shoulder, and season it with salt, pepper, and grated nutmeg; roll it, and give it an oblong shape, then tie it up, and put it into an oval stewpan, with a piece of butter, and stew it over a slow fire; let it take a fine light colour, then add a glass of water, and sprinkle it with a little salt, adding a bay-leaf; place fire above and below till a glaze is formed. Dress the shoulder on the dish, and drain the butter, detaching what remains with a spoonful of broth; and pour the gravy on the veal.

Turkish Kebobs.—Take lean meat, cut it into pieces about an inch square, and a quarter of an inch thick; rub these pieces with a little curry stuff, and put them upon skewers, with half a shalot between each. Dip the skewered meat into the yolk of an egg, and then into bread crumbs, mixed parsley, sweet herbs, salt, and cayenne; dip them again in the egg, and a second time cover them with bread crumbs. Put these sticks of meat on a spit, and roast them, basting them with a little salad oil. Serve them up brown, with or without sauce.

Minced Veal.—Cut the veal in small pieces, and put it in a stewpan with some *béchamel* sauce, a little milk, and a small quantity of floured butter, a small piece of lemon peel, and warm. Serve with bread sippets.

Neck of Veal Braised.—Put a little lean bacon or ham into a stewpan, with an onion, two carrots, two heads of celery, and a glass of sherry or Madeira; lay on them the neck and a little water, and stew until it is tender. Strain off the liquor, mix a little butter and flour in a stewpan until brown, stir some of the liquor in, and boil it up; skim it, and use a little lemon, and serve with the meat. The bacon must be browned in a salamander.

Beef or Veal en Roulade.—This is a German dish. Take a piece of beef, veal, or mutton, and cut it into thin slices; beat them, and spread one of the sides of each slice with anchovies, parsley, basil, the whole chopped very fine; add salt, pepper, and grated nutmeg; cut as many pieces of bacon as you have grated meat, and of the same length; place them on the edge of the latter, and roll up the whole, so that the slice of bacon may be in the centre; tie them up with a string, and put them into a saucepan with some melted butter; when they are well browned take them out, put into the fat a spoonful of flour, let it brown, and then add some *bouillon*, pepper, and salt. Put the *roulades* (from which you have taken the string) into this sauce to finish; add a few slices of lemon, and serve hot.

What the Germans call kloes is a sort of *quenelle*, composed of flour, or the crumb of bread soaked in milk, of rice or semolina, cooked in water, *bouillon*, or milk, according as it is intended to make a savoury dish or sweet *entremet*. Kloes are made with meat, fowl, sweetbread of veal, and kidneys cooked in *bouillon gras*; they then serve to garnish soups, *ragoûts*, and vegetables.

Beef Olives.—Cut slices of beef of about a quarter of an inch thick, lay on each piece a forcemeat of crumbs of bread, shalot, a little suet or dripping, pepper, and salt. Roll each piece separate, and fasten with a skewer; put them into a stew-pan, with some gravy, and stew till tender. Serve with slices of lemon.

Meat Sanders.—Mince beef or mutton small with onion, shalot, pepper and salt, adding a little gravy; put into scallop shells or tins, with a little gravy, making them about half full; fill up with mashed potatoes; put a little fat on the top of each, and brown in a Dutch oven.

Meat Cecils.—Mince any kind of meat, add crumbs of bread, onions, shalot, lemon-peel, salt, nutmeg, a couple of anchovies boned, and a small piece of butter; mix well, and make into balls, with an egg; sprinkle over them crumbs of grated bread, and fry them brown.

Calf's Head Hashed.—Cut the head up into slices, flour them, and put them into a stewpan, with a little of the liquor the head was boiled in, or some stock, with two blades of mace, a salt-spoon of salt, and flour to thicken. Let it simmer, and before serving add a dessert-spoonful of lemon juice.

A Scotch Haggis.—Make the haggis bag perfectly clean; parboil the drought, boil the liver very well, so as it will grate, dry the meat before the fire; mince the drought and a pretty large piece of beef very small; grate about half the liver; mince plenty of the suet and some onions small; mix all these ingredients very well together, with a handful or two of the dried meal; spread them on the table, and season them properly with salt and mixed spices; take any of the scraps of beef that is left from mincing, and some of the water that boiled the drought, and make about a chopin (*i.e.*, a quart) of good stock of it; then put all the haggis meat into the bag, and that broth in it; then sew the bag; but be sure to put out all the wind, before you sew it quite close. If you think the bag is thin, you may put it in a cloth. If it is a large haggis, it will take at least two hours boiling.

Australian haggis is sometimes made in a bason, and crust put over it, and then baked in an oven, which is a very good way of preparing this celebrated Scotch dish. This mode preserves the gravy far better than the usual way of boiling.

Dr. Kitchener states that he extracted the above *verbatim* from Mrs. M'Ivor, a celebrated Caledonian professor of the culinary art, who taught and published a book of cookery at Edinburgh, A.D. 1787, and it has been copied since Kitchener's second publication of it into almost all the works we have read, without acknowledgment.

Haricot Mutton.—Fry in a pan a sufficient quantity of mutton, cut in slices. When nearly done take the meat out, and fry of a brown colour equal quantities of turnips and carrots, cut into small pieces, and a few onions. When done put the mutton and vegetables in a stewpan, with a small quantity of stock, and pepper and salt; simmer and serve. A good haricot is never watery or full of gravy.

Curry.—Cut meats, fowls, or rabbits into small joints, and fry them brown in a pan with an onion chopped up. When half done take them out and put them into a stewpan, with two table-spoonfuls of curry stuff and a dredge of flour, and let it simmer with the juice of half a lemon, a table-spoonful of butter, and a little ketchup. The Bengal, Malay, or Madras curries are excellent and wholesome dishes; but a curry in a deluge of broth, with meats floating about like so many islands, is an abomination.

PRAWN CURRY AT CEYLON.—A sort of grand servitor of the house, in a specially white cotton garment and an extra big tortoise-shell comb, arranged the table in a style that only needed some orange blossoms and tinfoil to look like a small wedding; and when I took my preliminary sip of sherry I found it almost incumbent to make a little pleasant speech to myself, and return thanks in a proper soliloquy. The prawns were sublime. I seem to forget the accessories of sauce and vegetables. Dr. Johnson once said of a lady that she had been so well dressed that he could not recollect what she had on: and my prawns were just as well dressed as that lady. Half an hour was spent in a dreamy enjoyment of a dry curry and Amontillado, my white attendant quietly looking on like a benign spectre. Talking would have spoiled the thing. I pointed to a slender-stemmed wine glass, of the substance of a soap bubble, and waved my hand with a gesture of confidence, as Captain Cook might have done to a Polynesian savage. The tortoise-shell comb bowed gracefully, as divining my desires, and moved away as gently as a tortoise-shell cat. The wine was rich as ever ripened on a volcano. With delicately deferential, but quietly decisive manner, the spectre removed the *débris* of the first course. Green cocoa-nut curry was the next item in the programme. The first spoonful threw me into a paroxysm of astonishment and delight; my bosom throbbed, and I think a tear fell on my fourth plate. A little slow music would at this juncture, perhaps, have tranquillised the system. A melodious gurgling alone broke the silence. Sparkling St. Peray of 1811, the year of the great comet, candied pine-apple, jack fruit, marischino, mango jam, cigars, and coffee, are all that I can clearly recollect afterwards, except that my ghostly guardian extended my legs on the telescope chair, undid my necktie, and sprinkled me with rose water.—*Austral, in "Once a Week."*

Curries may be made of any lean meats, or of any kind of fish, lobsters, crayfish, prawns, or oysters, or vegetables. An Indian prawn curry is reckoned the best made, and potatoes alone curried are very good indeed. A Malay curry is superior to either those of Bengal or Madras, and a dish of this kind is not full flavoured without tomatoes and scraped cocoa-nut, with some of the milk. Acids or pickles are taken with curry and ham.

Stewed Rump-steaks.—Take two pounds of steaks, and put them into a stewpan with just sufficient water to cover them, and let them simmer for half an hour; then add six large onions whole, with a little pepper and salt, a carrot cut up, and some thickening, consisting of two table-spoonfuls of flour and some ketchup, and a tea-spoonful of mustard. Let it simmer for an hour longer, and the steaks will be done. They must be sufficiently cooked, and at the same time not "done to rags," or they are spoilt.

À la Mode Beef.—Take ten pounds of lean beef of any kind, cut it into small pieces, put two ounces of beef dripping and a couple of onions into a stewpan. As soon as it is hot, flour the meat and put it into the pan; keep stirring it about. When it has been some few minutes in the pan, dredge it with flour, and cover it with boiling water. Skim it when it boils, and put in one drachm of black pepper, two of allspice, and four bay leaves. Set the pan by the side of the fire, and let it simmer for three hours. When you find the meat sufficiently tender serve it in a tureen; and when cold it ought to jelly.

Hashed Beef.—Cut the beef in slices, and put it into a stewpan, with an onion, and a little water or stock. Let it simmer, then add a little flour thickening, with ketchup and other sauce. Let it simmer for a quarter of an hour, and serve with bread or toast sippets.

Stewed Ox Cheek.—Put the cheek into a stewpan, with two onions, two cloves, three turnips, three carrots cut up, two bay leaves, a couple of heads of celery, and a little allspice, pepper, and salt, with a few sweet herbs. Let it simmer for three hours, and skim it frequently. Take out the cheek, and melt an ounce of butter in a stewpan, add to it a half-pint of the soup, and thicken it with some flour and a table-spoonful of ketchup, tarragon vinegar, and a wineglass of port wine, with a little cayenne, and let it come to near a boil. Serve with the head on a dish, divided, and the soup in a tureen.

BLANCHING is sometimes performed previous to meats being dressed, by putting the article in cold water, when it is gradually brought to boil, and the article taken out and plunged into cold water, where it is left until it is quite cold. It is used to impart whiteness, plumpness, and softness to the article blanched. At the same time the operation lessens the nutritive qualities of the meat by abstracting a portion of the soluble saline matter which it contains, especially the phosphates, and thus deprives it of one of the features which distinguish fresh meat from salt.

SWEETBREAD.—The thymus gland of the calf. When boiled it is light and digestible; but when highly dressed and seasoned it is improper, both for dyspeptics and invalids.—*Pereira*.

Ox Tails Stewed.—Divide them at the joints, and serve the same as the head.

Stewed Giblets.—This is a very good dish, dressed in the same manner as the ox head.

Lamb à la Poulette.—Blanch any part of a quarter of lamb, put it into a saucepan with a bit of butter, and a spoonful of flour; when well mixed pour over it by degrees two or three glasses of boiling water, in order that it may mix well with the butter. When quite smooth put in the lamb, with pepper, salt, a bunch of mixed herbs, and some small onions. Stew the whole gently, and half an hour before serving add some mushrooms; take out the meat, skim the fat off the sauce, and serve.

Leg of Lamb, with Green Peas.—Stew a leg of lamb in a simmer of stock until half done, when add some seasoning of pepper, salt, a little ketchup, and a pint of green peas. Put it again on the fire, and simmer till done. This dish can be garnished with fried eggs.

Lamb's Head, Fry, and Sweetbread.—Good, whichever way they are dressed.—(*See Sheep's Head and Fry.*)

Prussian Cutlets.—Chop up some veal, with a little fat, add two spoonfuls of shalot, one of salt, half a one of pepper, a little nutmeg. Chop the whole, to give the shape of a cutlet; egg well with bread crumbs. Fry it of a light brown, and serve with any sauce you please.

Bacon, with Green Peas or Beans.—Put a pint of well-boiled peas or beans into a stewpan, with six spoonfuls of brown sauce, three of brown gravy, two onions, and a little parsley. Let it boil ten minutes; have ready about a quarter of a pound of lean bacon cut into pieces, add it to the peas or beans, season with an ounce of butter, and stew fifteen minutes, and serve.

Breast of Veal, with Green Peas.—Cut the breast into pieces, and fry of a light brown, with a shredded onion. When browned put the pieces into a stewpan, with a little stock, and allow it to simmer. When nearly done add a quantity of green peas, with pepper, salt, and the juice of half a lemon, or a little vinegar. Keep the cover of the stewpan off, and serve as soon as the peas are done.

Simple Dish of Mutton.—Put a few steaks of mutton on to simmer for an hour, with a quarter of a pound of maccaroni, and a little water; season with pepper, salt, cayenne, and chutney, and a table-spoonful of vinegar, or the juice of half a lemon.

An unexceptionable Devil.—This is a favourite dish with the epicure after he has sacrificed sufficiently to the jolly god, and requires a little stimulant; or it may be partaken of with great *gusto* at a hunting breakfast. Mind you, a dry devil is as different from a wet one as are the poles asunder, and it is with the latter that we have now to do. Cut into joints cold turkey, fowl, or ducks—we won't say game, for it destroys their flavour. Put the joints in a pan, with a moderate quantity of butter, and the best salad oil, with the following sauces:—mushroom ketchup, Harvey or Worcester, superlative and Chili vinegar, along with mustard, pepper, salt, and chutney, a moderate amount of cayenne, a few pickles cut in small pieces. Warm thoroughly, and serve hot, both from the fire and the sauce.

An Irish Stew.—Take two pounds of mutton cut into fair pieces, and four pounds of potatoes; peel the potatoes and cut them in half; six onions peeled and sliced. First put in the bottom of the saucepan a layer of potatoes, and then some of the meat and onions, a small spoonful of pepper, and two of salt. This dish must simmer, but not boil, for a couple of hours, when it will be found "vary delicious," as the Scotchman said when he ate the wrong end of the asparagus. Some use a little ham, but it overcomes the flavour of the mutton. The potatoes must not be too mealy, or they will mash together.

A Toad in a Hole.—A pudding pie—a piece of meat baked in a dish of batter—is mentioned by Taylor in 1630. How this dish came to be called "a toad in a hole" we are unable to divine.—*Things Not Generally Known.*

Marrow Bones.—Let the bones be sawn even. Put paste at the ends, and boil them until they are done, which will require nearly two hours. Serve on toasted bread, and send up a silver marrow-spoon and napkin for the helper to use. The dish must be sent up hot; cold marrow is decidedly objectionable.

MADE DISHES.

Cold Meat, with Poached Eggs.—Cut slices of beef or mutton of equal thickness, and either broil, fry, or brown, in an oven before the fire. Lay them in a dish to keep warm, while you poach eggs and mash potatoes; or you may fry potatoes and greens. Place the vegetables on the dish, the meat on the top, and garnish with the poached eggs.

Tripe Stewed.—Put the tripe into a stewpan, with onions whole (at least a dozen), and some sweet herbs. Add a pint of milk or stock, and let it simmer for a time. Add an ounce of butter mixed with flour, white pepper, salt, and a little spice. Some use a little white wine, but it overcomes the palate, and is hardly a favourite; but *chacun à son goût*.

Tripe is by no means a fashionable food, but it is easy of digestion, and is good whatever way it is cooked, whether boiled, stewed, fried, forced, roasted, or in a pie. If tender, fried in butter is one of the best ways of cooking it.

Côtelettes à la Soubise.—Take ten cutlets, or more, according to your party; do not pare or shape them, and take care that each cutlet has a bone. Lard them, and season your larding before you use it. Stew them in good braise for three or four hours. When done put them on a tin plate, with another cover on it, on which you place a weight to make the cutlets a good shape. When they are cold trim them neatly and fry them. When you serve them, place them either in a crown, or one bone over the other in a sort of pyramid, with small stewed onions round, and in the middle a purée of onions.

Mutton cutlets can also be served with chicory sauce, or turnips, mushrooms or cucumber strewed and served round, or with a purée of either in place of the onions.

Stewed Beef.—The rump, or any part of the beef, will make an excellent stew. The way to proceed is as follows:—Take three or four pounds, and trim it; add sweet herbs chopped fine, a little shalot, and spice whole; add a little bacon cut in slips; lard the beef, and rub it over with the herbs and spices, flour, and a small bit of butter. The beef can either be stewed or baked in an oven. It is an excellent dish, either hot or cold; and, in serving it up, it may be garnished with pickles. This, again, is a braise.

Brazilian Stew.—Take shin or leg of beef; cut it into slices of two or three ounces each; dip it in good vinegar; and, with or without onions, or any other flavouring or vegetable substances, put it into a stewpan, without water. Let it stand on the hot hearth, or by a slow fire, for two, three, or four hours, when it will be thoroughly done, will have yielded plenty of gravy, and be "as tender as a chicken." Care must be taken that the heat is moderate. This is the Brazilian mode. Leg or shin of beef makes the richest and most nutritious stew, and any other meat or fish may be so dressed. A pound and a half of leg of beef, without bone, so dressed, and plenty of vegetables, will dine four persons luxuriously.

Rinoles.—Take short paste, roll very thin, and cut it into small round pieces. Put into them some hashed meat, or forcemeat, and gather up the paste over it; moisten the edges, and press them securely together.

Fry them in a piece of very hot fat, drain them, and serve them hot. A rinole may be made in the napkin in the shape of a pate.

Croquettes de Veau, ou de Volaille.—Mince two pounds of veal, chicken, or turkey. Melt ten ounces of butter in a stewpan; when hot add a table-spoonful of fine flour, and mix; beat the yolks of two eggs, with a little milk and the juice of a lemon; mix it with the flour and butter by degrees; then add the minced meat, with a tea-cupful of stock; season with pepper, salt, and a little nutmeg grated, and a little lemon-peel. Stir it together, and let it boil till of proper thickness. Pour it into a basin till cold. Grate some bread on a pasteboard; cut the mince into pieces of the same size, and roll them lightly in the bread crumbs. Have ready beaten the yolk of an egg or two; dip the croquettes into this, and roll them again in the bread crumbs, making them a neat shape —like a pear, which looks well. Have some lard melted, put the croquettes in, and fry them a light brown; drain them on a colander, and keep them hot. Serve with garnished parsley.

Fricassée de Poulet.—Cut the chickens into small pieces, after they are semi-boiled; then put them into a stewpan, with a piece of butter, a bunch of sweet herbs, some mushrooms, chives, two shalots; add a little flour, a glass of white wine, the same of pale stock; season with salt and pepper, and stew for half an hour slowly. Take out the herbs, &c., and add to the sauce the yolks of three eggs, to which add a spoonful of vinegar and the same of stock.

ANCIENT MANNER OF DRESSING FOWLS.—Artemidorus, in his "Dictionary of Cookery," tells us:—"Boil a fat hen of the common poultry kind, and some young cocks just beginning to crow, if you wish to make a dish fit to be eaten with your wine. Then taking some vegetables, put them in a dish, and place upon them some of the meat of the fowl, and serve it up. But in summer, instead of vinegar, put some unripe grapes into the sauce, just as they are picked from the vine; and when it is all boiled, then take it out before the stones fall from the grapes, and shred in some vegetables."—*The Deipnosophists.*

THIRTEEN TO DINNER.—There is a prejudice, generally, in the pretended danger of being the thirteenth at table. If the probability be required, that out of thirteen persons of different ages one of them shall at least die within a year, it will be found that the chances are about one to one that one death at least will occur. This calculation, by means of false interpretation, has given rise to the prejudice, no less ridiculous, that the danger will be avoided by inviting a greater number of guests, which can only have the effect of augmenting the probability of the event so much apprehended.—*Quetelet, on the Calculation of Probabilities.*

IX.—SAUCES.

The palate's grown callous almost to disease;
Who peppers the most is surest to please.—Goldsmith.

Melted Butter.—As this is the constituent of almost all English sauces, and, according to the wily Talleyrand, the only one we use, it is necessary that it should be well made—neither too thick nor too thin. Cut about two ounces of butter into pieces, put it into a stewpan, with a dessert-spoonful of flour and two table-spoonfuls of milk; when well mixed add six table-spoonfuls more water, hold it over the fire, and let it simmer till *thick*, turning it one way. No branch of cookery is so easily performed, yet how seldom do we have it well made—generally a watery fluid, from sheer neglect.

It was an observation of a gourmet—of a late learned judge (Baron Hullock)—"that he was an excellent and learned man—he had always the best melted butter ever tasted." And the "Almanach des Gourmands" avers "that a delicious sauce will cause you to eat an elephant." As a rule, never pour sauce of any kind over any dish, as we have known persons prefer salt with pudding. It is related of Dr. Johnson that he used lobster sauce with plum pudding. Tastes are widely different, as much so as faces. *Chacun à son goût.*

Clarified Butter.—Put the butter in a stewpan, over a clear fire; when it is melted skim off the butter-milk, which will swim at the top; then pour off the butter into a basin to cool.

Burnt Butter.—Put butter into a pan; when it becomes brown add a little vinegar and pepper and salt.

Oiled Butter.—Put butter into a pan, and let it gradually melt till it comes to an oil. This oiled butter may be used for frying fish, instead of Florence oil, and is excellent for salads or frying.

Anchovy, Harvey, sauce à la Soyer, lemon, caper, parsley, fennel, shalot, chervil, Basil, Burnet, cress, and egg sauce, are merely these several ingredients added to melted butter.

Gooseberry Sauce.—Top and tail and scald half a pint of green gooseberries, drain them, and put them to the same quantity of melted butter; a little lemon or ginger is an improvement.

Tomato Sauce.—Take fifteen ripe tomatoes, cut them in half, and squeeze them; put them into a stewpan, with a capsicum and a few spoonfuls of gravy; simmer for an hour, run them through a sieve; add pepper, salt, and onion cut small, or a shalot.

Onion Sauce.—Take two dozen onions and peel them, put them in salt and water for an hour, and then boil them until tender; drain them, and chop them up. Put them in a clean saucepan, with some butter and flour, half a tea-spoonful of salt, and about half a pint of milk (cream would be richer), and simmer till done.

Sage and Onion Sauce.—Chop fine an ounce of onion and half an ounce of green sage leaves, put them into a stewpan, with a little water; simmer for ten minutes; then put in a tea-spoonful of pepper and salt and an ounce of bread crumbs; mix together; then pour in a pint of gravy or broth, and simmer a little longer. Excellent for roast pork or ducks.

Mint Sauce.—Wash a small quantity of fresh mint with a little parsley, pick the stalks out, mince them fine, and put in a sauceboat, with a tea-spoonful of moist sugar, and a quarter of a pint of vinegar. If mint cannot be procured this sauce can be made with mint vinegar.

Apple Sauce.—Pare and core six baking apples, put them into a saucepan, with a table-spoonful of cold water; let them simmer until done; add a little butter and sugar to sweeten them.

Rice Sauce.—Boil a little rice in a pint of milk, add onion and white pepper and salt. Rub it through a tamis sieve, and, if necessary, thicken it with cream.

Sauce Robert.—This is one of the most simple and excellent of sauces, and is called after a French cook of the name. It is very good with either pork, poultry, or mutton. Put a quantity of flour into a dry pan, and brown it. When browned cut a couple of onions up and brown them; then add a table-spoonful of ketchup, a little pepper and salt, a tea-spoonful of mustard, the juice of half a lemon, or a table-spoonful of vinegar, and half a pint of stock; let it simmer for ten minutes.

Wine Sauce for Venison, Hare, or Kangaroo.—A quarter of a pint of port wine or claret, or dark Sydney wine; the same quantity of good gravy, and a table-spoonful of currant jelly; warm up, and serve.

Sharp Sauce for Venison, Hare, or Kangaroo.—Put into a saucepan half a pint of the best white wine vinegar, and a quarter of a pound of white sugar; let it simmer, and serve.

Sauce for Fried Meat.—When meat of any kind has been fried in fat in a pan—whether chops, steaks, or cutlets—when they are done remove them, and pour out of the pan all but a couple of table-spoonfuls. Mix up, say half a pint of flour and water, pour it into the pan, and let it simmer until done; add a table-spoonful of ketchup. This is very savoury if properly made.

Bread Sauce.—Boil two onions, cut in parts, in milk until reduced to pulp. Pour the milk on stale bread, and cover it close. In half an hour put it into a saucepan, with a piece of butter, and add a very small quantity of flour; add pepper and salt, and let it simmer for ten minutes.

Sauce au Roi.—Mix two quarts of vinegar, a pint of soy, and a pint of walnut ketchup, with six cloves, six shalots, and a quarter of an ounce of cayenne pepper; let it stand for use.

Kelly's Sauce Piquante.—This is the sauce of an epicure, whose name it bears. Put a table-spoonful of parsley leaves, and the same of capers, into a mortar, and pound them; add a table-spoonful of fresh mustard, and three hard yolks of eggs, and properly mix the whole. Then add six anchovies, boned and forced through a sieve, a table-spoonful of vinegar, two of oil, and a finely-chopped shalot, and mix the whole. When to be used, stir the sauce into half a pint of melted butter or strong gravy.

Wou-Wou Sauce.—Chop some parsley leaves fine, and add two or three pickled walnuts or cucumbers. Put into a pan a bit of butter; when it has melted stir in a table-spoonful of flour, and about half a pint of broth, a table-spoonful of vinegar, the same quantity of ketchup, or port wine, and a tea-spoonful of mustard. Let it simmer till thick, and then add the parsley leaves and pickles.

Poor Man's Sauce.—Pick a handful of parsley leaves from the stalks, mince them very fine, strew over them a little salt; shred fine half a dozen young green onions, add them to the parsley, and put them into a sauceboat, with three table-spoonfuls of oil and five of vinegar; add some black ground pepper and salt; stir together, and serve. Pickles of any kind may be added, cut small, or grated horseradish.

Dr. Kitchener says, that the rich sometimes order the peasants' fare, as a variety. According to Dryden—
"The rich, tired with continual feasts,
For change, become the next poor tenant's guests;
Drink hearty draughts of ale from plain brown bowls,
And snatch the homely rasher from the coals."

Sauce for Roast Wild Ducks.—One salt-spoonful of salt, one ditto of cayenne, one dessert-spoonful of lemon-juice, one ditto of ketchup, two ditto of Harvey, three ditto of port wine, and the same of claret. To be mixed, warmed, and poured over, before the dish comes on the table. Keep away all fat from the bird when done.

Steak Sauce.—Pound an ounce of black pepper, half an ounce of allspice, an ounce of salt, and an ounce of grated horseradish and shalots. Put these articles to a pint of mushroom ketchup, and let them infuse for a month.

Bèchamel Sauce.—The name of the *maitre d'hotel* of Louis XIV. was Bèchamel, and this sauce is named after him, for he it was who first compounded it. Put into a saucepan a piece of butter, onions, and a carrot shred, some parsley and mushrooms; set it on the fire; put in three spoonfuls of flour, half a pint of cream, salt, white pepper, and nutmeg. Keep it stirred until it boils. Let it simmer for half an hour, then strain, and it is fit for use. When ready to serve add a small piece of fresh butter.

Sauce à la Maitre d'Hotel.—Take a piece of butter, a little flour, parsley and chives chopped small; put all into a saucepan, with half a glass of water, a little salt and pepper. Just before serving, set on the fire; keep turning it till all the ingredients are well incorporated; then add the juice of a lemon, and serve.

Sauce à la Rimolade.—Put into a sauceboat a shalot, chervil, chives, a head of garlic, all chopped very fine; salt and pepper; beat it up with mustard, oil, and vinegar.

Dr. Kitchener's Sauce Superlative.—Claret and port wine, a pint each; the same of mushroom ketchup; half a pint of walnut liquor; pounded anchovies, four ounces; fresh lemon-peel finely pared, one ounce; sliced shalots, an ounce; scraped horseradish, an ounce; allspice and black pepper, half an ounce; cayenne, one drachm; curry-powder, three drachms; celery seed, bruised, one drachm. Put into a wide-mouthed bottle, and shake every day for a fortnight.

Universal Sauce.—Into a pint of broth put a glass of white wine, salt, pepper, grated lemon, a bay leaf, and a spoonful of lemon juice. Let them macerate by the side of the fire for ten hours; and when served, pour over either game, fish, or vegetables, or send to table in a sauce-boat.

French Shalot Sauce.—Chop fine some shalots, boil them in vinegar, with pepper and salt to taste. About a wine-glassful of vinegar will be sufficient. Add some good stock, thickened lightly.

Sauce Blonde.—Roll about two ounces of butter in flour, moisten it with pale stock, and season it. This delicate sauce is often used in place of white sauce.

Dutch Horseradish Sauce.—Scrape some horseradish fine, put it in a stewpan, with some stock; let it stew; add some flour, butter, and a little vinegar.

Roux.—Melt a piece of butter in a saucepan, to which add as much flour as will give the sauce proper consistency; when it becomes of a brown colour, add the other ingredients which your sauce is made from.

Thickening.—Beat some eggs, separate the yolks from the whites, beat up the yolks with a spoonful or two of the sauce or soup you intend to thicken. Stir it till the mixture is complete; remove the saucepan from the fire, and pour the contents by degrees into the same, turning it with the other hand all the time; set it again on the fire in order to thicken it, still keeping it stirred, and on no account let it boil.

Turtle Sauce.—Put into a pan a pint of beef gravy thickened; add a wine-glassful of sherry, the juice and peel of a lemon, a few leaves of basil, a shalot divided, a few grains of cayenne, and a little essence of anchovy. Let them simmer for five minutes, and strain through a tammy.

This is a very good accompaniment for other dishes besides turtle.

Quin Sauce.—Two wine-glassfuls of port, two of walnut pickle, four of ketchup, half a dozen pounded anchovies, a few shalots sliced and pounded, a table-spoonful of soy, and half a drachm of cayenne. Let these ingredients simmer for ten minutes, and strain it into bottles for use.

Poivrade Sauce.—Put a bit of butter as big as an egg into a stewpan, with two or three onions, carrots, and turnips cut in slices, a clove of garlic, two shalots, two cloves, a bay leaf, thyme and basil; keep turning them in the pan until they get a colour; shake in some flour, and add a glass of red wine, a glass of water, and a spoonful of vinegar, with a little pepper and salt. Boil half an hour, skim and strain it.—*La Cuisinière Bourgeoise.*

Bonne Bouche, for goose, duck, or roast pork.—Mix a dessert-spoonful of mustard, a salt-spoonful of salt, and a little cayenne in a large glassful of port wine or claret; pour it on the meat just before serving. A tablespoonful of ketchup may be added.

ANCIENT SAUCES.—And the Lydians were also the first people to introduce the use of the sauce called caruca, concerning the preparation of which all those who have written cookery books have spoken a good deal—namely, Glaucus the Locrian, and Mithœcus, and Dionysius, and the two Heraclidæ (who were by birth Syracusans), and Agis, and Epœmus, and Dionysius, and also Hegesippus, and Erasistratus, and Enthydemus, and Criton; and besides these, Stephanus, and Archytas, and Acestius, and Acesias, and Diocles, and Philistion; for I know that all these have written cookery books. And the Lydians, too, used to speak of a dish which they called *candaulus*; and there was not one kind of candaulus, but three, so wholly devoted were they to luxury. And Hegesippus, the Tarentine, says, that the candaulus is made of boiled meat and grated bread, and Phrygian cheese, and aniseed, and thick broth; and it is mentioned by Alexis, in his "Woman all Night; or, the Spinners;" and it is a cook who is represented as speaking:—

A. And, besides this, we now will serve you up
  A dish whose name's candaulus.
B.   I've ne'er tasted
  Candaulus, nor have I heard of it.
A. 'Tis a most grand invention, and 'tis mine;
  And if I put a dish of it before you,
  Such will be your delight that you'll devour
  Your very fingers e'er you lose a bit of it.
  We here will get some balls of snow-white wool.
    *   *   *   *   *   *
  You will serve up an egg well shred, and twice
  Boiled till it's hard; a sausage, too, of honey;
  Some pickle from the frying-pan, some slices
  Of new-made Cynthian cheese; and then
  A bunch of grapes, steep'd in a cup of wine;
  But this part of the dish is always laugh'd at,
  And yet it is the mainstay of the meal.
B. Laugh on, my friend; but now be off, I beg,
  With all your talk about candauli, and
  Your sausages, and dishes, and such luxuries.
        Athenæus, literally translated by Yonge.

MEDICAL.—The faculty the stomach has of communicating the impressions made by the various substances that are put into it is such, that it seems more like a nervous expansion from the brain than a mere receptacle for food.—*Waterhouse.*

X.—GRAVIES.

"I will play the cook."—TITUS ANDRONICUS.

Beef Gravy.—Put into a stewpan a slice of bacon or ham, with four or five pounds of gravy beef cut into pieces, a carrot, an onion, a couple of cloves, and a head of celery. Put a quart of water to it, or a little more, and let it simmer for three hours, and strain through a tamis.

Savoury Gravy.—Made in the same way as beef gravy, with a larger proportion of sweet herbs and lemon peel, a bay leaf and shalot.

Veal Gravy.—Cut three pounds of veal into slices, with a small quantity of ham or bacon, and simmer in the same manner as beef gravy.

Brown Gravy.—Cut onions into a stewpan, about six or eight, depending on their size, with an ounce of butter. Set it on a slow fire, and turn the onions until lightly browned. Now stir in gradually half an ounce of flour, with a little stock, and pepper and salt, simmer for a short time, and add a table-spoonful of ketchup.

Garlic Gravy.—Cut a pound of beef into small pieces, pepper and salt it, and put it into a stewpan, with a couple of carrots, and four cloves of garlic, sliced, a quarter of a pound of ham, and a little water. Put it over a slow fire, and turn the meat when it sticks. When it is browned, dredge it with flour, and add a quart of stock, a bunch of sweet herbs, a little spice, and the slice of a lemon. Let it simmer for an hour, take off the fat, and strain.

Gravy for Roast Meats.—Joints of mutton or beef—if the meats are mellow and juicy—require no gravy, other than a little hot water, with a little salt in it, poured over the meat.

Shalot Gravy.—A few drops of shalot vinegar, to a pint of gravy, will give one of the finest flavours in cookery.

Giblet Gravy.—A rich gravy may be made from giblets by letting them simmer for about three hours, with an onion, pepper and salt, and a thickening of a little flour, with the squeeze of a lemon.

To Clarify Gravy.—Put on the stock in a stewpan, break an egg, and use the white and the shell; beat them together, put them into the stock, stir it with a whisk. When it has simmered for a short time, strain through a tamis.

Gravy without any Meat.—Mix half a pint of beer, the same quantity of water, with pepper, salt, lemon peel, a couple of cloves, and two spoonfuls of walnut or mushroom ketchup, together. Flour and skin an onion or two, and fry it in butter until brown. Then put the mixture into a stewpan, and simmer it for a quarter of an hour, and it is fit for use.

GENTEEL ECONOMY.—A certain lady, whose taste is equal to her economy, was under the necessity of asking a friend to dinner. The following is a bill of fare, and expense of each dish which was found on the table:—

	s.	d.
At top, 2 herrings	0	1
Middle, 1½ oz. of butter, melted	0	½
Bottom, 3 mutton chops, cut thin	0	2
One side, 1 lb. small potatoes	0	½
On other side, pickled cabbage	0	½
Fish removed, two larks, plenty of crumbs	0	1½
Mutton removed, French roll boiled for pudding	0	½
Parsley for garnish	0	½
	0	7

The dinner was served up on china, looked light, tasty, and pretty; the table small, and the dishes well proportioned. We hope each newly-married lady will keep this as a lesson; it is worth knowing how to serve up seven dishes, consisting of a dish of fish, mutton, couple of birds, pudding, vegetables, and sauce, for *sevenpence!*—*Newspaper Scrap.*

XI.—THE COOK.

"We have seen good families in England of the name of *Cook*, or *Coke*. I know not what they may think, but we may depend on it that they all originally sprang from some real or professional cooks, and that they need not be ashamed of their extraction, any more than the *Butlers, Parkers, Grooms*, &c."—*Pegge*.

The *status* of the cooks of our day is far below their vocation. The wages of female cooks range from £15 to £40 per annum in England. We recollect seeing in the London *Times*, a few years since, a police case, in which the cook of the establishment of that most charitable lady, Miss Burdett Coutts, figured, and the wages that she sought to recover from her mistress were £40 per annum; so we may assume that that is top pay for a female cook in England. In the Australias this is nearly the minimum wages of almost all house servants. Men cooks in the mother country, if they are professionals, of course receive higher salaries; but how few there are who are able to pay cooks above £20 per annum! The *Edinburgh Review* (vol. lix., page 536) tells us that of the sixteen millions of people who inhabit England there are but 108,000 who keep men servants, 152,000 who pay duty on horses, and 26,000 who possess the luxury of a four-wheeled carriage; so we may infer that only the "upper ten thousand" employ regular cooks. We believe that nearly as many are employed in the Australias. We are informed that Carême, when *chef* to George IV., had the *promise* of a salary of £1,000 per annum [the London aldermen were in the habit of giving enormous prices for his state *pâtes*], and that the Earl of Sefton paid Ure £300 per annum, and left him £100 a year at his death. What Francatelli received in royal service we do not know. Soyer made more by his works than he did by his labour, and the "Art of Dining" has it that his execution was not equal to his conception. The British public are bound, however, to respect his memory, as his conduct in going to the Crimea to superintend the hospital *cuisine*, and his visiting Ireland during the famine, to reform the cookery there, was beyond all praise. We believe it to be a fact that the celebrated *chef* to the late Marquis of Abercorn refused to accompany the Duke of Richmond as lord-lieutenant to Ireland, at a salary of £400 per annum, on learning that there was no Italian Opera in Dublin. So much for the stars of the profession; now for the commonalty. Pity the sorrows of a poor cook at £15 per annum, who is serving under "the Limited Liability Act" as to tea and sugar. She must be neat and clean, orderly in habit, good tempered, obliging, and respectful; she must keep the kitchen tidy and have everything in its place, and a place for everything; she is, moreover, required to *think*, and to cook breakfasts, luncheons, and dinners without a fault, and to make pap, broth, and gruel between the *heats*, as they say in horse-racing; she must be ready to cook a hot supper when necessary, as the master, or mistress, or Master Tom, Dick, and Harry can't bear cold things; she will be also required to do a great deal of nursing, must be up late and early, and on no account take snuff, neither must she be seen with a pipe (if Irish), or indulge to excess in gin or beer, nor have any followers in the shape of cousins of the masculine gender. What is she to do under the circumstances? Pack up her traps, without delay, and slope for the colonies, where she will be better paid, better fed, better treated, have tea three times per diem, and find a husband very soon after she arrives!

Apropos of a cook's great qualification, according to M. Brillat Saverin, and of every master and mistress who can pay the wages of one :—

APHORISM.—*Of all the qualities of a cook the most indispensable is punctuality;* and there is another essential that must never be lost sight of—that of cleanliness, which Scripture authority tells us is next to godliness.

In 1842, a poor fellow was taken before the authorities of Paris for begging in the street. He had studied the science of cookery under the celebrated Carême, and was the inventor of the delicious *saumons truffes à la broche:* he attributed his poverty to the decline of cookery from a science to a low art! We remember to have read that cooks, in nine cases out of ten, after ministering to the luxury of the opulent, creep into holes and corners, and pass neglected out of the world.—*Hints for the Table.*

A COOKS' REFUGE.—Why not organise an asylum for decayed cooks of good character? We are quite willing to contribute a large number of copies of this work for their benefit; but the only drawback to that offer might be that they would realise nothing. To show the rate of wages in England, we have extracted the following advertisements from late numbers of the London *Daily Telegraph* and *Morning Star* newspapers :—

WANTED, a COOK, about twenty-five years of age, in a family, twenty miles from London. Must understand Baking and Dairy. Wages £14, everything found.—Address prepaid, stating all particulars, to A. M., care of Mr. Young, Baker, Fore Street, Upper Edmonton, Middlesex, N.

WANTED, a GENERAL SERVANT, in a private family, a few miles from town; must be active and cleanly, and have good testimonials. Wages £8.—Apply at 247, High Street, Poplar.

NURSERY GOVERNESS.—A situation as NURSERY GOVERNESS, in London, WANTED, by a young lady, aged eighteen. Can teach French perfectly, the piano, drawing, and is a good needlewoman. As it would be her first situation, she would accept £12 per annum and laundry expenses.—Address Ruth, Post-office, Sussex Place, Hyde Park.

WANTED, IN-DOOR PORTER. Wages £12 per annum. — Apply, after three o'clock in the afternoon of this day, to Mr. Garrard, Laceman, 56, Westbourne Grove, Bayswater.

THE COOK AND THE DOCTOR.—If the administration of animal food, in a wholesome and agreeable form, is like life from the dead, how long shall any of the homes of England be without it? There will be good meals in every house when there is a good cook there. If we cannot put good dinners upon all tables, we may proceed a long way towards putting a cook into every house in England. Let us have a kitchen attached to every girls' school, and schools for cookery in every town, and the nation will be nearer than it has ever been yet to being well fed, which is the same thing as saying that the children will grow up well, the men and women will wear well, and the aged will go down to their graves in comfort. This will not be disputed by doctor or nurse, gentle or simple; and if it be true, almost everybody may save and fortify life by teaching, or getting taught to one or more future wife, mistress, or maid, the simple, pleasant, and inestimable art of spreading the household table.—*Harriet Martineau.*

XII.—CONDIMENTS:

Substances taken with the food, to season or improve its flavour, or to render it more wholesome or digestible. The principal condiments are common salt, vinegar, lemon-juice, spices, aromatic herbs, oil, butter, sugar, honey, and sauces. Most of these, in moderation, promote the appetite and digestion, but their excessive use tends to vitiate the gastric juice and injure the stomach.—*Cooley.*

Cayenne.—This is the pounded seed of the capsicum. It is a tropical plant, and is grown in the East and West Indies, and America. That produced and grown at Norfolk Island cannot be exceeded for flavour and strength.

Cinnamon: the under bark of a species of bay tree, which is extensively grown on the Malabar Coast. It possesses a fine aromatic flavour.

Cassia.—The bark of cassia is produced from a similar tree to cinnamon, but it is not so full flavoured.

Allspice, the production of a tropical plant, much used in cookery.

Ginger is grown in the East and West Indies. It is a fine stomachic, and useful in many ways.

Cloves.—These are the buds of an Indian tree, not arrived at maturity, and they afford a beautiful flavour when used for any purpose.

Nutmeg is the fruit of a tree, grown more numerously in the Molucca Islands, and is used very extensively in cookery. It is highly aromatic.

Elecampane has always been esteemed in the domestic herbal, as its leaves are aromatic and bitter. The root is used to flavour confectionery cakes, which bear its name. It is a tonic.

Mace: the slight shell that covers the nutmeg. It is used in a similar way.

Mustard can be cultivated anywhere. It is of a pungent nature. Its preparation is with cold water; if hot water is used, it destroys its pungency. Durham mustard has a proverbial reputation. The moderate use of this condiment is considered wholesome. The French add vinegar, and other additions to it, and dispose of it in bottles in a liquid state, and not dry, as we do.

Falstaff tells Poins, in the "Second Part of Henry the Fourth," that "his wit is as thick as Tewkesbury mustard," the town of that name being a great place for this condiment in the days of Shakespeare.

MUSTARD.—Why buy this, when you can grow it in your garden? The stuff you buy is half drugs, and is injurious to health. Your mustard would look brown instead of yellow; but the former colour is as good as the latter; and as to the taste, the real mustard has certainly a much better than that of the drugs and flour which go under the name of mustard.—*Cobbett.*

Onions are a bulbous root much used in cookery, and are considered a strengthening food, and a stomachic. There are many varieties of onions, and of the same description of plant, viz., garlic, shalot, leek, olives, and the cream-bole. The potato-onion, grown by planting sets, is an earlier kind, and is more mild and useful than any sorts. Potato-onions, stewed properly, and served with roasts of any kind, are viewed with considerable favour by lovers of gastronomy. Soups made of this vegetable are considered highly restorative to the system.

GARLIC.—Garlic has, of all our plants, the greatest strength, affords most nourishment, and supplies most spirits to those who eat little flesh, as the poorer people seldom do in the hotter, and especially the more eastern climates; so that the labour of the world seems to be performed by the force and virtue of garlic, leeks, and onions, no other food of herbs or plants yielding strength enough for such labour.—*Sir William Temple on Health and Long Life.*

Marjoram.—This is one of the sweet herbs used in the *cuisine*. There are many sorts—the pot-marjoram, the sweet-marjoram, and the common.

Savory.—This plant is used dried and bottled. There are two kinds, the winter and summer.

Basil.—There are two kinds of basil—the sweet and the least, and it is a herb in every-day use.

Sweet basil, called rayhan in Persia, and generally found in churchyards.—*Notes to "Lalla Rookh."*

Thyme.—This is another of the sweet herbs, and is in great request by the cook. The lemon-thyme is the most flavoured, and the common the least so.

Pennyroyal is not much in request, and is sometimes used where mint cannot be procured.

Sage.—This is a very important herb where pork, geese, or ducks are concerned; not omitting some dry for pea-soup. The best kind for cookery is the sort possessing a tinge of purple.

Parsley.—There are three varieties: the common, the broad-leaved, and the curled. The common is the best flavoured, but the curled is most in request for garnishing. It will keep well dried, but may be obtained fresh all the year.

Tarragon.—This herb is duly appreciated by connoisseurs, but neglected by the commonalty. It is highly aromatic and full of flavour.

It is a curious fact, strikingly exemplified in the history of condiments, that such articles as are, in the first instance, disagreeable to the palate are those for which we afterwards acquire the strongest partiality, and which even become necessary for our comfort; whereas the frequent repetition of flavours that are originally grateful is very apt to produce a sense of satiety, or even of disgust.—*Dr. Bostock's "Pharmacologia."*

Clary: a plant of the same kind, and used as a flavour to different dishes.

Fennel is used particularly with fish. It is a pretty garnish.

Celery.—This vegetable is eaten plain, and cooked as sauce for different joints; it is also made to flavour soups and made dishes.

Borage is not much used in cookery, as its flavour is a little bitter.

Horseradish is used sliced or grated, especially with roast beef and beef-steaks; but its agreeable pungent flavour soon evaporates. In Sweden the Chinese horseradish is cultivated, and oil obtained from it. Horseradish is not very dissimilar from the poisonous monkshood, or aconite, which has been the cause of many deaths. The outer resemblance of the roots is slight, but when the two roots are scraped, monkshood is succulent, and soon turns pink, while horseradish retains its colour. The taste of monkshood is bitter, while that of horseradish is pungent. The cook should at once be taught the difference between the two roots.

Chervil.—The flavour of chervil is pleasant, and it may be employed in made dishes to advantage, as well as in soups and salads.

Capers.—This is the mere bud of a shrub, grown in the north of Europe, salted and pickled. It is an excellent addition to fish and boiled meats.

Nasturtiums.—These seeds are used as capers occasionally, and they are pickled and used in salads.

Barberries are natives of England; they have a pleasant acid flavour, and make good pickles or preserves.

Gherkins are pickled, and also used as an addition to salads and made dishes.

Beet-root.—This root makes most excellent winter salad when dressed with pepper, oil, and vinegar, and they are elegant garnish for many dishes.

Mushrooms.—Having already entered into the detail of making ketchup, and cooking this edible fungi, we have little more to say. There are several species of *agaraci* so much resembling the mushroom proper, that the cook must be wary, or fatal results may happen from the use of the poisonous varieties.

Morils: a species of mushroom, of an agreeable flavour, that might be more often used with different dishes.

Truffles are a fungus, of a round oblong form, of the *cryptogamia*, or mushroom tribe, found in the earth, about a foot below the surface, by trained dogs and pigs; and the best are of a blackish brown colour. They are nourishing and stimulant to the system. The finest are found in Perigord in France, and they are obtained in Carolina in America, and in some parts of England. The French dish of *dinde aux truffes* (turkey with truffles) is considered by gourmets as one of the first dishes in gastronomy. M. Brillat Savarin, the author of the "Philosophy of Taste," whom we have so often quoted, declares (and we are bound to defer to his authority)—"La truffe est le demait de la cuisine."

Bay.—This is a species of laurel, and the leaves are used to flavour custards, and other dishes: but the cook must be cautious not to use the leaves of the cherry-laurel, which are poisonous.

Saffron: a root, the flowers of which are merely used for colouring yellow; extensively used in cookery in the East, as well as in Spain and Portugal. It takes 40,000 flowers to yield a pound, and it was used as a colouring matter in early days, as the bard has it—"I must have saffron, to colour the Warden pies."

Anglica, commonly called angelica, is the stalk of a plant, used in the confectionery line for preserving, as well as being candied.

Vanilla is the produce of a climbing tree, and its pod. It is employed to give a perfume to different articles of confectionery; and is elsewhere observed on.

Sugar is the expressed juice of the cane of its name, and is used extensively in the *cuisine*. In France it is prepared mostly from beet-root, and the sugar assumes the appearance of honeycomb. The moderate use of sugar gives a mellowness to different dishes. In America a large quantity of sugar is obtained from the sap of the maple. Honey was used instead of sugar until the fifteenth century; and beverages were made of it, called mead, metheglin, pigment, and moret.

Sugar is the sweet constituent of vegetable and animal products.—*Ure.*

Orange is a fruit grown in all warm climates. The juice is a sweet acid of a pleasant nature.

Avenzoar magnifies the juice of a pomegranate, if it be sweet, and especially rose-water, which he would have to be used in every dish: which they put in practice in those hot countries about Damascus, where (if we may believe the relations of Vertomannus) many hogsheads of rose-water are to be sold in the market at once, it is in so great request with them.—*Burton's "Cure of Melancholy."*

Orange Flowers: a distillation from the flower, much used in cakes and confectionery.

Verjuice is the expressed juice of the unripe grape, fermented. In England the juice of the crab-apple is so termed. It is often used for various dishes in preference to vinegar.

Olive is a fruit of the tree of the same name. It is pickled for use; and the olive pressed, produces the valuable vegetable oil so much used.

Arrowroot.—This is the powder of a tree grown in tropical climates, and is used as a thickening; it is also boiled for invalids, being highly nutritious.

CONDIMENTS.

Tapioca is a starch, produced from the roots of the cassava plant. It is used in a similar manner to the arrowroot.

Salsop is the root of a plant grown in the East, where it is used as an article of food; it is also taken as a drink by invalids.

Sago is the pith of the palm-tree, and is prepared in a similar way to tapioca.

Soy we have elsewhere observed on, so that we do not require to elaborate on its qualities.

Chutney is a condiment that we have also given the recipe for making, in another place.

Curry-powder: an Indian condiment of a very wholesome and agreeable kind; in daily use at every meal in the East.

Lemon.—The expressed juice of the lemon is a most wholesome and pleasant acid. It is extensively used in cookery and confectionery, as well as for various kinds of drinks. If persons would consult their health, it would be even more generally used than it is.

Lime is a large species of the lemon kind, and its expressed juice is even more acid than the lemon.

Citron.—The juice of the citron is sweeter, and the peel of the fruit is used largely, in a candied state, for puddings and cakes.

Vinegar is the fermented liquor of wine and beer, and is a useful and necessary article in common life. Pyroligneous acid is obtained from wood, and is very useful in preserving meat from being tainted, and if used in moderation on bacon and hams, gives the articles a smoky flavour, and preserves them from the hopper, or bacon fly.

Salt.—There is no condiment in such general use as salt, and with many individuals the deprivation of it would not only affect their health, but would render their food nauseating and indigestible. Nothing improves the growth of various animals so much as its moderate use. Salt is, next to bread, the most important necessary of life. The consumption in Great Britain alone, exclusive of Ireland, is 180,000 tons per annum. Previously to 1823 there was an oppressive tax of 15s. per bushel on salt in England; and during its continuance the retail price was $4\frac{1}{2}$d. per lb. It is now only one halfpenny per lb. It is the chief condiment in all countries, and with every civilised people.

Salt in bread is important; the French use less than we do. The ancient laws of Holland sentenced men to be kept on bread unmixed with salt, and in a moist climate the punishment was a severe one.

UNLEARNED.—We have not given the names of the above condiments according to Linnæus, nor in their "natural order"—which we could easily have done—for the reason that we are desirous of making this little work "more useful than ornamental."

XIII.—SAVOURY PIES AND PUDDINGS.

Pies.—" Well, though, I've heard you say," said George, "that Jenny was a pretty fair cook."
"So I did," said Aunt Chloe, "I may say dat. Good, plain, common cookin' Jenny 'll do : make a good pone of bread, bile her taters *far*. Her corn cakes isn't extra, not extra, now, Jenny's corn cakes isn't, but then they's far. But Lor, come to the higher branches, and what *can* she do ? Why, she make pies—sartain she does ; but what kinder crust ? Can she make your real flecky paste, as melts in your mouth, and lies all up like a puff ? Now, I went over thar when Miss Mary was gwine to be married, and Jenny, she jest showed me de weddin' pies. Jenny and I is good friends, ye know : I never said nothin' ; but go along, Mas'r George ! Why, I shouldn't sleep a wink for a week if I had a batch of pies like them ar ; why, dey wan't no 'count 't all."—*Uncle Tom's Cabin.*

Rump-Steak Pie.—Cut two pounds of rump-steaks into pieces ; chop very fine a few shalots, and mix them with half an ounce of pepper and salt mixed. Strew some of the mixture on each layer of steaks, and so on until the dish is full. Add a mushroom ketchup and thickening, with a few hard-boiled eggs. A few oysters is an improvement. The paste is elsewhere given.

Chicken, rabbit, fowl and ham, lamb, fish, partridge, quail, and pigeon are made in a similar way. The general mode is to stew the meats before putting them into the crust. Oyster, lobster, crayfish, chicken and ham, veal and mutton patties are made in a like way. With a partridge or pigeon pie, place a beef-steak over as well as under the birds. The Strasburg pâtes, made from geese livers, have a world-wide reputation.

Game Pie for Christmas.—Take a pheasant, a hare, a capon, two pigeons, and two rabbits ; bone them and put them into the paste in the shape of a bird, with the livers and hearts, two mutton kidneys, forcemeat and egg balls, seasoning, spice, ketchup, and mushrooms, filled up with gravy made from the different bones, and bake sufficiently.—*London Salters' Company's Books in the Reign of Richard II.*

Raised Pies.—Take a pound and a half of the best lard, and three quarters of a pint of new milk. Boil them together, stir the boiling mixture into four pounds of flour ; knead the paste well, and set it down before the fire for twenty minutes before using. To raise the crust of a pie, you must make your paste warm, roll it out, and mould it in a mould. When cold take it off, and fill it up with pork or veal, which must be cut up small, seasoned with white pepper, salt, and dried sage, put on the top, and egg if you like. Fancy leaves can be laid on the top, to make it ornamental. Bake well.

Any kind of meat, poultry, or game may be put into raised pies. Sometimes the crust is made hard and ornamental in a mould called a timbale (to raise the crust of a pie in this way without a mould is rather a difficult manipulation) ; and on other occasions the crust is made for eating. Raised pies of vegetables alone are an exquisite dish.

Sea Pie.—Make a thick crust, as for a pudding ; line a dish with it, put in a layer of sliced onions, then a layer of salt beef cut in slices, a layer of potatoes sliced, a layer of pork, and another of onions. Strew pepper over all, and cover with the crust, and tie with a cloth, well floured, so that it will not stick when done. Boil for a couple of hours, and serve.

<small>In large dinners, two cold pies of game or poultry are often sent to table with the first course, and allowed to remain between the courses. By this means, the epicure and dainty eater always has something before him. The pies are not in the way, but improve the appearance of the table.—*Ude.*</small>

Devonshire Squab Pie.—Lay mutton-chops, or mutton, at the bottom of the dish; on the meat strew some onions, with pepper, salt, a little sugar, and half a tea-cupful of water. Place on the top apples and potatoes, in layers, cut thin; cover the sides and top of the dish with crust, and bake well.

<small>In Devonshire and Cornwall the facility offered for baking is great, from the quantity of furze; and the use of pies is so general, that there is a proverb, "that the devil will not come into Cornwall, for fear of being put in a pie."</small>

French Vol-au-vent.—Prepare puff paste; make an under-crust of short paste as thick as a penny piece; moisten it a little, and over this crust put some puff paste, well rolled. Put these two crusts, thus placed over each other, at the bottom of a pie-dish; cover it with a lid the size intended for the *vol-au-vent*. Cut the puff paste all round the lid, and brush the surface with the yolk of an egg; with a knife cut the *vol-au-vent* within an inch and a half of the edge; that is, strike the knife into the paste three-quarters of its thickness, to form the cover. Bake it in a moderate hot oven, and when the crust is well browned take it out. Fill it with whatever you like; *ragoût* of fowl, fish, veal, or any mortal thing, for the *vol-au-vent* bears the name of the *ragoût* it is filled with. If the puff paste is made at seven turns, according to the mode *à la Soyer*, it should rise in baking more than four times its height, if put into the oven an inch thick.

<small>*Vol-au-vent* may be used for fruit as well as meat.</small>

Beef-steak Pudding.—Take two pounds of rump-steak, and cut into seasonable pieces; and cut into shreds two or three onions. Paste the pudding-basin with good crust, not too rich nor too poor. Put the meat into the basin, with some pepper and salt, and a dozen oysters, with a little thickening, composed of mushroom ketchup, flour and water, and mustard. Simmer for an hour and a half, and serve in the basin; or turn it out, if the gravy in the pudding can be retained.

<small>Connoisseurs prefer a beef-steak pudding to a beef-steak pie; and mutton, veal and ham, kidney, sausage, fowl, fish, and game puddings may be served in a similar way.</small>

Yorkshire Pudding (*under roast beef or mutton*).—Put six table-spoonfuls of flour into a basin, with a little salt, and stir in gradually a pint of milk to make a thin batter, and mind it is not lumpy. When it is well mixed, put in three eggs, well beaten up, and a little more milk. Place it under the meat, so that the dripping may fall on it. Serve as free from fat as possible.

Pease Pudding.—Soak the peas for ten or twelve hours; tie them loosely in a cloth, leaving room for them to swell, and simmer for a couple of hours. When tender, drain them; rub them through a colander with a wooden spoon; add an ounce of butter, one egg, beat up, and pepper and salt to taste. Beat them well together, tie lightly in a cloth, and boil for half an hour.

To be served with corned beef or boiled pork.

THE DANGER OF MEAT PIE.—All learned toxicologists and chemists appear to have forgotten the important fact that, if a meat pie is made without a hole in the crust, to let out certain emanations from the meat, colic, vomiting, and other symptoms of slight poisoning will occur. I have known two instances of large parties being affected in this manner from eating pies that had no hole in them.—*Correspondent of "Lancet."*

LIVING IN THE REIGN OF HENRY VII.—The records of the Percy family, in the time of Henry VII., show that the permanent household numbered 166 persons, and the average of guests was fifty; and the whole of the washing for these 216 persons was, for one year, 40s., a sum probably equal to £40 in the present day, most of which was for the chapel linen. From midsummer to Michaelmas was the only time they indulged in fresh meat; and the instructions say—"My lord has on his table for breakfast, at seven in the morning, a quart of beer and wine, two pieces of salt fish, six red herrings, four white ones; and on flesh days, half a chine of beef or mutton boiled." At dinner, men ranking as knights had a table-cloth, which was washed once a month. They had no napkins, and the fingers were extensively used in feeding. Until the thirteenth century straw was the bed of kings; and before that date the king and his family slept in the same chamber. The first change was to throw a coverlet over the sleeper; then another was used, and the persons undressed, their linen being substituted for blankets. Beatrice says she would "as lief sleep in the woollen," which shows that such a thing was done even in Shakespeare's time.—*W. Tite, F.S.A.*

XIV.—POULTRY.

Balthazar: Small cheer and great welcome make a merry feast.
Antipholus of Ephesus: Ay, to a niggardly host, and more sparing guest:
But though my cates* be mean, take them on good part;
Better cheer may you have, but not with better heart.
Comedy of Errors.

Turkey Braised.—Monsieur le Jacque has earned some celebrity by the invention of this dish, and the following distich speaks to the advantage of the *braise*:—

"Turkey boiled
Is turkey spoiled,
And turkey roast
Is turkey lost;
But turkey *braised,*
The Lord be praised!"

The turkey is trussed and stuffed in the usual manner. The bottom of a stewpan is covered with slices of bacon, chopped carrots, onions, sweet herbs, salt, pepper, allspice, and mace. On these ingredients lay the turkey, with its breast downwards, and over the bird place a layer of the same materials. Cover the top close, and put the pan in an oven, or on a hot-plate, for three or four hours, until it is done. Only let the dish gently simmer in its own steam, and it will become mellow and tender to a degree.

This is the French *braise,* and any joint cooked in a similar way acquires a tenderness and flavour, like the French *potage;* a single spoonful of which will lap the patient

---

* Dishes of meat.

in Elysium; and while one drop remains on the tongue, each other sense is eclipsed by the voluptuous thrilling of the lingual nerves.

Fowl in Batter.—Truss the fowl, then make a forcemeat thus:—Chop fine a handful of mushrooms, a little rasped bacon, a few bleached artichoke bottoms, a few truffles, a little beef suet, an anchovy, and parsley. Mix these together, with bread crumbs, pepper, salt, and mixed spice. Put a lump of butter into a stewpan; when it is warm add the mixture, and let it fry a little; moisten it with a glass of white wine, and after it has stewed a quarter of an hour take it off the fire, and add the yolks of two eggs. Put this forcemeat into the body of the fowl, cover it with paper, and roast. When the fowl is half done, remove the paper. In the meantime have a light batter made, with a little salt and grated nutmeg in it. Baste the fowl with it, so as to give it a thin coating. When the first coating is dry, add a second and third, until a delicate coat of the batter is formed of a light-brown colour. Serve with sauce of any kind, thickened with cream.

The above is a refined, delicate, and expensive mode of dressing a fowl.

Canards à la Braise.—Lard a pair of ducks, and place them in a stewpan, breasts downwards, in which you must lay a couple of slices of bacon or ham, with two onions sliced, salt, pepper, and a glass of claret or port; let it stew gently, and when done serve with sauce; either morels, capers, or artichokes may be sliced and added, with a small quantity of *consommé* or stock.

Political canard is a literary dish, very often served up at the Antipodes by the local Press. M. Quetelet, in the *Annuaire de l'Académie Française*, attributes the first application of the term *canard*, or hoax, to Norbet Cornelissen, who gave out this hit at the ridiculous pieces of intelligence in the public journals.

Stewed Duck, with Olives.—Give the duck a round form; rub it with lemon, and brown it in a pan with butter; when it has taken a good colour add some stock; when nearly done scald some olives, stone them, without breaking the olives, into the sauce in which the duck was cooked, and serve the duck with olives round it.

A colonial lady, a few years since, not having the advantage of a work on the *cuisine*, ordered a dish of this kind, and it came to table with the olives unstoned, to the wonder of a Cardinal Richelieu, were he present. The duck looked, for all the world, as if the unskilful hand had merely spilt the olives over it on the passage from the kitchen to the refectory. In this dish some prefer to cut the duck into joints before commencing its preparation.

Fowls, with Ragoût of Oysters.—Make a forcemeat, and add to it one dozen oysters; fill the craw of the fowls with it, truss them, and put on their breasts thin slices of bacon with writing paper over it; roast them; make some gravy, and put into it some oysters, a little ketchup, and the juice of a lemon; thicken with flour and butter; take away the bacon and paper, and serve the fowls in the gravy.

Pigeon Compôte.—Truss four pigeons as for boiling; grate some bread; scrape some bacon, or cut it into small slices; chop some thyme, parsley, and onion, and some lemon-peel; grate some nutmeg, and season with pepper and salt. Mix it up with an egg. Put this forcemeat into the craw of the pigeons, lard the breasts, and fry them brown. Afterwards place them in a stewpan, with some stock, and simmer them for three-quarters of an hour; thicken the gravy with a piece of butter rolled into some flour, serve with forcemeat balls, and pour the gravy over the pigeons.

Poulet à Moi.—Put a fowl, breast downwards, in an earthen pan with a cover; shred over it a small onion, a table-spoonful of chopped parsley, and two sticks of celery; fill in the hollow with a pound of sausages. Pepper, salt, and cayenne to taste. Cover it close; put in the oven just after breakfast and forget it till dinner. If it should be forgotten till night, take off the cover before putting it away in the larder, and in the morning turn it out in a mould of jelly. If the celery is bought, i.e., long gathered, add a little water. If you have no sausages, add lumps of butter and more water.

This is the kind contribution of a colonial lady, under the signature of "N. M. A.," and it will be found an unexceptionable dish.

Roast Turkey.—Turkey, like sucking-pig, requires great attention in roasting, and after having been properly trussed and stuffed with veal stuffing. The time of roasting will depend on the size of the turkey. Pork sausages, ham, pork, or bacon, are generally served with roast turkey, and sometimes forcemeat balls; and egg, bread, oyster, celery, or gravy sauce. Turkey may be stuffed with forcemeat of veal mixed with sausage-meat, liver, parsley, and chives, chopped fine.

A turkey is improved by roasting it covered with bacon and paper; to be taken off a short time before it is done, to brown. Chestnuts roasted, grated, or sliced, and truffles or mushrooms, stewed and sliced, are both an addition and improvement to forcemeat for turkeys. Chestnuts, stewed in brown gravy, are the correct thing to be served with this dish. The turkey did not arrive in England till A.D. 1524, about the fifteenth year of the reign of Henry VIII. According to *Baker's Chronicle*,

"Turkies, carps, hoppes, piccarell, and beere,
Came into England all in one year."

The truffled turkeys of Perigueux have acquired a world-wide notoriety. They are sold in Paris for £2 and £3 each, and one of them forms an exquisitely delicious roast, that, we are told, would throw Heliogabalus into ecstacies. Truffles are a food worthy of kings—an ambrosia fit for the gods. An immense trade in truffles is carried on in Perigueux. Truffled turkeys, capons, chickens, pheasants, and partridges, also truffled pies—pies that will keep a year—are exported from Perigueux to all parts of the world. These pies are made in tureens, and may be seen at the windows of the Italian warehouses in London, labelled "*pâte de faisan aux truffes;*" or, "*pâte de bécasse aux truffes;*" and so forth. The trade has enriched the naturally poor city of Perigueux, and the whole province. The truffle will not only impart its delicate flavour and fragrance to the meat, but will preserve it sweet for a long time. A truffled turkey will keep sweet a month.

Boiled Turkey.—Boiling a turkey is a very common mode of dressing it, and, if nicely done, makes an agreeable dish. It should be trussed, with the liver and gizzard in the wings, well dredged with flour, and fastened in a napkin, having previously filled the crop with forcemeat made of crumbs of bread, parsley, pepper, salt, nutmeg, lemon-peel, anchovy, oysters chopped, shredded mushrooms, a little suet, butter, and bound together with an egg. In the water in which the turkey is boiled put the juice of three lemons, two ounces of butter, and a handful of salt. Let it simmer. Serve with celery, oyster, or brown sauce.

Fowls are roasted and served in the same style as a turkey; only they do not take so long to roast. Bread sauce or fried bread-crumbs are a correct addition.

Goose.—Roast goose is a common but favourite dish. It must be well stuffed with onion, sage, bread-crumbs, pepper, salt, and a little cayenne; with the liver, and the yolk of an egg. It must be well done, and served up with apple sauce; and garnish the dish with cut lemons.

Roast goose is served up on Michaelmas Day in England because it is the day that Queen Elizabeth heard of the defeat of the Spanish armada, and her chivalrous Highness ordered the dish to be invariably on the table afterwards; but other writers contend that this dish was eaten on Michaelmas Day in the time of Edward IV., before the armada was thought of. In France they eat goose on St. Martin's Day, Shrove Tuesday, and Twelfth Day; and in Denmark on St. Martin's. We recommend the reader to eat it whenever he can get it, for it is a very good dish, and very palatable boiled, with sauce Robert. According to "Notes and Queries," the common expression of "cooking your goose" is thus explained:—

"THE KING OF SWEDEN'S GOOSE.—The King of Sweden coming to a towne of his enemys with very little company, his enemys, to slight his forces, did hang out a goose for him to shoote; but perceiving before night that these few soldiers had invaded and set their chiefe hoults on fire, they demanded of him what his intent was. To whom he replied, 'To roast your goose.'"

It is a curious illustration of *de gustibus non est disputandem*, that the ancients considered the swan as a high delicacy, and abstained from the flesh of the goose as impure and indigestible.—*Mowbray.*

When he fed on roasted goose he was more vigorous, both in body and mind, than with any other diet.—*Dr. Hack's Experiments on Diet.*

Ducks.—Roast in the same way as geese, and serve up in a similar manner.

Cold Turkey, Goose, Fowl, &c.—Cut them in quarters; beat up an egg, with some grated nutmeg, pepper, salt, and parsley fine, a few sweet herbs, and crumbs of bread; mix all together, and cover the fowl, &c. Fry in a pan until well warmed; thicken a little gravy with flour and ketchup, lay the poultry fry on the dish, and garnish with slices of lemon.

Sir Humphry Davy was a great epicure, and took unusual pains with the chemistry of the kitchen. He gives us two culinary hints of the advantages of a Norwegian dinner —to roast fowls with plenty of parsley in their interior; and to abstract the unwholesome juice of the cucumber it must be placed in slices in salt and water before it is used.

Hashed Poultry or Game.—Cut into joints, and flour them with a little pepper, salt, and mustard. Put into a stewpan with a pint of broth, or stock, and a couple of shredded onions; let the joints simmer, and add a little more thickening, if necessary, and a table-spoonful of vinegar. Serve, and garnish with toasted bread sippets. If this dish is attended to, the above recipe carefully followed, and the poultry not over-done, there is hardly any dish more savoury or digestible.

Dindon aux Legumes.—Wrap round the turkey prepared for roasting some slices of bacon, and dress it of a pale colour; then prepare a purée of chicory, celery, or turnips; celery is preferable; put the roast turkey into it, to give the purée a flavour, and serve; or stew the vegetables, and surround the turkey in the dish.

Fowl à la Marengo.—Cut up a fowl as for fricassee, and put it in a stewpan; first the legs, as they take longer doing, and then the other parts, with a little salt, and a quantity of Lucca oil. Let the joints brown, and, when half done, add some fine herbs, with pepper and cayenne. It may be eaten with sauce, and the dish garnished, but if the fowl is tender it will require no addition, except a slice of ham or bacon.

This dish is a *braise*, and it is a matter of history, that after the great fight at Marengo, the Emperor Napoleon's cook was obliged to use salad oil instead of butter. The general was so pleased with the *cuisine* that he ordered this kind of fare frequently afterwards, and hence fowl *à la Marengo* is a favourite *plat* in France to this day. Simple viands are in request by the sovereigns of our day. George IV. generally dined alone in the private *salle à manger* at Windsor Castle. A roast fowl was the favourite dish of William IV., with a black bottle of sherry, contrary to Cardigan propriety; and at the grand banquet given to our gracious Queen at Guildhall by the City authorities in 1837, her Majesty partook solely of turtle and roast mutton, with only a little sherry and claret. George III. lived like an ascetic, for fear of gout, and ate with rapidity, like Napoleon I.—so much so, that those persons who dined with him could not satisfy their appetite unless by continuing their meal after their sovereign had finished, which was opposed to the old etiquette. He was so sensible and considerate that, when dining with the Queen, he would say to his attendants, "Don't regard me, take your own time." Queen Charlotte enjoyed herself at table, and manifested a judgment in wine, which her royal husband rarely drank.

Roast Goose à la François.—Take a hundred chestnuts, and put them on the fire in a *poêle* with holes; after having taken off the first skin, put them again in the *poêle* till you remove the second skin. Chop half the chestnuts, and put them into a stewpan with half a pound of sausage-meat, the liver chopped, a little butter, some parsley, chives, shalot, and a clove of garlic, finely chopped. Put this on the fire for a quarter of an hour, then stuff the goose with it, and roast. Put the rest of the chestnuts into a stewpan, with a glass of wine, a little stock, pepper, and salt; when done serve round the goose.

Chestnuts are difficult of digestion in a raw state, but when cooked they are otherwise. In France they are much used in cookery and confectionery, and in Italy they are sold at the corners of the streets, dressed in various ways, as well as made into bread and puddings.

Poulard à la Montmorency.—Lard the fowl, and stuff it with the liver, cut in pieces, some bacon, and hard eggs; stew it in pale stock, with flour browned in butter, some onions, carrots, and a few fine herbs; reduce the sauce to a glaze, and serve with the fowl.

Fowls Stewed.—Fowls may be divided in joints and stewed in Béchamel sauce, or done in cream, with white pepper, salt, and an onion cut in shreds, and served with the dish garnished with slices of ham or bacon, and lemon or bread sippets.

THE BRIDGE OF JENA AND COLUMN OF AUSTERLITZ SAVED FROM DESTRUCTION BY A DINNER.—The Count von der Gotz, formerly one of Blucher's aide-de-camps, being entreated by Prince Talleyrand to interfere to prevent the bridge of Jena and the Austerlitz column being destroyed in Paris, Blucher's answer was very characteristic. "I have determined on blowing up the bridge," he wrote, "and I cannot conceal from your Excellency how much pleasure it would afford me if M. Talleyrand would previously place himself upon it." From this, as well as from the schemes of plunder, the Duke (Wellington) alone had sufficient influence to dissuade the fiery Prussian. He accomplished his purpose by a combination of argument and hospitality, of which the evidence is as curious as it is characteristic. One letter written on 9th July, 1815, pointed out that to destroy public monuments would be subversion of the capitulation. In another short note, he (the Duke) invites Blucher to dine with him at Very's, and announces the speedy arrival of the Emperor of Russia and King of Prussia. Blucher could not take hold against the good cheer, and the bridge of Jena and the pillar of Austerlitz were both saved.—*Gleig's "Life of the Duke of Wellington."*

Stewed Pigeons.—Pigeons are very excellent stewed in brown sauce, with whole potato-onions, which are milder and of finer flavour than the common onion.

CARVING.—There are certain choice cuts or delicacies, with which a good carver is acquainted: among them are the sounds of cod-fish; the thin or fat of salmon; the thick and fins of turbot, a portion of the liver and roe to each person; the fat of venison, lamb, and veal kidney; the long cuts and gravy from "the Alderman's walk" of a haunch of venison or mutton; the Pope's eye in a leg of mutton; the ribs and neck of a pig; the breast and wings of a fowl; back pieces, ears, and brain of a hare; the breast and thighs (without the drum-sticks) of turkey and goose; the legs and breast of a duck; the wings, breast, and back of game.—*Hints for the Table.*

XV.—PUDDINGS AND PIES.

But his neat cookery! He cut our roots in characters;
And sauc'd our broths, as Juno had been sick,
And he her dieter.   *Guiderus in "Cymbeline."*

Plum Pudding.—

Christmas comes but once a year,
So let it come cheerily;
Every face in smiles appear,
Not an hour pass wearily.

We give Dr. Kitchener's way of making this national Christmas pudding, for it is an undoubted fact that his mode was the means of no less than eighteen different recipes, with only a little more boil, which is erring on the right side:—Beef suet, chopped, six ounces; Malaga raisins, stoned, six ounces; currants, washed and picked, eight ounces; bread crumbs, three ounces; flour, three ounces; eggs, three ounces; sixth of a nutmeg, small blade of mace, and same quantity of cinnamon, pounded fine; half a tea-spoon of salt; sugar four ounces; candied lemon, one ounce, and the same of citron, with half a pint of milk. Beat the eggs and spice together, mix the milk with them by degrees, then the rest of the ingredients. Dip a clean linen cloth into boiling water, and put it in a hair sieve; flour it a little, and pour in the mixture, tie it up close, put it into a saucepan containing six quarts of boiling water. Keep a kettle of boiling water alongside of it to fill up your pot as it wastes. Be sure to keep it boiling *six* hours, at least.

The noble poet gave the requisite ingredients on one occasion to a foreign cook, and forgot to tell him of the cloth, so that the pudding appeared in a liquid state. This is akin to a story told on the early use of teas. A person from the East gave out a quarter of a pound of tea, and desired his servant to send up a cup. The leaves came up served, and the water that boiled them was thrown away. In England the plum pudding is frequently brought in enveloped in flames from any alcoholic spirit, and its advent on the table is hailed with joyous glee by children, and sometimes by those of

1. Christmas Pudding.
2. Raised Pie.
3. Jelly of Two Colours.
4. Open Jelly with Whipped Cream
5. Pancakes.
6 & 7. Mixed Fruits.

larger growth. The boar's head was another accompaniment of Christmas cheer, which, we believe, is still kept up at the Universities, and the forms and ceremonies of its introduction have been graphically and pleasingly told by Irving and others:—

> "*Caput apri defero,*
> *Redens laudes Domino.*
> The boar's heade in hande bring I,
> With garlandes gay and rosemary;
> I pray you all sing merrily,
> *Qui estis in convivio.*
>
> "*Caput apri defero,*
> *Redens laudes Domino.*
> The boar's heade, I understande,
> Is the chief service of the lande;
> Like wherever it be founde,
> *Servite cum cantico.*"

We like these quaint old customs and ceremonies, and hope they will be always kept up in the old country. In the Colonies it cannot be expected: besides, there is an insuperable objection—the heat of summer is discouraging to festivity. Old customs, manners, feasts, and dishes, as well as old songs and music, should be preserved, as they tend to keep together time-honoured remembrances, and the descendants of Englishmen at the Antipodes look on them all with filial respect. Why was Eton Montem abolished, and why cannot it be revived? We, at a distance, never heard any cause or reasons assigned for its abolition. Its continuation and existence as a species of Protestant carnival might, or might not, have been

> "More honoured in the breach
> Than the observance."

What is the difference, we should be glad to know, between the collection for the Grecians, after the speeches on St. Matthew's day, who are leaving Christ's Hospital for the Universities, and the former "salt money," raised by the forms and ceremonies of chivalry for the captain of Eton for a similar purpose? When the athletic sports of boxing, hunting, shooting, cricket, racing, rowing,* running, and walking, are discouraged, and roast beef, plum pudding, and the loving cup are no longer partaken of, we fear that we shall witness signs of the decadence of one of the greatest nations of the world, and our national character will sink into chronic insignificance. A writer of a work of this nature has reminded us that Bickerstaffe, in the "Tatler" in the reign of Queen Anne, asserts it as a received axiom of that Augustan age, that the men who fought the battles of Cressy and Agincourt derived their sinews of war from the substantial English fare of those early times; and records, with humiliation, the enervating effects which are supposed to have followed on the introduction of so dainty and effeminate an article of food as mutton, and the foreign confections of our Continental neighbours. In new countries we would have athletic sports, pastimes, and games encouraged by legislative enactment, and yearly games of an Olympic character held; for these contests, in the best days of Greece, were not only confined to manly sports, but music and poetry were encouraged, and the orators were crowned with garlands of wild olive: and surely there is room for improvement in the latter respect, both in the mother country and the colonies. If Olympic games were introduced in the latter, the Hellenic rule as to competitors would have to be relaxed. We are *running* into a disquisition on a subject that we have a strong feeling on, although almost foreign to our work, so that we had better "hark back" to the theme of cookery.

Plum Pudding Sauce.—Having given Dr. Kitchener's recipe for plum pudding, we are bound to give his sauce: a glass of sherry, half a glass of brandy, and two tea-spoonfuls of white sugar, a little grated lemon-peel, mixed with a quarter of a pint of *thick* melted butter, and nutmeg grated on the surface.

The Abingdon Pudding.—One pound of raisins, nicely stoned; one

---

* We are glad to perceive, by the late English papers, that our countryman, Mr. Green, has not, in this manly sport, dishonoured the land of his birth, and that the British public duly appreciated and admired the pluck of the Australian champion, in going the semi-circumference of the world to pull a race.

pound of currants washed and picked; one pound of beef suet, freed from skin and finely chopped; eight ounces of bread crumbs, sifted through a colander; two ounces of flour; half a pound of moist sugar, good brown; six eggs, well whisked; half an ounce of candied lemon; half an ounce of candied orange; the peel of one lemon, chopped fine; the juice of half a lemon; a nutmeg, grated; a thimbleful of salt; a wine-glass of brandy. Mix the whole thoroughly together, and have ready a well-buttered mould or basin; pack in, place over it a dusting of flour, and tie down with a buttered paper and strong cloth, and boil gently for six hours.—*Cassell's Illustrated Family Paper.*

Brown and Polson's Soufflé Pudding.—Put six ounces of Brown and Polson's patent corn-flour into a stewpan, with six ounces of best white sugar, and mix well with a quart of milk, and four ounces of fresh butter, a pinch of salt, and a few drops of essence of vanilla or lemon; stir it well until it boils. Then work in the yolks of six eggs; and the whites, whisked into a froth, are to be lightly incorporated with the butter; pour into a buttered pie-dish, and bake in a moderately heated oven for half an hour; sugar the top, and serve when risen.

Soufflés must be served as soon as done, or otherwise their goodness evaporates.

Petits Puits d'Amour.—Take puff paste and roll it out about half an inch thick; stamp out what will be used, work it up again and roll it the same thickness; then stamp out smaller pieces to correspond with the larger ones; stamp out the centre of the smaller rings; brush over the others with white of an egg; place a small ring on the top of every large circular piece of paste; egg over the tops; and bake sharp for less than a quarter of an hour. Sift sugar over them, and put them back in the oven to colour, then fill in the rings with preserves; dish them up and serve. French pastry is made into a thousand different shapes, all depending on the confectioner's taste and ingenuity.

PETITS PUITS D'AMOUR GARNIS DES CONFITURES.—A classical and well-known dish for part of the flank of a second course.—*Notes to "Don Juan."*

Pastry is digested with difficulty, in consequence of the oil which it contains; puddings from their heaviness, that is, closeness of texture. In proportion as they are light, they become digestible.—*Mayo.* The simple cure for their heaviness is to make them with Jones's patent flour.

Pancakes.—More than one author has said that the man, woman, or child was unknown who did not like pancakes, and *Mrs. Caudle* only objects to the price of eggs. They are made as follows:—Make a light batter of three spoonfuls of flour, three eggs, well beaten, a little salt, and small sprinkling of ginger. Fry in thin layers in a pan, and turn. The tossing of a pancake is easily acquired. They are rolled and served with sugar and lemon. Some persons mix flour with the butter, but it is quite unnecessary. Jams are sometimes served with pancakes, instead of sugar.

Naleskikes (*Polish Pancakes*).—Beat up eight eggs, and mix them with a pint and a half of milk or cream, two ounces of melted fresh butter, some grated nutmeg, lemon-peel rasped upon loaf sugar, a little salt, and ten ounces of flour, and make the whole into a smooth batter. Put into a frying-pan some butter or lard, and when it boils pour in some of the latter, and sprinkle in a few currants; fry nicely, and sprinkle the pancake with sugar; roll it with a two-pronged fork, and serve hot.

Pink Pancakes.—Boil a large red beetroot until it is very tender, then peel it, cut it into thin slices, and pound it to a pulp in a marble mortar; add the yolks of five eggs, two table-spoonfuls of flour, four of cream, powdered sugar, nutmeg, and a wineglass of brandy. Rub the whole into a batter, and fry the pancakes with lard. Serve hot, garnished with sweetmeats.

PANCAKES ON SHROVE-TUESDAY.—Taylor, the water poet, writing in 1630, says:—"Shrove-Tuesday, at whose entry in the morning all the whole kingdom is unquiet; but by the time the clock strikes eleven, which, by the help of a knavish sexton, is commonly before nine, then there is a bell rung called 'the pancake bell,' the sound of which makes thousands of people distracted, and forgetful either of manners or humanity; and there is a thing called wheaten flour, which the cooks do mingle with water, eggs, spice, and other tragical and magical enchantments; and then they put it, by a little and little, into a frying-pan, with boiling suet, where it makes a confined dismal hissing, like Lethean snakes in the reeds of Acheron, Styx, or Phlegethon, until at last, by the skill of the cook, it is transformed into the form of a flip-jack, called a pancake, which, with ominous incantations, the ignorant do devour very greedily."—*Things not Generally Known.*

Fritters are made with the batter a little thicker, and more of it is run into the pan. Apples, pears, and peaches are sliced thin, and mixed with the batter and fried, and sometimes raisins and currants—all depending on taste. Peach fritters are delectable eating.

Sweet Omelette.—Beat the yolks and whites of three eggs separate; grate on them a little ginger, with salt, and add a little cream or new milk. Fry the omelette, and serve with white sugar.

Mother Eve's Pudding.—
  If you would have a good pudding, observe what you're taught:
  Take two pennyworth of eggs, when twelve for the groat;
  And of the same fruit that Eve had once chosen,
  Well pared and well chopp'd, at least half a dozen;
  Six ounces of bread (let your maid eat the crust),
  The crumbs must be grated as small as the dust;
  Six ounces of currants from the stones you must sort,
  Lest they break out your teeth and spoil all your sport;
  Five ounces of sugar won't make it too sweet;
  Some salt and some nutmeg will make it complete:
  Three hours let it boil, without hurry or flutter;
  And then serve it up, without sugar or butter.

An excellent plain plum pudding may be made by substituting raw grated carrots for eggs; it is light, nice, and looks a rich pudding. This is the recommendation of a housewife of known culinary ability. We have read that other persons propose snow and small beer as substitutes for eggs, while Kitchener declares that "they will no more answer the purpose than substitutes for sugar or brandy." We incline to the latter opinion.

Green Apricot Pudding or Tart.—The apricots must be simmered in sugar and water before they are put into the pudding or tart. The pudding will be made from short crust, and the tart from either short or flaky crust, the directions for making which appear elsewhere. The apricots may be taken and put into the tart or pudding with a small quantity of syrup.

<small>The *Quarterly*, an excellent authority on matters relating to the *cuisine* (except as to saw-dust bread and clasp knives), and from whose valuable pages we have liberally extracted, informs us that a green apricot pudding is the best article in the pastry line that can possibly be made; and we defer to that opinion, with considerable doubts in favour of cold gooseberry tart, with cream *ad libitum*.</small>

Apple Puddings and Pies.—These kind of puddings and pies are, after plum puddings, also a national dish. The sort of fruit for cookery, according to all writers on pomology, should be juicy, full of flavour, and apt to pulp when done. The crust for puddings and pies we have given elsewhere, and in using the fruit a little lemon is an improvement to their flavour, or a few quinces cut up. They are served with cream and white sugar; in truth, we hardly know anything better than a nice apple dumpling made properly.

<small>The editor of "Hints for the Table" states a fact that we are desirous of giving further publicity to, in the hope that it will receive attention from those of the fair sex now living in "single blessedness." It is, that once upon a time "a clever man chose his wife by making an apple pudding." Who can doubt his sense and discernment? Love at first sight will become exploded, and love at first taste will now take its place. The drapery misses—that is, ladies furnished, on credit, with articles of attire, to be repaid on marriage—will fall into desuetude, and those young ladies who can work into proper shape an apple pudding will most properly be in request at the temple of Hymen.</small>

Currant Dumplings.—For each dumpling take three table-spoonfuls of flour, two of finely-minced beef suet, and two of currants; a little salt, and as much milk or water as will make a batter of the ingredients. Tie in a well-floured cloth, and boil for an hour. They can be served plain, or with sweet sauce.

<small>They may be made thick and boiled separately with meat without a cloth.</small>

Marrow Pudding.—Grate a penny loaf into crumbs, pour on it a pint of boiling cream, or milk. Cut very thin a pound of beef marrow; beat four eggs well; add a wineglass of brandy or sherry, with sugar and nutmeg to taste. Mix all well together, and either boil or bake for three-quarters of an hour. Cut two ounces of candied citron thin, and, when served up, stick the pieces all over it.

Light Dumplings.—We are not going to give a recipe for yeast dumplings; but, instead, we shall describe dumplings made from Jones's patent flour, which are not quite so light, but far more wholesome and digestible. Mix lightly Jones's patent flour, with milk (cold) or water, and as soon as mixed put them into boiling water; when done, take out, and serve, with melted butter and sweet sauce. They won't take much more than five minutes boiling.

<small>Yeast dumplings are made in a similar way, only allowing them to rise after the flour, salt, and lukewarm water are mixed.</small>

Soufflé de Pomme de Terre.—Take a pint of cream, a quarter of a pound of sugar, six spoonfuls of potato flour, four yolks of eggs; dilute the flour with the eggs and cream; add a piece of butter the size of an egg, and a little lemon-peel; put this mixture on the fire; let it boil a few minutes, stirring it; allow it to cool; then add six yolks of eggs, beat all together, whisk the whites of four eggs, mix them quickly and lightly with the rest; put all in a pan and bake; serve quickly.

Magnum-bonum plums are only fit for tarts and sweetmeats. *Magnum* is right enough; but as to *bonum*, the word is completely misapplied.—*Cobbett.*

Cheesecakes.—Put two quarts of new milk into a stewpan, set it near the fire, and stir in two table-spoonfuls of rennet, or less quantity of the patent rennet; let it stand until set—this will take about an hour. Break it well when set, pour off the whey, and put the curd to drain; when dry add four ounces of sugar, three ounces of butter, to be oiled; stir them well together; beat the yolks of four eggs in a basin, with a little nutmeg grated, lemon-peel, and a glass of brandy; add this to the curd, and stir well together. Line tins with paste, and bake.

CHEESECAKES.—Chrysippus of Tyana, in his book entitled "The Art of Making Bread," enumerates the following species and genera of cheesecakes:—The terentinum, the crassianum, the tulianum, the sabellicum, the clustron, the julianum, the apicianum, the canopicum, the pelucidum, the cappodocium, the tubybium, the maryptum, the plicium, the guttatum, the montianum. "This last," he says, "you will soften with sour wine, and if you have any cheese you may mash the montianum up half with wine and half with cheese, and so it will be more palatable." Then there is the clustrum tabonianum. There are also mustacia made with mead, mustacia made with sesame, crustum puricum, gosgloanium, and paulianum.—"*Athenæus*," translated by *Yonge.*

Lemon, orange, and almond cheesecakes may be made in a similar way, only using those fruits more largely; and the almonds must be well pounded.

College Puddings.—Beat up four eggs with two ounces of flour, a little nutmeg and ginger, and three ounces of white sugar. Beat to a batter, then add six ounces of suet, chopped fine, six of currants, well washed and cleaned, with a glass of white wine or brandy. Bake in an oven or patty-pan, or they are good boiled, served with wine sauce.

Baked Rice Pudding.—Boil six ounces of rice, and, when done, put it in a dish, and pour on it a well-made custard, and bake quickly in an oven.

Sago, Arrowroot, and Ground Rice Puddings.—These are excellent cold in summer, boiled in milk and run into shapes, sweetened and flavoured. Serve with cold custards, cream, or preserves of any kind.

Ure writes that the uses of arrowroot are well known and acknowledged. It is the most elegant and richest of all the feculas. Liebig places the powers of arrowroot, as a nutriment to man, in a remarkable point of view, when he states that fifteen pounds of flesh contain no more carbon for supplying animal heat, by its combustion into carbonic acid, than four pounds of starch.

Moost Aye; Save-all Pudding or Pie.—Put scraps of bread in a saucepan, with a little milk; then break in three eggs, three ounces of sugar, a little nutmeg, ginger, and allspice, and stew well together. This pudding may be either boiled or baked; a few currants are an improvement.

PUDDINGS AND PIES.

The Bakewell Pudding.—Cover a dish with thin puff paste, put a layer of any kind of jam, about half an inch thick, then take the yolks of eight eggs and ten whites, half a pound of sugar, half a pound of butter melted, and almond flavour to taste, beat all well together; pour the mixture into a dish, an inch thick, and bake an hour in a moderate oven.

This is rather an expensive pudding, but it is a far-famed one in the old country.

Batter Pudding.—Break three eggs into a basin, with a salt-spoon of salt, beat them well, then add about four ounces of flour, and, by degrees, half a pint of milk and a little powdered ginger. Boil in a cloth or mould well floured, or bake. Serve with sweet sauce.

Suet Pudding or Dumplings.—Chop six ounces of suet fine, put it into a basin, with six ounces of flour, two ounces of bread crumbs, and a tea-spoonful of salt; stir well together, beat up two eggs, and add to them six table-spoons of milk, put by degrees into the basin, and stir well together. Divide into dumplings, or boil in a cloth floured. Boil an hour.

Suet dumplings are very good boiled with meat, and made without either eggs or milk.

Bread and Butter Pudding.—Wash and clean two ounces of currants, get ready four or five layers of bread and butter, put the latter in the dish, and between the layers put the currants, and over all put in a custard. Bake about three-quarters of an hour.

Spring Pudding.—Peel and wash three dozen sticks of rhubarb, put into a stewpan with a little lemon, cinnamon, and moist sugar to sweeten; set it over the fire to marmalade; when done put paste round a dish, insert the rhubarb, and bake.

Vermicelli or Macaroni Pudding.—Boil sufficient vermicelli or macaroni to fill three-fourths of your pie-dish, with a little sugar, butter, and spice, on the top of which put a custard, and bake.

Nottingham Pudding.—Peel and core six pudding apples, leaving the apples whole, place them in a pie-dish, and pour over them a light batter; bake about three-quarters of an hour, and serve with sweet sauce.

Boiled Custard.—Put a quart of milk into a stewpan, with the peel of a lemon cut thin, a little grated nutmeg, a bay or laurel leaf, a stick of cinnamon; set it over a quick fire, and mind it does not boil over; when it boils set it beside the fire, and simmer ten minutes; break the yolks of eight and the whites of four eggs into a basin, beat them well, then pour in the milk a little at a time, set it on the fire again, and stir it with a wooden spoon; let it have one boil, pass it through a tamis; when cold, add a little brandy or white wine, and serve in cups.

Baked Custard is made more simply, by adding milk to eggs well beaten, and grating on the top, before being put into the oven, some nutmeg. The flavour of lemon may be added, but it is better without.

Fruit Pies or Tarts.—Gooseberries, damsons, morello cherries, currants mixed with raspberries, plums of all kinds, cranberries, and mulberries, should be fresh picked and washed. Lay them in the dish, with the centre highest, and half a pound of moist sugar to a quart of fruit; rub the edges of the dish with yolks of eggs, cover with paste in the usual way, and bake in a quick oven. For icing, beat up the whites of two eggs to a froth, lay it over the pie or tart, sift over it pounded sugar, and return it to the oven to set.

The Cup in a Pie.—The custom of placing an inverted cup in a fruit pie, the cook will inform us, is to contain the juice while the pie is baking in the oven, and to prevent it boiling over; and she is, moreover, certain in her theory, because, when the pie is withdrawn from the oven, the cup will be found full of juice. When the cup is first put into the dish it is full of cold air, and when the pie is placed in the oven this air will expand by the heat and fill the cup, and drive out all the juice and a portion of the present air it contains, in which state it will remain until removed from the oven, when the air in the cup will condense, and occupy a very small space, leaving the remainder to be filled with juice; but this does not take place till the danger of the juice boiling over is passed. If a small glass tumbler is inverted in the pie, its contents can be examined into while it is in the oven, and it will be found what has been advanced is correct.—*Gower's "Scientific Phenomena of Domestic Life."*

Nesselrode Pudding.—Blanch about forty chestnuts in boiling water, remove the husks and pound them in a mortar, adding a little syrup. Then rub them through a fine sieve, and mix in a basin, with a pint of syrup made from a pound of sugar clarified, and flavoured with vanilla, a pint of cream, and the yolks of a dozen eggs. Set this mixture over the fire, and keep stirring it, and just as it begins to boil take it off and pass it through a tamis. When it is cold put it into a freezing-pot, adding a glass of maraschino, and let the mixture set; then add an ounce of citron, two ounces of currants, and two ounces of stewed raisins; the whole thus mixed, add a plateful of whipped cream to the whites of three eggs beaten to a froth, with a little syrup. When the pudding is frozen, put it into a pine-apple mould, close the lid, place it again in the freezing-pan, cover over with pounded ice and saltpetre, and let it remain until required for table; then turn out the pudding and serve.

The above is one of the most fashionable and aristocratic of puddings made, and was reckoned a *chef d'œuvre* of the celebrated Carême.

Aunt Nelly's Pudding.—Chop half a pound of suet fine, mix with it half a pound of flour, half a pound of treacle, a few shreds of candied lemon-peel, three table-spoonfuls of cream, and two eggs well beaten; beat the ingredients well, put it into a buttered basin; tie it down with a cloth, and boil for a couple of hours.

Almond Puffs.—Blanch and pound two ounces of sweet and four of bitter almonds, melt two ounces of butter, dredge in two table-spoonfuls of flour, and add two ounces of sugar and the pounded almonds. Beat the mixture well, and bake in a moderate oven. Turn them out on a dish, the bottom of the puff uppermost, and serve.

Alma Pudding.—Beat half a pound of butter to a cream, strew in by degrees half a pound of powdered sugar, and mix both together; then dredge in half a pound of flour, add a quarter of a pound of currants, and moisten with four eggs well beaten; when all the ingredients are well stirred and mixed, butter a mould that will hold the mixture, tie it down with a cloth, put the pudding into boiling water, and boil for a couple of hours; when turned out, put on it some powdered sugar, and serve.

Bachelor's Pudding.—Pare, core, and mince four ounces of apples, add to these four ounces of currants well cleaned, four ounces of grated bread, and two ounces of sugar; whisk three eggs, beat them up with the rest of the ingredients, and when all are thoroughly mixed put the pudding in a buttered basin, tie it down with a cloth, and boil for a couple of hours.

This is said to be the pudding that the young lady made that induced the gentleman "to pop the question," which was duly responded to, as told in the addenda to one of the preceding recipes.

Barberry Tart.—Pull the barberries from the stalks, and put the fruit into a stone jar in boiling water, and let it simmer until the fruit is soft; then put it into a preserving-pan, with the sugar—a pound of sugar to a pound of fruit—and boil gently for fifteen minutes; line a tartlet-pan with paste, bake it, and when the paste is cold fill in with fruit.

Coburg Pudding.—Mix six ounces of flour to a smooth batter with a pint of new milk, add six ounces of sugar, six ounces of butter, six ounces of currants, six eggs, a little brandy and grated nutmeg, and when well mixed put it into moulds; bake for an hour, turn the puddings out in a dish, and serve with sweet sauce.

Indian Pudding.—Pare, core, and cut four large apples into slices, put them into a saucepan with some grated nutmeg, two table-spoonfuls of sugar, and a tea-spoonful of minced lemon-peel; stir them over the fire until soft, have ready some crust, roll it out thin, spread the apples over the paste; sprinkle over the apples six ounces of currants and three-quarters of a pound of minced suet, roll the pudding up, closing the ends, tie it in a floured cloth, and boil a couple of hours.

Half-pay Pudding.—Chop a quarter of a pound of suet fine, mix it with a quarter of a pound of currants well washed, a quarter of a pound of stoned raisins, a quarter of a pound of flour, the same of bread-crumbs, two table-spoonfuls of treacle, and half a pint of milk; beat up the ingredients until they are well mixed, put them into a buttered basin, and boil for a couple of hours.

Rowley Poley; or, Dog in a Blanket.—Make a light suet crust, and roll it out thin, spread the jam equally over it, leaving a small margin of paste without any, where the pudding joins; roll it up, fasten the ends securely, and tie it in a floured cloth, and boil for two hours.

Baked Lemon Pudding.—Beat four eggs to a froth, mix them with four ounces of sugar and a quarter of a pound of warmed butter; mix well together, putting in the strained juice and grated rind of a lemon.

Line a shallow dish with paste, and bake in a moderate oven for half an hour; turn the pudding out, and strew over it sifted sugar.

Lemon puddings, cheesecakes, and dumplings may be made in a similar way.

Sussex Dumplings.—Mix a pound of flour, a little salt, and water to a paste, form into small round dumplings, drop them into boiling water, and boil for half an hour. They may be served with roast or boiled meat, and, if with the latter, boiled in the same water.

Poor Clergyman's Pudding.—Put a quarter of a pound of flour, a quarter of a pound of suet, the same of currants, and a quarter of a pound of raisins stoned, a table-spoonful of moist sugar, half a tea-spoonful of ginger, and a little salt; put the mixture into a pudding-cloth, and boil for two hours, or a little more. Turn the pudding out of the cloth, and serve with sifted sugar.

Marlboro' Pudding.—Four ounces of butter melted, four ounces of sugar, and four eggs well beaten; mix all well together, line the dish with paste and a layer of preserve, and bake half an hour.

Plum Broth.—Plum broth or porridge was eaten as soup at Christmas, at St. James's, during the reign of George III., and a portion of it was sent to the different officers of His Majesty's household. It was composed of veal, beef, sugar, lemon, oranges, sack, hock, sherry, raisins, currants, prunes, cochineal, nutmeg, cinnamon, and cloves—an odd *olla podrida.*

> *Jacopo Foscari.* That melody, which out of tones and tunes
> Collects such pasture for the longing sorrow
> Of the sad mountaineer, when far away
> From his snow canopy of cliffs and clouds,
> That he feeds on the sweet but poisonous thought,
> And dies. You call this *weakness!* It is strength,
> I say; the parent of all honest feeling.
> He who loves not his country, can love nothing.—*The Two Foscari.*

Popular lyric poetry should be encouraged. The Scottish patriot, Fletcher of Saltoun, was right when he put forth the aphorism as to the mode of ruling a community: "Give me the making of a people's songs and ballads, and let who will make their laws." History informs us that "La Marseillaise" gave an immense impulse to the first French Revolution. Rousseau writes, that the "Ranz des Vaches," a Swiss patriotic air, was forbidden to be played to the troops under pain of death; so stirring was its effects, reminding them of the fate of their home; while Englishmen, whether of the old country, or native born, glory in the national songs of Fatherland. It is notorious that the naval poetry of Dibdin did the State more service in the time of the war, than the bonus for enlistment offered by the country. We are running into a disquisition on a subject almost foreign to our work, so that we had better "hark back" to the theme of cookery.

XVI.—PASTRY.

Shallow. He shall answer it: some pigeons, Davy, a couple of short-legged hens, a joint of mutton; any pretty little tiny kickshaws, tell William Cook.—*2nd Part Henry IV.*

Puff Paste.—As a general rule, puff paste requires one pound of butter to every pound of flour, half a salt-spoon of salt, and a little lemon-juice, with about a quarter of a pint of the coolest water. Ure and Soyer give these proportions; although very passable, crust may be made with half the quantity of butter. The latter *cuisinier* tells us to put the flour on the paste-board, make a hole in the centre, in which put the yolk of an egg, the lemon-juice, and salt; mix the whole with cold water (in summer the water must be either iced or cooled) into a flexible paste with the right hand, and handle it as little as possible; then squeeze all the buttermilk from the butter, wring it through a cloth, and roll out the paste; place the butter on this, and fold the edges of the paste over, so as to hide it; roll it out again to the thickness of a quarter of an inch, fold over one-third, over which again pass the rolling-pin; then fold over the other third, thus forming a square; place it with the ends, top, and bottom before you, and repeat the rolls and turns twice again, as before. Flour a baking-sheet, put the paste on this, and let it remain in a cool place for half an hour; then roll twice more, turning it as before; place it again in a cool place for a quarter of an hour, give two more rolls, making seven in all, and it is ready for use.

The richer the pastry is made, the more laminæ of butter it contains, the more unwholesome.

Good Short Crust.—Half a pound of butter, the yolks of two eggs, two ounces of sugar, and about a quarter of a pint of milk; rub the butter into the flour, add the sugar, and mix the whole as lightly as possible to a smooth paste with yolks of eggs well beaten and the milk.

Butter Crust, for Boiled Puddings.—Allow about six ounces of butter or clarified dripping to each pound of flour, or half of each quantity; work the flour to a paste with half a pint of water, roll out the crust rather thin, place the butter over it in small pieces, dredge over it some flour, and fold the paste over; repeat the rolling, and the crust is ready for use.

Suet Crust, for Pies or Puddings.—The quantity in proportion will be six ounces of beef suet to every pound of flour, with half a pint of water. Chop the suet fine, and rub it well into the flour, work the whole to a paste with the water, roll it out, and it is ready for use. It is a great improvement, before using the suet, if it were pounded with a small quantity of dripping, or even oil used. This suet crust is much more digestible, and, of course, more wholesome, than the flaky crust made from butter.

Ude's Royal Paste, au Choux.—Take a stewpan large enough to hold four quarts of water, pour half a pint of water in it, with a quarter of a pound of fresh butter, two ounces of sugar, a little salt, and the peel of a lemon; let them boil until the whole is properly melted. Then take some very dry flour and pass through a sieve. Take the lemon-peel out with a ladle, and throw a handful of flour into the preparation while boiling; take care, however, not to put more flour than the liquor can soak up. Stir with a wooden spoon until the paste can be easily detached from the stewpan, and then take it off the fire. Now break an egg into this paste, and mix it well; then break a second, which also mix. Do not put more eggs than the paste can absorb, but you must be careful not to make this preparation too liquid. It is almost certain that about five or six eggs will be wanted for the above quantity; then form them *en choux*, by which is meant, in the shape of a ball, an inch in circumference. As this paste swells very much, you must dress it accordingly, putting the *choux* on a baking-sheet, at an inch distance from each other, in order that they may undergo a greater effect in the oven. Brush them over, as usual, with the *doune*, or egg-wash, to which has been added a little milk. Put them into an oven moderately hot, but do not open the oven till they are quite baked, otherwise they would flatten, and all attempts to make them rise again would be found to be useless; next, dry them, sometimes you may glaze them, or not. To detach them from the baking-sheet, apply the sharp end of a knife, and take them off gently. Then make a small opening in the side of the *choux*, into which put with a tea-spoon such sweetmeats as you think proper, and send them up dished *en buisson*.

Mrs. ——'s Pastry.—Take flour, and butter, and dripping enough to make the crust—half butter and half dripping, and to one pound of flour put half the weight of butter; rub the flour and butter well together; then beat up one or two eggs, with sufficient warm water to mix the flour; roll *once*.

This is the recipe of an elegant Australian lady, whose fair hands could fabricate by this simple mode crust infinitely superior to any professional daubing; and as a matter of course, its intrinsic goodness was wonderfully enhanced if the eater was acquainted with the maker.

Puffs.—Mix two table-spoonfuls of flour with a quarter of a pint of cream, two eggs well beaten, some grated nutmeg, four bitter almonds pounded, two tea-spoonfuls of ratafia, and an ounce of butter beaten to a cream. Bake these ingredients in small buttered cups for half an hour, turn them out in a dish, and serve immediately with sweet sauce poured over them.

Tourtes à la Crême.—Put a pound of flour on a paste-board, make a hole in the middle, and put in a quarter of a pint of thick cream and a pinch of salt; mix it lightly, and let it stand half an hour; then put in it half a pound of butter, at five times, letting it stand a quarter of an hour twice; then make it into several cakes; feather with yolk of egg, and bake.

Brioches.—Make a paste with half a pound of flour and a little hot water, with a spoonful of yeast; wrap up this paste in a cloth, and put it in a warm place, for twenty minutes in summer and an hour in winter; then put a pound of flour on the board, mix the paste that you have leavened with it, and three-quarters of a pound of butter, five eggs, a little water, and a few grains of salt. Knead all together three times; then wrap up warmly, and let it remain nine or ten hours. Then cut the paste into pieces, the size you wish to make your brioches: mould them into the form you wish, egg them over, and bake small ones half an hour; those of a larger size an hour and a half.

Baba.—Made with the brioche paste. Add thereto the size of a nut of saffron in powder, a quarter of a pound of the best raisins stoned, and double the quantity of currants, sugar, and some slices of candied citron cut in small pieces; mix and knead all together. Let the paste be soft and well mixed; put it into a buttered pan, and let it stand eight hours in winter and four in summer; then, without touching it, let it bake in a slow oven for an hour. It will be done enough when it has taken a good colour.

Spanish Puffs.—Put into a saucepan half a pint of water and a quarter of a pound of butter; stir it until it boils, and mix with it four table-spoonfuls of flour; stir it together, and add six yolks and four whites of eggs, two at a time; let it cool, and, with a dessert-spoon, drop it into boiling clarified dripping or lard. If the puffs are to be flavoured with ginger, a tea-spoonful of powdered ginger may be added.

Flan.—Mix a table-spoonful of flour with a table-spoonful of brandy or orange-flower water, eight yolks of eggs, and a little salt; when well mixed, add a quarter of a pound of sugar to a pint of milk, which pour over the eggs, stirring all the time; put the mixture into a buttered tart-pan, and bake in a moderate oven; powder it with sugar and serve.

A GOURMAND ABROAD.—Three stout, middle-aged men, evidently well to do in the world, were travelling together on a pleasure trip. One of them incessantly *talked eatables*. Like—with a difference—the fairy-tale damsels, who with every word dropped a diamond on a rose, this worthy man spoke but to enunciate, in a tone of immense relish, "Soup—gravy—turtle—capital pie!—steaks done to a turn, with the juice in!—glorious goose!—splendid *sassages!*—oysters stewed in cream!"—and all this with such a watery smacking and sucking of the lips, and an unctuous gabble in the voice, that, as a neighbour, he was more to be dreaded, if possible, than the second of the triad, who volunteered long narratives of dyspepsia and other maladies.—*Mrs. Meredith's "Over the Straits."*

XVII.—BASTINGS AND DREDGINGS.

DIET.—It follows that, in our climate, a diet of animal food cannot, with safety, be exclusively employed. It is too highly stimulant; the springs of life are urged on too fast, and disease necessarily follows. There may, nevertheless, exist certain states of the system which require such a preternatural stimulus; and the physician may, therefore, confine his patient to an animal regimen with as much propriety as he would prescribe opium, or any other remedy. By a parity of reasoning, the exclusive use of vegetable food may be shown to be inconsistent with the acknowledged principles of dietetics, and to be incapable of conveying a nourishment sufficiently stimulating for the active exertions which belong to our present civilised condition.—*Paris.*

The rarest ways of dressing of all manner of roast meats, either flesh or fowl, by sea and land, and divers ways of breading or dredging meats, to prevent the gravy from too much evaporating.

Dredgings.—
1. Flour mixed with grated bread.
2. Sweet herbs dried and powdered, and mixed with grated bread.
3. Lemon-peel dried, or orange-peel mixed with flour.
4. Sugar finely powdered, and mixed with pounded cinnamon and flour, or grated bread.

5. Fennel seeds, corianders, cinnamon, and sugar, finely beaten and mixed with grated bread or flour.

6. For young pigs: grated bread or flour mixed with beaten nutmeg, ginger, pepper, sugar, and yolk of eggs.

7. Sugar, bread, and salt mixed.

Bastings.—
1. Fresh butter.
2. Clarified suet.
3. Minced sweet herbs, butter, and claret—especially for mutton and lamb.
4. Water and salt.
5. Cream and melted butter—especially for a flayed pig.
6. Yolk of eggs, grated biscuit, and juice of oranges.—*May's* "*Accomplished Cook.*" London, 1665.

Garnishes.—Boiled parsley is the universal garnish for all kinds of cold meat, poultry, fish, butter, cheese, &c. Horseradish is the garnish for roast beef, and with fish it is used alternately with sliced lemon. Lemons sliced are used for fowl and fish, as well as veal and calf's head. Carrot sliced for boiled beef. Barberries for game. Red beet for cold meat and fish. Fried smelts are used as a garnish for turbot, or any large fish. Sausages or forcemeat balls for turkey or fowl. Lobster, coral, and parsley to boiled fish. Fennel for mackerel and salmon. Currant jelly is used as a garnish to bread and custard pudding. Seville oranges for wild ducks and teal. Mint for lamb, and pickles for some meats and stews. Nasturtiums and other flowers to pastry, custard, and jelly.

Egg-snow Trifle.—This is a garnish for made-dishes or pastry. Whites of eggs must be beaten up to a froth in a vessel perfectly free from moisture of any kind, or grease. The whisk must be well done, and then ladled a spoonful at a time into boiling water. It will immediately set into a beautiful firm and white sponge, having the appearance of snow, and is used as frost-work to surround dishes of all kinds. Great care must be taken in the manipulation, and we need not say that the eggs must be fresh.

DALLAWAY'S SERVANTS' MONITOR.—1. Do everything in its proper time. 2. Keep everything to its proper use. 3. Put everything in its proper place.

XVIII.—MACARONI AND VERMICELLI.

Macaroni is a dough of fine wheat flour, made into a tubicular or pipe form, of the thickness of goose-quills, which was first prepared in Italy, and introduced into commerce in the name of Italian or Genoese paste. The wheat for this purpose must be ground into a coarse flour, called *granu* or *semoule* by the French, by means of a pair of light millstones, placed at somewhat greater distance than usual. This *semoule* is the substance employed for making the dough.—*Ure.*

To Dress Macaroni.—Put the quantity required on the fire to boil, either in milk or water, with a little salt; when done, take the macaroni out of the liquid, and put into a tin dish that will fit into a toaster or salamander. Have ready cheese grated, or cut up into suitable small pieces sufficient cheese, which place on the macaroni, with a small quantity of butter and a few bread-crumbs. Put a little salt in, with grated cheese on the top. Brown before the fire, and serve hot. Let the consumer use either pepper or cayenne, according to fancy; put none in the dish.

EXCELLENT FOOD.—The above is a simple recipe for macaroni; but it is good in any way, whether in stews or in soups, or plain boiled, with melted butter. Vermicelli is the same in every respect, only smaller in the pipe, and is used in puddings and soups in a like manner, and its name implies that it is tortuous in shape, like worms. There is nothing more nutritious to adults and children than macaroni or vermicelli, as they are both made from the gluten of the best Southern wheat.

XIX.—PICKLES.

Such boiled stuff, as well might poison poison.—Iachimo in " Cymbeline."

It is necessary that we should allude to these sponges of vinegar, as Dr. Kitchener designates them, which are often very indigestible. Make a brine of salt and water, lay the article to be pickled in soak for a day; take it out, and use good vinegar, and to every quart put an ounce of black pepper, the same of mustard-seed, half an ounce of ginger, and a few shalots. Boil it, and put over the article to be pickled. Walnuts, nasturtiums, mangoes, melons, capsicums, cucumbers, chillies, tomatoes, cauliflower, artichokes, French beans, mushrooms, red cabbage and white, samphire, horseradish, apples and peaches, marrows and pumpkins, and every mortal thing, in fact. We recommend the piccalilli made from curry-powder, ginger, mustard, rubbed well together with salad oil, and a large proportion of cayenne. The evidence of the *Lancet* commissioner (Dr. Hassall) and Mr. Blackwell (of the eminent firm of Crosse and Blackwell) went to prove that the pickles sold in the shops are nearly always artificially coloured, and are thus rendered highly unwholesome, if not actually poisonous. The thrifty manager is therefore recommended to make her pickles at home, if " her lord and master " is fond of them; or try the following:—

Apple and Onion Compound.—Mince fine equal quantities of apples and onions, after peeling both and coring the former, and add a little cayenne, and sufficient vinegar to cover the mixture. A very good relish for a chop, or steak, or cold meat; and far more wholesome than any kind of pickles.

THE OLD SCHOOL.—Mrs. Raffald's "Cookery," published in 1806, states that, to render pickles green they should be boiled with copper pence, or allowed to remain for twenty-four hours in a copper saucepan. We fear that the natural colour of vegetables cannot be preserved without the aid of some deleterious agent. Ure tells us that, " The peculiar and beautiful green colour which has been frequently imparted to pickles, is due, in nearly all cases, to the use of a salt of copper. This is in the highest degree injurious, and cannot be too strongly deprecated." The recipe we have above advised to the housewife is that usually termed *piccalilli*—certainly the most wholesome. It is made as follows: ginger, powdered, curry-powder, and mustard, of each two ounces, well mixed, and diluted with three or four table-spoonfuls of salad oil, then add a little cayenne pepper, and the requisite quantity of vinegar. Pour it warm on the article that you are desirous of pickling. This pickle will be well flavoured and thick, and more digestible than any made from plain vinegar.

XX.—SALADS.

We cannot reasonably expect tranquillity of the nervous system whilst there is disorder of the digestive organs. As we can imbibe no permanent source of strength but from the digestion of our food, it becomes important, on this account, that we should attend to its quality, quantity, and the periods for taking it, with a view to ensure its proper digestion.—*Abernethy.*

There is nothing more wholesome than vegetable salads, and there is no question that they promote digestion, when eaten with moderation. Lettuce, endive, cold potatoes, mild raw onions, and beet, when properly dressed, with good vinegar and the best salad oil, not forgetting pepper, both red and black, are excellent in their way. We have read that some years since an *artiste* made professional visits to the houses of the nobility and gentry of London for the purpose of dressing salads. He rode in his carriage, after the manner of fashionable physicians, and his *fee* was one guinea. The materials he provided himself, and he would allow no one to witness his compounding. His preparations were not always the same, but suited to the palate of his employers; and during the season he realised from forty to fifty guineas per day. He was an Italian by birth, and he adopted the proverb of his country—" *En salada, ben salata, hoc aceto, ben oleata* "—which tells us what we all know, that a salad should be well salted, with much oil, and little vinegar. Subsequently the 1s. 6d. mixture compounded by Batty, which would make a dozen salads, spoiled the foreigner's trade, and he was obliged to " shut up." Dr. Paris writes : " I have generally found condiments useful, and that dressed lettuce is less likely to ferment in the stomach than that which is eaten without them." Oil is known to have such an effect in checking fermentation, and the vinegar is not found to promote it. The lettuce contains a narcotic principle, and the effect of this is, in a great measure, obviated by a vegetable acid. There is no better recipe for dressing them than the poetical one of the Rev. Sydney Smith, which may be varied, by leaving out the anchovies, and using instead the same quantity of cream :—

" Two large potatoes, passed through kitchen sieve,
Unwonted softness to the salad give,
Of mordant mustard add a single spoon ;
Distrust the condiment which bites so soon ;
But deem it not, thou man of herbs, a fault
To add a double quantity of salt ;
Three times the spoon with oil of Lucca crown,
And once with vinegar procured from Town.
True flavour needs it, and your poet begs
The pounded yellow of two well-boiled eggs.
Let onion atoms lurk within the bowl,
And, scarce suspected, animate the whole ;

And, lastly, on the flavoured compound toss
A magic teaspoon of anchovy sauce.
Then, though green turtle fail, though venison's tough,
And ham and turkey are not boiled enough,
Serenely full the epicure may say,—
'Fate cannot harm me. I have dined to-day!'"

The fastidious declare it a mistake ever to wash lettuces; it destroys their crispness, and that it is more correct to eat the insects than to allow water to approach them.

Spanish Salad.—Take the lettuce, or any other salad that is to be procured, and tear the leaves off from the stem. Put into a bowl equal quantities of vinegar and water, a tea-spoonful of pepper and salt, and four times as much oil as vinegar and water; mix well together. Chop small on a plate any fine herbs that can be got, especially tarragon and chervil. Immediately before eating pour the sauce over the salad and herbs.—*Ford's " Spain."*

French Salad.—Cut half a pound of cold beef into thin slices, which put into a salad bowl, with a couple of lettuce cut into pieces; season with half a tea-spoonful of salt, one spoonful of vinegar, three of good salad oil, and a tea-spoonful of black pepper, with a little garlic or a shalot cut up fine; mix well together. The French use large quantities of oil and black pepper with their salads, and make them from cold potatoes, white chicory, kidney beans, and various kinds of vegetables.

We are told that Galen, in the decline of life, suffered much from morbid vigilance, until he had recourse to eating lettuce every evening, which cured him.

Lobster and Crayfish Salad.—Cut lobster or crayfish into small pieces, and add the yolk of an egg, boiled hard, a mealy potato, a table-spoonful of vinegar, two of oil, a dessert-spoonful of mustard, half a tea-spoonful of salt, the same of cayenne, and then slice into pieces a couple of medium-sized lettuces. A table-spoonful of cream may be added. Mix the whole well together.

To make a proper salad, *four* different characters are said to be required:—A *spendthrift* for oil; a *miser* for vinegar; a *counsellor* for salt: and a *madman* to stir the different ingredients together.

Horseradish Salad, for Roast Beef.—Moisten scraped horseradish with a small quantity of vinegar, add a little moist sugar, a spoonful of mustard, and the yolk of an egg, with a dust of cayenne; soften the whole with cream to the consistence required. A first-rate relish for beef, hot or cold.

Onion Salad.—Mild onions, cut in thin slices, and dressed with pepper and cayenne, and three parts of the best salad oil to one of vinegar, are good, and a fine stomachic.

Cucumber Salad are dressed plain in a similar way, and require a large portion of oil and pepper to make them digestible.

Meat Salads.—Any kind of meat, fish, or fowl, cut up small and added to a salad, make a light, pleasant, and wholesome meal, especially in hot weather. Mustard and cress, radishes, chicory, chives, &c., are all proper of their kind to be added to the articles we have previously quoted for the making of salads.

Parmentier's Salad Vinegar.—Shalots, sweet savory, chives, and tarragon, of each three ounces, two table-spoonfuls of dried mint leaves, and the same of balm; beat together in a mortar, and put them into a stone gallon bottle; fill up with strong white wine vinegar, cork it securely, and let it stand a fortnight exposed to the sun, then filter it.

GOOD ADVICE.—Persons in health, who feel a craving for salad, may indulge in the enjoyment of it to a great extent with perfect impunity, if not with positive benefit. Oil, when mixed in salad, appears to render the raw vegetables and herbs more digestible. Vinegar likewise promotes the digestion of lettuce, celery, and beetroot. Endive is very wholesome, strengthening, and easy of digestion; but, when strong seasoning is added to it, it becomes an epicurean sauce.—*Mayo.*

XXI.—OYSTERS.

Fool. Canst tell how an oyster makes his shell?
Lear. No.
Fool. Nor I neither.   *King Lear.*

We think we ought to devote a paper to oysters, as they are recommended by the faculty as affording much nourishment, and are easy of digestion. The French allow the British oysters to be superior to their own, according to "Le Manuel de l'Amateur des Huîtres;" but Mackay, in his "Letters from the United States," informs us that nowhere are there such fine oysters and so plentiful as at New York. Indeed, Mackay's description is sufficient to make "one's mouth water," if there is any meaning in such an expression. In the hotels at New York oysters are to be had at all hours, either from the shell, as they are commonly eaten in England, or cooked in twenty—or, for all I know to the contrary, in forty or a hundred—different ways. Oysters pickled, stewed, baked, roasted, fried, and scalloped — oysters made into soups, patties, and puddings—oysters with condiments, and without condiments—oysters without stint or limit, fresh as the fresh air, and almost as abundant, are daily offered to the palates of the Manhattanese, and appreciated with all the gratitude which such a bounty of nature ought to inspire! The most esteemed oysters in England are the *natives;* but the coasts everywhere abound with the common sorts, and the Irish oyster fisheries, as well as the Scotch, are highly esteemed. The southern colonies produce this delicious and wholesome bivalve in perfection, and those from Tasmania are unequalled in goodness and flavour. The Romans of old commenced their repasts with a few oysters obtained from the British coast, which custom is continued to the present day by the nation, who understand better than most peoples the cookery of food, and the requirements for the table: hence the common aphorism, "As many Frenchmen as many cooks."

Boiled Oysters.—Take four oysters, wash them clean—that is, wash their shells clean—then put your oysters into an earthen pot, with their hollow sides down; then put this pot, covered, into a great kettle with water, and so let them boil. Your oysters are thus dressed in their own liquor, and not mixed with water.—*Swift's Letters.*

Oysters Stewed.—Put a pint of oysters into a stewpan, with their own liquor; add to the liquor a quarter of a pint of cream or milk, some mace and cayenne, and a little salt; when it boils stir in an ounce of butter mixed smoothly with a little flour, then put in the oysters, bearded or not, as you choose. A few moments' simmering is sufficient, and when ready to serve add a little lemon-juice.

Oysters Roasted.—Place the oysters in their shells between the bars of a fire, or over a clear fire. In five minutes they will be done.

Oysters Fried.—Make a batter of eggs, milk, and flour, season it with pepper and salt, dip the oysters into the batter, which ought to be rather thick, and fry them of a light brown. A little nutmeg and bread-crumbs should be added to the seasoning.

Oyster Sauce.—Put three dozen bearded oysters into half a pint of melted butter. Let them just come to the boiling point, then put the whole into a basin. Strain the liquor from them; add sufficient milk and a little mace and cayenne. Set by fire to become hot, but not to boil. With rump-steaks or roast poultry, too much butter destroys the oysters' flavour.

Oyster Patties.—Put paste into patty-pans, and cover them, with a bit of bread on each; bake them, and by the time they are done have ready the following to fill them with on taking out the bread:—Take off the beards of the oysters, cut the other parts in small bits, put them into a small saucepan, with a little nutmeg, white pepper and salt, lemon, cream and a small quantity of the oyster liquor. Simmer for a few minutes, and fill the patty-pans. Some prefer the oyster put into the patty, and baked with the crust.

Oysters Marinaded.—Put the oysters into a saucepan for a few minutes, to blanch with their liquor, take them out, lay them on a linen cloth to drain; next place them for an hour in lemon-juice or vinegar, pepper and salt, and a little nutmeg; dip them into batter, and fry them.

Oysters Scalloped.—Open the shells carefully, and let the oysters remain in the scallop-shell; put some butter, bread-crumbs, and a little mace into the shells, and brown in a Dutch oven before the fire. Send them to table hot. They may be treated in a similar way and baked.

In Europe, oysters and French *chablis* is the correct thing, either at lunch or the commencement of a *recherché* repast; and in the Colonies the *chablis* may be exchanged for Blake's kaleedah, and the comparison "may be odorous," as "Mrs. Malaprop" has it.

Oysters Broiled.—Take them from the shells and beard them, and put them with their liquor into scallop-tins, with a little pepper and butter. Put the shells upon a gridiron, over a good fire, and serve them when plump and hot. Squeeze a little lemon-juice on them as they come from the fire.

If you wish to cleanse and fatten oysters for the table, place them on their flat sides in a pan or tub, which fill up with salt water, or, if fresh, with a handful of salt in it. Five ounces to the gallon is the proportion. This water should be changed every twenty-four hours, and a handful of flour, barleymeal, or oatmeal, with the same quantity of wheaten bran, added. In about a week they will be eatable. The poet tells us that—

> "Eggs, oysters too are amatory food,
> But who is their purveyor from above?
> Heaven knows, it may be Neptune, Pan, or Jove."

Oyster day, on St. James's day (July 25, old style), came in in London; and there is a popular notion that whoever eats oysters on that day will never want money for the rest of the year. Yet this does not accord with another popular conceit in Butter's "Dry Dinner," 1599: "It is unseasonable and unwholesome in all months that have not an r in their name to eat an oyster."—*Notes and Queries.*

Omelettes aux Huîtres.—Scald some oysters, and put two-thirds in a stewpan, with a little butter, and moisten them with some of their own liquor and some *coulis*, with a little pepper. Take care the oysters are well done; break a dozen eggs, season them with salt, parsley, chopped, and pepper; then have some sippets of bread, about the size of half-a-crown; give two or three blows of a knife to the oysters that remain, and put into the beaten eggs, with some cream; beat them all together, and pour your omelette into a pan, with melted butter; stir it till well done; put the oysters and their sauce in the dish; roll your omelette in the fryingpan, and serve in the middle of the ragoût of oysters.

Oyster, Lat., *ostrea*, "an oyster." This name is generally understood to signify the species of ostracean bivalve called *ostrea edulis*, which is one of a numerous genus, characterised by an equivalve shell, composed of two irregular lamellated valves, of which the convex or under one adheres to rocks, piles, or the shell of another individual. The animal is unprovided with either a byssus or foot; it is the best flavoured of its class, and has, consequently, been always much esteemed.—*Brande.*

XXII.—WATER.

In general, the number of rainy days is greatest near the sea, and decreases in proportion the farther we penetrate into the interior. On the eastern side of Ireland it rains 208 days in the year; in the Netherlands, 170; in England, France, the North of Germany, and the Gulf of Finland, on 152 to 155 days; in the plateau of Germany, on 131; and in Poland, on 158 days; while on the plains of the Volga, at Kaseán, it rains on 90; and in the interior of Siberia, only on 60 days of the year. In Western Europe it rains on twice as many days as in Eastern Europe; in Ireland on three times as many days as in Italy and the South of Spain.—*Johnston's "Physical Atlas."*

In many parts of England, and almost throughout the Australias, nothing is felt so much as the want of pure water. It is required for every purpose in life, and that which is the purest is obtained from the atmosphere. Rain water is of all others the softest. Brande tells us, "that, of all water, rain water, carefully and cleanly collected, is most pure." Dr. Paris writes that rain water is the purest natural water, being produced, as it were, by natural distillation. A house with a slate or corrugated iron roof would always supply more than sufficient water for the establishment without filtration. The average fall of rain is generally known in the part of the country, and the catch could be easily calculated from the area of roof available. The mean quantity of water that falls yearly in the world is about thirty-four inches, so says Dr. Thomson. The superficies of the roof have only to be calculated, and the supply may be known with great accuracy. In such cases water rates are unnecessary, and you obtain a purer supply. The city of Venice, with an immense population, is thus supplied. Surely, then, the expense of a few pounds would well repay the inestimable boon of having on hand a large quantity of this most necessary blessing of life.

THE CISTERNS OF VENICE.—The collection and preservation of water are becoming of national importance. The inhabitants of Venice (120,000), placed in the midst of a salt lake, communicating with the sea, derive their supply of water from the atmosphere. The greatest part of the rain is collected in 2,077 cisterns, of which 177 are public, and 1,900 belong to private houses. As these cisterns may serve as models, a detailed account, furnished to M. Grimaud by M. Saloxdori, the engineer of the municipality of Venice, has been laid before the French Academy of Sciences, and is printed in their "Comptes Rendus." An excavation is made in the earth, in the form of a reversed truncated pyramid, to the depth of three mètres (nearly ten feet), the earth being supported by walls of oak or other strong wood, on which is laid a thoroughly compact layer of clay, great care being taken to exclude air. At the bottom is placed a circular stone, hollowed in the middle; on this is put a hollow cylinder (like an ordinary well), constructed of dried bricks, well adjusted, those at the bottom only being pierced with conical holes. The space round the cylinder is filled with well-washed sea sand. At the four corners at the top are put four stone boxes, with stone lids pierced with holes. These boxes rest upon the sand. The rain from the roofs of the houses falls into these boxes, and, after filtering through the sand, enters the hollow cylinder, and then becomes a limpid water, pure to the last drop.—*Illustrated London News.*

NATURAL WATER PURIFIERS.—Mr. Warrington has for a year past kept twelve gallons of water in a state of admirably balanced purity by the action of two gold fish, six water snails, and two or three specimens of that elegant aquatic plant known as *balis perea sporalis.* Before the water snails were introduced, the decayed of the voluperia caused a growth of slimy mucus, which made the water turbid, and threatened to destroy both plants and fish. But under the improved arrangement, the slime, as fast as it is engendered, is consumed by the water snails, which reproduce it in the shape of young snails, whose tender bodies again furnish a succulent to the fish; while the voluperia plants absorb the carbonic acid exhaled by the respiration of their companions, fixing the carbon in the growing stems and luxuriant blossoms, and refreshing the oxygen—during sunshine, in visible little streams—for the respiration of the snails and the fish. The spectacle of perfect equilibrium thus simply maintained between animal, vegetable, and inorganic activity, is striking and beautiful; and such means may possibly hereafter be made available on a large scale for keeping tank water clean and sweet.—*Quarterly Review.*

RAIN FALL IN IRELAND.—You would hardly believe what a rainy country Ireland is. I have here statistics as to the rain fall of Ireland, and I find we have actually had in 1862, 221 days—rather more than seven months—of rain in Ireland.—*Sir Robert Peel.*

RAIN WATER.—The cottage of the writer is covered with corrugated iron, with felt under as a non-conductor of heat. The rain water is led by spouting into iron tanks, and it is always as pure and pellucid as it is possible to be, without any filtration. There is more water on the premises than can be consumed, without the payment of rates, or the trouble of drawing it from a stream or well, and every house can be thus easily supplied. Dr. E. S. Hall, in his paper on "The Climate and Health of Tasmania," published at the last London Exhibition, states that, for the last seven years, the number of days in which rain fell in Tasmania has been recorded; the mean of six years being 137·63; but 1861 had 167 rainy days, being eight more than 1859, previously the highest.

XXIII.—SAUSAGES.

*The sausage made of beef
Is fit for London thief;
The sausage made of pork
Is eaten but at York.—The Razor Grinder.*

If the reader is wise he will always abstain from eating sausages, unless he knows of their manufacture, should he not be desirous of partaking of the man who, Dickens cleverly informs us, was chopped into sausage meat, and all that remained of him was his buttons. It is a positive and notorious fact in all parts of the world, that every kind of unwholesome meat is minced into sausages. Who would ever think of putting good meat into sausages when the mince and sage will effectually smother the flavour of putrid stuff? We have given elsewhere a recipe for black hog's puddings. We now give a few modern ways of making at home a very favourite relish, with the aid of a twenty-five shilling machine:—

Sausages.—To each pound of pork allow a pound of veal and one pound of fat—that is, two parts lean to one part of fat. Mix them well, and allow a pound of bread-crumbs, thyme, parsley, an ounce of sage, two heads of leeks, a little garlic or a shalot, chopped fine, with pepper, salt, and nutmeg. To each pound allow one egg, the yolks and whites separate; beat both well, mix in the yolks, and as much of the whites as necessary to moisten the bread, and add all the ingredients together.

Worcester Sausages are made of beef, suet, and allspice, with other herbs.

Mutton Sausages.—To each pound of mutton add a pound of beef suet, and anchovies, for relish, chopped fine, and what seasoning you choose. Herbs or not, as you please.

Veal Sausages.—Veal sausages are made like Oxford sausages, except bacon is used instead of sage.

Savoury Sausages.—Salt a piece of lean beef and pork with common salt, a little saltpetre, sugar, black pepper, and allspice, for two days. Season with pepper, cayenne, garlic. and a shalot; and mince fine and put into clean gut. Smoke them. When wanted for use they may be boiled and eaten cold.

Saveloys.—These are a fine relish, cleanly and properly prepared, and are good either hot or cold. The proportions are as follows: Pork, free from bone and skin, three pounds; salt it with an ounce of saltpetre, and half a pound of common salt for about forty-eight hours; then mince it fine, and add three spoonfuls of pepper, a dozen leaves of sage, and a pound of grated bread; mix well; fill the skins, and boil or bake them slowly: or the ingredients may be made flat and round, without being put into skins, and cooked in that manner, after being mixed with beaten eggs, in order to bind the meat together.

Oxford Sausages.—Take one pound and a half of pig meat, cut from the griskins, without any skin; half a pound of veal, and a pound and a half of beef suet. Mince these meats very finely, then mix them with a dessert-spoonful of powdered sage, pepper, and salt, to taste, and the well-beaten yolks and whites of four eggs. The whole should be well beaten together, as much depends on the mixing.—*Theodore Hook in " Peter Priggins."*

French Sausages.—The meat is cut into pieces and rubbed with garlic. It is then put in a mortar and pounded until it becomes a paste, when it is sprinkled with brown sugar, and worked up again. It is now worked up with the following ingredients :—Two parts of salt, and one of saltpetre, are well pounded with allspice, mace, and white pepper, and a small quantity of preserved bay-leaf. The meat being now laid on the table, and rolled out, strips of lard are laid on it with peppercorns. The sausages are then rolled, placed in pickled chitterlings, tied very tight at each end, and hung up to dry. They have a fragrant taste, which, and their tenderness, as they are not boiled, makes them particularly *piquante* and *recherché*.

Sausage Rolls are an excellent variety of relish, which is merely the sausage meat enveloped in paste, in any shape you wish; but we say again, beware of those ready made, unless you know where and by whom.

AN AMERICAN COOK—AUNT CHLOE.—A cook she certainly was, in the very bone and centre of her soul. Not a chicken, a turkey, or duck in the barn-yard but looked grave when they saw her approaching, and seemed evidently to be reflecting on their latter end; and certain it was that she was always meditating on trussing, stuffing, and roasting, to a degree that was calculated to inspire terror in any reflecting fowl living. Her corn-cake, in all its varieties of hoe-cakes, dodgers, muffins, and other species too numerous to mention, was a sublime mystery to all less practised compounders; and she would shake her fat sides with honest pride and merriment, as she would narrate the fruitless efforts that one and another of her compeers had made to attain her elevation.—*Uncle Tom's Cabin.*

XXIV.—BREAD AND BREAKFAST CAKES.

One of the most important, if not altogether the most important article of food, unquestionably is bread; and although barley, oats, and other cereals are sometimes used by the baker, wheat is the grain which is best fitted for the manufacture of that article, not only on account of the larger amount of gluten or nitrogeneous matter which it contains, and that can only be found in other edible grains, but also on account of the almost exact balance in which the nitrogeneous and non-nitrogenous constituents exist in that cereal, and owing to which it is capable of ministering to all the requirements of the human frame, and of being assimilated at once, and without effort to our organs; whence the name of the "Staff of Life," which is often given to it, wheat being like milk, a perfect food.—*Ure.*

To Make Bread.—The following is said to be a good bread recipe: Put a bushel of flour into a kneading trough. Mix a pint of yeast thoroughly with as much milk-warm water; make a deep hole in the middle of the flour, and pour the yeast and water into it; then take a spoon and work it round the edges of this body of moisture, so as to bring into it by degrees flour enough to make a thin batter, which must be well stirred for a minute or two. Throw a handful of flour over the surface of this batter, and cover the whole with a cloth thickly folded to keep it warm. Set it by the fire, regulating the distance by the state of the weather and the season of the year. When the batter has risen enough to make cracks in the flour, form the whole mass into dough, thus:—Begin by strewing six ounces of salt over the heap; and then beginning round the hole containing the batter, work the flour into it, pouring in milk-warm water or milk as it is wanted. When the whole mass is moistened, knead it well, mould the loaves, let them rise for twenty minutes, and put them into an oven that has been previously heated. The length of time will depend on the size of the loaves. The baking in an ordinary oven will require about an hour for a four pound loaf, fifty minutes for a three pound, and so on in proportion.

This important article of food is made of the flour of different grains; but it is only those which contain gluten that admit of conversion into a light or porous and spongy bread, of which wheaten bread furnishes the best example.—*Brande.*

PERSIAN BREAD.—Certainly the women of Yezd are the handsomest women in Persia. The proverb is, that to live happy, a man must have a wife of Yezd, eat the bread of Yezdecas, and drink the wine of Shiraz.—*Tavernier.*
Keep him at least three paces distant who hates bread, music, and the laugh of a child.—*Jean Caspar Lavater.*

Unfermented Bread.—Unfermented bread is made without yeast, by using muriatic acid and carbonate of soda. Flour, three pounds; bi-carbonate of soda, four drachms; hydrochloric acid, five drachms; salt, one drachm; water, twenty-four ounces.—*The Critic.* Another:—Flour, seven pounds; bi-carbonate of soda, one ounce; tartaric acid, three-quarters of an ounce; and water, two quarts.—*Lloyd's Weekly Paper.* As soon as either of these ingredients are mixed, they must be immediately put into the oven. We have tried these recipes, and they answer the purpose of making the bread light; but the taste is not palatable.

French Bread.—French bread is made from four pounds of fine flour, a quart of lukewarm milk, salt, one quarter of a pound of melted butter; mix the fluids together, and add three beaten eggs, handling it as little as possible; let the dough rise, and mould it into shape. Bake in a quick oven.

The French use eggs, milk, and butter as ingredients for their fancy bread, and are in the habit of adding ammonia to the dough, which, during its evaporation in the oven, raises it, and thus adds to its sponginess.

Brown Bread.—This is far more easy of digestion than the very white bread. To three pounds of flour add one pound of rye flour, and the same quantity of yeast and salt, as previously given, and bake longer.

Cottage Bread.—Put into a pan fourteen pounds of flour; add to a quart of warm water a quarter of a pint of good yeast; make a hole in the flour, pour in the water and the yeast, stir it well with a wooden spoon until it forms a thickish paste, throw a little flour over, and leave it in a warm place. In about an hour it will have risen, and burst through the covering of flour; then add more warm water, and three teaspoonfuls of salt. Until it forms, when kneaded, a rather stiff dough, it cannot be too much worked. Then let it remain, covered with a cloth, an hour. After a time, divide it into loaves and bake for an hour and a quarter.

In making home-made bread an increase of weight equal to a fifth is said to arise if bran water is used for working the dough.

Belvidere Cakes.—Take one quart of flour, four eggs, a piece of butter the size of an egg; mix the butter with the flour, beat the eggs together with cold milk; then pour gradually into the flour, add a teaspoonful of salt, work it for a few minutes, cut the dough the size of a breakfast-plate, and bake in a quick oven.

Pandarus: Ay! to the leavening; but here's yet in the word. Hereafter to the kneading, the making of the cake, the heating of the oven, and the baking; nay, you must stay the cooling too, or you may chance to burn your lips.—*Troilus and Cressida.*

Rice Cakes.—Breakfast cakes are made sometimes from rice, which are easily digestible. Put half a pound of rice to soak over night; early in the morning boil it very soft, drain it from the water, mix with it a quarter of a pound of butter, and set it away to cool. When cold stir in a quart of milk, and add to it a little salt; beat up six eggs and mix with half a pint of flour; stir the eggs and flour into the rice and milk. Having mixed the whole, bake it on the girdle in cakes the size of a dessert-plate, butter them, and send to table hot.

Rolls.—Take nine ounces of flour, and an ounce and a half of butter, and rub them together; then take four spoonfuls of yeast, half a cup of milk, the yolk of one egg beaten, and mix them together; pour on them the flour, and water, and butter, working them lightly with the hand.

The finest and best baked bread is that which is made of farina, abounding in gluten; for this latter body, rising in large blisters by the dilatation of the gases imprisoned within it, allows each feculent grain to participate in the communication of the heat, and to burst as it would by boiling. Hence, after panification, if the paste has been well kneaded, we do not find a single grain of fecula entire.—*Raspail's "Organic Chemistry," by Henderson.*

Dr. Dauglish proposes a new system of making "aërated bread." The distinguishing characteristic is to do away with the old plan of fermentation by yeast and hand kneading. For yeast, Dr. Dauglish substitutes carbonic acid gas, which produces all the effects on the flour to turn it into bread. The machinery occupies little space, and is managed by one man, and every sack of flour, by this method, will yield five 4lb. loaves more than the present process of fermentation. The process is simple, and consists of a gas holder and a generator, an air pump, suitable to condensed elastic fluids, a mixing vessel, and a water vessel in connection with it. The flour is first of all emptied from the granary down a long shoot into the mixer, which is a hollow sphere of cast iron, constructed so as to resist an internal pressure of 100lbs. to the square inch. The mixer is then closed so as to be air-tight, and all the air is pumped out until a vacuum of about 27lbs. to the square inch is produced. This done, the carbonic acid gas is admitted into the water through a pipe passing from the reservoir to the

BREAD AND BREAKFAST CAKES. 75

water vessel, which is above the mixer, and communicates with it, and the condenser is set to work until a pressure of 90lbs. is produced. Two sacks of flour will take from 28 to 30 gallons of water, according to the quantity, and about ten minutes will be occupied in thoroughly aërating this quantity of water. According to a well-known rule, the 30 gallons of water will take in as many gallons of gas, and the vacuum in the mixer is also charged with gas, though this is afterwards returned to the reservoir to be used again. The salt is infused in the shape of brine, through a separate pipe, at the rate of 4lbs. of salt to a sack of flour. The water is turned into the flour, and the process of mixing commences, which is performed by half a dozen iron blades made to revolve rapidly inside the iron vessel on an axis turned by the steam-engine, and in seven or eight minutes the two sacks of flour and the thirty gallons of water are turned into dough, as light and as well kneaded as the most expert journeyman baker, with an hour's violent exertion, can effect. The whole process lasts half an hour, and the bread is now ready for the oven. The cost is about three shillings per sack, while the baker, by the hand system, is put down at four shillings.

Muffins.—Five eggs, a quart of milk, two ounces of butter, a tea-spoonful of salt, two large table-spoonfuls of yeast, and enough flour to make a stiff batter; warm the milk and butter, cover the mixture, and set it to rise in a warm place. When it has risen sufficiently grease your baking-iron and muffin rings. Bake them a light brown; tear them asunder, and butter.

According to "Things Not Generally Known," in the old times of Henry VIII., in the regulations for his Highness's household (the kings of those days not being called Majesty), there was a regulation that enacted punishments for the adulteration of food, which, if carried out in our day, according to Dr. Hassall, would involve the imprisonment of a very numerous class. "His Highness's baker shall not put alums in the bread, or mix rye, oaten, or bean flour with the same, and if detected shall be put in the stocks." It is to be regretted that, as far as the public health is concerned, the same law is not now in force.

Crumpets.—To a pound and a half of flour add three pints of milk, two table-spoonfuls of yeast, and two eggs; mix the milk lukewarm, beat it into a batter, and let it stand until it rises into bladders; then bake on polished iron in the tin rims.

Scones.—Flour, two pounds; bi-carbonate of soda, quarter of an ounce; salt, quarter of an ounce; sour buttermilk, one pint, more or less. Mix to the consistence of light dough, roll out about half an inch thick, or less, and cut them in any shape you please; bake them on a girdle, turning, to brown on each side.

Potato Rolls.—Boil two pounds of potatoes, mash them, and work them with an ounce of butter and as much milk as will pass them through a colander; mix with the potatoes half a pint of yeast, and a quarter of a pint of lukewarm water. Pour the whole on two pounds of flour, knead it well, let it stand before the fire to rise, and make it into rolls. Toast and butter them after baking.

Oat Cakes.—Soak a pound of oatmeal in a pint of buttermilk, rub a quarter of an ounce of carbonate of soda and a little salt in half a pound of flour, and mix with the oatmeal; roll out any thickness, and bake in a moderate oven.

Scotch Shortbread.—Rub one pound of butter and twelve ounces of fine sugar into two pounds of flour, with the hand, make it into a stiff paste with four eggs; roll it out to double the thickness of a penny-piece, cut it into cakes, pinch the edges, stick slices of candied lemon-peel and carraway comfits on the top, and bake on plates in a moderate oven.

Soda Cakes.—Six ounces of butter rubbed into one pound of flour, half a pound of sugar, half a pound of currants, three-quarters of an ounce of carraway-seeds, a tea-spoonful of soda dissolved in a little warm water, and mixed with new milk to make a pint. Bake an hour, putting it in the oven as soon as possible after mixing.

Buttermilk Breakfast Cakes.—Take half a pint of buttermilk, add to it sufficient flour to make it into dough, in which a tea-spoon half full of bi-carbonate of soda is well mixed. Bake quickly, and butter hot. The only requisite in these cakes is to put them in the oven or on the girdle as soon as the soda and buttermilk have come in contact.

About the middle of the last century hardly any wheat was used in the northern counties of England. In Cumberland, the principal families used only a small quantity about Christmas. The crust of the goose pie, with which almost every table in the country is then supplied, was, at the period referred to, almost uniformly made of barley meal. —*Eden on the Poor.*

In many parts of England it is the custom for private families to bake their own bread. This is particularly the case in Kent, and in some parts of Lancashire. In 1804 there was not a public baker in Manchester, and their number is still limited.— *M'Culloch's Commercial Dictionary.*

For some time public attention has been drawn to an odious fraud committed by a great many bakers in the north of France and of Belgium—the introduction of a certain quantity of sulphate of copper into their bread. When the flour was made from bad grain, this adulteration was very generally practised, as was proved by many convictions and confessions of the guilty persons. When the dough does not rise well in the fermentation, this inconvenience was found to be obviated by the addition of blue vitriol, which was supposed also to cause the flour to retain more water. The quantity of blue vitriol added is extremely small, and it is never done in the presence of strangers, because it is reckoned a valuable secret. Lime-water has been recommended by Liebig as a means of improving the bread made from inferior flour, or of flour slightly damaged by keeping. It was tried with success at Glasgow in 1855, still we should deprecate the use of lime-water. To allow articles of food to be tampered with, under any circumstances, is a dangerous practice, and Liebig himself has said that chemists should never propose the use of chemical products for culinary preparations.—*Ure's Dictionary.*

A SCHOLAR BAKING HIS "DAILY BREAD."—I was told an amusing story of an Oxford man shepherding down in Otago. Some one came into his hut, and, taking up a book, found it in a strange tongue, and inquired what it was. The Oxonian (who was baking at the time) answered that it was "Machiavellian Discourses upon the First Decade of Livy." The wonder-stricken visitor laid down the book and took up another, which was, at any rate, written in English. This he found to be Bishop Butler's "Analogy." Putting it down speedily, as something not in his line, he laid hands upon a third. This proved to be "Patrum Apostolicorum Opera," on which he saddled his horse and went right away, leaving the Oxonian to his baking.—*Butler's "First Year in the Canterbury Settlement."*

Sally Lunns.—Two pounds of fine flour, two table-spoons of yeast, with a little warm water. This must be put to rise in half an hour. Put two ounces of butter and the yolk of an egg in as much new milk as will make it a proper stiffness. Mix all well up, and, when risen, bake in a quick oven.

The bun so fashionable, called Sally Lunn, originated with a young woman of that name at Bath about thirty years ago. She cried them in a basket, with a white cloth over it, morning and evening. Dalmer, a respectable baker and musician, noticed her, bought her business, and made a song and set it to music on behalf of Sally Lunn. This composition became the street favourite; barrows were made to distribute the nice cakes. Dalmer profited thereby, and retired; and to this day the Sally Lunn cakes claim pre-eminence in all the cities of England.—*Hone's "Every-day Book."*

Corn Cakes.—Two cups of Indian corn meal, one cup of flour, two eggs, large spoonful of melted butter, two small tea-spoons of cream of tartar, one of soda, and one of sugar; mix and bake.

ECONOMY.—How wasteful, then, and indeed, how shameful, for a labourer's wife to go to the baker's shop; and how negligent, how criminally careless of the welfare of his family must the labourer be who permits so scandalous a use of the proceeds of his labour! . . . Give me, for a beautiful sight, a neat and smart woman, heating her oven and setting in her bread! And if the bustle does make the sign of labour glisten on her brow, where is the man that would not kiss that off rather than lick the plaster from the cheek of a duchess?—*Cobbett.*

Superior Cakes.—Mix with Jones's patent flour, a little butter, and moisten with new milk; bake on the girdle, and butter hot. Nothing so simple to make, and none so wholesome or nutritious for the breakfast table. We strongly recommend them; as the quack advertiser has it, "one trial will prove the fact."

Yorkshire Cakes.—Melt in a pint of milk four ounces of butter; add two pounds of flour, three table-spoonfuls of yeast, and two eggs well beaten. Let rise. Then knead them lightly, and make into cakes. Let them rise on the tins before you bake them, which do in a moderately heated oven.

Pulled Bread.—When an ordinary loaf is half baked, take it out of the oven, and tear it into small-sized pieces, of irregular shape, and bake them brown and crisp. They form crust for cheese, or may be used as a substitute for wine-biscuits. Many persons prefer crust, and in this mode their taste is easily gratified.

WHITE BREAD.—He had prepared for me a simple, but hospitable repast, of which fruits from his own garden, the white bread of Olyra, and the juice of the honey-cane, formed the most costly luxuries.—*The Epicurean.*

Breakfast Rolls.—Mix with a pound of flour a little salt, two ounces of butter, an ounce of sugar, and two eggs, well beaten up, with half a pint of milk, lukewarm, and two table-spoonfuls of yeast; let the dough rise, and then make it into six rolls, and set them to rise again, and then bake in tins.

Northumbrian Breakfast Cakes.—Rub well into a pound of flour four ounces of butter, a little salt, a tea-spoonful of sugar, and a proportionate quantity of milk or cream; knead it well together, and bake on a girdle. When done, open the cakes, and butter; send them up hot to the breakfast-table, enveloped in a napkin.

These cakes are made constantly at a private house in Tasmania, the inmates of whom came from "bleak Northumbria," and are always first-rate.

Italian Bread.—Make a stiff dough, with flour and six table-spoonfuls of sugar, three eggs, well beaten, two ounces of fresh butter, and a little grated lemon-peel; mix them in a pan, with a wooden spoon, and, if the dough is not firm, add more flour and sugar. Then turn it out of the pan, and work it slightly; cut it into the shape of round long biscuits, and glaze them with the white of an egg.

Barley Bannocks.—Mix barley-meal with water and a little salt; then roll them out into a paste, three quarters of an inch thick, divide it into cakes, and bake in an oven or on the girdle of a light brown colour.

BARLEY BREAD.—Barley bread has a sweetish, but not unpleasant taste; it is, however, rather viscid, and is less nutritive, as well as less digestible, than wheaten bread. It is common to mix pea-meal with the barley, which certainly improves the bread. Rye bread is of a dark brown colour, and is apt to lie heavy on the stomach; it is also liable to create ascecency and purging; but it appears to be highly nutritive. In some of the interior counties of England, where bread is often manufactured from oatmeal, there is a mode of preparing the meal by making it sour; the bread, instead of being hard, is thus rendered of a soft texture, and, from its moderate acidity, is wholesome to strong persons; but invalids should, if possible, avoid it. In bread, however, this grain is more usually in an unfermented state, or it is made into flat thin cakes, which are baked or roasted. The *bannock*, *class bread*, and *riddle cakes*, are the names which such productions have received. The *bannock* is oaten bread made into loaves. It is evident, from the health and vigour of the people who use this grain as a principal article of that it must be nutritive; but the stomach will require some discipline before it can digest it.—*Paris on Diet*.

American Puffets for Tea or Breakfast.—One pint of cold milk, that has been boiled, a quarter of a pint of yeast, half a pound of butter, half a pound of sugar, and five eggs, to be made into a stiff paste, which must be put on the baking-tin to rise, and, without taking off, be baked in the usual manner.

Unfermented Bread (*another way*).—White meal, three pounds, avordupois; bi-carbonate of soda, four and a half ounces, troy; hydrochloric acid, five drachms; water, thirty fluid ounces; salt, two-thirds of an ounce, troy. Bread made in this manner contains nothing but flour, common salt, and water. It has an agreeable natural taste, keeps much longer than common bread, is more digestible, and is much less disposed to turn sour. — "*Instructions for making Unfermented Bread*," *by a Physician*.

The French, who particularly excel in the art of baking, have a great many different kinds of bread. Their *pain bis*, or brown bread, is the coarsest of all, and is made of coarse groats, mixed with a portion of white flour. The *pain de métiel* is a bread made with rye and barley flour, to which wheat flour is sometimes added also. The *pain de blanc* is a kind of bread between white and brown, made of white flour and fine groats. The *pain blanc*, or white bread, is made of white flour, shaken through a sieve after the finest flour has been separated. The *pain mollet*, or soft bread, is made of the finest flour, without any admixture. The *pain chaland*, or customers' bread, is a very white kind of bread, made of pounded paste. *Pain chapelé* is a small kind of bread, with a well-beaten and very light paste, seasoned with butter or milk. This name is also given to a small bread, from which the thickest crust has been removed with a rasp. *Pain cornée* is a name given by the French bakers to a kind of bread made with four corners, and sometimes more; of all the kinds of small bread this has the strongest and firmest paste. *Pain de la reine*, Queen's bread, *pain à la Sigorie*, *pain chapelé*, and *pain cornée* are all kinds of bread differing only in the lightness or thickness of the paste. *Pain de gruau* is a small white bread made now in Paris from the flour separated after a slight grinding from the best wheat. Such flour is in hard granular particles.—*Ure*.

Milk Cuits (American).—Two pounds of flour, sifted; half a pound of butter; two eggs, six wine-glasses of milk and two of yeast. Cut the butter into the milk, and warm it lightly in the stove; sift the flour into the pan and pour the milk and butter into it. Beat the eggs and pour them in also, lastly the yeast. Mix all well together, flour your pasteboard, put the dough on it and knead it. Then cut the dough in small pieces and knead them in round balls. Stick the tops of them with a fork, lay them in butter-pans, and set them to rise. They will be probably light in an hour. When they are light, put them in a moderate oven and bake them.

Apple Bread (French).—Take apples and flour, in the proportion of two parts of flour to one of apples mashed well together, and add a quantity of yeast, and allow it to rise a sufficient time. Very little water is required if the apples are juicy.

In the country in France they make an excellent bread from flour and apples, baking it in long loaves, and they are very sweet and wholesome.

Manchets (fine White Rolls).—The manchets are used in the Universities of Oxford and Cambridge to this day, and the following recipes for their make appears in Nares' " Glossary : "—

LADY OF ARUNDEL'S MANCHET.—Take a bushel of white wheat flour, twenty eggs, three pounds of fresh butter; then take as much salt and barm as the ordinary manchet; temper it together with new milk pretty hot, then let it lie the space of half an hour to rise, so as you may work it into bread, and bake it. Let not your oven be too hot.—*True Gentlewoman's Delight*, 1676.

Take a quart of cream, put thereto a pound of beef suet minced small, put it into the cream, and season it with nutmeg, cinnamon, and rose-water; put to it eight eggs and but four whites, and two grated manchets; mingle them well together, and put them in a buttered dish, bake it, and being baked, scrape on sugar, and serve it.—*The Queen's Royal Cookery*, 1713.

Colonial Damper.—This bush fare is simply composed of flour and water, with a little salt, made into flat round pieces on bark, and baked in the ashes. All old colonists are expert in making damper. "Tea, damper, and mutton," is a colonial institution, as the weary bushman is fully aware of.

THE CAMP OUT.—At length their preparations were made. The fire burned up, the pot was on to boil, the flour, kneaded into a heavy dough, was placed to bake in the ashes until the dough mass should have acquired the consistency that entitled it to its appropriate name of damper. Gilbert's mug was made a tea-pot for the occasion; and the two friends, thoroughly wearied, lit their short black pipes and reclined against their saddles, watching with considerable satisfaction the cooking of a savoury mess which was to constitute their meal.—"*Good for Nothing,*" *in Fraser.*

Ash Cake.—Scald the meal, and put it in little heaps to cool, then mix it with more water (warm) into dough, and mould it into flat cakes rather larger than a breakfast saucer. These are baked as follows:— Open a place in the side of a wood fire on the hearth, and having put in the cakes, each between two cabbage leaves, lay them on the hot hearth, sprinkle some ashes lightly over first, then put hot coals on the top, and if these appear to cool fast, remove them from time to time, and replace them with hotter coals from the fire.

Johnny Cake.—This is made in the same manner as ash cake, and baked before the fire; first on one side, and then on the other.

Pone Cake.—Made in the same way as the ash cake, and baked in a utensil much used in America, and in some parts of England—a round kettle standing on legs, with a lid fitting down, so that you may put hot coals on the top as well as under. This and the girdle should be in every labourer's cottage.

We are indebted for the three last recipes to Cobbett's "Cottage Economy;" and we presume the latter utensil is the modern camp oven.

We exhaust the space we have allotted to bread and breakfast cakes with the following hints to enable the housewife to select flour:—

1. Look at its colour: if it is white, with a straw-coloured tint, it is a good sign; if white with specks, the flour is not good.
2. Examine its adhesiveness. Wet and knead it a little: if it works dry and elastic, it is good; if it works soft and sticky, it is poor.
3. Throw a small lump of dry flour against a dry and smooth surface; if it falls like powder, it is bad.
4. Squeeze some of the flour in your hand: if it retains the shape given it by pressure, that is a good sign.

The Adelaide (South Australia) silk-dressed flour, and the best American barrelled flour of good brands, are the most economical, as they absorb considerably more water than the generality of other flours. The London *Bakers' Gazette*, of 1849, asserted a self-evident truth—the finer the flour the more bread can be made of it.

HOME-MADE AND BAKERS' BREAD.—Home-made good bread is full of flavour—that of the baker comparatively tasteless. The former is firm, of a strong, compact substance, goes far, and keeps well (from three days to three weeks), and, indeed, improves after the three first days; the latter is light, very white and spongy, does not satisfy the appetite, and can scarcely be kept in an eatable condition for four days.—*Magazine of Domestic Economy*.

XXV.—THE DESSERT.

A word of doubtful etymology, signifying the last service at dinner, consisting of fruits and confections, &c. The modern dessert is probably equivalent to the *mensæ secundæ* of the Romans. If we believe Congreve, the term came into use by the French about the commencement of the seventeenth century, and was soon adopted into, and naturalised in most of the European languages. In all the countries of Europe the splendour of the dessert has ever since the period of its introduction kept pace with the progress of refinement and civilisation; and by many *gastronomes* the qualities and arrangement of a dessert are looked upon as the most valid test of all that is Attic in taste, and refined in elegance.—*Brande*.

There is no question that Professor Brande is correct in the above definition of a dessert, as nothing adds so much to a banquet, or the most common dinner party, than that the last service should be perfect of its kind. The amphitryon must see that this course is properly served and assorted. The arrangement is a mere matter of taste, perhaps display; but we have now only to enumerate the essentials, viz., cakes, biscuits, and conserves of every possible variety; ices, and fruits of every kind—pine apples, grapes, melons, strawberries, raspberries, cherries, plums, peaches, apricots, pears, apples, medlars, filberts, walnuts, chestnuts, oranges, shaddocks, figs, dates, and many tropical varieties, not forgetting—

> The simple olives, best allies of wine,
> Must I pass over in my bill of fare?
> I must, although a favourite *plat* of mine
> In Spain, and Lucca, Athens, everywhere;
> On them and bread 'twas oft my lot to dine.

In olden times it was the fashion in summer time, we may presume, always to take the dessert in the summer-house in the garden. We are reminded of this in the "Second Part of Henry IV.," when Shallow tells Falstaff, Silence, Bardolph, Davy, and the Page—

"Nay, you shall see mine orchard; whence, in an arbour, we will eat a last year's pippin of my own grafting, with a dish of carraways, and so forth. Come, Cousin Silence, and then to bed."

The celebrity of Mazagong is owing to its mangoes, which are certainly the best fruit I ever tasted. The parent tree, from which all those of this species have been grafted, is honoured during the fruit season by a guard of sepoys; and in the reign of Shah Jehan couriers were stationed between Delhi and the Mahratta coast, to secure an abundant and fresh supply of mangoes for the royal table.—*Mrs. Graham's "Journal of a Residence in India."*

The mangusteen, the most delicate fruit in the world; the pride of the Malay Islands. —*Marsden.*

A LUXURY.—Frozen water-melon is all the rage among the epicures at Washington. The melon (select a first-class one in the start at first) subjected to the freezing process should be buried in pounded ice, perhaps twelve hours previous to use, and packed away carefully in the coolest place attainable. When again brought to light the melon shows an even coating like dew upon its surface, and on being cut (lengthwise, by all means), a smart crisp detonation precedes the knife in its process, when the fruit is in perfect condition. Then carve, and eat ad libitum.—*Washington Evening Star.*

THE FIG.—This fruit, even in a perfectly dry state, is about as nutritious as rice. In the moist state, as imported, the fig will go considerably further in feeding and fattening than an equal quantity of wheaten flour.—*J. F. W. Johnston.*

XXVI.—GAME.

The effect of keeping game is not only to make it tender, but likewise to bring out its flavour, which tends in another way to promote digestion. Nothing is more tasteless than a pheasant cooked too soon, or has a finer flavour after hanging a proper length of time. No doubt, the flavour, while it gratifies the palate, assists digestion, by sympathetically exciting the stomach.—*Mayo on the "Philosophy of Living."*

Haunch of Venison Roasted.—

The haunch was a picture for painters to study,
The fat was so white, and the lean was so ruddy.—*Goldsmith.*

Take a haunch of venison and set it before a slow fire, taking care to paper it to prevent its scorching. Baste it well with salt and water at first, but afterwards use clean dripping or butter, dredge it with flour, and when it is done it will be frothed and browned on both sides. Wrap a white paper ruffle round the knuckle-bone, and send it to table with plain gravy; serve with currant jelly. If the venison has hung long, the outer skin had better be removed. Unless the venison is very tender and fat, a haunch of good mutton, dressed in the same way, and kept, is preferable.

Venison Pasty.—A shoulder boned makes a good pasty, but it must be beaten and seasoned, and the want of fat supplied by that of a fine well-hung loin of mutton, steeped twenty-four hours in equal parts of rape, vinegar, and port. The shoulder being sinewy, it will be an advantage to rub it well with sugar for two or three days, and when it is to be used, wipe it extremely clean from it and the wine. Cut the meat into pieces two inches square, and put them into a stewpan with two gills of port wine, one of claret, a few shalots, some pepper, salt, mace, and allspice, and enough stock to cover it; let it simmer until three parts done. Take out the meat you intend for the pasty, and put into a deep dish with a part of the liquor, then cover the pasty an inch thick with paste, and bake for two hours, and before it is sent to table pour in a sauce made from the liquor the venison was stewed in, free from fat; add some pepper, salt, the juice of half a lemon, and half a gill of port wine or claret, and a little thickening.

"Cervus," in a late number of the *Field,* asks for a good recipe for venison pasty. We recommend the above.

Kangaroo Pasty, made in a similar way, is even more palatable.

To Cook Kangaroo.—Take the hind-quarters, above the kidney. Cut off the tail, also the legs, at the first joint from the back; having discarded the feet, cut up the remainder of the legs with the tail to stew for gravy, of which you will require, when done, a pint or more; add to the gravy meat a small onion sliced, a few peppercorns, and one or two bay leaves. Let it stew till all goodness is out of the meat; then strain. Make a good stuffing, as for turkey, with a large cupful of grated bread, half as much shred suet, some thyme, parsley, and a small portion of onion, chopped very fine; and either half a pound of sausage-meat, or a little finely-shred ham or bacon; season with pepper and salt, and mix well with one or two eggs. Be *liberal* in the quantity of the stuffing. Put into the aperture of the body as much as it will hold, and make the rest into balls about the size of pullets' eggs. You *may* lard the kangaroo, but it is very good without, if covered with a caul of sweet mutton suet while baking. It requires long cooking. You may very safely let it stay in the oven a full half hour after you think it done, to have it thoroughly cooked. Serve with some of the gravy—having added to it some mushroom ketchup, and a little flour and butter. Have currant jelly to eat with it; some persons like ham or bacon instead. Hashed with the remaining gravy, the kangaroo is often nicer than it was the first day.

Kangaroo Steamer.—Cut the meat off the hind-quarters, take away the skin, and mince, pound, or grind the meat in a sausage mill, not set finely; set it aside until next day, and prepare the gravy meanwhile; for this you can use the bones, skin, tail, or part of the fore-quarter, well bruised and hacked up, and slowly simmered with three pints of water and a small onion till reduced to little more than one pint. Do this the day before you want to serve the steamer, and strain off the gravy to be cold. Next day take a pound (or more, if liked) of nice fat bacon, free from rust, cut it into dice, add it to the minced meat, and stir all well into the cold gravy (which should be a jelly, if good); let the whole warm gradually, and simmer slowly until cooked. Season to your palate, being careful not to add much salt, if any, as the bacon salts it. A spoonful or two of mushroom ketchup and a dredge of flour will improve the flavour and consistency of the steamer. Serve with sippets of toasted bread, and if you would have a "steamer superlative," garnish round with nicely-fried balls of the same forcemeat as directed for the roast kangaroo.

The two preceding recipes are from the pen of an Australian lady, who combines in her own person the desideratum of literary ability with becoming attention to household affairs.

Kangaroo Steamer (*Prize Recipe*).—Take the most tender part of the kangaroo, being careful to remove all the sinews. Chop it very fine, about the same quantity of smoked bacon (fat); season with finely-powdered marjorum, pepper, and a very little salt. Let it *steam*, or *stew*, for two hours; then pack or press tight in open-mouthed glass bottles; the bung must be sealed down, and the outside of the bottles washed well with white of egg, beaten; preserved in this way it will keep *good* for twelve months or more. When needed for use, the vessel containing the preserve should be put into a saucepan of cold water, and allowed to boil for fifteen minutes (if a large bottle); when dished, pour a little rich brown gravy over it, flavoured with mace, salt, and pepper; garnish with forcemeat balls. If required for immediate use, half an hour will cook it sufficiently; no gravy will be necessary. Forcemeat balls without bacon will be found a great improvement.

Mrs. Sarah Crouch, the lady of the respected Under-Sheriff of Tasmania, obtained a Prize Medal for the above at the Exhibition of 1862, and has allowed us to make public the recipe. The dish was partaken of by the guests of the Acclimatisation Society, at the London dinner of that year, Lord Stanley in the chair. Several speakers commented on the goodness of the "steamer." Sir John Maxwell, a first-rate judge, pronounced it excellent, as a stew, and said that he should like to see it introduced into the Navy. It is understood that Prince Napoleon, one of the first gastronomers of the day, was desirous to acclimatise the kangaroo to France, for the sake of the *cuisine* the animal affords.

Melville's "Australasia" has it, that the flesh of the kangaroo is, perhaps, the most nutritious and most easily digested of any known to man!

Roast Kangaroo (*Author's Recipe*).—The hind quarters of a medium-sized brush kangaroo is to be larded with bacon, and put down to roast. It must be well basted, and stuffed with good veal stuffing. Make some forcemeat balls and put in the dripping-pan to warm; serve with some good gravy, properly made, and currant jelly. The kangaroo, in being roasted, can be basted with either good dripping or milk—the latter is best. This dish must be well but not over-done.

Meat and game are larded as follows:—A strip of bacon is inserted in a larding needle—a short steel needle, with a spring opening instead of an eye, so that the bacon is introduced—and when passed through a part of the meat the slit opens and it is left there.

A batter for roast kangaroo or hare may be made thus—with two spoonfuls of salad oil, a couple of eggs, a little cream and salt. Baste the kangaroo or hare with it at the time of roasting.

ENCOUNTER WITH A GIGANTIC OLD MAN KANGAROO, OR BOOMAR.—As John Thomas Patterson, of Sugar-loaf Flat, Tarlo, was proceeding on horseback through the bush in the vicinity of his residence, he was attracted by the yelping of three or four of his dogs near to a thick piece of brushwood, and riding up, he came upon them attacking an immense old man kangaroo. One of the dogs was already dead, rent asunder by the claws of the monster, and two others were also wounded, and were still tackling it. No sooner did the kangaroo espy Patterson than it jumped at him and threw its forepaws round the horse's neck. Fortunately the youth had a loaded pistol with him, which he drew and fired, the ball striking the kangaroo on the left shoulder, and passing out through its back. By this means one of the animal's paws was disabled, but with the other it showed fight, and Patterson being unable to make any impression on his assailant with the blows of the pistol, for he had not another charge, endeavoured to get the stirrup out of the spring-bar, so as to use it at the end of the leather as a weapon. Whilst doing this the kangaroo, with its disabled paw, slightly wounded his hand. At length Patterson got the stirrup-leather loose, and hitting the animal on the temple with all his force, he succeeded in stunning it. With several other well-directed blows he succeeded in killing it. The kangaroo was of enormous size, measuring no less than 9 feet 6 inches from the tip of its tail to its ears. The tail itself measured 15½ inches round at the butt, and the skin and tail weighed 29½ lbs. When sitting on its haunches the animal was fully 7 feet in height, and weighed 150 lbs.—*Goulburn Chronicle.*

Kangaroo Steamer (*Author's Recipe*).—This is a simple species of braise, and, as its name imports, the meat is steamed. Cut the meat in pieces of about a quarter of an inch square, and put it into a pan with a well-covered lid, with a spoonful of milk, an onion shredded into small pieces, and some pepper and salt to taste. When it has been on the fire a short time add about a tenth in quantity of salt pork, or bacon cut to the same size as the kangaroo, with a spoonful of ketchup. Serve hot, with jelly.

But of all the dishes ever brought to table, nothing equals that of the steamer. It is made by mincing the flesh of the kangaroo, and with it some pieces of pork or bacon. The animal has not any fat, or scarcely any, in its best season. When the meat is chopped up, it is thrown into a saucepan, and covered over with the lid, and left to stew or steam gently by the fireside. It is, from this method of cooking, called a "steamer." People generally put a spoonful of water in the pot when they place it on the fire; but this is unnecessary, as the flesh soon floats in its own rich gravy. It only requires pepper and salt to render it delicious. No one can tell what a steamer is unless it has been tasted; it indeed affords an excellent repast; and it is surprising that the steamer, preserved in tins, has not yet been exported to England.—*Australia, by Melville.*

KANGAROO.—Usually mild, inoffensive animals, they are sometimes stirred up to wrath when brought to bay by dogs; and there are two instances on record, in the Bothwell district, of "boomers" (forester kangaroos) having seized men in their arms, and carried them for some distance, and then flung them violently down. I have seen the haunches of a boomer which weighed ninety-six pounds, and stood seven feet high. The average weight of a "brush" kangaroo is about eighteen to thirty pounds; the "wallaby" is still less. The latter are taken in large numbers, by means of wire-snares.—*Hull.*

The kangaroo was supposed to be an Australian word by Captain Cook, who first used it, and described the remarkable animal to which it is applied, yet it is strange that no such term is to be found in any Australian language.—*Crawford.*

Roast Emeu.—This is very unctuous sort of food, and much resembles coarse beef in flavour. At the early establishment of the colony it was generally partaken of, but we cannot recommend it to the epicure, unless he has the sailor's digestion elsewhere alluded to. In the first settlement of Hobart Town, and, we believe, Sydney, kangaroo was purchased into the public stores at a shilling a pound, and served out to the only two classes of inhabitants—the military and the bond—then in being, with a few officers. Emeu can either be roasted or boiled.

The emeu has almost entirely disappeared in Tasmania, and other native game are scarce. The forest kangaroo (the larger species) are very rare, and are now preserved as much as possible. The smaller sorts of brush and wallaby are still numerous. Peafowl have become wild and plentiful in some districts, as well as a small kind of deer. At a late meeting of the Acclimatisation Society at Melbourne, a letter was read from

M. Rammel, of Paris, stating that Prince Napoleon was desirous of stocking his estate at Mendon with kangaroo; and another communication was received from M. Rufy de Lawson, director of the Acclimatisation Garden of the Bois de Boulogne, suggesting a shipment of kangaroo, as they would fetch £10 per pair at Paris. While we are penning these remarks, a vessel, the Racer, has just left Launceston in Tasmania for New Zealand, with the following, as part of her cargo:—12 kangaroos, 12 dogs, 24 cats, 42 horses, 150 pigs, 400 fowls, 100 ducks, 100 geese, 100 turkeys, 4 peacocks, eggs, potatoes, hay, oatmeal, bricks, and timber.

THE EMEU.—The Emeu is peculiar to Australia. For a long period, and even to the present time, this bird has been called "the New Holland Cassowary," but we consider the name of "Emeu" to apply exclusively to the New Holland bird. We have, therefore, the cassowaries of the Asiatic Islands and of New Britain, a supposititious species in New Holland, and the emeu, confined solely to the Australian continent. The emeu crops herbage, like the cow or the horse, and feeds upon various fruits. The flesh is eaten by the settlers, and by some is preferred to the kangaroo; the rump part is considered as delicate as fowl, the legs coarse, like beef, but tender when the animal is young. The fibulæ of the legs are used as ornaments by the blacks. The best time to hunt these birds is at an early hour in the morning, when they are seen cropping the tender grasses. They are swift of foot; but as soon as the dogs reach them, which is not until they are completely tired out, they are speedily overthrown and killed.— "*Gatherings of a Naturalist in Australia,*" *by Bennett.*

Jugged Hare or Kangaroo.—Cut the hare or kangaroo into pieces; then cut up a pound of bacon into small squares, and fry it in a pan for five minutes; then add the hare or kangaroo, and stir them in a stewpan until a little brown; then add some flour, pepper, allspice, onions, and a little winter savory. Moisten the stew with a pint of stock, and allow it to simmer for half an hour. Serve with currant jelly and sharp sauce.

Venison or Kangaroo Hashed.—Cut the meat in slices. Put it in a stewpan, with a small quantity of stock gravy, a gill of port wine, a table-spoonful of ketchup, some lemon, with salt and cayenne in moderation. Let it simmer. Serve in a hot dish—silver, pewter, or crockery, according to your circumstances. Serve with currant jelly sauce.

Roast Wombat (*Tasmania*).—This animal feeds on grass and roots, and its flesh is eaten roasted; some persons like its flavour, others, again, decry it. It is also cooked in steaks. Native porcupines are cooked in a like way.

A friend, and an author, too, writes:—"A pleasant and grateful impression on my memory has a roasted porcupine, which I breakfasted on, on the top of a mountain near the Big Lagoon, in Tasmania, about five-and-thirty years ago; and, if any epicure will hunt kangaroo on foot for two days fasting, and then try a roasted porcupine on a frosty morning, he will very likely have discovered a new pleasure."

Mutton Birds (*Bass's Straits*).—These birds are procured in great numbers in the Straits, by the sealers, and are salted for use, but we can't say we should like them as a relish. The eggs are good, and largely used, and the feathers are made into beds of rather a fishy odour.

THE MUTTON BIRD.—I found that nothing had been done, as all the natives were away mutton-birding on the islands in the straits. The mutton bird (*tec-te*) is a species of puffin, that builds in holes in sand-banks on sea-girt islands. They are very fat and rich, and greatly prized as food by the Maoris, who preserve them in great numbers by salting and smoking them, trading any surplus they obtain, beyond what is necessary for their own consumption, to the natives farther to the northwards, in which case they are packed in bags made of kilp. The mutton-bird harvest is therefore of great importance to them, and the first party of natives had only just returned from it, reporting that they had this year been very unsuccessful, and the remainder of those belonging to this kaiyk would arrive in a few days.—*Extract from Dr. Hector's* "*Geological Expedition to the West Coast of Otago.*"

Pan Jam.—This dish used to be made from kangaroo tails. Roast them in the ashes with the skin on. When nearly done, scrape them well, and divide at the joints. Then put them into a pan, with a few slices of fat bacon, to which add a few mushrooms, pepper, &c. Fry gently, and serve. First-rate tack.

The flesh of the boomah (kangaroo) is extremely tough and coarse-grained; but, nevertheless, is full of rich brown gravy, and certainly makes most delicious soup; so does its nether appendage, which, from its containing a considerable quantity of glutinous matter, bears a great resemblance to, but far outrivals in quality, the celebrated ox-tail.—"*Thirty-three Years in Tasmania and Victoria,*" *by Lloyd.*

The tail of the forest kangaroo in particular makes a soup which, both in richness and flavour, is far superior to any ox-tail soup ever tasted.—*Wentworth's* "*New South Wales.*"

Slippery Bob.—Take kangaroo brains, and mix with flour and water, and make into batter; well season with pepper, salt, &c.; then pour a table-spoonful at a time into an iron pot containing emeu fat, and take them out when done. "Bush fare," requiring a good appetite and excellent digestion.

The above dishes of pan jam and slippery bob were supplied by an "old hand" of Tasmania, for "new chums" of thirty years' standing never heard of these dishes, much less have partaken of them.

BUSH COOKERY.—Here I was first initiated into the bush art of "sticker-up" cookery, and for the benefit of all who go "a-gipsying," I will expound the mystery. The orthodox material here is of course kangaroo, a piece of which is divided nicely into cutlets, two or three inches broad and a third of an inch thick. The next requisite is a straight clean stick, about four feet long, sharpened at both ends. On the narrow part of this, for the space of a foot or more, the cutlets are spitted at intervals, and on the end is placed a piece of delicately rosy fat bacon. The strong end of the stick-spit is now stuck fast and erect in the ground, close by the fire, to leeward, care being taken that it does not burn. Then the bacon on the summit of the spit, speedily softening in the genial blaze, drops a lubricating shower of rich and savoury tears upon the leaner kangaroo cutlets below, which forthwith frizzle and steam and sputter with as much ado as if they were illustrious Christmas beef grilling in some London chop-house under the gratified nose of the expectant consumer. "And, gentlemen," as dear old Hardcastle would have said, if he had dined with us in the bush, "to men that are hungry, stuck-up kangaroo and bacon are very good eating." Kangaroo is, in fact, very like hare.—*Mrs. Meredith's* "*Home in Tasmania.*"

Beef or mutton cooked in this manner, at a pic-nic, would be a good dish for such a party.

Canvas-back Ducks.—The fame of the canvas-back ducks of America, fed on the wild parsley grown in Chesapeake Bay, has reached all parts of the world. In delicacy of flavour and richness of flesh they are said to have no equals in the "wide, wide world." We can give no special directions for their cookery, and we may presume that, like beauty unadorned, they require no additions, but are simply served up hot, in their own "natural aroma," to borrow the expressive observation of Lady Morgan.

Swainson is very eulogistic on the canvas-back duck, and describes it as the ortolan of the duck family, and the turtle of the swimming birds.

Ortolans.—These birds are of a scarce kind. They are procurable in Belgium, but are found occasionally in England. When sufficiently fat for eating, they must not be bruised in their death, but very delicately handled. The feathers must be picked with great care and attention.

They are singed, and not drawn, put in a case, soaked in the best oil, and broiled over a slow fire. In a few minutes they will swim in their own fat. The most delicate mouths can masticate the bones, without the least inconvenience.

To an epicure, ortolans are the most delicious of morsels, and are infinitely superior to roast pig, of which Charles Lamb had so favourable an opinion.

ORTOLAN.—The name given in France and England to a species of *frangillidæ*, greatly esteemed for the delicacy of its flesh, when in season. It is the *ortolano* of the Italians, and the *fettammer* of the Germans. The ortolan is a native of Northern Africa; but in the summer and autumnal months it resorts to Southern Europe, and frequently migrates to the central, and even the northern parts. There are large establishments in Italy and the south of France for feeding these birds, the flesh of which is styled by Prince Musignano, *carne squisita.—Brande.*

THE AMERICAN BOBLINK.—I have shown him only as I saw him at first, in what I may call the poetical part of his career, when he is in a manner devoting himself to elegant pursuits and enjoyments, and was a bird of music and song, and taste and sensibility, and refinement. While this lasted he was saved from injury: the very schoolboy would not fling a stone at him, and the merest rustic would pause to listen to his strain. But mark the difference. As the year advances, as the clover blossoms disappear and the spring fades into summer, he gradually gives up his elegant tastes and habits, doffs his poetical suit of black, assumes a russet, dusty garb, and sinks to the gross enjoyments of common, vulgar birds. His notes no longer vibrate on the ear; he is stuffing himself with seeds of the tall weeds on which he lately swung and chanted so melodiously. He has become a *bon vivant, a gourmand;* with him, now, there is nothing like the joys of the table! In a little while he grows tired of plain, homely fare, and is off on a gastronomical tour in quest of foreign luxuries. We next hear of him, with myriads of his kind, banqueting among the reeds of the Delaware, and grown corpulent with good feeding. He has changed his name in travelling. Bob-lincon no more: he is the *reed-bird* now, the much sought for tit-bit of Pennsylvanian epicures, the rival in unlucky fame to the ortolan! Wherever he goes, pop—pop—pop! every unlucky rusty firelock in the country is blazing away. He sees his companions falling by thousands around him. Does he take warning and reform? Alas! not he. Incorrigible epicure! again he wings his flight. The rice swamps of the south invite him. He gorges himself among them almost to bursting; he can scarcely fly for corpulency. He has once more changed his name, and is now the *rice-bird* of the Carolinas. Last stage of his career: behold him, spitted, with dozens of his corpulent companions, and served up, a vaunted dish, on the table of some southern gastronome!—*Washington Irving's " Chronicles of Wolfert's-roost."*

Paon (Peacock) Revêtu.—Instead of plucking this bird, take off the skin with the greatest care, so that the feathers do not get detached or broken. Stuff it with what you like, as truffles, mushrooms, livers of fowls, bacon, salt, spice, thyme, crumbs of bread, and a bay-leaf. Wrap the claws and head in several folds of cloth, and envelope the body in buttered paper. The head and claws, which project at the two ends, must be basted with water during the cooking, to preserve them, and especially the tuft. Before taking it off the spit, brown the bird by removing the paper. Garnish with lemon and flowers. If to come on the table cold, place the bird in a wooden trencher, in the middle of which is fixed a wooden skewer, which should penetrate the body of the bird, to keep it upright. Arrange the claws and feathers in a natural manner, and the tail like a fan, supported with wire. No ordinary cook can place a peacock on the table properly. This ceremony was reserved, in the times of chivalry, for the lady most distinguished for her beauty. She carried it, amidst inspiring music, and placed it, at the commencement of the banquet, before the master of the house. At a nuptial feast, the peacock was served by the maid of honour, and placed before the bride.

There is a paucity of native game at New Zealand; the kinds are only wild ducks and quail. The large wingless bird, the moa (*dinornis elephantopus*) is extinct. It would have been a rather difficult task to describe the cookery of such a gigantic bird, belonging to the struthious family, with feet like an elephant, thirteeen feet in height, and large in proportion.

Guinea Fowl.—This bird is said to unite the flavour of the turkey and pheasant. It must be well attended to in the cooking, properly stuffed, and basted. It is decidedly a game bird in every sense, and requires attention in its being well served. Slices of ham and interminable basting are essential to its cookery.

Wild Ducks and Teal.—The wild ducks of England and Australia are dressed in the same manner. Keep them sufficiently, and roast them rather under-done, not forgetting to baste well. Serve with lemon and port wine sauce, and cayenne pepper. A novice would use melted butter, but it is quite contrary to the school of M. Brillat Savarin, who advises the roast with snipe and truffles. The black and mountain duck of Tasmania, when well done, are excellent feeding, as well as the wood duck, often to be seen perched on trees, near water.

When carving wild ducks, be sure to slice the breast, and pour over the cuts a few spoonfuls of sauce, composed of port wine, or claret (warmed), lemon-juice, salt, and cayenne pepper. The manner in which this is done is said to be the criteriæ of gentlemanly habits and practice.

Pheasants, Partridges, and Quails.—The first of these birds is plentiful in England, and several kinds of the latter are so in the colonies. They are best roasted. Let them hang for a short time, not too long; draw, singe, and truss them; put them down to a clear fire, and let them be quickly done. Baste them incessantly, and serve with bread sauce, or good brown gravy. These birds are first-rate in a pie, with a little bacon or ham; but as to boiling them, or placing them in puddings or ragoûts, or *salmi*, or soups, we don't admire such a mode of dressing them. The most desirable *cuisine* is to lard them slightly, and roast.

Pheasants, Partridges, and other Game, en papillotes.—Split the birds in halves, and stew them in butter, until nearly half done. Make a sauce of the butter, with mushrooms, chopped parsley, a few herbs and shalots; add a little flour, salt, and spice; with some stock, and a glass of wine; stew this sauce, and pour it over the halves of the birds: then wrap them in paper, and broil for about fifteen minutes. Serve in the paper, with the sauce as an accompaniment.

Black Cock and Red Grouse are dressed in a similar way to a pheasant; served with toast and lemon, and as little fat as possible. The fire must be bright, and the birds not over-done. A few minutes before serving, make some toast, squeeze over it a little lemon, and then lay it in the pan; place the birds on this toast for the table, and serve with a minimum amount of melted butter.

Woodcock and Snipe are dressed with the trail, to absorb the *gout*,

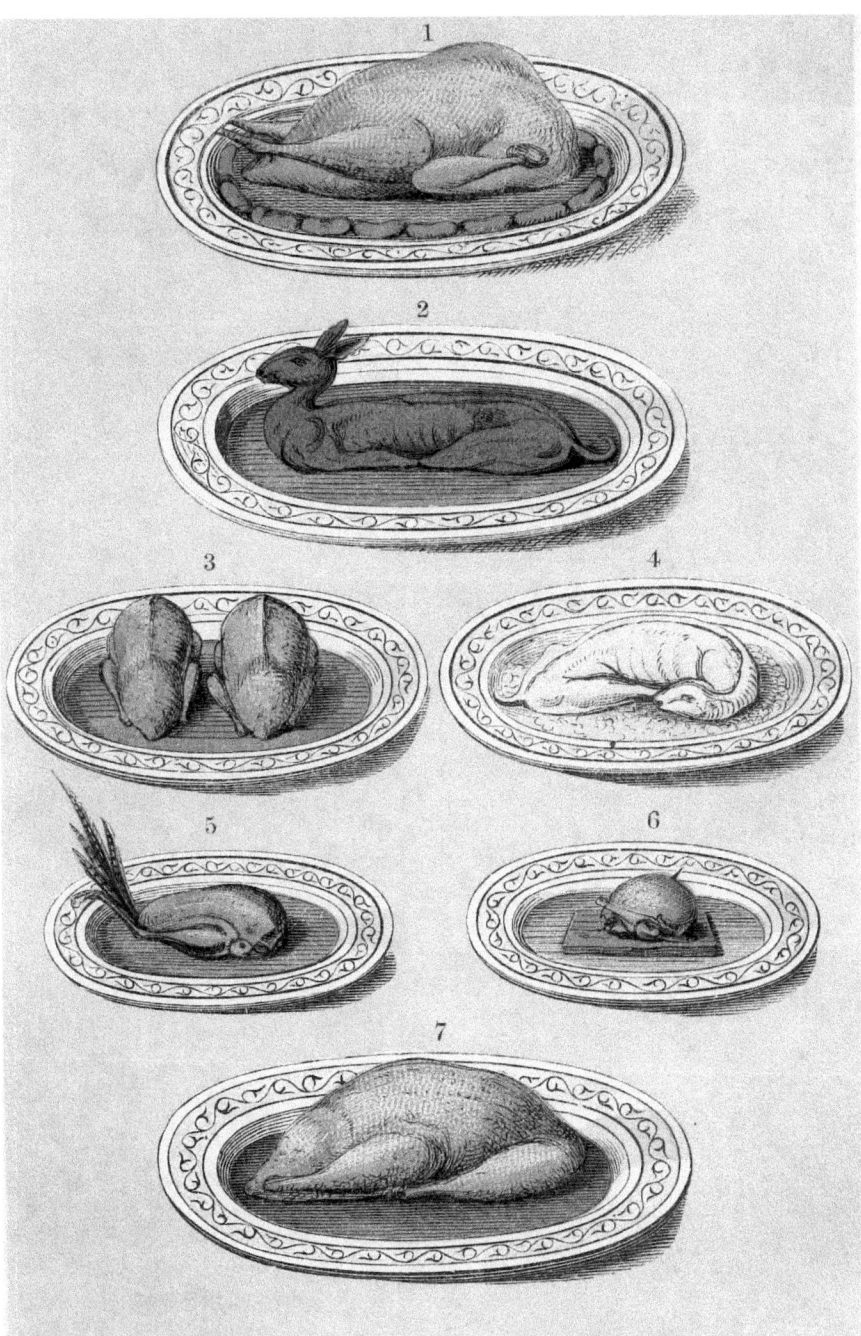

1. Roast Turkey and Sausage.
2. ,, Hare.
3. ,, Ducks.
4. Boiled Rabbit.
5. Roast Pheasant.
6. ,, Woodcock.
7. Roast Goose.

on toast, according to the sportsman's rule. If over-done they are spoiled.

Hare.—There is nothing better than hare well cooked, and there is hardly any dish so insipid and bad if improperly done; and the grand detail is the basting. Some fill the belly with forcemeat; but if the hare is tender, don't do so. Put it down to roast, like all meats, away from the fire at first, but afterwards draw nearer, and keep eternally basting with milk or cream, and subsequently with butter. Mince the liver, and flour the hare well when nearly done, so as to raise a froth on the joint; serve hot, with red currant jelly. Jugged and hashed hare are favourite dishes; but there is no cooking like the roast, and the continuous and interminable basting.

HARE.—In fact, how light of digestion we feel after a hare! How tender its processes after swallowing! What chyle it promotes! How ethereal—as if its living celebrity were a type of its nimble coursing through the animal juices! The notice might be longer. It is intended less as a natural history of the hare, than a cursory thanks to the country "good unknown." The hare has many friends, but none sincerer than *Elia* (Lamb).

THE HARE.—We must now speak of the hare. Concerning this animal, Archistratus, that author so curious in his dishes, speaks thus:—

> "Many are the ways, and many the recipes,
> For dressing hares; but this is best of all:
> To place before a hungry set of guests,
> A slice of roasted meat fresh from the spit,
> Hot, season'd only with plain, simple salt,
> Not too much done. And do not you be vexed
> At seeing blood fresh trickling from the meat,
> But eat it eagerly. All other ways
> Are quite superfluous; such as when cooks pour
> A lot of sticky, clammy sauce upon it,
> Parings of cheese, and lees, and dregs of oil,
> As if they were preparing cats'-meat."
>
> *"Athenæus," translated by Yonge.*

Rabbits are dry meat, only fit for pies or curries; and excellent served as the latter; indeed, lean meats always are best for this Indian dish.

Wild Pigeons (*Australia and New Zealand*).—These birds are very fine eating, stuffed, larded, and served up with sauce; or they are excellent stewed, with onions, in a rich gravy. Cook them as a grill, with moderation, on a slow fire; put a bit of butter on them, and serve hot, with the juice of a lemon and a little cayenne.

Wattle Bird (*Australia*).—These birds, when in good order, are very fine eating, either dressed plain, or served up in the same way as ortolans.

Turkey Bustard (*Australia*): a very fine bird, nearly the size of the common turkey. Must be kept sufficiently, and dressed in a similar way to its namesake. They vary in weight from twelve to twenty-four pounds. The flesh is rather dark, but, well cooked, it is superior food. Gould describes the Australian bustard as of the order *Otis Australasianus*. There is another species of turkey in Australia—the wattled tallegalla (*Tallegalla lalliami*), which is not so plentiful as the bustard, and smaller in size.

Black Swan (*Australia*).—The cygnets of the black swan are dressed in the same manner as the white species. When young they are tender, and if properly roasted, with good sauce, they are eatable; and that is all we can say.

The dun-bird, larks, ruffs and reeves, godwits, plovers, and wheatears, are all game, and are dressed in the general way of roasting.

Tainted Game.—To render tainted game fit for table use, wrap it in a cloth, so as to prevent any dust getting into it; when this has been done, put it in cold water, and throw in a fire-shovelful of hot charcoal. Allow the game to remain in the water for about five minutes. Take it out, and wipe dry. All the offensive smell will have been deodorised. Animal charcoal is superior to vegetable for this purpose. The game, as a matter of course, must be cooked *instanter*. Any kind of meat or fish may, by this simple process, be rendered fit for the palate, or it may be boiled with a little charcoal in the pot.

A THINKING JUDGE.—When M. Brillat Savarin, judge of the Court of Cassation, and an amateur gastronomer, was in America, once, on his return from a shooting excursion, in which he shot a wild turkey, he fell into conversation with Jefferson, who began relating some interesting anecdotes about Washington and the war; when, observing the *air distrait* of M. Brillat Savarin, he stopped, and was about to go away. "My dear sir," said the gastronomer, "I beg a thousand pardons, but I was thinking how I should dress my wild turkey."—*Quarterly Review*.

Salmis of Game.—Take off the legs, wings, and breasts of as many under-done partridges as you intend to use. Remove the skin from them very carefully. Prepare a sauce as follows:—Put into a stewpan, with a bit of butter, a few slices of ham, four or five shalots, a dried carrot, a few mushrooms, a little parsley, sprig of thyme, a bay-leaf, two cloves, three or four peppercorns, and some allspice. Fry the vegetables slightly, then add two wine-glassfuls of sherry, four or five spoonfuls of brown gravy, and a spoonful of mushroom ketchup. When these ingredients are in the stewpan, add the parts of the bird not intended to be eaten, and let them simmer for a couple of hours; then season with pepper and cayenne; skim off the fat and add a lump of sugar. When this is dissolved, strain this gravy over the wings, legs, and the breast of the partridge, which must be put into a clean saucepan. Let it simmer by the fire until the meat is saturated with the sauce, and serve with fried bread sippets.

It will be seen that this fashionable salmis is a species of *braise*, a kind of hash of a *recherché* kind, and the French are first-rate hands at serving up this dish; they use, with the same, Chablis wine, and the French mustard (*moutarde de maille*), diluted with Tarragon vinegar and a little oil. It is necessary that the game, whether pheasants, partridges, or woodcocks, should be under-done before put into the salmis, for birds done to rags are not eatable. Kangaroo dressed as a salmis is unexceptionable.

XXVII.—CARVING.

You should praise, not ridicule your friend, who carves with as much earnestness of purpose as though he were legislating.—*Dr. Johnson.*

One of the most important acquisitions in the routine of daily life is to know how to carve well. Every person who mixes with society at all is likely to be called on at any moment to perform this office; to refuse to undertake it savours of ill-nature and selfishness; and to perform it in an awkward and bungling manner is painful and unpleasant for lookers-on, and exceedingly humiliating to the operator. The best mode of becoming an adept in carving neatly and expeditiously is to dine at hotels and taverns where there is a *table d'hôte* or ordinary, and daily assist in cutting up the dishes prepared for the public dinner. Carving is not to be considered alone as an accomplishment to be displayed at the tables of others; it is, in fact, a very requisite branch of domestic management, and highly important in an economical point of view, for it is notorious that a joint of meat ill carved will not serve nearly so many persons as it would if it were properly carved. But this requires a certain amount of tact and judgment to cut fairly, and to observe an equitable distribution of all dainties, so as to give general satisfaction. In the first place, whatever is to be carved should be set in a dish sufficiently large for turning it, if necessary; but the dish itself should not be moved from its position, which should be so close before the carver as only to leave room for the plates. The carving-knife should be light, sharp, well tempered, and of a size proportionate to the joint, strength being less required than address in the manner of using it. The carver must carefully avoid all clumsiness of attitude and deportment: squaring the elbows, tucking up the coat-sleeves, dropping the knife and fork, splashing the gravy, and overturning glasses, are evidences of awkwardness and ungracefulness on the part of the carver. To carve standing is considered vulgar; and to obviate this, the seat of the carver should be raised to the requisite height. In carving, the eye must be employed as well as the hand: there is an art in discovering when a person's plate needs replenishing without appearing to be too solicitous; and there is also a tact and delicacy in recommending some particular dainty, which you have reason to think will be acceptable.—*The Dictionary of Daily Wants.*

MANGLING.—The words so often seen in out-of-the-way places of populous towns apply with full force to the bad carver—"Mangling done here." The editor of the above Dictionary recommends the novice to learn carving by frequenting hotels; but we would suggest that he should take a few lessons at the ham and beef shops. The dinners *à la Russe* require no carving on the part of the Amphytrion, and that is the only advantage in their favour; but *Fraser* dissents, for he makes Mr. Macborrowdale exclaim:—"At the last of these Siberian dinners at which I had the misfortune to be present, I had offered me, for two of my rations, the tail of a mullet and the drumstick of a fowl. Men who carve behind screens ought to pass a competitive examination before a jury of gastronomers. Men who carve at table are drilled by degrees into something like tolerable operators by the mere shame of the public process."

XXVIII.—FISH.

As food, fish are undoubtedly wholesome and nutritious, although less so than the flesh of animals or the grain of cereals. Of all the substances used as aliments by man, fish are, however, most liable to run into a state of putrefaction, and therefore should be eaten when perfectly fresh, or, if not recently taken, then only when they are in a state of good preservation by any of the ordinary methods employed for the purpose. Those that are the whitest and most flaky when cooked, as cod, flounders, haddock, hake, soles, turbot, whiting, &c. are the most easily digested; and those abounding in oily matter, as eels, herrings, mackerel, salmon, &c., are most nutritious, though the most likely to offend the stomach. Salt-water fish are said to be more wholesome than river fish, but without sufficient reason. Salted fish are hard of digestion, unless when carefully cooked and well masticated. The frequent use of fish as an aliment is said to promote the sexual feelings, but not the increase of population, unless a sufficiency of other food is taken at the same time. As one of the components of a mixed diet the value of fish is indisputable. Acid sauces and pickles are the proper additions to fish, from their power of retarding the progress of putrefaction, and of correcting the relaxing tendency of large quantities of oil and butter.—*Cooley's "Practical Receipts."*

Broiled Bream.—When at the sea-coast, on fishing excursions, it has been one of my customs to eat of the various fishes I could either catch or purchase, that are not in general use for the table. With the example of Izaak Walton before me, I will venture to suggest a mode of preparing a sea bream which materially improves its more ordinary flavour:— When thoroughly cleaned, the fish should be wiped dry, but none of the scales should be taken off. In this state it should be broiled, turning it often; and if the skin cracks, flour it a little, to keep the outer case entire. When on table, the whole skin and scales turn out without difficulty, and the muscle beneath, saturated with its own natural juices, which the outside covering has retained, will be found of good flavour.— *Yarrell's " British Fishes."*

Anchovies.—*Hors d'œuvre* of anchovies upon a plate. In the middle place the anchovies, cut in fillets, and lay them transversely. Around them place a wreath of parsley or other minced garnish, and upon them quarters of hard egg. Serve with oil.

According to "*La Nouvelle Cuisine Economique*," the head of the carp is the best part of that fish, being *le morceau d'honneur*, and which, for that reason, the author adds, "*Doit être offert à la personne la plus considerée.*"

<blockquote>Rust in anchovies, if I'm not mistaken,
Is as bad as rust in steel, or rust in bacon.—*Young's " Epicure."*</blockquote>

To Pot Fish.—Any kind of fish may be potted, as well as lobster, crayfish, prawns, &c. Pull the fish to pieces, and pick out every bone; mix with a little butter, cayenne, pepper, salt, mace, oil, and vinegar; place the fish in pots, and pour clarified butter over it.

Potted fish and potted meats (done in a similar way) are an excellent accompaniment at a breakfast, luncheon, or picnic.

New England Chouder (*American*).—Cut a haddock, cod, or any other solid fish, into pieces three inches square; pound a pound of fat salt pork in strips into the pot, set it on the fire and fry out the oil; take out the pork and put in a layer of fish, over that a layer of onions, in slices, then a layer of fish with slips of salt pork, then another layer of onions, and so on alternately until your fish is consumed; mix some flour with as much water as will fill the pot, season with black pepper and salt to taste, and boil for half an hour. Have ready some crackers (Philadelphia pilot bread, if you can get it), soaked in water until a little softened; throw them into your chouder five minutes before you take it up. Serve in a tureen.

A correspondent in the "Magazine of Domestic Economy" asserts that it is a well-known fact, not only in our own country but in every part of the world, especially on the North American continent, that ichthyophagists, or feeders on fish, who dwell on the sea-coast, are a hardy, well-conditioned, and healthy race of men.

Lampreys.—Cleanse the fish, remove the tough membrane from the back, put the lampreys into a stewpan, and cover them with strong beef gravy; add a dessert-spoonful of mixed allspice, mace, and cloves, in powder, a spoonful of salt, a few grains of cayenne pepper, a gill of port wine, the same of sherry, and a table-spoonful of horseradish vinegar; cover the pan, and stew gently till the fish are tender; then take them out, and add to the same two anchovies beaten to paste, and the juice of a lemon; boil it up and strain it, and, if requisite, thicken it with butter and flour. Warm the lampreys in this sauce before serving. Garnish with slices of lemon and sippets of toasted bread.—*Cuisine at the "Hop Pole," Worcester.*

The lamprey was a pet fish with the ancients. Antonia, the wife of Drusus, hung the gills of a lamprey with pearls and earrings; Licanius Croesas fed his lampreys in a vivarium; and Quintius Hortensius is said to have wept at the death of his dear fish. One of our kings (Henry I.) died from eating too largely of lampreys. By ancient custom, the city of Gloucester, as a token of their loyalty, present a lamprey pie annually at Christmas to their sovereign; this is sometimes a costly gift, as lampreys at that season can scarcely be procured at a guinea a piece.

Fish—How to Choose, How to Dress.—We much question whether the ancients could better the above recipe for dressing lampreys, which mine host of the "Hop Pole," Worcester, adopts; indeed, the most ill-flavoured fish, after undergoing such an ordeal, must be received with respect by any piscatory feeder.

Conger Soup, in the Jersey Mode.—Take five pounds of conger to three pints of water; cut the former into small pieces, and place them in a boiler with the water, until the liquid is reduced to two-thirds of its original quantity; then strain it; add to it the same quantity of new milk there is of soup, and warm this up again; throw in some green peas, which should be boiled up in the soup until thoroughly done, and then serve the peas and soup together.—*Piscator.*

Any fish soup may be made in the above manner, substituting weak stock for milk, and other vegetables and herbs for green peas.

Trumpeter (*Tasmania*).—This is, without exception, the finest-flavoured fish in the Southern Hemisphere, and it is said to rival the turbot in delicacy. It is sometimes caught up to forty pounds weight, but one of about five or six pounds is the proper size for the piscamous *gourmet*, who will have it boiled in salt water, and served with plain melted butter, for a pungent sauce overcomes the delicate taste of the fish. Trumpeter is good fried, and salted, and smoked; but the simple boil is by far the most sensible mode of dressing this fish.

Strangers visiting Tasmania invariably call for this fish, and they are to be had in perfection at the "Ship," " "Derwent," and Webb's hotels, Hobart Town, kept by hosts Butler, Watkins, and Webb, who are sensibly alive to the propriety of its being well served. Why it was called trumpeter we cannot say; but, as the great bard has it, "there is nothing in a name."

All fish must be well and thoroughly cleansed; and, to do this effectually, they must be slitted sufficiently open to be properly washed. The flavour of fish is much improved by adding a little salt and vinegar to the last water through which they are passed. The sound milt and roe should be carefully cleaned and preserved. The latter made into patties are very superior, and duly appreciated by the *gourmet*. Persons of the old Hebrew faith are particular in the preparation of their food. They use salad oil in the frying of their fish, which is to be recommended.

Crimping Salmon.—The fish is first stunned by a blow on the head, then cut cross-wise just below the gills, and crimped by cutting to the bone on each side, so as almost to divide him into slices. He is next put into a cold spring for ten minutes, and then put slice by slice into a pot of salt and water, boiling furiously, time being allowed for the water to recover its heat after the throwing in of each slice; the head is left out, and the thickest pieces are thrown in first. The fat of the salmon, being mixed with much albumen and gelatine, is extremely liable to decompose, but is kept cool by the spring; and by the boiling salt and water, which is of a higher temperature than that of common boiling water, the albumen is coagulated, and the curdiness is preserved; and the crimping, by preventing the irritability of the fibre from being gradually exhausted, seems to preserve it so hard that it breaks under the teeth, while a fresh fish, if not crimped, is generally tough. This may improve small fish, but will cause a large, fine-fed fish to eat too dry and brittle. To choose crimped salmon, see that it rises at the edge of the cuts, and that the muscle is well contracted between them, which should develop the flakes, and appear firm and elastic.—*Sir Humphry Davy.*

A FISH DINNER.—Tancred was going to give them a fish dinner! A what? A sort of banquet, which might have served for the marriage feast of Neptune and Amphitrite, and be commemorated by a constellation, and which ought to have been administered by the Nereids and the Naiads; tureens of turtle, pools of water souchet, flounders of every hue, and eels in every shape, cutlets of salmon, salmis of carp, ortolans represented by whitebait, and huge roasts, carved out of the sturgeon.—*The New Crusade.*

The attempts to introduce salmon into the Australian colonies have hitherto been unsuccessful, as the ova have died on the passage; but, by the last accounts, Mr. Youl, a Tasmanian gentleman resident in London, has made some experiments by preserving the ova in ice, and it fructified after being immersed in ice for one hundred and twenty days; so there is now every prospect of the fish being brought out successfully. In France the piscicultural establishments are eminently successful; so much so that the price of salmon has been reduced there from three and four shillings to sixpence per pound: but, as in days of yore, they manage these matters better in France.

WHALE STEAKS.—In passing along the street we saw strips of whale flesh, black and reddish-coloured, hanging outside the gable of almost every house to dry, just as we have seen herrings in fishing villages on our own coasts. When a shoal of whales is driven ashore by the boatmen, there are great rejoicings among the islanders, whose faces, we were told, actually shine for weeks after their season of feasting. What cannot be eaten at the time is dried for future use. Boiled or roasted it is nutritious, and not very unpalatable. The dried fish which I tasted resembled tough beef, with a flavour of venison. Being "blood meat," I would not have known it to be from the sea; and I have been told that, when fresh and properly cooked, tender steaks from a young whale can scarcely be distinguished from beef-steak.—*Symington's "Pen and Pencil Sketches of Faroe and Iceland."*

Salmon Cutlets.—Salmon cutlets are dressed somewhat *à la Maintenon*, as follows: cut them in slices, rub them with salad oil, and season with cayenne pepper and salt; wrap them in paper, and fry in boiling fat. When nearly done, lay them in their paper shrouds, on a gridiron, to dry; or place them in a hot oven for a similar purpose.

Caper sauce is a superior sort of accompaniment to any kind of fish.

Crayfish.—Boil, in a pint of milk, two blades of mace, one onion, sliced, cayenne, and salt, with lemon, a little butter and flour, and a gill of cream, and serve with crayfish.

This was considered a *recherché* dish at a mayor's feast in Tasmania.

The Austrian trout, bred in the rivulets of the Alps, are very good. They are served either fried or boiled, and when in good condition have the firmness of the white of an egg. Trout are excellent slit open, and sprinkled with cayenne and salt, and broiled for breakfast. Cold fish may be dressed as a salad, or the fillets may be warmed with white sauce for a side-dish. A fish omelette, well made, is excellent fare. Perch are delicate and easy of digestion, either in water souchet or fried in batter. They are recommended to invalids who have debilitated stomachs.

Herrings.—The flesh of herrings is so delicate that no cook should attempt to dress them otherwise than by broiling or frying. Let the herring be placed upon the gridiron, over the clearest of fires, and when sufficiently embrowned, let him instantly be transferred to the hottest of plates; eat him with mustard sauce, in the kitchen if you can. The male or soft-roed herring is always the best, when in proper season.—*Hints for the Table.*

It is not, therefore, improbable, that certain cutaneous diseases may be produced, or at least aggravated, by fish diet; and, in hot countries, this effect may be questionable. The priests of Egypt may, therefore, have been prohibited from eating fish, upon just principles, in order that the leprosy might be averted; and the great legislator of the Jews was, no doubt, influenced by some such belief when he framed his celebrated prohibition, Lev. xi. 9—12.—*Paris on Diet.*

Caviare, the prepared roe of the sturgeon. Caviare is made and consumed largely in Russia, and exported to all parts of the world, less to England than elsewhere. The membranes of the roe being removed, the grains are washed in vinegar, dried in the air, salted, and packed. It is eaten raw, with oil and lemon-juice.

Caviare has a bitter taste, and is by no means palatable: having partaken of it once, we have no desire to repeat the dose; nor should we recommend it to the reader. Caviare was used as a luxury in the time of Charles II., and it is one of the most valuable of Russian exports, the sales reaching nearly two millions sterling. There is no accounting for tastes in the appreciation of caviare, as it is oily and indigestible According to Brande, on the Continent a kind of caviare is made of the hard roe of the carp, which is considered equal in flavour to the sturgeon, and finds favour in the eyes of the Jews, who reject caviare made from the sturgeon, which, being a fish without scales, is forbidden by the Levitical law, and is consequently an abomination to all true Israelites.

To Boil Turbot.—Soak the fish in cold water a couple of hours before you dress it, with some salt in it; then score the skin across the back. Put a handful of salt into a fish-kettle with cold water, lay your fish on a strainer, and when coming to the boil, skim it well. Then set the kettle on the side of the fire to simmer for about fifteen minutes; supposing the fish to be about eight pounds, if the water gallops, the fish will break to pieces; rub some of the red spawn of the lobster through a sieve, and sprinkle over. Garnish with parsley, lemon, and horseradish; or it may be served with fried smelts. Lobster or crayfish sauce is an accompaniment.

Ude says that a turbot kept a few days eats far better than a fresh one. It may be so; but, according to medical authority, it is not so wholesome: of that fact there can be no doubt. Carême tells us, in a voice of authority, that boiled turbot ought to be garnished with a boiled lobster, and this lobster in its turn is to be garnished with smelts, fastened with silver skewers. Brande writes, that turbot is the best, and, excepting the halibut, largest of our flat fishes; it is the type of the sub-genus *rhombus* of Cuvier. It is taken either by the troll-net, or, in deep water, by the many-hooked line baited with the common smelt or small gar-fish. A preference is given in the London markets to the turbots caught by the Dutch, who are estimated to have drawn for this supply not less than £80,000 a year.

Boiled Cod.—Wash and clean the fish, and rub some salt on the inside. Put the fish in the kettle, so that it may be covered; put in a handful of salt, and then put in the fish. A small fish will be done in about fifteen minutes, and a larger one will take longer time. Garnish the dish with the roe and liver.

The carver's reputation depends upon the equitable distribution of the sound, the jelly part of the jowl, and the tongue, which are esteemed highly by pisciverous eaters.

To REMOVE THE MUDDY TASTE FROM FISH (*German*).—As this flavour exists only on the skin of the fish, and becomes communicated to the body only on being first boiled, it will be sufficient, before dressing such as are taken from ponds or stagnant water, to put them alive into a tub, and pour fresh water over them, adding half a handful of salt, stirring it well up among the fish, and finally rinsing them with cold fresh water.—*Scheibler.*

To Fry Fish.—

> The King's Bench reports have cook'd up an odd dish—
> An action for damages, *Fry* versus *Fish*;
> But sure, if for damages action would lie,
> It certainly must have been *Fish* versus *Fry!*—*The Morning Chronicle.*

Fish may be fried either with or without bread crumbs. Wash the fish thoroughly, and dry them well. Prepare some bread crumbs, by rubbing stale bread through a colander; or oatmeal may be used instead. Beat an egg up, and use it on the fish on both sides. Put clarified fat or salad oil into the pan, and then put in the fish, which must literally boil in the fat. When done, take them off and dry them; serve with a napkin laid on the dish, or without a napkin.

FISH GRAVIES.—Gravies for fish are seldom thought of; and yet in many instances they are a great improvement, and really a valuable acquisition, particularly to those who dislike the oleaginous batter. The heads, bones, and other parts of the fish, which would otherwise be thrown away, or a cheap kind of fish, with the aid of a little butter or dripping, an onion or two, and a portion of herbs, with the addition of a glass of wine, ketchup, lemon, and cayenne, will make a perfect gravy, far superior to the eternal melted butter. Acids are most wholesome with any kind of fish.

To Stew Fish.—When the fish have been well washed, lay them in a stewpan, with half a pint of claret or port wine, and a quart of stock or gravy, a large onion sliced, and a few cloves and a little mace; cover the stewpan, and let it simmer for about twenty minutes, according to the size of the fish; take the fish out, and lay it on a hot hearth in a dish; thicken the liquor that it was stewed in with a little flour, and season with pepper, salt, anchovy, and mushroom ketchup, and chilli vinegar. When it has boiled about ten minutes, either pour it over the fish or return the fish into the stewpan to warm.

The flesh of any fish is in the highest perfection, or in season, as it is called, during the period of the ripening of the milt and roe. After it has deposited the spawn, the flesh becomes soft, and loses a great deal of its peculiar flavour. This is owing to the disappearance of the oil or fat from the fish, it having been expended in the function of reproduction.—*Fleming's Phil. of Zoology.*

Maigre Fish.—Put the fish into a stewpan, with a shredded onion, a few cloves, allspice, and pepper; just cover it with boiling water; let it simmer for about twenty minutes; strain the liquor into another pan, leaving the fish to keep warm, until the sauce is ready; rub well together as much butter and flour as will thicken. To each pint of sauce add a glass of wine, a little ketchup and anchovy, and cayenne; let it simmer for a time, and pour over the fish; garnish with sippets of bread toasted or fried.

This is a very palatable mode of dressing fish for those whose religious tenets do not allow of eating meat on *maigre* days.

Salt Fish.—Salted fish generally requires soaking, according to the time they are salted. Put it into plenty of cold water, and let it simmer till done. Egg sauce and boiled beet are an accompaniment, with yolks of hard-boiled eggs.

Twice-laid, for Fast-days, is made from any kind of fish, either fresh or salt, mixed with mashed potatoes, with a little butter, and browned before the fire, in the proportion of about one-fourth fish to three-fourths potatoes. This is a very acceptable dish to Catholics on *maigre* days.

Small Fish, Fried.—Clean them well, and let them dry; fry them plain or egg them; put plenty of dripping or lard into the pan, and as soon as the fat boils put them in and brown them; they will hardly take a couple of minutes. Drain them in a hair sieve, and serve.

Lobsters, &c.—Lobsters, crayfish, crabs, prawns, and shrimps—these may be eaten *au naturel*, made into sauce, or potted; if the latter, the meat is all picked out and pounded in a mortar, with a little mace, cayenne, butter, black pepper, and salt. The crab is highly esteemed by epicures, and is eaten with the second course, according to the diction of the late editor of the "Original."

Lobsters and other shell-fish should be killed before being boiled.

Luxurious lobster-nights, farewell,
For sober, studious days!
And Burlington's delicious meal,
For salads, tarts, and pease!
—Pope's "*Farewell to London,*" 1715.

Whitebait.—The fish should be dressed within an hour after being caught, or they are apt to cling together. They are kept in water, from which they are taken by a skimmer as required; they are then thrown upon a layer of flour contained in a large napkin, in which they are shaken until completely enveloped in flour; they are then put into a colander, and all the superfluous flour is removed by sifting; the fish are next thrown into hot lard, contained in a copper cauldron, or stewpan, placed over a charcoal fire; in about two minutes they are removed by a tin skimmer, thrown into a colander to drain, and served up instantly, by placing them on a fish-drainer, in a dish. The rapidity of the cookery is of the utmost importance; and if not attended to, the fish will lose their crispness, and be worthless. At table, lemon-juice is squeezed on them, and they are seasoned with cayenne pepper; brown bread and butter is substituted for plain bread, and they are eaten with iced champagne or punch.—*Dr. Pereira on Diet.*

WHITEBAIT.—Whitebait, without which there would be no vessel, and, in the minds of a great many people, no Greenwich; whitebait, which Theodore Hook called " curled paper fried in batter;" which most people sneer at as nothing, and which everybody eats with delight, are caught where the water is a little brackish, generally between Barking and Greenhithe, with a net thirty feet long and twelve feet wide. This net is cast at daylight, either at high or low water, and remains two feet below the surface until nearly the ebb or flow, as the case may be. At the commencement of the spring, whitebait first appear, but not in large quantities, as these are old fish who escaped last year's netting. About the middle of April the young fry, perfectly transparent, arrive, and, in the first week in May, come to perfection. So it continues for a couple of months; then gradually whitebait get larger and larger, and about the close of September are lost sight of altogether. There is a specialty for dressing bait, and the fisherman who, assisted by his son, for upwards of a score of years has supplied the vessel, not only catches the whitebait, but cooks them. On a glowing coke fire is placed a large frying-pan full of boiled lard; the fish, first thoroughly sifted with flour, are placed in a cloth, which is plunged into the hissing fat. Cook is a perfect salamander, utterly impervious to the frightful heat, which makes strangers wink and beat a hasty retreat. He takes the handle of the frying-pan, and turns it from right to left, peering in at the seething mass. In two minutes the cooking is accomplished, and the fish are emptied out of a cloth on to a dish. Ye who would take your whitebait in perfection, get permission to eat it in the kitchen.—*All the Year Round.*

At the last festival of the Acclimatisation Society, held at St. James's Hall, London, Mr. Bernal Osborne responded to the toast of " the House of Commons ;" and in doing so, said that one of the dishes with which the company was regaled was the white soup of the Channel Islands. It appeared that this delicious soup was made of the conger-eel—a creature so despised that the starving Irish have refused to add flavour and nutriment to their potatoes by boiling with them a salted steak of the conger (laughter). Among the dishes served were the yam, or *Dioscorea Batatas lucioperia*, grenoilles, or edible frogs, pepper-pot, Chinese lamb, roasted whole, with pilaff and kuscoussoo, *poulete à l'emancipation des negres*, and ostrich eggs. There were, besides the usual wines, Greek, Hungarian, Australian, and Californian sorts.—*Home News.*

Boiled Flounders.—Wash and clean them well, and cut the back side of them, the same as you do turbot; then put them into a kettle, with cold water and salt: when it comes to a boil, skim them; let them simmer for five minutes, and they are ready.

Eaten with plain melted butter, you have the flavour of the flounder, which, like many other delicate fish, is overpowered by powerful sauce.

Eels.—Clean them well, wipe them dry, and fry them until brown. Have ready some beef gravy, or stock, about a quart; put the eels into it when cold, and let it simmer for about fifteen minutes. Take them out of the stewpan, and place them in a deep dish. Thicken the sauce with flour, and put into it two table-spoonfuls of port wine, and one of ketchup; let it simmer for about ten minutes; then pour on the fish.

> The Kennett swift, for silver eels renown'd;
> The Lodden slow, with verdant alders crown'd. *Pope.*

Eels are very good plain fried, or made into a pie; indeed, any kind of fish made into a pudding or pie is excellent, only the *cuisinier* must not omit the gravy or thickening, and a little acid is an improvement. The muddy taste of fish may be obviated by parboiling them in salt and water. The conger-eel, stewed in brown gravy, with a pudding in its belly, or dressed in cutlets, is first-rate; and eel or fish pies, when baked, should have the top crust removed, and be filled up with cream, which will amalgamate with the gravy and make good sauce.

Fish Soup (*Another Recipe*).—Under the head of "Soups" we have given one recipe for making fish soup, but we have now to glean another one. Take about five pounds of fish—assorted kinds—cut them into pieces, and fry until half done; then place them in a boiler, in about a quart of water or weak broth, having first seasoned the pieces of fish with cayenne, common pepper, and salt, a bundle of sweet herbs, and parsley; let the whole stew for about three hours, so that all the goodness may be extracted from the fish. Whilst stewing, fry a couple of onions, well coated with flour, in the fat the fish was previously fried in, then put them into the soup; thicken it with a little flour and butter, and ketchup, soy, and sauce. Strain the contents through a hair sieve, and, when cold, take off the fat. When wanted for use, warm it up, and add macaroni or vermicelli.

To Stew Lobsters the Irish Way.—Cut and break a boiled lobster, but not into small pieces, then, having ready, prepare a mixture of mustard and vinegar, seasoned with cayenne; put this, with the lobster, and a good-sized piece of butter, into a stewpan; keep the cover close for about five minutes, then put in a glass of sherry or madeira, and let it boil for about five minutes more; then serve it up, garnished with sliced lemon. In Ireland this savoury meal is often prepared in the same apartment in which it is eaten, being cooked in a machine called a *dispatcher*, which has a spirit lamp under it, and is dressed in the presence of the company, whose appetites are greatly excited by the agreeable odour it emits whilst the cooking process is progressing. Mr. Michael Angelo Titmarsh, in his "Irish Sketch-book," speaks in the highest terms of this dish; he also informs us that porter is drank with it, and whisky punch afterwards.—"*Fish,*" *by Piscator.*

Other Fish.—We have not entered into the detail of dressing the various other kinds of fish—soles, haddock, ling, red and grey mullet, shad, tench, trout, gudgeons—the latter are said to come up to the smelt in flavour if properly fried—pike, carp, perch, and gurnard. The *Quarterly* has it that the former fish, if bled in the tail and gills when taken, die much whiter, which is a comfort to themselves, and that they look better at table. Mackerel must not be washed, but wiped dry. The plaice, when in good order, is a delicious fish. The basse was extolled of old, and is in favour in Cornwall. The skate must be kept to get rid of its rankness, and broiled. The hake is dressed in cutlets, and fried with egg and bread crumbs, and the ruffe is eatable if cooked in a similar way. Dr. Mayo tells us fish of different kinds vary in digestibility. The most digestible is whiting, boiled; haddock next; cod, soles, and turbot are richer and heavier; eels, when stewed, notwithstanding their richness, are digestible. Ling is, perhaps, the most digestible river fish; salmon is not very digestible, unless in a fresher state than that in which much of it reaches the London market.

Recipe to Prepare Fat to Fry Fish.—Carefully pick ten pounds of beef suet, when ready put it into an iron pan to melt; as soon as melted add five pounds of fresh butter and three pounds of hog's lard. The moment the whole is in a boiling state, throw in two turnips, four carrots, an onion stuck with cloves, a bunch of parsley, half a dozen shalots, a small bit of thyme, two bay-leaves, and a little sweet basil. Let the herbs and roots fry until they are dried up. Strain the melted fat through a sieve, and, when nearly cold, stir in some baysalt and some whole pepper, and put in jars for use. The oftener this fat is used the better it becomes. To fry fish nicely, the frying-pan should always be full, and the fat strained into the jar the moment the process of frying is done.

HINTS.—Cooks generally, after frying fish, throw away the fat—an extravagance to be reprehended. A knife applied to fish is likely to spoil the delicacy of its flavour; so that it should be helped with a silver slice or trowel, and be eaten with a silver fork and bread, or a fish-knife. Fried fish should never be sent to table covered, because the steam that rises is condensed by the cover, and falls back on the fish, which thereby becomes soddened, and loses its crispness and flavour. Boiled fish is improved by a little vinegar being put into the water, an onion, and a few sweet herbs.

XXIX.—FORCEMEAT AND STUFFING.

Solitary dinners, I think, ought to be avoided as much as possible, because solitude tends to produce thought, and thought tends to the suspension of the digestive organs.—*Walker.*

The ability of the cook is always determined by his or her forcemeats and stuffing. We can describe the latter, and can only hint at the ingredients of the former, for they may be said to comprise Legion. Every variety of meat: hams, tongues, crumbs of bread, flour, dripping, and herbs, spices, curry-powder, anchovies, prawns and crabs, eggs and sauces—in truth, forcemeat may be made from any and every thing. The great desideratum is to allow the taste of no one article to overpower the others, or otherwise it is decidedly imperfect in its composition. Stuffing and forcemeat has been always considered as the *chef d'œuvre* of the *cuisine*, for a bad cook cannot manipulate good forcemeat: such a circumstance would be a culinary paradox.

Plain Forcemeat.—Take an equal quantity of meat and beef suet; mince and chop small; add pepper, salt, cloves, pounded lemon-peel, and nutmeg, grated, parsley and sweet herbs, a little shalot and onion, a few bread crumbs, grated fine, and yolk of egg sufficient to work it light; roll it into balls. If for roast meat, put them in the dripping-pan to brown; for white sauce, boil them; for brown sauce, fry them.

Forcemeat Balls for Fish, Soups, &c.—Beat the flesh and soft parts of a medium-sized lobster or crayfish, half an anchovy, a large piece of boiled celery, the yolk of an egg, hard-boiled, a little cayenne, mace, salt, and pepper, with two table-spoonfuls of bread crumbs, two ounces of butter, and two eggs, well beaten up; make into balls, and fry of a light brown.

Stuffing-balls for Hashes.—Three-quarters of a pound of bread crumbs, half a pound of beef suet, finely chopped; add a little lemon, thyme, parsley, marjoram, and savory, also chopped, nutmeg, mace, pepper, and cayenne; mix with two well-beaten eggs, and divide into small balls, and fry them dry. They will keep good several days.

Stuffing for Veal, Turkey, Fowl, &c.—Mix a quarter of a pound of beef stuffing in marrow, the same weight of bread crumbs, two drachms of parsley, an onion, sweet marjoram, grated nutmeg, pepper and salt; pound them with the yolks and whites of two eggs. They can be made into balls or sausages, and floured when so required. They may be fried or boiled.

Veal Forcemeat.—Four ounces of lean veal, two ounces of bread crumbs, two ounces of suet, and some parsley and sweet herbs, an onion, and spice. Pound in a mortar, break into it the yolk of an egg, mix all together, and season with pepper and salt. A little ham, bacon, or salt tongue would make it more savoury.

Goose and Duck Stuffing.—Chop fine two ounces of onion, an ounce of green sage, four ounces of bread crumbs, the yolk and white of an egg, and a little minced apple and cayenne.

Stuffing for Hare or Kangaroo.—Two ounces of beef suet, chopped fine, three ounces of bread crumbs, some parsley, shalot, marjoram, thyme, nutmeg, pepper, salt, a little cayenne; mix these ingredients thick with the yolk and white of an egg.

Forcemeat Balls for Turtle or Made Dishes.—Pound some beef or veal, and a third of its weight in butter; put into a stewpan the same weight of bread crumbs, moistened with milk; add chopped parsley and shalot, rub them in a mortar until they form a smooth paste, put it through a sieve, and, when cold, pound and mix all together, with the yolks of three eggs, boiled hard; season with salt, pepper, and curry-powder, add the yolks of two eggs, rub together and make small balls. Put into the soup a few minutes before it is served.

Egg Balls.—Four eggs, boiled till hard. When they are cold put the yolks into a mortar, with a small quantity of salad oil, a tea-spoon of flour, some chopped parsley, a little salt and cayenne. Rub them well together, roll into small balls, and boil two or three minutes.

SEASONINGS. — Antiphanes, in his "Leacas," gives the following catalogue of seasonings:—

"Dried grapes, and salt, and eke new wine,
Newly boiled down, and assafœtida,
And cheese, and thyme, and sesame,
And nitre, too, and cinnamon seed,
And sumach, honey, and marjoram,
And herbs, and vinegar, and oil,
And sauce of onions, mustard, and capers mix'd,
And parsley, capers, too, and eggs,
And lime, and cardamums, and th' acid juice
Which comes from the green fig-tree; besides lard,
And eggs, and honey, and flour, wrapp'd in fig-leaves,
And all compounded in one savoury forcemeat."
"*Athenæus*," translated by *Yonge*.

DIET.—There is not so much harm proceeding from the substance itself of meat, and quality of it, in ill-dressing and preparing, as there is from the quantity, disorder of time and place, unseasonable use of it, intemperance, over-much or over-little taking of it. A true saying is, "*Plures crapula quam gladius* (this gluttony kills more than the sword); this *omnino rantio, et homicida gula* (this all-devouring and murdering gut)." And that of Pliny is truer:—"Simple diet is the best. Heaping up of several meats is pernicious, and sauces worse: many dishes bring many diseases." Avicen cries out, that "nothing is worse than to feed on many dishes, or to protract the time of meals longer than ordinary: from thence proceed our infirmities; and 'tis the fountain of all diseases, which arise out of the repugnancy of gross humours."—*Burton's* "*Anatomy of Melancholy*," 1651.

XXX.—CIDER AND PERRY.

Let me efface the first term—epicurism, which is so injuriously and so falsely applied to the philosopher, from whom it takes its name, and let me not confound his refined moral system with the indulgence in sensual enjoyments of those professing themselves epicureans.—*Lady Blessington*.

Cider and perry are the fermented juice of the apple and the pear, and they are a very ancient beverage, as Pliny calls them "the wine of apples and pears." The rennets are the best kind of apples for cider, as their specific gravity is greater than any other. Apples are classed into bitter, sweet, and sour. The bitter are the best for cider, as the juice is the richest in sugar, ferments most readily, and keeps best after fermentation. As a general rule, apples and pears for cider and perry are not the kinds in table use, so the farmer must decide, in planting an orchard, for what purpose he intends to make it available. The process of making cider and perry varies in different places. The first operation is the collection of the fruit, which are generally left for a fortnight in a barn to mellow, and the unsound fruit are separated, as they impart a bad flavour to the liquor, and impede its clarification. The expression of the juice is the next step; the fruit is crushed in mills containing fluted cylinders of hard wood or cast-iron. The general practice is to sprinkle the pulp with a quarter of its weight in spring water, and allow it to remain in wooden tubs or cisterns for twelve or fourteen hours, during which time the fermentation commences. The pulp is then run through haircloth or coarse canvas bags, and subject to pressure. The *first* liquor is the best. The juice is then placed in casks, and kept full, so that the yeast may froth over. After a week the sediment will subside, when the liquor is racked off into clean casks, and stored for use. When about to be bottled, if not clear, it should be clarified. When wanted for immediate use, a small lump of white sugar should be put in each bottle. Both cider and perry are far more wholesome than the foreign wines that are generally drugged for the English market. The vast variety of New Jersey champagne cider is far superior to inferior champagne. The following is a good recipe for cider of this class:—

Good pale vinous cider, one hogshead; pale proof spirit, three gallons; honey or sugar, fourteen pounds. Mix well, and let them remain together in a temperate situation for a month, then add three pints of orange-flower water, and in a few days fine it down with half a gallon of skimmed milk. This is very pale. (We are indebted to "Cooley's Practical Receipts" for the above.) Like everything else, cider is adulterated, and the generality of this liquor is merely water, treacle, and alum, mixed with a moiety of the real article of an inferior kind, and called "Devonshire Cider." As for perry, when pure, it is a pleasant and wholesome liquor, and is often taken for champagne by persons who profess to be connoisseurs and judges.

CLEANLINESS.—I have more than once expressed my conviction that the humanising influence of habits of cleanliness and of those decent observances which imply self-respect—the best, indeed, the only foundation of respect for others—has never been sufficiently acted on. A clean, fresh, and well-ordered house exercises over its inmates a moral no less than a physical influence, and has a direct tendency to make the members of a family sober, peaceable, and considerate of the feelings and happiness of each other; nor is it difficult to trace a connection between habitual feelings of this sort, and the formation of habits of respect for property, for the laws in general, and even for those higher duties and obligations the observances of which no laws can enforce.—*Dr. Southwood Smith.*

XXXI.—GINGER:

The dried rhizoma of *zingiber officinalis*, a native of the East Indies, and abundantly cultivated in America, and the West India Islands, whence Europe is chiefly supplied. It is a good stimulant, and carminative, and the fresh root preserved makes an agreeable, warm, and not unwholesome sweetmeat. The acrimony of ginger appears to reside in a peculiar attractive matter, which is soluble in alcohol; hence a spirituous tincture contains the virtues of the root.—*Brande.*

The medical properties of this very useful plant are much neglected. It is an aromatic stimulant of considerable power, and its action on the nervous membrane is great. When chewed it relieves toothache, rheumatism of the jaw, and relaxed uvula. When received into the stomach, it promotes digestion in languid habits, and relieves flatulent colic. Gouty subjects are much benefited by ginger, and it formed the basis of the once celebrated Portland powder. For such persons, preserved ginger, taken at dessert, after a mixture of viands, is most beneficial, the finest being that in small round tender pieces, sent from the West Indies.

Ginger tea is an excellent stimulant for languid habits. Some headaches are relieved by applying to the forehead a poultice of scraped ginger and hot water. Ginger-beer often disagrees with persons, owing to the sugar; for, if made without it, it agrees with such persons well. Ginger, it should be remembered, however, loses much of its efficacy with age, so that old pieces are worthless.—*Things not Generally Known.*

LORD GULOSETON.—"A new friend," said he, as we descended into the dining-room, "is like a new dish; one must have him all to oneself, thoroughly to enjoy and rightly to understand him."

"A noble precept," said I, with enthusiasm. "Of all vices, indiscriminate hospitality is the most pernicious. It allows us neither conversation nor dinner, and, the mythological fable of Tantalus, gives us starvation in the midst of plenty."

"You are right," said Guloseton, solemnly; "I never ask above six persons to dinner, and I never dine out: for a bad dinner, Mr. Pelham, a bad dinner is a most serious—I may add *the* most serious calamity."

"Yes," I replied; "for it carries with it no consolation. A buried friend may be replaced; a lost mistress renewed; a slandered character be recovered; even a broken constitution restored; but a dinner, once lost, is irremediable; that day is for ever departed; an appetite, once thrown away, can never, till the cruel prolixity of the gastric agent is over, be regained. '*Il y a tant de maîtresses* (says the admirable Corneille), *il n'y a qu'un dîner.*'"—*Pelham.*

XXXII.—CONFECTIONERY.

That our great king himself doth woo me oft
For my confections.   *The Queen in "Cymbeline."*

Caramel.—Put a pound of the finest powdered loaf sugar into a pan, with half a pint of water and the white of an egg. Whisk the mixture till it boils, taking off the scum as it rises. Let it boil five minutes, then run it through a tamis; put it again on the fire and boil it up. When it has reached caramel height, it must be taken off. To ascertain the latter, when the syrup has become thick, dip into it the handle of a spoon, and immediately put it into cold water: if the sugar on it becomes crisp, it is done. To spin a basket or any other ornament, when the caramel begins to cool take some up with a spoon, and run it cleverly in thin threads over the mould, which must have been oiled. The French are most expert in the mysteries of sugared ornaments.

Snow Trifle.—This has an elegant appearance on the table, and is simply prepared. Whip the whites of eight eggs until they form a very thick froth. Put a pint and a half of milk on to boil, and when it boils place on its surface as many table-spoonfuls of the whipped whites of eggs as will stand on it without touching each other. As each spoonful becomes cooked and assumes the appearance of snow, take it off and put on another, until all the whipped eggs are done. As you take off the snow from the milk, put it on a hair sieve to drain. When all the snow is done, add to the milk a bit of lemon-peel, and sugar enough to sweeten it well. As soon as it has acquired the flavour of the lemon-peel, stir into it the yolks of eight eggs beaten up with a table-spoonful of orange-flower water; when of proper consistency, but not so thick as cream, pour it into a cream-dish. After it is cold, put the snow on the surface to make the sauce.

Snow Cream.—Put into a stewpan four ounces of ground rice, two ounces of sugar, a few drops of essence of lemon, with two ounces of butter; add a quart of milk; boil for about twenty minutes, until it is smooth, but not too thick. Pour it into a mould, or basin, which has been rinsed with butter, to let it set and cool.

Italian Cream.—An elegant dish. Boil a pint and a half of milk, and when it is boiling infuse the peel of an orange and lemon until the milk is flavoured. Put in a little salt, three ounces of pounded lump sugar, and the yolks of six eggs; add a sufficient quantity of isinglass, dissolved, to make it tenacious; put it into moulds until cold. To take it from the mould, dip a cloth in hot water, and rub round the mould; the cream will then turn out entire.

French Cream.—Dilute a dessert-spoonful of arrowroot or potato starch in a small quantity of cold water; put a pint and a half of milk to boil in a saucepan. When it boils, add a little salt, three ounces of pounded white sugar, and the diluted arrowroot or starch. When the milk has sufficiently thickened, put to it the yolks of eight eggs, well beaten, and a table-spoonful of orange-flower water. Stir the whole sufficiently, and pour into a cream-dish.

Lemon Cream.—Make a quart of good lemonade sweet. When so made, strain it, and put it into a stewpan over the fire. Add the yolks of eight eggs, well beaten up, and stir the cream well. Put it into cream-glasses, or a cream-dish; if to be put in moulds, add a small quantity of dissolved isinglass.

Custards.—Take a pint and a half of milk, and put it on the fire in a clean saucepan; when it boils add a bit of lemon-peel, a couple of peach-leaves, a salt-spoonful of salt, and two ounces and a half of powdered white sugar. Let the milk simmer until it has acquired the flavour of the lemon-peel and peach-leaves, but keep stirring it all the time, or it will burn. Use a wooden spoon for this purpose. Have the yolks of eight eggs ready beaten up, put them into the milk, and stir the whole over the fire until the custard is thick. If it boils or becomes too hot it will curdle. When cold put into glasses.

Vanilla Custards are made in a similar way, only leaving out the lemon-peel and peach-leaves, and pour in four drops of essence of vanilla, or boiling a drachm of vanilla, cut into bits, with the milk. Coffee custards, chocolate, tea, and other flavouring ingredients, are added to the milk and eggs, and take the name of the article used.

Blanc-mange.—To one quart of milk add an ounce of isinglass, a quarter of a pound of the best sugar, a quarter of an ounce of cinnamon, a little grated nutmeg, half the peel of a lemon, and a bayleaf; simmer over a slow fire till the isinglass is dissolved, and strain it through a napkin into a mould for the table. It can be coloured or flavoured any way, as long as no ingredient is used that does not curdle the milk.

Arrowroot Blanc-mange.—To a quart of new milk add a quarter of a pound of arrowroot, sweetened to taste; add a little cinnamon water or lemon for flavour; stir it well on the fire, and boil for about fifteen minutes; pour it into a mould to cool. When served add milk, cream, jam, or a custard over it. Rice used instead of arrowroot, boiled until soft, and served with jelly or jam, is equally good.

Trifle.—We disapprove of brandy in trifles, and advise sherry wine. Put in the trifle-dish four sponge biscuits and a quarter of a pound of macaroons and ratafias; cover the dish with these, and soak into them a quarter of a pint of sherry; when soaked sufficiently pour in a pint of custard, then a layer of raspberry jam, and cover with whipped cream well frothed.

Apple Trifle is made up in a similar manner, by a pulp of apples being placed at the bottom of the trifle-dish, flavoured with sugar and lemon. Mix half a pint of milk, half a pint of cream, and the yolk of an egg; give it a scald over the fire, with a little sugar in it; let it cool, then cover the apples with it, and put a whip on the top.

Calves' Feet Jelly.—Take four calves' feet, and slit them in two, and wash them in lukewarm water. Put them into simmer for six hours in sufficient water to cover them; and when reduced to half the quantity, after skimming it, strain it through a sieve, and skim off all the oily part on the top of the liquor. Put the liquor in a stewpan to melt, with a pound of lump sugar, the peel of two lemons, the juice of six, six whites of eggs, and shells beat well together, and a bottle of sherry; whisk the whole together until it simmers for half an hour; and strain through a jelly-bag. If the weather is warm, it will require icing or cooling. Sheep's trotters make very delicate jelly, but not so firm as the calves' feet. They require a little isinglass to set them firm.

Meringues.—Take the whites of eight eggs, and whisk them up to a strong froth; then stir in half a pound of white sugar, as lightly as possible. Flavour them with any essence you please; lay them on white paper the shape of half an egg; sift fine preserved sugar on them, and blow off all that does not stick. Bake them on a board on a slow oven; when of a pale brown, they are done. Take them off the paper, and beat in the under part with a spoon, to form a hollow, and dry them; fill them with cream, or any preserved fruit, and stick two together, which will form an egg shape.

Apple Jelly.—Put a pound and a half of apples, after being pared and cored, in a quart of water; boil them till the apples are in pulp, and put them into a hair sieve to drain. To every pint of juice add half an ounce of isinglass, the juice and peel of a lemon, sugar to taste; boil ten minutes. Pass it through a flannel bag into a mould.

Nougat.—Take a pound of sweet almonds; blanch them; cut each almond into four or five slices; dry them on a slow fire, taking care not to let them burn. Put into a pan three-quarters of a pound of sugar in powder, when melted through put in the almonds hot; mix them well together, and put a layer round a buttered mould; smooth them round equally with a lemon. When small let it cool; and if not quite hard when cold, put your shapes into a cool oven to dry. The shapes should be of tin, to turn out, and first oiled; it should be of about an inch thick. This is also eaten as a *bon bon*.

German Cream.—Take a pint of wine, put in sugar to taste; a little cinnamon, and boil it half an hour; mix it lukewarm with the yolks of eight eggs, strained after being well beaten. When cool, put it in a bowl, in a saucepan of hot water till done enough, and then pour it into the dish on which you serve it, cold, garnished with slices of lemon.

Constantinople Rouge Roquelocum.—Dissolve sugar in as strong a syrup as can be made. Colour some red, and have flat, square shapes. Pour the syrup in hot, and strew almonds cut in four, after being blanched with pistachios cut small, let it cool; and if not quite hard when cold, put your shapes into a cool oven to dry. The shapes should be of tin, to turn out, and first oiled; it should be of about an inch thick. This is eaten as a *bon bon*, and is excellent.

Jaune-mange.—Dissolve an ounce of isinglass in half a pint of boiling water; beat the yolks of six eggs, and mix them with half a pint of sherry, the juice of a lemon, and sugar to taste. The peel of the lemon should be rubbed on some of the sugar to extract the flavour. Stir all well together, and boil ten minutes. Strain, and put in a mould for shape.

Lemon Sponge.—Take half an ounce of isinglass; dissolve it in a little boiling water; then take the juice of eight lemons, and put sugar to your taste. Whisk it together until it becomes a sponge; then wet the mould and put it in; when set, turn it out. The mixture ought to be nearly cold to whisk well.

Everton Toffy.—Put half a pound of butter and half a tea-cupful of water into a pan; add three pounds of good moist sugar, the grated peel of one lemon; boil in water till it becomes brittle, and then pour on a tin.

Barley Sugar.—Put clarified syrup, containing rasped lemon-peel, into a saucepan with a lip as for melting butter, and boil it to caramel height, carefully skimming as it boils. Have ready a marble slab, well buttered, and pour the syrup on it of the thickness required for the sticks of barley sugar. Twist every stick at each end when hot, and it will assume the form required.

Barley-sugar Drops are made in a similar way to the foregoing;

but, instead of making it into sticks, drop them on the marble in round pieces.

Acidulated Drops.—Put a quantity of pounded loaf sugar, with some rasped orange-peel, into a saucepan; add a quantity of orange-juice, to give it flavour. Dry the whole over the fire, until it is of a proper consistence; then drop the confection from the point of a knife on clean paper.

Sugar-plums and Comfits.—Make these confections at home, unless you wish to be poisoned with those generally so highly coloured, and sold at the shops. The deleterious admixtures of colouring matter, in the general run of confectionery, has been over and over again exposed by scientific medical men, but all to no purpose. Sugared almonds, and comfits of every kind, can be easily made, for they are merely paste, sugar, and fruit.

Crême à l'Eau.—Grate a rind of a lemon, and add to it, with sugar, a pint of water; boil, and then add the yolks of eight eggs, well beaten; when cool, put in a bowl in a saucepan of hot water, till done enough, and pour into the dish on which you serve it, garnished with slices of lemon.

Vanilla Ice (German).—Boil half a pound of sugar into a syrup; add one quart of good cream, and, having tied up half a drachm of bruised vanilla in a muslin slip, boil the whole together; having beaten up four or five yolks of eggs, add them to the cream; press the vanilla, and take the slip out, and place it in a refrigerator to cool.—*Madame Scheibler.*

Vanilla is used very much in confectionery as a flavouring ingredient. It is the *epicudrum vanilla* of Linnæus, and is a creeping shrub of the orchis tribe, growing in Peru, Mexico, and the tropical parts of America. The pods are dried and preserved in tinfoil for exportation. They would thrive well in Queensland, Australia. It is worth about £4 per pound.

Russian Charlotte.—Place in a mould, in a circle, some ladies' finger cakes, and let them lie closely together; line the sides of the mould with them by placing them upright. Pour into the middle a whipped cream; turn it upside down in the dish. If made in warm weather, it must be iced.

Currant and Raspberry Jelly.—Take two pounds of ripe currants and a pound of raspberries, put them on a stone in a preserving-pan, with a spoonful of water; slightly mash them with a wooden spoon, and strain them through a napkin. Mix this juice with sugar and a little isinglass, boil and skim, and put it in a mould to set.

Orange, rose, violet, and lemon jellies may be made in a similar way, as well as rum, cherry brandy, annisette, curaçoa, maraschino, and any kind of wine, which article used will give the name to the jelly.

Caledonian Cream.—This favourite cream may be made as follows:—Two tea-spoonfuls of white sugar, one ditto of raspberry jam, the whites of two eggs, and the juice of one lemon. Beat well for half an hour, and serve up, sprinkled with fancy biscuits.

Ice Cream.—Put the cream into a pan, then stir in the sugar by degrees, and, when all is well mixed, strain it through a sieve; put it into a tin that has a close cover, and set it in a tub. Fill the tub with ice broken in small pieces, and strew round the ice a quantity of salt, taking care that none of the salt gets to the cream. Scrape the cream down with a spoon, as it freezes round the edges of the tin; while the cream is freezing stir in gradually the lemon-juice or the pulp of a pint of mashed strawberries or raspberries. When it has frozen, dip the tin into lukewarm water, take out the cream, and fill the glasses.

We have given the above recipe; but, in preference, we recommend the freezing-vase, elsewhere alluded to, by Simpson; for he propounds, in a pamphlet, the different modes of making strawberry, raspberry, currant, pine apple, and lemon-ice creams, and the following water ices, viz., lemon, orange, pine apple, cherry, currant, strawberry, raspberry, and vanilla. Were we to give these modes in detail, we almost fancy we should bring ourselves within the purview of the charge the celebrated *Alabama* is accused of—piracy.

Devonshire Clouted Cream.—The milk, put into the pan one morning, stands to the next; then set the pan on a hot hearth; put this over a stove for about twenty minutes; it will be done when bladders rise on its surface. It must not boil, but be moved from the fire, and placed in a cool plate, when the cream is taken off the surface.

The above is the celebrated Devonshire clouted cream, which has been rendered famous by one of Moore's favourite songs being parodied in its praise:—

"The gems may be rich, and the gems may be rare;
But this I solemnly do declare:
There is nothing on earth, or in poets' dreams,
So rich and so rare as your Devonshire creams."

CLOUTED OR CLOTTED CREAM.—The cream produced on the surface of milk, by setting a pan of new milk on a hot hearth, is so named. It is chiefly used as a kind of *entremet*, and when mixed with new milk, is eaten along with fruit pies, strawberries, raspberries, &c. It is also eaten without milk, and spread upon bread.—*Brande*.

Devonshire Junket.—Put lukewarm milk into a bowl, and turn it with rennet; then add some clouted cream, sugar, and cinnamon on the top, without breaking the curd; then drain the milk, and add a little wine or brandy. When turned, put sugar and nutmeg on the top, and serve.

Icing for Cakes.— Take one pound of sugar; put into a pan; break in the whites of six eggs, and as much powder blue as will lie on a sixpence; beat it well with a wooden spoon for ten minutes, then squeeze in the juice of a lemon, and beat it till it becomes transparent. Set the cake you intend to ice in an oven or warm place for five minutes; then spread over the mixture as smooth as possible. A plain ice, or ornament the cake with fancy articles of any description.

Corstorphine Cream.—Corstorphine cream is called from a village of that name near Edinburgh; it is made by putting the milk of three or four days together, with the cream, into a vessel, and allowing it to remain there until it becomes sour and coagulated. The whey is then drawn off and fresh cream added; and when it is brought to table it is eaten with sugar, and, in the strawberry season, with that fruit.

Gooseberry Fool.—Blanch a quart of gooseberries, closely covered with sufficient water to pulp them; beat six eggs, and add them to a pint of cream—some use milk—a table-spoonful of orange-flower water, spice and sugar to sweeten; stir it over a fire till of a proper thickness; dish, and sift powdered white sugar on the top.

Gooseberry Trifle.—Proceed as above with a quart of gooseberries, and pass them through a sieve; then place them at the bottom of a dish; add sugar and a little nutmeg. Mix half a pint of cream with the same quantity of milk, and the yolk of an egg; scald it over the fire, and stir it; add a little sugar, and let it cool. Pour over the gooseberries a whip made the day before of a pint of cream, two eggs, lemon-peel to flavour a little, and sugar.

Suèdoise of Peaches.—Pare and divide four ripe peaches, and let them simmer for about five minutes in a syrup made with the third of a pint of water and three ounces of white sugar; lift them out carefully into a deep dish, and pour half the syrup over them, and into the remaining half put a couple of pounds of ripe peaches, and boil them to marmalade. Lift the other peaches from the syrup, and reduce it by boiling more than half. Spread a deep layer of marmalade in a dish, and arrange the peaches round it, and fill the places with the marmalade; place the half of a blanched peach kernel on each, pour the reduced syrup equally over the surface, and form a border round the dish with macaroons; or, instead, candied citron, sliced thin, and cut into leaves with a paste-cutter. A little lemon-juice added is a great improvement.

Syllabub.—Whipped syllabub is made of a strong whip, as for trifle; then mix a pint of cream, with half a pint of wine; sugar and flavour with the juice and grated peel of a lemon, and a little cinnamon. Stir briskly, and fill the glasses sufficiently to put some of the whip on the top of each glass. Staffordshire syllabub is made in a similar way, with a pint of cider, and a glass of brandy and grated nutmeg; and Somersetshire is made from port wine and sherry, and over the top is strewed grated nutmegs and different kinds of comfits. Lemon syllabub is made in a similar way, with the squeezed juice of half a dozen lemons.

Swiss Cream.—Flavour with lemon-peel a pint of cream; add six ounces of white sugar, put the cream and sugar into a saucepan, and, when simmering, add, by degrees, two tea-spoonfuls of flour; let it simmer for five minutes, stirring it all the time; pour it out, and when cold mix with it, by degrees, the juice of two lemons. Take a quarter of a pound of macaroons, put them in a dish, and pour over them a glass of white wine; then part of the cream, then the macaroons, and cream again; ornament the dish with sliced citron or iced lemon-peel.

Spanish Cream.—Boil in half a pint of water an ounce of isinglass till dissolved; strain, and mix with it a quart of cream or good milk; if cream, do not use so much isinglass; stir it over the fire till it comes to a boil; when a little cooled, add gradually the beaten yolks of six eggs and a glass of white wine. Pour it into a deep dish, sweeten with loaf sugar, stir it till cold, and then put it into a shape. In lieu of the wine, it may be flavoured with the peel of a lemon.

Spanish Flummery.—Scald a quart of cream with a little cinnamon or mace, mix this gradually into half a pound of rice flour, and stir it over a gentle fire until it is of the thickness of jelly. Sweeten it to taste, and pour it into cups or shapes. Turn it out when cold, and serve up. Cream, wine, or preserves eat well with it; or it may be eaten alone, as preferred.

DINING IN STATE.—With growing reverence for the sage, we attended the hermit of Bellyfulle back to his cell. "In half an hour," said he, graciously smiling, "it will be dinner time. Half an hour," he repeated with musical emphasis, as he passed into his chamber. Having profitably employed the time with cold water, we then, refreshed yet hungry, sought our host. The hermit awaited us. He had put aside his cloak of the morning, and was again wrapped in his old damask gown. He perceived that we observed the change. "My custom, sir," he said; "I never yet could dine in full dress. The digestive organs, sir, abominate close buttoning, and do their work sulkily, grumblingly. No, sir: a man in full dress may chew and swallow, but he never dines. The stomach cannot honestly perform its functions in state." We smiled; whereupon the hermit, with a grave, sly look, asked, "Will you answer me this question?" We bowed affirmatively. "Do you think it is in the power of mortal man to give a fair, wise, learned judgment upon any dish or sauce soever, the said man being, at the time of tasting, in tight boots? Sir, it is impossible."—*Chronicles of Clovernook.*

XXXIII.—FONDU.

Where, where? Art thou come? Why, my cheese, my digestion, why hast thou not served thyself into my table so many meals?—*Achilles, in "Troilus and Cressida."*

Four eggs well beaten, three ounces of butter, three ounces of cheese, and a gill of cream; mix well, and bake for twenty minutes in small shapes or in a dish. Serve hot, for cold fondu is unbearable.

Another Recipe.—Beat up the yolks of eight eggs together with a quarter of a pound of melted butter, and half a pound of grated cheese, of good flavour; mix the ingredients with the whites of the eggs whisked to a froth. Bake in small dishes and serve hot.

IMPORTANT.—According to the gastronomical adjudication of our friend, the French judge (M. Brillat Savarin), this dish must be served in silver, or metal, so as to preserve the caloric heat, and along with the fondu must be handed round choice Burgundy, or Australian white wine, if the Amphitryon has such liquor; if not, port, or a small ale-glass of real Burton.

XXXIV.—DINNER ACCORDING TO COUNT D'ORSAY.

Ford. Well, I promise you a dinner.—*Merry Wives of Windsor.*

It is said that the Count was without a rival as a connoisseur in the dining art, except Mr. Walker; we therefore insert the *menu* of a banquet given by Lord Chesterfield on his quitting the office of Master of the Buckhounds, the bill of fare of which was furnished by the Count. The dinner took place at the Clarendon, a few years since, and the party consisted of thirty, and the price was six guineas per head. The extract is taken from the "Art of Dining." Ude tells us that "Cookery in England, *when well done*, is superior to that of any country in the world;" but the same remark may be applied to the *cuisine* anywhere. Count D'Orsay's bill of fare was in the French language, but, for the general reader, we have given the English version of it as far as possible:—

FIRST SERVICE.

SOUPS: Spring, Queen, turtle.
FISH: Turbot (lobster and Dutch sauce),
Salmon (Tartar fashion, that is, with a *sauce piquante*—acid sauce),
Gurnet (Cardinal fashion),
Cod fritters,
Whitebait.
REMOVES: Fillet of beef (in the Neapolitan fashion),
Turkey, flavoured with shalots,
Macaroni, in a high silver dish,
Haunch of venison.
ENTREES: Chicken rissoles,
Oyster patties, lamb cutlets,
A thick soup of mushrooms,
Lamb cutlets dressed with asparagus tips,
Veal fricandeau, with sorrel,
Sweetbreads, pierced with thin strips of bacon fat, and tomato sauce,
Pigeon cutlets (Dunell fashion),
A mixture of vegetables and minced pheasants,
Duckling fillets (Bigarrade fashion),
Richelieu sausages,
Pulled fowl, with truffles,
Raised mutton pie.
SIDE DISHES: Round of beef, ham, salade.

SECOND COURSE.

ROASTS: Capon, quails, turkey poults, green goose.
SIDE DISHES: Asparagus, haricot beans in the French fashion,
Lobster salad,
Mixed jelly (omnium gatherum jelly),
Plovers' eggs in jelly,
Russian Charlotte,
Maraschino jelly,
Marble cream,
Basket of pastry,
Rhubarb tart (light pastry),
Apricot tart (close or solid pastry),
Basket of meringues (called, vulgarly, sugar eggs),
Dressed crab,
Salad au jelantine (we fancy must be a misprint for salade en jalantine. Galantine is a fashion of arranging salad or poultry with herbs and jelly),
Mushrooms, with herbs.
REMOVES: Vanilla soufflé (*i.e.*, beaten up—whipped),
Nesselrode pudding,
Adelaide sandwiches,
Foudu (melted cheese).

(*Pièces moditers* are the ornamental articles of confectionery.)

N.B.—Fricandeau is a piece of meat (generally veal) *sauté*—*i.e.*, cooked—in a peculiar manner, partly in a frying-pan and partly in a stewpan, with very rich sauce, and stuck full of little pieces of the fat of bacon, and with some kind of vegetables round it—peas, spinach, or sorrel.

PUBLIC DINNERS AT ATHENS.—The public dinners at the Prytaneium, of which the archons and a select few partook in common, were either first established, or perhaps only more strictly regulated, by Solon. He ordered barley cakes for their ordinary meals, and wheaten bread for festival days, prescribing how often each person should dine at the table. The honour of dining at the Prytaneium was maintained throughout as a valuable reward at the disposal of the Government.—*Grote's " History of Greece."*

XXXV.—APPERT'S MODE OF PRESERVING FRUIT OR VEGETABLES.

The article must be put into wide-mouthed glass bottles. The finest corks must be used; the bottles dry; and when corked, they must be air-tight. The bottles being thus corked, put them into a saucepan, fill it with cold water, and set it on the fire, and boil the bottled articles in the *bain marie*. Then remove the saucepan from the fire, and let it get almost cold before taking out the bottles. Dip the cork in resin, and put the bottles in the cellar. To avoid any breakage the heat of the *bain marie* might produce, it is necessary only to fill the bottles to within two inches of the necks, and not even so high if the bottle only contains liquid. The articles to be preserved ought to be gathered in the proper season, that they may be neither too green and watery, nor too dry; they should also be quite fresh. In wet seasons vegetables require a quarter of an hour's less boiling in the *bain marie* than in dry seasons.

Mr. Appert's book, 12mo, 1812, is a most useful family work, but we believe out of print.

DRINKING AT MEALS.—It is injurious to drink much at meals. Those who take a large quantity of liquids during dinner generally eat more than those who drink less. The sensation of thirst depends upon the quantity of aqueous fluid circulating in the blood. It has been found by physiologists that the most severe thirst of animals is appeased by injecting watery fluids into the blood. A moderate quantity of liquid should be taken at dinner; too large a portion acts injuriously by diluting the gastric fluid. Persons whose diet is more animal than vegetable require more liquid during their meals. Drinking before a meal is pernicious, whilst by drinking during a meal the digestive process is promoted. Those also who eat fast require more drink than do others; for, as Dr. Philips says, the food is swallowed without a due admixture of saliva, and forms a dry mass in the stomach.—*Winslow's "Health of Body and Mind."*

XXXVI.—VEGETABLES.

One of the greatest luxuries, to my mind, in dining is to be able to command plenty of good vegetables. Excellent potatoes, smoking hot, would alone stamp merit on any dinner; but they are as rare on state occasions so served, as if they were the cost of pearls.—*Walker.*

Potatoes.—If this vegetable is very mealy it must be steamed. There is no other mode of cooking the best Tasmanian black potatoes. In steaming them, all that the cook has to do is to peel them before they are put into the steamer, and when done remove the steamer from off the saucepan. If they are boiled, they are placed in the water with a little salt, and allowed to simmer until they are done, which is known by forking them. When boiled, they may be fried again whole, or cut up with greens. Potatoes are often used mashed and browned, with a small quantity of butter or milk; but a vegetarian does not generally like pappy potatoes. A favourite *plât* of ours is this vegetable cut green, and fried in fat until done, of about an eighth of an inch in thickness. Roast potatoes under meat is another mode, and baked potatoes with meat are equally good. The mealy sort baked in the ashes, and sent to table with their jackets on, is a common mode of cooking them. Potato scones are a very nice way of dressing them: mash the potatoes with a little milk, keeping them as dry as you can; add an egg well beaten, a sprinkling of flour, and fry them of a light brown. Potato pie is made by putting a few chops or slices of mutton at the bottom of a pie-dish, on the meat a little gravy or thickening, and fill up the dish with potatoes sliced green, with salt, and bake. This is a simple and very good dish indeed, assuming that the vegetables are of the right sort. If potatoes are watery, in boiling them put a dessert-spoonful of lime in the water, and that will make them mealy. New potatoes are well cleaned with a flannel rubber, and boiled until tender.

KEEPING POTATOES.—The following mode of preserving potatoes for ten months from the time of their being taken up, by Mr. M'Cormack, land steward to the Earl of Charlemont, obtained the prize from the Royal Dublin Society a few years since :—

First, the species of potato with which I am acquainted for long keeping is the apple (either red or white), and those, in the present state of my information, should always be preferred for that purpose. Secondly, they should be planted in March, or, at the farthest, the middle of April, from the circumstance of their taking a longer time in the ground to mature the crop than any other potato I know of. And next in importance is to avoid putting them in any way exposed to the southern sun. I should prefer for the purpose a close place, surrounded with large trees, but not under their drops, for the cooler the situation is in which they are pitted the better, provided that no water can lodge in the pits or about them. The potatoes produced were taken out of the ground in November, and pitted in a situation where neither the morning nor the midday sun had much influence upon them, the solar heat from the south and east being intercepted by two plantations. The potatoes have been taken out of these pits by the middle of March to the potato-house, which is also in a great degree overshadowed by large trees, and the roof on the south side nearly covered with ivy. Here they remained to the 4th of June, turning them carefully over with a wooden shovel every fortnight, but not picking off any of the buds that were produced, which by this system were very few indeed. By the 4th of June I had six cwt. of apple potatoes selected for experiment, two cwt. of which I put upon a loft over the potato-house, with a louvre window facing to the north, which admitted all the changes of atmospheric air, &c.; two cwt. more I put in a coal-room under the same loft, to which, however, there was frequent access. The remaining two cwt. I put in a vault, which is immediately under the grotto of Marino, which adjoins the gardens. This vault is, however, on a level, or nearly so, with the surrounding surface on the garden side, the whole building completely overshadowed by large trees, evergreens, &c. I placed a thermometer in the vault, and immediately after the potatoes were removed from it (the potato-house) on the 4th of June, the degree of heat in the vault at twelve o'clock at noon was 52°, at six o'clock in the afternoon 52° also. Another thermometer in the open air, on the same day, at twelve o'clock at noon, was 72°; at six in the afternoon, 61°. I continued to observe that in the vault, from the circumstance of its being completely overshadowed with trees, &c., the degree of heat was always the same, whether the day was warm, cold, or changeable. My conclusions are:—First, that a temperature of 52° is the atmosphere potatoes will keep best in; secondly, that the atmospheric changes of heat, cold, and moisture, light and darkness, are all productive of vegetation; and the more these alternate changes can be avoided or counteracted by keeping a low and an even temperature, the better and the longer will the potato keep.

THE POTATO AT A DISCOUNT.—Dr. Mapother, at the last meeting of the Dublin Royal Society, read a valuable paper on improving the diet of the Irish labourers. He agreed with Cobbett that potatoes had been the curse of Ireland. From potato diet to starvation was but a step. The prevalence of scrofula and consumption he ascribed to this national food. The ash of the potato is remarkably poor in lime and magnesia—materials of the first importance in building the framework of the body. He considered the health and well-being of the Irish peasantry demanded animal food. They could easily be supplied by South America. [Why not from Australia?] The meat is cut in slices, dipped in brine and dried in the sun. When soaked for use, it increases threefold in size, and can be sold for threepence per pound. Capt. Henry stated that he farmed his own land, and that he had established a mess for his labourers with a satisfactory result. He saw his labourers crouched under the hedges eating their miserable meal of potatoes. He employed a good cook, obtained the best meat and vegetables, and now supplies an abundant, well-dressed dinner for threepence each to the men, and twopence each to the women and children. The numbers thus fed amounted to 200. Dr. Mapother recommended the use of peas and beans; one pound of peas would form as much muscle as fifteen pounds of potatoes. Mr. Pollock's men, in the county of Galway, are fed on peas porridge, and they found that it took a long time before the appetite returned. The leguminous seeds are particularly rich in lime and in phosphoric acid—that great constituent of the nobler parts of man, the brain, and the locomotive organs.—*Condensed from Irish Newspapers.*

HOW TO CHOOSE A GOOD POTATO.—The finest, mealiest, and most nutritious potatoes are always denser and heavier than the soft and waxy. By taking advantage of this difference in their specific gravity, the light and inferior potatoes are made to swim on the surface of a solution of salt, while the heavy and good sink to the bottom. By this simple contrivance the dry and mealy potatoes are separated from the soft and waxy in the most effectual manner, with the most scientific exactness, and by a process that cannot err. Let the potatoes be first washed clean in fresh water; and as all vegetables should be washed in salt and water for the dislodgment of the slugs or insects, a tub of salt and water ought to be kept in readiness in every garden for the purpose, and in this the potatoes can be proved. If replenished once a week it will be found sufficient.—*Scottish Farmer.*

DIFFERENT WAYS OF COOKING POTATOES.—*Mrs. Rundell* prefers steaming in plenty of water, and, when half done, some cold water and salt thrown in, and then left in the pot over the fire. *Mrs. Glasse.*—Boil in as little water as possible, without burning the saucepan. *Mrs. Acton.*—The potatoes to be peeled, and boiled slowly; when done, salt thrown over, and the pot shook violently, so that they are not broken. *M. Soyer.*—If potatoes are steamed, salt should be thrown into the water, and not on the potatoes; and, when done, remove the steamer, and also the cover.—The fisherman simply boils his potato in the salt water of the sea, and by this mode can dress them as well as any other.

Reader, if you are at all subject to dyspepsia, beware, oh! beware of waxy or watery potatoes. Mealy potatoes are those that are nutritious, as they contain the greatest amount of gluten, which is the important consideration. The *Quarterly* states that a club committee were specially called together to select a cook. There were two candidates, an Englishman, from the Albion, and a Frenchman, recommended by Ude; an eminent divine was deputed to examine them, and the first question he put to each was, "Can you boil a potato?"

Green Peas.—Green peas are reckoned early in the season a great delicacy, and they are a wholesome vegetable. They require plenty of water, and when done must be removed from the fire. Drain them on a hair sieve, and put them in the dish with the least bit of butter. A sprig of mint boiled with them is usually sent up with the peas.

Beans are sometimes boiled with a small piece of bacon; if by themselves, they need the addition of parsley and butter.

Most vegetables being more or less succulent, require their full proportion of fluids for retaining that state of crispness and plumpness which they have when growing. On being cut or gathered the exhalation from their surface continues, while from the open vessels of the cut surface there is often great exudation or evaporation, and thus their natural moisture is diminished, the tender leaves become flaccid, and the thicker masses or roots lose their plumpness. This is not only less pleasant to the eye, but is a real injury to the nutritious powers of the vegetable, for in this flaccid and shrivelled state its fibres are less divided in chewing, and the water which exists in vegetable substances in the form of their natural juices, is directly nutritious. The first care, therefore, in the preservation of succulent vegetables is, to prevent them from losing their natural moisture.—*Edinburgh Cyclopædia.*

Spinach.—This vegetable must be well cleaned, and boiled quick. Put a little salt in the water, and, when well done, strain it well from the water. Poached eggs, with fried bread as a garnish, is frequently served with spinach.

Asparagus.—Great care must be observed in boiling asparagus. They must be tied in bundles of the same size and length, and put into the boiling water with a little salt. When done it is taken out of the pan and served on toast.

Vegetable Marrow.—This is an excellent vegetable in any way it may be dressed, whether fried, boiled, or stewed. There are numerous varieties, some tasteless, others full of flavour. On one occasion we cultivated a small oblong kind, the taste of which was so like asparagus, that it was an impossibility to tell it in flavour from the latter esculent. True and Jerusalem artichokes, sea-kale, nettles, cabbage, greens, savoys, cauliflower, broccoli, parsnips, turnips, carrots, French beans, mangold-wurzel, and radish-tops, are all boiled in a similar way until tender, and not allowed to sodden in the water. Turnips, after boiling, are mashed, and served in that state, with a piece of butter added to them. A small bit of charcoal boiled with vegetables will counteract their bitter taste, or a little sugar will answer the same purpose. Haricot beans are best parboiled in one water, and finished in another boiling water. In boiling vegetables never keep the lid on the saucepan. Vegetables assist the stomach in digesting food, such as pork, goose, and wild fowl. The acid in apple sauce, the lemon-juice and vinegar, are all assistants to digestion; as we have the high authority of Dr. Mayo, "that the palate has suggested, and philosophy has approved, of the association."

CABBAGE.—According to ancient poetry, translated, cabbage is an antidote to the effect of drink :—

"Last evening you were drinking deep,
So now your head aches. Go to sleep;
Take some boil'd cabbage when you wake,
And there's an end of your headache."

The Egyptians are said to eat boiled cabbage before the rest of their food to this time.

The onion—though said to form one of the connecting links between an alimentary root and a condiment, must be considered valuable on account of its stimulating matter —certainly contains a considerable proportion of nourishment. This appears evident in its boiled state, by which process its acrimony is exhaled, and a sweet mucilage separated. Sir John Sinclair says that it is a well-known fact, that a Highlander, with a few raw onions in his pocket, and a crust of bread, or some oat cake, can travel almost to an incredible extent, for two or three days together, without any other food. The French are fully aware of the quantity of nourishment this plant affords; hence the soup, à l'oignon, is considered by them as the best of all restoratives. As a stimulant to the stomach and bowels, the onion, in a raw state, is certainly of value, and this is much enhanced by its diuretic qualities. The leek, garlic, and shalot are of the same species, and possess qualities of the same nature.—*Paris on Diet.*

Asparagus à la Français.—Boil some asparagus, and chop the heads and tender parts of the stalks, together with a boiled onion, into small pieces; add a little salt and pepper, and the beaten yolk of an egg; beat up, and serve on sippets of toasted bread, with melted butter poured over.

Purées.—This is generally the French preparation of vegetables, and we shall only give one recipe, for the mode is merely to pulp the vegetables through a sieve, and add a little stock or butter. Purées, when served with meat, are *entremets*; if they are served alone, they should be accompanied with fried or toasted bread.

Purée of Green Peas.—Take two quarts of shelled green peas; put them into boiling water, and let them boil with a little parsley, chives, and salt; strain them, and rub them through a sieve; add a little butter or gravy; warm them up again, and serve.

Purées may be made of the pods of peas, of dried peas, beans, haricots, onions, celery, pumpkin, succory, turnips, carrots, lentils, and every vegetable that grows, and sometimes of meats, which come on the table pappy and spiced, so that one does not know from the taste what he is eating. We cannot recommend them.

All kinds of vegetables are excellent stewed. Marrows, carrots, peas, cauliflowers, and onions, either in white sauce or brown gravy, are very correct accompaniments to

meats; the mildness of the latter vegetable when thus cooked is well known, although we are told in *All's Well that Ends Well,* "Mine eyes smell onions; I shall weep anon." Stewed celery is an addition to various roast joints, and is made as follows:—
Take off the outside and the green ends of the celery, boil them in water till tender, put in a slice of lemon, a little mace, thicken with butter and flour. Beat up an egg or two, grate in some nutmeg, mix with a table-spoonful of cream, put to it half a cupful of gravy or stock, and let it simmer until sufficiently thick. Serve hot, as every dish should be.

THE TARO.—Among its vegetables, too, is found the "taro" (*arum esculentum*). It formed the staple of food, and is still very generally used. This succulent root was sometimes cooked, but was more generally pounded into a semi-fluid mess, and allowed partially to ferment, when it was called *poi.* Among the reasons which made some Hawaiians object to visiting England was that *poi* could not be obtained here. It is so productive, that it has been said, a *taro* pit a few yards in length will supply food for one man throughout the year.—"*Historical Account of the Sandwich Islands,*" *by Hopkins.*

Macédoine of Vegetables.—Take an equal quantity of carrots and turnips, cut them of the size of almonds, peel a dozen button onions, put all in a saucepan with a piece of butter; let them brown gently, add a little gravy and some mushrooms, young beans, French beans, haricots, and some Brussels sprouts (the last must be parboiled), some asparagus plants, and the tops of a cauliflower, with a teaspoon of sugar; let them all boil gently; just before serving thicken the sauce with a little flour, and serve.

HOW TO PRESERVE VEGETABLES.—Gather the vegetables when at maturity, string them on twine, and suspend them under a roof of rather low temperature, so that you may not dry them too fast. When you find them getting a little crisp, you may pack them in a box, and keep them in a dry, airy place, and you will find them ready for use. I have succeeded with the following:—White beet, red, white, and green cabbage, spinach—the larger the leaf the better, as you get a large quantity with the same trouble. Spinach answers admirably; indeed, you can prepare any description of vegetable, and have them ready for consumption, so that it will require a keen taste to know the difference between them and those freshly plucked from the garden. Boil them in the ordinary way, adding a little soda, to bring out the colour. By doing as described you may have, when the hot winds are blowing, and every sign of vegetable gone, your vegetable garden flourishing in your pantry, every variety in full bloom, independent of showers or irrigation.—*Correspondent to the "Pastoral Times" (New South Wales).*

Potatoes, in whatever condition, whether spoiled by frost, germination, &c., provided they are raw, constantly afford starch, differing only in quality—the round grey ones the most, a pound producing two ounces.—*Parmentier on "Nutritive Vegetables."*

THE POTATO.—Next to bread there is no vegetable article the preparation of which, as food, deserves to be more attended to than the potato.—*Sir John Sinclair's "Code of Health."* The potato is the cause of the moral and physical degeneration of the nations that use it.—*Professor Mulder.* Since the days of Cook the New Zealanders have lived upon potatoes, the lowest species of human food.—*Dr. Thomson's "New Zealand."* The well known root of the *Solanum tuberosum.* Many methods at different times have been tried for preserving potatoes in an unchangeable state, and always ready to be dressed as a wholesome and nutritious dish, but none equal to Mr. Daones Edwards, for which he obtained a patent in 1840.—*Ure.* Its use as a subordinate and subsidiary species of food is attended with the best efforts, producing both an increase of comfort and security; but there are certain circumstances inseparable from it which would seem to oppose the most formidable obstacles to its advantageous use as a *prime* article of subsistence. . . . We are inclined to estimate the yearly value of the produce of potatoes in the Empire at twelve millions.—*M'Culloch's "Commercial Dictionary."* The vegetable kingdom affords no food more wholesome, more easily procured, easily prepared, and less expensive than the potato.—*Kitchiner.* Amongst the farinaceous aliments the potato holds a distinguished rank; but its digestibility greatly depends on its kind, and the nature of the cookery to which it is subjected.—*Paris.*

"Who shall decide when doctors disagree,
And soundest casuists doubt, like you and me?"

XXXVII.—TOASTED CHEESE.

> Happy the man that has each fortune tried,
> To whom she much has given and much denied;
> With abstinence all delicacies he sees,
> And can regale himself on toasted cheese.—*King.*

If toasted cheese is to be ate in perfection, the cheese must be mild, not too poor, nor too rich. There must be fitted into the toaster six or eight movable small tin dishes. Have them of silver, if you can afford the expense. The least bit of butter is put in the tin, at the bottom, with the cheese; or a little ale; it is then exposed to the fire until done. This dish must not be attempted unless it can be served hot; and on such an occasion, if perfection is aimed at, ceremony must be disregarded. Even to wait for pepper, salt, and mustard, is time that cannot be spared by the real *gourmet* on this *plât*. The caution of the author of "Vanity Fair" would apply with full force to toasted cheese:— "My dear fellow, don't let us speak a word until we have finished this dish!" or the observation of Lord Guloseton in "Pelham," after sitting down to dinner:—"My dear friend, this is no time for talking; let us eat."

CHEESE.—Old cheese taken in small quantities after dinner is a good digester. The only *post-prandial* item at the Beef Steak Society is a stew of cheese in a silver dish.

A BUMPKIN AT DINNER.—
> Hodge to the squire's once went to dine,
> And drank his fill of beer and wine;
> Next day, being asked how he had fared,
> Says he, "D'you know I summut stared,
> That arter guttlin' soup and fish,
> An' wenson in a silver dish,
> Plumpoodden, an' sich things as these,
> They brout me in plain bread and cheese.—*Punch's Almanack.*

Welsh Rabbit, or Rarebit.—Toast a slice of bread on both sides, and butter it; toast a slice of mellow cheese on one side, and lay that next the bread, and toast the other with a salamander; rub mustard over, and serve hot and covered.

XXXVIII.—JONES'S PATENT FLOUR.

"Taste and try" will alone ensure success in cookery; and a few years' experience is better than a volume on the art. A medical man once asked Ude why cooks had not weights and measures as apothecaries? To which Ude replied, "We taste our recipes, whereas doctors seldom taste those they are mixing; wherefore they must have exact measures."—*Rationale of Cookery in* "*Things not Generally Known.*"

We are indebted to Cooley's "Practical Receipts" for this mixture, and can vouch for its goodness, and the ease with which bread is made from the different ingredients. The reason it is not more generally, nay, we say universally, used we cannot divine, when the best authority—the *Lancet*—has written that it is "the greatest invention of the age;" and we apprehend that the editor of that publication is no quack. The use of this flour would save England two millions of quarters of corn per annum, which are now lost in carbonic acid gas and defective manipulation. It can only be made properly from the finest kiln-dried flour, and is invaluable for cakes, puddings, pastry, biscuits, and fancy bread. It is economical, as it requires more water to make into dough, and there can be no adulteration. Cooley is justly indignant that it is not more generally used; and he writes, that Englishmen appear to prefer alumed bread, with headache, dyspepsia, and indigestion, to a clear head and vigorous digestion. Jones's patent flour, in the country, on board ship or yacht, or at the diggings, is most necessary and valuable. The London *Times* has lately published an able article on the advantages of baking bread on board of our men-of-war, and the boon of such a diet to our seamen. No doubt of it; and if soft bread was served out, even twice a week, to our soldiers and sailors in war time, they would be the better for it. An Englishman cannot fight unless he is well fed. The French men-of-war have large ovens, and fresh bread is baked for the crew daily. Why should our men be subject to the eternal boil every day of their lives? We would have "My lords" put on this boiling diet for a time, to see how they would like it. The Americans *whipt* the world for flour, and the South Australians *whipt* the Americans, as their flour is acknowledged to be infinitely superior. Why do not the Board of Admiralty give a fillip to the colonies by calling for tenders for victualling their fleets? Nowhere is flour and beef so cheap, and a victualling-yard could easily be called into existence. Is circumlocution or red-tape the only objection? If economy is to be considered, this would at once be effected. Adelaide exported in the first six months of 1863 no less than 30,000 tons of the finest flour, and, as a consequence, has obtained the enviable position of being the granary of the Southern Hemisphere. Launceston, in Tasmania, comes next in order, and yet "*Mr.* Mother Country," to use a term of the late Charles Buller's, will not assist his offspring at a great pecuniary saving to himself. The finest flour has been selling at Adelaide and Launceston during the past year at £10 per 2,000 pounds. Borwick's and every other baking powder may hide their diminished heads in comparison with Jones's patent flour. Borwick advertises that the Queen has ordered the use of his powder in the Royal kitchen; but Her Majesty will do so no more after a trial with the patent flour, as it will effectually supersede the baking mixture, both in the palace of the Sovereign and the cottage of the poor. The reader may naturally think that we are employed in the Holloway style—to puff. By no means; we only came across the recipe by mere chance, and have not the pleasure of knowing Mr. Jones. Let any one peruse with attention what a talented lady and excellent house-manager writes on this subject; but, before doing so, let us give the proportions:—

Flour	one cwt.
Tartaric acid	ten ounces and a half.

Mix, and after a day or two add

Bicarbonate of soda...	twelve ounces.
Lump sugar	half a pound.
Salt	one pound and a half.

Thoroughly mix and pass through a dressing-machine or sieve. Less salt will do.

"Twamley, February 7th, 1862.

"Dear Mr. Abbott,—I think you may like to have my evidence, as that of a practical bush housewife, in favour of the new bread recipe, which you published in the *Advertiser* of January 13th, and I am happy to give my testimony as to its great value in a country household.

"During the past fortnight I have used it frequently, and the bread I have made (for I did not leave the test of the new plan to servants) is so much preferred by us all to any fermented by the old method, that the 'yeast keg' will soon become an obsolete institution in our house.

"I find that the 'patent corn flour' mixed accurately by the recipe (except that I omit half the salt), makes lighter, whiter, and sweeter bread than flour worked with yeast; and if mixed lightly with skim-milk instead of water, it is particularly delicate and nice, especially in twists, rolls, or small loaves.

"Most country housekeepers, however notable, have at some unlucky time or other experienced the annoyance of finding that the yeast, or, as servants often call it, 'the rising,' would *not* rise; and then how miserably the batch of hard, dark, lead-like dough sat, a horrid incubus, on the stomachs and tempers of the family and dependants! Such an event may be wiped from the catalogue of household grievances by this excellent invention. The quickness of the process is a great advantage, as when the oven is hot it is time enough to begin the bread, which is mixed and made up in five minutes, if the flour be kept ready, and is so good that few stale fragments or old crusts will find their way to the pig-trough, that omnivorous receptacle of unsavoury viands. Long experience has confirmed my old conviction, that the truest economy is to have eatables so good of their kind, that the consumers shall have no inclination to waste them. The worst food is always the most expensive; and so 'Jones's patent flour,' or, as it is known with us, the 'Abbott's bread' (which is a name savouring of well-furnished refectories and goodliest fare), is a right thrifty as well as a dainty device.

"The thanks of every housewife in the island who has—and where is she who has not?—suffered the pains and penalties of a 'bad baking' are due to you for giving publicity to the recipe for the 'patent flour.' It will prove a '*Housekeepers' heavy bread, indigestion, and grumblings relief bill,*' and pass into the code of domestic enactments by a large majority of votes, among which pray record mine, and believe me very truly yours,

"Ed. Abbott, Esq." (Signed) "L. A. MEREDITH.

EXPENSE.—The only objection to using this flour in the Colonies is the high price of soda and acid. In England bicarbonate of soda is about twopence per pound, and tartaric acid, one shilling and sixpence. In the Colonies the retail price is two and five shillings respectively by chemists, and eightpence and three shillings and sixpence by grocers. Now, to make bread of one hundred weight of flour at the grocers' price would come to four shillings and twopence, and if yeast or barm were used, the cost would be about one shilling for a quart of yeast, four pounds and a half of salt, and fourteen pounds of potatoes. But with cakes, pies, and puddings, even with the high price of soda and acid, the use of Jones's patent flour is by far the cheapest in reality, and has the advantage of easy digestion.

XXXIX.—MILK.

Health, beauty, strength, and spirits, and I might add all the faculties of the mind, depend on the organs of the body; when they are in good order, the thinking part is most alert and active, the contrary when they are disturbed or diseased.—*Dr. Cadogan on Nursing Children.*

Milk has been so often analysed that it would seem no further facts could be elicited regarding this important liquid. Professor Boedecker, however, has just completed a series of experiments conducted on quite a new principle. The question he proposed to himself was whether milk obtained at any hour of the day always presented the same chemical composition or not; and he has arrived at the result that the milk of the evening is richer by 3 per cent. than that of the morning, the latter containing only 10 per cent. of solid matter, and the former 13 per cent. On the other hand, the water contained in milk diminishes by 3 per cent. in the course of the day; in the morning it contains 89 per cent. of water, and only 86 per cent. in the evening. The fatty particles increase gradually as the day wears on. In the morning they amount to 2·17 per cent.; at noon, to 2.63; and in the evening, to 3·42 per cent. This circumstance, if true, would be very important in a practical point of view. Let us suppose a kilogramme of milk to yield only the sixth part of its weight of butter; then the milk of the evening may yield double that quantity. The caseous particles are also more abundant in the evening than in the morning; from 2·24 they increase to 2·70 per cent., but the quantity of albumen diminishes from 0·44 to 0·31. The serum is less abundant at midnight than at noon, being 4·19 per cent. in the former case, and 4·72 in the last.—*Galignani.*

"To THE EDITOR OF THE 'TIMES.'

"Sir,—I trust that a sense of justice will ensure the insertion of the following brief remarks.

"Under the heading 'Milk,' your impression of yesterday contains some observations on the analysis of that article, and among them the following passage occurs:—

"'Milk has been so often analysed that it would seem no further facts could be elicited regarding this important fluid. Professor Boedecker, however, has just completed a series of experiments, conducted on quite a new principle. The question he proposed to himself was, whether milk obtained at any hour of the day always presented the same chemical composition or not, and he arrived at the result that the milk of the evening is richer by 3 per cent. than that of the morning, the latter containing only 10 per cent. of solid matter, and the former 13 per cent.,' &c.

"These observations are not new; they have been long since anticipated; so that whatever merit or importance is attached to them, does not belong to Dr. Boedecker.

"In my report on the adulteration of milk, published in the *Lancet* in 1851—that is, eleven years since—I gave the results of the analysis of a number of samples of morning and afternoon milk, obtained from different cows, and from these it appeared that while ten samples of morning milk furnished collectively 77½ per-centages of cream, the average of the whole being 7¾, the same number of samples of afternoon milk, taken from the same cows, gave 96½ per-centages, the average being 9½. The curd in the first series of samples amounted to 693, and in the second to 810 grains.

"Thus I have found the difference to be even greater than that stated by Dr. Boedecker.

"But, further, at the period referred to, I made the somewhat singular observation that the composition of milk varies still more at different periods of even the same milking, the milk last drawn from the udder being always much richer than that first abstracted. Thus while eight samples of the afternoon milk first drawn furnished 61½ per-centages of cream, that last removed amounted to no less than 141½ per-centages.

"These facts are pregnant with practical importance. Upon this part of the subject I must not enlarge, but will merely refer to the common practice which prevails for invalids to procure their glass of milk from the cow. The milk thus obtained must, as we have seen, be of the most uncertain composition, according as it is first or last milk drawn. If the former, it will be exceedingly poor in cream, &c.; and if the latter, exceedingly rich. "ARTHUR HILL HASSALL, M.D.

"Wimpole Street, Dec. 27, 1862."

COAGULATED MILK.—An excellent and wholesome dish as an *entremets*, or for children, is made from new milk coagulated with patent rennet, and ate with a little wine, sugar, and nutmeg. For youth and young children, there is no food so nutritious and wholesome as bread and milk; chemists aver they are both perfect as food in themselves. According to the analysis of Berzelius, he found in milk—water, 928·75; cream and curd, 28; sugar of milk, 35; chloride of potassium, 1·70; phosphate of potassa, 6; lactic acid, lactate of iron, and acetate of potassa, 6; earthy phosphates, 0·30; total, 1,000.

XL.—CHUTNEY.

Indian Chutney.—
> The qualms or ruptures of your blood
> Rise in proportion to your food;
> And if you would improve your thought,
> You must be fed as well as taught.
> Your stomach makes your fabric roll,
> Just as the bias rules the bowl.—*Prior.*

Take two pounds of green tamarinds, and stone them; two pounds of unripe mangoes, two pounds of salt, two pounds of ginger roots, one pound of onions, one pound of garlic, and one pound and a half of raisins, stoned; well pound them, and add to six parts of good vinegar. Jar them for use.

English Chutney.—A very near imitation of the Indian may be made from two pounds of apples, peeled, cored, and pounded; a quarter of a pound of green mint chopped fine, the juice of two lemons, half a pound of bird's-eye chillies, half a pound of salt, a quarter of a pound of onions, and the same of garlic, with a small quantity of vinegar. If you cannot procure the green chillies, use cayenne.

PARLIAMENTARY DINNER AND DEBATES.—He must say that, as far as he could recollect, the debates in that House were conducted with more order and with much fuller attendance between seven and half-past nine o'clock, when simple mutton chops were served for their dinner, than at present, when something like a French dinner was attempted.—*Mr. Osborne, in the House of Commons, on the Dining-room Debate.*

XLI.—TOAST.

Buttered Toast.—
> Rather than fail, they will decry
> That which they love most tenderly;
> Quarrel with minc'd pies, and disparage
> Their best and dearest friend, plum porridge:
> Fat pig and goose itself oppose,
> And blaspheme custard thro' the nose.—*Hudibras.*

How is it that buttered toast is so much better done at public inns than at private houses? The bread should not be cut thicker than about a quarter of an inch, and toasted with attention, not omitting the browning of the crust. When toasted it must not be left, but buttered on both sides at once, and kept warm. Some persons have the crust cut off, while other admirers of buttered toast like the crust to remain on.

Dry Toast.—Dry toast must be made from bread a day old. Have it evenly browned, and, when done, stand by itself or put in the toast-rack. The admirer of dry toast generally likes it as crisp as possible.

NEW BREAD.—New bread is an article of food most difficult of digestion. Everything which, by mastication, forms a tenacious paste is indigestible, being slowly pervaded by the gastric juice. Even bread sufficiently old, which it never is until it is quite dry, is frequently oppressive if taken alone and in considerable quantity. The sailors' biscuit, or bread toasted, often agrees better with a weak stomach than bread in other states.—*Dr. Philip.*

XLII.—A DINNER FROM THE "ORIGINAL."

It is a mistaken notion that good cookery is expensive; on the contrary, it is the cheapest. By good cookery we make the most of everything; by bad cookery, the least.—*Ude.*

The party will consist of seven besides myself, and every guest is asked for some reason, upon which good fellowship mainly depends; for people brought together unconnectedly had, in my opinion, better be kept separate. Eight should be the golden number, never to be exceeded without weakening the efficacy of concentration. The dinner is to consist of turtle, followed by no other meat but grouse, which are to be succeeded by apple fritters and jelly, pastry on such occasions being quite out of place. With the turtle, of course, there will be punch; with the whitebait, champagne; with the grouse, claret; the two former I have ordered to be particularly well iced, and they will all be placed in succession on the table, so that we can help ourselves as we please. I shall permit no other wines, unless perchance a bottle or two of port, if particularly wanted, as I hold a variety of wines a great mistake. With respect to the adjuncts, I shall take care there is cayenne —with lemons cut in halves, not quarters—within reach of every one, for the turtle; and that brown bread and butter in abundance is set at the table for the whitebait. It is no trouble to think of these little matters beforehand, but they make a vast difference in a convivial entertainment. The dinner will be followed by ices, and a good dessert; after which coffee and one glass of liquor each, and no more, so that the present may be enjoyed rationally, without inducing retrospective regrets. If the master of a feast wishes his party to succeed, he must know how to command, and not let his guests run riot according each to his own wild fancy. Such, reader, is my idea of a dinner, which I hope you approve; and I cannot help thinking if Parliament were to grant me £10,000 a year in trust, to entertain a series of worthy persons, it would promote trade and increase the revenue more than any hugger-mugger measure ever devised.—*Extract from the "Original," by Thomas Walker, M.A., Cambridge, a police magistrate of London.*

INDIGESTION.—People very commonly complain of indigestion; how can it be wondered at when they seem, by their habit of swallowing or bolting their food wholesale, to forget for what purpose they are provided with teeth? In America this abominable practice obtains to a greater degree than in any other country, so travellers inform us.

XLIII.—THE HUNDRED GUINEA DISH.

Two things which are very necessary to a perfect dinner are noiseless attendants, and a precision in serving the various dishes in each course, so that they may be all placed on the table at the same moment. A deficiency in these respects produces that bustle and delay which distract many an agreeable conversation, and spoil many a pleasant dish.—*Tancred; or, the New Crusade.*

This dish was devised by Soyer for the Exhibition banquet, given by the Lord Mayor of York, in 1850, to Prince Albert, whom Tennyson so poetically calls, "Silent father of our kings to be." In a work on Cookery such a dish should find a place as a curiosity. The lamented Prince is no more:

"We have lost him—he is gone;
We know him now: all narrow jealousies
Are silent, and we see him as he moved—
How modest, kindly, all-accomplished, wise!"—

taken from us in early life, realising the classic saying from Herodotus, that "those whom the gods love die young;" but nowhere is his memory held in greater respect than in the Colonies; for he was a man whom they may, without any adulatory compliment, say, "We ne'er shall look upon his like again."[*] As the husband of our Queen, having no political position, he gave his time to the honourable pursuits of agriculture and the encouragement of the arts, evincing Attic taste of no ordinary calibre, and showing a marked contrast to many of the same rank and station, who have wasted their lives and destroyed their health in ignoble pursuits. Moreover, Prince Albert's character in the common relations of our being, as partner and parent, has afforded a praiseworthy example for imitation to the nobility, the gentry, and the commonalty of England, as well as their respective equals in the Colonies. The honoured and respected guest as well as the great *cuisinier* have gone to "that bourne from whence no traveller returns;" or, to use still more simple and affecting language, to where "the weary are at rest." But the list of articles that formed the celebrated dish and their cost remain—"*Sic transit gloria mundi.*" The death of a relation or of an esteemed person in a high position must always carry "the wise who think" to the beautiful lines of Gray, that the immortal Wolfe said, previously to the fight that decided the fate of Canada, he would rather have written, than conquer the French, which he did next day, and died in the arms of Victory:—

"The boast of heraldry, the pomp of power,
And all that beauty, all that wealth e'er gave,
Await alike th' inevitable hour—
The paths of glory lead but to the grave!"

---

[*] This was written long before the account reached the Colony of the same words being used on the Prince Consort's Memorial at South Kensington, as many colonists can testify who perused this work in MS.

THE HUNDRED GUINEA DISH.

		£	s.	d.
5 Turtle heads, part of fins, and green fat		34	0	0
24 Capons (the two small *noix* from middle of back only used)		8	8	0
18 Turkeys—the same		8	12	0
18 Poulards—the same		5	17	0
16 Fowls—the same		2	8	0
10 Grouse		2	5	0
20 Pheasants—*noix* only		3	0	0
45 Partridges—the same		3	7	0
6 Plovers		0	9	0
40 Woodcocks—*noix* only		8	0	0
3 Dozen quails, whole		3	0	0
100 Snipes—*noix* only		5	0	0
3 Dozen pigeons—*noix* only		0	14	0
6 Dozen larks, stuffed		0	15	0
Ortolans, from Belgium		5	0	0
The garnish, consisting of cocks' combs, truffles, mushrooms, crayfish, olives, American asparagus, *croustades*, sweetbreads, *quenelles de volaille*, green mangoes, and a new sauce		14	10	0
		£105	**5**	**0**

If an epicure were to order such a dish only, he would be charged for the whole of the above-mentioned articles.

We append to these remarks on the late Prince Albert an extract from an English newspaper, showing that even the Royal family of England are most properly brought up to domestic pursuits; indeed, the sketch thus drawn by the British periodical is worthy of the attentive perusal and example of every circle, high or low, in England and Australasia:—

EMPLOYMENT OF THE QUEEN'S FAMILY.—At the seaside residence of Queen Victoria, in the Isle of Wight, a large portion of the pleasure ground is appropriated to the young princes and princesses, who have each a flower and a vegetable garden, greenhouse, hot-houses, and forcing-frames, nurseries, tool-houses, and even a carpenter's shop. Here the Royal children pass many hours of their time. Each is supplied with a set of tools marked with the name of the owner, and here they work with the enthusiasm of an amateur and the zeal of an Anglo-Saxon. There is no branch of gardening in which the Royal children are not at home. Moreover, on this juvenile property is a building, the ground-floor of which is fitted up as a kitchen, with pantries, closets, larders, and dairy, all complete in their arrangements; and here may be seen the young princesses, arrayed in their aprons and cooking jackets, floured to the elbows, deep in the mysteries of pastry making, like rosy farm-girls; cooking the vegetables from their own gardens, preserving, pickling, baking, sometimes to partake among themselves, or to distribute to the poor of the neighbourhood, as the result of their own handiwork. The Queen is determined that nothing shall remain unlearned by her children; nor are the young people ever happier than while thus engaged. Over the domestic establishment is a museum of natural history, furnished with curiosities collected by the young party in their rambles and researches—geological and botanical specimens, stuffed birds and animals, articles of their own construction, and whatever is curious or interesting, classified and arranged by themselves. Here the most exalted and purifying tastes are cultivated. Here Nature, common to all, is studied and admired; while beyond this, a capability of entering into the condition of the people, and a sympathy for their labours, is acquired by a practical knowledge of what labour is; and though we need scarcely suppose that the Royal children weary themselves as those who gain their bread by the sweat of their brow, yet even in their moderate digging and working they must learn the better to appreciate the results of labour in the luxuries surrounding them. This is a picture of which the English nation may justly be proud. There is not such another Royal family on the face of the earth.—*Christian Witness.*

THE QUEEN.—A foreign courier, who attended the Queen and the late Prince Consort, has been dispatched to Coburg to make preparations for the reception of her Majesty, who proposes, during the summer, to visit a spot hallowed to her, being the birthplace of her beloved husband. There is something particularly touching in every action of our revered Sovereign connected with the death of the Prince. Her visits to the mausoleum that contains his ashes; her attention to old and faithful servants; her works of mercy in cheering the dying hours of some valued attendant; her anxiety to carry out every scheme suggested or approved of by the Prince; her liberality in retaining all the officers of his household—speaks volumes in favour of her Majesty's sense of duty and kindness of heart. Among other traits of the Queen may be mentioned that, in Kensington Palace, where her early years were passed, there exists an apartment in which a doll's baby-house, kitchen, drawing-room, and bed-room are fitted up with furniture peculiar to such juvenile buildings, but, unlike most baby-houses, large enough to admit a child of eight or ten years of age. Occasionally the Queen visits this apartment, recalling, probably, happy hours of childhood.—*Court Journal.*

A ROYAL ENTERTAINMENT.—The Report of the Royal Reception Committee of the City of London, appointed to carry out the entertainment given by the Corporation to the Prince and Princess of Wales in June, 1863, has published a synopsis of the expense. The entire cost was £15,054. Artificers' charges, £3,591; toilet articles, perfumery, &c., £208; supper, &c., £1,680; decorations after sale, £3,591; wines, &c., £584; care of plate, £60; china and glass, £205; music, £117; printing, £431; lighting and illuminations, £207; miscellaneous, £1,163; gratuities to officers, £508. The expenditure incurred in 1837, when the Queen honoured the Corporation with her presence at Guildhall, was £8,157.—*Home News.*

ART EDUCATION OF CHILDREN.—Let us here mention, that we have found the children of the Sovereign of Great Britain at nine in the morning at the Museum of Practical Art; and on another occasion, at the same hour, amidst the Elgin marbles—not the only wise hint to the mothers of England to be found in the highest place. Accustom your children to find beauty in goodness, and goodness in beauty.—*The Builder.*

XLIV.—SPORTSMAN'S DINNER; OR, ATHLETES' FOOD.

Time was when John Bull little difference spied
'Twixt the foe at his feet and the friend at his side:
When he found (such his humour in fighting and eating)
His foe, like his beefsteak, the sweeter for beating.—*Moore.*

This important meal—dinner—should consist of roast beef or mutton, or, occasionally, a boiled leg of mutton may be allowed as a change; but veal, pork, and salt beef, or bacon should be avoided, also goose, duck, and wild fowl generally. Roast fowls, or partridges, or pheasants are very good food. Hare is too apt to be accompanied by high-seasoned stuffing, without which it is scarcely palatable. Nothing is better than venison, when come-atable, but it should be eaten without seasoned sauce or currant jelly. As to vegetables, potatoes may be eaten, but very sparingly—not more than one or two at a meal; cauliflower and broccoli only as an occasional change, and no other vegetable is allowable. Bread may be given *ad libitum*, and about a pint to a pint and a half of good, sound, home-made beer. If this does not agree, a little sherry and water or claret and water may be allowed with the meal, and a glass or two of the former wine, or of good sound port, after dinner. When the training is continued for any length of time, and the previous habits of the party have accustomed the stomach to it, I have found the occasional use of white fish—such as cod or soles—a very useful change. Nothing disorders the stomach of man more than keeping to one diet; "*toujours perdrix*" is enough to tire any one even of so good a fare; and this is constantly to be borne in mind by the trainer. The round he can make is not very extensive, but let him by all means stretch it to the utmost limits of which it is capable. It is even desirable to give an occasional pudding, but it should always have bread for its foundation. A good cook will always make a very palatable pudding of bread, with a little milk and an egg or two, and this served up with fresh green gooseberries boiled, or any common preserve, is by no means disagreeable to the palate or unwholesome to the stomach; but let it be only as a change, not as otherwise useful. The grand articles of diet are beef and mutton, with bread or porridge, and, if the stomach and palate would accept them gratefully, no change would be necessary, but as they seldom will, the best plan is not to attempt too much.—"*British Rural Sports*," by *Stonehenge*.

ARROWROOT.—Arrowroot forms an agreeable, non-irritable article of diet, for invalids and children, in the form of cakes, biscuits, or puddings; or boiled with milk or water, and flavoured with sugar, spices, lemon-juice, or wine, at pleasure. For young children, a little carraway or cinnamon-water is to be preferred. It is especially useful in irritation or debility of the stomach, bowels, or urinary organs, and in all cases in which a demulcent or emollient is indicated. It must not, however, be employed to the entire exclusion of other food, as, being destitute of the nitrogenous elements of nutrition, it is incapable alone of supporting life. Arrowroot jelly is prepared by first rubbing the powder up with a very small quantity of cold water, and then gradually adding the remainder boiling, stirring well all the time. Beef tea, veal broth, or milk may be used instead of water. Some persons boil it for a few minutes. This jelly is flavoured with a little genuine port wine and nutmeg, and is almost a specific in cases of simple diarrhœa arising from habit or debility.—*Cooley*.

XLV.—DINNER PARTY PRECEDENCE.

Good suitor, let us dine, and never fret.—Luciana, in the "Comedy of Errors."

There is really no precedence for commoners. A colonel in the army, a captain R.N., and a deputy lieutenant (not a J. P.), all rank the same, according to the dates of their commissions; and custom in dinner parties gives them precedence to clergymen, though not in the court returns of a *levée*. It is customary to give commoners rank according to their social position, say as regards wealth or acknowledged talents in their country. Esquire is only indefinite from every one assuming to themselves the title. Barristers, colonels, majors, captains, M.A.'s, magistrates, and deputy-lieutenants are esquires by right of title. Attorneys, yeomen, &c., are simply gentlemen, and liable to serve on sessions, grand juries, special juries of assizes, and the offices of constable and overseer. I apprehend " Country House" will find few heart-burnings amongst his male guests. The "dear ladies" feel it most, and then let them hark back to the covers of Sir B. Burke. A baronet's daughter or grand-daughter takes precedence of a commoner's daughter or grand-daughter. Officers on half-pay always retain their rank; and military field officers, by a new regulation, do so, although they have sold out of the army.—*Eboracum.*

The term "esquire" is not (as "Country House" supposes) indefinite and undefined. Men are esquires by birth, office, or creation. An esquire by birth is one, or the son of one, entitled to bear arms; so Admiral Rous is H. J. Rous, Esq., commonly called the Honourable H. J. Rous. A justice of the peace is an esquire by office, and a barrister an esquire by creation. In H. Blackstone's Reports there is a case where the court refused to hear an affidavit in which a barrister was not entitled esquire. With reference to his dinner party, colonels, post-captains, serjeants, and doctors of the three learned professions, hold equal rank according to the date of their commissions, patents, or degrees. Clergymen rank with esquires. Therefore the colonel and post-captain would go first according to the date of their commissions; then would come the clergyman, the J. P., and the barrister, as each was ordained, created, or called to the bar; Crœsus, if a merchant engaged in business, would not necessarily be an esquire; *e.g.*, the late Jemmy Wood, of Gloucester, was only Mr. Wood, or, on an affidavit, James Wood, Gent. It is the use of the term only that is indefinite and undefined.— *J. W. Slade in the "Field," country gentleman's newspaper.*

THE BRAISE.—Meat should be half-cooked (braised) before it is put into paste; as should also forcemeat used in savoury meat pies.

XLVI.—SUPPERS AND LUNCHEONS.

Would that the cook were of my mind.
Don John in "*Much Ado about Nothing.*"

We say little respecting the above, because we consider them unnecessary and unwholesome. A person who partakes of a luncheon cannot possibly enjoy his dinner; and any one eating supper must loathe his breakfast, which ought to be the principal meal of the day. The utmost limit that we can advise in either case is a glass of sherry and a biscuit. "Nimrod" writes, that a hot luncheon is a most destructive meal; and half the young men who lose their health or their lives in the East Indies, are destroyed by the excitement of hot luncheons, followed by still hotter dinners. Hook describes a stand-up supper, in "Gilbert Gurney," as "tables against the wall, covered with cold negus and warm ice, where men, women, and children take perpendicular refreshment, like so many horses with their noses to the manger."

SUPPERS: the evening meal, the last meal of the day. Supper is generally an unnecessary meal, and when either heavy or taken at a period not long before that of retiring to rest, proves nearly always injurious, preventing sound and refreshing sleep, and occasioning unpleasant dreams, nightmare, biliousness, and all the worst symptoms of imperfect digestion. Cases of sudden death during sleep, arising from the stomach being overloaded with undigested food, are far from rare. The last meal of the day should be taken at least three hours before bed-time. Even when it consists of some "trifle," as a sandwich or biscuit, an interval of at least an hour should elapse before retiring to rest. In this way restlessness and unpleasant dreams will become rare.—*Cooley.*

You must not *indulge* in "filthy beer," nor in porter, nor eat *suppers*—the last are the devil to those who swallow dinner.—*Byron to Moore,* 1817.

TASTES DIFFER.—Suppers were the *ne plus ultra* of human invention; it could go no further, and was obliged to degenerate. Dinner is too much a matter of business, it is a necessity; now, a necessity is too like a duty ever to be pleasant; besides, it divides the day instead of winding it up. I do not think, moreover, that people were ever meant to enjoy themselves in the daytime.—*Miss Landon.*

EDIBLE SNAILS.—In a former letter I mentioned the reputation the snail enjoyed in Ireland as a remedy for arresting the progress of consumption. As the snail just now is attracting a large share of the attention of your readers, it may be interesting to them to know how they are prepared when used as a cure. I have had the receipt from a lady, the daughter of a clergyman in the west of Ireland, who has prescribed the remedy with great success. She writes:—"The snails used for the broth, as you call my fine syrup, are the common large brown things that creep about the gardens carrying their houses along with them. They are collected and placed on a large dish and plentifully sprinkled with dark sugar; then another dish is turned over them to prevent them running away; and next morning the syrup which has been made during the night is to be drained off and bottled, and a table-spoonful is to be taken three times a day. A little lemon-peel may be added to flavour the broth. The same snails should not be sugared twice. It is really a good thing, but, of course, will not cure in a day." I have spoken to a lady who attributes her own recovery from consumption to the use of this receipt—cod-liver oil having failed to strengthen her; and a lady from the county of Tipperary tells me she knows snails boiled in veal broth to have effected a perfect cure in a consumptive patient. The subject is, I think, well worthy of attention and inquiry.—*Correspondent in the "Field."*

XLVII.—HOME-MADE WINES AND CORDIALS.

Lord Palmerston (who as Minister has been accustomed to employ his pleasantries as *passatonnerres* for troublesome visitors) one day related the following anecdote to a deputation of gentlemen, who waited on him to urge the reduction of the wine duties. Referring to the question of adulterations, "I remember," said his lordship, "my grandfather, Lord Pembroke, when he placed wine before his guests, said, 'There, gentlemen, is my champagne, my claret, &c. I am no great judge, and I give you this on the authority of my wine merchant; but I can answer for my port, for I made it myself.'"—*Hints for the Table.*

Now if Lord Palmerston had honoured us with his grandfather's mode for the manufacture of port, we should have been much obliged to him, for there is little doubt but that many home-made wines are infinitely superior to the foreign "made up" for the English market, and from thence exported to the Australias; but as we have not been so fortunate as to obtain Lord Pembroke's recipe, we are obliged to have recourse to a few of our own.

Raisin Wine, with Frontignac Flavour.—Boil twelve pounds of Malaga raisins in twelve gallons of water till they are quite absorbed, then take them out, extract the stones, and return the pulp to the water. Pour on twenty-four pounds of loaf sugar, and ferment it with half a pint of yeast. When the fermentation begins to subside, tie up in a muslin bag half a peck of elder-flowers, and suspend the bag for some days in the liquor; then remove it, and when clear draw off and bottle.

Grape Wine.—Take any given quantity of ripe grapes, macerate and strain them, add two gallons of water to one gallon of juice, and three pounds and a half of loaf sugar. Let it ferment for six weeks. Clear it with white of eggs or isinglass, and barrel it. Some brandy must be added; a little crude tartar is an improvement.

Elder Wine.—Pick and shred twenty-four pounds of raisins, and cover them with three gallons of boiling water, stir the liquor every day, and add three pints of elderberry juice and one pound of sugar. Let it ferment its usual time, then close the cask, and bottle. Elderberry wine may be made from the berries alone, with a proportionate quantity of sugar and brandy.

Elderberry Wine (*Another Mode*).—To six gallons of berries add seven of water, and a quarter of a pound of allspice, two ounces of ginger, and a few cloves. Boil for half an hour, squeeze the berries through a sieve, adding to every gallon three pounds and a half of sugar. This quantity will about fill a nine-gallon cask. The sugar being added, boil until the liquor becomes pretty clear, taking off the scum. Put it into the cask, and remove it to a cool place; when it becomes lukewarm, ferment it by toasted bread being dipped in thick yeast. When the fermentation has subsided, bung up the cask; it will be fit to drink in three months, and will keep for years.

Cherry Wine.—Pound morella cherries in a mortar, and let them be be in a cool place for twenty-four hours. Press the pulp through a fine tin strainer, and to every quart of juice add a pound of loaf sugar. Allow it to ferment the proper time, and add a little brandy.

Raspberry Wine.—To every quart of raspberries put the same quantity of water, bruise, and let them stand two days; strain off the liquor, and to every gallon put three pounds of loaf sugar. Put the liquor in a cask, and, when ready to bottle, add a table-spoonful of good brandy to each bottle.

Raspberry and Currant Wine.—Bruise three pints of fruit, and add one quart of water; let it stand, and after twenty-four hours strain the liquor, and put to every quart a pound of the best sugar. It will work of its own accord. Put a bottle of brandy to every five gallons; keep it for a time and bottle it.

Pink Champagne.—Dissolve nine pounds of loaf sugar over the fire in three gallons of water, remove the scum. Have ready picked a gallon of red and white currants, and pour over them the boiling liquor. Let it stand until cool, then add a tea-cupful of yeast; allow it to ferment for two days, then put it in a cask, and add some isinglass or white of egg to clear. Bung up the cask, but don't do this too soon, or there will be an explosion. When ready for bottling add a small lump of sugar to each bottle.

THE EARL OF DERBY AND THE WINE MERCHANT.—A forward and pushing wine merchant, on a late occasion, sent a sample of his wine to the Earl of Derby, stating at the same time that it was a cure for the gout, and after a short time wrote to his lordship soliciting an order. The earl laconically replied "that he had tasted the wine, but preferred the gout!"—*Newspaper paragraph.*

White Champagne.—Pour three quarts of water to one gallon of fruit, and let the mixture stand a week, after the gooseberries have been well macerated; then strain through a sieve, and add to every gallon of liquor four pounds of loaf sugar, or the best crystallised sugar. Let the fermentation go on for several days, then pass the liquor through a jelly-bag into the cask, leaving it open until the fermentation has nearly subsided, but not quite. When the fermentation is in the latter state, bung the cask up, having previously inserted a small quantity of brandy. Let it remain twelve months, and then bottle, and you will have excellent wine. The great difficulty is to know when to bung up, for if you do it too soon, the cask will explode—and crashing work such an event is; if too late, the wine will not be brisk. Mind, the fruit must be unripe, just on the turn.

It has been stated that Lord Haddington, a first-rate judge of wines, had a bottle of gooseberry and a bottle of Epernay champagne once placed before him, and that his lordship mistook the home-made for the *genuine* article, as Jonathan has it.

Ginger Wine.—Boil half a pound of bruised ginger and fourteen pounds of loaf sugar in six gallons of water; pour the liquor on the rind of a dozen lemons. Let it stand until cool, and then add the lemon-juice and half a cup of yeast. Let the fermentation proceed; and before you bottle the wine, add a pint of brandy. An old lady's specific for many ailments.

Lemon and Orange Wine.—Boil ten pounds of loaf sugar in four gallons of water for half an hour, and pour the liquor on the rind of eighteen oranges and lemons; squeeze the fruit, and boil it in a syrup with two pounds of white sugar; mix the syrup with the liquor, and let it cool. Ferment with a little yeast. When the fermentation subsides, bung it down, and bottle in three or four months.

We could elaborate these wine recipes with rhubarb-leaf, carrot, turnip, parsnip, birch, cowslip, mead, apple, plum, and every kind of fruit and vegetable; but we abstain from so doing, leaving the choice to the "gude huswii."

CORDIALS.

Cherry Bounce.—To six pounds of morella cherries add three pounds of loaf sugar and two ounces of powdered bitter almonds; pour over them two quarts of the best brandy. Let it remain steeped, and afterwards bottle according to taste. Some prefer the cherries entire remaining in the brandy; others strain away both fruit and kernels.

Noyeau.—Blanch and pound two pounds of bitter almonds, and put to them a gallon of brandy, with two pounds of white sugar and a little spice. Stir it, and let the spirit remain in the almonds for a month, when the noyeau may be bottled for use.

Ratafia.—Blanch two ounces of peach, apricot, or other kernels, and put them in a bottle. Dissolve half a pound of white sugar-candy in a cup of cold water, and add to the brandy after it has stood a month on the kernels. Strain, and bottle for use.

Rum Shrub.—Put the juice of oranges, three pints, and a pound of white sugar to a gallon of rum. Let it remain in a cask for a few weeks, and it will be fit for use.

Brandy and currant shrub may be made as above, as well as raspberry, peach, apricot, and other fruit brandies, and gooseberry, lemon, blackberry, currant, and ratafias, made from other fruit, for they are nothing more than the flavour of the fruits added to sugar syrups.

Tasmanette.—In making jam—mulberry, Aldridge plum, morella, and quince—after the sugar has been added, skim off and strain the surplus syrup. Keep in a dry place till all are ready; then add a tablespoon of vinegar to every pint.

The above recipe was kindly furnished the author by Mr. Allport, of Aldridge Lodge, Tasmania, and the liqueur obtained a medal at the last International Exhibition in the mother country.

Cyprus Wine (*Imitation*).—To ten quarts of syrup of elderberry add eighty pints of water, two ounces of ginger, and two ounces of cloves, and boil together; add a few bruised grapes and strain.—*Bibliothèque Physio-Economique.*

Grape Wine (*Colonial*).—To a gallon of water add a gallon of grapes (bruised), and let them stand a week without stirring. Draw it off fine, and to every gallon of wine add three pounds of loaf sugar. Then put it in a cask; do not bung it until the fermentation has ceased. Add a bottle of brandy to every ten gallons of wine; it will keep for two or three years. Bottle it on a clear day in July or August (Australian time). Try it previously; and if not fine, dissolve an ounce of isinglass and put in the cask, and let it remain for two or three weeks. You need not clear the fruit from the stems unless you choose; and if you desire the wine effervescent, the fruit should not be quite ripe. Fine moist sugar answers the purpose of white, but it heightens the colour, though rather less is required. If fruit is plentiful, use but little water; and of course fruit to make up the quantity of the liquid.

The above recipe has been obligingly furnished by a barrister, a member of the Tasmanian bar, whose wine (home manufactured) has local repute and prestige for its flavour and goodness.

Common Grape Wine.—Take any quantity of sound, ripe grapes; with a common cider press, press out the juice, put it into barrels, cover the bung lightly; after fermentation has ceased, cork it; place it in a cellar or house. In twelve months you will have a good wine, which improves by age. Let it stand on its lees.—*Scientific American.*

NOTE.—The journal from which the above recipe was taken states that when the vine disease appeared, the common eatable mushroom entirely disappeared. In the districts of Maçon, Lyons, and the banks of the Rhone, which were great sufferers from the disease, this vegetable has again appeared.

RECOMMENDATIONS.—
1. Grind your own wheat; make your own yeast and bread, or use Jones's patent flour

2. Make your own port, especially if you can procure Lord Pembroke's recipe, or purchase from a respectable firm.
3. Avoid green pickles; *i.e.*, pickles artificially coloured.
4. Avoid bright-coloured peppers, spices, sauces, anchovies, and herrings.
5. Purchase spirits and beer of large dealers and brewers.
6. Avoid coloured confections, especially those green, blue, or red.
7. Weigh and measure your purchases when brought home. You will be then sure of full weight if the articles are good, and be more able to detect the bad.

XLVIII.—TABLE-CLOTHS AND NAPKINS.

The comfort of napkins at dinner is too obvious to require comment, while the expense can hardly be urged as an objection. If there be not any napkins, a man has no alternative but to use the table-cloth, unless (as many do) he prefer his pocket-handkerchief—a usage sufficiently disagreeable.—*Hints on Etiquette.*

The napkins used at dinner, breakfast, and at all meals, are not only essentially necessary, seeing beards are so fashionable,* but they add materially to the appearance of the table. Napkins are usually of linen damask, 28 in. by 30 in. The fold is a matter of taste. The French mode is to place them in the shape of a fan, while the English custom is to form them as a shoe, placing the bread inside, the most desirable way. "The Practical Housewife" describes the manner of folding the *Mitre*, the *Exquisite*, the *Collegian*, the *Cinderella*, the *Flirt*, the *Neapolitan*, and the *Favourite*, with descriptive wood-cuts of these different forms. Table-cloths are formed of the same materials as napkins, and many families use slips, which are removed with the dinner. Good light, moderate temperature, snow-white linen, clean plate, and beautiful glass are necessary appendages to the dinner table. Fish and potatoes served up in napkins, will be always *comme il faut*, as well as patties, *vols-au-vent*, and savoury pies. With hot dishes of these kinds, the napkins must be warmed in cold weather.

SUBSTITUTE FOR CREAM IN TEA OR COFFEE.—Beat the white of an egg to a froth, put to it a small piece of butter, and mix well. Then turn the tea or coffee to it gradually, so that it may not curdle. If carefully done, this is an excellent substitute for cream, and it softens the tea or coffee nearly equal to milk.

---

* Apropos of *beards*, Beatrice, in "Much Ado about Nothing," says:—"He that hath a beard is more than a youth, and he that hath no beard is less than a man; and he that is more than a youth is not for me; and he that is less than a man, I am not for him." Who would not wear a beard?

Those who have the sense and courage to wear the natural comforter, which gives warmth without pressure—the beard—improve their chances for a sound throat, a clear head, and a long life.—*Harriet Martineau on Dress, in " Once a Week."*

XLIX.—TEA.

*Now stir the fire, and close the shutter fast,
Let fall the curtains, wheel the sofa round;
And while the bubbling and loud-hissing urn
Throws up a steamy column, and the cups
That cheer but not inebriate wait on each,
So let us welcome peaceful evening in.—Cowper.*

There are two varieties, viz., the *thea nigra* (black), and *thea viridis* (green). Brande writes, that tea, taken in moderation, especially as we use the infusion, with sugar and milk, is strengthening and invigorating; it also appears to possess certain stimulating and narcotic properties. The black kinds appear the most wholesome, and the finest kind we ever drank was scented Souchong. M'Culloch asserts that tea is a narcotic, as much so as even opium, but that it is the least pernicious of all narcotics. It is a favourite beverage with Englishmen both at home and abroad; but it must not be indulged in to excess, as it produces watchfulness, and is hurtful to the nerves. Green tea in the morning is slightly injurious, and must not be taken by hypochondriacal or hysterical persons. The way it is prepared for use is simply to pour boiling water on the leaves, and not allow it to stand too long. Never pour water on the leaves a second time; if you want more tea, use a second teapot. Newnham, on the "Medicinal and Dietetic Property of Tea," maintains, that in a state of *sthenic* excitement of the brain and nervous system—as that produced by alcoholic stimulants, or by intense and long-continued application of the mind to any particular object of literary research—tea will act as a remedy; whereas, on the contrary, in cases of diminished excitement, morbid vigilance and nervous disturbance will follow its potation. Swift tells us, to such an extent is modern epicurism carried, that the world must be encompassed before a washerwoman can sit down to breakfast; while Cobbett exclaims, "The drink which has come to supply the place of beer has, in general, been *tea*. It is notorious that tea has no useful strength in it; it contains nothing nutritious; it is known to produce want of sleep, and to weaken the nerves." According to a late letter from the *Times'* correspondent in India, we are soon to be supplied with tea largely from that part of the empire.

Black is the natural colour of the tea plant. The preparation of green tea is made in this wise:—It is brought to Canton and other towns unprepared, as Bohea (*sanshung*), and is thrown into a hemispherical iron pan, kept hot. The leaves are constantly stirred till they are thoroughly heated, when they are dyed, by adding to each pound of tea one spoonful of gypsum, one of turmeric, and two or three of Prussian blue. The leaves instantly change into a blueish green, and, after being well stirred for a few minutes, are taken out, being shrivelled by the heat. They are now sifted; the small, longish leaves fall through the first sieve, and form young hyson; the roundest, granular ones fall through last, and constitute gunpowder, or *choo-cha*.

TEA IN RUSSIA.—The Russians attribute the superiority of their tea to the fact that it is sent overland from China, and does not get spoiled by the sea air. I should be inclined to think that the real reason is that it comes from provinces in China near the Russian frontier, where there is a better growth of tea than in the provinces from which comes the article we use. I think, also, that they understand infusing the tea better than we do. They drink it as soon as the boiling water is poured on it, whilst we allow it to stand until it becomes as black as one's hat, and as bitter as hops. The gentlemen mostly drink their tea in tumblers, without milk, sometimes adding a slice of lemon; whilst the ladies take it in cups, with any amount of cream. We were afterwards, especially when travelling on the Moscow and Nijni railroads, surprised at the large and constant use of this beverage at all hours of the day and night; but we very soon became as large consumers of it as the native Russians themselves. Indeed, after a night in the railway carriage, we found a tumbler of tea in the early morning more exhilarating than the "blest sherbet," and more refreshing than even hock and soda-water. When at St. Petersburg, we bought a small quantity of a fine sample of caravan tea, for which we paid at the rate of thirty-eight shillings the pound (about ten dollars); but, of course, this was one of the fancy sorts, and not that which is in common use, which costs about six shillings and sixpence the pound. At the shop where we bought this tea, we were informed that they had some as high as seventy shillings the pound. As we were accompanied by a resident in the city who always dealt there, we knew that we were not being victimised.—*Bentley's Miscellany.*

Physiology of Tea-Drinking.—Tea is indeed a great fact in our present mode of life. It has been the making of an additional meal among us since the good old days, when people lived on three meals a day. Justice has scarcely been done to the magnitude of the change which has happened since the time when gentlemen—ay, and ladies too—took beer to their early breakfast; when they dined at eleven, supped between five and six, and went to bed at ten. Tea and coffee have been the principal cause of this revolution.—*The Lancet.*

Lovers of tea and coffee are, in fact, rarely drinkers; and hence the use of these beverages has benefited both manners and morals. Raynal observes that the use of tea has contributed more to the sobriety of the Chinese than the severest laws, the most eloquent discourses, or the best treatises on morality. Paris writes, "In enumerating the advantages of tea, it must not be forgotten that it has introduced and cherished a spirit of sobriety; and it must have been remarked by every physician of general practice, that those persons who dislike tea generally supply its place with alcoholic liquors." Ure states that the quality of tea depends much on the season when the leaves are picked, the mode in which it is prepared, as well as on the district in which it grows. Green tea, it is stated, is coloured by the application of an extract of indigo, of Prussian blue, and gypsum; and the fine odour which renders the "flowery" kinds remarkable is derived from the leaves of *olea fragrans*, a species of camellia, and other similar plants. The most remarkable products in tea are—1st, tannin; 2nd, an essential oil, to which it owes its aroma, and which has great influence on its commercial value; 3rd, a crystalline substance, very rich in nitrogen—*theine*—which is also met with in coffee (whence it is frequently termed *caffeine*), and which is found in Guarana, a remedy highly valued by the Brazilians. Besides these three, M. Mulder extracted from tea eleven other substances, which are usually met with in all leaves. The same chemist found, in the various kinds of tea from China and Java, a little less than half per cent. of their weight of theine. Dr. Stenhouse, in a recent investigation, obtained from 1·37 to 0·98 theine from 100 parts of tea. An accurate knowledge of the amount of the nitrogenous principles contained in tea being of the utmost importance, he first determined the total amount of nitrogen contained in the leaf, in order thus to have a safe guide when subsequently isolating the substances between which this nitrogen is distributed. On determining the nitrogen by M. Dumas' process, he obtained the following numbers:—

	Nitrogen in 100 parts Tea dried at 230°
Pekoe tea	6·58
Gunpowder tea	6·15
Souchong tea	6·15
Assam tea	5·10

This amount of nitrogen is far more considerable than has been detected in any vegetable hitherto analysed. These experiments prove, therefore, the existence of from 20 to 30 per cent. of nitrogenous substances in tea, while former analyses scarcely carry the proportion to more than three or four hundredths. The observations of Liebig afford a satisfactory explanation of the cause of the great partiality of the poor, not only for tea, but for tea of an expensive and superior sort. At a meeting of the Academy of Sciences, in Paris, lately held, M. Peligot read a paper on the chemical combinations of tea. He stated that tea contained essential principles of nutrition, far exceeding in importance its stimulating properties, and showed that tea is, in every respect, one of the most desirable articles in general use. One of his experiments on the nutritious qualities of tea, as compared with those of soup, was decidedly in favour of the former.

Black Tea.—Many years ago a spirited Chinese merchant, who, no doubt, saw well enough that black and green teas could be made easily from the same plant, had a crop of *black* teas made in the Ning-chow district, and brought to Canton for sale. This tea was highly approved of by the foreign merchants of that port, and was bought, I believe, by the house of Messrs. Dent and Co., and sent to England. When it got home, it found a ready sale in the market, and at once established itself a black tea of the first class. Year by year after this the demand for this tea steadily increased, and was readily supplied by the Chinese. At the present time the Ning-chow districts produce black tea only, while in former days they produced green. If proof were wanting, this would appear sufficient to show that black or green teas can be made from any variety of the tea plant, and that the change of colour in the manufactured article depends entirely on the mode of manipulation.—*Fortune's* "*Residence among the Chinese.*"

THE EMPEROR KIENHONG'S IMPERIAL EDICT FOR DRINKING TEA (*Translated by Sir John Barrow, in his* "*Travels in China*").—"On a slow fire set a tripod, whose colour and texture show its long use; fill it with clear snow water; boil it as long as would be necessary to turn fish white, and crayfish red; throw it upon the delicate leaves of choice tea, in a cup of yooé (a particular kind of porcelain); let it remain as long as the vapour rises to a cloud, and leaves only a thin mist floating on the surface. At your ease drink this precious liquor, which will chase away the causes of trouble. We can taste and feel, but not describe, the state of repose produced by a liquor thus prepared." Kienhong, after having reigned the term of sixty years, resigned his throne to his son. He died 1799.

TEA MAKING.—In making tea, always use the best and softest water, and on no account let it remain long after the goodness and flavour is extracted from the leaves. Tea was first introduced into England in 1650. An entry appears in the diary of Mr. Pepys, secretary to the Admiralty:—"September 26, 1661.—I sent for a cup of tea (a Chinese drink), of which I never drunk before!" and now, according to *Cassell's Family Paper*, the annual consumption of tea in the world is set down at one billion, five hundred and fifty-five million, one hundred thousand pounds; Great Britain consuming seventy-eight million pounds, and Australia and the Cape seven million pounds!

L.—DINNER CEREMONIAL.

Antipholus of Ephesus. You are sad, Signor Balthazar. Pray God our cheer
May answer my good will, and your good welcome here.
Balthazar. I hold your dainties cheap, sir, and your welcome dear.
Antipholus. O Signor Balthazar, either at flesh or fish,
A table full of welcome makes scarce one dainty dish.
Balthazar. Good meat, sir, is common: that every churl affords.
Antipholus. And welcome more common; for that's nothing but words.
Comedy of Errors.

We have extracted the following remarks from the *Quarterly Review* on the "Codes of Manners and Etiquette:" vol. v., 1837, which are of interest to the giver of dinners as well as the guests:—

"In Germany dinner parties are of rare occurrence, except in the capitals and among the higher classes, whose habits and manners are nearly the same all over Europe. But dinner parties are now quite common in France, and an infinity of rules regarding them are included in the French books on etiquette. We extract the following comprehensive paragraphs from a chapter of the 'Code,' entitled, 'Theorie du Diner en Ville':—

"'When all the guests assembled in the drawing-room have been presented to one another by the master of the house, and dinner is announced, he rises, invites the company to follow him into the dining-room, and gives the example by leading the way. You ought not to rise till after the Amphitryon, and each gentleman offers his hand to a lady, to conduct her to her cover, on which her name is inscribed. So soon as all are seated the host helps the soup, a heap of plates being placed for that purpose on his left; these he sends round, beginning with his left-hand neighbour. The servants take away the empty plates, upon which each leaves his spoon. We might here detail a number of trifling usages that one is bound to observe; but to know these it is only sufficient to have dined twice in good company. Politeness requires that the gentleman placed next a lady should save her every sort of trouble, keeping watch over her plate and glass. Placed in the centre of the table, the Amphitryon must not lose sight of any of his guests; it is he who carves, or causes to be carved by some expert friend, the more important dishes in their order; from his hand nothing is to be refused, and all ceremonies would be an awkward want of tact.

"'During the first course, every one drinks as he likes. During the second, the Amphitryon, in circulating the finer wines, requests you to take a glass. It would be uncivil to refuse; but you are not bound to take a second unless you like. So soon as the dessert appears, the rights and duties of the host lose much of their importance; all he has left to do is to give such a tone to the conversation as that all may take a part in it. It is still he, however, who gives the signal for leaving the table. All then rise together, and leave the eating-room for the drawing-room, where coffee is ready. This time the master of the house goes last. At the moment when the coffee is handed round, the drawing-room presents an aspect of joyous disorder: knots of talkers have got together—the physiognomies of all wear an air of satisfaction and self-complacency—each, armed with his cup, inhales the boiling mocha. Ere long the circle is formed, the conversation becomes general, the card-tables are set. Politeness requires you to remain an hour at least after a comfortable dinner. When you have your whole evening at your disposal, it is as well to devote it to your Amphitryon.'

"The injunction to gentlemen to take care of their fair neighbours is of universal applicability; but we would not recommend too close an attention to their glasses or their plates. A distinguished maximist says that whenever you ask a lady to take wine, you should fill her glass to the brim, in spite of her protestations, and look the other way till she has emptied it. Without going the full length of this philosopher's assumption, it stands to reason that, the number of glasses women allow themselves being limited, they should be full."

The reviewer proceeds to remark on the dinner-hour: "Germany, where the dinner-hour is generally one. In Italy it is five; in Paris, six; in London, half-past seven or eight. It is the custom to rail in good set terms against the prevalent fashion in this particular, but with little reason, for it is hardly possible to give oneself up to the full enjoyment of a convivial meeting until the business of the day has been despatched; and it should be remembered that when people dine early they require suppers, which are equally injurious to health. There is another reason. During the summer months women unconsciously betray a consciousness that daylight is unfavourable to charms which have undergone a course of London balls, or are no longer in the first freshness of youth, and can seldom be got to present themselves in a drawing-room before eight."

Ale and porter are rigidly proscribed, on European authority, as the *ne plus ultra* of vulgarity. We presume from this that Lord Mulgrave's novels do not enjoy an extended circulation in America; for in one of these a gallant attempt is made to disabuse the public as to beer. "Is not that a fashionable novelist opposite?" says an exquisite. "Well, I'll astonish the fellow. Here, bring me a glass of beer." What is still worse, the interdict has extended to port.

CLUBS.—Mrs. Gore writes that clubs are not bad things for family men. They act as conductors to the storms hovering in the air. The man forced to remain at home, and vent his crossness on his wife and children, is a much worse animal to bear than the man who grumbles his way to Pall Mall, and not daring to swear at the club servants, or knock about the club furniture, becomes socialised into decency. Nothing like the subordination exercised in a community of equals for reducing a fiery temper. The *Original* informs us that clubs are favourable to temperance; it seems that when people can freely please themselves excess is seldom committed. The 17,322 dinners at the Athenæum in '32, cost, on an average, 2s. 9¾d, each, and the wine for each person consumed was a fraction over a pint. Expenses are discouraged. The *Quarterly* states that on one occasion the Iron Duke was charged fifteenpence for dining off a joint at the Senior United Service, and that his grace bestirred himself to have the odd three-pence struck off; the motive being not to sanction the principle of an overcharge.

LI.—SOY.

Thought is the stomach of the mind; learning is mental eating and digestion; schools mental eating-houses; teachers mental cooks; insane people those whose mental stomachs have been deranged.—*Schulz Schulzenstein.*

There is very seldom any genuine soy to be obtained. The vulgar idea is that this condiment is generally made in the East from pounded cockroaches, well spiced. The principal place where soy is obtained is in Japan. It is a rough plant, growing to the height of six feet, and is called by Linnæus the *dolchicos soja*. The pods produce a kind of bean, which is salted and fermented for use. There is nothing more relishing than this liquid when real; but that usually sold is manufactured in the neighbourhood of London from not the very best materials. The Chinese are great consumers of soy, and would give more for the article than any price to be obtained in the European market. Very tasty stuff may be made from one pound of salt, two pounds of dark brown sugar, fried and browned over a fire; then add two pints of boiling water, a quarter of a pint of essence of anchovies, and a few herbs. Boil, and when cold, bottle, and fancy you are eating the real tropical *dolchicos*.

COCKROACHES.—Sailors have a notion that soy is made from cockroaches. The Chinese at Canton have a large soy manufactory, and they are particularly solicitous to obtain cockroaches from the ships. Cockroaches are used in fish baiting by the Chinese. Mr. Webster, surgeon of H.M.S. Chanticleer, states that salt and water, substituted with cockroach juice, has all the flavour and qualities of soy.—*Things Not Generally Known.*

LII.—BREAKFAST.

"I strut to the old café, Hardy, which yet
Beats the field at a *déjeûner à la fourchette*.
There, Dick, what a breakfast! Oh, not like your ghost
Of a breakfast in England, your curst tea and toast;
But a side-board, you dog, where one's eye roves about
Like a Turk's in the harem, and thence singles out
One *paté* of larks, just to tune up the throat;
One's small limbs of chickens, done *en papillote*;
Or one's kidneys, imagine, Dick, done with champagne!"
The Fudge Family in Paris.

This matutinal meal should be remarkably well served, and the articles good of their kind. The housekeeper or mistress of the establishment has an infinite variety to choose from. Meats—cold, of different kinds—poultry, pies, ham, tongue, and game. Hot fish, and broiled chops and steaks, eggs and bacon, omelettes, poached and boiled eggs, toast, muffins, marmalade, butter, jams, and honey, not omitting delicious cakes, made on a girdle from Jones's patent flour, which, buttered hot, are light, wholesome, and nutritious. Tea, coffee, and fruits assorted. The Americans are first-rate hands at the display and fixings they put on the table; but we believe that the Scotch exceed all other nations, in the variety at this repast, and the goodness of the viands. Coffee is the liquid for this meal; eschew tea by all means, unless for an exercise or a journey, and then a glass of mild ale is not to be disregarded. For training to obtain a good wind in walking, running, boxing, riding, or rowing, there is no breakfast more wholesome than oatmeal porridge, so says *Rural Field Sports*, and it is very good tact to commence the breakfast with a plateful on any other occasion. The cookery of it is very simple, but rarely well done—either too thick or thin. The Scotch mode of making it is to allow the water to boil, and then to put the meal in by degrees. We prefer the common way of mixing the meal with cold water, so that it should not be lumpy, putting it on the stove to simmer, until done, with a little salt. When it has boiled sufficiently, it will, on being put on a cold plate, with a little milk in it, set hard, and this is the best criterion of its being done. Gruel is made in a similar way, with the addition of wine, sugar, and spice.

Breakfast has been considered the meal of *friendship*, and dinner that of *etiquette*.

The *carte* of a well-appointed breakfast is as follows:—On a table, where everything should be neat and simple, there should be as many different kinds of rolls as the person who prepares them is able to make. These should differ from each other as much in form as in taste, and on the side table there should be some cold dishes, such as fowls, pheasants, partridges, tongue, ham, cold pâtes, &c. Few persons are displeased at seeing a slight sprinkling of hot dishes, as mutton kidneys, new-laid eggs, eggs and bacon, boiled cutlets, larks *à la minute*, devilled fowl, &c.; in fact, all that is generally considered as constituting a *déjeûner à la fourchette*, observing that the hot meats ought not to be served till the guests are at table. Tea (green and black separately), coffee, and chocolate, should also be served.—*Ude.*

BREAKFAST.—This is, perhaps, the most national, and not the least important of our meals; for, since many hours must have intervened since the last meal, the stomach ought to be in a condition to receive a fresh supply of aliment. As all the food in the body has, during the night, been digested, we might presume that a person in the morning ought to feel an appetite on rising. This, however, is not always the fact; the gastric juice may not be secreted in any quantity during sleep, while the muscular energies of the stomach, although invigorated by repose, are not immediately called into action; it is therefore advisable to allow an interval to commence the meal of breakfast. The solidity of our breakfast should be regulated by the labour and exercise to be taken, and to the time of dining.—*Paris.*

A couple of poached eggs, with a few fine dry fried collops of pure bacon, are not bad for breakfast, or to begin a meal.—*Digby's Closet of Cookery*, 1669.

LIII.—ICE.

In the warmer climates of Europe an ice-house, or an ice-safe (refrigerator) is a necessary appendage to every respectable dwelling, not merely for the purpose of pleasing the palate with iced beverages, but to enable the residents to preserve their provisions (fish, meat, game, milk, butter, &c.) in a wholesome state from day to day.—*Cooley's "Practical Receipts."*

The greatest luxury in hot weather is ice, and where that cannot be obtained recourse must be had to Simpson's portable freezing vases, which are sold at a moderate price at the manufactory; and it is surprising that they are not more used in the colonies. The vase is most simple of its kind, and the freezing mixture, warranted to keep in any climate, is 34s. per cwt. At inns there is nothing more delightful to the traveller than to have cool wines and water. To see the butter on the breakfast-table in a fluid state, when one of these patent butter-coolers can be purchased for a guinea, and the expense of the freezing power only comes to a penny, betrays sheer laziness on the part of the housekeeper. We recollect the breakfasts at the hotels at Sydney, on a late visit, which were "first chop" except the liquid butter. No public or private establishment should be without a portable freezing-vase; and if they are not to be had in the Colonies, a cheap and powerful freezing mixture may be obtained by pulverising glauber salts finely, and placing it at the bottom of a glass vessel. Equal parts of sal-ammoniac and nitre are then to be finely powdered and mixed together, and subsequently added to the glauber salts, stirring the powder well together to dissolve the salts; a degree of cold will be produced frequently below zero of Fahrenheit. It is said that nitrate of ammonia, phosphate of soda, and diluted nitric acid will on the instant produce a reduction of temperature amounting to eighty degrees. It is desirable to reduce the temperature of the substances previously, if convenient, by placing the vessels in water, with nitre powder thrown in occasionally. Professor Brande informs us that when five parts of powdered nitre, and five parts of powdered sal-ammoniac are mixed with sixteen parts of water, the thermometer falls in the mixture from fifty degrees to about ten degrees, so that in this way a degree of cold much below the freezing point of water may be artificially and cheaply obtained. How simple is the latter recipe! Where ice is to be had, a "refrigerator" or portable ice-safe will preserve ice and furnish space for cooling provisions, wine, butter, &c., for any time required, and a small-sized one, costing £4 10s., will consume only fifty pounds of ice weekly. Simpson, of Oxford Street, London, is the best maker.

ICE-HOUSE.—An ice-house should not be regarded as an object of mere luxury; in the southern countries of Europe it is considered, among people of easy circumstances, as an indispensable appendage to a country house. During the dog days, especially at those periods and in those districts where the *sirocco* blows, a lassitude and torpor of body and mind supervene, with indigestion, or total loss of appetite, and sometimes dysenteries, which are obviously occasioned by the excess of heat, and are to be prevented or counteracted by the use of cold beverages. By giving a tone to the stomach, iced drinks immediately restore the functions of the nervous and muscular systems when they are languid, while they enable persons in health to endure, without much inconvenience, an atmosphere so close and sultry as would be intolerable without the remedy.—*Ure.*

SABOTIERE.—The apparatus for making ices called *sabotière* is composed of two principal parts—a part which is indented towards the top and covered; and the *sabotière* or inner vessel, slightly conical, which is inserted in a pail, on which it rests by a projecting border or rim. This vessel is closed at the bottom like a cup, and open at the top to admit the creams to be iced. It is closed at the top by a cover furnished with a handle and a hook, which fastens it to the rim of the vessel. This apparatus works as follows: The freezing mixture is turned into the pail, and the creams to be iced into the inner vessel; its cover is then fastened by the hook, and the vessel is set into the pail among the freezing liquid; then taking the whole by the handle of the *sabotière*, an alternate motion of rotation is given to it for about a quarter of an hour, when the cream is sufficiently frozen. The cover is opened from time to time, and the mixture well stirred with a spoon adapted to the purpose. The freezing mixture must be renewed every fifteen or twenty minutes.

ICE.—The ice shipped from America to England is obtained from Fresh, Spy, and Wenham ponds, near Boston. The ice is beautifully transparent, and free from air cells, and is usually cut in blocks a foot thick. Nearly 200,000 tons are shipped from Boston, and 20,000 tons for New York. The American consumption is nearly 300,000 tons.—*Hunt's "Merchants' Magazine."*

The following table is taken from "Ure's Dictionary," consisting of frigorific mixtures, having the power of generating or creating cold without the aid of ice, sufficient for all useful purposes, in any part of the world, at any season:—

Mixtures.	Parts.	THERMOMETER SINKS. Deg. to Deg.	DEG. OF COLD PRODUCED. Deg.
Nitrate of ammonia	1	from +50 to + 4	46
Water	1		
Muriate of ammonia	5	" +50 " +10	40
Nitrate of potash	5		
Water	16		
Muriate of ammonia	5	" +50 " + 4	46
Nitrate of potash	5		
Sulphate of soda	8		
Water	16		
Sulphate of soda	3	" +50 " − 3	53
Dilute citric acid	2		
Nitrate of ammonia	1	" +50 " − 7	57
Carbonate of soda	1		
Water	1		
Phosphate of soda	9	" +50 " −12	62
Dilute nitric acid	4		
Sulphate of soda	8	" +50 " − 0	50
Hydrochloric acid	5		
Sulphate of soda	5	" +50 " + 3	47
Dilute sulphuric acid	4		
Sulphate of soda	6	" +50 " −10	60
Muriate of ammonia	4		
Nitrate of potash	2		
Dilute nitric acid	4		
Sulphate of soda	6	" +50 " −14	64
Nitrate of ammonia	5		
Dilute nitric acid	4		

Carre and Co.'s patent economical freezing apparatus, for which the prize medal was awarded by the Exhibition of 1862, as well as a gold medal by the French *Société d'Encouragement*, will produce a pound of ice at an expense of less than a farthing; will cost (including packing and accessories) not more than £6, and is invaluable in warm climates.

LIV.—PRESERVES AND CONSERVES.

As the last taste of sweets is sweetest last.—*Gaunt, in "Richard II."*

In making jams, jellies, or conserves of any kind, be sure to use the best sugar. It is bad economy to make them of an inferior article. There is another rule which we would press on the attention of the housewife—for jams, never commence to boil fruit and sugar together. Boil the fruit first for about twenty or twenty-five minutes, and then put the sugar in, and boil, or jump it, as it is called, quickly. Jelly cannot be made to set firm and hard unless this mode is followed. A brass preserving pan, rather shallow, with handles to it, is the best, but we have eaten good jam made in an iron pot. As a rule, a pound of sugar to a pound of fruit or juice is about the correct thing. This quantity may be reduced a *little* with sweet fruits. We shall only describe one mode, and then proceed to the next subject.

Red Currant Jelly.—Put the fruit on the fire or hot plate, with a table-spoonful of water at the bottom of the pan, and boil for twenty to twenty-five minutes, and pass the juice through a flannel jelly bag. To every pint of juice add a pound of sugar of the best kind. Return it to the pan, and boil quickly for a little better than ten minutes, or until the preserve sticks to the spoon. It is then done, and you have only to run it into pots or jelly glasses. Cover with paper, steeped in spirits of any kind, and use bladder for top covering.

The above is the mode of making jelly, and it can be applied to strawberries, white currants, raspberries, black currants, blackberry, cranberry, gooseberry, apple, pear, apricot, peach, quince, or, indeed, any fruit, with this difference, that if the fruit is not juicy, a little water must be added in the preserving pan.

Raspberry Jam.—Weigh your fruit, and put it in the preserving pan to simmer or boil, in the same way as jelly. When the fruit has set, add a pound of sugar for each pound of fruit. Let it boil ten or twelve minutes, skim occasionally, and when it sticks to the spoon it is fit for the jar or pot.

Every kind of jam and marmalade is made in this way—green gooseberry (the best of any), currants, plums (the stones being taken out and the kernels added); same with peaches, nectarines, and apricots. With apples, pears, and quinces, they must be peeled and cored, and a little lemon-juice added; cherries, oranges, strawberries, and rhubarb. If the fruit is dry, such as apples and quinces, a little water must be used.

Colonial Jam and Molasses.—Take any quantity of mangold, wash and pare them; then grate on a coarse grater, and express the juice through a cheese cloth; add to the juice obtained about one-third of its bulk of grated carrot, and simmer gently for about forty-eight hours; a drop or two of essence of lemon or vanilla will improve it. The treacle is simply the juice of mangold evaporated to a proper consistence over a slow fire.—*Hobart Town Advertiser.*

To Keep Gooseberries and Damsons.—Pick the fruit, not too ripe, and put them into wide-mouthed bottles; cork them gently; put them in the oven—not over-warm—until they have shrunk a third of their weight. Take them out of the oven, tighten the corks, and rosin them down close.

BOTTLING CHERRIES.—To every pound of fruit for tarts through the winter, add six ounces of loaf sugar. Fill the jars with fruit; shake the sugar over, and tie down with two bladders, as there is danger of one bursting through the boiling. Place the jars in a boiler of cold water, and, after the water has boiled, let them remain three hours; take them out, and, when cool, put them in a dry place, where they will keep over a year. We have tried this receipt for several years, and never knew it fail. The fruit makes delicious puddings.—*Correspondent in the "Field."*

To Preserve Apples, Pears, and Quinces.—Peel and core them, and cut them in thin slices; dry them in the sun. When used in pies or puddings, soak them sufficiently in lukewarm water, and the flavour of the apple will be found excellent. Apples, gooseberries, and other fruit may be preserved for winter use, by putting the fruit dry in earthern jars, and the jars placed in a pan of water over a hot plate until the water boils. Then take the jars from the fire, and fill them up with boiling water; cover them with bladders while hot, and place them where they are to remain until wanted.

Preserved Ginger.—If green ginger cannot be procured, take some large pieces of the common ginger, and simmer it in water until tender, and when done put in cold water. Take it out and drain; and to equal quantities in weight of ginger add white sugar (sugar-candy is best); let the sugar be clarified, and put to the ginger. Simmer constantly, until the sugar has penetrated right through the ginger. The sugar must not be put to the ginger too hot, or it will shrink, and not take the sugar. By proceeding carefully, the housewife will make a preserve quite equal to that for which the Chinese are so famous.

Compotes.—These are simply fruits stewed in syrup, for which the French are justly famous; and sometimes a little wine or brandy is added to the liquor.

Compote of Apples.—Cut your apples in halves or quarters, according to their size; put them in to stew with sufficient water and sugar to taste; add a glass of wine, and a little lemon acid; simmer, and, when sufficiently done, serve in their own syrup.

Compotes of pears, currants, cherries, plums, gooseberries, peaches, apricots, strawberries, raspberries, quinces, and chestnuts, are served in the same way.

Syrups.—These are French preparations of fruit, &c., to mix with water for a cooling beverage at *soirées* or balls. Water and sugar are the component parts of all syrups, except, as a " Manual of French Cookery " observes, the syrup of punch, which should have a strong proportion of alcohol. We give the recipe for the most fashionable of all syrups.

Syrup d'Absinthe (*Wormwood*).—Put in a basin two ounces of the tops of wormwood, and pour over it four quarts of boiling water; let it steep four hours on a hot hearth; then strain the decoction through linen; beat the white of an egg, melt two pounds of sugar, and simmer until done. Bottle for use.

The *poculum absinthiatum* was regarded in remote ages as a wholesome beverage, and the wormwood was, moreover, supposed to act as an antidote against intoxication.

Syrup of cherries, strawberries, mulberries, raspberries, apples, vinegar, gum arabic, capillaire, sweet almonds, currants, marsh-mallow roots, and punch, are made in a similar manner.

To Preserve Gooseberries Whole (*Another Recipe*).—The gooseberries must be full grown, but not ripe. Top and tail them, and put the fruit into wide-mouthed bottles; gently cork them with new corks; put them into a pan of boiling water—a French *bain marie* is the thing—and let them remain in the water until they have shrunk to a fourth; then beat the corks in tight, and resin the tops; set the bottles in a dry place, and they will keep for winter use for pies and puddings.

JAMS AND JELLIES.—Jelly and jam can be prepared from the tender leaf-stalks of the red rhubarb, their flavour being equal to currant jelly. Blackberry jelly is good in tarts. Baked pears, of fine colour, make an excellent dish for the dessert; and barberries are good preserved. The white bullace is good preserved in sugar; the *magnum bonum* plum is flavourless for eating, and only fit for preserves. The Victoria plum is one of the best in England, by repute, for eating and preserving, and is likely to preserve its good qualities for years to come. The British-made fruit, jams, and jellies, lose their fine flavour in crossing the Line to the Colonies, and become hard and tasteless. The Tasmania jams have acquired a repute in the Colonies for their goodness and fine aroma, and the demand for them is very great.

LV.—PRESIDENCY AT DINNER.

"It is not difficult to foresee that this department (cookery) of philosophy must become the most popular of all others, because every department of human beings is interested in its success. If science can really contribute to the happiness of mankind it must be in this department. The real comfort of the majority of men in this country is sought for at their own firesides; how desirable, then, it becomes to give every inducement to be at home, by directing all the means of philosophy to increase domestic happiness."—*Sylvester, on "Domestic Economy."*

1st. Always hurry the bottle round for five or six rounds, without prosing yourself or permitting others to prose. A slight fillip of wine inclines people to be pleased, and removes the nervousness which prevents men from speaking; disposes them, in short, to be amusing and to be amused.

2nd. "Push on, keep moving," as young Rapid says. Do not think of saying fine things—nobody cares for them any more than for fine music, which is often too liberally bestowed on such occasions. Speak at all ventures, and attempt the *mot pour rire*. You will find people satisfied with wonderfully indifferent jokes, if you can hit the taste of the company, which depends much on its character. Even a very high party, primed with all the cold irony and *non est tanti* feelings, or no feelings, of fashionable folks, may be stormed by a jovial, rough, round, and ready president. Choose your text with discretion, the sermon may be as you like. Should a drunkard or an ass break in with anything out of joint, if you can parry it with a jest good, and well; if not, do not exert your serious authority, unless it is something very bad. The authority even of a chairman ought to be very cautiously exercised. With patience you will have the support of every one.

3rd. When you have drunk a few glasses to play the good fellow and banish modesty (if you are unlucky enough to have such a troublesome companion), then beware of the cup too much. Nothing is so ridiculous as a drunken president.

Lastly. Always speak short, and *skeoch doch na skiel*—cut a tale with a drink.

"This is the purpose and intent
Of gude Schir Walter's testament."—*Walter Scott.*

A MODERN DINNER.—On a late occasion Prince Napoleon gave at Paris a grand dinner, at which several dishes were Chinese, some of the wine drank was from Siam (having been sent by the King of that country to the Prince), and one of the guests was a Chinese mandarin. Among the dishes were swallow's-nest, cooked in the Nankin mode; fins of a shark, fried; *oluthuries à la mandarine*; the interior of a sturgeon, *à la bocto genaire, aux rondelles de bauboux; oluthuries* in salad, with pheasant jelly; rice, *des immortels*; fowls, with Japanese curry; spinach, with *balichuo*, such as was esteemed at Rome under Augustus; rice in the Chinese fashion; ordinary India curry.—*Hints for the Table.*

LVI.—CAKES.

Dost thou think, because thou art virtuous, there shall be no more cakes and ale?—
Sir Toby Belch, in "Twelfth Night."

Twelfth Cake.—The ingredients of a fair-sized cake may be:—Two pounds of flour, two pounds of white sugar, two pounds of butter, eighteen eggs, four pounds of currants, washed and cleaned, half a pound of almonds, blanched and cut into pieces, one pound of candied orange and lemon-peel, half a pound of citron, half a nutmeg, grated, half an ounce of mixed spice, and a gill of brandy. Put the butter into a stewpan, and work it smooth with a wooden spatula, and mix it, with the sugar and spice, in a pan for a time. Then break in the eggs by degrees, and beat the mixture; stir in the brandy, and then the flour, and work it a little; add the fruit, sweetmeats, and almonds, and mix all lightly together. Put it in a hoop, and bake on a baking-tin for four hours. When nearly cold, ice it.

Bride or Wedding Cake: made in a similar way, with a pound of raisins.

In Yorkshire and other parts of England the bride cake is cut into little square pieces, thrown over the bride and bridegroom's head, then put through the ring nine times, and afterwards laid under the pillows at night to cause young persons to dream of their lovers. The custom of introducing cake after a rich entertainment is very ancient; but the cakes or *mustacea* of the Romans were very different compositions.

They consisted of meal, aniseed, cummin, and several other aromatics. Their object was to remove or prevent the indigestion which might occur after a feast. A cake was, therefore, constantly introduced for such a purpose after a marriage entertainment, and hence the origin of the "bride cake," which in modern times is an excellent invention for *producing* instead of *curing* indigestion.—*Old Magazine.*

Plain Pound Cake.—Made in a like manner, with a pound of butter, a pound of sugar, and nine eggs. Beat separately, and baked in the same way as the twelfth cake, with less time.

Common Seed Cake.—Take two pounds and a half of flour, and half a pound of white sugar; put it into a bowl, and make a cavity in the centre, and pour in half a pint of lukewarm milk, and two tablespoonfuls of yeast. Set it in a warm place for an hour; then melt to an oil half a pound of fresh butter, and add to the other ingredients, with an ounce of carraway seeds, and warm milk to make it a middling stiffness. Put it into a round tin, and allow it to rise again a short time, and then bake.

A Rich Cake.—Take two pounds and a half of Jones's patent flour, add to it a pint and a half of cold milk, a pound of butter, oiled, a pound of sifted sugar, a pound of currants, a quarter of a pound of lemon and orange-peel, and a little grated nutmeg, cinnamon, and allspice. Put these ingredients in a round tin and bake an hour. This cake may be iced or ornamented.

Queen Cakes.—One pound of sugar, one pound of butter, eight eggs, one pound and a quarter of flour, two ounces of currants, and half a nutmeg. Mix the butter with sugar and spice, then add half the eggs, and beat for a few minutes, add the rest of the eggs, and work for five minutes longer; stir in the flour and currants, when bake in shapes.

Plain Sponge Cake.—One pound of flour, one pound of sugar, and eight eggs. Beat the yolks and the whites of the eggs separate sufficiently, then add the two together, and put in the sugar. When mixed, add the flour by degrees; a few drops of essence of lemon is an improvement. Butter a dish and bake.

Shrewsbury Cakes.—Rub together one pound of white sugar, one pound of fresh butter, and a pound and a half of flour. Mix it into a paste, with half a gill of milk and one egg beaten. Let it lie half an hour, roll it out thin, cut it into cakes, and bake them in a moderate oven.

Victoria Cake.—Take the yolks of twelve eggs, leaving out the whites of six, one pound of white sugar, the juice of one lemon, and the peel of two cut very fine; whisk these ingredients together for half an hour, and then add twelve ounces of flour. The cake must be put in the oven and baked an hour.

Passover Cakes.—Make a stiff paste with biscuit-powder, milk, and water, add a small piece of butter, the yolk of an egg, and a little white sugar. Cut it into pieces, mould with the hand, and bake in a crisp oven. To make them without butter, warm a quarter of a pint of milk, flavoured with a little salt; mix four eggs with half a pound of Hebrew or "matso" flour, and a dessert-spoonful of white sugar; mix with a tea-cupful of milk, and bake in a tin.

PASSOVER CAKES.—Seven days shall ye eat unleavened bread; even the first day ye shall put away leaven out of your houses: for whosoever eateth leavened bread from the first day until the seventh day, that soul shall be cut off from Israel.—Exod. xii. 15.

Ginger and Lemon Cakes.—To two pounds of flour add a pound of good sugar, one ounce of best ginger, well mixed with the flour; have ready three-quarters of a pound of lard or butter, melted, and four eggs well beaten; mix the lard and eggs together, and stir in the flour, which will form a paste; roll out in thin cakes, and bake in a moderately-heated oven. Lemon biscuits are made the same way, by substituting essence of lemon instead of ginger.

There is a wonderful difference in these cakes made with plain flour and Jones's patent flour. The superiority of the latter in cakes and puddings is very great indeed.

Banbury Cakes.—Put a gill of warm milk to a pound of flour, and three spoonfuls of yeast; when it has worked a little, mix with it half a pound of currants, washed and cleaned, a quarter of a pound of orange and lemon-peel, cut small, and an ounce of mixed spice; mix the whole together with half a pound of honey; roll out some paste thin, and make it in the form of an oval; put into each the quantity of the mixture, close it round and soft, sugar over, and bake.

Bath Buns.—Rub half a pound of butter into a pound of flour; beat up six eggs, and add them to the flour, with two table-spoonfuls of yeast. Mix them together with half a cupful of lukewarm milk; set it to rise; then add six ounces of white sugar, and a few carraway-seeds; mould into buns; put on the top of each six or eight carraway comfits, and bake.

Italian Macaroons. — Blanch a pound of Jordan or Valencia almonds; pound them fine with the whites of four eggs; add two pounds and a half of the best white sugar, and pound all together; add the whites of six more eggs, and bake; adding slips of blanched almonds on the top of each macaroon before putting in the oven.

The old English recipe of 1618 shows that macaroons were composed of sugar and almonds, and they were formerly called March-panes, said to be derived from the celebrated epicure, Marcus Apicius; while other authorities aver that they were sacred to Mars, and stamped with a castle. March-pane was an invariable accompaniment in the desserts of our ancestors, and we believe is now used at the old universities.

Ratafia Cakes.—These cakes are made in a similar way to the macaroons.

Almond Sponge Cake.—Pound in a mortar one pound of blanched almonds, with the whites of four eggs; then add one pound of sifted white sugar, some grated lemon-peel, and the yolks of twelve eggs; work them well together, beat to a froth the whites of the dozen eggs, and stir them into the other ingredients, with a quarter of a pound of flour; put the mixture in a mould, and bake an hour; take the cake out of the mould, and set it on a sieve.

Orange Gingerbread.—To two pounds of flour add a pound and three-quarters of treacle, six ounces of candied orange-peel, cut small, three-quarters of a pound of moist sugar, one ounce of ground ginger, and one ounce of allspice. Melt half or three-quarters of a pound of butter, mix the whole well together and lay it by for six hours. Roll it out into pieces in the form of chequers, and bake an inch apart; rub them over with a brush dipped in yolk of eggs and milk. When baked, rub over a second time.

Gingerbread Nuts.—Mix two pounds of flour, three-quarters of a pound of sugar, two pounds of treacle, half a pound of candied orange-peel, cut small, an ounce and a half of ginger, an ounce of ground allspice, carraways, and corianders mixed, and three-quarters of a pound of butter, oiled. Mix all together, and set it aside for six hours, then roll it out in pieces the size of a walnut. Press them flat and bake.

Plain Buns.—To two pounds of flour put half a pound of moist sugar, make a cavity in the centre, and stir in half a gill of good yeast, half a pint of lukewarm milk, with enough flour to thicken it. Let it rise for half an hour or more, then melt half a pound of butter lukewarm, stir it into the other ingredients with enough warm milk to make it a soft paste, throw some flour over it, and let it rise for three-quarters of an hour. Have ready a baking-tin, mould the buns into sizes, and bake. When drawn from the oven, milk them over.

Cross Buns.—Made similar to the above, only crossed when baked, and an ounce of spice added to the mixture.

Hot cross buns are, in England, intimately associated with our observances of Good Friday. Winclemann relates the discovery of two perfect buns at Herculaneum, each marked with a cross, within which were four other lines. Hesychius describes the *bonn* as a kind of cake, with a representation of ten horns. Descending to the earlier Catholic times, we find that buns were the *eulogiæ*, or consecrated loaves, made from the dough whence the host was taken, and given by the priests to the people. They are marked with the cross, as our Good Friday buns are.—*Fosbroke.*

Seed Buns.—Made as above, with half an ounce of carraway-seeds added for the spice.

Plum Buns.—Made the same way as plain buns, with a small quantity of spice, and a quarter of a pound of currants, washed and picked.

Comfit Buns.—A pound and a half of fresh butter, to be melted in a little warm water, and three-quarters of a pint of good yeast added, with a wine-glassful of rose-water. This is poured on two pounds of flour, mixed with three-quarters of a pound of sifted sugar; knead the whole into a light paste, with half a pound of carraway comfits. Make it into buns, and put a few comfits on the top of each, and bake.

In the recipes for all buns and cakes, where yeast is directed to be used, if Jones's patent flour is used, the yeast is quite unnecessary.

Scotch Buns.—Take two pounds of flour, one pound of raisins, stoned and cut, and one pound of currants. Add three ounces of orange-peel, the same of citron, and of almonds blanched and cut; mix together. Take some mixed spice, and add. Make a hole in the flour, and break in three-quarters of a pound of butter; pour warm water on the butter to soften it; then work the flour and butter together; add a quarter of a pint of yeast; work it smooth. Cut a third part of the paste for sheets; spread out the rest of the paste on the table, and put the fruit in. Pour about half a gill of yeast over the fruit and paste, and work together. Then make it round; roll out the sheet in a circular form; lay the bun in the middle, and gather the sheet round it; roll it out the desired thickness; run a fork through in different parts, down to the bottom, and pinch it on the top. Flour double paper, and put the bun on it, and give a cut round the side. Mind it does not run in the oven, and bake moderately.

Derby Cakes.—Rub half a pound of butter into a pound of flour, put half a pound of currants, half a pound of sugar, and one egg; mix all together, with a quarter of a pint of milk; cut them into round cakes, and bake.

Rout Cakes.—Two pounds of flour, one pound of butter, one pound of sugar, and one pound of currants; wet them with three eggs beaten, half a pint of milk, two glasses of white wine, and one glass of brandy. Work them together, and bake in a tin plate.

Scotch Fancy Cakes.—Rub half a pound of butter into a pound and a half of flour, then break four eggs into an earthen pan, with three quarters of a pound of sugar; whisk them for five minutes, then make a print with your butter and flour, pour in the eggs and sugar, and add half a gill of cream. Mix all into a dough, cut into pieces two inches across, and an eighth of an inch in thickness, then cover your tins with wafer paper; lay your cakes on it, and bake.

Portugal Cakes.—One pound of flour, one pound of white sugar, and one pound of fresh butter. Work it well up until it crumbles; then add ten eggs and half a pound of currants, with a little white wine. Bake in tins only half filled.

Bordeaux Cake.—Roll paste out less than a quarter of an inch thick, and cut it into six or seven portions of equal size; lay them on buttered tins floured, and bake them in an oven until they are firm and crisp, and of a pale brown. When they are cold, spread upon each a different kind of choice preserve, and pile the whole evenly in the form of a cake. The top may be iced and decorated.

Mrs. Hill's Cakes.—A pound of flour, a pound of sugar, a quarter of a pound of butter, the yolks of two eggs, and the peel of two lemons, cut very small; to be rolled into thin cakes; they can be baked in the oven after the bread is drawn.

Rice Cake.—Half a pound of ground rice, half a pound of white sugar, and four eggs. Beat the eggs separately, and then the whole ingredients together for some time, and bake in a mould.

Jenny Lind Cake.—One pound of flour, a quarter of a pound of butter, a quarter of a pound of moist sugar, and a little spice, to be mixed with two tea-spoonfuls of soda in three-quarters of a pint of fresh-churned buttermilk; candied peel to taste, and bake.

Easter Cake.—Two pounds of flour, one pound of butter melted, half a pound of currants, one pound of moist sugar, four yolks of eggs, a table-spoonful of brandy; add a little cinnamon.

Chantilly Trifle Cake.—Take a savoury cake of the size required. Cut off the top, and scoop out the inside to about three-quarters of an inch from the edge, having about the same thickness at the bottom. Put it on the dish on which it is to be served, and pour about half a pint of sherry wine over the sides and bottom of the cake; as it soaks in, pour it over until it has absorbed. Just before serving fill the cake with whipped cream, flavoured with vanilla or lemon, or a little brandy and wine. The edge of the cake may be garnished with preserved fruits or blanched sweet almonds, cut in thin slices lengthways, and stuck round. Custard may be substituted for the cream in filling the cake.

Ginger, Currant, and Cinnamon Cake.—Rub six ounces of butter into four pounds of flour; make a paste, and add one pound of sugar, an ounce and a half of volatile salts, four eggs well beaten, and as much butter as will make into dough; divide it into three equal parts, add to one half an ounce of ground ginger, to another two ounces of currants, and to the third half an ounce of ground cinnamon. Bake on buttered tins, and sprinkle the top with sugar.

Handsome Tipsy Cake.—Provide some sponge cakes, place four close upon the dish upon which the cake is to be served, spread over them a thick layer of jam; upon this place three sponge cakes close together, spread over a thick layer of jam, and complete the pyramid with one. Pour over the whole three glasses of sherry, so that the cakes may absorb all the wine; when this is done, add two glasses of brandy slowly, so that in absorbing the spirits, the cakes do not become too moist and break. Make a rich custard and pour over the whole.

Rock Cakes.—Half a pound of butter, half a pound of sugar, one pound of flour, three eggs, and half a pound of currants. Beat the butter to a cream, then beat up the eggs thoroughly, and mix in with the butter and sugar, after which stir in the flour very gradually, and lastly the currants. Keep a little of the white of egg out to froth the top with. Drop the buttons on buttered paper, and bake quickly.

Gateaux d'Epice.—The following are the ingredients:—Treacle, a pint; butter, half a pound; powdered ginger, an ounce; powdered cinnamon, an ounce; allspice, a quarter of an ounce; candied lemon-peel, chopped fine, two ounces; tincture of vanilla, six drops; flour as much as necessary. The treacle being placed over the fire, the butter is added, and successively all the other things but the flour; let them, when well mixed, take a single boil, stirring them, and then let them cool. When cold, mix in, with a wooden spoon, enough flour to make it into a pretty stiff paste; butter a tin baking-dish, and lay on it with the spoon the paste, in the size necessary to form the nuts; set the tin in the oven, and bake. When cold they are hard, if done.

By following the above recipe, the good housewife will make what are considered the ne plus ultra of French gingerbread nuts.

Marlborough Cakes.—Beat eight eggs and one pound of ground sugar well; then by degrees mix in one pound of flour and two ounces of carraway seeds, and bake in tin pans in a quick oven.

Maids of Honour.—Take the curd of a quart of milk, and drain dry; then rub it through a sieve into a pan, mix with it four ounces of butter, eight ounces of ground white sugar, the yolks of four eggs, and one mealy potato of medium size; when well mixed, add one ounce each of sweet and bitter almonds (using the strained juice of a lemon to prevent their oiling while being pounded), the rind of one lemon grated, some nutmeg, and a wine-glass of brandy, and stir in with the rest. Line the pans with puff paste, fill them with the mixture, and bake.

Richmond "Maids of Honour" are delicious cheesecakes, peculiar to Richmond and Surrey, and doubtless named from its regal days, when Richmond had its royal palace and court. It is stated that one thousand pounds was once paid to the fortunate possessor of the receipt for making this cheesecake, with the goodwill of the business said to have been originally established in Hill-street, Richmond. George III. had his tables at Windsor Castle and Kew regularly supplied with these cheesecakes.—*Things not Generally Known.*

Theodore Hook, in "Gilbert Gurney," tells the lady at dinner that cheesecakes were called, at the place where they were dining, "maids of honour," and a "gooseberry tart" a "gentleman usher" of the black rod. The feminine was *sold*, for she ordered a "gentleman usher" to be brought in cold, amidst the laughter of the company.

Pikelets.—Put half a pint of milk and the same quantity of water into a saucepan, with an ounce of butter, two lumps of sugar, and a little salt; stir it over the fire till rather warmer than new milk, then beat up the yolks of two eggs and the white of one, and add a table-spoonful of yeast. Put them into a jug and mix the whole together; then add one pound of flour, and stir it in free from lumps. Let the jug remain by the fire to rise; rub a little butter on the baking-iron, then pour on the batter to bake.

Jersey Wonders.—Take two pounds of flour, six ounces of butter, six ounces of white sugar, a little nutmeg, ground ginger, and lemon-peel. Beat eight eggs, and knead them well together; a taste of brandy is an improvement. Roll them out the thickness of your wrist, cut off a small slice, and roll it into an oval, about four inches long and three inches wide, not too thin; cut ten slips in it, but not through either end, there will be then three bands. Pass the left one through the aperture to the right, and throw it into a skillet of boiling dripping or lard. You can cook three or four at a time. In about ten minutes turn them with a fork, and you will find them browned, and swollen or risen in two or three minutes more. Remove them from the pan to a dish, when they will dry and cool.

Christmas Yule Cake.—Take one pound of fresh butter, one pound of sugar, one pound and a half of flour, two pounds of currants, a glass of brandy, one pound of sweetmeats, two ounces of sweet almonds, ten eggs, and a quarter of an ounce of cinnamon. Melt the butter to a cream, and put in the sugar, stir it light, adding the allspice and cinnamon; take the yolks of the eggs and work them and the whites separate. The paste must not stand to chill, or it will be heavy. Work in the whites gradually, then add the orange-peel, lemon, and citron; cut in strips, add currants and almonds, which must be well mixed in; then add the flour and brandy. Bake in a tin hoop, in a hot oven for three hours, and paper the bottom to prevent its being burnt.

Hanover Cakes.—Beat the yolks of eight eggs and the whites of four well together, then add a pound of finely-powdered white sugar, the rind and juice of two lemons; beat them well together with a pound of blanched almonds, coarsely bruised, and three-quarters of a pound of flour; shape and put them on a tin to bake.

The Whig.—Rub a quarter of a pound of fresh butter into two pounds of flour till none of it is visible, then add half a pint of warm cream and a quarter of a pint of good yeast; mix the whole into a light paste, and set it to rise; have ready some grated nutmeg, mace, and cloves, a quarter of an ounce of carraway-seeds, and a quarter of a pound of fine sugar. When the dough has risen these ingredients must be worked into it. The paste is then rolled out thin, and divided into cakes. These were crossed in olden times. Put the cakes on tins to rise, and then bake.

Scotch Cake.—To a pound and a half of flour, the same quantity of butter, and the same quantity of white sugar, six ounces of blanched sweet almonds, three-quarters of a pound of candied orange-peel, half a pound of citron, cut small, half a nutmeg grated, a tea-spoonful of carraway-seeds, twelve eggs (the yolks and whites well beaten separately); beat the butter to a cream, add the sugar and eggs gradually, mix the flour by degrees, and then the sweetmeats, almonds, and spice; lastly, stir in a glass of brandy; butter the hoop or tin, and pour in the cake so as to nearly fill it; smooth the top, and strew over it carraway comfits. Bake in a moderate oven.

Galette.—Work lightly three-quarters of a pound of butter into a pound of flour, add a salt-spoonful of salt, and make it into a paste with the yolks of two eggs, mixed with a tea-cupful of cream or water; roll round, three-quarters of an inch thick, score it in small diamonds, brush yolks of eggs over the top, and bake it for about half an hour in a quick oven. It is usually eaten hot, but it is served cold also.

This is a very favourite cake in *la belle France*.

Treacle Parkins.—One quart of oatmeal, three pounds of treacle, three-quarters of a pound of sugar, a little butter and flour, sweetmeats or carraways *ad libitum*. Mix all together, then roll it out thin, and cut into round cakes. Bake in a tin. Wholesome and excellent for children.

Good Things.—Sussex, in England, is said to be celebrated for *six* good things: A Chichester lobster, a Selsey cockle, an Arundel mullet, a Pulborough eel, an Amberley trout, and a Rye herring.

LVII.—APPLES.

Apples are gold in the morning, silver at noon, and lead at night.—*Old Saying.*

Baked Apples.—The French have a capital way of managing these fruits (the French crab), and we think you will be of opinion, after trying it, that Easter pippins are amongst the housekeeper's most useful store. 1. Scoop out the inside of the apple by the stalk, leaving the eye unpierced. 2. Fill the hole with fresh butter. 3. Place the apple on a plate (not tin), crown downwards. 4. Sprinkle it thickly with powdered sugar. 5. Set it to bake very slowly in an oven. 6. Eat it before it cools. This was probably invented by Pomona herself—that is to say, if the lady had a kitchen, and anything better to eat than roasted acorns.—*Gardeners' Chronicle.*

Apples à la Cremona.—The apples are cut into small squares, and strewed over with half their weight in sugar and a few pieces of lemon-peel, and after remaining covered up until the next day, lightly dropped into a small stewpan, with three or four table-spoonfuls of cider or perry, and simmered gently until they become clear; they are then taken out, and when cold built in a wall-like form round a small china or glass dish, and the syrup being poured into the middle, the strips of lemon are placed on the top.

Dried Apples.—The apples are placed in a cool oven, six or seven times in succession, and flattened each time by gentle pressure, gradually applied, as soon as they are soft enough to bear it; after which they are taken out, and as soon as cold put on clean dishes or glass plates. The sour are the best sort for baking. If the process is well managed the appearance of the prepared fruit is very rich, and the flavour delicious.

Fruit, &c.—To preserve fruits in a dry state various plans are adopted. Pears, apples, plums, &c. should be gathered in a sound state, altogether exempt from bruises, and plucked in dry weather before they are fully ripe. One mode of preservation is to expose them in an airy place to dry a little for eight or ten days, and then lay them in dry sawdust or chopped straw, spread upon shelves in a cool apartment, so as not to touch each other. Another method consists in surrounding them with fine dry sand in a vessel which should be made air-tight, and kept in a cool place. Some persons coat the fruit, including the stalks, with melted wax; others lay the apples, &c., upon wicker-work shelves in a vaulted chamber, and smoke them daily during four or five days with vine branches or juniper wood. Apples thus treated and afterwards stratified with dry sawdust, without touching each other, will keep fresh for a whole year. The drying of garden fruits in the air, or by a kiln, is a well-known method of preservation. Apples and pears of a large size should be cut into thin slices. Dried plums, grapes, and currants are a common article of commerce, coming from Greece, Spain, and the Mediterranean.—*Ure.* Tasmania is an apple-producing country. Her exports are about 130,000 bushels yearly: and we have known the French crab keep sound, fresh, and plump in appearance for upwards of two years, without any preparation whatever.

American Dried Apples.—The apples (or pears), after being peeled, are cut into eighths, the cores extracted, and then placed in the sun, or in a kiln or oven, until they are quite dry and hard. In this state they may be kept for two or three years. For use, the fruit is cracked in water, and after being drained boiling water is poured on it; after standing for a few minutes it may be used as fresh fruit. The water it has soaked in is an excellent substitute for fresh juice, and should be poured into the pie-dish with the apples. In this way a cheap and constant supply of apples and pears may be had all the year round for pies and puddings almost equal to fresh fruit. Some kind of plums and prunes may be dried and preserved in a similar mode.

Worth Knowing.—One quart of wheat flour weighs 1lb., avoirdupois; one quart of Indian meal, 1lb. 2oz.; one quart of butter, 1lb. 1oz.; one quart of lump sugar, 1lb.; one quart of white powdered sugar, 1lb. 1oz.; one quart of best brown sugar, 1lb. 2oz.; ten average eggs, 1lb.—*Newspaper paragraph.*

LVIII.—BISCUITS.

A well-known variety of hard, dry, unleavened bread, made in thin, flat pieces. Those prepared for seamen are composed of flour and water only. When a few carraway seeds are added, they are commonly called Abernethy's biscuits. Fancy biscuits generally contain sugar and butter, to which almonds, carraways, and other articles are frequently added. The word biscuit is borrowed from the French, and implies twice baked.—*Cooley.*

Captain's Biscuits.—To three pounds and a half of flour add a quarter of a pound of butter and a pint of milk; mix them together till they make a hard, even dough, cut it into pieces, and roll it into paste half an inch thick. Mould them into shape, and bake in a crisp oven.

Carraway Biscuits.—To three pounds of flour add two ounces of butter, rubbed into the flour, half a pound of sugar, one ounce of carraway seeds, half an ounce of ground coriander seed, half a tea-spoonful of carbonate of soda, and a table-spoonful of arrowroot; mix the whole together, and make a stiff paste with warm milk, cut into thin cakes, prick with a fork, and bake.

Hard Biscuits.—Warm two ounces of butter in as much milk as will convert a pound of flour into a stiff paste. Beat it smooth, and roll them out thin, cut them into round biscuits, prick them with a fork, and bake.

Hard biscuits are remarkably wholesome and digestible. We are told that Marcus Antonius made it a rule to eat a hard biscuit the moment he got up.

Crisp Biscuits.—Mix a pound of flour, the yolk of an egg, and some milk into a stiff paste; beat it well, and knead it smooth, roll the paste thin, and bake.

Sweet Biscuits.—Beat eight eggs to a froth; add a pound of white sugar, and the peel of a grated lemon; whisk the whole well together then add a pound of flour and a tea-spoonful of rose-water. Divide it into biscuits, sugar them over, and bake in tins.

Brighton Biscuits.—Mix together one pound of flour, one drachm of carbonate of ammonia in fine powder, four ounces of white sugar, one ounce of arrowroot, four ounces of butter, and one egg; add new milk, so as to form a stiff paste; then beat the mass with a rolling-pin; roll it out, and bake.

Biscuits à la Française.—Beat up the yolks of four eggs, with one pound of sugar; whip the whites separately, and, when they are well frothed, mix them with the yolks and sugar, and stir in half a pound of flour, lightly; have ready some tin moulds, buttered; put in the biscuit paste, filling the moulds only half; throw some sugar over them, and bake.

Biscuit Drops.—Beat up the whites and yolks of six eggs separately, with a spoonful of rose-water; to which add six ounces of powdered loaf sugar. Beat the whole well, and add one ounce of bruised carraway seeds, and six ounces of flour. Drop them on wafer-paper, and bake in a moderate oven.

Devilled Biscuits.—Soak the common ship's biscuit, or the captain's biscuit, for a quarter of an hour in lukewarm water. Toast them, and butter well; add cayenne and anchovy, or herring paste, and hold before the fire in a cheese-toaster for a few minutes.

Oatmeal Biscuits.—One pound of the finest oatmeal, half a pound of butter, half a pound of loaf sugar, and two eggs. Pound the sugar, and mix all the ingredients into a stiff paste, with cold water. The eggs are not to be beaten for these biscuits. Make the paste into small balls; flatten them, and bake on tins.

Savoy Biscuits.—Six eggs, with three ounces of white sugar, lemon-peel, and four ounces of flour. Beat the eggs first, then mix the other articles, and drop on paper. When they have been a short time in the oven, sprinkle a little sugar over them.

Wexford Biscuits.—Rub ten ounces of butter into four ounces of flour, and three ounces of white sugar, the yolks of two eggs, and a table-spoonful of brandy; roll the paste out thin, and cut, with a cutter, into round shapes. Egg over the tops of each with the white of the eggs, and sift on white sugar. Bake in a quick oven.

Lemon Biscuits.—These are simply and easily made. To one pound of flour add six ounces of good sugar; have three-quarters of a pound of lard or butter melted, and two eggs well beaten; mix the lard and eggs together, and stir in the flour to form a paste; add about eight drops of essence of lemon; roll out into thin cakes, and bake in a moderately heated oven.

Invalid Biscuits.—Melt three-quarters of a pound of butter in a pint of new milk, and pour it on three-quarters of a pound of white sugar; when cool, put in half a dessert-spoonful of yeast, and a whole one of carraway seeds; add flour sufficient to make it into a stiff paste to roll thin; prick and cut into shapes, and bake them.

Norfolk Biscuits.—Three-quarters of a pound of butter, three pounds and a half of flour, and a quarter of a pint of yeast; melt the butter with water, knead it well, and bake on buttered paper—an ounce for each biscuit.

Soda Biscuits are made from the finest flour and a small quantity of carbonate of soda.

Sponge Biscuits.—Add the whites and yolks of eight eggs, well beaten, to a pound of finely-pounded sugar; then add a pound of fine flour, and the rind of two lemons grated. Put it into shapes; sift some white sugar over them, and bake in tin moulds for some time.

Almond Biscuits.—Take four ounces of sweet and two ounces of bitter almonds; blanch and beat them till smooth, then add one pound of loaf sugar, mix all together; beat the white of an egg to a froth and mix it with the rest; bake in lumps on wafer-paper, to prevent their sticking. A quick oven is necessary, and they should be done of a light brown.

Biscuits (*to keep for use*).—Biscuits to be kept for any length of time must be well and sufficiently baked, and preserved in tin, so as to exclude the air, or they may be preserved in bags that have been soaked in saltpetre and dried.

Cracknels (*American*).—Mix with a quart of flour half a nutmeg, grated, the yolks of four eggs, beaten with two spoonfuls of rose-water; make into a stiff paste, with sufficient cold water; then roll in a pound of butter, and make them into cracknel shapes; put them into a kettle of boiling water, and boil them until they can swim; then take them out, and place them in cold water; when hardened, lay them out to dry, and bake on tin plates.

And take with thee ten loaves, and *cracknels*, and a cruse of honey, and go to him: he shall tell thee what shall become of the child.—1 Kings xiv. 3.

Biscuits (originally biskets) of various kinds were in use in the sixteenth and seventeenth centuries, among which that most in repute was called Naples biscuit, from the place where it was first made. It occurs in the Carpenters' Company's books in 1644.—*The New Metamorphosis. Note to the New Edition of " Nares' Glossary."*

Ure's "Dictionary" (late edition by Hunt), informs us that there are no less than eighty fanciful names for biscuits, all expressive of articles in different forms, appearance, and taste, made of the same materials, with but little variation in the proportion in which they are used, the principal ingredients being flour and water, butter, milk, eggs, and carraway, nutmeg, cinnamon, or mace, or ginger, essence of lemon, neroli, or orange-flour water; called, in technical language, "flavourings."

LIX.—OLD TUSSER'S GOOD AND BAD HUSWIFERY.

Weak alchoholic drinks gently stimulate the digestive organs, and help them to do their work more fully and faithfully; and thus the body is sustained to a later period of life. Hence poets have called wine, "The milk of the old," and scientific philosophy owns the propriety of the term.—*Johnston's "Chemistry of Common Life."*

I.
Ill huswifery lieth
  Till nine of the clock;
Good huswifery trieth
  To rise with the cock.

II.
Ill huswifery tooteth
  To make herself brave;
Good huswifery looketh
  What household must have.

III.
Ill huswifery trusteth
  To him or to her;
Good huswifery lusteth
  Herself for to stir.

IV.
Ill huswifery careth
  For this, nor for that;
Good huswifery spareth
  For fear, yet wot not.

V.
Ill huswifery pricketh
  Herself up in pride;
Good huswifery tricketh
  Her house as a bride.

VI.
Ill huswifery one thing
  Or other must crave;
Good huswifery nothing
  But needful will have.

VII.
Ill huswifery moveth
  With gossip to spend;
Good huswifery loveth
  Her household to tend.

VIII.
Ill huswifery wanteth,
  With spending too fast;
Good huswifery canteth,
  The longer to last.

IX.
Ill huswifery easeth
  Herself with unknown;
Good huswifery pleaseth
  Herself with her own.

X.
Ill huswifery brooketh
  Mad toys in her head;
Good huswifery looketh
  That all things be fed.

XI.
Ill huswifery bringeth
  A shilling to nought;
Good huswifery singeth
  Her coppers full frought.

XII.
Ill huswifery rendeth
  And casteth aside;
Good huswifery mendeth,
  Else would it go wide.

XIII.
Ill huswifery sweepeth
  Her linen to gage;
Good huswifery keepeth
  To serve her in age.

XIV.
Ill huswifery craveth
  In secret to borrow;
Good huswifery saveth
  To-day for to-morrow.

XV.
Ill huswifery pineth
  (Not having to eat);
Good huswifery dineth
  With plenty of meat.

XVI.
Ill huswifery letteth
  The devil take all;
Good huswifery setteth
  Good brag of a small.

Mrs. Partington on Markets.—Mrs. Partington says she can't understand these 'ere market reports. She can understand how cheese can be lively, and pork can be active, and feathers drooping—that is, if it's raining; but how whisky can be steady, or hops quiet, or spirits dull, she can't see; neither how lard can be firm in warm weather, nor iron unsettled, nor potatoes depressed, nor flour rising, unless there had been yeast in it, and sometimes it wouldn't rise then.—*Newspaper paragraph.*

LX.—DRESS AND MANNERS AT A DINNER PARTY.

The finest linen, plenty of it, and country washing.—*Beau Brummel.*

Art. 1. Before leaving your house to go to a dinner, ball, or *soirée*, consult your glass twenty times, and scrupulously scrutinise each part of your *toilette*, thus assuring yourselves that there is nothing in contradiction *to your age*, or the exterior that nature has given you.

Art. 2. All men cannot be as handsome as Adonis, but they may at least endeavour not to appear uglier than they can help.

Art. 3. If you have little eyes, without lashes, and bordered with red, wear blue spectacles. A man may have bad eyes, it is absurd to have them very bad.

Art. 4. If you are diminutive, ugly, without grace or *tournure*, give up all intention of presenting yourself in society. You would be the butt of a thousand pleasantries; all the wit in the world would not save you.—French " *Code Civil.*"

Without altogether denying the wisdom of these admonitions, and fully admitting to the noble author of " Don Juan " that

Somehow, those looks
Make more impression than the best of books;

we must, notwithstanding, take the freedom to state that plain men, nay, even ugly little fellows, have met with tolerable success among the fair. Harry Jermyn, who carried all before him in his day, is described, in Grammont's "Memoirs," as of small stature, with a large head and thin legs; and the redoubtable Prince de Condé had equal or greater disadvantages of person to contend against. Wilkes's challenge to Lord Townsend is well known: " Your lordship is one of the handsomest men in England, and I am one of the ugliest; yet give me but half an hour's start, and I will enter the lists against you, with any woman you choose to name, because you will omit attentions on account of your fine exterior, which I shall double on account of my plain one." He used to add that it took him just half an hour to talk away his face: a strong proof, if true, of the sagacity of the French proverb: " Avec les hommes l'amour entre par les yeux; avec les femmes, par les oreilles;" for if ever man exceeded the privilege—dont jouissent les hommes d'être laids—(the phrase is De Sevigné's) it was Wilkes. He was so exceedingly ugly that a lottery-house keeper once offered him ten guineas not to pass his window whilst the tickets were drawing, for fear of his bringing ill luck upon the house. Balzac says that ugliness signifies little, provided it be *à laideur interessante*—Mirabeau's, for example, who desires a female correspondent, who had never seen him, and was anxious to form some notion of his face, to fancy a tiger marked with the smallpox. We rather think the whole philosophy of the matter is to be found in the concluding lines of Spenser's description:—

> " Who rough, and black, and filthy did appear;
> Unseemly man to please fair lady's eye,
> Yet he of ladies oft was loved dear,
> When fair faces were bid standen by:
> Oh, who does know the bent of woman's fantasie?"

Indissolubly connected with the topic of personal appearance, is the momentous one of dress; and it would be difficult to give a better illustration of its importance than an anecdote related of Gerard, the famous French painter. When a very young man he was the bearer of an introduction to Lanjuinais (the distinguished leader of the Girondists), and in the carelessness or confidence of genius he repaired to the (then) Imperial Councillor's house very shabbily attired. His reception was extremely cold; but in the few remarks that dropped from him in the course of conversation, Lanjuinais discovered such striking proof of talent, good sense, and amiability, that on Girard's rising to take leave, he rose too, and accompanied his visitor to the ante-chamber. The change was so striking, that Girard could not avoid an expression of surprise. "My young friend," said Lanjuinais, anticipating the inquiry, "we receive an unknown person according to his dress, we take leave of him according to his merit!" Napoleon was deeply impressed with the effects producible by dress, and on all important occasions kept a scrutinising eye on the personal appearance of his suite. A remarkable instance (related in the "Code Civil") occurred on the morning of his interview with Alexander of Russia, on the Niemen. Murat and General Dorsenne arrived at the same moment to take their places in his train; Murat, as usual, all epaulette, aigrette, lace, orders, and embroidery—Dorsenne in that elegant and simple costume which made him the model of the army. Napoleon saluted Dorsenne with a smile of marked favour; then, turning sharply round upon Murat, he said, "Go and put on your marshal's dress; you have the air of Franconi's." Goethe, the autocrat of German literature for nearly half a century, entertained similar sentiments; and during his dynasty at Weimar, an ordinary stranger's reception there depended very materially on the dress.
—*Extract;* " *Code of Manners and Etiquette,*" *Quarterly Review, vol.* 59, 1837.

A gentlewoman being at table, abroad or at home, must observe to keep her body straight, and lean not by any means with her elbows, nor, by ravenous gesture, discover a voracious appetite; talk not when you have meat in your mouth, and do not smack like a pig, nor venture to eat spoonmeat so hot that the tears stand in your eyes, which is as unseemly as the gentlewoman who pretended to have as little a stomach as she had a mouth, and therefore would not swallow her peas by spoonfuls, but took them one by one, and cut them in two before she could eat them. It is very uncomely to drink so large a draught that your breath is almost gone, and are forced to blow strongly to recover yourself; throwing down your liquor as into a funnel is an action fitter for a juggler than a gentlewoman. Thus much for your observation in general; if I am defective as to particulars, your own prudence, discretion, and curious observations will supply.—*The Ingenious Gentlewoman's Delightful Companion,* 1653.

COOKING DEPOT.—The "First Edinburgh Cooking Depôt" is situated in Dickson's Close, 118, High-street, a short way below the Tron Church. It is open from seven in the morning till six at night, and offers a breakfast consisting of a bowl of porridge, bowl of milk, cup of coffee or tea, and a slice of bread and butter, for 3d., and a dinner, which is to be had between the hours of one and four, consisting of broth or soup, bread, meat, potatoes, and plum, rice, or macaroni pudding, for 4½d. A cup of coffee or tea, a glass of sherbet or raspberry, &c., at 1d. each, can also be had at any time. Every article is guaranteed of the best quality, and any can be had separately; but the dinners and breakfasts, as such, are supplied only at the stated hours. The entrance to this establishment is not all that could be wished, but the hall itself is large, airy, and well-lighted; the viands appear to be really what they profess to be in regard to quality; in respect to quantity the portions are ample; and the service is prompt and sufficient, though wanting a little in the style of the Glasgow depôts—a homely style enough though that be. Mr. Buchanan is, we believe, well pleased with the patronage he has obtained, and contemplates the early opening of another large hall, mainly with a view to improving his accommodation for females, at present rather scanty.—*The Scotsman.*

LXI.—BEER.

Beer and wine met at Waterloo; wine, red with fury, boiling over with enthusiasm, mad with audacity, rose thrice against that hill on which stood a mass of immovable men—the sons of beer. You have read history; beer gained the day.—*Esquiros.*

Englishmen, all over the world, are a beer-drinking people, and they keep up the habit in the Colonies. There are extensive breweries in all the cities and inland towns of Australia. Tooth's brewery, at Sydney, is a large establishment, and so is Atkins's, at Melbourne; but the ale they make is very inferior to that of the Degraves, in Tasmania, now carried on by Mr. James Milne Wilson. This ale is now very much called for in Melbourne; and even Messrs. Allsop, of Burton-on-Trent, must look to their well-earned laurels, or else the Tasmania ale will supplant their bitter beer in the Indian market. This latter English firm have lately finished the largest brewery in the world, and their ales are deservedly in great repute. The *Lancet*, an excellent authority on such matters, informs us " that these bitter beers differ from all the other preparations of malt, in containing a smaller amount of extractive matter, thus being less viscid, and saccharine, and consequently more easy of digestion; they resemble, indeed, from their lightness, a *wine of malt* rather than an ordinary fermented infusion, and it is very satisfactory to find that a beverage of such general consumption is entirely free from every kind of impurity." The Messrs. Walker, Button, Scott, and James and Co., have large brewing establishments in Tasmania, and they are contending for the lead in the pale ale race; but at present " Wilson's brew " is, by universal consent, the favourite beverage, and has distanced his competitors; but Walker's bitter beer is highly esteemed; it may yet take the lead. Both kinds are exported to Sydney and Melbourne, and the public are benefited by a fair trade rivalry. The last beer brewed by Wilson has obtained the name of the " Golden tip ale," from its being made from very superior yellow hops. One of the firm in London lately went to a large hop merchant, and asked the price of a number of pockets for Tasmania. The merchant took the purchaser to a part of his store, and pointed out an inferior article, with which he said he supplied the Colonies; but that did not satisfy the applicant, who was then shown the best variety, which he purchased largely; and these were the hops used in the beer last in demand in Tasmania:—

> "Lo! too—Sir John Barleycorn is here!
> Stout, sound, and sparkling as his beer—
> That beer we love so well.
> Hear how his merry tale and joke
> The laughter of the crowd provoke,
> And jovial echoes swell."

The historical Nelson motto is peculiarly appropriate to the best brewer—*palmam qui meruit ferat*. The great heat in the Australias is prejudicial to brewing and malting, but Tasmania, being situate in a milder climate, has an advantage; besides, she is a large hop-growing country, which gives her a superiority over her sisters. As beer is more or less connected with eating, we are bound to give some short recipes for family brewing, although it will be seen, by dinners elsewhere described, that to a refined epicure malt at meals is decidedly a vulgar beverage. No one but a parvenu imbibes beer with choice viands; with those of a commonplace character we may presume such drink is permissible. Poor old Cobbett—all honour to him, for he was the type of a plain-spoken Englishman—did a world of good by teaching the poor how to brew in a kettle, on the same principle as tea-making. If you put into a tea-kettle a handful of malt, and fill it up with hot water, not quite boiling, and continue adding water, and pouring it out till it becomes tasteless, the strength of the malt will thus be extracted, just like the strength of the tea-leaves. The malt-tea boiled with a few hops, and when cooled to about blood-heat, having a little yeast added to it, to make it ferment, will produce you a quantity of ale and beer according to the strength you have made it. Apply this principle, which is the whole art of brewing, and you cannot be far out. A peck of malt and four ounces of hops will produce ten quarts of ale better than you can purchase, and for this purpose you require a large kettle and two pans. For a larger quantity you must have a mash-tub and oar, a sieve, and two coolers, a wicket-hose, a spigot and faucet, with two nine-gallon casks. These will cost about £2 new, and you may brew four bushels of malt with them, and allowing four pounds of hops, this will yield nine gallons of the best ale, and nine more of excellent table-beer. Beer, in London, is adulterated by almost every publican, and this truth is verified by the fact that the price which the publican pays the brewer would not leave a sufficient profit, unless adulteration took place. We wonder that more stringent laws are not made to prevent the sale of so much poisonous compounds; but it is satisfactory to make known that Dr. Hassall, when treating on this subject, states "that no case of adulteration can be proved against any of our great London brewers." Families would do well, therefore, to have their beer at first hands, or brew themselves, and the following is an excellent recipe for a small quantity:—

To Make Strong Beer or Ale.—Twelve bushels of malt to the

hogshead for beer, and eight for ale; for either pour the whole quantity hot, but not boiling, on at once, and let it infuse three hours, being covered; mash it in the first half-hour, and let it stand the remainder of the time. Run it on the hops, previously infused in water; for strong beer, three-quarters of a pound to a bushel; if for ale, half a pound. Boil them with the wort two hours from the time it begins to boil. Cool a pailful to add two quarts of yeast to, which will prepare it for putting to the rest when ready next day; but if possible, put them together the same night. Tun as usual. Cover the bung-hole with paper when the beer has done working; and when it is to be stopped, have ready a pound and a half of hops dried before the fire, put them into the bung-hole, and fasten it up. After the beer or ale has run from the grains, you can make table-beer of a similar quantity. This ale and beer will keep for years.

NOTE.—Our housekeeper tells us that a poor widow in his neighbourhood fitted up a brewery for the sum of 1s. 6d. A butter-tub, price 9d., is her mash-tub, three half-tubs of smaller size (at 3d. each) are her coolers. With these she brews half a bushel of malt at a time, and declares that she finds her home-brewed ale "very comfortable indeed."—*Home-brewed Ale by a Housekeeper*, 1804.

The cheap beer sold in many taverns in London is made by dividing the contents of two butts between three butts, and adding a bladder of porter extract (technically called P. E.) to each. This P. E. is a mixture of powdered coculus, roasted quassia, Spanish juice, pearlash, burnt sugar, &c., boiled up with treacle and sugar to the consistence of a thin extract, and put into bullocks' bladders.—*Medical Circular*.

Sugar Beer.—Very good sugar beer is made from eight pounds of brown sugar, a pound and three-quarters of hops, and six gallons of water. Pour boiling water on the sugar, and boil the hops; and when cool, add half a cup of yeast.

Sugar Beer without Yeast.—Boil from a quarter to half a pound of hops, according to taste, in two and a half gallons of water. Strain the water from the hops on six pounds and a quarter of brown sparkling sugar to dissolve it. Bruise and boil a quarter of a pound of ginger, add to it two and a half gallons of cold water, and fill up a five-gallon keg. Put in the tap, and bung it up tight; in a week the beer will be fit to drink, and continue brisk to the last.

SIFTINGS BEER.—A very pleasant and sharp drink is made in many parts of the Colonies by simply pouring boiling water on bran, adding sugar, and yeast to ferment; and before it has quite done working, bottling it for use.

A late writer states, that Belgium has for ages been celebrated for its beer. The finest is brewed in Louvain, where 200,000 casks are made annually, and that this liquor is more drank in Bavaria than any other country. The late king was so fond of this drink as to be personally acquainted with the interior of every beer-shop in his capital, and when you see a Bavarian peasant not working, you are sure to find him with a beer-can in his hand. Yet there is no sign of poverty in the country, nor any drunken people to be seen, so that, according to this theory of domestic economy, a country is more or less prosperous according to the malt liquor imbibed by its inhabitants. The Continental peasants have carried their habits to America, where the lager beer is made and in general use. A Tasmanian colonist travelling on the Continent of Europe has described to us the Vienna beer as remarkably pure, good, wholesome, and reasonable in price.

PORTER.—Before the year 1730 the malt liquors in general use in London were ale, beer, and twopenny; and it was customary to call for a pint, or tankard, of half-and-half, *i. e.*, half of ale and half of beer. In course of time it also became the practice to call for a pint, or tankard, of *three-threads*, meaning a third of ale, beer, and twopenny; and thus the publican had the trouble to go to three casks, and turn three cocks, for a pint of liquor. To avoid this inconvenience and waste, a brewer of the name of Harwood conceived the idea of making a liquor which should partake of the same united flavours of ale, beer, and twopenny. He did so, and succeeded, calling it *entire*, or *entire butt*, meaning that it was drawn entirely from one cask or butt; and as it was a very hearty and nourishing liquor, and supposed to be suitable for porters and other working-people, it obtained the name of PORTER.—*Paris.*

Lager Beer.—The Bavarian lager beer, slowly fermented, is highly appreciated. Ure writes that considerable interest among men of science in favour of the Bavarian beer process has been excited since the appearance of Liebig's " Organic Chemistry." In the introduction to this admirable work he says, " The beers of England and France, and for the most part those of Germany, become gradually sour by contact of air. This defect does not belong to the beer of Bavaria, which may be preserved at pleasure in half-full casks, as well as full ones, without alteration in the air. This precious quality must be ascribed to a peculiar process employed for fermenting the wort, called in German *unterghärung*, or fermentation from below, which has solved one of the finest theoretical problems. We will endeavour to condense the mode of manufacturing this renowned lager beer. For the winter beer the worts are brought down to about 50° F., and the beer is transferred to the fermenting tuns at from 54° to 59° F. For the summer *lagerbier* the worts must be brought down in the cooler at from 43° to 45°, and put into the fermenting tubs at from 40° to 43°. A few hours afterwards, while the wort is still at the temperature of $63\frac{1}{2}°$, a quantity must be made, called *vorstellen* (fore-setting) in German, by mixing the proportion of *unter-life* (yeast) intended for the whole brewing with a barrel or a barrel and a half of the worts in a small tub called the *gahr-tiene*, stirring them well together, so that they may uniformly run into fermentation; the *lobb* is in this state to be added to the worts. The *lobb* is known to be ready when it is covered with a white froth from one quarter to half an inch thick, during which it has to be well covered up. The wort in the tun should, in the course of from twelve to twenty-four hours, exhibit a white froth round the rim, and even a slight whiteness in the middle; after another twelve or twenty-four hours the froth should appear in curls; and in a third like period these curls should change into a frothy brown mass. In from twenty-four to forty-eight hours the barm should have fallen down in portions through the beer, so as to allow it to be seen in certain points. In this case it may be turned over into the small ripening tuns in the course of five or six days. But when the worts have been set to ferment at from 41° to 43°, they require from eight to nine days. The beer is transferred, after being freed from the top yeast by a skimmer, by means of the stop-cock near the bottom of the large tun. It is either first run into an intermediate vessel, in order that the top and bottom portions may be well mixed, or into each of the *lager* casks, in a number series; like quantities of the top and bottom portions are introduced. In the ripening cellars the temperature cannot be too low. The best-keeping beer can never be brewed unless the temperature of the worts at setting, and, of course, the fermenting vault, be as low as 50° F. In Bavaria the Government take great pains to improve this national beverage, by encouraging the growth of the best qualities of malt and barley; and Government inspectors are apppointed to see that no deleterious substances are used. Zimmermann assumes the merit of having introduced Carrageen moss as a clarifier into the making of beer. He says one ounce is sufficient for twenty-five gallons of beer, and that it operates not only in the act of boiling with the hops, but in that of cooling, as also in the squares and casks before the fermentation has begun. The German test of clarification with the topers is, when they can read a newspaper while a tall glass beaker of beer is placed between them and the candle. M. Zimmermann professes to have also discovered an unexceptionable solvent in tartaric acid, one pound of which dissolved in twenty quarts of water, is capable of dissolving two pounds of ordinary isinglass, forming finings which may be diluted with water at pleasure.

The *lagerbier* once introduced in the Australasian Colonies would, without doubt, supersede all other brewings; and for this reason we have bestowed much of our limited space in its mode of manufacture.

ALL FOR BEER.—Listen to the conversation of Bavarians; it turns on beer. See to what the thoughts of the exile recur—to the beer of the country. Sit down in a coffee-house or eating-house, and the waiter brings you beer unordered; and when you have emptied your glass, replenishes it without a summons. Tell a doctor the climate of Munich does not agree with you, and he will ask you if you drink enough beer. Arrive at a place before the steamer or train is due, and you are told you have so long to drink beer. Go to balls, and you find it replaces champagne with the rich, and dancing with the poor. I once went to a servants' ball, and stayed there some time; but when I came away, dancing had not began, and all the society were sitting still as ever in drinking beer.—*Wilberforce's " Social Life in Munich."*

Berlin, White, or Pale Beer (*Wess-bier*).—This is the national beverage of Prussia Proper, and is brewed from one part of barley malt and five parts of wheat malt, mingled, moistened, and crushed between rollers. This mixture is worked up first with water at 95° F., in the proportion of thirty quarts per *scheffel* of the malt, to which pasty mixture of seventy quarts of boiling water are forthwith added, and the whole is mashed in the tun. After it has been left there a little to settle, a portion of the thin liquor is drawn off by the tap, transferred to the copper, and then for each bushel of malt there is added to it a decoction of half a pound of Altmark hops, separately prepared. This hopped wort, after half an hour's boiling, is turned back, with the hops, into the mash-tun, of which the temperature should now be 162° F., but not more. In half an hour the wort is to be drawn from off the grains, and pumped into the cooler. The grains are afterwards mashed with from forty to fifty quarts of boiling water per *scheffel* of malt, and this infusion is drawn off, and added to the former malt. The whole mixture is set at 66° F., with a due proportion of top yeast or ordinary barm, very moderately fermented.

Potato Beer.—The potatoes, being well washed, are to be rubbed down by a grating cylinder into a hopper, and then they are crushed and ground into pulp. For every *scheffel* of potatoes eighty quarts of water are to be put with them into a copper and made to boil. Crushed malt, to the amount of twelve *scheffels*, is to be worked about in the mash-tub, with ninety gallons (English) of cold water, to a thick pap, and then six barrels (English) of cold water are to be suddenly introduced, with constant stirring, and left to stand an hour at rest. The potatoes having been meanwhile boiled to a fine starch paste, the whole malt mash, thin and thick, is to be speedily ladled into the copper, and this mixture is to be stirred for an hour, taking care to keep the temperature at from 144° to 156° F. all the time, in order that the *diastase* of the malt may convert the starch present in the two substances into sugar and dextrine. This transformation is made manifest by the white pasty liquid becoming transparent and thin. Whenever this happens the fire is to be raised, to make the mash boil, and to keep it at its heat for ten minutes. The fire is then withdrawn, the contents of the copper are to be transferred into the mash, worked well there, and left to settle for half an hour; during which time the copper is to be washed out, and quickly charged once more with boiling water. The clear wort is to be drawn off from the tun, as usual, and boiled as soon as possible with the due proportion of hops, and the boiling water may be added in any desired quantity to the drained mash for the second mashing. Wort made in this way is said to have no flavour whatever of the potato, and to clarify more easily than malt wort, from its containing a smaller proportion of gluten relatively to that of saccharine.

We have condensed the foregoing recipe from Ure's "Dictionary," and in reference to the potato beer, we should state that Zimmermann thinks it is quite equal, if not superior, to pure malt beer, both in appearance and quality.

Professor Brande gives the quantity of alcohol (of the specific of 825 at 60) by measure contained in 100 parts, as follows:—

    Brown stout ... ... 6·80
    London porter ... ... 4·20
    Small beer ... ... 1·28

We must conclude this notice of malt liquors with an anecdote from the "Quarterly," which is *beery*. Madame Pasta, when in England, was asked by a literary lady of high distinction whether she drank as much porter as usual, "No, mia cara, prendo *half-and-half*, adesso."

ALE.—Lord Bacon attributed anti-consumptive virtues to ale; and Dr. Hodgkin asserts that the invalid who has been reduced almost to extremity by severe or lingering illness, finds in well apportioned draughts of sound beer one of the most important helps to his recovery of health, strength, and spirits. This is when drank in moderation, but if taken to excess, sleepiness follows its use, showing that the narcotic principle of the hop produces an effect upon the brain. In seven cases out of ten, malt-liquor drunkards die of apoplexy or palsy; thus is a liquor abused, which, if taken in moderation, is wholesome; so much so, that Sydenham, in his last treatise, writes, "A draught of small beer is to me instead of a supper." While the great bard makes Autolycus say, in the *Winter's Tale*, that "A quart of ale is a dish for a king." Jackson, the celebrated trainer—

"Men unpractised in exchanging knocks
Must go to Jackson ere they learn to box"—

affirmed that, if any person accustomed to wine, would try malt liquor for a month, he would find himself so much the better for it that he would soon take the one and abandon the other. Herodotus states, that in early history the art of making a fermented liquor from barley was discovered by the Egyptians. Dr. Paris writes, "The liquor called ale was originally made of barley, malt, and yeast alone." We are told by one of the oldest

English writers on medical subjects (Andrew Boorde) that those who put in any other ingredient "sophisticated the labour. It is," he says, "the natural drink of an Englishman; but beer, on the other hand, which is made of malt, hops, and water, is the national drink of the Dutchman, and of late is much used in England, to the great detriment of many Englishmen." As the climate of England is not congenial to the growth of the vine, this species of liquor is perhaps more universal than in any other country, and it has therefore been denominated *vinum Britannicum*. Every prudent housewife should sing or say, in the homely language of Burns,

" We'll make our maut, and we'll brew and drink,
We'll laugh, sing, and rejoice, man."

LXII.—EGGS.

My honest friend, will you take eggs for money?—*Old Play*.

The eggs of birds are nutritious, and easily digestible, and when lightly cooked by boiling, and eaten with a little salt, are admirably adapted as an aliment for the sick and delicate. When boiled hard or fried, they are rendered less digestible, and possess no advantage in this respect over butcher's meat. A new-laid egg beaten up in a cup of tea, coffee, or chocolate, is an excellent ingredient in the breakfast of a person with a poor appetite, and is very supporting. A glass of wine, beer, or porter similarly treated, along with a biscuit, has been recommended as a light and nutritious luncheon or supper, well suited to the debilitated or dyspeptic. Raw eggs are powerfully anti-scorbutic, and from containing a large quantity of iodine and the phosphates, are superior to cod-liver oil in all the cases in which this last is ordered, occurring in persons with delicate or irritable stomachs. These good qualities are, however, lost, if they are boiled longer than two minutes for a small one, and three minutes for a large one, or are eaten with much salt. The addition of fresh salad oil vastly increases their medicinal virtues. A fresh egg contains about the same amount of nourishment as one and a half ounces of fresh meat, and one ounce of wheaten flour, but in a more digestible form.—*Cooley's " Practical Receipts."*

Omelette aux Fines Herbes.—Take three eggs, well beaten, one shalot, parsley, and a little ham or bacon, chopped very fine all together, with a little cayenne and salt to taste. Put two ounces of butter into the frying-pan, and when it boils pour in the batter and fry. It will take about five minutes. Serve with brown gravy, vinegar, and cayenne.

Sweet Omelette.—Proceed as above and omit the herbs, add a tablespoonful of milk, a spoonful of sugar, and a little salt. Fry of a light brown and serve with sifted sugar over them.

OMELETTES.—Their proper *cuisine* is a task that requires care and attention. It has been said that no one could suit the taste of the Hero of Blenheim and Malplaquet so well as Sarah, first Duchess of Marlborough. As a general rule, when eggs are used on any occasion, the whites and yolks must be separately whisked; but Miss Leslie thinks otherwise, so we transcribe her directions:—"Those who do not know the right way to beat eggs complain much of the fatigue, and, therefore, leave off too soon. There will be no fatigue if they are beaten with the proper stroke, and with wooden rods, and in a shallow, flat-bottomed earthen pan. The coldness of the pan retards the lightness of the eggs. For the same reason do not use a metal egg-beater. In beating them do not move the elbow, but keep it close to the side. Move only the hand at the wrist, and let the stroke be quick, short, and horizontal; putting the egg-beater always down to the bottom of the pan, which should therefore be shallow. Do not leave off as soon as the eggs are in a foam—they are then only beginning to be light—but persist till after the foaming has ceased, and the bubbles have all disappeared. Continue till the surface is as smooth as a mirror, and the beaten egg is thick as a rich boiled custard; for till then it will not be really light. When white of egg is to be used without any yolk, it should be beaten till it stands alone on the rods, not falling when held up."—*Leslie's "Confectioner."*

Boiled Eggs.—Put the eggs into boiling water, and let them take about three minutes. They are said to be good for clearing the voice.

Poached Eggs.—This is a very difficult operation in cookery. It has been said that one of the London clubs in want of a cook, put the first preliminary question—"Can you boil a potato?" But a more proper query would be—can you poach eggs properly? To proceed—put in a stewpan a pint of water, with half a table-spoonful of salt, and three of vinegar; when simmering break in the eggs, and let them remain until the yolk is set. Serve on toast or spinach. If the cook cannot do this well, he had better have recourse to a tin stand, which contains a receptacle for each egg, and the stand is immersed in the pan containing boiling water until the egg is sufficiently done.

The lightest mode of preparing eggs for the table is to boil them only as long as is necessary to coagulate slightly the greater part of the white without depriving the yolk of its fluidity.—*Dr. Pearson's " Mat. Alim."*

Eggs Dressed with Oil.—This is by far the most simple way of dressing eggs, and the most nutritious. Pour into a Dutch oven or cheese-toaster two table-spoonfuls of salad oil. Break the eggs into the tin, which ought to take out, and when the yolk is set send up the tin, with the eggs in it, hot.

Fried Eggs.—Break the eggs into a pan with boiling fat, and spoon some fat over them; mind the yolks are not done hard.

The egg, as a whole, is richer in fat than beef. It is equalled in this respect, among common kinds of food, only by pork and by eels. The white of the egg is, however, entirely free from fat; and it is a very constipating variety of animal food, so that it requires much fat to be eaten along with it when consumed in any quantity, in order that this quality may be counteracted. It is, no doubt, because experience has long proved this, in the stomachs of the people, that "eggs and bacon" have been a popular dish among Gentile nations from time immemorial.—*J. F. W. Johnston.*

Eggs au Miroir.—Spread a piece of butter upon a dish that can be set on the fire, break the eggs over it, adding salt, pepper, and two spoonfuls of milk; place it on a slow fire, with a red-hot shovel over it, and serve when the eggs are set.

Eggs à l'Ardennaise.—Beat to a froth the whites of six eggs which have been seasoned as for an omelette, pour this froth into a buttered baking-tin, and pour across it four spoonfuls of cream, dropped into it at equal distances, the yolks whole; bake, but not too briskly, and serve.

Eggs for Salad.—Eggs for salad require to boil for six minutes, and, when done, put them into cold water to harden.

Omelette Soufflé.—Put the yolks of six eggs into a basin and the whites into another, with a little rasped lemon-peel, a spoonful of orange-flower water, some powdered sugar, and a little salt; whip the yolks into a froth; mix the yolks and whites lightly together; then put a lump of fresh butter into an omelette pan, and, when it boils, pour the omelette into the pan; when the bottom of it has become firm, turn it over into the dish to be baked in, the sides of which may be raised with paper. Bake it in an oven or before the fire. The moment it has risen, it must be sent to table, or it will sink. This is a far-famed Parisian dish.

The cookery aphorism is peculiarly applicable to all *soufflés*—"Better the guests wait a little for the dish, than the dish, when done, wait for the guests."

Omelette aux Confitures.—Beat up the yolks and whites of six eggs separate; add to the yolks a little grated lemon-peel; then add the whites, and beat the whole well together, adding a little cream, two spoonfuls of orange or apple marmalade, apricot or gooseberry jam, currant jelly, or any preserve. Fry and finish in the same way as a sugar omelette.

The French are said to have several hundred modes of dressing eggs; but the more simple manner they are cooked the more nourishment they afford, according to medical authority. The most delicate eggs are those of the turkey, guinea-fowl, and plover.

To Keep Eggs.—Eggs varnished with lac and spirits of wine will keep good for twelve months according to M. Reumeur; while M. Gagne states that a paste made of lime, salt, and cream of tartar, in the proportion of one bushel of lime, two pounds of salt, and eight ounces of cream of tartar, adding a sufficient quantity of water, will keep eggs fresh for two years. It is said that they will keep eight or ten months in dry salt. Ure writes, that eggs coated with gum-arabic, and packed in charcoal, will keep good for a year; and that lime-water, or milk of lime, is another eligible mode. For long sea voyages, the surest mode of preserving eggs is to dry up the albumen and yolk by first triturating them into a homogeneous paste; then evaporating this in an air stove, or a water bath, heated to 125 degrees, and putting up the dried mass in vessels which may be made air-tight. When used, it should be dissolved in three parts of cold or tepid water.

NATIVE EGGS.—The ibis, or bran's eggs, have been procured in great numbers. These eggs are of a white colour, rather sharp at one end, and about the size of a turkey's egg. The albumen is, however, quite different from that of any other egg, being, even when boiled, pellucid, gelatinous, and fat in appearance, and very small in quantity compared with the yolk. On the whole this egg may be pronounced not particularly palatable, and will never be used except as a makeshift, when neither hen nor duck eggs can be procured.—*Sydney Morning Herald*

DINNER IN THE MANNER OF THE ANCIENTS. — This here, gentlemen, is a boiled goose, served up in a sauce composed of pepper, loyage, coriander, mint, rue, anchovies, and oil! I wish, for your sakes, gentlemen, it was one of the geese of Ferrara, so much celebrated among the ancients for the magnitude of their livers, one of which is said to have weighed upwards of two pounds; with this food, exquisite as it was, did the tyrant Heliogabalus regale his hounds. But, I beg pardon, I had almost forgot the soup, which, I hear, is so necessary an article at all tables in France. At each end there are dishes of the sulacubacia of the Romans; one is made of parsley, pennyroyal, cheese, pine tops, honey, vinegar, brine, eggs, cucumbers, onions, and hen livers; the other is much the same as the *soup maigre* of this country. Then there is a loin of boiled veal, with fennel and carraway seeds, in a pottage composed of pickle, oil, honey, and flour; and a curious hashis of the lights, liver, and blood of a hare, together with a dish of roasted pigeons. Monsieur le Baron, shall I help you to a plate of this soup?—*Peregrine Pickle.*

LXIII.—MAGICAL DRINKS.

Hecate.—And now about the cauldron sing,
Like elves and fairies in a ring,
Enchanting all that you put in.—*Macbeth.*

The professors of ancient as well as modern magic found powerful auxiliaries in the soporific drugs and poisonous beverages which derange the intellectual as well as the physical condition of man. The waters of Lethe, and the beverage of Mnemosyne, which killed Timochares in three months after he quaffed it in the cave of Trophonius, are examples of the soporific and stupefying drinks of the ancients. The *nephentes* of Homer, the *hyoscyamus datura*, the *solanum*, the *potomantis*, the *salatophyllis*, and the *archamenis* of Pliny, the *ophinsia* of the Ethiopians, and the *muchamore* of Kamschatka, were all the instruments of physical and intellectual degradation. The Old Man of the Mountain, in the time of the Crusades, is said to have enchanted his youthful followers by narcotic and exhilarating draughts. The Hindoo widow is supposed to ascend the funeral pile physically as well as morally fortified against pain. The victims of the Inquisition, similarly prepared, are said to have frequently slept in the midst of their torments; and M. Taboureau assures us that the merciful gaolers make their prisoners swallow soap dissolved in water (the vehicle, doubtless, of more powerful medicaments) to enable them to bear the agonies of torture.—*North British Review.*

An Intelligent Dinner Companion.—Coleridge once dined in company with a person who listened to him and said nothing for a long time, while he nodded his head to the remarks made at the appropriate time, and Coleridge set him down as intelligent. At length some apple dumplings were placed on the table, and the listener had no sooner seen them, than he burst forth, "Them's the jockies for me!" Coleridge adds, "I wish Spurzheim could have examined the fellow's head."—*Table Anecdotes.*

LXIV.—WINES.

The Frenchman lives under a clear sky, drinks a brisk and joyous wine, and lives on food which keeps his senses in constant activity. The Englishman, on the contrary, dwells on a damp soil, under a sun which is almost cold, swills beer and porter, and consumes a quantity of butter and cheese.—*Pelet's "Napoleon in Council."*

As good eating requires equally good drinking, it is necessary that we should say something on wines. The antiquity of their existence is referred to in Genesis ix. 20 :—" And Noah began to be a husbandman, and he planted a vineyard; " and a modern Latin poet describes the vine as a gift from Heaven, to console mankind for the miseries entailed on them by the Deluge. So writes M'Culloch. The wines generally used are port, sherry, claret, champagne, Madeira, hock, and Marsala. Most of these wines are *doctored* for the English market by adulteration. To such an extent is this trade carried, that, within a given time, the Channel Islands received 210 pipes from Oporto, and managed to export to London 2,072 pipes; so that the Jersey folks made one pipe of real port into ten spurious ones. Dr. Gorman, in his evidence before the select committee of the House of Commons, stated—

> That no natural sherry came to this country; no wine house will send it. The article you get is a mixed article. If they gave you the natural produce of Xeres it would not suit you; in all probability you would say it was an inferior wine. Our taste is artificial, because we are not a wine-drinking people.

Brande informs us that sherry, of a due age, and in good condition, is a fine, perfect, and wholesome wine—free from excess of acid, and possessing a dry, aromatic flavour and fragrancy; but, as procured in the ordinary market, it is of fluctuating and anomalous quality, often destitute of all aroma, and tasting of little else than alcohol and water. The clarets of France, Château Margaus, Haut Buon, Latour, Larore, and Lafitte—these are the Medoc wines—are all of high repute; while the inferior sorts—M'Culloch says in his "Dictionary"—are shipped at Bordeaux as low as £2 per hogshead. Champagne was pronounced by the faculty of Paris, in 1778, to be the finest of all wines. The question whether the wines of Champagne or Burgundy were entitled to the preference, was agitated during the reign of Louis XIV. with extraordinary keenness. The Rector of the University of Beauvais published a classical ode, in which champagne was eulogised, and its superiority vindicated, with a spirit, vivacity, and delicacy worthy of the theme. The citizens of Rheims were not ungrateful to M. Coffin, but they liberally rewarded him with an appropriate and munificent donation of the wine he had so happily panegyrised. M. Gréneau wrote an ode in praise of Burgundy; but, unlike its subject, it was flat and insipid, and failed to procure any recompense to its author. There is generally a good supply of claret in bond in the docks in London. Its price varies from £12 for the inferior, to £50 for the superior growth. What are called shipping clarets may be bought from £5 to £10 per hogshead. The finest case clarets sell in bond at about 50s. per dozen; but well-flavoured wine may be bought in bond at 15s. or 16s. per dozen. When the Russian army of invasion passed through Champagne, they took away with them 600,000 bottles; but M. Moet considered himself a gainer by the loss, as his orders from Russia have more than doubled every year since. The wine sovereigns at Epernay used to be M. Moet and Madame Cliquot. The former died in 1841, aged eighty years. The King of Prussia was so fond of the lady's champagne, that he received, in consequence, the *soubriquet* of King Cliquot. M. Moet employed 200 workpeople, and kept a stock of three millions of bottles of wine. Every stranger visiting the establishment is invariably presented with a bottle of the best wine as a present. Professor Brande states that champagne should never be drank until its active effervescence is over, for its body and flavour is concealed by the carbonic acid. The poet Crabbe has written—

> Champagne the courtier drinks, the spleen to chase;
> The colonel, Burgundy; and port, his grace.

Good port wine, duly kept, is, when taken in moderation, one of the most wholesome of vinous liquors. It strengthens the muscular system, assists the digestive powers, accelerates the spirits, and sharpens the mental energies. In *excess*, it is, perhaps, the most mischievous of wines, and most likely to produce those permanent derangements of the digestive organs which follow the habitual use of distilled spirits.—*Brande.*

The Burgundy wines are remarkable for richness of flavour and perfume; a red wine of that kind (Chambertin), history has it, was the favourite drink of the great conqueror of Europe, as well as Louis XIV. When a French regiment on the march comes in sight of the Clos Vougeot, in Burgundy, the commanding officer orders a halt and a presentation of arms, as an honour to the grape.* Sauterne and Barsac are light wines, well flavoured, and will keep a long time. The Johannesberger stands at the head of the wines of the Rhine; and next in order is Steinberger. They do not arrive at maturity for five or six years, and will keep twice that period. Tokay,† so called from a town in Hungary, is the first of the liqueur wines, and Malmsey Madeira comes afterwards. The Hockheimer, or hock, is made from a few vines that grow near Hockheim, on the Maine. Scharrberger and Greenhauser are called the nectars of the Moselle. The Laubenheim and Heerstein, as well as the other delicate Moselle wines, are used for the table. The best German red wine is the Asmanshausen. In 1836 the Duke of Nassau sold the finest cask in his cellar for £500, at the rate of £1 4s. per bottle. The Italian wine is Marsala. The Cape of Good Hope wines are inferior, except the luscious Constantia. Port wine is the produce of the upper Douro, and requires time to fit it for the table; but it is soon made so, and to have on its bottles the crust of age. Spain produces an enormous quantity of wine, which is not suitable to the English market. Mr. Porter estimated that—good, passable, and bad—it amounted to 120,000,000 gallons; but Sir E. Tennent states that, except in Andalusia and a few other places, its manufacture is so imperfect, its qualities so peculiar, and its flavour so extraordinary, from carelessness, dirt, and other qualities, it is not in demand in England. The Montillado of Spain is a wine which appears to depend for its character on a white soil, containing seventy per cent. of carbonate of lime; and the Manzanilla is the produce of red earths, somewhat sandy. From unknown causes, it is certain that there are wines raised in a few districts that no art or care has hitherto succeeded in producing of equal goodness in other places, such as Tokay, Constantia, Johannesberger, the best clarets, Burgundy, and champagne.

---

* BURGUNDY.—In richness of flavour and perfume, and all the more delicate qualities of the juice of the grape, they rank as the first in the world; and it was not without reason that the Dukes of Burgundy, in former times, were designated as the princes *des bons vins.—Henderson.*

The best of the red wine of Champagne are those of Verzy, Verzenay, Maily, Bouzy, and St. Basle. The Clos St. Thierry, in the vicinity of Rheims, produces wine which unites the colour and aroma of Burgundy to the lightness of champagne.

† TOKAY. — A wine made at Tokay, in Hungary; it is luscious, and yet has an agreeable quickness of flavour. It is usually more or less turbid, and is the only wine which is preferred in that state, and consequently agitated before it is poured into the glass.—*Brande.*

The vine, when transferred to a different soil, loses its characteristics. It has been found that vines from Spain, France, and Germany transplanted to the Cape of Good Hope and Australia have, in no one instance, produced wine assimilating to the original plant; and the same result has occurred with European wines transplanted to America. The richest vines, as a general rule, have been grown on the sites of extinct volcanoes. The produce of the celebrated Lafitte vineyard, near Bordeaux, was sold in the year 1848 at 4,000 francs per tun, while the wines in the neighbourhood only realised 200 francs. The proprietors of a vineyard, which is only separated from that of Lafitte by a narrow gully, expended a large sum in endeavouring to improve their ground and assimilate it to Lafitte. They did not succeed, and were ruined. The costly Clos Vougeot grows only on a farm of eighty acres of land. Romanée Conti is but six and a half; and the famous Mont Rachel of the Côte d'Or is distinguished into three classes, of which one sells at less than two-thirds of the other two. Yet these qualities, writes Henderson, are produced from vineyards separated from one another by a foot-path. Sir Emerson Tennent, on "Wine— Its Uses and Taxation," tells us that only one small valley in Madeira produces the Malmsey; and at the Cape of Good Hope, there is only one Constantia vineyard. Liebig, in his "Organic Chemistry," has the following remarks on the Vougeot:—"It is well known that wine and fermented liquors generally contain, in addition to alcohol, other substances which could not be detected before their fermentation, and which must, therefore, have been formed during that process. The smell and taste which distinguish wine from all other fermented liquors are known to depend upon an ether of a volatile and highly combustible acid, which is of an oily nature, and to which the name of *œmanthic æther* has been given." The most expensive wine is Vernuth, made in Austrian Germany. Madeira used to be a fruity and generous wine, but the vine disease ("the *oidium Tuckeri*") has caused sad destruction.* Teneriffe is far inferior to Madeira. A pipe of Madeira was fished up near Antwerp in 1814, where it had lain in the water since 1778, and sold to Baron Rothschild for nearly its weight in gold. Dry Lisbon and Bucellas, white wines, are deservedly in high repute. The American wines,† Catawba, grown in Virginia and Missouri, and the Isabella, are highly spoken of. The Catawba is delicious in flavour, and more devoid of

---

* BARON LIEBEG ON THE VINE DISEASE.—A French landholder in the department of the Indre, whose vines were severely attacked by oïdium, had asked my advice about a remedy, the sulphur being no longer of any use. I advised him to manure his vineyards with wood ashes and phosphates. Last October he sent me a document, signed by a number of persons who had seen his vines. It declared that those which had been manured with ashes and phosphates had produced healthy fruit in abundance, while others close by, which had not received these manures, were the prey of oïdium.

† Light, dry wines, such as hock, claret, Burgundy, Rhenish, and hermitage are, generally speaking, more salubrious than the stronger varieties, as port, sherry, or Madeira. Claret, in particular, is the most wholesome wine known; champagne, except in cases of weak digestion, is one of the safest wines that can be drunk. Its intoxicating effects are rapid, but exceedingly transient, and depend partly upon the carbonic acid which is evolved from it, and partly from the alcohol, which is suspended in this gas, being applied rapidly and extensively to a large surface of the stomach.—*Macnish.*

alcohol than any other wine. This vine was noticed by Major Adlum, who found it growing near Washington in 1826, and the grape is of a peculiar musty taste. It has been immortalised by Longfellow :—

> "For richest and best
> Is wine of the West,
> That grows by the beautiful river,
> Whose sweet perfume
> Fills all the room
> With a benison on the giver."

Ure tells us, that two millions of gallons of wine are made in the (dis) United States, from 7,000 acres of vines, of the value of three millions of dollars. The wines of Australia Proper obtained a high meed of praise at the French Exposition, the Camden wines being much prized, and no one can deny that our Gallic friends are the best judges. The South Australian wines are the Shiraz, the Verdeilho, the Pineau, the Muscat, the Reisling, and the Montura. The South Australian grapes are the largest in size of any of the Australias; but the finest fruit do not ferment the best wines. The wines made in New South Wales (Australia) are free from acidity, fruity in flavour, devoid of spirit, and mellow on the palate. Although no poet has spoken their praise, they will soon force themselves on public notice. We have used M'Arthur's Camden, Blake's Kaludah, and Lindeman's Cawarra, and cannot decide which is the superior; but it is only justice to the latter to say, that the manufacturer was awarded a first-class medal at the last International Exhibition. No less than sixty different samples of colonial wines from the elder colony were shown at the Exhibition, of whom the M'Arthurs produced twenty-five sorts. One of the family received the honour of knighthood after the French Exhibition, and if it was given on account of the wines produced, the higher title should have been bestowed, for the Australias owe the immense wool export of this day entirely to this respected family. We hope that it will not be considered a digression, when we ask—Who is so justly entitled to the consideration of the Sovereign, and the honours that flow from Her Majesty in the dispensation of the royal prerogative, as those, who, by any means, contribute largely to the exports and imports of the empire; to the employment of the people in the arts, manufactures, and commerce, and thus directly add to the wealth, the renown, and the greatness of the mother country? There is a curious custom-house anomaly at present in operation. One of the Australias cannot use the wine of the adjoining colony without paying a similar duty to that exacted from wines of foreign growth. The interchange of articles grown in each colony should be free and unfettered.* Hen-

---

* ANCIENT WINES.—The wines of Lesbos and Chios among the Greeks, and the Falernian and Acuban among the Romans, have acquired an immortality of renown. Great uncertainty, however, prevails as to the nature of these wines. Dr. Henderson thinks that the most celebrated of them all, the Falernian, approached, in its most essential characters, near to Madeira. In preparing these wines, the ancients often inspissated them till they became of the consistence of honey, or even thicker. These were diluted with water previously to their being drunk; and, indeed, the habit of mixing wine with water seems to have prevailed much more in antiquity than in modern times.—M'Culloch's "Com. Dic."

derson, in his "History of Wines," informs us that a stony or gravelly soil is preferable to all others, that hills are preferred to plains, and that in rainy seasons the produce will be increased, but that the grapes will be poor and insipid. It requires a hilly and dry climate to produce good dry wines; so that we may anticipate that Australia Proper will become a wine country, and that the climate of New Zealand will be too moist for the purpose. Mr. Boothby, the compiler of the South Australian statistics, states that last year 20,000 gallons were exported, and that, in his opinion, the wine will become a great export. The acreage in vines was 4,777.

> Cool the wine, Doris. Pour it into the cup
> Simple, unmixed with water. Such dilutition
> Serves only to wash out the spirit of man.
> *Translation from Diphilus in the Greek Anthology,*
> *"Fraser's Magazine."*

The following is a table, showing the quantity of alcohol (of the specific gravity of 825·60) by measure contained in 100 parts of the respective wines, Australian and American excluded :—

	BRANDE.	JONES.
Marsala	25·09	21·1
Port	22·96	23·2
Madeira	22·27	19·7
Sherry	19·17	24·7
Teneriffe	19·79	
Lisbon	18·94	
Bucellas	18·49	
White Hermitage	17·43	13·2
Claret	15·20	11·1
Malmsey	16·40	
Burgundy	17·84	13·2
Hock	12·08	13·0
Johannesberger, 1788	8·71	
Barsac	13·86	
Champagne	12·01	14·8
Cote Rotie	12·32	
Tokay	9·88	

Dr. Bence Jones's is a later calculation than Brande's by forty years. The sherry is now stronger. The port much the same. The Marsala weaker. The Burgundy and claret have less alcohol in their composition, and the wines of the Rhine about the same strength.

The author of the "Art of Dining" gives this good advice :—"The wines which may be deemed indispensable at a complete English dinner —which, consequently it is of paramount importance to have good—are sherry, champagne, port, and claret. The palate is confused and made indiscriminating by a greater number, although anything good of its kind will always be welcome as a variety." Shakespeare, in "As You Like It," says, that "good wine needs no bush," as in days of yore vintners always hung up a bush in front of their houses, an ivy bush being held sacred to Bacchus. There is a little matter that it would not be *comme il faut* to forget. White wines are taken with white meats, and red wines with brown meats. Champagne should never be stinted at dinner, for there is nothing adds more to the success of a party than a profusion of the sparkling Ay, the perfumed Avise, or the limpid Sillery; these being the wines Viscount Chelsea favourably reported on. Besides, another advantage to be derived from a bountiful supply of the wines of the Marne, the ladies are generally prevailed upon to take an extra glass. When they have left the dinner table, the masculine sex may revel in the stronger Hermitage, Cote Rotie, or Clos Vougert; and, before we leave the subject of wines, we must call the attention of the Amphitryon to the poet's reminder:—

> I hate a lingering bottle,
> Which with the landlord makes too long a stand,
> Leaving all claretless the unmoistened throttle;
> Especially with politics on hand.

NOTE.—Since the above was written, the report of the jury upon the wines and spirits exhibited in 1862 has been issued, and as nearly 8,000 samples had to be carefully examined, the lateness of the report is satisfactorily accounted for. Respecting the samples submitted from the Australian colonies, the jury say:—"We find these wines of the character of the German wines; others again more resembling the French wines, while some have the substance and body of the wines of Spain. With care and time there is every prospect of the colonies becoming the great wine-growing countries of that part of the world."

At the Great Exhibition in Paris in 1851, wine made from the muscat grape, at Camden, ranked high among the best wines of the Continent; and it has, as well as other wines grown in the Hunter River district and other parts of the colony, obtained like favourable mention at the Great Exhibition of 1862 in London. As Sir R. Bourke's opinion on any subject will be held in respect in New South Wales, I may here insert a passage from one of his letters to me on the defect he noticed in the mode of making wine in the colony:—

"It seemed to me," he says, "what was wanting was to cultivate the vine so as to obtain the ripening of the fruit later in the season. I noticed the neglect of this salutary precaution at the vintage of Sir John Jamison, at Regentville, and elsewhere, near Sydney. Coming in, as the fruit did, at the very hottest season of the year, it was impossible to moderate the fermentation and preserve the strength of the liquor. I have no doubt this defect might easily be corrected. The grapes were, I think, the finest I ever tasted; and, by paying attention to this and other points which experience will inculcate in the cultivation of the grape and the manufacture of wine, New South Wales must assuredly become a great and abundant wine-producing country."—*Therry's " New South Wales and Victoria."*

VICTORIAN WINES.—A late important sale of wines grown and manufactured in the Sandhurst district, took place at the Shamrock Hotel, Pall Mall. The wines submitted were the produce of Mr. George Bruhn's vineyard, at the Emu Creek, and were some of them awarded prizes at the Bendigo Agricultural and Horticultural Shows, in 1861, 1862, and 1863. Seventy-five casks, comprising upwards of 3,000 gallons, were offered. The Reisling and Scyras were most approved of; and the Chasselas and Hambro' were generally of a superior flavour. The wines were superior to the Tering wines offered for sale in Melbourne. No. 5 Reisling was sold at 6s. 9d., for transmission to England. The white wine averaged 4s. 8d. per gallon, and the red, 6s. 5d. Mr. Bruhn expects next year to have 6,000 gallons of wine, superior to that now disposed of.—*Extract from the Bendigo Advertiser.* The first of a series of further sales of Australian wines, which attracted a large attendance, was held. Of the Victorian wine (free of duty), Chasselas realised 4s. 6d. per gallon; Gonais, 5s.; Tokay, 7s.; Pinean

M

Blanc, 7s.; Hermitage, 7s; and Burgundy, 5s. 6d.—*Melbourne Argus.* Mr. Soloman offered for sale wine from the vineyard of Mr. Gehrig, senior. The Malbec realised 13s.; Brown Muscadel, 11s. 6d.; Aucurot, 8s. 6d.; Tokay, 6s. 6d; Reisling, 6s.; and Black Hamburgh, 6s., per gallon. Advices from London inform us that Reisling, grown by Mr. Henry Rau, sold for 29s. 6d. Shubach has refused £500 for 500 gallons of his Reisling.—*Albury Advertiser.* The yield of wine for 1862 was at the rate of 182 gallons per acre—a near approach to the average of the French vineyards—190 gallons. —*Maitland Mercury.* Mr. Wyndham's celebrated Australian wines are the Dalwood and the Bukkulla.

COLONIAL WINES.—The Melbourne journals of a late date announce a sale of wines by the Barnawartha Company, held near Albury, in New South Wales, when the following high prices were obtained, showing either extraordinary competition or a superior quality of the article:—Brown sherry, 6s.; white muscat, 8s.; Malbec, 12s.; brown muscat, 14s.; Hermitage, 15s.

> Good wine's the gift which God has given
> To man alone beneath the heaven;
> Of dance and song the genial sire,
> Of friendship gay, and soft desire;
> Yet rule it with a tighten'd rein,
> Nor moderate wisdom's rules disdain;
> For when uncheck'd there's nought runs faster—
> A useful slave, but cruel master.
> *Panyasis, in Yonge's " Deipnosophists."*

VICTORIAN WINE.*—Messrs. De Dollon and La Moile have lately embarked in the sale of colonial wine in William Street, Melbourne. Their cellars are 90 feet in length, by 40 feet wide, and 15 in height, and hold 12,000 gallons. The temperature of the cellar is kept from 62 degrees to 66 degrees. The cellars at present contain of red wines, hermitage, Burgundy, muscat, and claret; and of white wines, Chasselas, Sauterne, Barsac, Tokay, and Ponillac. The hermitage is the best of the red variety, and is a full-bodied, strong wine, obtained from a judicious blending of different wines with shiraz. The next highest class is the Burgundy—a fine wine, which only requires age to come to perfection. The muscat is a luscious wine. Of the white wines, the Chasselas is the best, and is rapidly rising in public favour. It is popularly known as the D C B brand, and the demand for it is considerable. It is made from M. De Dollon's vineyard at Hanthorn. The Sauterne, Tokay, and Barsac are of a superior kind, and of the vintage of 1863—Messrs. De Dollon and La Moile having only entered into business in the latter year. The vignerons from whom the principal portion of the wines was obtained, were M. Dardel and M. Chollet, of the Barrabool Hills. About 5,000 gallons, however, were brought from M. De Dollon's own vineyard, which he planted about four years ago. Its extent exceeds twenty-five acres, and contains seven varieties of grape. The celebrated hermitage was manufactured from the vineyard of M. Dardel. Messrs. De Dollon and La Moile do not fortify their wines with any spirituous compounds, as the admixture only spoils the juice of the grape; but, by a skilful blending of the different wines, they strive to impart a superior character to their production. The sale of wine is very considerable, an earnest of what the wine trade will become when properly developed, and assisted by wise and prudent legislation. In countries where wine is the principal drink of the inhabitants, there is little or no intoxication; and besides, in a sanitary point of view, the juice of the grape being more wholesome than the liquors imported from Europe, its consumption should be encouraged in preference to that of the compounds known as brandy, rum, or ale.—*Illustrated Melbourne Post.*

In Hungary the smallest proprietor possesses his vineyard; for the water is so bad that wine is the common beverage of all; nevertheless, with all its cheap and overflowing produce, the country is essentially a sober one.—*Szemere on Hungarian Wines.*

PURE WINE.—" Verily, the righteous shall dwell among delights; seated on couches, they shall behold objects of pleasure; thou shalt see in their faces the brightness of joy. They shall be given to drink of pure wine, sealed; the seal whereof shall be musk, and to this let those aspire who aspire to happiness: and the water therewith shall be Tasnim, a fountain whereof those shall drink who approach unto the Divine presence."—" *Koran*," chap. lxxxiii.

---

* The folly of legislation cannot be carried further, than by Victoria imposing a duty of 1s. 6d. a gallon on **Tasmanian beer**, and Tasmania exacting a duty of 2s. a gallon on **Victorian wine**!

LXV.—NUTRITION.

With us, no public meeting is valid without a dinner; no party leader is chartered in public estimation till his services have been anticipated or acknowledged, and his public principles pledged amidst circling bumpers and convivial cheers. Even charity obeys the same law, and the beneficent institutions for the sick, and the lame, and the blind find increase of prosperity in their annual celebrations.—*Mayo.*

Table showing the average quantity of nutritive matter in 1,000 parts of several varieties of animal and vegetable food :—

Blood	... 215	Wheat	... 950	Apples	... 170
Beef	... 260	Rice	... 880	Gooseberries	190
Veal	... 250	Barley	... 920	Cherries	... 250
Mutton	... 290	Rye	... 792	Plums	... 290
Pork	... 240	Oats	... 742	Apricots	... 260
Brain	... 200	Potatoes	... 260	Peaches	... 200
Chicken	... 270	Carrots	... 98	Grapes	... 270
Cod	... 210	Turnips	... 42	Melons	... 30
Haddock	... 180	Cabbage	... 73	Cucumber	... 25
Sole	... 210	Beetroot	... 148	Tamarind	... 340
Bones	... 510	Strawberries	100	Almonds	... 650
Milk	... 72	Pears	... 160	Morels	... 896
White of Eggs	140				*Brande.*

Approximate relation of nutritive or nitrogenous to calorifiant matter :—

Milk food for a growing animal	1 to 2
Beans	1 to 2½
Peas and linseed	1 to 3
Scottish oatmeal	1 to 5
Wheaten flour, semolina, Indian corn, barley, food for an animal at rest	1 to 8
Potatoes	1 to 9
East India rice	1 to 10
Dry Swedish turnips	1 to 11
Arrowroot, tapioca, sago	1 to 26
Starch	1 to 40

These proportions will consequently vary considerably according to the richness of the grain or crop, and hence, similar tables which have been subsequently published by others will be found to differ in some of the details from the preceding data; but the facts now stated, given as an approximate, are, probably, as good averages as could be selected.—*Thomson,* " *Medico Chirurgical Trans, and Expe.* : *Researches on Food.*"

In the last edition of Ure, there is a very able article on "Nutrition," from the same pen as the above, and we regret that our limited space prevents us from transferring the whole paper to our pages. The writer commences by observing that nutrition, or the process for promoting the growth of living beings, occupies a most important position in the study of physiology, and in the important practical question of health. The consideration of the subject of nutrition comprehends the nature of nutriment or food, and its change into blood, and into the solids and fluids of the animal structure. Food is required in proportion to the wear and tear of the body. The waste which the animal system thus undergoes varies with the age, and the labour to which the animal is subjected. Hippocrates knew that children are more affected by abstinence than young persons; these more than the middle-aged; and the latter more than old men. The primary and original food of man, whatever speculators may say to the contrary, is milk—a fluid of purely animal origin. If those who are to regulate diet are not guided by scientific knowledge, and do not exercise their judgment, they might be inclined to draw from this fact the inference, that the proper nutriment of the man is animal food. This deduction might be defended with some show of reason, to the exclusion of a vegetable diet. We are sorry we cannot follow the writer further, but if the reader is anxious to do so, we have only to refer him to "Ure's Dictionary," iii., 257, article "Nutrition."

LEGISLATURE.—The House of Commons, in its character of a first-class club, considers itself badly fed. A select committee, appointed to consider the question, has decided that the kitchen department is not so good as it ought to be, and gives the keeper of the refreshment rooms till July to reform, under penalty of being superseded. The present purveyor, who has been ten years in office, says it is not his fault. Members cannot order their dinners, because they cannot tell when they will want them, and after a great speech scores of legislators rush out, all screaming for food at once.—*Liverpool Albion.*

LXVI.—LIQUEURS.

A neat glass of *parfait amour*, which one sips
Just as if bottled velvet tipp'd over one's lips.—*Moore.*

The *Quarterly Review* has it, that *parfait amour* has gone out of fashion altogether—*i. e.*, the liqueur under that name—and that maraschino is now the proper *chasse* for the *gastronomes*, even in preference to curaçoa. The witty scribe states, that ladies sip maraschino with such evident signs of enjoyment that, once upon a time, when a certain eminent diplomatist was asked by his *voisine*, at a *petit souper*, for a female toast to parallel with the masculine one of "Women and wine," his excellency gave, "Men and maraschino," which elicited general applause. Now, a fair one differed with the writer on this occasion, and thought that such a sentiment would have come with far better taste from the lips of her excellency. The Grand Chartreuse is said to be the most famous liqueur made on the Continent of Europe. Kirschwasser is in high favour in Germany; but English cherry brandy, when properly compounded, is quite equal to any foreign importation whatever as a *chasse café.* Its effects are astonishing as a "jumping powder" before a hunt, and it steadies the sportsman's aim in the stubble-field, as the unfortunate nut-brown partridges ought to know. Foreign curaçoa may be so closely imitated by the following that a good judge may be deceived:—

Put six ounces of thin-cut Seville oranges into a quart bottle, with a pint of genuine whisky; cork it tightly, and let the rind infuse for ten or twelve days, when take out the peel, and fill up the bottle with clarified syrup; shake it well, and let it remain for three days. Then pour a tea-spoonful of the liqueur into a mortar, and mix with it a drachm of powdered alum, and the same quantity of carbonate of potash; pour this into the bottle, shake it well, and the curaçoa will be bright and well-flavoured. Kirsch, or, as it is called in Germany, kirschwasser (cherry-water), is made in large quantities in the Black Forest and in Switzerland. In France, it is made exclusively in Franche Comtè, the centre of the trade being at Fougerolles (Haut Saône). As soon as the cherries are ripe, the trees are beaten by the peasants with poles, and the fruit is picked up and thrown into tubs. The juice is pressed out; after which the stones are taken out of the mass, broken, and the kernels are put into the cherry juice. After the whole has undergone fermentation, it is distilled. The bouquet of the kirsch is owing to the prussic acid in the kernels. According to Le Normand, kirschwasser is "downright poison."

Martinique Noyeau.—Put into a stone jar—

Preserved quarns and their syrup, or jelly of that fruit	$\frac{1}{2}$ lb.
Oil of sweet almonds	1 oz.
Sweet almonds, beaten fine	1 ,,
Bitter ditto	1 ,,
Preserved ginger and its syrup	2 ,,
Cinnamon and cloves (bruised) each	$\frac{1}{2}$,,
Nutmeg and pimento	$\frac{1}{3}$,,
Jamaica ginger	$\frac{1}{2}$,,
Candied lemon and citron, of each	1 ,,
White sugar-candy (powdered)	14 ,,
Proof spirit of wine	5 quarts.

Boil the oil with a little brandy, and mix it with the almonds, when beaten to a paste with orange-flower water. Stop up the jar securely, and let it remain in a warm room, or the sun, shaking it often, for a fortnight. Keep it in the tun for twelve months, then strain it, and filter repeatedly until it is as clear as spring water. Rinse phials or half-pint bottles, with any white wine, drain them and fill. Cork and seal well. In six months it will be fit for use, but will improve greatly by age.—*Robinson.*

Tears of the Widow of Malabar.—To ten pounds of spirit (pale brandy) add four pounds of white sugar, and four pints of water, adding four drachms of powdered cinnamon, forty-eight grains of cloves, and the same quantity of mace. Colour with caramel.

The Sighs of Love.—Spirit, water, and sugar, as above. Perfume with otto of roses, and slightly colour with cochineal.

Absinthe.—Take of the tops of wormwood, four pounds; root of angelica, calamus aromaticus, aniseed, leaves of dittany, of each one ounce; alcohol, four gallons. Macerate these substances during eight days, add a little water, and distil by a gentle fire, until two gallons are obtained. This is reduced to a proof spirit, and a few drops of the oil of aniseed added.

Ratafia is the generic name, in France, of liqueurs compounded with alcohol, sugar, and the odoriferous or flavouring principle of vegetables. Bruised cherries with their stones are infused in spirit of wine to make the ratafia *de Teyssère*. The liquor being boiled and filtered, is flavoured, when cold, with spirit of noyeau, made by distilling water off the bruised bitter kernels of apricots, and mixing it with alcohol. Syrup of bay, laurel, and galanga are also added.—*Ure*.

The foreign liqueurs are principally maraschino de Zara, Amsterdam, curaçoa, pine-apple ditto, kirschwasser, kümmel, anisette de Bordeaux, cherry ratafia, eau de vie de Dantzic, Dantzic cherry brandy, Copenhagen ditto, aqua d'oro, and aqua d'argento, crême de noyeau (red and white), vanille, rose and Venus, l'amour, d'absinthe, de Canelle, fine orange, d'Ananas, de thé, and de café.

SPIRITUOUS LIQUEURS.—As a liqueur, Hennessy and Co.'s cognac is deservedly in high favour in the Colonies, from the purity and goodness of the spirit; and it is known from their label of the "battle-axe" crest, registered at Stationers' Hall, London. Also Kinahan's celebrated Irish LL whisky, which is a potent though mild spirit, and is held in delight by every connoisseur—the attraction of every festive board; the corks of which liqueur have a ducal coronet impressed on them, from the time that a lord-lieutenant of that rank honoured it with his patronage. Then we have Browning's, and Crosse's and Blackwell's Old Tom; Sir Robert Burnett's glass-stoppered ditto; Hay's old islay; and Cambleton's whisky; Thin and Kirkleston's, and Meehan's old Irish; Martell's, The United Vineyard Company's, and Otard, Dupuy, and Co.'s brandies.

LXVII.—COFFEE.

Coffee—which makes the politician wise,
And see through all things with his half-shut eyes—
Sent up in vapours to the baron's brain
New stratagems, the radiant Lock to gain.—*Pope*.

We are of accord with many authors, that coffee promotes digestion and exhilarates the spirits; that, drank in moderation, especially if combined with sugar and milk, it is one of the most wholesome beverages known. It must be fresh roasted and fresh ground, and a common percolator is, of all the modes of preparing it, the most simple. Use the best coffee—have it ground, if not burnt on the establishment—and put into the percolator one part in twelve of good chicory. Chicory is by no means unwholesome, but mind it is not adulterated. The extent to which the system of adulteration is carried in every consumable article is a disgrace to the trading community, and a reflection on the age in which we live. Medical writers tell us chicory is reputed to be alterative, attenuant, diuretic, febrifuge, hepatic, resolvent, and tonic. When taken to excess, it has a tendency to excite diarrhœa, according to Pereira. Pour on the coffee *boiling* water, and you have the real thing. The chicory gives the coffee a fulness, but, if too much is used, the flavour and aroma of the coffee is overpowered and lost. The French *café au lait* is a small quantity of coffee, and a large proportion of milk made hot, and sweetened to taste.

Coffee, like tea, has certainly an anti-soporific effect on many individuals. It imparts an activity to the mind which is incompatible with sleep; but this will rarely occur if the beverage is taken for several hours before our accustomed period of repose. It seems to be generally admitted that it possesses the power of counteracting the effects of narcotics; and hence it is used by the Turks with much advantage in abating the influence of the inordinate quantities of opium they are accustomed to swallow. When our object is to administer it as a promoter of digestion, it should be carefully made by infusion; decoction dissipates its aroma.—*Paris on Diet.*

M. Payen proves that coffee, slightly roasted, contains the maximum of aroma, weight, and nutrition. He declares coffee to be nutritious, as it contains a large quantity of azote, three times as much nutriment as tea, and more than twice the nourishment of soup. Chicory contains only half the nutriment of coffee.

A late number of "L'Année Scientifique," by Louis Figuier, contains an able article, showing that the use of coffee tends to prolong life. The property which coffee possesses of rendering the produce of the secretions more aqueous, leads Dr. Petit to recommend it as an agent for combatting the gout, gravel, and calculous affections. M. Trosseau, in his treatise on "Materia Medica and Therapeutics," states, the above-named complaints are all unknown where the consumption of coffee takes place.

The Eastern nations are great coffee drinkers, and the small berry of Mocha, in Arabia, is considered the finest kind of the *coffea Arabica*. The Turks are both great smokers and drinkers of coffee; it is tolerated by the Koran precepts of temperance, and universally used by all Islamites.

The roasting of the berry to a proper degree requires great nicety; the virtues and agreeableness of the drink depend upon it, and both are often injured by the general method. Bernier says, when he was at Cairo, where coffee is so much used, he was assured by the best judges, that there were only two people in that great city who understood how to prepare it in perfection. If it be under-done, its virtues will not be imparted, and, in use, it will load and oppress the stomach; if it be over-done, it will yield a flat, burnt, and bitter taste, its virtues will be destroyed, and, in use, it will heat the body and act as an astringent.— *Moseley.*

MAHOMETANISM.—At present the use of coffee is generally tolerated, if not granted, as is that of tobacco, though the more religious make a scruple of taking the latter, not only because it inebriates, but also out of respect to a traditional saying of the Prophet (which, if it could be made to be his, he would be a prophet indeed), that in the latter days there should be men, who would bear the name of Moslems, but should not be really such, and that they should smoke a certain weed, which should be called tobacco. However, the Eastern nations are so addicted to both, that they say a drink of coffee and a pipe of tobacco are a complete entertainment; and the Persians have a saying, that coffee without tobacco is meat without drink.—*Preliminary Discourse, Sale's "Koran."*

The coffee, as dispensed at the Café de Paris, at Melbourne, in Victoria, was unexceptionable in flavour, and served hot. The *garçon* brought in a large-sized white stone china cup and saucer, and after putting before the visitor, on a little marble table, a small basin of white crystallised sugar, the grains of which sparkled in the gaslight, proceeded to pour simultaneously into the cup two jets of coffee and milk from silver ewers. We question whether the city on the banks of the Seine could supply mocha better made or served, and for the same price—sixpence.

The most esteemed coffee is that of Mocha. It has a small and a rounder bean; a more agreeable taste and smell than any other. Its colour is yellow. Next to it in European reputation are the Martinique and Bourbon coffees. The former is larger than the Arabian, and more oblong; it is rounded at the ends; its colour is greenish; and it preserves almost always a silver-grey pellicle, which comes off in the roasting. The Bourbon coffee approaches nearest to the mocha, from which it originally sprung. The St. Domingo coffee has its two extremities pointed, and it is much less esteemed than the preceding.—*Ure.*

COFFEE BENEFICIAL.—Coffee is said to be an antidote to the gout and rheumatism. A case is mentioned in the "Pharmaceutical Journal," of a gentleman having had the gout for twenty years who was completely cured by the use of coffee. In asthma it has been found particularly serviceable, and it is extolled in gangrene of the extremities in drunkards. Calculous complaints are scarcely known in France and Turkey, where coffee is the principal beverage of the people. M. Devereaux was cured of gout of twenty-five years' standing, accompanied by chalk stones, by taking coffee freely (Du Four); and Sir John Floyer was cured of asthma, after sixty years of suffering, by the like simple means. "I have myself seen several cases in which coffee was really useful" (Laennec). Brande writes, that coffee is exhilarating, and operates on many persons as an aperient, owing to the caffeine contained in it. Vanilla gives coffee a perfumed flavour; and, according to "Le Manuel de l'Amateur de Café," isinglass or hartshorn shavings are used to clarify it; but this addition injures the aroma. Plenty of good cream with coffee is highly nutritious. The "Medical Reporter" says, that a consumptive patient, under treatment, is now taking cream with better effect than was experienced under the cod-liver oil previously tried. This latter journal further observes, "Our advice is, for all who have, or think they have, consumption, to adopt a cream diet. Eat the pure cream abundantly, as much of it as the stomach will digest well, and we doubt not that it will prove as effective as the finest cod-liver oil that can be bought;" and, the editor should have added, far more agreeable to take. Dr. Livingstone tells us, that sugar is cultivated in the Shore Valley, as well as many parts of Africa near the Zambesi, and that it may be purchased at a halfpenny per pound!

LXVIII.—STOVES.

La bonne cuisine se fait toujours à petit feu.—*Dialogues sur la Gastronomie.*

We must say a few words on stoves, as they are intimately connected with the *cuisine*. The "Curiosities of London" has it, that the kitchen range which is used for the Lord Mayor's dinner is some sixteen feet long, and seven feet high. For a small establishment the best range is that called the "Newark," and for a large family, the "Improved Leamington Kitchener" is recommended. The first range merely contains an oven, boiler, and open fire-place. The latter is a very complete affair, and has an open fire-place, hot-plate, boiler, and movable roaster; which will bake bread and pastry in first-rate style. The prices of these articles are from fifty shillings to twenty guineas; but the cooking stoves that we would recommend beyond all others are those made in America. They are portable, require no fixing, and vary in price from five to fourteen pounds. They are a perfect cure for a smoky chimney, and are decidedly the best, in every way, for a warm climate, as a person may use them without being burnt by the fire. Meat baked in their ovens cannot be distinguished by the taste or flavour from that roasted in front of an open fire; provided the joint is basted occasionally. The open iron surface on the top of the stove has room for stewpans and kettles. They have a variety of names. The one used by the writer is called "The Golden State," and bears on it as makers the names of "Johnson and Fuller, Broadway, New York." Hill, of Silver Street, Trowbridge, advertises the "Leamington Prize Kitchener" at a more reasonable rate than any other ironmongery establishment, as far as we know. The common American tin baking-oven, that heats before the fire by a reflector, and costs six or eight shillings, is admirable for a small family, as it will bake rolls, pies, or meat to perfection, if properly attended to.

PORTABLE OVENS.—An expert bushman can bake a good loaf in an iron pot, or a pie in a camp oven; but, for a fire-place, the revolving ovens are a useful and necessary article. They are suspended in front of the fire by a worsted string, or bottle-jack, and in this mode will bake bread, cakes, pies, &c., in a very perfect manner. They will bake a four-pound loaf in an hour and a quarter, the only care being that it is always on the turn. The saving in families in grinding their own wheat and baking their own bread is very great—without considering the better article they thereby have, and the proper habits of domestic economy promoted in the household; besides, home-made bread is, according to medical authority, far more wholesome and nutritious than the bakers', which has been elsewhere stated.

LORD MAYOR'S DINNER.—The dinner at Guildhall, on Lord Mayor's Day, is a magnificent spectacle. The Lord Mayor and his distinguished guests advance to the banquet by sound of trumpet; and the superb dresses and official costumes of many of the company (about 1,200), with the display of costly plate, is very striking. The hall is divided. At the Upper, or Hustings Tables, the courses are served hot; at the lower tables the turtle only is hot. The baron of beef is brought in procession from the kitchen into the hall, in the morning, and being placed upon a pedestal, at night is cut up by the City Carver. The kitchen wherein the dinner is dressed is a vast apartment. The principal range is sixteen feet long, and seven feet high, and a baron of beef (three cwt.) is roasted by gas. There are twenty cooks, besides helpers. Some forty turtles are slaughtered for 250 tureens of soup; and the serving of the dinner requires about 200 persons, and 8,000 plate changes. Next morning, the fragments of the great feast are doled out at the kitchen gate to the city poor.—*Curiosities of London.*

LXIX.—WHY ANIMALS TO BE EATEN MUST BE KILLED.

The Irish are very hospitable, and are remarkable for the novelty and point of their convivial toasts; so much so, that an Irish squire was known to spend half of his day in inventing toasts and the other half in drinking them.—*Nimrod.*

It is universally understood that animals which die from disease are not fitted for our markets. It is also understood that when cattle are over-driven their meat is notably inferior to that of healthy animals, unless they are permitted to recover their exhausted energies before being slaughtered. Why is this? The first and most natural supposition respecting those which die from disease is that their flesh is tainted; but it has been found that prolonged agony or exhaustion are quite as injurious, though in these cases there is no taint of disease. Mr. Claude Bernard propounds the following explanation:—In all healthy animals, no matter to what class they belong, or on what food they subsist, he finds a peculiar substance, analogous to vegetable starch, existing in their tissue, and especially in their liver. This substance he calls *glycogene*, *i. e.*, the sugar former. It is abundant in proportion to the vigour and youth of the animal, and disappears entirely under the prolonged suffering of pain or disease. This disappearance is peculiarly rapid in fish, and is always observed in the spontaneous death of animals; but when the death is sudden none of it disappears. He finds that a rabbit, for example, which he killed after suffering pain for five or six hours, exhibits no form whatever of this sugar-forming substance, and its flesh has a marked difference in flavour. The same remark applies to exhausted, over-driven animals; their muscles are almost deficient in glycogene, and yield in water a far larger proportion of soluble principles than the same muscle in a normal state. Mr. Bernard finds, moreover, that animals which are suffocated lose more of the sugar-forming substance than similar animals killed in the slaughter-house. To this let us add the fact that the blood of over-driven animals will not coagulate, or coagulates very slowly and imperfectly, and we shall see good reason for exercising some circumspection over the practices of our meat markets.—*Cornhill Magazine.*

POETICAL.—When my spirits are low, for relief and delight
    I still place your splendid memorial in sight;
    And call to my muse, when care strives to pursue,
    Bring the steaks to my mem'ry, and the bowl to my view.
—*Captain Morris, at the Beefsteak Club, in 1835, at the age of ninety, on being presented with a silver bowl.*

LXX.—DINNERS À LA RUSSE.

Anybody may dine, but very few know how to dine so as to ensure the greatest quantity of health and enjoyment.—*Walker.*

In some establishments this form of dining is observed. The dishes are placed on the side-table, and the servants carve and hand round what is required. The table is ornamented with the dessert, the glass, plate, an epergne or plateau of plate, and flowers of a choice kind in vases. The table has a pleasing appearance, but it is scarcely a favourite mode for an Englishman, who likes to see the cut taken from the dish. Dinners *à la Russe* are merely a refined adaptation of the cheap ham and beef shop, where you are served with a plateful at a time, and we venture with deference to express such an opinion. The strict etiquette of a Russian dinner is, that the guests are seated, and the master and mistress of the feast remain standing—it being their business to wait on the company, and to see that the servants do their duty. Nothing can escape their observation: your plate is never empty, and your glass always full; you are literally crammed, according to swinish rule. This mode requires first-rate servants, and plenty of them. The *menu*, or bill of fare in the French language, elegantly embossed, is placed beside each guest. The late King of Hanover had the name of the cook, by whom each dish was dressed, printed on rose-coloured paper on the *carte*, like the programme of a concert, with the name of the performers. The author of the "Art of Dining," evidently a first-rate connoisseur, writes that opinions are undecided as to dinners *à la Russe;* but that on *one* occasion, in a country house in Northumberland, he saw them most pleasingly put in practice. Let us alter the poet's lines by one word—

"For forms of *dinners* let fools contest; Whate'er is best administer'd is best."

When the Abbé de Pradt was sent by Napoleon to gain over Poland to his cause, the Emperor told him at parting, "*Tenez bonne table et soignez les femmes.*" There was no injunction as to the mode, and the advice shows a man having a master mind.

"G. H. M.," in the London *Times*, wrote about two years ago in deprecation of the English style of cookery, and laudatory of the dinner *à la Russe*. The *Illustrated Times* informs us that during the past year a banquet was given to M. Rouher at Willis's Rooms, and that it was the most perfect public dinner ever served in England, proving that "G. H. M." was a master of the culinary art. The *menu* contained printed instructions as follows:—" Here dry champagne is preferable;" again, "No champagne allowed with the ducklings."

REASONS IN FAVOUR OF A RUSSIAN DINNER.—*Mr. Macborrowdale:* You are a man of taste, Mr. Gryll; that (roast beef) is a handsomer ornament of a dinner-table than clusters of nosegays, and all sorts of uneatable decorations. I detest and abominate the idea of a Siberian dinner, where you just look on fiddle-faddles, while your dinner is behind a screen, and you are served with dinner like a pauper. *The Rev. Dr. Opimian:* I quite agree with Mr. Macborrowdale. I like to see my dinner; and herein I rejoice to have Addison on my side, for I remember a paper in which he objects to have roast beef placed on a sideboard. Even in his day it had been displaced to make way for some incomprehensible French dishes, among which he could find nothing to eat. I do not know what he would have said to its being placed altogether out of sight. Still, there is something to be said on the other side. There is hardly one gentleman in twenty who knows how to carve; and as to ladies, though they did know once on a time, they do not now. What can be more pitiable than the right-hand man of the lady of the house, awkward enough in himself, with the dish twisted round to him in the most awkward possible position, digging in unutterable mortification for a joint which he cannot find, and wishing the unanatomisable *volaille* behind a Russian screen with the footman?—*Gryll Grange, in " Fraser's Magazine."*

LXXI.—GERMAN SOUR-KROUT.

It was suggested to a distinguished *gourmet* what a capital thing a dish all fins (turbot fins) might be made. "Capital," said he; "dine on it with me to-morrow." "Accepted!" Would you believe it? when the cover was removed, the sacrilegious dog of an Amphitryon had put into the dish, Cicero "*De Finibus!*" "There is a work all fins," said he.—*Bulwer.*

Take some full-grown cabbages, cut them in very thick slices, and put them in layers, of about two fingers' thickness, in a tub, and sprinkle each layer with juniper-berries; for twenty cabbages use two pounds of salt. When the tub is full, put on a cover which exactly fills the tub; put on the cover a weight of forty or fifty pounds, and put the tub in a moderate heat. The cabbage sinks when fermentation begins. and the liquor rises to the surface over the cover. When it smells sour, the fermentation has begun; then put the tub into the cellar, keep it covered, and let the pickle cover the sour-krout. Cover it close each time any is taken out. When you use it, wash it in warm water, and stew it in butter or fat. Serve with ham, pickled pork, or sausages. There will be no scurvy on board ship if sour-krout is used occasionally.

Salting is employed for certain fruits, as small cucumbers, or gherkins, capers, olives, &c. Even for peas such a method is had recourse to for preserving them a certain time. They must be scalded in hot water, put up in bottles, and covered with saturated brine, having a film of oil on its surface, to exclude the agency of the atmospheric air. Before being used they must be soaked for a short time in warm water, to extract the salt. The most important article of diet of this class is the *saur-kraut*, sour herb or cabbage, of the northern nations of Europe, which is prepared simply by salting, a little vinegar being formed spontaneously by fermentation. The cabbage must be cut in small pieces, stratified in a cask along with salt, to which juniper-berries and carraway-seeds may be added, and packed as hard as possible by means of a wooden rammer. The cabbage is then covered with a lid, on which a heavy weight is laid. A fermentation commences, while a quantity of juice exudes and floats on the surface, which causes the cabbage to become more compact, and a sour smell is perceived towards the end of the fermentation. In this condition the cask is transplanted into a cool cellar, where it is allowed to stand for use during the year; and indeed where, if well made and packed, it may be kept for years.—*Ure.*

TURKISH COOKERY.—They have many dishes which are indeed worthy of the greatest epicure, and I shall not consider my Oriental mission terminated to my satisfaction till I see in the bills of fare of France and England their purée de volaille au ris, tomates, et concombres, and purée de Bahamia aromaticée à la crême, by the side of our potages à la reine, tortue, Julliene, and mulligatawny; near our whitebait, red mullets aux herbes, oyster pilaff, mackerel, salad, &c., and with our roast beef, saddle-back of mutton, and haunch of venison, their sheep, lamb, or kid, roasted whole, and the monster and delicious kebab; by our entrées of suprême de volaille, salmis, and vol-aux-vents, their doulmas kioffee, sis kebabs, hahar-ram bouton, pilaff au cailles, &c.; with our vegetables, their Bahamia, fried leeks and celery, partligan bastici, and sakath kabac bastici; with our macédoines, jellies, charlottes, &c., their lokounds, mouka halibi, Baclara gyneristi, ekmekataire; their coffee, iced milk, and sherbet; in fact, all their principal dishes might, with the best advantage, be adapted and Frenchified and Anglicised. Not so their method of serving, in which they mix sweet and savoury dishes throughout the repast; and still less likely their eating with their fingers. . . . . . I became acquainted with the principal officer of His Sublime Majesty's household, called the Hachji Bachji, or General-in-Chief of the Culinary Department. He has under his command, in the various palaces, about 600 men cooks, and had, in the time of Sultan Mahmoud, upwards of 1,000. Having expressed a wish to become acquainted with some of the principal Turkish dishes, and the way in which the dinner was served, he not only gave me the required information, but invited me to a dinner *à la Turc*, at the new palace of Dolina Batchi. We were only four guests. About seventy small dishes formed a luxurious bill of fare, which, after the Turkish fashion, were partaken of quickly, as the Moslems only taste a mouthful of each dish which may take their fancy. He then informed me that the repast was a *fac-simile* of the dinner daily served to the Padiscah, who took his meals alone.—*Soyer to the "Times," from Constantinople.*

LXXII.—STRASBOURG PIES.

In a club, nothing is so prejudicial as bad carving. A joint, ill carved at first by one, is always disregarded by the other members; and frequently, from this circumstance, a joint of great weight and price is no longer presentible, and is left to the loss of the establishment.—*Ude.*

The Patés de foie gras, for which Strasbourg has been so long celebrated, were commonly said to be principally made from the livers of geese, subject to great torture, by being fed to repletion, but without water, before a fierce fire, until their livers became enlarged with disease. Hence epicures began to feel some qualms of conscience for indulging in these luxuries obtained by such cruel means, when Alexis Soyer, the famed *cuisinier*, visited Strasbourg, and, in a letter to the *Courier du Bas Rhin*, says: "After having carefully examined the subject, I can declare that there is not one word of truth in the general belief. Up to the age of eight months," he adds, "the geese are allowed to feed at full liberty in the open air. They are then brought to market, and purchased by the persons whose occupation it is to fatten them for killing. They are placed in coops, and fed, for about a month or five weeks, three times a day with wheat, and allowed as much water as they please. Each bird eats about a bushel of corn during the process of fattening, the water of Strasbourg, it is said, contributing to increase the volume of the liver. When sufficiently fat they are killed, having been treated with the greatest attention and humanity during the whole period of their incarceration, and entirely removed from any unusual heat."—*Things Not Generally Known.*

DIGESTION.—A good digestive system is the basis of other parts, including the brain. It sustains mental application, and seems to be a principal condition of good animal spirits, and the hearty temperament. It naturally, although not necessarily, leads to the love of good eating, and must therefore be taken along with the alimentative organ in determining the epicurean propensity. As regards the power of mental labour, a good digestion is even of more importance than good muscles.—*Bain, in "Fraser's Magazine."*

LXXIII.—HERRING AND ANCHOVY PASTE.

Athenæus maintains, with great truth, that cookery is an important element in the advancement of civilisation, and that crudity of food and thought are interdependent.—*The Lancet.*

If the reader is fond of herring or anchovy paste, let him not purchase the artificial coloured compounds under this head sold in pots, but make it himself, and he will have the articles unadulterated. It will not look so well, perhaps, but it will be much more wholesome. Soak herring or anchovies in warm beer or water, then take out all the bones and skins, and pound them with a small quantity of butter, some good cayenne, and a little vinegar, and pot them. A little powdered mace may be added. Meats, fowl, game, fish, ham, and salt meats are potted in a similar way.

Darteneuf. Alas! poor Apicius, I pity thee much for not having lived in my age and my country. How many good dishes have I ate in England that were unknown in Rome in thy days?

Apicius. Keep your pity to yourself—how many good dishes have I ate in Rome, the knowledge of which has been lost in these latter degenerate days? The fat paps of a sow, the livers of scari, the brains of phenicopters, and the tripotatum—which consisted of three sorts of fish for which you have no names—the lupis marinus, the myxo, and the muraenus.—*Dialogues of the Dead.*

LXXIV.—ORANGE-FLOWER WATER.

At this instant the slaves appeared, bearing a tray covered with the first preparative of the feast. Amidst delicious figs, fresh herbs strewed with snow, anchovies, and eggs, were ranged small cups of diluted wine sparingly mixed with honey. As these were placed on the table, young slaves bore round to each of the five guests (for there were no more) the silver basin of *perfumed water* and napkins edged with a purple fringe.—*The Last Days of Pompeii.*

Orange-flower water has been a favourite perfume in England since the reign of James I. It occurs in Copley's "Wits, Fits, and Fancies," 1614; and in the "Accomplished Female Instructor," 1719, is the following recipe:—

Take two pounds of orange-flowers, as fresh as you can get them, infuse them in two quarts of white wine, and so distil them, and it will yield a curious perfuming spirit. Orange butter was made, according to the "Closet of Rarities," 1706, by beating up new cream, and then adding orange-flower and red wine, to give it the colour and scent of an orange.—*Things Not Generally Known.*

UTOPIAN, VERY.—At the hours of dinner and supper, the syphogranty, being called together by sound of trumpet, meet and eat together, except only such as are in the hospitals, or lie sick at home. Yet after the halls are served no man is hindered to carry provisions from the market-place, for they know he does that for some good reason, yet none does it willingly, since it is both an indecent and foolish thing for any to give themselves the trouble to make ready an ill dinner at home, when there is a much more plentiful one made ready for him so near at hand. All the uneasy and sordid services about these halls are performed by the slaves; but the dressing and cooking of their meat, and the ordering of their tables, belong only to the women, which goes round all women of every family by turns.—*Utopia; or, the Happy Republic.*

LXXV.—VEGETABLE ESSENCES AND TINCTURES:

Pharmaceutical preparations, generally consisting of certain remedies dissolved in rectified or proof spirits. Tinctures are generally made by digesting bruised or pulverised vegetable substances in the spirit, either at common temperature, or aided by heat.—*Brande.*

The flavour or extract of cayenne, lemon-peel, celery, ginger, allspice, nutmeg, cloves and mace, cinnamon, marjoram, and herbs of any kind, may be obtained by infusing the different ingredients in rectified spirits or brandy, and allowing them to steep for a month or more, and then straining the liquor for use. There is one important matter that must be strictly looked to—the various articles must be good of their kind, and not adulterated. By this mode the flavour of any kind of herbs may be obtained, or sweet herbs, such as marjoram, thyme, savory, mint, balm, hyssop, or pennyroyal, may be gathered and dried for winter use, either in a Dutch oven in the sun, or in a room where there is plenty of draught. Citron, orange, and lemon-peel may be similarly preserved.

Herbs, cabbages, &c., may be kept a long time in a cool cellar, provided they are covered with dry sand. Cabbages should be scalded in hot water previously to drying, and all such plants when dried should be compactly pressed together, and kept in air-tight vessels. Tuberous and other roots are better kept in an airy place, where they may dry a little without being exposed to the winter's frost.—*Ure.*

ECONOMY IN LIVING.—Poverty is relative, and therefore not ignoble; neediness is a positive degradation. If I have only £100, I am rich as compared with the majority of my countrymen. If I have £5,000 a year, I may be poor as compared with the majority of my associates, and very poor compared with my next-door neighbour. With either of these incomes, I am relatively poor or rich; but with either of these incomes I may be positively free from neediness. With the £100 a year I may need no man's help; I may, at least, have my "crust of bread and liberty." But with £5,000 a year I may dread a ring at my bell; I may have my tyrannical masters in servants whose wages I cannot pay; my exile may be the fiat of the first long-suffering man who enters a judgment against me; for the flesh that is nearest my heart, some Shylock may be dusting his scales and whetting his knife. Nor is this an exaggeration. Some of the neediest men I have ever known have a nominal £5,000 per annum. Every man is needy who spends more than he has; no man is needy who spends less. I may so ill-manage my money that, with £5,000 a year, I purchase the worst evils of poverty—terror and shame. I may so manage my money that, with £100 a year, I purchase the best blessings of wealth—safety and respect. Man is a kingly animal. In every shade which does not enslave him, it is not labour which makes him less loyally lord of himself—it is fear.— *Sir E. B. Lytton, in " Blackwood."*

In Russia, the berry of the mountain ash is made use of to flavour jellies, wine, brandy, and other articles, to which it imparts a most agreeable bitter.—*Mark Lane Express.*

LXXVI.—HAMS, BACON, AND SALT MEAT.

Killing swine.—*Macbeth.*

The pigs should always be killed in the afternoon, if possible, and hung up until next morning, when they must be cut up. If the weather will allow of their hanging a few days, so much the better. The bacon and hams must be well rubbed with coarse salt, in which a small quantity of saltpetre must be mixed, and allowed to remain twenty-four hours to drain, after which they must be put into the following pickle:—Four pounds of salt, one pound and a half of white sugar, and two ounces of saltpetre to every two gallons of water, to be boiled, and allowed to get cold, making sufficient to cover the quantity you intend to have. There is no further trouble with them, except to turn them while in the pickle, and they must remain in it, according to size, from a fortnight to three weeks. You will find them rich and fine flavoured. They can be smoked afterwards, if desired. The pickle will last some time, if re-boiled and skimmed. A small quantity of bicarbonate of soda used with the salt mellows the meat. The proportionate quantity of soda, in curing bacon, is about similar in amount to the saltpetre used, which will effectually prevent rust, and it has the effect of making hams more mellow.

The above is the mode adopted by an amateur, who is a good judge of such matters, and who cures excellent bacon, hams, and pig's cheeks; but we prefer the following simple plan:—

Hams.—If the weather will allow it, let them hang for a few days. Mix in proportion one ounce of black pepper, one ounce of allspice, one ounce of saltpetre, half a pound of salt, and half a pound of sugar with a quart of beer; boil them together, and pour them hot on the hams, and turn them in this pickle for three weeks. Let the ham drain, and brush it over with pyroligneous acid, and sprinkle over it some sharps, bran, or pollard. Or the following recipe:—One pound and a half of brown sugar, two pounds and a half of salt, and half a pound of saltpetre; rub it dry on the hams, bacon, and cheeks, and turn every day for the first ten days, and afterwards every other day. Use the acid, and bran it as before. When a pig is killed the hog's lard must be carefully melted and run into jars, and the prudent housewife will not allow the time to pass for making sausages or black puddings, to do which proceed as follows:—

Black Puddings.—The blood must be stirred with salt until cold. Put a quart of it to a quart of grits or boiled rice, and soak some bread in milk. Clean the grits well with salt and water. Chop winter savory, thyme, pennyroyal, pepper, and salt, and a little ground spice; mix these about with three pounds of beef suet, or the fat of the pig; add six eggs well beaten up. Then add the rice, or grits, and bread, and fill your skins. White puddings are made in a similar way with cream, without the blood, but are far inferior in taste or goodness.

SALTING.—The meat should be rubbed well with common salt, containing about 1-16th of saltpetre, and 1-32nd of sugar, till every crevice has been impregnated with it; then sprinkled over with salt, laid down for twenty-four or forty-eight hours, and, lastly, subject to pressure. It must be next sprinkled anew with salt, packed into proper vessels, and covered with the brine obtained in the act of pressing, rendered stronger by boiling down. For household purposes it is sufficient to rub the meat well with good salt, to put it into vessels, and load it with heavy weights, in order to squeeze out as much pickle as will cover its surface. If this cannot be had, a pickle must be poured on it, composed of four pounds of salt, one pound of sugar, and two ounces of saltpetre dissolved in two gallons of water. M. Fitch patented the use of a liquid containing two cwt. of common salt to the product of distillation of two cwt. of wood, adding sugar, treacle, and saltpetre. Some people drive the salt by force of pressure, some by centrifugal motion. Milk has been preserved by the use of carbonate of soda, preventing acidity. Alum has been patented, for shell-fish especially.—*Ure.*

WESTPHALIA HAMS.—These usually come by way of Hamburg, and owe their fine flavour to their being "cold smoked." The hams are hung in the upper part of the building; the smoke is generated in the cellar, and carried up to the smoking-room through tubes. During its ascent it deposits all moisture, and when it comes in contact with the hams it is both dry and cold, so that no undue change occurs in the meat while being smoked.—*Newspaper paragraph.*

Mild Pickle.—The following is an excellent mild pickle, and meat put into it will remain mellow, and not briny, for months at a time:— Water, four gallons; salt, a quart and a half; saltpetre, a wine-glassful; boil and skim.

If meat is required for early use dry salting is the most expeditious mode, in the following proportions:—Two pounds of salt; one ounce and a half of saltpetre; one ounce good moist sugar; rub in and turn occasionally.

COOKING HAMS.—A ham of ten pounds should be boiled slowly, in a pot without a cover, and that for the space of nearly two and a half hours. To ascertain if sufficiently boiled, try if the skin will come readily off, and if so it is fit for use. Before sending it to table, the ham is generally subjected to a little ornamental dressing. We do not refer to the ornamenting and covering of the bone with a net or cut paper, but the browning where the skin has been removed. There are two ways of doing this. In the one you cover the surface with bread-crumbs, and keep it in the oven until it attains the proper colour. In the other, you sprinkle sugar on the ham, and pass a red-hot iron over the surface, and thus impart to it that rich, glossy brown which so many admire.—*Scottish Farmer.*

Soyer recommends that, in order to retain the juices in corned meat, when intended to be eaten cold, the joint should, when taken off the fire, be plunged into ice-water, or water as cold as can be procured.

The Empress of Russia's Brine.—In Europe the Russian pork has a name for its goodness and quality, which is supposed to be owing to the pickle in which it is preserved. That named after the Empress is prepared as follows:—Boil together, over a slow fire, six pounds of common salt, two pounds of powdered loaf sugar, three ounces of saltpetre, and three gallons of water; skim it while boiling; and, when cold, pour it over the meat, every part of which must be covered with the brine. Small pork will be sufficiently cured in four or five days, and hams intended for drying, in two weeks. This pickle may be used frequently if boiled up, skimmed, and more ingredients used. Before putting the meat into the water, wash it well, and dry it. This pickle will efficiently cure hams and tongues, and any kind of salted provisions—only don't keep it in brine too long; whereas in the mild pickle, in the previous recipe, meat may be immersed for months.

PRESERVING WITH VINEGAR, SUGAR, &c.—Vinegar dissolves or coagulates the albumen of flesh, and thereby counteracts its putrescence. The meat should be washed, dried, and then laid in strong vinegar: or it may be boiled in the vinegar, allowed to cool in it, and then laid aside with it in a cool cellar, where it will keep sound for several months. Meat will also keep fresh for a considerable period when surrounded with oil, or fat of any kind, so purified as not to turn rancid of itself, especially if the meat be previously boiled. This process is called potting, and is applied successfully to fish, fowls, &c. Meat may be also preserved by boiling in its own gravy, or embedding in fat ("Plowden's Patent," 1807), or in animal jelly.—*Ure.*

Mutton Hams.—The *Journal des Connoissances Usuelles* gives the following method of curing mutton hams:—It is necessary that the mutton should be fat; it cannot be too much so. Two ounces of sugar must be mixed with an ounce of common salt, and half a spoonful of saltpetre. The meat must be well rubbed with this mixture, and then placed in a pan. It must be beaten and turned once a day for ten days, and then dried and smoked. Rashers cut thin, and served hot, will satisfy the palate of the most fastidious epicure; or the hams are first-rate cold, after having been previously *simmered* sufficiently. As a general rule, never *gallop* any meat in boiling water, unless you desire to make it tough, and utterly destroy the flavour of the joint.

French hung Beef.—The bones are removed from the meat, and it is put in a pan, and well rubbed with a pickle composed of a pound of salt, two ounces of saltpetre, an ounce of sal prunella, and half a pound of coarse brown sugar, well mixed together. It is covered with parsley, shalots, thyme, bay-leaves, marjoram, sweet basil, winter savory, a little coriander-seed, a table-spoonful of juniper berries, and three cloves of garlic. It is turned every day for ten days in the brine, and the herbs put on the top; afterwards hung up and smoked. When boiled, a little vinegar must be put in the water, a couple of onions cut, a few cloves, some nutmeg, and herbs. When done, let it remain in the same liquor until cold.

Dutch Beef is cured in a similar manner, being first well rubbed with brown sugar, and then a pound of salt is mixed with a quarter of a pound of saltpetre, and an ounce of juniper berries. The beef is well rubbed in with this mixture in the pan for ten days. It is then pressed, and afterwards dried and smoked. Boil it in a cloth, and do not remove it until cold.

Beef Hams.—Select a leg of beef, that cannot be too fat, and rub it well with saltpetre and salt; then make a pickle of an ounce of bay-salt, an ounce of saltpetre, a pound of coarse brown sugar, and a pound of common salt. Rub this well in every day for a week, and then every other day for about three weeks; then roll it in bran or sawdust, and smoke.

These kinds of hams are made very extensively in Australia, and it is a wonder that they are not largely exported.

THE SALT BEEF OF VICTORIA.—Some interesting proceedings have lately taken place at the office of Messrs. Dalgetty, merchants, at Melbourne, in connection with the experiment of packing Colonial beef in casks and submitting it to the test of a voyage to England and back. This experiment was suggested by the Council of the Board of Agriculture, and two Melbourne firms entered into competition in the matter, each submitting three tierces of beef properly packed, two tierces being sent the voyage, and the remainder retained in the colony. The six tierces were opened in the presence of three judges—Captain Henry, of the Omar Pacha; Captain Norman, H.M.S. Victoria; and Mr. Bignill. Mr. Matson, the secretary of the Board of Agriculture, and other gentlemen of practical experience were present. A portion of the meat from each cask was boiled, and the judges pronounced it to be delicious in taste, colour, and condition. There was no perceptible difference between that voyaged to England and that portion retained in the colony. The nautical captains said the beef was far superior to any they received as ships' stores. Nothing can be more satisfactory than the result of this interesting test.—*Condensed from the "Melbourne Herald."* In another part of this work we have directed further attention to the circumstance of the ease with which the fleets and vessels of the mother country could be supplied with provisions from these colonies, at a most cheap and reasonable rate, and the urgency of a victualling yard being improvised somewhere in the Southern Hemisphere. The day will come when this idea will be carried out. South Australian and Launceston flour can be procured, the best in the world, at £10 per 2,000 lbs.; and by the above experiment, Mr. Bignill offers to supply excellent beef at from £3 to £3 10s. per tierce, when an inferior article was charged in England from £6 to £6 10s. How is it possible for circumlocution to get over these facts? The *Melbourne Argus* states:—"The casks that stood the test of the voyage to England and back with the salt meat were made of the silver wattle, imported from Tasmania." Australians should turn their attention to the French, as a late number of *La France* announces the arrival at Paris of a large consignment of salt meat from Buenos Ayres, being a first attempt to open a permanent trade in that article. The immense number of horned cattle which feed on the vast plains of Buenos Ayres may thus provide a cheap kind of food for the poor in France, and on that account the plan has been encouraged by the Emperor. The meat sent over this time has been approved of by the *Conseil d'Hygiène* (or Board of Trade); and the price, it is believed, will not exceed thirty centimes per pound. If this be true, an immense sale of the article may be anticipated.

Brighton Hunting Beef.—The beef is first put into spring water, and allowed to remain there a few hours. On being taken out and well drained, a few ounces of powdered saltpetre are well rubbed into the meat. This must be repeated two or three times. Some common salt is next rubbed in several times for the next twenty-four hours. Then a mixture of a quarter of a pound of allspice and two ounces of pepper is rubbed into the meat for another twenty-four hours. The beef must remain ten days in the pickle, turned every day. It is then baked in a pan for four hours, covered with crust, and round the bottom of the baking-pan.

Salt Mutton (*French Fashion*).—If it be a leg, bone it, put it into a pan and pour over it a *marinade* made of oil, vinegar, salt, pepper, garlic, onion, thyme, a bay-leaf, and parsley. Let it *marinade* three days, and roast it. It may be stewed, and any part of mutton is good dressed in this mode.

Kangaroo Ham (*Prize Recipe*).—Take a quarter of a pound of fine Liverpool salt, add three ounces of coarse brown sugar, and one ounce of pounded allspice; mix them well together, then rub the whole well on and down the leg bone; let them lay in the pickle for a fortnight, rubbing them every other day. If not required for immediate use they may be hung up to dry; in this state they will keep good for years. When required for the table, chop off the bone close to the meaty part, cut slightly the sinew over the knee-joint, and bind it round; steep in cold water for twelve hours or more before using, then place it in a saucepan of cold water on a slow fire, and let it boil only ten minutes, drawing it aside until the water is nearly cool. When dished, pour over a rich brown gravy, flavoured with mace, salt, and pepper. Garnish with forcemeat balls, adding to the usual ingredients a little smoked bacon very finely chopped; a slice of boiled pork or ham is an agreeable addition.

The above recipe obtained a prize medal at the London Exhibition of 1862, and was kindly furnished the author by Mrs. Crouch, who was awarded the distinction.

Can that which is unsavoury be eaten without salt? or is there any taste in the white of an egg?—*Job* vi. 6.

The Best Way to Cook a Ham.—Put the ham in cold water to soak for twenty-four hours before boiling; scrape it well, then place in your copper, well covered with *cold* water, let it come to boil *slowly*, and after it has boiled for *twenty minutes* take all the fire from under the copper,* and let it remain until the water is cool, or until it is convenient to remove it out of the water. This will apply to any weight of ham.

To Dress a Ham for Table.—When skinned, chop parsley (free from grit, but not wetted or washed) impalpably fine, scatter it over the ham,

---

* If the ham is boiled in a pot, remove the same off the fire and let it stand to cool.

then grate a whole nutmeg over it. This will keep it almost any length of time, and adds a nice flavour.

To Cure a Round of Beef in Hot Weather, or if needed for Immediate Use.—Rub in thoroughly a rather large quantity of *fine* Liverpool salt, with a little saltpetre, then place it over a tub or pan of water on two sticks, placing a good quantity of salt on the upper side; turn it once after twelve hours, laying additional salt on the turned-*up* side. It will be cured in twenty-four hours. Should it be required at once, with a small squirt or syringe, if cold brine be at hand, it might be squirted into *all* the crevices, and then it could be cooked in twelve hours. If beef is not required in a hurry, a little sugar and less salt very much improves the flavour. This applies to curing hams.

The three last recipes were kindly furnished by a lady, whose mode of salting beef and dressing hams for the table has been much approved of, so much so; that she has supplied the *modus operandi* to several excellent gastronomical judges.

FEMALE REQUIREMENTS.—It should never be forgotten that household service is the only school that many a woman ever passes through, and to many a woman it is a pernicious school. If she has never learned to save in the midst of plenty, she cannot begin to save under the pressure of small means. As she has never had reason for turning small things to account—to make the most of odds and ends—she is often reduced, and reduces her husband, to a recurring necessitude of one day's feasting and three or four days' fasting, with an intermediate day of scraps; and she is utterly ignorant of the thousand ways of dressing vegetables with a little meat or fish, so as to make the absence of a more substantial dish unregretted. And this happens in a million homes in a country which has, on the whole, the finest fish, the richest and most succulent meats, and produces or imports poultry, eggs, and butter, to an extent which precludes their excessive dearness at any season. And while this happens to us, the French peasant, with far lower wages, with fewer materials of food, is making savoury dishes and healthy condiments out of the simplest produce of the field and the moor. Who can wonder, then, that while an English army is half-starved, despite numerous appliances and supplies, a French army feeds itself out of the rudest of Nature's gifts? Miss Burdett Coutts, and Lord Ashburton, who took the lead which she has so well followed, will have earned the gratitude of the country if they have done nothing more than set people thinking about the amelioration of their cookery, and lead high teachers to consider that the art of feeding is really a science which affects the wellbeing of twenty million citizens of England, and may often affect the existence of some quarter of a million soldiers abroad; and our social reformers will do well by following her example, and teaching the people of England that which, to the majority of them, is still a great secret—what food to buy, and how to cook it.—*The London "Times."*

LXXVII.—KETCHUP.

To speak, then, of the knowledges which belong to our English housewife, I hold the most principal to be a perfect skill in cookery. She that is utterly ignorant therein may not, by the laws of strict justice, challenge the freedom of marriage—because, indeed, shee can perform but half her vow—shee may love and obey, but shee cannot cherish and keepe her husband.—*Markham's "English Housewife,"* 1637.

Mushroom Ketchup.—*Syn.: Catchup, catsup, katchup, ketchup.* Sprinkle mushrooms, fresh gathered, with common salt for three days, then squeeze out the juice, and to each gallon add cloves and mustard-seed of each half an ounce; allspice, black pepper, and ginger bruised, one ounce; boil sufficiently. The above is from Cooley's

"Practical Receipts," and if followed with attention, cannot be improved; some persons use a little brandy, but any such spirit destroys the delicate flavour of the mushroom. Oyster, pontac, tomato, walnut, anchovy, caper, and cockle are each additions to the real ketchup, and take their names. There is nothing so useful in cookery as good ketchup; and we strongly advise the housewife to make it herself, as those purchased ready-made can seldom be depended on. It is a most valuable addition to soups, joints, and indeed every dish. Bottles of the best kind are required to hold it. Nothing in the shape of copper, lead, or pewter must be allowed to touch it; a plated copper spoon left in a bottle of ketchup for any time will render its contents poisonous. Dangerous fits of vomiting, colic, and diarrhœa have resulted from the neglect of this latter precaution. The majority of the ketchups retailed is a bad compound of liver and fish-roes, seasoned with pepper and drugs, not of the most healthful kind. Mushrooms are excellent, whatever way they are cooked: they may be fried, boiled, or done on toast in an oven before the fire, with a little butter put over them; or they may be stewed. As an accompaniment to chops, steaks, or roast meats or poultry, they are never out of place, and are always most *recherché* fare. What an addition and zest they give to the braise!

Camp Ketchup.—Take of old beer two quarts; white wine, one quart; anchovies, four ounces. Mix, and heat to the boiling point; remove it from the fire, and add three ounces of peeled shalot, half an ounce of mace, nutmegs, ginger, and black pepper. Macerate for fourteen days, and strain.

Cucumber Ketchup: made from ripe cucumbers, in the same way as mushroom ketchup. Very luscious and rich. Mixed with cream or melted butter, it forms an excellent white sauce for fowls, &c.

Marine Ketchup.—Strong beer, one gallon; anchovies, a pound and a half; peeled shalots pounded, one pound; half an ounce of mace, mustard-seed, and cloves; bruised pepper and ginger, a quarter of an ounce; mushroom ketchup and vinegar, one quart. Proceed in the same manner as camp ketchup.

Wine ketchup, oyster ketchup, pontac ketchup, walnut ketchup, and tomato ketchup are made in a similar way. Chili vinegar is used with the latter, and it makes an admirable relish.

DIFFERENT MODES OF EATING.—European nations use knives, forks, and spoons. The Hindoos eat their rice with their right hand; and the Chinese use two chopsticks, about half the thickness of lead pencils, but rather longer, and it is astonishing the dexterity with which they will feed with this simple aid, and even pick up a grain of rice. The Turks use their fingers, and generally with pieces of bread absorb the gravy of their little dishes. The Persians commence and end their repasts with coffee; and the generality of their dishes is an odd admixture of pillau, boiled fowl, raisins, melons, and fruits, and boiled meats, closely resembling the Turks. The Chinese are great fish-eaters, and anything in the shape of shark, dog-fish, or any coarse kind, they salt and preserve, and parties of these sons of Ham are found in the colonies contiguous to the gold fields, curing fish for their countrymen. Their birds'-nests and similar dishes are simply glutinous compounds. The Germans are very primitive in their cookery. A *table d'hôte* dinner commences with *potage au riz* and grated cheese; then plain boiled beef and sour-crout; boiled carp, and savoury puddings, swimming in oiled butter; Dutch cheese, pears, biscuits, with coffee and liqueur. The Viennese are many of them great epicures, and the Hungarians commence their repast with salted tongue, and the dinner ends with the roasts. At Wurtemburg the sausages are prepared from various materials. Blood, liver, bacon, brains, milk, bread, and meat are mixed together, with salt and spices. The mixture is then put into bladders, and being boiled, is smoked. The *Saturday Review* writes, that the Romans made little use of cattle as food; and the fattening of cattle for this purpose was unknown to them. Pliny mentions the use of beef, roasted, or in the shape of broth, as a medicine; but not as food. Plautus speaks of beef and mutton as sold in the markets; but amidst the immense variety of fish, flesh, and fowl, we hear little of the above meats in the Roman larder. Fish and game, poultry, venison, and pork are often mentioned as elements of a luxurious banquet; but undoubtedly the common food of all classes was vegetables flavoured with lard, or bacon. The warriors of Homer waxed strong and mighty on roast beef; but Regulus and Cincinatus "filled themselves," as Lord Macaulay would say, with beans and bacon. The cattle slain in sacrifice furnished, we must suppose, a special banquet for the epicure. Such, perhaps, were among the peculiar delicacies of the "suppers of the pontiffs." Bechman, in his "History of Inventions," tells us, that among the Romans, all articles of food were cut into small morsels before being served at table, and this was the more necessary, as the company did not sit at table, but lay on couches towards it, consequently could not well use both their hands for eating. For cutting meat, persons of rank kept in their houses a carver; he was designated the *scissor, carpus*, or *carptor*. Dr. Johnson asserts that the Scotch Highlanders knew nothing about dinner-knives till after the Revolution. Butler describes the dagger of one of the Hudibras heroes as—

> "A serviceable dudgeon,
> Either for fighting, or for drudging.
> When it had stabbed, or broke a head,
> It would scrape trenchers, or chip bread;
> Toast cheese or bacon; though it were
> To bait a mouse-trap, 'twould not care."

LXXVIII.—VINEGAR.

There are only two bad things in this world—sin and bile.—Hannah More.

Boil eleven gallons of water and fourteen pounds of sugar for twenty minutes; then pour it into a vessel to cool; when milk-warm, add yeast, and let it ferment. Place it in a warm place, and in a few months you will have good vinegar.

Wine and ale vinegar is made in a similar way, by continuing the fermentation; and, after the vinegar is ripe, you may have shalot, horseradish, chili, cayenne, cucumber, gooseberry, or any other fruit or vegetable, by merely adding the flavouring ingredients.

There is another mode of keeping up a stock of vinegar for family use, which is a very simple operation. Have a barrel to hold from thirty to forty quarts; then boil two quarts of good vinegar, pour it into the barrel, stop the bung-hole, and roll it about well. Half fill the barrel with light French wine, and leave it for a time in a warm place. At the end of a week boil two more quarts of vinegar, pour it into the barrel, and fill it up with wine and set it by. The vinegar may be used in a month, and it will acquire strength by keeping. If the vinegar should at any time be getting weak, add two quarts of vinegar to the cask, after boiling. For fifteen years a barrel of vinegar has been thus kept up, and found to improve every year.

VINEGAR.

VINEGAR.—This term is applied to various modifications of the acetic acid. The simplest mode of obtaining vinegar is to excite a second or acetous fermentation in wine. In this case oxygen is absorbed, a variable proportion of carbonic acid gas is generally evolved, and the alcohol of the wine passes into acetic acid. Very good vinegar is also made from strong beer, or from a wort of infusion of malt prepared for the purpose, or from a decoction of common raisins, or from a mixture of about one part of brandy with eight of water, and some sugar and yeast.—*Brande.*

Chili Vinegar.—Put an ounce of cayenne pepper, or the same quantity of the green birds'-eye chillies, to a pint of vinegar, and allow the infusion to remain a month. You may filter it if you please, or not.

Tarragon, basil, cress, mint, cucumber, garlic, shalot, horseradish, celery, and other ingredients, steeped in plain vinegar, will give out the several flavours, according to the vegetables used. Disciples of the epicurean school prefer the flavour of the tarragon and shalot.

Vinegar in Twenty-four Hours.—The whole philosophy of the manufacture of vinegar is included in the word oxydation. The alcohol contained in cider, beer, or wine, combining with the oxygen of the atmosphere, becomes acetic acid, which, in a diluted state, is vinegar. The methods usually pursued in the domestic manufacture of this article are, to say the least of them, susceptible of improvement. The conversion of good cider into vinegar, by exposure to the air in casks, requires weeks and even months to accomplish, because only a small surface is exposed at one time to the oxydising action of the atmosphere. By exposing a large surface of the liquor to the atmosphere, oxydation takes place with corresponding rapidity, and the process may be completed in from twenty-four to twenty-eight hours. The method of accomplishing this rapid acetification, which has long been known to scientific men and manufacturers, may be pursued in private houses without difficulty, as follows:—Take a clean flour barrel, and bore auger holes all around the sides and in the bottom; set it over a tub or open cask, and fill it lightly with beech shavings which have been soaked in vinegar. On the top of this barrel, which is open, lay two strips of wood, and rest on these a pail filled with cider, beer, or the like; procure fifteen lengths of cotton wicking, about thirty inches long, which, after dipping in the liquid, arrange round the side of the pail at regular intervals, so that one end of each will be hanging in the cider and the other hanging down outside, and below the bottom of the pail. By means of these wicks the pail will be gradually emptied of its contents, which, trickling over the shavings, will be exposed to the air, absorb oxygen, and finally be received in the tub beneath. By returning the liquor into the pail above, and suffering this trickling process to be repeated two or three times, a splendid vinegar will be obtained. The whole secret of the process lies in the mechanical increase of surface accomplished by the shavings.—*Scientific American.* The above process will be rendered much more efficient by being performed in a room heated to 80° or higher. The whole apparatus should be covered with a tight hogshead, without a head, turned upside down. Without this, the loss by evaporation will be great.—*Californian Farmer.*

Sugar, Cider, Fruit, and Beer Vinegars.—An excellent vinegar may be made for domestic purposes by adding to a syrup, consisting of one pound and a quarter of sugar for every gallon of water, a quarter of a pint of good yeast. The liquor being maintained at a heat of from 75° to 80° F., acidification will proceed so well that in two or three days it may be racked off from the sediment into the ripening cask, where it is to be mixed with one ounce of cream of tartar and one ounce of crushed raisins. When completely freed from the sweet taste, it should be drawn off into bottles, and closely corked up. The juices of currants, gooseberries, and many other indigenous fruits, may be acetified either alone or in combination with syrup. It will keep better than malt vinegar, on account of the absence of gluten; and at the present low price of sugar will not cost more, when fined upon beech chips, than a shilling per gallon.—*Ure.*

THE PHILOSOPHERS AT DINNER.—No wonder that these dinners had the reputation of being the best in London, nor that there should have been a great desire to dine at the Royal Society Club. It was the opinion of a distinguished aristologist that "a great deal of English spirit is owing to good dinners; and that as long as men are emboldened by good cheer they are in no danger of becoming slaves." We are indebted to a French *savant* for a picture of the philosophers at dinner a century ago, which, making every allowance for high colouring, is probably sufficiently faithful to be accepted as true. It is drawn by M. St. Fond, who travelled in England in the middle of the last century, and dined at the club on the occasion of the Elector Palatine being admitted in the Royal Society:—We sat down at five o'clock. The dinner was truly English, for there were no napkins. Grace was said by the astronomer, Maskelyne, after which we set to. The dishes consisted of huge joints of beef and mutton, roasted and boiled, and abundant supplies of potatoes and other vegetables, which each person seasoned as he pleased with the different sauces on the table. The viands were liberally watered (*arrosé*) with great potations of a kind of strong beer, called porter, drank out of pewter pots, which are preferred to glasses, because they hold a pint. This prelude over, the cloth was removed, and the table covered, as if by magic, by numerous crystal decanters filled with excellent port, Madeira, and claret. Several wine glasses were placed before each guest, and drinking was prosecuted vigorously, the desire to drink being encouraged by various descriptions of cheese, which were rolled from one end of the table to the other in mahogany boxes mounted on wheels. Toasts were now given, the first being for the health of the Royal family, then that of the Elector Palatine and the visitors, and, finally, each member of the club drank the health of his brother members, one by one, for it would be considered a great want of politeness to drink the health of more than one person at a time. When this formality terminated, champagne was introduced, which had the effect of putting every one in good humour (*d'egager tout le monde*). Tea followed the champagne, served with bread and butter and toast, and this was succeeded by coffee, which was very inferior to the tea. In France it is the custom to drink only one cup of excellent coffee; the English drink five or six cups of a vile decoction they call coffee. Brandy, rum, and other spirituous liquors wound up this philosophical banquet, which terminated at half-past seven. We then went to a meeting of the Royal Society, everybody being—but we prefer here using M. St. Fond's own words: "*Fort gris mais d'une gaieté décente.*"—*Fraser's Magazine.*

LXXIX.—THE DINNER HOUR.

Luciana. Dromio, go, bid the servants spread for dinner.—*Comedy of Errors.*

The proper hour for dinner is laid down by Thomas Cogan, a physician, in a book entitled the "Haven of Health," printed in 1584, as follows:—

"When foure houres bee past after breakfast, a man may safely take his dinner; and the most convenient time for dinner is about eleaven of the clocke before noone. The usuall time for dinner in the universities is at eleaven, or elsewhere about noone."

Grace at meat was often said in metre in the time of Shakespeare. In the play of "Timon of Athens" there is an instance of a metrical grace, by Apemantus (Act I., Scene 2). Dr. Johnson says that metrical graces are to be found in the primers; but Archdeacon Nares could not meet with them.—*Things not Generally Known.*

The time for dinner, according to an old saying, is, for the rich, when they can get an appetite; and for the poor, when they can get food. We append the grace alluded to in the above remarks:—

APEMANTUS' GRACE.

Immortal gods! I crave no pelf,
I pray for no man but myself:
Grant that I may never prove so fond,
To trust a man on his oath or bond;
Or a harlot for her weeping;
Or a dog that seems a-sleeping;
Or a keeper with my freedom;
Or my friends if I should need 'em.
Amen. So fall to 't:
Rich men sin, and I eat root. [*Eats and drinks.*

ENGLISH AFTER-DINNER CUSTOM.—There was one thing the Emperor did not like, nor did he hesitate to say so: the length of time passed by the English at their repasts. He, whose restless activity would not allow him, when alone, to spend more than a few minutes at table, would not consent to remain there for hours with the English. The Admiral (Cockburn) soon perceived that his national customs must yield to such a guest, and when dinner was finished, rose, and, with his staff, stood until Napoleon had left the room, offering him his hand if the motion of the vessel were unsteady, and then returned to indulge his English habits with his officers.—"*History of the Consulate and the Empire,*" *by Thiers.*

ARISTON.—According to the lexicons, the Greek for dinner is *ariston*, and therefore, for the convenience of terms, and without entering into inquiry, critical or antiquarian, I call the art of dining *Aristology*, and those who study it, *Aristologists.—The Original.* Socrates, who afterwards turns out to be the builder of the State, descends to the Peiras, in company with Glaucon, the son of *Ariston*, for the purpose of performing his devotions to Artemus, and beholding the Bendidia, a splendid festival in honour of that goddess.—*Analysis of Plato's Republic, by J. A. St. John.*

A very great personage in a foreign, but not remote country, once mentioned to the writer of these pages that he ascribed the superiority of the English in political life— in their conduct of public business and practical views of affairs—in a great measure to that "little half-hour" that separates, after dinner, the dark from the fair sex. The writer humbly submitted, that if the period of disjunction was strictly limited to a "little half-hour," its salutary consequences for both sexes need not be disputed; but that, in England, the "little half-hour" was apt to swell into a time of far more awful character and duration.—*Coningsby.*

LXXX.—ELIZABETHAN LIVING.

The art of feeding is a science which affects the well-being of twenty million citizens of England.—*The London "Times."*

It is the vulgar idea that Queen Elizabeth's maids of honour breakfasted on beef-steaks and ale, and that wine was such a rarity as only to be sold by apothecaries as a cordial. The science of good living was as well understood in those days as now, though the fashion might be somewhat different. The nobility had French cooks, and among the dishes enumerated we find not only beef, mutton, veal, lamb, kid, pork, rabbit, capon, pig, but also red or fallow-deer, and a great variety of fish and wild fowl, with pastry and creams, Italian confections and preserved fruits, and sweetmeats from Portugal; nay, we are told even of cherries served at twenty shillings per pound. The variety of wines can hardly be exceeded at present; for a writer of Elizabeth's time mentions fifty-six different kinds of French wine, and thirty-six Spanish and Italian wine, imported in England.—*Mrs. Jameson.*

FRENCH COOKS.—The best French cooks are from Picardy, then Flanders, Burgundy, Courtois, Lorraine, the Parisian last but one, and the Norman last of all.-*Mercier's Tableau de Paris.*

LXXXI.—DIGESTION.

God sends us meat; who sends cooks the proverb has saved us the trouble of guessing.—*Almanach des Gourmands.*

The following articles are digested in the times indicated:—

	hs.	mts.
Rice (boiled)	1	0
Apples (ripe)	1	30
Sago (boiled)	1	45
Bread, cabbage with vinegar (raw), boiled milk and bread, milk (cold)	2	0
Potatoes (roasted), and parsnips (boiled)	2	30
Baked custard	2	45
Apple dumpling	3	0
Bread, corn (baked), and carrots (boiled)	3	15
Potatoes and turnips (boiled), butter and cheese	3	30
Tripe and pigs' feet	1	0
Venison	1	35
Oysters (undressed), and raw eggs	2	3
Turkey and goose	2	30
Eggs (boiled soft), beef or mutton (roasted or boiled)	3	0
Boiled pork, stewed oysters, eggs (hard boiled or fried)	3	30
Domestic fowls	4	0
Wild fowls, pork (salted and boiled), suet	4	3
Veal, roasted pork, and salt beef	5	30

—*Beaumont.*

EATING.—The propriety of eating slowly ought always to be remembered. The great Napoleon was a fast eater; from the moment he and his guests sat down to the time the coffee was served was not more than forty minutes. The habit of eating fast, writes the *Quarterly*, is supposed to have paralysed him on two of the most critical occasions of his life, the battles of Borodino and Leipsic, which he might have converted into decisive and influential victories by pushing his advantages as he was wont. On each of these occasions he was known to have been suffering from indigestion. On the third day at Dresden, too, the German novelist, Hoffman, who was present in the town, asserts that the Emperor would have done much more than he did but for the effects of a shoulder of mutton stuffed with onions! The poet describes a hurried meal in the following terms:

But hark! the chiming clocks to dinner call;
A hundred footsteps scrape the marble hall.
The rich buffet well-coloured serpents grace,
And gaping Tritons spew to wash your face.
Is this a dinner? This a genial room?
No, 'tis a temple, and a hecatomb.
A solemn sacrifice, performed in state,
You drink by measure, and to minutes eat.
So quick retires each flying course, you'd swear
Sancho's dread doctor and his wand was there.
Between each act the trembling salvers ring,
From soup to sweet wine, and God bless the King.
In plenty starving, tantalised in state,
And complacently help'd to all I hate,
Treated, caress'd, and tired, I take my leave,
Sick of his civil pride from morn to eve.
I curse such lavish cost and little skill,
And swear no day was ever pass'd so ill.—*Pope's Moral Essays.*

LXXXII.—CONVIVIAL MAXIMS FROM THE "PHYSIOLOGY OF TASTE."

According to the laws of conviviality, a certificate from a sheriff's officer, a doctor, or an undertaker, are the only pleas admissible for absence. The duties which invitation impose do not fall on the persons invited, but, like all other social duties, are reciprocal. As he who has accepted an invitation cannot disengage himself from it, the master of the feast cannot put off the entertainment on any pretence whatever. Urgent business, sickness, not even death itself can dispense with the obligation which he is under of giving the entertainment, for which he has sent out invitations, which have been accepted; for in the extreme cases of compulsory absence or death, his place may be filled by his friend or executor.—*Le Manuel des Amphitryons.*

Article 1. Let not the number of the guests exceed twelve, that the conversation may be constantly general.

We differ with M. Brillat Savarin, and think Disraeli's number of *nine* far preferable, and accord with Kitchener in objecting to *thirteen*, when there is only dinner for *twelve*. Walker's limit is *eight*.

2. Let them be so selected that their occupations shall be varied, their tastes analogous, and with such points of contact that there shall be no necessity for the odious formality of presentations.

3. Let the eating-room be luxuriously lighted, the cloth remarkably clean, and the atmosphere at the temperature of from 16 to 18 of Réaumur.

4. Let the men be *spirituels* without pretension, the women pleasant without too much coquetry.

5. Let the dishes be exceedingly choice, but limited in number, and the wines of the first quality, each in its degree.

6. Let the order of progression be for the first (the dishes) from the most substantial to the lightest, and for the second (the wines) from the simplest to the most perfumed.

7. Let the act of consumption be deliberate, the dinner being the last

business of the day; and let the guests consider themselves as travellers who are to arrive together at the same place of destination.

8. Let the coffee be hot, and the liquors chosen by the master.

9. Let the saloon be large enough to admit of a game of cards for those who cannot do without it, and so that there may notwithstanding remain space enough for post-meridian colloquy.

10. Let the party be detained by the charms of society, and animated by the hope that the evening will not pass without some ulterior enjoyment.

11. Let the tea be not too strong; let the toast be scientifically buttered, and the punch carefully prepared.

12. Let not the retreat commence before eleven, but let everybody be in bed before twelve.

If any one has been present at a party uniting these twelve requisites, he may boast of having been present at his own apotheosis.

The heat of a dining-room should not be more than 62° of Fahrenheit.

LUXURY.—By repute, the celebrated Mr. Beckford, of Fonthill, was the most luxurious individual known in modern days. He it was that carried out the idea invented by Louis XIV., of the *tables volantes*. Mr. Beckford seldom entertained company, yet his table was invariably most gorgeously arranged. He used often, it is said, give orders for a superb dinner for twelve, and sit down alone to it, attended by twelve servants, each in full dress, eat of one dish, and send all away. Mr. Beckford had no bells; the servants waited in the ante-rooms. This would not do for Byron, who tells us—

"Turkey contains no bells, yet men dine."

Mr. Beckford's solemn state is equal to that which occurred at Arundel Castle, as detailed by an American writer, who was rather surprised, at a party of thirty, to see as many servants in the Howard livery waiting at table. M. Ude left the service of an English nobleman on one occasion, solely because he could not have a servant to carry up every dish; so writes the "Quarterly." The Romans considered flowers essential and necessary to their festal entertainments, and at their desserts: and modern fashion has followed suit with effect, for nothing tends to set off a table so much as choice and fragrant floral ornaments.

LXXXIII.—YEAST.

Every one who has reached the middle of life must have had occasion to observe how much his comfort and his powers of exertion depend on the state of his stomach, and will have lost some of his original indifference to rules of diet. The hour of dinner should be neither too late nor too early; if too late, the system will have been exhausted for want of it, will be weakened, and the digestion enfeebled; if too early, the stomach will crave another substantial meal, which, taken late in the evening, will not be digested before the hours of sleep. A person who breakfasts at nine should not dine later than six.—*Mayo*.

The preparation of yeast as a ferment is of some moment in the country, where no brewery is near. We therefore insert a recipe for

Good Potato Yeast.—Take about twelve full-sized potatoes, and, when boiled, mash them. Then boil a handful of hops and three tablespoonfuls of sugar in six pints of water. When nearly cold, mix the whole with about half a pint of stale yeast. Set it near the fire to work; it is ready for use when done working, and will keep a fortnight.

The above recipe, with common attention, makes most excellent bread, only it requires some pure yeast to commence with.

The following correspondence appeared some few years since in the London *Times* in reference to this subject:—

How to Make your own Yeast.—

"TO THE EDITOR OF THE 'TIMES.'

"Sir,—As you have succeeded in giving instructions to your readers how to grind their own wheat, and where to get an oven to bake it, to render your services complete I send you the following recipe for yeast. The new system will be incomplete without it. That the housekeeper may be independent both of the brewer and that compound called German yeast, I will give it you in plain language:—

"Monday morning boil two ounces of the best hops in four quarts of water for half an hour, strain it, and let the liquor cool down to new milk warmth, then put in a small handful of salt and half a pound of brown sugar; beat up one pound of the best flour with some of the liquor, and then mix all together.

"On Wednesday add three pounds of potatoes boiled and then mashed, to stand till Thursday; then strain it and put it into bottles, and it is ready for use.

"N.B.—It must be stirred frequently while it is making, and kept near the fire. Before using shake the bottle well up. It will keep in a cool place for two months, and is best at the latter part. The beauty of this yeast is that it ferments spontaneously, not requiring the aid of other yeast; and if care be taken to let it ferment well in the earthen bowl in which it is made, you may cork it up tight when bottled. I put mine into Seltzer-water bottles, and this quantity will fill four. I have used it now for many months, and never had lighter bread than it affords, without any failure.—Yours, &c., "D. S. Y."

[*Times*, October 22, 1855.]

"TO THE EDITOR OF THE 'TIMES.'

"Sir,—There appeared lately in the *Times* a letter signed 'D. S. Y.' containing directions for making yeast. I have most carefully followed them in every particular, and the result has been a total failure.

"In a time when it is of the utmost importance to increase the supply of good wholesome bread, and there are mills for grinding and ovens for baking at home, it would be a great boon to all those who know the constant difficulty of procuring yeast to discover some way of making it. If any of your numerous readers could send a recipe for insertion in your columns, it would be, I am sure, thankfully received by many, and by none more so than "Your obedient servant, "H.

"January 17."

[*Times*, January 21, 1856.]

"TO THE EDITOR OF THE 'TIMES.'

"Sir,—In reply to 'H' in the *Times* of this morning, and dated January 17th, I beg to say that I have copied the following recipe from your paper in September or October last. I have used it ever since with invariable and complete success.

"If the recipe is the same as that alluded to by 'H,' there must have been some fault in preparing it, as I have never found it fail. I make bread three times a week with it for my family.

"The bread takes a considerable longer time to rise in the sponge, and also after being made into dough, than that made by ordinary yeast, and is better by being baked in a tin. "M. H."

(The recipe enclosed.)

"TO THE EDITOR OF THE 'TIMES.'

"Sir,—In answer to your correspondent 'H' the following I consider an undoubted recipe, and one in constant use in Cornwall, where yeast is difficult to be procured.—I am, sir, your obedient servant,

"January 21. "DOUGH.

"Put one handful of hops to three quarts of water, and let it boil two hours; then strain the hops away, mixing a pint of flour with the liquor, and while hot a tea-cupful of moist sugar; let it stand and get lukewarm, then work it with a tea-cupful of yeast, stirring it often; let it stand one day, and then put it into jars for use.

"Quantity—one quart of the above to one bushel of flour."

[The *Times*, January 21, 1856.]

Artificial Yeast.—Mix two parts of fine flour of pale barley malt with one part of wheat flour; stir fifty pounds of this mixture gradually into one hundred quarts of cold water, with a wooden spatula, till it forms a smooth pap. Put this pap into a copper over a slow fire; stir it well till the temperature rise to fully 150° to 160°, when a partial formation of sugar will take place, but this sweetening must not be pushed too far; turn out the paste into a flat cooler, and stir it from time to time. As soon as the wort has fallen to 59° Fahr., transfer it to a tub, and add for every fifty quarts of it one quart of good, fresh beer-yeast, which will throw the wort into brisk fermentation in the course of twelve hours. This preparation will be good yeast, fit for bakers' and brewers' uses, and will continue fresh and active for three days. It should be occasionally stirred.—*Ure.*

Patent Yeast.—Boil six ounces of hops in three gallons of water for three hours; strain it off, and let it stand ten minutes; then add half a peck of ground malt, stir it well up, and cover it over; return the hops, and put the same quantity of water to them again, boiling them the same time as before, straining it off to the first mash; stir it up and let it remain four hours, then strain it off, and set it to work at 90°, with three pints of patent yeast. Let it stand about twenty hours; take the scum off the top, and strain it through a hair sieve; it will then be fit for use. One pint is sufficient to make a bushel of bread.

GERMAN YEAST.—It is well known that a large proportion of the bread prepared for family use is raised from what is called German yeast, a noxious compound, imported weekly into Hull, in quantities really astonishing, and where, I am credibly informed, tons of it are thrown into the sea from having become alive; yet this is used by the great majority of bakers over the kingdom to produce the bread for our vast population, who little suspect the slow poison they are daily and unconsciously consuming.—*Manchester Guardian.*

Cobbett's Yeast Cakes.—Provide seven pounds of Indian corn meal, three and a half pounds of rye flour, three ounces of hops, and one gallon of boiling water. Separate the hops by the hand, strew and boil them in the water for half an hour, then strain the liquor into an earthen vessel, put in the rye while hot, stirring quickly as the fermentation commences. Next day, when it is working, put in the Indian meal, stirring it well. Before all the meal is added, it will become a stiff dough. Knead it well, and roll it out as you would a pie-crust, to the thickness of the third of an inch. Cut it into cakes with a tumbler; place these cakes in the sun to dry. Turn them every day until they are hard; keep them in a dry place. When you bake, take a couple of these cakes, break them and put them into warm water over-night. Let the vessel containing them stand near the fire; they will dissolve. Use the liquid for setting your sponge, just as you would the yeast of beer. White pea-meal or barley-flour will do as well as Indian meal.

Mr. Cobbett states in his "Cottage Economy," that the best bread he ever ate in his life was lightened with these cakes.

LA BELLE FRANCE.—The south of France is the great larder of Paris. Thence we have from Provence the exquisite pale truffle and oil, pure and colourless as water; *pâtés*, led on by the sublime *pâté de foix gras;* the *poulard truffé* of Perigord; the unbrandied claret of Bordeaux; the liqueurs of Marseilles; the nougat of the same emporium; the oranges of Hyères; the muscat of Lunel; the ortolans, quails, *verdiers, becfigues,* the olives, figs, anchovies, almonds, fruits, dried and preserved in jelly, *en compote,* in brandy and out of it, and other countless delicacies.—*Hints for the Table.*

LXXXIV.—A BACHELOR'S DINNER, ACCORDING TO SOYER.

Some people have a foolish way of not minding, or pretending not to mind, what they eat. For my part, I mind my stomach very studiously and carefully, and I look upon it that he that does not mind his stomach will hardly mind anything else.—*Dr. Johnson.*

"The dinner having thus began with six oysters, a glass of Chablis, or, if preferred, white hermitage, or even Moselle, the soup is then placed on the table; this ought to be of a light kind, and should turtle be preferred it ought to be light and transparent. With the soup a glass of sherry or Madeira is the best accompaniment. At the same time as the soup is placed on the table so are the fish, the sauce, and the potatoes on the sideboard. The fish, if boiled, should be accompanied by hock or white Burgundy; if baked or stewed, with claret of a light kind. The next course should consist of a boiled and roast remove, and two *entrées.* To those who know artistically how to eat a dinner, it may appear strange when I tell them that I have known those who have considered themselves *gourmets* commence this course with the *entrées*. The plan which ought to be followed is to begin with the boiled, and, if your appetite is good, to slightly touch the roast, partaking of wines according to the nature of the dish; for instance, boiled poultry with oyster sauce, return to Chablis; lamb, with caper sauce, to hock or Moselle; roast mutton, light claret; roast beef, sherry or Madeira. The two substantials having been disposed of, the palate has now arrived at that degree of perfection (supposing the wines partaken of to have been good of their kind, for nothing destroys the reputation of a good dinner more than bad wines), in which the art of the cook, as displayed in his *entrées*, now engages the attention of the guests. These *entrées* should be as different as possible, and also differ from the roast and boiled. With the *entrées*, whatever their nature, it is generally the custom to partake of champagne. This, when the ladies are at the table, I do not object to, as they are not supposed to be professors in the science of eating, but with the real epicure it is a *sin* I cannot pardon. The wine to be partaken of depends upon the nature of the *entrée*, but should never be of that luscious description as to overpower the delightful sensation produced by the *plat*. These having been removed, their places should be occupied by two dishes of nicely-roasted game and four *entremets*—as, for instance, woodcocks and pheasants, or even a fine larded capon and wild fowl, and one savory, one vegetable, and two sweets as *entremets*. With the roast I prefer claret or red Burgundy; with the *entremets* may be served champagne. These *entremets* should display the skill of the professor, not in a way that anything about them cannot be partaken of, but that what they are made of may delight the sight as well as the taste. The roast should be removed with two dishes, containing either a *soufflé*, a pudding, or something of that sort. These being disposed of, I would have the dessert placed on the table, with the cheese handed round, and at the same time a loving cup, or, if that is not to be obtained, a tankard full of the same liquid. Port wine *may* be partaken of with the dessert. The plates should be changed as often as possible, and not left, as at present, to receive a collection of orange and apple peel, and other refuse. During the time that this is being partaken of—say twenty minutes or half an hour, or even longer, so much depending upon the Amphitryon and his guests—the coffee ought to be introduced, and the table should be immediately cleared, or the guests go into the drawing-room, should the unhappy bachelor happen to have one, and the remainder of the evening may be passed according to the disposition and taste of the party, such as music, cards, &c.; and I am afraid the enjoyment of the evening would not be complete without cigars."

A GREAT MAN NOT SO PARTICULAR AS DR. JOHNSON.—The Duke dined one day in Paris with M. Cambacères, one of the most renowned *gourmets* in France. The host having pressed a *recherché* dish upon the Duke, asked eagerly, when the plate was cleared, how he had liked it. "It was excellent," replied the Duke; "but to tell you the truth, I don't care what I eat." "Good heavens!" exclaimed Cambacères; "don't care what you eat! Why, then, did you come here?"—*Anecdote of the Duke of Wellington.*

COMING LATE TO DINNER.—Jack Sippit never keeps the hour he has appointed to come to a friend's dinner; but he is an insignificant fellow, who does it out of vanity. He could never, he knows, make any figure in company, but by giving a little disturb-

once at his entry, and therefore takes care to drop in when you are just seated. He takes his place, after having discomposed everybody, and desires that there may be no ceremony. Then does he begin to call himself the saddest fellow, in disappointing so many places as he was invited to elsewhere. It is the fop's vanity to name houses of better cheer, and to acquaint you that he names yours out of ten dinners which he was obliged to be at that day. The last time I had the fortune to eat with him, he was imagining how very fat he should have been, had he eaten all he has ever been invited to. But it is impertinent to dwell upon the manners of such a wretch as obliges all whom he disappoints, though his circumstances constrain them to be civil to him. But there are those that every one would be glad to see who fall into the same detestable habit.—*The Spectator.*

LXXXV.—CHOCOLATE.

Thus, at the outset, he was gastronomic, discussed the dinner from the soup to the Stilton, criticised the cutlets, pronounced upon the merits of the mutton, and threw out certain vague hints that he would one day astonish the world by a *little volume* on cookery.—*Major Monsoon in "Charles O'Malley."*

Chocolate is a rich breakfast beverage. Do not grate it, but cut the quantity required, and boil it in water. To an ounce of chocolate put an ounce and a half of boiling water; add cream or milk. Do not allow it to boil over if you desire the flavour to be preserved, and it must not be boiled a second time. The prepared homœopathic cocoa is highly spoken of as an excellent preparation for an early meal, wholesome, devoid of fatty matter, and digestible. Messrs. Fry and Son's homœopathic cocoa is recommended for invalids and persons subject to dyspepsia. Messrs. Fry, of London and Bristol, were awarded medals at the Exhibitions of London, Paris, and New York, so that their preparation has a world-wide celebrity.

COURTESY AT DINNER.—Some hosts are sadly wanting in attention to their guests. A Lord Lyttelton, one of this class, was very absent in company. His lordship one day pointed out a particular dish and asked for it, calling it by another name. A gentleman at table was about to tell him of his mistake. "Never mind," whispered another; "help him to what he asked for, and he will suppose it is what he wanted."—*Table Anecdotes.*

LXXXVI.—CURRY POWDER.

A gay French marquis came accidentally on the celebrated Descartes enjoying himself in eating an excellent dinner. "What! do you philosophers eat dainties?" asked the former. When the latter replied, "Do you think that God made good things only for fools?"—*Life of Descartes.*

Indian servants differ in the relative quantities of the different ingredients used in the manufacture of curry stuff. They invariably make it as they want it, from the best ingredients. We have even seen it made in this way on board Indiamen. The powder sold at the shops is invariably adulterated; there may be exceptions, but they are rare; for if the articles are dearer when singly purchased than the curry stuff, it is impossible for the latter to be pure, that's certain. In a book in our collection, "The Cook," by Read, the author says that no cayenne is to be used in curry powder. We fancy a Bengalee or Malay would laugh at such a foolish recommendation. The following are our proportions:—Mustard seed, one ounce and a half; coriander, four ounces; turmeric, four and a quarter ounces; black pepper, two and a half ounces; cayenne, one ounce and a quarter; ginger, half an ounce; cinnamon, cloves, and mace, each, quarter of an ounce. To be well pounded and mixed, and kept in a stoppered bottle in a dry place.

OIL v. BUTTER.—One day a certain *bon vivant* abbé came to Fontenelle, who lived within a month of a hundred years. The abbé was fond of asparagus dressed with butter, but Fontenelle preferred it dressed with oil. The latter said that for such a friend there was no sacrifice he would not make, and that he should have half the dish of asparagus which he had ordered for himself, and, moreover, that half should be dressed with butter. While they were thus conversing together, the poor abbé fell down in a fit of apoplexy, upon which Fontenelle instantly scampered down-stairs and bawled out to his cook, "The whole with oil—the whole with oil, as at first!"—*Table Anecdotes.*

LXXXVII.—BITTERS.

Some physiologists will have it that the stomach is a mill; others, that it is a fermenting vat; others again, that it is a stewpan; but, in my view of the matter, it is neither a mill, a fermenting vat, nor a stewpan, but a stomach, gentlemen, a stomach.—*Hunter's Lectures.*

Make your own bitters as follows, and we can vouch for their superiority:—One ounce and a half of gentian-root, one ounce and a half of lemon-peel, one ounce and a half of orange-peel. Steep these ingredients for about a month in a quart of sherry, and then strain and bottle for use. Bitters are a fine stomachic, but they must be used with caution.

Bitters and tonics are often confounded, whereas there is a great difference between them. When weakness proceeds from excess of irritability, these bitters are beneficial; because all bitters are poisons, and operate by stilling, and depressing, and lethargising the irritability. But where weakness proceeds from the opposite cause of relaxation, then tonics are good; because they brace up and tighten the loosened string. Bracing is a correct metaphor. Bark goes near to be a bitter and a tonic; but no perfect medical combination of the two properties is yet known.—*Coleridge.*

GENTIANA LUTEA, the common yellow gentian, which is said to owe its name to Gentius, King of Illyria, who introduced it as a medicine 170 years before Christ. The roots of the plant are collected and dried by the peasants of Switzerland, the Tyrol, and the Auvergne. The bitter of the gentian is agreeable and aromatic; it is much used in medicine, and has, on some occasions, been employed instead of hops in beer.—*Ure.*

LXXXVIII.—COPPER SAUCEPANS.

To be eaten in perfection, the interval between meat being taken out of the stewpan and its being put into the mouth must be as short as possible; but ceremony, that most formidable enemy of good cheer, too often decrees otherwise, and the guests seldom get a bit of an *entremet* till it is half cold.—*Kitchener*.

The precise danger from the use of copper saucepans imperfectly tinned is far from being generally understood. It appears that the acid contained in stews, as lemon-juice, though it does not dissolve the copper by being merely boiled in it a few minutes, nevertheless, if allowed to cool and stand in it for some time, will acquire a sensible impregnation of poisonous matter, as verdigris, or the green band which lines the interior of the vessel. Dr. Falconer observed, that syrup of lemons boiled fifteen minutes in copper or brass pans did not acquire a sensible impregnation; but if it was allowed to cool and remain in the pans for twenty-four hours, impregnation was perceptible, even to the taste, and was discovered by the test of metallic iron. This fact was further confirmed by the researches of Proust, who states, that in preparing food or preserves in copper, it is not till the fluid ceases to cover the metal, and is reduced in temperature, that the solution of the metal begins.—*Christison on Poisons*.

CAUTION.—Persons cannot be too cautious in using copper saucepans, and they should be often examined. Many cases of poisonings have occurred from the verdigris having become mixed with food. In 1829 a gentleman was poisoned in Paris by eating soup warmed in a copper saucepan; and in 1837 the family of a nobleman in the same city died from eating stew which had been allowed to get cold in a copper pan. The French are more fond of using copper saucepans than we are.

LXXXIX.—COOKERY FOR THE DESTITUTE.

There is no reason why the poor man's mess of porridge should not be made as savoury and wholesome, and be prepared with as much care and cleanliness, as the more costly viands of the rich.—*Paper on "Charity Soups."*

Dr. Kitchener tells us that a gallon of good broth may be made for fourpence, as follows:—Put four ounces of Scotch barley and four ounces of sliced onions into five quarts of water, boil gently for one hour, and pour it into a pan; then put into the saucepan two ounces of beef or mutton dripping, and three ounces of fat bacon; when melted, stir into it four ounces of oatmeal, rub these until you make a paste, which add to the barley broth, and season with black pepper, salt, &c., and it is ready.

On a larger scale 1,000 quarts of soup may be made at twopence halfpenny per quart, by using the following ingredients—viz.:—210 pounds of beef (fore-quarters), 90 pounds legs of beef, 3 bushels of peas, 1 bushel of flour, 12 bunches of leeks, 6 bunches of celery, 12 pounds of salt, and 12 ounces of black pepper.—*The Morning Post*, 1840.

"The Art of Dining" informs us that Soyer is more likely to earn his immortality by his soup kitchen than his soup; he is one of the best authorities, therefore, for cheap soups. We extract a recipe from the "Culinary Campaign," in which good soup for the poor may be made at three farthings per quart, as follows:—To 100 gallons of water add

	£	s.	d.
12 pounds of solid meat, at 4d., or 16 pounds of meat with bones	0	4	0
3 pounds 2 ounces of dripping	0	1	0
12 pounds of onions, sliced	0	0	8
6 pounds of leeks } 6 pounds of celery } 8 pounds of turnips }	0	3	1
37 pounds and a half of flour (seconds)	0	7	0
25 pounds of pearl barley, soaked	0	6	9
9 pounds of salt	0	0	3
1 pound 7 ounces of sugar	0	0	9
	£1	3	6

Indian corn meal, oatmeal, and vegetables of every kind, simmered with a small quantity of meat or fish, make most nutritious food for the poor, and the expense is trifling.

Frugal cookery, based on the most economical principles, is of essential consequence to those who have little money to spend. The most nourishing meats are often the cheapest. With a good manager, a shilling or two laid out in the coarser parts of beef and mutton, would be far more profitable, and more nutritious, than buying butter and cheese. Meat goes furthest when made into soup and stews. A pound of meat even, boiled, or rather simmered, with oatmeal or rice, will make a nourishing meal for a whole family. Ox's head and feet, sheep's head and trotters, and cow's heel, are most strengthening, and only require a little more care in the preparation. Give an Englishman a pound of meat: the chances are, that two to one, he rushes to the frying-pan, and frizzles all the goodness out of it. How different the Frenchman proceeds: he has recourse to the *pot au feu*, and, with the assistance of every kind of vegetable that he can lay his hands on, he will have ready, in a few hours, the most savoury of dishes, and the most digestible; hence the common saying, "as many Frenchmen, as many cooks." Why should there not be national schools of cookery, and prizes given to those who would economise and make meat go further than it does at present? Let but a hundredth part of the money that is now expended in powder and ball practice be appropriated to this purpose, and the nation would be materially benefited. We have no wish to decry the Volunteer mania— far from it; but we do contend, that the poor generally would be better cared for by a movement that had cookery for its basis; for the meat now wasted by improvident *cuisine* would support twice the number of Great Britain's population; and, in this case, we should hear of no cases of starvation in the mother country. In the Australias, among the industrious classes, *meat* three times a day is a matter of course, besides butter *ad libitum*. In the earlier days of the colonies, with all classes, "tea, mutton, and damper" was the universal fare, damper being nothing more than flour and water, with a little salt, smothered in wood ashes until done. There is an alteration in Colonial cookery for the better, and great room for further improvement.

Cheap Cookery.—There is something much more practical and promising in Mr. Corbett's recent establishment of cheap cooking-houses in Glasgow. His aim is to provide the food commonly in use among the working classes, cooked in a simple but efficient manner, and sold at the lowest rate compatible with a distinct profit on the articles prepared. Thirteen of these houses have been already fitted up, and are now in operation in Glasgow, and thus far they have succeeded singularly well. A breakfast of porridge, milk, coffee, and roll, with butter, may be had for threepence; separate rations of soup, potatoes, bread-and-butter, or bread-and-cheese, coffee, tea, porridge, eggs, &c., may be obtained any hour during the day for one penny. At the chief branches a fourpenny halfpenny dinner is served, comprising a basin of broth, a plate of meat (either hot or cold), an ample supply of potatoes, and a slice of capital plum pudding. The houses are plainly, but neatly fitted up, and have a very cheerful aspect. They are inundated with customers; and ultimately they must exercise a most important and favourable influence upon the domestic management of the operatives who frequent them. The economical advantages must be very great. The men will there learn, and that in the most pleasant fashion, the advantage, both to the pocket and palate, of properly cooked food. They will also learn what rightly prepared food is. The women will be taught the need of becoming acquainted with the modes of concocting such palatable food, if they would maintain their domestic power. If at first they may seem to weaken the home tie, in the end they will strengthen it. If the husband prefers his meal at the eating-house, to the neglect of his wife and family, it will be for the wife to show that he may have more comfortable, as well as well-cooked and as cheap, food at home. This is practicable, if women will learn how. When women have fully mastered the lesson— one, by the way, of wider application than to operatives only—a step in civilisation will have been gained, which will show in increased health, increased prosperity, and happier domestic hearths. Let us hope, then, that Mr. Corbett's successful experiment in Glasgow will find many imitators elsewhere.—"*The Lancet*" *on Culinary Civilisation.*

Glasgow appears to be taking the lead in cheap and good dinner and refreshment establishments. In addition to Mr. Corbett's great cooking depôt for the working classes, which now shows gross receipts to the amount of £35,000 per annum, there is a luncheon-room, of a unique kind. Persons unacquainted with Langs', would pass it by as a mere confectioner's shop; but the initiated know better: they know it as one of the best-regulated refreshment places in Europe; in fact, it is without a parallel, and might be taken as a model by all the railway refreshment rooms of the kingdom.—*Home News.*

HINTS TO EMIGRANTS.—Married women, more deeply versed in ball-room gossip than in the arts of boiling and frying, should set their faces against emigration, unless they intend to turn over a new leaf. Unmarried girls may emigrate, but they must condescend to become useful as well as agreeable. Many good, honest settlers have been ruined by having fine ladies for wives.—*Thomson's "New Zealand."*

XC.—DINNER PARTIES IN THE SIXTEENTH AND SEVENTEENTH CENTURIES.

So soon as dinner's done, we'll forth again.—*Timon of Athens.*

When a feast is made ready, we are told, " the table is covered with a carpet and a table-cloth by the waiters, who, besides, lay the trenchers, spoons, knives and little forks, table-napkins, bread, with a salt-cellar. Messes are brought in platters, a pie in a plate. The guests being brought in by the host, wash their hands out of a laver or ewer, over a hand-basin or bowl, then they near the table on the chairs. The carver breaketh up the good cheer and divideth it. Sauces are amongst roast meat in saucers. The butler filleth strong wine out of a cruise, or wine-pot, or flagon, into cups or glasses, which stand on a cupboard, and he reacheth them to the master of the feast, who drinketh to his guests."—*Wright's Domestic Manners and Sentiments.*

A Richmond Dinner Three Hundred Years Ago.—We find, in the Lansdowne manuscripts, that about Christmas, 1509, certain officials of the court of King Henry VIII. dined together at the village of Shene, now called Richmond, and that, at the end of the entertainment, my host of the "Star and Garter," with many salutations, handed to them the following bill :—

For brede	... ...	12d.
Ale	... ...	3s. 4d.
Wyne	... ...	10d.
Two lignes moton	...	8d.
Maribones	... ...	6d.
Powdered beef	... ...	5d.
Two capons	... ...	2s.
Two geese	... ...	14d.
Five conyes	... ...	15d.
One legge moton	... ...	4d.
Six plovers	... ...	18d.
Six pegions	... ...	5d.
Two dozen larkes	... ...	12d.
Salt and sauce	... ...	6d.
Buter and eggs	... ...	10d.
Warden and guyees	...	12d.
Herbes	... ...	1d.
Spices	... ...	2s. 4d.
Floure	... ...	4d.
White cuppes and cruises		6d.
Amounting to one pound sterling.		

—*Hints for the Table.*

PRIMITIVE COOKERY.—The science of cookery was in a primitive state among the New Zealanders, for, being destitute of vessels capable of resisting fire, the cookery of the whole race, except those being near the boiling springs of Rotoma and Taupo, was limited to steaming and roasting. The former was done in an oven, made by digging a hole in the ground, according to the size of the banquet, into which burning firewood, and stones about the size of an orange, were put, and then covered slightly over. When the stones were red-hot one-half were taken out, food put in, water sprinkled on to generate steam, and the whole covered with fresh leaves, hot stones, and earth.—*Thomson's "New Zealand."*

XCI.—MOSSES.

Cookery is an art appreciated by only a few individuals, and which requires, in addition to a most studious and diligent application, no small share of intellect, and the strictest sobriety and punctuality.—*Ude.*

Carrageen Moss (*Choudrus Crispus*).—This Irish moss is soothing and strengthening to the stomach. It is cooked by being cleaned sufficiently in water, and then boiled; or a decoction of it may be taken by those subject to pulmonary complaints. It is a very economical substitute for isinglass in orange, lemon, or savoury jellies, or blanc-mange. It is cooked in a similar way to laver, and served with meat of any kind. It is a most nutritious vegetable, if it can be called such. It is the pearl moss, and the decoction or jelly is a useful and popular demulcent and emollient: often employed by cooks and confectioners. It is excellent for clarifying beer and wines, or for any purpose where isinglass is used; and, according to Zimmermann, when combined with tartar emetic, a little of it goes a great way in clearing worts. It is found in the Australias, but its usefulness is not generally known.

Ceylon Moss (*Plocaria Candida*).—This moss is exported from the islands of the Indian Archipelago, forming a portion of the cargoes of nearly all the junks. It is stated by Mr. Crawford, in his "History of the Indian Archipelago," that on the spots where it is collected, the prices seldom exceed from 5s. 8d. to 7s. 6d. per cwt. The Chinese use it in the form of jelly with sugar, as a sweetmeat, and apply it in the arts as an excellent paste. The quantity of nitrogen contained in these plants is remarkably large, and will, of course, account for the high nutritive value ascribed to them.—*Ure.*

Dr. Macgowan, of Ningpo, forwarded, through Sir John Bowring, the following algæ, which he thus names and transcribes:—

Tan-shivin grass, so named from the place, on the coast of Formosa, whence it is procured. It is used for making *yang-tsai* (ocean vegetable).

Nin-mau (ox-hair) grass: made into an iced jelly, and sold in the streets in hot weather, sugared.

Hâi-tai (sea-tape).—It is usually boiled with pork.

Tsz-tsai (purple vegetable).—Eaten to give a relish to rice.

Fah-tsai (hair vegetable).—Boiled either with animal or vegetable articles.

Ki-tsai (hen-foot vegetable).—Cooked with soy or vinegar. Sea-tape, from Japan: it is preferred to the former.—*Society of Arts' Journal.*

A PROPER HOST.—Mr. Canning's fund of animal spirits, and the extreme irritability of his temperament, were such as to hurry him, *nolentum volentum*, into the full rush and flush of conviviality. At the latter period of his life, when his health began to break, he would sit down, with an evident determination to be abstinent—eat sparingly of the simplest soup, take no sauce with his fish, and mix water with his wine;

but as the repartee began to sparkle, and the anecdote to circulate, his assumed caution was insensibly relaxed, he gradually gave way to temptation, and commonly ended by eating of everything, and taking wine with everybody—the very *beau-ideal* of an Amphitryon.—*Quarterly Review.*

XCII.—MINCEMEAT À LA SOYER.

Evans: I will make an end of my dinner; there is pippins and cheese to come.
Merry Wives of Windsor.

Take four pounds and a half of beef suet, which skin and chop very fine; have also a quarter of a pound of candied lemon and orange-peel, the same of citron, a pound and a half of lean cooked beef, and three pounds and a half of apples, cored and peeled, and chopped fine, and put into a large pan, with four pounds and a half of currants, well washed and picked, two ounces of mixed spice, and two pounds of moist sugar. Mix the whole well together, with the juice of eight lemons, and a pint of brandy; place it in jars, and tie down for use. A pound and a half of raisins, well stoned and chopped, may be added to the above.

AMERICAN MINCEMEAT.—Take pieces of vegetables and cold meat; mash the vegetables, and chop the meat fine. Warm it with gravy or dripping. Fry, and slice a few apples, and mix with it, with a little sage. After it has been sufficiently warmed, lay it on slices of toasted bread, and serve.

MONASTIC LIVING.—The kitchen and feasting at the Monastery of Alcobaca is thus described by Mr. Beckford:—The kitchen was magnificent; through the centre of the immense and groined hall, not less than sixty feet in diameter, ran a brisk rivulet of the clearest water, flowing through pierced wooden reservoirs, containing every sort and size of the finest river fish. On one side loads of grain and venison were heaped up, on the other vegetables and fruits in endless variety. Beyond a long line of stoves extended a row of ovens, and close to them hillocks of wheaten flour, whiter than snow, rocks of sugar, jars of the purest oil, and pastry in vast abundance, which a numerous tribe of lay brothers and their attendants were rolling out and puffing up into a hundred different shapes, singing all the while as blithely as larks in a cornfield. The banquet is described as including exquisite sausages, potted lampreys, strange matters from the Brazils, and others still more strange from China (viz., birds' nests and sharks' fins), dressed after the latest mode of Macao, by a Chinese lay brother. Confectionery and fruits were out of the question here; they awaited the party in an adjoining still more sumptuous and spacious saloon, to which they retired from the effluvia of viands and sauces. On another occasion, by the aid of Mr. Beckford's cook, the party sat down to one of the most delicious banquets ever vouchsafed a mortal on this side of Mahomet's paradise. The *macédoine* was perfection, the ortolans and quail lumps of celestial fatness, the *sautés* and *béchamels* beyond praise, and a certain truffle cream was so exquisite that the Lord Abbot personally gave thanks for it.

XCIII.—LEMON-JUICE.

Among the minor causes, no doubt, excess in eating and drinking has a great effect in multiplying cases of indigestion, which effect is augmented by the inferior and base quality of many articles of diet in general consumption, such as bakers' bread and brewers' beer. It is not many years since it was as common for families to make their own bread, and brew their own beer, as it is now to have these articles from the tradesman. My readers will perceive that I do not wish to represent these changes as principal causes of the present malady, but they are causes, and probably have greater effect than is commonly supposed. It must be recollected that these are articles of *daily* consumption, and therefore, if injurious, their deleterious operation, although in the beginning silent, yet is sure, and annually increasing.—*Graham on Indigestion.*

Cut off the peel of the lemons, and squeeze them until all the juice is out into a basin; then strain it through muslin. Have ready dry bottles, fill them with the juice until near the top. Pour into the bottles after a teaspoon of olive oil. Cork them, and place them upright in a cool place. Dry the peel, and string it for use. When you require to use the juice, open the bottle, and put in a skewer, with some cotton at the end, which will absorb the oil, and you will find the juice as good as when first bottled. No family should be without plenty of lemon-juice. It is useful for so many purposes. It is a refrigerant, and antiscorbutic, and makes an excellent summer drink, not forgetting its use in the different kinds of punch elsewhere detailed. In cure for scurvy it has no equal, and in acute rheumatism and gout, according to the united testimony of Owen, Rees, Babington, and numerous Continental practitioners, it has been taken with great success. It has no equal as flavouring for sauces, meats, and biscuits, and there is no pudding so wholesome or so easily made as a lemon one.

THE SYMPOSIACS.—These were table entertainments of the ancients, and were part of the education of the times, their discourses being commonly the canvassing and solution of some question, either philosophical or philological, always instructive, and usually pleasant; for the cups went round with the debate, and men were merry and wise together, according to the proverb. Plutarch says that one Lamprias, a man eminent for his learning and a philosopher, disputed best, and unravelled the difficulties of philosophy with most success, when he was at supper and well warmed with wine.—*Dryden.*

XCIV.—AL FRESCO PARTIES, OR PIC-NICS.

There, on a slope of orchard, Francis laid
A damask napkin, wrought with horse and hound,
Brought out a dusky loaf, that smelt of home,
And, half cut down, a pasty, costly made,
Where quail, and pigeon, lark and leveret, lay
Like fossils of the rocks, with golden yolks
Imbedded and injellied.—*Tennyson.*

These kind of gatherings are favourites everywhere in the summer, and it requires an adept at the organisation and providing of every requisite. Disraeli informs us, in "Coningsby," that, in the country, 'tis the coquette that provides amusement, and plans the *pic-nic;* that she is the stirring element amid the heavy congeries of social atoms; the soul of the house, the salt of the banquet. Amiable being! This picture is, no doubt, a truthful sketch of every-day life. Cold roast and boiled corned meats, poultry, game, pies of every kind and variety, not forgetting a moving dessert. Bread, cakes, biscuits, fruits, and wines; ginger-beer, soda-water, and bottled ale *à discretion;* salads, "sticker up" meats, roasted potatoes, and various condiments. Who would not be a gipsy on such an occasion, if the company are agreeable, and especially *one* possessing, to the consideration of the masculine sex,

"The nameless charms unmask'd by her alone;
The light of love, the purity of grace;
The mind, the music breathing from her face?"

PIC-NICS.—The origin of pic-nics has been traced to Charles, Prince of Wales, afterwards Charles I., who, in the year 1618, gave such a party, and invited the marquises, lords, knights, and squires to bring every man his dish of meat.—*History.*

XCV.—LIST OF BRITISH FISH.

Water Souchy.—This may be prepared from most kinds of fish, but perch, tench, and flounders are best. The principal thing in preparing water souchy is to extract every particle of goodness from one kind of fish to make a rich soup to dress those whose bodies are to be eaten. To do this you must take one-half the weight and quantity of the fish, and boil them in a mash in about a couple of quarts of water and some broken parsley, until the greater portion of the flesh of the fish may be strained with the gravy through a colander, after which add a little parsley, chopped fine, and place the remainder of the fish in the liquor; season with pepper and salt, and let the fish stew until done. Fish souchy is simply a batch of fish divided into two parts, the goodness of one of which, with herbs, is extracted to dress for the table the other moiety.

Alick.
Atherine.
Barbel.
Bass.
Black bream.
Bream, fresh water.
Bukar.
Bull.
Bull trout.
Burbot.
Carp.
Chad.
Char.
Chub.
Cod.
Codling.
Conger eel.
Crab.
Crayfish.
Crucian.
Dab.
Dace.
Dogfish.
Dory.
Drizzle.
Eel.
Fin-beared ling.
Flounder.
Forked hake.
French sole.
Garfish.
Grayling.
Grey gurnard.
Grey mullet.
Gudgeon.
Gurnard.
Gwiniad.
Haddock.
Hake.
Herring.
Halibut.
Lamprey.
Launce.
Lemon dab.
Ling.
Lobster.
Mackerel.
Minnow.
Morgay.
Mullet, red.
Mussel.
Oyster.
Parr.
Perch.
Pike.
Pilchard.
Plaice.
Pollish ranlin.
Pollish whiting.
Prawns and Shrimps.
Rayon, gilt head.
Ray.
Redback.
Roach.
Ruffle.
Salmon.
Salmon-peel.
Sandflack.
Scad.
Scaldfish.
Shad.
Smelt.
Sole.
Sprat.
Sturgeon.
Tench.
Topkud.
Torsh.
Trout.
Turbot.
Vendua.
Weever.
Whiffle.
Whitebait.
Whiting.
Wrasus.

Music at Dinner.—And, therefore, can there be a greater wrong committed on the cook than the common injury of dining to music? It is abominable. Once—I well remember it—I chewed to the clangour, and crash, and thunder of a military band. Well, sir, the dinner was excellent—admirable as a dinner; but I have no more judgment than a beast if I had any other taste in my mouth save the brass of the trumpets and the tough parchment of the drum-heads. Silence, profound and solemn, is due to the first hour of dining.—*Douglas Jerrold.*

XCVI.—SOUTH AUSTRALIAN FISH

Full many a partrich hadd he in mewe,
And many a bream, and many a luce in stewe.—*Chaucer.*

Snapper—weighing from 2lbs. to 10lbs.
Mullany, or Murray cod—10lbs. to 70lbs. This is a fresh-water fish found in the rivers of Australia. The flesh is rather soft. It produces isinglass, and requires attention in the dressing. The following is an account of its discovery:—

The river is rich in the most excellent fish, procurable in the utmost abundance. One man, in less than an hour, caught eighteen large fish, one of which was a curiosity from its immense size and the beauty of its colours. In shape and general form it most resembles a cod, but it was speckled over with brown, blue, and yellow spots, like a leopard's skin; its gills and belly a pure white; the tail and fins a dark brown. It weighed, entire, 70lbs.—*Oxley on the "Lachlan,"* 1817.

Baker, or mud fish—from 8lbs. to 50lbs. Rather rare. A highly-prized fish for the table.
Native herring, or ruff. A small but delicate fish.
Guardfish. Of a similar character.
Salmon—2lbs. to 4lbs. Highly esteemed.
Bream—2lbs. to 4lbs. Very good eating, and excellent stewed.
Mullet and whiting—½lb. to 1lb. Very delicate, white flesh, and good.
Soles. Large ones are occasionally procurable.
Flathead. A very firm fish, and makes unexceptionable soup.
Snook and mackerel. Rare.
Silver fish and flounders. Rather small, but of fine flavour.
Crayfish—2lbs. to 8lbs.
Crabs. Very fine and large.
Oysters. Fine.
Shrimps. Very good.
Cockles and whelks. The white variety and of a large kind.

A PARISIAN FIGURATIVE DINNER.—Accordingly we all three once more entered the *fiacre*, and drove to the celebrated restaurateur's of the Rue Mont Orgueil. Oh, blissful recollections of that dinner! how at this moment you crowd upon my delighted remembrance! Lonely and sorrowful as I now sit, digesting with many a throe the iron thews of a British beef-steak—*more Anglico*—immeasurably tough—I see the graceful apparitions of *escallopes de saumon* and *laitances de carpes* rise in a gentle vapour before my eyes! breathing a sweet and pleasant odour, and contrasting the dream-like delicacies of their hue and aspect with the dire and dure realities which now weigh so heavily on the region below my heart! And thou, most beautiful of all—thou evening star of *entremets*—thou delightest in truffles, and gloriest in a dark cloud of sauces—exquisite *foie gras!*—have I forgotten thee? Do I not, on the contrary, see thee—smell thee —taste thee—and almost die with rapture of thy possession? What, though the goose, of which thou art a part, has, indeed, been roasted alive by a slow fire, in order to increase thy divine proportions—yet has not our *Almanach*—the *Almanach des Gourmands* —truly declared that the goose rejoiced amid all her tortures, because of the glory that her awaited? Did she not, in prophetic vision, behold her enlarged and ennobled *foie* dilate into *pâtés* and steam into *sautés?*—the companion of truffles—the glory of made dishes, the delight, the treasure, the transport of gourmands! Oh! exalted among birds!—apotheosised goose, did not thy heart exult even when thy liver parched and swelled within thee, from that most agonising death; and didst thou not, like the Indian at the stake, triumph in the very torments which could alone render thee illustrious?—*Pelham.*

XCVII.—TASMANIAN FISH.

One of the greatest curiosities here (Strasburg) is the fish market. The fish are offered to purchasers *alive*, being preserved in large water-tanks. I am assured that upwards of fifty kinds are occasionally exposed for sale, embracing every variety, from a sprat to a sturgeon! Mr. Mac acknowledged the thing was very pretty-looking. But for eating, God help him! he had no ambition. He was easily pleased. Give him a Galway turbot, a Boyne salmon, a Toone eel, or even a Ban trout, and he could live for a day or two with a Catholic family; but then he was no epicure.

The fellow's intolerable. He hits me now and again, and pretty hard; and here he had me confoundedly. If Apicius himself were choosing a fish dinner, where could he match Mr. MacDermott's selection?—*Grant's " Flood and Field."*

The Derwent (Tasmania) teems with fish of the finest quality; indeed, we question whether any river in the world surpasses it; and when the salmon is introduced—which there is now every prospect of being carried to a successful issue—Apicius, or even Mr. Mac Dermott, might be easily pleased.

Salt Water:—

Trumpeter—weighing from 1lb. to 40lbs.—We have elsewhere expatiated on this fish, which is superior to any in the adjacent colonies. The choicest are from six to eight pounds. Boiling is the course recommended. The belly part is almost too luscious for some palates, but to others is the epicurean tit-bit. Smaller fish fried are very good; and kippered *à la* salmon, it is an excellent relish.

Bass Trumpeter, $\frac{1}{4}$lb. to 6lbs.—This has no resemblance to the above; it is, however, more plentiful; and the flesh is firm and good, either fried or boiled. The Jewish community buy large quantities of this fish, and, cooked in their peculiar way, it is excellent.

Ling, 1lb. to 8lbs.—By no means a common fish; but it more than equals its English namesake. Boiled, it eats firm, and cuts flaky, like the cod.

Horse Mackerel, 1lb. to 4lbs.—Good, but rather coarse; it has two sharp bony ridges on each side, for three or four inches from the tail; is marked with vivid blue stripes. We suspect it is a toneta.

Mackerel—$\frac{1}{2}$lb. to 2lbs. Has only recently been observed on the eastern coast. It is more like the English fish, and can be procured in large quantities; it is sold at mackerel price, "three a shilling." Good eating.

Perch (black)—$\frac{1}{2}$lb. to 8lbs. ⎫
Perch (red)—$\frac{1}{2}$lb. to 5lbs. ⎬ Choicest, three to four pounds. All very handsome fish, plentiful, and good eating; but rather bony.
Perch (silver)—$\frac{1}{2}$lb. to 5lbs. ⎭

Perch (white), or "talking fish"—2oz. to 8oz. Affords excellent sport to the angler. When pulled out of the water it utters two audible squeaks, hence its second name. It is a true perch in shape, but nearly as flat as a flounder; excellent eating, fried or boiled.

Magpie fish—½lb. to 1lb. Marked with black and white bands, and spots resembling marble. Very good eating; not common.

Trevally or snotgall—½lb. to 6lbs. This fish, in the estimation of connoisseurs, is next to the trumpeter; by some it is preferred, not being so luscious. The flesh is firm and flaky; boiled, fried, or smoked, it is equally good.

Mullet—3oz. to 1½lb., the Tasmanian herring. The largest are usually caught with a rod and line, and the flesh is juicy and well-flavoured; grilled or fried is the best way of cooking. The flavour is quite equal to the caller herring when caught by the angler, but they lose much of this when netted and heaped in large quantities in the boats for market.

John Dory—½lb. to 2lbs. A very handsome red fish, not very common; good eating. There is another nondescript fish, with a head like a duck's bill or platipus, body perch-shaped, called by this name, weight, from 5lbs. upwards. Capital eating, but rarely captured in the nets.

Gurnet—2lbs. to 3lbs. There are two sorts of this fish, one has scales, the other not; the head is formed of a series of bony plates; both are good eating.

Jew Fish—3lbs. to 4lbs. Not common, but a very good boiling fish.

Snapper—10lbs. to 12lbs. Scarce here, only occasionally caught.

Parrot Fish—1lb. to 3lbs. Three or four varieties, differently marked in various tints of colours resembling the feathers of the bird. All very handsome to look at, and good eating, but not often in the market.

Salmon—½lb. to 16lbs. A coarse fish, in shape only resembling somewhat its English namesake. At times it is not fit for human food, and numerous slight cases of fish poisoning have occurred from eating of it. The fishermen say it is when the moon is at the full, but we rather think that, like the English mackerel, if not cooked soon after it is caught it begins to putrefy. It is very plentiful, and from its cheapness much in demand with the poorer classes; boiled with fennel, or soused in some of the liquor it was boiled in, with spice and vinegar, it forms a wholesome meal when in good order.

Bream—1lb. to 5lbs. Very excellent eating; makes a good pie; particularly the one called fresh-water, which is, in reality, the same fish, only caught at a different season. Bream pie was, with "the monks of old," an esteemed luxury. A writer in *Fraser* laments that their recipe is lost.

Whiting—2oz. to 1lb. Scarce, but very good eating.

Conger Eel—20lbs. to an immense weight. Plentiful, but rarely sold in the market, people fancying they are sea-serpents or snakes. A junk baked, stuffed with veal-stuffing, or fried in cutlets, is not to be despised.

Flathead—3oz. to 4lbs. Fine, white, and firm eating; the best fish we have for soup. Very plentiful; excellent fried.

Rock Cod—3ozs. to 10lbs. The flesh is soft, but it should be cleaned and salted as soon as possible after it is caught, and left in the salt for twelve hours before cooking. The larger boiled and the smaller fried are good eating, their flavour being very delicate.

Skate—1lb. to 40lbs. The flaps only are used; those of about two to ten pounds are preferable. The flesh is good, but it is not a favourite with many.

Hapuka, or Arboukir—10lbs. to 104lbs. Belongs to the New Zealand coast, but is frequently caught here. The flesh is coarse, and we never heard any one speak in its favour. The poorer classes do not take to it, a sure sign that much cannot be said for it.

Carp — 4lbs. to 10lbs. A beautiful fish, of a dingy red colour; the scales iridescent. Excellent eating. Seldom in market.

Flounder—2ozs. to ½lb. Plentiful, and as fine as the English sole. Some are as large as a dinner-plate, but they usually run about the size of a small cheese-plate and under. On the northern side this fish is watery and muddy in flavour; but in Hobart Town it is in great estimation, and deservedly so.

King Fish — 4lbs. to 18lbs.⎫ Both jack-shaped. Very plentiful at cer-
Barracouta— 3lbs. to 10lbs.⎭ tain seasons. Much in demand with the poorer classes, as a fine fish is sold for sixpence, weighing five or six pounds. They are often salted and smoked, and excellent eating, however cooked.

Gar, or Guard Fish—a few ounces. Called in England the piper. It is from a foot to eighteen inches long, and as narrow as a sand-eel; of a light brownish grey, and nearly transparent. Excellent eating.

Shellfish :—

Crayfish (*vulgo*, Crawfish)—1lb. to 7lbs. Very fine. Sold in immense quantities, and a favourite from high to low; is in season about eight months of the year.

Crown crabs—1lb. to 8lb. Not often in market, but very fine.

Oysters—all sizes. The smaller and choicest at present come from the east coast, the larger from Southport, but above Hobart Town beds are now forming. Volumes have been already written respecting this fish; suffice it to say ours are very good and plentiful.

Scallops, similar to those caught in England, plentiful on the sandy beaches, but rarely brought to market.

Mussels, very fine and large. As they are to be gathered by every one they are not brought to market. Occasionally poisonous, we suspect, when gathered off piles in the harbour, or far beyond low-water mark, as the sun in hot weather half cooks them when exposed high up on the beach.

Cockles, whelks, and periwinkles, procurable as easily as the above. One solitary individual has hawked cockles about for many years, but the *penny*-winkle man, with his musical "London cry" of "winkety, wink, wink, wink," has not reached our hemisphere.

Shrimps. Our Hobart Town supplies are obtained from Launceston (the northern side of the island), where they are plentiful.

Lobsters—very small. Small lobsters are to be got also at Launceston. Our crayfish prevents our feeling the want of this delicacy.

Fresh Water :—

Eels—½lb. to 5lbs. Very abundant and fine.

Sandfish, or fresh-water flathead—1oz. to 3ozs. Very delicate eating.

Mullet, or cucumber fish. When pulled out of the water this fish smells exactly like a cut cucumber. It is a herring, affords excellent sport to the angler with a fly, and is caught in most of the rivers and rivulets in the island. It is highly esteemed and a delicate fish. Above New Norfolk, at the Falls, they are caught in large quantities during the season, and at the Bush Hotel, New Norfolk, they are served in perfection. Many parties visit this locality expressly to partake of these fish; and some day New Norfolk will be as celebrated for this delicacy as Blackwall for its "whitebait." The trip up the river, about thirty miles, by steamer is delightful.

Trout, or black fish, and silver bellies—2 to 8 inches long. These abound as above; thirty or forty dozen can be caught in a day's sport; fried they are good, but dressed like the small sand-eels sold in England, they are delicious. The trout exactly resembles its English namesake in shape and spots, but has no scales.

Lobsters abound in the creeks, and even on marshy ground. They are black like the English, very pugnacious, and for two or three months of the year, when cooked, eat like fine prawns.

We have above, we believe, given for the first time a complete list of the edible fish of Tasmania, but not as a naturalist would, by giving them a scientific nomenclature. To a naturalist a vast field of study is open; we could name more than one hundred fish (no doubt, some edible, but too dangerous to experiment on) to be caught in this river, some the most extraordinary in shape and colour. Hardly a week elapses but some new species is exhibited at King's, our colonial fishmonger, that has been captured in the nets. We must, however, name one, the toadfish, simply to caution our readers from eating it. Many years ago, two or three persons in one family at New Town lost their lives, and all were seriously ill who partook of this fish; while only a few months back an elderly female lost her life from eating one of these fish, which she had picked up on the beach in the same locality. The fish is so remarkably ugly, and has a leathery sort of jacket, that we are surprised at any one attempting to cook it.

Large quantities of some of the fish we have enumerated are salted and smoked, and exported to the other colonies. The trade, we believe, might be much extended; and as we have elsewhere written, a Chinese firm in Victoria has had an agent here some two or three years who purchases and prepares fish of all descriptions—but principally, we believe, crayfish and dogfish, the latter not eaten with us—for his celestial brethren. We have not ventured to procure any of his recipes to enrich our book, not relishing the appearance of their so-called delicacies.

NOTE.—The lovers of pisciculture will read with interest the following *précis* of the salmon question, as between the mother country and Tasmania, which has been obligingly furnished the compiler by a gentleman connected with the official department through which the arrangements have been made for the reception of the ova of the king of fish:

SALMON IN TASMANIA.—Should the arrangements now in active operation by the Tasmanian Government, through commissioners in the colony and friends and agents in England, for the introduction of salmon ova, prove successful, in a very few years our rivers and tributary streams will be abundantly stocked, and fisheries fully established throughout the island.

In 1860 an unsuccessful though well-directed effort was made to introduce ova *viâ* Melbourne to these waters. The experiment was entrusted to one well versed in piscicultural matters, who failed, through no fault of his management.

A second attempt in 1862, though under the charge of an able and experienced pisciculturist, Mr. Ramsbottom, Jun., a son of the celebrated Clitheroe, propagator of fish, also failed, owing to the unsuitable class of vessel in which the ova was shipped.

A third trial is now being made, and there is no doubt entertained of its being carried to a prosperous issue.

Previous experiments have added considerably to a better knowledge of the requirements necessary to ensure complete success, and the information so acquired has, *with subsequent discoveries*, brought about the most satisfactory and promising results—results highly encouraging to all engaged or interested in so important an undertaking.

It has been established, by actual tests, that the ova taken, at the proper season, from the parent fish can be hatched in boxes prepared for its reception, after being kept in ice 124 days; so that if a vessel freighted with ova in ice makes even a tardy or lengthened passage, the experiment can scarcely be endangered, unless, indeed, from the most adverse and unforeseen causes.

It is expected that Mr. Ramsbottom, Jun., will leave England with his charge in all December, as no exertion has been spared to secure a suitable ship, with all necessary requirements and appliances.

The vessel once in the Derwent, the ova will be immediately transferred to the artificial breeding ponds prepared for its reception. Of these there are two sets, in different, but equally eligible, localities.

The first is on the North West Bay River, situate in a most picturesque and beautifully wooded country, about fourteen miles from Hobart Town, and consists of two refining ponds, one 30 feet by 27 feet, and one 25 feet by 12 feet, sloping gradually towards the middle, and of an average depth of 4 feet; two breeding ponds, 28 feet by 3 feet each, sloping to a depth of about 6 inches, with protecting basins at different elevations connected by falls. These ponds are paved with channel stones, and are supplied with a continuous flow of the most pure water from the river, by covered troughing, 20 chains in length, with sluices and movable gratings to regulate the supply which enters each pond by small feeders. The cutting from the breeding boxes debouches at once into coast water.

Ponds of a like description have been constructed at the River Plenty, on the Derwent, about twenty-seven miles from the metropolis.

Both these rivers are very fine streams, tortuous, and brisk running, with *gravelly bottoms*, admirably adapted for spawning beds, and possessing in numerous places deep pools, well shaded by rocky declivities and steeply-wooded banks.

Practical judges have pronounced the coast and river waters of Tasmania to be in every way adapted for the propagation of salmon. The temperature is much below the maximum in which salmon cease to propagate; the thermal condition of our rivers not differing from those of the west and south of Ireland during the summer season in the latter country.

In order to the preservation of the fish, temporary provision has been made by Act of Council to secure it against the depredations of man, and it is a pleasing fact that the breeding grounds selected and our rivers are much more free from its natural enemies than the rivers of Britain.

"The English and Australian Cookery Book" will, therefore, in its future editions, contain recipes setting forth the antipodean mode of cooking, boiling, potting, broiling,

collaring, currying, kippering, and pickling, that most delicious of the finny tribe, whose "body, broad and muscular, gradually tapers to the tail and ends in a crescentic curve."
—*James A. Youl.*

THE SALMON OVA.—After several unsuccessful attempts the ova has at last safely arrived in Tasmania, and been deposited in the place prepared for its reception. The arrival of the ova is an important event in the annals of Australia, and it has been celebrated accordingly. Henceforth, we may reasonably expect that the king of fishes will increase and multiply in all the colonies. This fortunate transmission has been achieved chiefly owing to the continuous industry and praiseworthy perseverance of Mr. Youl, the agent for the colony in London; the advice and attention of the Messrs. Ramsbottom, of Clitheroe; the practical aid of Mr. Frank Buckland, of piscatory renown; the generous liberality of Messrs. Money Wigram and Sons, the owners of the Blackwall liner, Norfolk, in bringing it out gratuitously; the assistance of the Victorian Government, in its transhipment by the Victoria, and its handsome monetary contribution to the undertaking. These several parties deserve honourable mention in future Colonial history. We regard with fear the result of the Acclimatisation Society's introducing into the Tasmanian rivers that most voracious fish, the Murray cod; for we think the consequences would be injurious to the propagation of the salmon. "Piscator" tells us that the *salmonidæ*, or salmon tribe, are the very aristocracy of fishes, and of these the salmon, the acknowledged king of the fresh-waters, ranks pre-eminently first. The period of these fish coming in and out of season is determined in a great degree by that at which they deposit their spawn. When the rudiments of roe first show themselves the fish is usually in greatest perfection. The best proof of the condition of a salmon is a small head, a thick shoulder, a great roundness and breadth over the back, and continued thickness down to the tail. When a salmon comes in from the sea, it is often covered with small parasitical insects, which, so far from denoting ill health, affords a certain proof of the excellence of the condition.

TASMANIAN FISH.—Of other fish, the finest are taken on the Hippolyte Bank, near Port Arthur, from which albicore (arbouker) weighing from 1lb. to 170lbs. (104lbs.), and trumpeters from 1lb. to 50lbs. (25lbs.) weight, are brought by the fishermen. They sell for about threepence a pound.

King-carp (salmon, so called) of the white species, and sometimes weighing ten pounds, mullet, perch, and garfish are also taken in large quantities in the various bays, while an hour in the evening frequently rewards the fisher in the Derwent with a heavy basket of rock-cod, flatheads, perch, &c.

The red gurnard, the silver fish, and flounders are taken in large quantities at George Town, and are sold in Launceston at a low price. At Fingal, in the clear stream of the South Esk, herrings are taken with a rod and fly, and in the month of April they can be taken by hand in the mill-race at Millford. They are also caught in large numbers at New Norfolk, at the Ouse Bridge, and at the Cataract at Launceston. Eels are abundant and of large size in all the deep and sluggish rivers of the island, and are taken by thousands, of fine flavour and of large size; at certain seasons from the Bothwell mill-ponds, and sent in light carts to Hobart Town. They sell for about fourpence a yard in Bothwell. In the South Esk, and in most of the rivulets in the colony, a diminutive trout, about three or four inches long, is taken in considerable numbers. Shrimps are taken at George Town and sent over per coach to Hobart Town, where they are sold for sixpence a quart. Hobart Town supplies Launceston and the interior with fine crayfish. Oysters are protected by local laws, and while in season, *i. e.*, from April to October, are very fine. The South Port oysters are frequently fifteen inches in circumference. Other shell-fish are plentiful, and are retailed about the streets by the city Arabs, boys who, as Scott says, "have no ambition beyond the cockle-trade."—*Hull's "Forty Years' Experience in Tasmania."*

A Tasmanian Picnic.—
    Anon he led that Royal pair
      And goodlie companie
    Into a tent, where stood a board
      So filled, you plain mote see
    That Master Cook had mastered well
      His task of cookerie;

For there was store of viands good—
  Beef, mutton, lamb, and veal;
And tongues, and hams, and sucking-pigs,
  As fat as e'er did squeal.
There hens and cocks, and bubbly-jocks
  Were plucked, and stuffed, and trussed;
And puddings crammed so full of plums,
  The cook "was sure they'd bust!"
And on a lordly dish, upraised,
  The lure of every eye,
In tempting glory was displayed
  A noble warden-pie.
That very pie the warden made—
  As he had sworn to do—
[Or if he didn't, it was wrong,
  And I'm mistaken too.
The recipe is in his Book,
  At Section Ninety-two.]

—*Extract from the "Revels of Rokesby," in a late number of the "Hobart Town Advertiser," on the occasion of the annual ploughing match at Clarence, in Tasmania, under the patronage of the Warden (the author holding that office) and Municipal Council, in 1863, at which the Governor and Mrs. Gore Brown were present.*

XCVIII.—NEW ZEALAND FISH.

Many estates are spent in the getting,
Since women for tea forsook spinning and knitting,
And men for punch forsook hewing and splitting.—*Poor Richard.*

One hundred different species of fish have been described by naturalists as frequenting the coasts; and this list is apparently very imperfect, seeing that the natives have enumerated to me many more they are in the habit of eating. Next to the shark, which renders bathing dangerous in the summer, the hapuka is the largest New Zealand salt-water fish. One hundred pounds is no unusual weight for an hapuka. Immense shoals of fish visit the bays and inlets during the summer, and various edible shell-fish abound in the sands along the beach. Flying fish are frequently observed in close proximity to the coast.

In the lakes of New Zealand are a large number of delicate fish, not unlike whitebait, called inanga; and in the rivers and lakes there are numerous eels, occasionally weighing fifty pounds. These are the only two kinds of fresh-water fish which can properly be said to form a part of the food of the natives. The lamprey (*pipiharu*) is, properly speaking, a salt-water fish, which enters the river to spawn. The fresh-water mussel and the crayfish are plentiful in some parts.

Every fish found in the surrounding sea is eaten by the natives, except the shark—from which teeth are obtained for ornaments—portions of the stingaree, and one or two red-coloured fish, which are said to be poisonous.

Fresh-water eels, frequently of great size, and small fish, suitable for food, are numerous in the rivers and lakes.

Fish are eaten after being stewed, roasted, or dried. Crayfish, and several small fish, are eaten alive—a custom settlers have pointed out as a remnant of cannibalism, all the time forgetting that swallowing an uncooked oyster is an analogous act.

Eels, dogfish, snapper, mackerel, and several other fish, are preserved in various ways for winter food. In effecting this the entrails are sometimes extracted, and the fish are frequently dipped in sea-water and dried in the sun. At other times the fish are half cooked, then dried in the sun, or exposed to a slow smoky fire for several days. In this last process the fat does not escape, and the flavour of the fish is not lost. Preserved fish keep good for several months; shell-fish also furnish much food. The pipi and cockle were the most esteemed, and at certain seasons places where shell-fish abounded were tapued (held sacred). Shell-fish were preserved for winter food in the same way as other fish, and kept on strings.

The intimate knowledge the New Zealanders possess of the habits of fish, and their success in fishing, are indirect proofs that much of the ancient food of the people was derived from this source. The largest villages are on the sea-coast, and all the settlements in the interior are within easy access of some productive lake, eel weir, or arm of the sea. Like the Saxons, the New Zealanders reckon eels the finest of all fish.

NEW ZEALAND WAR.—We applied to a *pakeha maori* for an account of the New Zealand fish, and he referred us to Thomson's "New Zealand, Past and Present, Savage and Civilised," from the pages of which excellent work the above extracts have been taken. We also append some of the quaint remarks of our esteemed correspondent :— "About the cookery I have no notion; indeed, the attention of the Europeans in this country is chiefly at present taken up with the consideration of how not to get *cooked* themselves—a thing not unlikely to happen to some before the war is over. I *could* give you some information as to how a *man* should be cooked and *dished*, but this I suppose you don't care to put in your book, and I only know it not as a *cook*, but as one of the proper accomplishments of a Maori warrior, which every gentleman of the old school is supposed to be versed in." Cannibalism at New Zealand has ceased; therefore the witty remark of Sydney Smith to Dr. Selwyn, on his departure for that land, is no longer appropriate. The advice was for the bishop to receive the chiefs with the following speech: "I deeply regret that I have nothing on my table suited to your taste, but you will find plenty of cold curate and roasted clergyman on the side-table."—*Lady Holland's Memoirs of Sydney Smith.* Responsible Government, in a country where there are a large number of intelligent aboriginal inhabitants, the rightful owners of the soil, is "a mockery, a delusion, and a snare." The natives can understand a Government being carried on by the Queen and her nominees, but they cannot comprehend a Government by the majority of the European settlers. The present war going on at New Zealand is much to be deplored; the settlement and civilisation of the country will be retarded. Better far to purchase the land ten times over than such a hostile conflict of races should occur, which must be written in blood, waste millions of money, and afford no attainable glory to the soldiery engaged. On the contrary, according to Dr. Thomson, 58th Regiment—a military man most unlikely to give false colouring to the acts of the troops—at Oheani pa, in 1845, a British flag was taken, and the officers only saved themselves by ridiculous and undignified flight.—*Thomson's "New Zealand," vol. ii., p. 115.* That won't be the case with General Cameron. He will teach the unfortunate Maories that barbarism must give way to civilisation, and that it is far wiser on their part to place themselves quietly under British rule than to oppose it—to forfeit their broad lands and save their lives. At the same time, we are bound to say it may be necessary to assert, by force of arms, England's supremacy, after every possible effort has been made to negotiate by peaceable means. Has this been done? George IV. told the late chief Hongi, that he would not send soldiers to New Zealand, lest the natives should be deprived of their country. So Honi Heki informed Her Majesty, by letter, shortly before his death. That event will now come to pass; and the statesmanlike language of Lord John Russell seems far from realisation: "To rescue the inhabitants of New Zealand from the calamities of which the approach of civilised men to barbarous tribes has hitherto been the almost universal herald, is a duty too sacred and important to be neglected, whatever may be the discouragements under which they may be undertaken." "What has this to do with your book on the *cuisine?*" naturally asks the reader; to which query we only rejoin, that it bears very much on the "political kettle of fish," now commencing to boil over in the adjoining Maori colony.

XCIX.—VICTORIAN FISH.

The *cuisine* of a woman of refinement, like her dress or her furniture, is distinguished, not for its costliness and profusion, but for a pervading air of graceful originality. She is quite sensible of the regard due to the reigning fashion of the day, but her own tasteful discrimination is always perceptible. She instinctively avoids everything that is hackneyed, vulgar, and common-place, and uniformly succeeds in pleasing by the judicious novelties she introduces.—*Extract from the Preface to the "Jewish Manual," by a Lady.*

Salt Water :—
Red mullet—2lbs. to 4lbs. Very delicate and good eating.
Land ditto—½lb. to 3lbs. Ditto.
School ditto—¼lb. to 1lb. Ditto.
Whiting—¼lb. to 1lb. A first-rate table fish.
Snapper—½lb. to 40lbs. Very good dinner fish.

At Western Port, in October, the "schnapper" is found in quantity, and in the same month the salmon, but so absurdly unlike the king of English fishes, that we must Latinise him for want of English as *Centropristis Georginanus*. In the same month, pike, or *sphynæna Nova Hollandiæ*. There is mullet, *alias Dajanus Diemensis*; whiting, not unlike the English namesake, *Siligo punctata*; two kinds of flatheads—this kind appropriate and done into Latin as *Platycephalus Tasmanius* and *P. nematophthalmus*; kingfish, a decided usurper, as proved by *Sciæna Aquila*; barracoota, *Thyrsites atun*; ling, or shark-cod, *Lota breviuscula*; besides others too numerous to mention by scientific identification.—*Melbourne Paper.*

Guardfish—Small. Very delicate, and good eating.
Salmon—½lb. to 4lbs. Not in request.

The Colonial salmon, and the English fish of that name—the *Salmo salar of Linnæus*—are dissimilar in every possible respect. The Australian colonists have been endeavouring to procure the latter from the mother country for some time past. At the last meeting of the Acclimatisation Society, at Melbourne, the Governor, Sir Charles Darling, in the chair, the Council stated that the salmon claimed priority of notice, as it occupied the anxious attention, and as many previous difficulties were now removed by the experiments carried out successfully in London by the friends of acclimatisation, it may be confidently expected that before many months have passed Tasmanian waters will receive the first promised supply of British fish. Dr. Black seconded the adoption of the report, and in connection with the introduction of the salmon ova, he introduced to the meeting Dr. Officer, the Speaker of the Tasmanian House of Assembly, who would give them information on the subject. Dr. Officer expressed his pleasure at being present at that meeting, and regretted that he had not more to report on the proceedings of the Tasmanian Society. Of all the animals that could be introduced, the salmon was the most desirable, whether as an article of food or for sport. He briefly referred to the efforts that had been made to bring out the ova alive, and the experiments that had been tried for the preservation of the ova in ice boxes. From the last experiment it had been found that ova continued alive over 140 days after being placed in ice. The vessel that was to bring out the next supply would have an ice-house, containing fifty tons of ice, in which the boxes would be placed, and would not be opened during the voyage. He hoped the experiment would be made next year, and that the vessel might be expected to arrive in March next. He thanked the Victorian Society for the assistance it had afforded Tasmania in its acclimatisation efforts, and expressed a hope that before many years the salmon would prove an attraction in the sparkling waters of Tasmania. —*Melbourne Argus*. These societies work a vast deal of good, no doubt, but some of their proclivities are rather startling. At the meeting from which the above extract was taken, the chairman gave it as his opinion, that the boa constrictor was an elegant and interesting drawing-room pet; while he dissented from his predecessor, Sir Henry Barkly's regard for monkeys. Perhaps the former Governor of Victoria wanted the monkey introduced as food, for Sir Robert Schomburghk enumerates:—"The tapir, or maisuri; the capibara, or water paas; the labba; the aguti; the acuchi; the cairuni, or wild hog; the peccari, or Mexican hog; and deer of different species: other animals are the ant-eaters, armadillo, sloth, otters, several species of pole-cats and opossums. Numerous birds and varieties of monkeys people the otherwise solitary forest, and serve as food to the natives. The manati, lamantine, or sea-cow, is from time to time met with in the largest rivers; its flesh is white and delicate, and has been compared in taste to veal."—*Description of British Guiana*. As to the opinions of the two Governors —one being in favour of monkeys, the other proposing to acclimatise the boa constrictor —we think Swift's couplet will apply:—

> "Strange that such difference should be
> 'Twixt tweedle-dum and tweedle-dee."

Barracoota—4lbs. to 8lbs. Very good eating.
Skipjack—½lb. to 3lbs. Ditto.
Ruffy—Small. Exquisitely delicate.
Soles—Large ones occasionally. Very excellent eating.
Bream—2lbs. to 4lbs. Very good eating.
Butterfish—2lbs. to 5lbs. Next to snapper, for dinner.
Rock-cod—½lb. to 2lbs. Very excellent eating.
Ling—¼lb. to 2lbs. Scarce and good.
Black perch—½lb. to 6lbs. Very good eating.
Skate—5lbs. to 12lbs. Ditto.
Flathead—½lb. to 7lbs. Very excellent and firm fish, and superior for soup.
Mackerel—Ditto. Rare.
Silver fish—½lb. Fine flavoured.
Flounders—Occasionally large. Very palatable.
Crayfish—2lbs. to 8lbs. Very fine and delicate.
Crabs—Small.
Shrimps—Ditto.
Mussels, cockles, and whelks. Ditto.

MUSSELS.—The mussels of Blackenberghe are a great delicacy; they are caught on a bank; they are kept in clear water for two days, to clean, then in scalding water till they open; then a sauce of butter, parsley, and other fragrant herbs is poured over them, shells and all, and they are picked out, nominally, with a fork, but really with a finger and thumb, and eaten with brown bread and butter and Faro beer.—*"Clover" in Once a Week*.

Oysters—In embryo.

ARTIFICIAL BREEDING OF OYSTERS IN WESTERN PORT BAY, VICTORIA.—We have condensed from the *Melbourne Leader* an account of the formation of an oyster breeding establishment in Victoria. The Hon. Mr. Verdon, M.L.C., Mr. Rostron, of Moona Ponds, and Mr. James Putwain, late Inspector of Fisheries, are the parties who have entered into this undertaking, and the management is in the hands of the latter gentleman. A great deal has been written about what M. Costa and other French *savans* have done, under the patronage of the Emperor Napoleon, in the way of oyster breeding; but the enterprise of Mr. Putwain exceeds theirs, inasmuch as the French do not attempt to breed—they only remove the spawn. The bay of Western Port is a land-locked inlet, nearly circular in its upper part, and semi-circular towards the [sea. It is separated from Port Philip Bay by a neck of land about twenty to thirty miles in width. Mr. Putwain's system of breeding is based on the Italian, from which it differs in some respects. The breeding pond is situated at the extremity of Sandy Point. It was originally a shallow lagoon, but Mr. Putwain has had it deepened. The bottom of the pond is laid with bundles constructed of tea-tree saplings; these hurdles are securely fixed to the bottom of the pond, and on the top of them clean oyster-shells are placed, in order to attract and form a bed for the oysters that are to deposit their spawn. Mr. Putwain prefers a bed composed of oyster-shells. In France it has been found that the fish which cling to the fascines become deformed, and of a round shape; to give them their natural flatness, he adopts a horizontal bed. The hurdles are supplied by contract, at 1s. 1d. each, Mr. Putwain conveying them in his own vessels, making the cost about two shillings each. The work has been costly. From thirty to forty men have been employed for months in preparing the future cultivation grounds, and in the construction of ponds. The adventure has already cost £3,000, and it is calculated it will amount to £10,000 before any return is derived. The establishment owns five vessels, from seven to twenty tons each, which are employed in dredging and fetching the oysters, conveying the hurdles from various parts of the bay, and in dredging and clearing out the future beds. The first step in the process is to obey the famous direction of the culinary Mrs. Glasse *—first catch your oysters. The oyster caught is deposited in the breeding pond. The breeding season runs from October to December, a period of about three months. [In England oysters are permitted to be sold from August to May—the close months being May, June, and July. They cast their spat, or spawn, in May, when they are said to be sick; but begin to recover in June and July, and in August they are perfectly well.—*Supp. to "Encyc. Brit."* In Tasmania the law prevents the taking of oysters in the months of November, December, January, February, and March.] Mr. Putwain procures his oyster parents from Port Albert. A considerable supply is on hand, and already in the pond. The oyster is laid down with its *flat* side uppermost. The spawn, on being shed, floats on the water for nine days. As the spawn grows it waxes heavier, and sinks. Then, if left to the peace and quiet of nature, it rapidly advances in growth. In three weeks it will be visible to the naked eye as a minute shell; at six weeks it is removed to the cultivation beds; and at four months' old it is the size of a fourpenny piece. At three months, taken up from the beds in a mass, the little oysters are removed from each other by an oyster knife. When separated they are replaced again, and spread over the bottom. At the end of three years the well-grown oyster is fit for the market; but it is not until the fourth year that it is in the interesting condition of being parent to other broods. The oyster is one of the most productive of creatures. Hartwig ("Das Leben des Meeres") states that it produces during each summer of the year no less than one to two millions of young, the greater part of which perish during their wanderings. Instead of leaving its eggs at once to their fate, like the greater number of marine animals, the oyster retains them for some time in the folds of the paternal mouth-like structure between the gill-plates, where they are surrounded with slimy matter. After growing in this fashion, the microscopic larvæ, provided with a swimming apparatus and eyes, are carried by thousands from the mother's shell, and drifted about till they find a substance to which to attach themselves. The enemies of the oyster are principally the borer: (the bir), one of the echinidæ, or sea-urchins, and the starfish, or asteroids. The Government have given a lease of a track of five miles long and half a mile broad, covering a space of about 4,000 acres, at a nominal rental of a shilling an acre, for the speculation. We trust the enterprise will answer the expectations of those who have embarked their capital on the waters of Western Port, where there is shore enough to yield a supply of oysters sufficient to satisfy not only Melbourne, but the entire colony of Victoria, which, at present, receives a large importation of this valuable bivalve, principally from Tasmania. We hope that Mr. Putwain will meet with success in his interesting undertaking.

"'Tis not in mortals to command success,
But we'll do more, Sempronius—we'll deserve it."

Fresh Water :—

Murray Cod—½lb. to 100lbs. First-class dinner fish; its goodness not generally known. A fish of about 20lbs. should be slightly corned for a couple of days. Lay it on one side one day, and turn it; if this is done it will flake like English cod.

---

* Mrs. Glasse's "Cookery Book" was written by Dr. Hill.

RIVER CODFISH.—In 1835 an enormous head of one of these fish was presented to the Australian Museum by Mr. William Bowman. It was found entangled and struggling near the bank in a pond of the Cudgegong River, was killed, and brought on shore. It weighed upwards of 120lbs.—*Western Post.*

Eels—Average about 1lb. Very excellent eating, or for pies.

Native herring—Small. Found on the Yarra in the months of December, January, February, and March. Deliciously delicate, and smells like cucumber.

Golden bream—¼lb. to 3lbs. Murray River. Very excellent eating.

Silver ditto—Same size. Ditto, ditto.

Catfish, or Murray eel—Same size. Ditto, ditto

Black perch—Same size. Ditto, ditto.

Lobsters—Same size. Ditto, ditto, very delicate.

Native oysters—Small. Fresh-water, good.

Mussels—Small. Ditto, ditto.

THE GOURAMER.—Sir Henry Barkly, late Governor of Victoria, at present holding a similar position at the Mauritius, in writing to Dr. Black, the secretary of the Melbourne Acclimatisation Society, says:—"The value of this fish is over-estimated, as, like all fresh-water fish, it depends a good deal on the *sauce.*"

THE EVENING MEAL.—

  Another day is gone. The sun
   Has sunk behind yon mountain high,
  The little stars have just begun
   To light their bright lamps in the sky.
  Soft clouds of pink and yellow hue,
  Succeed to noon-day skies of blue.

  In every little cottage home,
   The wife prepares her husband's meal,
  She will no longer be alone;
   For round the cottage shadows steal,
  And looking out with cheerful face,
  She sees him come with quickening pace.

  The weary horse his work has done,
   And man has left his toil till morn;
  And all do hail the setting sun,
   As signal true of rest till dawn.
  The fields deserted, all are gone,
  And man and beast are trudging home.

  The meal is o'er, they kneel in prayer;
   Each little heart and voice unite
  To thank the good God for his care,
   And pray for rest till morning light.
  And then again, with one accord,
  Their voices sweet will praise the Lord.
    R. and A. Tasmania, in "*Wulch's Literary Intelligencer.*"

C.—FISH OF NEW SOUTH WALES—AUSTRALIA PROPER.

Gain as much knowledge *de l'art culinaire* as you can; it is an accomplishment absolutely necessary.—*Lady Frances Pelham to her Son.*

Snapper (salt water)—2lbs. to 10lbs. Good eating. Always in season.

Whiting   " —½lb. to 2lbs. Most delicate fish.

Black Bream " —2lbs. to 8lbs. Very good eating.

Mackerel (salt water)—1lb. to 3lbs. Ditto.
Guardfish   „   —2ozs. to ½lb. Good when young.
Jewfish   „   —5lbs. to 15lbs. Very good eating.
Flathead   „   —3lbs. to 10lbs. Ditto.
Mullet   „   —¼lb. to 6lb. Ditto.
Black-fish (salt and fresh water)—8ozs. to 1½lb. Not equal to other fish; taste muddy.
Oysters—unlimited supplies; consumption enormous.
Crabs—all sizes and weights—say ½lb. to 3lbs. Good eating.
Crayfish   ditto   ditto.   ditto.
Shrimps and Prawns—very delicate.
Cockles and Whelks.
Soles (salt water)—2ozs. to ½lb. Good eating.
Flounders   „   „   Ditto.   Always in season.
Murray River Cod fish (fresh-water)—2lbs. to 20lbs. Very good eating. Always in season.

Dr. Bennett, at the last meeting of the Acclimatisation Society, at Sydney, in New South Wales, read some notes on the river cod and perch, which we have condensed. The river cod, or cod perch (*gristes Peelii*), is justly esteemed as a well-flavoured and delicate fish, and certainly merits to be the first of the Australian fishes. He had seen the river cod very plentiful in the Yass, Tamut, and Murrumbidgee rivers—more so in the last—and they are known to exist in all rivers of the eastern and western ranges. It is a voracious fish. Their average length is nineteen inches, and the weight from three to eight pounds; and they are often taken from two and a half to three feet in length, and weighing from twenty to twenty-five pounds. Some have been taken from forty to seventy pounds, and one was reported as weighing one hundred and twenty pounds! The fish is named by the natives of the Murrumbidgee, *mewuruk*. In the stomachs of those he had an opportunity of examining, he observed species of shell-fish of the genus *unis*, or fresh-water mussel—a large and small kind; also a large species of river lobster (*astacus*), called *mungula* by the Aborigines. In the Turmut country there are supposed to be varieties of the river cod, named by the blacks *bewuck* and *mungee*. The river cod may be heard at night splashing and running about in the water frequented by them, but they are rarely seen in the daytime. He had no doubt that there are many fresh-water fishes inhabiting the rivers of Australia known but to a few, but which will, when tried, be found valuable as food. There was another fish caught in the Yass and other large rivers, called perch by the colonists, and *kupe* by the aborigines, and it was of excellent flavour, but not so delicate as the river cod.

Eels—¼lb. to 6lbs.
Rock Cod (salt water)—1lb. to 6lbs.
Murray River Cod Perch—4ozs. to 4lbs.

ICHTHYOLOGICAL.—We have been shown one of a number of pretty fish, diminutive in size, being not more than three inches long, that have been caught in the chain of ponds near the Yass on the road to Gunning. They have no resemblance to the cod or perch which are the inhabitants of the Yass and Murrumbidgee rivers. In the specimen we can trace no dorsal fin, and the body is broader and flatter than those of the fish we have spoken of. In appearance it recalls to our mind the bream of the "old country."—*Yass Courier*.

NEW FISH.—At a recent meeting of the Philosophical Society of New South Wales, Mr. Krefft read a paper describing a new fish in the Hawkesbury River, belonging to the genus *therapon*, named Pitt's perch (*Therapon Pittii*, Kr.), a specimen being exhibited:— "This fine fish abounds in the Hawkesbury and its tributaries; it is also found in many of the lagoons of the Richmond district. The Australian Museum is indebted to Mr. George Pitt, jun., for some very fine specimens of this delicious fish, which I have named in honour of my friend, who informs me that this perch is found in every part of the Nepean and Hawkesbury above Windsor. It has been caught as heavy as 5lbs. in weight. It may be caught with hook and line. With regard to the taste of this fish, I can bear witness that its flesh is excellent, far superior to the much-talked-of Murray cod, and well worth the attention of pisciculturists." Mr. Krefft writes up to the present time, "I have only captured four distinct species of fish in the Hawkesbury River —namely, Pitt's perch (*Therapon Pittii*), the sprat (*Megalops setipinnis*, Richardson), the Australian eleotris, or gudgeon of the settlers (*Eleotris Australis*, Kr. MSS.), and the so-called "smelt" (*Galaxias scrita*, Richardson). The two last species are common also in the fresh water of the neighbourhood; all are of excellent flavour, but the gudgeon and smelt of small size, and seldom caught for the table; the sprat is larger, and grows to about fifteen inches in length. This fish rises to a fly, it furnishes good sport, and a magnificent dish if fried crisp. It is necessary to fry the sprat well, owing to the numerous fine bones, which otherwise would not allow one to enjoy it.—*The Melbourne Yeoman.*

FISH AT BRISBANE.—We had the pleasure of inspecting a magnificent barramundi. The fish in question was a portly-shaped specimen, of some ten pounds weight, and a clear evidence of our piscicultural resources. The river at this season (summer) of the year swarms with barramundi and mullet, very different from the repulsive catfish hawked about our doors. Surely, something must be wrong when, in a climate like this, a town numbering a large and prosperous population cannot boast a fish-shop.—*Queensland Newspaper.*

We regret that several attempts have been made unsuccessfully to introduce, from the Mauritius into Australia, the valuable fish called the guaramier. Its advent into the Colonies would be very advantageous, for this fish is little inferior to the salmon in fineness of flavour, and it reaches nearly seventy pounds in weight.

LONG LIFE.—I have, in my life, met with two of above one hundred and twelve, whereof the woman had passed her life in service, and the man in common labour, till he grew old, and fell upon the parish. But I met with one who had gone a much greater length, which made me more curious in my inquiries. It was an old man, who begged usually at a lonely inn upon the road in Staffordshire, who told me he was a soldier, a hundred and twenty-four years old; that he had been a soldier in the Cales voyage, under the Earl of Essex, of which he gave me a sensible account; that, after his return, he fell to labour in his own parish, which was about a mile from the place where I met him; that he continued to work till a hundred and twelve, when he broke one of his ribs by a fall from a cart, and, being thereby disabled, he fell to beg. This agreeing with what the master of the house told me was reported and believed by all his neighbours, I asked him what was his usual food. He said, *milk, bread,* and *cheese,* and flesh when it was given him. I asked him what he used to drink. He said, "Oh, sir, we have the best water in our parish that is in all the neighbourhood." Whether he ever drank anything else? He said, yes, if anybody gave it him; but not otherwise. And the host told me he had got many a pound in his house, but never spent a penny. I asked him if he had neighbours as old as he; and he told me—but one, who had been his fellow-soldier at Cales, and was three years older; but he had been most of his time in good service, and had something to live on now he was old.—*Sir W. Temple's "Essays on Health and Long Life."*

CI.—SMOKING.

Sublime tobacco! which, from East to West,
Cheers the tars' labour or the Turkman's rest,
Which on the Moslem's ottoman divides
His hours, and rivals opium and his brides;
Magnificent in Stamboul, but less grand,
Though not less loved, in Wapping or the Strand;
Divine in hookahs, glorious in a pipe,
When tipped with amber, mellow, rich, and ripe;
Like other charmers, wooing the caress,
More dazzling when appearing in full dress;
Yet thy true lovers more admire by far
Thy naked beauties—give me a cigar!—*Byron.*

Smoking in moderation is by no means unwholesome; indeed, it has been pronounced a sedative. Like other indulgences in the world, there is every difference between its moderate use and its great abuse. A case was reported in the newspapers a short time ago, of a person having killed himself by excessive inhalations of the noxious plant; and for the sake of public example, it is a pity the fact was not duly reported, and "crowner's 'quest law" made known far and wide—"smoked himself to death."

The celebrated Dr. Parr was a great smoker, and invariably refused to dine anywhere unless he was allowed this indulgence. His answer was, "No pipe, no Parr." In the East Indies a *hookah* is used, and the smoke is inhaled through rose-water by a tube with an amber mouth-piece; and a special servant attends and takes charge of the smoking apparatus, who is termed the *hookah-burdar*. In Turkey the choice tobacco of Syria is smoked through the cherry-stick of a Turkish or Egyptian chibouque, or by means of the jasmine pipe of the Nargilly. Smoking is in general favour after meals in all countries, and we may therefore give it a short notice in a book on cookery. In the army and navy, not to say volunteers, and in the bush, a pipe is in request. With our allies, the Turks, whether on shore or on board their men-of-war, no visit is satisfactory unless "pipes and coffee" are introduced, as they are considered by all Eastern nations as the calumet of peace. Ure writes—it has been observed by Lane, the learned annotator of the "Arabian Nights" (and the observation has been confirmed by the experience of Mr. Layard, M.P., the explorer of Assyria), that the growth and use of tobacco amongst Oriental nations has gradually reduced the resort to intoxicating beverages; and Mr. Crawford, in a paper on the "History and Consumption of Tobacco," in the "Journal of the Statistical Society" for March, 1853, remarks, that simultaneously with the decline in the use of spirits in Great Britain, has been a corresponding increase in the use of tobacco. America produces annually about two hundred millions of pounds. Various are the kinds of the noxious weed, from the mild Latakia, the pungent Virginia, to the favourite Havannah, which Dr. Lyon Playfair assures us is the finest tobacco in the world, while Baroni, in "Tancred," claims pre-eminence for the Latakia, having smoked all. Marryatt, in one of his works, expresses a strong opinion of the *Nicotiana tabacum* in the following apostrophe:—

I love thee, whether thou appearest in the shape of a cigar, or diest away in sweet perfume enshrined in the meerschaum bowl.

A paper on "Tobacco," by H. E. Adams, headed—

You takers of tobacco and strong waters,
Mark this!—*Ben Jonson,*

is much more elaborate on the article of smoking. "Shepherd, where is your pipe?" asks Miss Amantia Dowsabel Higgins, as she rambled on the glassy meads all bespangled with daisies, while the air was musical with the tingling of sheep-bells, the singing of birds, the murmuring of bees, and other pleasing sounds of rural life. "Where is your pipe?" repeated the charming fair one, in the most mellifluous accents, to the gentle shepherd, whom she designated Corydon, of course anticipating that was the youth's baptismal appellation; when the following reply came from the bumpkin, who did not properly respond to the maiden's query:—

My name ain't Corry Dunn, he lives with Farmer Stubbles. My name's Tom Styles, miss, and I left my pipe at home, 'cos I ain't got no baccur.

The delicate sensibilities of the lady were so shocked—possessed, as she was, with a heart overflowing with love and poesy, liable to amatory impressions which she expected a response to, and not so loutish a reply—that Miss Amantia vanished.

MEERSCHAUM.—Syn., *écume de mer*; Fr. A silicated carbonate of magnesia. It has a specific gravity ranging between 2·6 to 3·4; is readily acted on by acids, and fuses before a powerful blow-pipe into white enamel. The finest qualities are found in Greece and Turkey. It is used by the Tartars in washing linen. Its principal consumption is, however, in the manufacture of tobacco pipes. The Germans prepare their pipes for sale by soaking them in tallow, then in white wax, and, finally, by polishing them in shave-grass. Genuine meerschaum pipes are distinguished from mock ones by the beautiful brown colour they assume after being smoked for some time. Recently, some of the pipemakers have produced a composition clay pipe, which closely resembles meerschaum in appearance, and is "warranted to colour well." This composition, which is comparatively valueless, is made into pipes of suitable patterns, which are frequently sold to the ignorant as meerschaums.—*Cooley.*

I shall now smoke two cigars, and get me to bed. The cigars do not keep well here. They get as old as a *donna di quarante anni* in the sun of Africa. The Havannah are the best; but neither are so pleasant as a hookah or chibouque. The Turkish tobacco is mild, and their horses entire—two things as they should be.—*Byron's Journal*, 1813. *Moore.*

SMOKING.—I should be forced to give it a place as one of the least hurtful of luxuries. It is on this ground, in fact, that tobacco holds so firm a position—that, of nearly every luxury, it is the least injurious. It is innocuous as compared with alcohol; it does infinitely less harm than sugar; it is in no sense worse than tea; and, by the side of high living, altogether it contrasts most favourably. A thorough smoker may, or may not, be a hard drinker; but there is one thing he never is—a glutton; indeed, there is no cure for gluttony, and all its train of certain and fatal evils, like tobacco. In England this cure has been effected wholesale. The friends of tobacco will add to these remarks, that their "friendly weed" is sometimes not only the least hurtful of luxuries, but the most reasonable. They will tell of the quiet which it brings to the over-worn body and to the irritable and restless mind. Their error is transparent and universal; but, notwithstanding, it is a practical truth, for, in their acceptation, tobacco is a remedy for evils which lie within its own domain, and, as a remedy, it will hold its place until these are removed.—*Dr. Richardson, in the "Social Science Review."*

A SMOKING PRINCESS.—At a ball recently given at Baden, by Madame de Behague, Princess Menschikoff, who regularly smokes half a dozen cigarettes in the course of the evening, was just about to place the perfumed paper to her lips, when the hostess prevented her proceeding further by warning her Excellency that the King of Holland, who was present, had a decided objection to the smoke of cigars. "But this is only a cigarette," replied the princess, sharply; "and no man on earth, even a king, has a right to object to the good will and pleasure of a lady." Thereupon, heedless of the annoyance of the good hostess, the princess put up her lips and puffed away. In an instant the king detected the obnoxious vapour. The whole company beheld the sudden colour in his cheek as he listened to the whispered observation by Madame de Behague, and few were there who did not sympathise with the indignation which had caused it. The king, by-the-by, disappeared from the room, giving his arm to the kind hostess; in another moment he was followed by the greater portion of the company, consisting of French, German, English, and Italian guests: none remained but the Russians and a few Danish dancers. Princess Menschikoff herself was amongst the last to leave; and it was not till the next day that it became known that a second band had been sent for, at a late hour, and that another set of dancers had been enjoying themselves in another saloon. The result has been a total division of society—the King of Holland strictly refusing to meet Princess Menschikoff in private society; and the persistence of the latter in driving his Majesty from every public place of amusement by means of her cigarette.—*Court Journal.*

CII.—SERVANTS.

*"Bear, and forbear," thus preached the stoic sages,
And in two words include the sense of pages.—Pope.*

Employers should be mindful that servitude—" labour—has its rights as well as its duties," and we would therefore entreat attention to the warning voice of the honoured British Judge, who shortly after inculcating the propriety of sympathy with our domestics, and thus giving effect to the golden rule of " doing as we would be done by," was suddenly stricken with death :—

"The crimes," he said, "I will not say exclusively, but in the far greater majority of these cases, come from those districts which are the most rich in mineral treasures, where wages are high, and where no temptation of want can for a moment be set up as an excuse or palliation for the crime; on the contrary, I have observed in the experience I have had of the calendar of prisoners tried at these assizes—an experience, many of you are aware, extending far beyond the period of my judicial labours—I have observed that in times of comparative privation crime diminishes, and that when wages are high, and are earned by a less degree of work, there is a strong temptation to spend them in various indulgences; and that crime is increased almost in proportion to the state of prosperity by which the criminals have been surrounded. This consideration should awaken all our minds, and especially the minds of gentlemen connected with those districts, to see in what direction to search for a remedy for so great an evil. It is untrue to say that the state of education—that is, such education as can be furnished by the Sunday-schools, and other schools in these districts—is below the general average. Then we must search among other causes for the peculiar aspect of crime presented in these cases. I cannot help thinking myself it may be in no small degree attributable to that separation between class and class which is the great curse of British society, and for which we are all, more or less, in our respective spheres, in some degree responsible, and which is more complete in these districts than in agricultural districts, where the resident gentry are enabled to shed around them the blessings resulting from the exercise of benevolence and the influence and example of active kindness. I am afraid we all of us keep too much aloof from those beneath us, and whom we thus encourage to look upon us with suspicion and dislike. Even to our servants we think, perhaps, we fulfil our duty when we perform our contract with them—when we pay them their wages, and treat them with the civility consistent with our habits and feelings—when we curb our temper, and use no violent expressions towards them. But how painful is the thought that there are men and women growing up around us, ministering to our comforts and necessities, continually inmates of our dwellings, with whose affection and nature we are as much unacquainted as if they were the inhabitants of some other sphere. This feeling, arising from that kind of reserve peculiar to the English character, does, I think, greatly tend to prevent that mingling of class and class, that reciprocation of kind words and gentle affections of the heart, that refinement and elevation of the characters of those to whom they are addressed; and if I were to be asked what is the great want of English society, to mingle class with class, I would say, in one word, the want is—the want of *sympathy*."

Mr. Justice Talfourd was seized with a fit of paralysis, which ended fatally, just at the conclusion of the utterance of the above noble sentiments, while addressing the grand jury, at the Stafford Assizes, on the 12th March, 1854. The *Household Words* of the 25th of that month bears testimony, in affecting terms, to the probity, learning, ability, and kindliness of disposition of the learned Judge; but it is due to this excellent and lamented man—who is now no more—as well as to society, that attention should be directed to this "address," so that the kindly sympathy as between masters and servants, should be, if possible, reciprocated in the Colonies as well as in the mother country.

The attention of servants is directed to the following Scriptural authorities for the performance of their relative duties:—
1. Love not sleep, but rise early (Prov. xx. 13).
2. Be not slothful (Prov. xviii. 9).
3. Let nothing be wasted (John vi. 12).
4. Be obedient and serve heartily (Col. iii. 22, 23).
5. Clean in person and dress (1 Peter iii. 3, 4).
6. Correct in manners, and not given to purloining (Titus ii. 9, 10).
7. Be civil to your fellow-servants (Ephes. iv. 32).
8. Be kind to them and they will be so to you (Matt. vii. 12).
9. Neither utter falsehoods nor tell tales (Prov. xi. 13; xiv. 5).
10. A quiet answer appeaseth wrath (Prov. xv. 1).
11. Wander not away from a good home (Prov. xxvii. 8).
12. Be content and satisfied with your calling (1 Cor. vii. 20).

THE TREATMENT OF OUR DOMESTICS.—Whatever uneasiness we occasion to our domestics, which neither promotes our service nor answers the just end of punishment, is manifestly wrong, were it only upon the general principle of diminishing the sum of human happiness. By which rule we are forbidden—
1. To enjoin unnecessary labour or confinement, from the mere love and wantonness of domination.
2. To insult our servants by harsh, scornful, or opprobrious language.
3. To refuse them any harmless pleasures;
And, by the same principle, also are forbidden causeless or immoderate anger, habitual peevishness, or groundless suspicion.—*Paley.*

DOMESTIC SERVANTS.—It is well known that the deeply and justly lamented Prince Albert gave his particular attention to the state of domestic servants, and delivered an able, instructive address to the Provident Society for their protection. The importance of this class is undeniable, and he represented them as the most numerous body of the servants of the Queen. A meeting was held upon the subject this summer, which I regretted being unable to attend; but there was a most instructive paper read, which gave rise to useful discussion, and it may be hoped that the subject will come before our social economy department. The importance of the subject may be estimated from this, that the number of domestic servants in England is calculated to be above a million, of whom one hundred thousand are in London, and ten thousand are out of place.—*Extract from Lord Brougham's eloquent "Address to the National Society of Edinburgh,"* 1863.

CIII.—PYROLIGNEOUS ACID.

Shepherd. Oh, man, there's something very auld wifish-like in publishing a book to tell olks how to devour vittles. There's nae mystery in that matter; hunger and thirst are simple, straightforward instincts, no likely to be muckle improved by artificial erudition; and I'll bet you a cheese to a kibbock (by-the-by, what for is't no coming ben, the bit Welsh rabbit?) that your frien's wark on diet will hae nae perceptible influence on the character o' the table during our age.—*Noctes Ambrosinæ.*

Dr. Wilkinson, in the *Philosophical Journal*, was the first person who applied pyroligneous acid in the curing of meat. If a ham had the reduced quantity of salt usually employed for smoke-dried hams, and was then exposed, putrefaction soon took place, where pyroligneous acid was not used. Even one-half of this reduced portion of salt is sufficient when it is used, being applied cold, and the ham is then effectually cured without any loss of weight, and retaining more animal juices. This acid communicates the same quality to the meat as the process of smoking. Hams, salmon, and fish of any kind are more effectually cured by this acid than any other process. Beef-steaks have been kept fresh for six weeks by merely covering the bottom of the plate with acid, and turning them daily. A little acid added to the pickle for salt meat improves its flavour. Herrings, cod, haddock, and other fish may be cured by the acid after a little salting. In Holland, the red colour imparted to fish is attributed to tobacco dissolved in a fluid not the most acceptable—urine. Dr. Wilkinson states that pyroligneous acid may be manufactured at a profit for about 3½d. per gallon.

The Legislature of Tasmania have lately passed a law allowing of the distillation from the woods of the colony of pyroligneous acid, and many colonists think it will become an article of export, as some of the indigenous timber was found to yield the acid in greater proportion than any other known woods. Professor Brande's description of the acid is as follows:—

The pyroligneous acid, freed from tar, is saturated with chalk or powdered slaked lime, filtered, and evaporated, by which an impure acetate of lime is obtained; this is gently heated, so as to destroy part of its empyreumatic matter without decomposing the acetic acid; it is then mixed with sulphate of soda, which yields, by double decomposition, sulphate of lime and acetate of soda; the acetate of soda is filtered off, the sulphate of lime heated, and re-dissolved and crystallised. In this way, a pure, crystallised acetate of soda is, by proper management, obtained, which is mixed in a retort or still, with a proper proportion of sulphuric acid and a gentle heat applied, which causes the strong acetic acid to distil over, and sulphate of soda remains behind. This acetic acid is in a high state of concentration; it is lowered by the addition of water, and if intended for the table, or domestic use, as a substitute for other forms of vinegar, it is usually coloured with a little burnt sugar. The charcoal, which is the residue of this distillation of wood, is of excellent quality; that employed in the manufacture of gunpowder is thus prepared. This manufacture of vinegar is now carried on upon a very large scale, and the greater part of the vinegar used for domestic purposes, and in the arts, in many of which it is largely consumed, is derived from this source.

TABLE ARRANGEMENTS, A.D. 79.—The reader understands that the festive board was composed of three tables—one at the centre and one at each wing. It was only at the outer side of these tables that the guests reclined; the inner space was left untenanted for the greater convenience of the waiters, or *ministri*. The extreme corner of one of the wings was appropriated to Julia, as the lady of the feast, and next to her, to Diomed. At one corner of the centre table was placed the Ædile; at the opposite corner the Roman senator. These were the posts of honour. The other guests were arranged so that the young (gentleman or lady) should sit next each other, and the more advanced in years be similarly matched: an agreeable provision enough, but one which must often have offended those who wished to be thought still young. The chair of Ione was next to the couch of Glaucus. The seats were veneered with tortoise-shell, and covered with quilts, with feathers, and ornamented with the costly embroideries of Babylon. The modern ornaments of Epergne or Plateau were supplied by images of the gods, wrought in bronze, ivory, or silver. The sacred salt-sellar and the familiar harles were not forgotten. Over the table and the seats a rich canopy was suspended from the ceiling. At each corner of the table were lofty candelabras, for, though it was early noon, the room was darkened; while four tripods, placed in different parts of the room, distilled the odour of myrrh and frankincense; and upon the abacus, or sideboard, large vases and various ornaments of silver were arranged, with much the same ostentation, but with more than the same taste, that we find displayed at a modern feast.—*The Last Days of Pompeii.*

CIV.—SCRAPS AND SAYINGS.

A green apricot tart is commonly considered the best tart that is made, but a green apricot pudding is a much better thing. A cherry dumpling is better than a cherry tart. A rhubarb pie is greatly improved by a slight infusion of lemon when eaten. A beef-steak pudding, again, is better than the corresponding pie; but oysters and mushrooms are essential to its success. A mutton-chop pudding with oysters, but without mushrooms, is excellent.—*The Quarterly Review.*

If you would avoid waste in your family, attend to the following rules, and do not despise them because they appear so unimportant. "Many a little makes a mickle."

See that the beef and pork are always under brine, and that the brine is sweet and clean.

Count towels, sheets, spoons, &c., occasionally, that those who use them may not become careless.

See that the vegetables are neither sprouting nor decaying; if they are so, remove them to a drier place, and spread them.

Examine preserves, to see that they are not contracting mould; and your pickles, to see that they are not growing soft and tasteless.

As far as possible, have bits of bread eaten before they become hard. Take care of those not eaten, for puddings.

Attend to all mendings in the house once a week; never put out sewing if it be possible to do it in your own family.

Make your own bread and cake. Some people think it is just as cheap to buy it of the baker or confectioner. It is not half so cheap, and, in the next place, your domestic or yourself may just as well employ their own time as to pay for that of others.

When ivory-handled knives turn yellow, rub them with fine sand-paper or emery; it will take off the spots and restore their whiteness.

When a carpet is faded, it must be dipped in salt and water to bring round the colour.

An ox gall will set any colour, silk, cotton, or woollen.

Tortoise-shell and horn combs last much longer for having oil rubbed on them occasionally.

Lamps will have a less disagreeable smell if you dip the wicks in strong vinegar, and dry them.

Britannia ware should be first rubbed gently with a woollen cloth and sweet oil, then washed in warm suds, and rubbed with soft leather and whitening.

Silver may be cleaned by warm suds, and then rubbed with soft leather.

Eggs will keep any reasonable length of time in lime-water properly prepared.

New iron must be gradually heated, or it is apt to crack.

Clean a brass kettle, before using it, with salt and vinegar.

Never wash marble mantelpieces with suds, as it destroys their polish.

Feathers should be thoroughly dried before being used.

Jamaica rum is better for the hair than Macassar oil.

Cream of tartar will cleanse white kid gloves.

Cheese will keep if covered carefully with paper.

Pulverised alum possesses the property of purifying water.

Woollens should be washed in very hot suds, and not rinsed; lukewarm water shrinks them.

Do not let knives be dropped into hot dish-water.

Keep your salt-spoons out of the salt, and clean them often.

Suet and lard keep better in tin than in earthen.

Suet will keep all the year round, if chopped and packed in a stone jar, covered with molasses.

It is poor economy to buy vinegar in small quantities.

If beer grows sour, it may be used to advantage in pancakes and fritters.

If you have a large family, keep white rags from coloured ones—"A penny saved is a penny got."

Keep an old blanket and sheet for ironing, and on no account allow any other to be used.

Have plenty of holders, that your towels may not be used on such service.

Have plenty of towels in the kitchen.

It is easy to preserve horseradish for winter use, by steeping it in vinegar, after being scraped.

Run the heels of stockings faithfully, and mend the holes. "A stitch in time saves nine."

Green tea is an excellent restorative of silk

Milk will remove ink-stains.

Butter should be potted down for winter use, and a stock of lard in the season.

It is a bad plan to allow clothes to remain too long dirty.

Care must be taken to have bacon and hams secured from the fly.

Herbs for kitchen use should be cut and dried, but not in the sun.

Soap purchased, and cut in slices to dry, will go twice as far as when bought new.

Onions must be bought in the season, roped, and hung up in a dry place.

Mind who sits next to you in an omnibus, and look out for garotters in the street.

Aged persons are enjoined to preserve an upright position, so as to keep their lungs in full play.

Buy a proper stock of apples, filberts, and walnuts for winter use.

Potatoes must be put by in a very dry store, with carrots and parsnips, for winter use.

The practice of scouring bed-rooms in the winter is productive of colds and coughs.

See the end from the beginning, and the whole way, before you begin.

Bed-covers should be provided to be laid over the beds when the rooms are being swept.

Brown holland covers for castors or liquor stands are very useful in preserving them from dust and fly marks.

Out of debt, out of danger.
Keep your shop, and your shop will keep you.
Lay in your stock of coals in the summer time.
Three removes are as bad as a fire.

> Early to bed and early to rise
> Makes a man healthy, wealthy, and wise.

A bit in the morning is better than nothing all day.
Good kale is half a meal.
Butter is gold in the morning, silver at noon, lead at night.
He that would live for aye must cart sage in May.
After cheese comes nothing.
You must drink, as usual, after an egg as after an ox.
He that goes to bed thirsty rises healthy.
Often and little eating makes a man fat.
Fish must swim thrice.
Drink wine, and have the gout; drink no wine, and have it too.
Young men's knocks old men feel.
Eat at pleasure, drink by measure.

> Cheese is a peevish elf,
> It digests all but itself.
> Drink in the morning staring,
> Then all the day be sparing.

Eat a bit before you drink.
Feed sparingly and dupe the physician.
Better be meals many than one too many.
Fish spoils water, but flesh mends it.
Apples, pears, and nuts spoil the voice.

Old fish, old oil, and an old friend.
Raw pullet, veal, and fish make the churchyard fat.
Of wine, the middle; of oil, the top; of honey, the bottom.
If you take away the salt throw the meat to the dogs.
Qui a bu boira. Ever drunk ever dry.
Bitter to the mouth and sweet to the heart.
Rise from dinner with an appetite, and you will not be in danger of sitting down without one.

Dr. Johnson's three rules of frugality:—
1. A man's voluntary expenses should never exceed his income.
2. Let no man anticipate uncertain profits.
3. Let no man squander against his inclination.

From Mrs. Child's "Frugal Housewife," and other Authors.

THE MILLETS.—The *seterias*, or close-seeded millets, yield Italian millet (*S. Italica*) This millet, called Raggy, in Madras, is considered by the natives of India one of the most delicious of cultivated grains. The Brahmins, indeed all classes of natives, particularly esteem it, and use the seeds for cakes and porridge, &c. It is good for pastry —scarcely inferior, says Ainslie, to wheat, and when boiled with milk makes a pleasant light dish for invalids.—*The Technologist.*

CV.—AIGUILLETTES.

To be able to carve well is a useful and elegant accomplishment. It is an artless recommendation to a man who is looking for a wife.—*Hints for the Table.*

Aiguillettes is a term in the *cuisine* applied to small dishes, from the articles of which they consist being mounted on silver needles or skewers, with ornamental tops; something akin to the Turkish *kebobs*. In a French dinner, they form one of the *hors d'œuvres*, or dishes handed around the table during the first course.

Aiguillettes de Ris de Veau (*Sweet-bread of Veal*).—Take three throat sweet-breads, boil in water ten minutes, pour off the liquor, add one onion, one carrot, one turnip, two bay-leaves, and a pint of stock; simmer twenty minutes, cut them into round pieces a little larger than a shilling, and season with salt and pepper; next, put them into a stewpan with an ounce of butter, dress them white, then dip each piece with a fork into a mixture of white sauce, yolks of eggs, and the juice of a lemon. When cold, run the skewer through the pieces, putting several on each skewer; dip them into egg well beaten, then into bread crumbs, and fry in hot lard. Serve on a napkin. *Aiguillettes aux huitres* (oysters), *de filets de sole* (soles), *de langue de bœuf* (ox-tongue), *de volaille à la John Fille* (fowl), are prepared in a similar way to the above, merely varying the sauces to be sent up according to the taste of the *gourmet*.

CLASSICAL EATING.—The Romans, in the luxurious period of their empire, took five meals a day—a breakfast, *jentaculum*; a dinner, which was a light meal without any formal preparation, *prandium*; a kind of tea, as we would call it, between dinner and supper, *meranda*; a supper, *cœna*, which was their great meal, and commonly consisted of two courses, the first of meats, the second what we call a dessert; and a posset, or something delicious after supper, *commissatio*.—*Adams's "Roman Antiquities."*

CVI.—PRESERVED MEATS.

HOUSEWIFERY: an ancient art, said to have been once fashionable among young girls and wives, but now entirely out of use, or practised only by the lower orders.—*Scrap.*

The reason why meat-preserving establishments have not been organised and carried out in the Australian provinces we cannot divine, seeing that the article to be made is cheaper than in any other British colony, and that it might become one of the most important industrial resources and exports of Australia. We have extracted from that valuable work, Ure's "Dictionary," the following condensed observations bearing on this subject:—

The great importance of preserved meats to a maritime nation like Great Britain is apparent, as these provisions, when sound, are a preventive of sea scurvy. The first successful attempt at preservation of unsalted meats is of French origin, and is due to the inventive skill of M. Appert. This gentleman, in the year 1810, received from the Board of Arts, at Paris, the sum of 12,000 francs for his discovery of a mode of preserving animal and vegetable substances, the results of which were tested in the French navy. M. Appert induced a M. Durant to visit London, and take out a patent, which was done in 1811. In the patent the claims were so wide that it was infringed. The claims included all kinds of fruit, meat, and vegetables, when subjected to the action of heat in closed vessels, more or less freed from air. It was, however, discovered that the British Society of Arts had, in 1807, presented a premium to Mr. Suddington for "a method of preserving fruit without sugar," which was the same as Appert's. The validity of Durant's patent was set aside; but the results were so satisfactory that the patent was purchased by Messrs. Donkin, Hall, and Gamble for £1,000, and that firm became the sole manufacturers of preserved meats. M. Appert could only use glass bottles, while Messrs. Donkin and Co., after many experiments, produced provisions preserved in tin. The method of Appert, as improved by Gamble, is to render the albumen of the meat or vegetable insoluble, and therefore scarcely, if at all, susceptible of the action of atmospheric oxygen. By this means the total exclusion of air from the tin cases is rendered unnecessary; for even if a small quantity of air remain in the case, it will exert no more influence than happens to a piece of coagulated albumen, or hard-boiled egg, which, as is well known, may be exposed to the air for years without sensible alteration, though in its uncoagulated state it putrifies. If, therefore, we desired in a few words to express the essential characteristics of Gamble's process, it could not be by referring to the exclusion of air, but to the thorough coagulation of the albumen, that we look for a satisfactory description. In this process, the meat, more or less cooked, is placed, with a quantity of gravy, in a tin vessel, capable of being hermetically sealed with solder. It is then heated, for some time, in a bath of muriate of lime, and the aperture neatly soldered up. After this, it is again exposed to the action of the heated bath, for a period which varies with the size and nature of the contents of the vessels; and to prove that this latter operation is really the most important of the whole, it sometimes happens that cans which have began to decompose are opened, re-soldered, and again submitted to the muriate of lime bath, with the most perfect success as regards the ultimate result. The system of Gamble has worked well, although there are occasional failures. Provisions have been kept in this way for twenty-six years. It was found by Sir John Ross, that a number of cases of preserved provisions left for many years upon Fury Beach, and exposed to varieties of temperature, were nevertheless perfectly sound and wholesome when opened. Mr. Solder, some few years since, adopted the idea originally conceived by Sir Humphry Davy, of enclosing cooked provisions in a complete vacuum. For this purpose, the provisions, slightly cooked on the surface, were enclosed in canisters, similar to those of Gamble's, but stronger, and provided with a small opening in the cover. At this moment a slight condensation was effected by the application of a cold or damp rag or sponge, and simultaneously with this the small opening was soldered up. In theory nothing could seem better adapted to insure success; but, from the Parliamentary disclosures, it is evident that the practical working of the invention was not satisfactory. Few vessels leave the ports of Great Britain without a supply from Messrs. Gamble and Co. The mode of preserving butcher's meat, fish, and poultry is as follows:—Let the substance to be preserved be first parboiled, or rather somewhat more, the bones of the meat being previously removed. Put the meat into a tin cylinder, fill up the vessel with seasoned rich soup, and then solder on the lid, pierced with a small hole. When this has been done, let the tin vessel thus prepared be placed in brine and heated to boiling point, to complete the remainder of the cooking of the meat. The hole in the lid is now to be closed perfectly by soldering, whilst the air is rarefied. The vessel is then allowed to cool, and from the diminution of the volume, in consequence of the reduction of temperature, both ends of the cylinder are pressed inwards and become concave. The tin cases, thus hermetically sealed, are exposed in a test chamber for at least a month to a temperature above what they are now likely to encounter, from $90°$ to $110°$ of F. If the process has failed, putrefaction takes place and gases evolved, which, in process of time, will cause both ends of the case to bulge, so as to render them convex instead of concave. But the contents of those cases which stand the test will infallibly keep perfectly sweet and good in any climate, and for any number of years. If there be any taint about the meat when put up, it invariably ferments, and is detected in the proving process. According to the last notice of that most useful institution, the Society for the Encouragement of Arts, Manufactures, and Commerce, the first intimation of which appears to the colonists in Saunders, Otley, and Morgan's "Oriental Budget," the sum of £70 has been placed at the disposal of the society, by Sir W. C. Trevelyan, Bart., to which they have added their prize medal, for the discovery of a process for preserving fresh meat better than any hitherto employed. This matter is of the most paramount importance to Australia, and we hope that some useful result will accrue from the competition for this prize.

DINNER.—Among the Romans this was rather considered as a refreshment to prevent faintness, than as a meal to convey nourishment. It consisted principally of some light repast, without animal food, or wine; but in modern times it is considered the principal meal, at which every species of luxurious gratification is indulged in. With regard to the proper period at which invalids should dine, physicians entertain but one opinion—it should be in the middle of the day, or about two or three o'clock. Sir A. Carlisle has justly observed, that it is thus best adapted to the decline of animal vigour, because it affords a timely replenishment before the evening waning of the vital powers, and which naturally precede the hours of rest; besides which, the custom tends to prevent intemperance; while late hours, and consequent state of exhaustion, demand or seem to justify an excessive indulgence in strong drinks and in variety of food.—*Dr. Paris on " Diet."*

CVII.—LAVER—(*Porphyra Laciniata*).

Point de légumes—point de cuisinière.—*French Culinary Adage.*

This is a species of reddish sea-weed, or *ulva*—the sea and river wort—and found on many pebbly beaches all over the world. The poor eat it in the Highlands of Scotland on bread, and the Irish use it sometimes instead of butter; but, with the rich, it is one of the dainties of the dinner-table, and served hot in a silver lamp dish. It is eaten with roast beef or mutton. The manner of its cookery is simple. It is stewed, with a little butter, the juice of a lemon, some cayenne pepper, with a spoonful of glaze. It would be a first-rate dish for the Celestials, and beat their birds' nests fare all to pieces. There is a gelatinous sea-weed—an *alga*—sometimes used for making jelly, to be found in the bay at the estuary of the Derwent, in Tasmania. We have never heard of its being cooked like the laver; perhaps it might be equally as good. It is, we believe, the *Laminaria potatrium*. In Dr. Hooker's botanical account of the sea-weeds of the Falkland Islands, he states, that the green, pink, and purple lavers of Great Britain were there found in great plenty.—*Sir James Ross's " Voyage to the Southern Seas."*

Broad-leaved Laver (*Ulva latissima*).—This is rarely used, being considered inferior to the *Porphyra laciniata* (laciniated purple laver). This *alga* is abundant on all our shores. It is pickled with salt, and sold in England as *laver*, in Ireland as *sloke*, and in Scotland as *slank*. The London shops are mostly supplied with laver from the coasts of Devonshire. When stewed, it is brought to the table, and eaten with pepper, butter or oil, and lemon-juice or vinegar. Some persons stew it with leeks and onions. The pepper dulse (*Laurencia pennatifida*), distinguished for its pungent taste, is often used as a condiment when other sea-weeds are eaten. Tangle (*Laminaria digitata*), so called in Scotland, is termed red-ware in the Orkneys, sea-weed in the Highlands, and sea-girdles in England. The flat, leathery fronds of this weed, when young, are employed as food. Mr. Simmonds tells us, "There was a time when the cry of 'Buy dulse and tangle' was as common in the streets of Edinburgh and Glasgow as that of 'Water-cresses' now in the metropolis."— *Society of Arts' Journal.*

DINNERS.—One of the greatest sources of complaint in society is the want of propriety in the conducting of entertainments in all their varieties, from the simple family dinner to the splendid banquet. For instance, a family dinner; a family dinner to which guests are admitted; a common dinner party; an entertainment; a bachelors' dinner; a ministerial dinner; and a dress dinner. Though these and similar other entertainments are distinct, yet the distinctions are not so strictly observed as those in other usages of society. At the plainest, as well as the most splendid of these entertainments, everything ought to be as good, and as well cooked, and nice as possible; but the style of service ought to be varied, rising from the simple, in elegant succession, to the sumptuous. For real taste does not indiscriminately present turtle and venison on every occasion; something more delicately palatable and less obtrusive is presented, with the zest of a fine mango, high-flavoured vinegars, well-made sauces, nice salads, and appropriate wines, with the charms of well-supported conversation, affording an uncloying feast throughout the year.—*Beau Villiers.*

CVIII.—BUTTER.

Unquiet meals make ill digestion.—*Old Saying.*

Butter is, perhaps, in more general use, and subject to greater variations in quality, than any other substance employed in domestic economy. It is consumed by every grade of society, and, when good, appears not only to be wholesome, but extremely nutritious. Some writers inveigh against the use of butter, as universally pernicious; but they might with equal reason condemn the vegetable oils, which form a considerable part of the diet in the southern climates, and seem to be beneficially intended by nature for that purpose. That butter may be improper in some bilious constitutions there can be little doubt; but the same objection tells against any other substance used as food; for instances are not uncommon of the most delicate and nutritious articles disagreeing with persons under certain circumstances, and who are of peculiar idiosyncrasy. To obviate all objections, it would be a commendable practice for the bilious, at breakfast, first to eat some dry bread—crust is better—and to chew it well before taking any butter. By these means such a quantity of saliva would be carried into the stomach as would be sufficient for the purpose of digesting the usual amount of oil and fatty matter taken with our food. —*Cooley's "Practical Receipts."* Butter was not used either by the Greeks or Romans in cooking or the preparation of their food, nor was it brought on the tables by way of dessert, as it is everywhere customary at present. We never find it mentioned by Galen or others as food, though they have spoken of it as applicable to other purposes; no notice is taken of it by Apicius, nor is there anything said of it in that respect by the authors who treat of agriculture, though they have given us very particular information with respect to milk, cheese, and oil. This, as has been remarked by others, may be easily accounted for by the ancients having accustomed themselves to the use of good oil; and in like manner butter is very little employed at present in Italy, Spain, Portugal, and the southern parts of France.—*Beckman.* Butter is very extensively used in this and most northern countries; that of England and Holland is reckoned the best. In London the butter of Epping and Cambridge is in the highest repute; the cows which produce the former feed during summer in the shrubby pastures of Epping Forest, and the leaves of the trees and numerous wild plants which there abound are supposed to improve the flavour of the butter. It is brought to market in rolls, from one to two feet long, weighing a pound each. The Cambridgeshire butter is produced from cows that feed one part of the year on chalky uplands, and in the other on rich meadows or fens. It is made up into long rolls like the Epping butter, and generally salted or cured before being brought to market; the London dealers having washed it and wrought the salt out of it, it frequently sells for Epping butter. The butter of Suffolk and Yorkshire is often sold for that of Cambridgeshire, to which it is little inferior. The butter of Somersetshire is thought equal to that of Epping; it is brought to market in dishes, containing half a pound each, out of which it is taken, washed, and put into different forms by the dealers of Bath and Bristol. The butter of Gloucestershire and Oxfordshire is very good; it is made up into half-pound packs or prints, packed up in square baskets, and sent to the London markets by wagon (? rail). The butter of the mountains of Wales and Scotland, and the moors, commons, and heaths of England is of excellent quality when it is properly managed; and though not equal in quantity, it often is confessedly superior to that produced by the richest meadows.—*Loudon's " Encyc. of Agriculture."* Considerable quantities of butter are made in Ireland, and it forms a prominent article in the exports of that country; generally it is very inferior to that of Britain; but this is a consequence rather of the want of cleanliness and attention than of any inferiority in the milk. Some of the best Irish butter brought to London, after being washed and repacked, is sold as Dorsetshire and Cambridge butter. The salt butter of Holland is superior to that of any other country; large quantities are annually exported. It forms two-thirds to three-fourths of all the butter we import, the rest being brought from Germany, Belgium, &c. The production and consumption of butter in Great Britain is very great. The consumption of the metropolis may be averaged at eight pounds for each person, and the population to amount to 2,300,000; the annual consumption would amount to 18,400,000 pounds, or 8,214 tons; to this may be added 3,000 tons for victualling ships and other purposes, so that the total consumption would be 11,200 tons, which, at 10d. per pound, would be £1,045,333. The average produce per cow of the butter dairies is estimated by Mr. Marshal at 168 pounds a year, but owing to improvements which have been lately made, the yield per cow is now 180 pounds, so that 140,000 cows are required to produce the supply for the London market.—*M'Culloch's " Commercial Dictionary."* In India butter is denominated *ghee,* and is mostly prepared from the milk of buffaloes: it is usually conveyed in dippers, or bottles made of hide, each of which contains from ten to forty gallons. *Ghee* is an article of considerable commercial importance in many parts of India. The Arabs are the greatest consumers of butter in the world. It is a common practice among all classes to drink every morning a coffee-cupful of melted butter or *ghee*, and they use it in an infinite variety of ways. The taste for it is universal, and the poorest individuals will expend half their daily income that they may have butter for dinner and butter in the morning. Large quantities are annually shipped from Cossier, Souakin, and Massonah, on the west coast of the Red Sea, for Djidda, and other Arabian ports.—*Burckhardt's Travels*. Butter is the fatty matter of milk, several salts, and water. The butter exists in the form of very small globules of nearly uniform size, quite transparent, and strongly refractive of light. Milk left in repose throws up the lighter particles of butter to the surface as cream. It was imagined that the butter was separated in the process of churning, in consequence of the milk becoming sour; but this is not the case, for milk rendered alkaline by bicarbonate of potash affords its butter fully more readily than acidulous milk. The best temperature for churning milk or cream is 53° F.; that of 60° is too high, and under 50° it is too low.—*Ure*.

FLATTERY AT MEALS.—So saying, my panegyrist took his place right over against me, and a cover being laid for him, attacked the omelette as voraciously as if he had fasted three whole days. By his complaisant beginning, I foresaw that our dish would not last long, and therefore ordered a second, which was dressed with such dispatch that it was served up just as we—or rather he—had made an end of the first. He proceeded on with the same vigour, and found means, without losing one stroke of his teeth, to overwhelm me with praises during the whole repast, which made me very well pleased with my sweet self. He drank in proportion to his eating, sometimes to my health, sometimes to that of my father and mother, whose happiness in having such a son as I he could not enough admire. In the meantime he plied me with wine, and insisted upon my doing him justice, while I toasted health for health—a circumstance which, together with his intoxicating flattery, put me in such good humour, that, seeing our second omelette half devoured, I asked the landlord if he had no fish in the house. Signor Corcuelo, who, in all likelihood, had a fellow-feeling for the parasite, replied, "I have a delicate trout, but those who eat it must pay for the sauce; 'tis a bit too dainty for your palate, I doubt." "What do you call too dainty?" said the sycophant, raising his voice; "you're a wiseacre, indeed! Know that there is nothing in this house too good for Signor Gil Blas de Santillane, who deserves to be entertained like a prince!"—*Gil Blas' Adventures at Pennaflor*.

CIX.—HEBREW REFECTION.

For thou art a holy people unto the Lord thy God, and the Lord has chosen thee to be a peculiar people unto himself, above all the nations that are upon the earth.
Thou shalt not eat any abominable thing.
These are the beasts that ye shall eat: the ox, the sheep, and the goat.—*Deut*. xiv. 2, 3, 4,

Palestine Soup.—Stew a knuckle of veal, a calf's foot, one pound of *chorissa*, and a large fowl, in four quarts of water; add a piece of fresh lemon-peel, six Jerusalem artichokes, a bunch of sweet herbs, a little salt and white pepper, a nutmeg, and a blade of mace. When the fowl is thoroughly done remove the white parts to preserve for thickening, and let the rest continue stewing till the stock is sufficiently strong. The white parts of the fowl must be pounded and sprinkled with flour or ground rice, and stirred in the soup after it has been strained, until it thickens.

Matso Soup.—Boil down half a shin of beef, four pounds of gravy beef—and a calf's foot may be added if approved—in four quarts of water, season with celery, carrots, turnips, pepper and salt, and a bunch of sweet herbs. Let the whole stew gently for eight hours, then strain, and let it stand to get cold, when the fat must be removed; then return it to the saucepan to warm up. Ten minutes before serving throw in the balls from which the soup takes its name, and which are made in the following manner:—Take half a pound of *matso* flour, two ounces of chopped suet, season with a little pepper, salt, ginger, and nutmeg; mix with this four beaten eggs, and make it into a paste; a small onion shred and browned in a dessert-spoonful of oil. The paste should be made into rather large balls, and care should be taken to make them very light.

Almondigos Soup.—Put a knuckle of veal and a calf's foot into two quarts of water, with a blade of mace and a bunch of sweet herbs, a turnip, a little white pepper, and salt. When sufficiently done, strain and skim it, and add balls of forced meat and egg-balls. A quarter of an hour before serving beat up the yolks of four eggs, with a dessert-spoonful of lemon-juice, and three ounces of sweet almonds, blanched, and with a spoonful of powdered white sugar. This mixture is to be beaten into the soup until it thickens, taking care to prevent its curdling.

Sauce à la Tartare.—Mix the yolk of an egg with oil, vinegar, chopped parsley, mustard, pepper, and salt. A spoonful of *pati de diable*, or French mustard, renders the sauce more piquante.

Egg Sauce.—A fine white sauce for boiled fowls, turkeys, or white *fricassées*:—Beat up the yolks of four eggs with the juice of a lemon, a tea-spoonful of flour, and a little cold water; mix well together, and set it on the fire to thicken, stirring it to prevent curdling. This sauce will be found excellent, if not superior, in many cases where English cooks use melted butter. If capers are substituted for the lemon-juice, this sauce will be found good both for boiled lamb or mutton.

A Fish Sauce without Butter.—Put on in a small saucepan a cup of water well flavoured with vinegar, an onion chopped fine, a little rasped horseradish, pepper, and two or three cloves, and a couple of anchovies cut small. When it has boiled, stir carefully in the beaten yolks of two eggs, and let it thicken until of the consistency of melted butter.

Fish Stewed White.—Put an onion, finely chopped, into a stewpan, with a little oil, till the onion becomes brown; then add half a pint of water, and place the fish in the stewpan, seasoning with pepper, salt, and mace, ground allspice, nutmeg, and ginger; let it stew gently until the fish is done, then prepare the beaten yolks of four eggs, with the juice of two lemons, a tea-spoonful of flour, a table-spoonful of cold water, and a little saffron; mix well in a cup, and pour it into the stewpan, stirring it carefully one way until it thickens. Balls should be thrown in about twenty minutes before serving. They are made in the following way:—Take a little of the fish, the liver and the roe, if there is any, beat it up finely with chopped parsley, and spread warm butter, crumbs of bread, and seasoning according to taste. Form this into a paste with eggs, and make it into balls of a moderate size. This is a very nice dish when cold. Garnish with sliced lemon and parsley.

Fish Soup.—Make a good stock, by simmering a cod's-head in water, enough to cover the fish; season it with pepper and salt, mace, celery, parsley, and a few sweet herbs, with two or three onions; when sufficiently done strain it, and add cutlets of fish prepared in the following manner:—Cut very small, well trimmed cutlets from any fish—sole or brill are, perhaps, best; stew them in equal quantities of water and wine, but not more than will cover them, with a large lump of butter, and the juice of a lemon; when they have stewed gently for about fifteen or twenty minutes, add them to the soup, which thicken with cream and flour. Serve the soup with the cutlets in a tureen. Forcemeat balls of cod's liver are sometimes added.

Fish Fried in Oil.—Soles, plaice, or salmon are the best kind of fish to dress in this manner, although other sorts are used. When prepared by salting or drying, have a dish ready with beaten eggs, turn the fish well over in them, and sprinkle it freely with flour, so that the fish may be covered entirely with it; then place it in a pan, with a quantity of the best frying-oil, at boiling heat. Fry the fish in it gently till of a fine, equal, brown colour. When done it should be placed before the fire for the oil to drain off. Great care should be taken that the oil should have ceased to bubble when the fish is put in, otherwise it will be greasy; the oil will serve again if strained off and poured into a jar. Fish preserved in this way is usually served cold, garnished with parsley.

Escobeche.—Take some cold fried fish, and place it in a deep pan; then boil half a pint of vinegar with two table-spoonfuls of water, a little grated ginger, allspice, cayenne pepper, two bay-leaves, a little salt, and a table-spoonful of lemon-juice; with sliced onions. When boiling, pour it over the fish; cover the pan, and let it stand twenty-four hours before serving.

Kugel and Cornmean.—Soak a pint of Spanish peas and one pint of Spanish beans all night in three pints of water; take two marrow-bones, and tie them together, to prevent the marrow from escaping, and put altogether in a pan; then take one pound of flour, half a pound of shred suet, a little grated nutmeg and ground ginger, cloves and allspice, one pound of coarse brown sugar, and the crumb of a slice of bread, first soaked in water, and pressed dry. Mix all these ingredients into a paste; grease a quart basin, and put it in, covering the basin with a plate; set it in the middle of the pan, with the beans, meat, &c. Cover the pan tightly down with coarse brown paper, and let it remain all the night and the next day (until required) in a baker's oven; when done, take out the basin containing the pudding, and skim the fat from the gravy, which must be served with soup. The meat, &c., is extremely savoury and nutritious, but it is not a very seemly dish for table. The pudding must be turned out of the basin; and a sweet sauce, flavoured with lemon and brandy, is a fine addition.

Salmon Pie.—Cut two pounds of fine fresh salmon in slices, about three-quarters of an inch thick, and set them aside on a dish; clean and scrape five or six anchovies, and halve them; then chop a small pottle of mushrooms, a handful of fresh parsley, a couple of shalots, and a little green thyme. Put these together into a saucepan, with three ounces of butter, a little pepper, salt and nutmeg, and tarragon; add the juice of a lemon, and half a pint of good brown gravy; and let the whole simmer, stirring it gently all the time: also slice six eggs boiled hard; then line a pie-dish with short paste, and fill it with alternate layers of the slices of salmon, hard eggs, and fillets of anchovies, spreading between each layer the herb sauce; then cover the dish with the paste, and bake in a moderately-heated oven.

Sour-krout.—Boil about seven or eight pounds of beef, either brisket or a fillet off the shoulder, in enough water to cover it. When it has boiled for an hour, add as much sour-krout as may be approved; it should then stew gently for four hours, and be served in a deep dish. The Germans are not very particular in removing the fat, but it is more delicate to do so.

Scalloped Fish.—Break the fish into pieces; pour over the beaten yolk of an egg; sprinkle with pepper and salt; strew with bread crumbs, chopped parsley, and grated lemon-peel; and squeeze in the juice of a lemon. Drop over a little warmed butter, and brown before the fire.

Smoked Beef.—As there are seldom conveniences in private kitchens for smoking meats, it will generally be the best and cheapest plan to have them ready prepared for cooking. All kinds of meat, smoked and salted, are to be had in great perfection at all the Hebrew butchers.

Chorissa.—That most refined and savoury of all sausages is to be procured at the same places. It is not only excellent fried in slices with poached eggs, or stewed with rice, but imparts a delicious flavour to stews, soups, and sauces, and is one of the most useful resources of the Jewish kitchen.

Impanada.—Cut in small pieces, halibut, plaice, or soles; place them in a deep dish, in alternate layers, with slices of potatoes and dumplings made of short crust paste, sweetened with brown sugar, seasoned well with small pickles, pepper, gherkins, or West India pickles; throw over a little water or butter, warmed, and bake it thoroughly.

Kinsmil Meat.—Place a small piece of the rump of beef, or the under-cut of a sirloin, in a deep pan, with three pints of vinegar, two ounces of carraway-seeds tied in a muslin bag, salt, pepper, and spices; cover it down tight, and bake thoroughly in a slow oven.

To Hash Beef.—The meat should be put on the fire in a little broth or gravy, with a little fried onion, pepper, salt, and a spoonful of ketchup, or any other sauce at hand; let it simmer for about ten minutes, then mix in a cup a little flour with a little of the gravy, and pour it into the stewpan to thicken the rest; sippets of toast should be served with hashes; a little port wine, a pinch of saffron, or a piece of *chorissa,* may be considered great improvements.

A-la-mode Beef, or Sour Meat.—Cover a piece of the ribs of beef, boned and filleted, or a piece of the round, with vinegar diluted with water; season with onions, pepper, salt, whole allspice, and three or four bay-leaves; add a cupful of raspings, and let the whole stew gently for three or four hours, according to the weight of the meat; this dish is excellent when cold. A rump-steak stewed in the same way will be found exceedingly fine.

Beef and Beans.—Take a piece of brisket of beef, cover it with water; when boiling, skim off the fat; add one quartern of fresh beans cut small; two onions, cut in quarters; season with pepper and salt, and when nearly done, take a dessert-spoonful of flour, one of coarse brown sugar, and a large tea-cupful of vinegar; mix them together, and stir in with the beans, and continue stirring for about half an hour longer.

Fricondelle.—Prepare cold veal or poultry, add a French roll soaked in white gravy, with sweet herbs, pepper, salt, parsley, and essence of lemon; mix all well with two or three eggs, and form it into shapes; sprinkle with crumbs of bread, and place in a frying-pan as deep as a shallow saucepan; when they have fried enough to become set, pour enough white gravy in the pan to cover the fricondelles, and let them stew in it gently; place them both in the same dish, and pour over any well-thickened sauce that may be selected.

Mutton Stewed with Celery.—Take the end of a neck of mutton, or a fillet taken from the leg or shoulder, place it in a stewpan, with enough water to cover it; throw in a carrot and a turnip, and season, but not too highly; when nearly done, remove the meat and strain off the gravy; then return both to the stewpan, with forcemeat balls, and some fine celery cut in small pieces; let all stew together till perfectly done, then stir in the yolks of two eggs, a little flour, and the juice of half a lemon, which must be mixed with a little of the gravy before pouring into the stewpan, and care must be taken to prevent its curdling.

Amnastich.—Stew gently one pint of rice in one quart of strong gravy till it begins to swell, then add an onion stuck with cloves, a bunch of sweet herbs, and a chicken stuffed with forcemeat; let it stew with the rice till thoroughly done, then take it up, and stir in the rice, the yolks of four eggs, and the juice of a lemon; serve the fowl in the same dish with the rice, which should be coloured to a fine yellow with saffron.

Fowls Stewed with Rice and Chorissa.—Boil a fowl in sufficient water or gravy to cover it. When boiling for ten minutes, skim off the fat, and add half a pound of rice and one pound of *chorissa* cut in about four pieces; season with a little white pepper, salt, and a pinch of saffron to colour it, and then stew till the rice is thoroughly tender. There should be no gravy when served, but the rice should be perfectly moist.

Chicken Pudding.—Line a basin with a good beef-suet paste, and fill it with chicken prepared in the following manner:—Cut up a chicken, lightly fry the pieces, then place them in a stewpan, with thin slices of *chorissa*, or, if at hand, slices of smoked veal. Add enough good beef gravy to cover them, season with mushroom essence or powder, pepper, salt, and a very small quantity of nutmeg and mace. Simmer gently for a quarter of an hour, and fill the pudding. Pour over part of the gravy, and keep the rest to be poured over the pudding when served in the dish. The pudding, when filled, must be covered closely with the paste, the end of which should be wetted with a paste-brush, to make it adhere closely.

Spiced Beef.—Take a fine thick piece of brisket of beef, not fat; let it lay three days in pickle, take it out and rub in a mixture of spices, consisting of equal quantities of ground allspice, black pepper, cloves, ginger, and nutmegs, and a little brown sugar. Repeat this daily for a week, then cover it with pounded dry sweet herbs, roll or tie it tightly, put it into a pan with a little water, and bake slowly for eight hours; then take it out, untie it, and put a heavy weight upon it. This is a fine relish when eaten cold.

A White Fricandeau of Veal.—Take four or five pounds of breast of veal, or fillet from the shoulder; stuff it with a fine-flavoured veal stuffing, and put it into a stewpan, with water sufficient to cover it; a calf's foot cut in pieces is sometimes added. Season with one onion, a blade of mace, white pepper and salt, and a sprig of parsley. Stew the whole gently until the meat is quite tender, then skim and strain the gravy, and stir in the beaten yolks of four eggs and the juice of two lemons, previously mixed smoothly with a portion of the gravy. Button mushrooms or pieces of celery, stewed with the veal, are sometimes added by way of varying the flavour. Egg and forcemeat balls garnish the dish. When required to look elegant it should be *pique*.

Descaides.—Take the livers of chickens or any other poultry; stew them gently in a little good gravy, seasoned with a little onion, mushroom essence, pepper and salt. When tender remove the livers, place them on a pasteboard, and mince them; return them to the saucepan, and stir in the yolks of one or two eggs, according to the quantity of liver, until the gravy becomes thick. Have a round of toast ready on a hot plate, and serve it on the toast. This is a very nice luncheon or supper dish.

Potato Shavings.—Take four fine large potatoes, and having peeled them, continue to cut them up as if in ribbons, of equal width; then throw the shavings into a frying-pan, and fry of a light brown; they must be constantly moved with a silver fork to keep the pieces separate. They should be laid on a glass to drain, and placed in the dish lightly.

Peas Stewed with Oil.—Put half a pint of peas into a stewpan, half a lettuce chopped small, a little mint, a small onion, cut up, two table-spoonfuls of oil, and a dessert-spoonful of powdered sugar, with water sufficient to cover the peas, watching from time to time that they do not become too dry; let them stew gently, taking care that they do not burn, till they are perfectly soft. When done they should look of a yellowish brown. French beans, broccoli, and greens, stewed in the above manner, will be found excellent.

Stewed Giblets.—Scald one or more sets of giblets; set them on the fire with a little veal or chicken, or both, in a good gravy; season to taste, thicken the gravy, and colour it with browning, flavour with mushroom powder and lemon-juice, and one glass of white wine; force-meat balls should be added a few moments before serving, and garnish with thin slices of hard-boiled eggs.

To stew Spanish Beans and Peas.—Soak the beans over night in cold water; they must be stewed in only sufficient water to cover them, with two table-spoonfuls of oil, a little pepper and salt, and white sugar. When done they should be perfectly soft and tender.

Chorissa Omelette.—Add to the eggs, after they are well beaten, half a tea-cupful of finely-minced *chorissa;* this omelette must be lightly fried on both sides, or the salamander held over long enough to dress the *chorissa.*

Melena Pie.—Mince finely cold veal or chicken, with smoked beef or tongue; season well, add lemon-juice, and a little nutmeg; let it simmer in a small quantity of good beef or veal gravy; while on the fire, stir in the yolks of four eggs, put it in a dish to cool, and cover it with a rich pastry and bake it.

Bola d'Amor.—The recipe for this much celebrated and exquisite confection is simpler than may be supposed from its elaborate appearance; it requires chiefly care, precision, and attention. Clarify two pounds of white sugar; to ascertain when it is of proper consistency, drop a spoonful in cold water, form it into a ball, and try if it sounds when struck against a glass; when it is thus tested, take the yolks of twenty eggs, mix them up gently, and pass them through a sieve; then have ready a funnel, the hole of which must be about the size of a vermicelli; hold the funnel over the sugar while it is boiling over a charcoal fire, pour the egg through, stirring the sugar all the time, and taking care to hold the funnel at such a distance from the sugar as to admit of the egg dripping into it. When the egg has been a few minutes in the sugar, it will be hard enough to take out with a silver fork, and must then be placed on a drainer; continue adding egg to the boiling sugar till enough is obtained. There should be previously prepared one pound of sweet almonds finely pounded and boiled in sugar, clarified with orange rose-water only; place in a dish a layer of this paste, over which place a layer of citrons cut in thin slices, and then a thick layer of the egg prepared as above; continue working thus in alternate layers till high enough to look handsome. It should be piled in the form of a cone, and the egg should form the last layer. It must then be placed in a gentle oven till it becomes a little set, and the last layer slightly crisp; a few minutes will effect this. It must be served in the dish in which it is baked, and is generally ornamented with myrtle and gold and silver leaf.

Superior Recipe for Almond Pudding.—Beat up the yolks of ten eggs, and the whites of seven; add half a pound of sweet almonds pounded finely, half a pound of white sugar, half an ounce of bitter almonds, and a table-spoonful of orange-flower water; when thoroughly mixed, grease a dish, put in the pudding, and bake in a brisk oven; when done, strew powdered sugar over the top, or, which is exceedingly fine, pour over clarified sugar with orange-flower water.

Sopa d'Oro; or, Golden Soup.—Clarify a pound of sugar in a quarter of a pint of water, and the same quantity of orange-flower water; cut into pieces the size of dice, a thin slice of toasted bread, or cut it into shapes with a paste-cutter; throw it, while hot, into the sugar, with an ounce of sweet almonds pounded very finely; then take the beaten yolks of four eggs, pour over the sugar and bread, stir gently, and let it simmer a few minutes. Serve in a deep glass dish, sprinkled over with pounded cinnamon.

Bola Toliedo.—Take a pound of butter, and warm it over the fire, with a little milk; then put it into a pan with a pound of flour, six beaten eggs, a quarter of a pound of beaten sweet almonds, and two table-spoonfuls of yeast; make these ingredients into a light paste, and set it before the fire to rise; then grease a deep dish, and place in a layer of the paste; then some egg prepared as for *bola d'amor;* then slices of citron, and a layer of egg marmalade; sprinkle each layer with cinnamon, and fill the dish with alternate layers. A rich puff paste should line the dish, which ought to be baked in a brisk oven; after which sugar clarified with orange-flower water must be poured over till the syrup has thoroughly penetrated the bola.

A Luction, or a Rachael.—Make thin nouilles paste, cut into strips of about two inches wide; leave it to dry; then boil the strips in a little water, and drain through a colander; when the water is strained off, mix it with beaten eggs, white sugar, a little fresh butter, and grated lemon-peel; bake or boil in a shape lined with preserved cherries; when turned out, pour over a fine custard, or cream, flavoured with brandy, and sweetened to taste.

Prenesas.—Take one pint of milk, stir in as much flour as will bring it to the consistency of hasty pudding; boil it till it becomes thick, let it cool, and beat it up with ten eggs; when smooth, take a spoonful at a time, and drop it into a frying-pan in which there is a good quantity of boiling clarified butter; fry of a light brown, and serve with clarified sugar flavoured with lemon essence.

Chejados.—Clarify a pound of sugar in half a pint of water, peel and grate a moderately-sized cocoa-nut, add it to the syrup, and let it simmer till perfectly soft, putting rose-water occasionally to prevent its becoming too dry; stir it to prevent burning. Let it cool, and mix it with the beaten yolks of six eggs. Make a thin nouilles pastry, cut it into rounds the size of a tea-cup, pinch up the edges deep enough to form a shape, fill them with the sweetmeat, and bake of a light brown. A rich puff paste may be substituted for the nouilles pastry if preferred.

Macrotes.—Take a pound of French roll dough, six ounces of fresh butter, two eggs, as much flour as will be requisite to knead together; roll it in the form of a long French roll, and cut it in thin long slices, set them at a short distance from the fire to rise, and then fry them in the best Florence oil. When nearly cold, dip them in clarified sugar, flavoured with essence of lemon.

Tart de Moy.—Soak three-quarters of a pound of savoury biscuits in a quart of milk; add six ounces of fresh butter, four eggs, one ounce of candied orange-peel, the same quantity of lemon-peel, and one ounce of citron; mix all well together. Sweeten with white sugar, and bake in a quick oven; when nearly done, spread over the top the whites of the eggs well whisked, and return it to the oven.

Green Stick.—Make into a stiff paste one pint of biscuit-powder, a little brown sugar, grated lemon-peel, six eggs, and three-quarters of a pound of warmed fresh butter; then prepare four apples chopped finely, a quarter of a pound of sweet almonds blanched and chopped, half a pound of stoned raisins, a little nutmeg grated, half a pound of coarse brown sugar, and a glass of white wine, or a little brandy. Mix the above ingredients together, and put them on a slow fire, to simmer for half an hour, and place in a dish to cool. Make the paste into the form of small dumplings, fill them with the fruit, and bake them. When put in the oven, pour over a syrup of brown sugar-and-water, flavoured with lemon-juice.

Haman's Fritters.—Take two spoonfuls of the best Florence oil, scald it, and, when hot, mix with it one pound of flour; add four beaten eggs, and make it into a paste; roll it out thin, and cut it into pieces about four inches square; let them dry, and fry them in oil. The moment the pieces are put into the frying-pan they must be drawn up with silver skewers into different forms, according to fancy. A few minutes is sufficient to fry them; they should be crisp when done.

Waflers.—Mix a cup and a half of thick yeast with a little warm milk, and set it, with two pounds of flour, before the fire to rise; then mix with them one pound of fresh butter, ten eggs, a grated nutmeg, a quarter of a pint of orange-flower water, a little powdered cinnamon, and three pints of warm milk. When the batter is perfectly smooth, butter the irons, fill them with it, close them down tightly, and put them between the bars of a bright clear fire; when sufficiently done, they will slip easily out of the irons.

Wafler irons can be obtained from any ironmonger of the Hebrew persuasion, or, indeed, of others.

Lamplich.—Take a pound of currants, the same quantity of raisins and sugar, a little citron, ground cloves and cinnamon, with eight apples, finely chopped. Mix all together. Then have ready a rich paste; cut into small triangles; fill them with the fruit, like puffs, and lay them in a deep dish; let the pieces be placed closely, and, when the dish is full, pour over one ounce of fresh butter, melted in a tea-cupful of clarified sugar, flavoured with essence of lemon, and bake in an oven not too brisk.

Staffin.—This is composed of the fruit, &c., prepared as above; but the dish is lined with the paste, and the fruit is laid with alternate layers of paste till the dish is filled. The paste must form the top layer; clarified sugar is poured over before it is put in the oven.

Passover Pudding.—Mix equal quantities of biscuit-powder and shred suet, half the quantity of currants and raisins, a little spice and sugar, with an ounce of candied peels, and five well-beaten eggs; make these into a stiff batter, and boil well, and serve with a sweet sauce. This pudding is excellent baked in a pudding-tin; it must be turned out when served.

Passover Fritters.—Mix into a smooth batter a tea-cupful of biscuit-powder, with beaten eggs, and sweeten with white sifted sugar; add grated lemon-peel, and a spoonful of orange-flower water, and fry of a light brown. The flavour may be varied by substituting a few beaten almonds, with one or two bitter, instead of the orange-flower water.

Passover Fritters (*superior*).—Mix into a smooth batter a tea-cup of passover biscuit-powder, with beaten eggs, and sweeten with white-sifted sugar; add grated lemon-peel, and a spoonful of orange-flower water, and fry of a light brown. The flavour may be varied by substituting a few beaten almonds, with one or two bitter, instead of the orange-flower water.

Siesta Cake.—Take one pound of butter, warm it over the fire with a little milk, pour it into a pan with a pound of flour, six eggs, a quarter of a pound of sweet almonds, finely powdered, and two table-spoonfuls of yeast; beat these ingredients well together into a light paste, and set it before the fire to rise. Butter the inside of a pan, and fill it with alternate layers of the paste, and of pounded almonds, sugar, citron, and

R

cinnamon. When baked and while hot, make holes through the siesta with a small silver skewer, taking care not to break it, and pour over clarified sugar until it is perfectly soaked through.

Butter Cakes.—Take equal quantities of butter and sugar, say half a pound of each, grate the rind of a lemon, add a little cinnamon, and as much flour as will form it into a paste, with spice and eggs; roll it out, cut it into small cakes, and bake. A piece of candied orange or lemon peel may be put on the top of each cake.

A Juditha.—Put some gooseberries into a saucepan with a little water; when they are soft, pulp them through a sieve, and add several well-beaten yolks of eggs, and sweeten with white sugar; have ready a shape of biscuit ice, or any other cream ice that may be preferred; take off a thick slice of the ice from the top carefully, and without breaking, so that it may be replaced on the ice. Scoop out a large portion of the ice, which may be mixed with the gooseberry cream, and fill up the hollow with it. Cover the shape with the piece that was removed, and serve. This is an elegant dish. The ice should be prepared in a sound mould. Brown bread ice is particularly well adapted to a Juditha.

A Plain Bola.—Take three-quarters of a pound of white sugar, three-quarters of a pound of fresh butter, two eggs, one pound and a half of flour, three spoonfuls of yeast, a little milk, and two ounces of citron, cut thin, and mix into a light paste; bake in a tin, and strew powdered sugar and cinnamon over it before baking. The above ingredients are often baked in small tins or cups.

Oil Twist.—Take half a quartern of dough, one gill of the best Florence oil, half a pound of currants, the same of moist sugar, and a little cinnamon; mix all well together, make it up in the form of a twist, and bake it.

"And if thy oblation be a meat offering baken in the frying-pan, it shall be made of fine flour with oil."—*Lev.* ii. 7.

Matso Cakes.—Make a stiff paste with biscuit-powder and milk and water; add a little butter, the yolk of an egg, and a little white sugar; cut into pieces, and mould with the hand, and bake in a brisk oven. These cakes should not be too thin.

Fried Matsos.—Soak some of the thickest matsos in milk, taking care they do not break, then fry in boiling fresh butter. This is a very nice method of preparing them for breakfast or tea.

An Excellent Recipe for a Fruit Charlotte.—Line a jelly-mould with fine picked strawberries, which must be first dipped into some liquid jelly, to make them adhere closely; then fill the mould with some strawberry cream, as follows:—Take a pottle of strawberries, mix them with half a pound of white sugar; rub this through a sieve, and add to it a pint of whipped cream and one ounce and a half of dissolved isinglass; pour it into the mould, which must be immersed in ice until ready to serve, and then carefully turned out on the dish and garnished according to fancy.

A Cake without Butter.—Beat well five eggs, to which add six ounces of flour; flavour with beaten almonds, and add, if liked, thin slices of citron; bake in a mould in a moderate oven.

Matso Diet Bread.—Simmer one pound of white sugar in a quarter of a pint of water, which pour hot upon eight well-beaten eggs; beat till cold, when add one pound of matso flour, a little grated lemon-peel, and bake in a prepared tin, or in small tins. The cake must be removed while hot.

Breakfast Cake.—Make a paste of half a pound of flour, one ounce of butter, a very little salt, too eggs, and a table-spoonful of milk; roll it out, but first set it to rise before the fire; cut it into cakes the size of a small cheese-plate, sprinkle with flour, and bake in a tin in a brisk oven, or on a girdle. They should be buttered hot, and served quickly.

The above recipes are from the pen of a lady, and although written for the "peculiar people" to which she belongs, we do not see why others should not use them occasionally, as a change, more especially as they are easy to make, and of a good practical quality; nay, we will go further, and assert that the Jewish *cuisine* is unexceptionable in flavour, and more wholesome than the generality of Christian dishes, from the acid invariably used in their composition. If the reader is sceptical on this point, "let him taste and try."

Mosaic Law.—The ecclesiastical precautions always adopted to insure the purity of the Passover diet, and that it should be composed of the best and simplest materials, are conducted with the severest scrutiny, in obedience to a written code, and are extremely minute and rigorous. The Passover food consists of a mixture of the finest flour with the purest water, to form biscuit, or unleavened bread; and it is eaten in reference to the Divine command to observe the Passover, in commemoration of the deliverance from the land of Egypt.—*Extract from the " Account of the Persecution of the Jews, at Damascus," by D. Solomons, Esq., Lord Mayor of London in* 1855.

CX.—DOMESTIC HINTS.

Rhenish wines are very wholesome and agreeable, drunk simply without other wines. I must not here pass over altogether the excellence of malt liquor, though it is rather difficult to unite the use of it judiciously with that of wine. When taken together it should be in great moderation; but I rather prefer a malt-liquor day exclusively now and then, by way of variety, or take it at luncheon. There is something extremely grateful in the very best table-beer; and it is to be lamented it is so rarely to be met with in the perfection of which it is capable.—*The Original*.

If you are particular in wishing to have a good joint from a butcher's, choose it yourself.

A short needle makes the quickest sewing.

If you desire to have health, admit plenty of light and air into your house.

It is bad economy to have inexperienced servants at low wages.

Nothing is so pernicious as sleeping in damp beds.
If the weather is doubtful, carry an umbrella.
Exercise in the open air is of the utmost importance to the human frame.
Never suffer your rooms to be littered, but keep your chairs and tables in their proper places.
Rub your own tables if you wish to be warm all day.
Weigh tea, sugar, and meat when they come in.
Dine late; it makes the day longer, and saves a supper.
Allow no perquisites; it makes the servants thieves.
Look now and then into your kitchen and larder, and always know what there is for dinner.
Be regular in keeping your accounts. It will secure your husband's esteem.
If you have daughters, teach them to knit and spin, and to keep the family accounts.
Love your own house better than your neighbour's.
Love your own wife, if you wish her to love you.
Keep no servants who have hangers on.
Dress modestly, but not fine, unless the world knows you can afford it.
Insure your life, and you will sleep the better for it.
Never enter an auction-room to buy things you don't want.
Keep no more servants than you can employ.
Never pay a tradesman's bill until you have cast it up.
Pay all your bills at Christmas, *if you can.*
If you owe money, be regular in paying the interest.
Be not a collector of books without reading them.
Commence to teach your children the rudiments of arithmetic.
Do not put much money in your children's pocket on going to school, as it is encouraging prodigality.
If you employ tradesmen in building, double the estimate.
Look for the deserving poor, and give them what you can spare.
A good servant considers his master's interest as his own.
Never be without a will, and alter it on the purchase of property.
If you lend a small sum, ask for it before it is forgotten.
If you are in trade, keep no more hands than you can support.
A summer-house and a winter-house have forced many a man to a poor-house.
Idleness travels very leisurely, and Poverty soon overtakes her.
Do not look down upon your neighbour because he is not so rich as yourself.
Nothing is so graceful as being courteous to our inferiors.
If you are not affluent, remember that a pin a day is a groat a year.
A gossip has no home.
Give alms only to the silent beggar.
If you keep a drunken servant, insure your house against fire, and yourself against the censures of your neighbours.

DOMESTIC HINTS.

If you are rich, be liberal in your expenses.

Never write a letter in a passion.

A woman who marries a gamester must never expect to have a good night's rest.

Waste not, want not.

Remember, in partaking of a luxurious meal, how many in the world there are who would be glad of the crumbs.

A glutton eats as much to-day as if he expected to die to-morrow.

Plant; you are only paying posterity what you have borrowed.

Give no advice unasked.

In the morning think what you are to do, and at night think what you have done.

The wisest are ignorant.

If you want to grow fat, keep your eyes open and your mouth shut.

Live to-day as if you were to die to-morrow.

Money got by industry is Heaven's gift.

Eating is the spur to industry; could we live without eating all the world would be idle.

Never leave what can be done to-day till to-morrow.

Good manners are learned by keeping good company.

Set your watch by a good clock every morning, and you will find a bad watch will go nearly as well as a good one.

Good breeding requires punctual engagements; a fool thinks otherwise.

No vice is more easily acquired than drunkenness.

Marry in haste and repent at leisure.

Mental inactivity is an evil more deplorable than inactivity of body.

Sound sleep is of importance to health.

A sooty chimney costs many beef-steaks.

One candle well snuffed will give as much light as two with neglected wicks.

The breath may blow out a candle, but an extinguisher will prevent a fire.

Ventilate your bed-rooms night and day.

See that nothing is thrown away that might nourish your own family, or a poorer one.

Never let the anticipation of a coming pleasure cause you to waste present moments.

Many lose half their lives by neglecting the present in regrets for the past, or vain anticipations for the future.

Keep the doctor from your doors as long as you can; but, when disease appears, don't trifle with it.

Disease is soon shaken by physic well taken.

Eat slowly, and you will never over-eat.

Keeping the feet warm will prevent the headache.

Late at breakfast, hurried for dinner, cross at tea.

Between husband and wife little attentions beget much love.

Always lay your table neatly, whether you have company or not.

Whatever you may choose to give away, always keep your temper.

Dirty windows bespeak to passers-by the characters of the inmates.—*Condensed from "Practical Housewife."*

THE COUNTRY GENTLEMAN OF THE REVOLUTION.—His table was loaded with coarse plenty, and guests were cordially welcome to it. But, as the habit of drinking to excess was general in the class to which he belonged, and as his fortune did not enable him to intoxicate large assemblies daily with claret or canary, strong beer was the ordinary beverage. The quantity of beer consumed in those days was enormous. For beer then was to the middle and lower classes not only all that beer now is, but all that wine, tea, and ardent spirits now are. It was only at great houses, or on great occasions, that foreign drink was placed on the board. The ladies of the house, whose business it had commonly been to cook the repast, retired as soon as the dishes had been devoured, and left the gentlemen to their ale and tobacco. The coarse jollity of the afternoon was often prolonged till the revellers were under the table. His wife and daughter were in tastes and acquirements below a housekeeper or a still-room maid of the present day. They stitched and spun, brewed gooseberry wine, cured marigolds, and made the crust for the venison pasty. From this description it might be supposed that the English squire of the seventeenth century did not materially differ from a rustic miller or ale-keeper of our time.—*Macaulay.*

Hares are only fit to be sent to table when they are young. In order to judge of this, feel the first joint of the fore-claw; if you find a small nut, the animal is still young. Should this nut have disappeared, turn the claw sideways, and if the joint cracks, that is a sign of its being tender.—*Ude.* Or if the ears feel tender and pliable, and the claws smooth and sharp, the hare is young.—*Dolby.* It is not fit for the ta immediately after being killed: by being kept a few days the flesh becomes tender, but dark coloured and rather unpleasant to the eye.—*Donovan's "Domestic Economy."*

CXI.—CLUBS.

GENERAL RULES FOR THE PREPARATION OF NUTRITIOUS BROTHS.—
1. Meat healthy, and sufficiently bled.
2. Earthenware pots in preference to metal ones, because the former are not such conductors of heat as the latter, and because, once warmed, a little hot ashes suffices to keep up the gentle ebullition which is desirable.
3. Water in such quantity as to be double the weight of the meat employed.
4. A sufficient quantity of common salt to facilitate the separation of the *albumen*, as well as its coagulation under the form of scum.
5. A temperature capable of keeping the mixture at ebullition point during the whole time that the scum is gathering at the surface of the liquid, from which it must be most carefully removed.
6. A lower and constant temperature after the preceding operation, in order that the liquid may merely simmer gently, so as to give time to the *mutative, colouring,* and *extractive* substances contained in the meat to unite and combine with the water in the order which accords with their solubility.—*Parmentier, "Code Pharmaceutique."*

To my club for a luncheon. A plate of prime, cold roast beef, excellent pickles, bread *ad libitum*, and a glass of good table-beer, very elegantly served, and all for sixpence! If I choose to add to it half a pint of sherry, my whole bill comes to eighteenpence. If, instead of ordering a plate of cold meat, I prefer a more ample meal—an early dinner, in fact—I sit down to a long table, on which are ranged cold beef, veal, ham, pickles of various kinds, and an abundance of confectionery, and I eat away until I am tired, at the cost of one shilling and sixpence, table-beer included. I am attended by two or three servants. No table can be more splendidly furnished with silver utensils of every description. I sit in a magnificent chamber, and when I have finished my repast I retire to a library, where a choice collection of standard works, books of reference, and maps, are at my command. The newest publications of the day—of any merit—are placed at one table, and upon another are all the morning newspapers. A writing-table, stocked abundantly with foolscap, letter and note paper, envelopes, pens and inkstands, tapers, sealing-wax, and club seals, is in the middle of the chamber, and placed in due order are various kinds of easy chairs and sofas, on which I may lounge, or read, or sleep, as I may think fit. Should the work or the debate which I have undertaken to explore be, as most of the debates now are, excessively prosy and stupid, on a little round table is a box of snuff to assist me in my endeavours to keep my eyes from closing up their shutters. Starting from one of these sleep-compelling chairs, I ask myself what o'clock it is? I need not trouble myself to extract my watch from my pocket, for there is a first-rate chronometer on the chimney-piece to answer the question. I am writing a note, and I forget the day of the month; on the same chimney-piece is a little square black board, with the date of the day on it in white letters. Is my epistle for the general or twopenny post? boxes for each are within a few paces of me in the same chamber. Do I want a frank? Ten to one but a peer or a commoner is sitting at the same table with me, and I would oblige him by asking him to expend an item of his diurnal privileges in my favour. Court guides, red books, navy and army lists, and directories of every kind are within my reach, if I be at a loss for an address; and if I want a quick and trusty messenger I have only to ring a bell, when, presto! he stands before me. The country newspapers, those of Ireland and Scotland, the foreign journals, the weekly, monthly, and quarterly periodicals are in another apartment, where I spend an hour or two culling sweets from every flower. By this time the evening approaches. Men are hastening in from all quarters to dine, and the savoury odours arising from soups and hot joints, and meat and fruit pies, assist not a little to improve a naturally good appetite. Then the example of so many men eating heartily, and tossing off their bumpers of port, champagne, claret, or burgundy, is, it must be owned, extremely seductive, especially if at my table I be joined by a friend or two, of no new date, with whom I can revive, as the generous grape warms our bosoms, the recollection of happy days spent together. Then we sit, grouped, in the midst of a splendid saloon crammed with familiar faces: we are served well, dining on a hot joint, abundance of vegetables, pastry, bread, butter, cheese, fruit, all of the best description; the cookery irreproachable; snow-white table-cloths and napkins, finger-glasses, toothpicks; any wine we choose to ask for; and, if we live with the moderation most conducive to health and comfort, we rise from table at an expense not exceeding three shillings and threepence! The use of the higher classes of wines will, of course, cause a higher bill. A larger apartment contains wash-hand basins, towels, hair brushes and combs, clothes' brushes, hat brushes, and other conveniences. Besides this there is a dressing room, where a member can have his things sent to him, in case he should happen to dine at any distance from home. In truth, the club is a home for him whenever he chooses so to consider it. He may look upon the servants of the establishment as his own; they are all as civil and obedient to him as if they were in his own house. He has no trouble in paying or managing them: they are men carefully selected for their good conduct and general intelligence. The order preserved throughout the whole establishment is admirable.—*London Saturday Journal.*

SUPERSTITION.—The superstition prevails everywhere against thirteen to dinner. There were thirteen at dinner one day at Madame Catalan's, when a French comtesse, who lived with her up-stairs, was sent for to remedy the grievance. Lord L—— said he had dined once abroad at Count Orloff's, who did not sit down to dinner, but kept walking about from chair to chair, because "the *haristiken* were at table, who he knew would rise instantly if they perceived the number *thirteen*, which Orloff would have made by sitting down himself."—*Moore's Diary.* Dined at ——. We were seated, *twelve* in number, when Hook arrived. He looked, at first, very black on finding himself the thirteenth; but being told that T——, the actor, was expected, immediately took his seat, and the evening passed off merrily enough. An anecdote was given in the course of conversation singularly corroborative of the superstition by which Hook was clearly at first affected. A party of twelve had just sat down, and one of the guests having observed a vacant chair, was remarking that he should hardly like to be the person destined to occupy that seat, when a tremendous double rap was heard, the door was thrown open, and *Mr. Fauntleroy* announced. He was hanged within the year!—*Life of Theodore Hook.*

CXII.—EDIBLE FOOD.

It is melancholy to find that, according to the authority of a certain great French author, " Cooks, half-stewed and half-roasted, when unable to work any longer, generally retire to some unknown corner, and die in forlornness and want."—*Blackwood's Magazine.*

The traveller Bell observed whole rows of badgers hung up for sale in China, just as rabbits are displayed in the English markets; and those who have partaken of the meat, especially of the European badger, report that it is excellent. Major Lloyd, in his " Field Sports of the North of Europe," remarks that its flesh is very eatable when parboiled in bay-seed water, or, still better, in salt water, and afterwards roasted and left to cool, and used for luncheons; but it must be the flesh of the young badgers. Of an allied species, the canajou of North America, the Hon. C. A. Murray relates in his " Travels ":—" We made our soup, and I boiled my badger; his own fat was all the basting he required, and when he was served up, we all agreed that we had never eaten better meat; it had but one fault, being so exceedingly fat, that it surpassed, in that respect, any pig or other animal I ever saw." Mr. Jordan gives his personal testimony that the flesh of the bedgehog is excellent; and a mole-catcher relates that he was in the habit of eating the moles he caught; and said that if folks generally knew how good they were, but few would fall to his share. The armadilloes are exceedingly foul feeders, yet all who have partaken of their flesh agree that one roasted in his own shell is most delicate eating. In tropical seas some of the shell-fish attain a great size; one species (*triducna gigas*) has been known to measure above two and a half feet in the longest diameter of the shell, and contains, of course, a proportionate quantity of food. A peculiar interest, however, attaches to some of those mentioned by classic writers, and to none so much as the different species of cuttle-fishes, which, though not valued on our coasts, are regularly sought for in other seas, and publicly exposed for sale in the markets. As in ancient times, these mollusks constitute now, on the shores of the Ægean, a valuable part of the food of the poor, by whom they are chiefly used. Hence the imprecation of the chorus, who, calling down on their victim the extremity of ill-fortune, desired that he might be reduced to a single cuttle-fish, and that a dog might come and snatch this last poor morsel from him, would be as well appreciated in a modern Greek coffee-house as among the original admirers of Aristophanes. The Romans, if we may judge from the culinary recipes of Apicius, regarded a cuttle-fish with more respect. "We can ourselves," says Professor Forbes, "bear testimony to their excellence; when beaten, to render the flesh tender, before being dressed, and then cut up into morsels, and served in a savoury brown stew, it makes a dish by no means to be despised; excellent in both substance and flavour." A modern Lycian dinner, in which stewed cuttle-fish formed the first, and roast porcupine the second course, would scarcely fail to be relished by an unprejudiced epicure in search of novelty. In the southern part of the United States, one species of crab is particularly valued just after having cast its shell and before the new one has become hard. It is thus referred to in "Hochelaga:"—"Among the delicacies of the sea, the soft crab is in great request; he is much like ours in shape, but wears only a silken doublet instead of a coat of mail, and, consequently, can be carved and eaten without the trouble of undressing him. It is, however, at only certain seasons of the year that his costume is suitable." This crab might seem sufficient to tempt an epicure. Another jointed or articulated animal is, to our ideas, the very reverse of tempting, yet so capricious is human taste that Indian children have been seen by Humboldt, "to draw out from the earth, and eat, millipedes, or scolopendras, eighteen inches long and seven lines broad." Many insects, properly so called, are used in the different states as food for man. The grub of the palm-weevil has long been in request in both Indies, and, when roasted, is considered very delicious. So, also, is the grub of a species of ceramboyx, which is eaten at Surinam, in America, and in the West Indies. The locust tribe, as they are the greatest destroyers of food, furnish, in return, a considerable supply of it to many nations. They are ground by the Arabs, made into cakes, and baked like bread; they are also boiled and then stirred with butter into a fricassée. Sparman informs us, that the Hottentots are highly rejoiced at the arrival of the locusts in their country, although they destroy all the verdure, eating them in such vast quantities as to get visibly fatter than before, and making of their eggs a brown or coffee-coloured soup. Clenard, in his letters quoted by Bochart, says that they bring wagon-loads of locusts to Fez, as a usual article of food. Perhaps no insects have been more celebrated than the cicadas; the ode addressed to one by Anacreon would, of itself, be sufficient to insure for it an immortality of fame. They belong to the tribe *tettigonia*; and, from the time of Homer, who compares the garrulity of age to the chirping of these insects, they have been celebrated by the poets. It is a curious fact that the polished Greeks nevertheless did not hesitate to *eat* them, and we are assured by Aristotle they were considered very delicious. These brief notices of edible insects may be concluded by a reference to the termites, or white ants. The Africans parch them in iron pots, over a gentle fire, and then eat them by handfuls, as we do comfits. Smeathman says he has several times eaten them dressed in this way, and thought them delicious, nourishing, and wholesome, resembling in taste sugared cream or sweet almond paste.

Fish would appear to have constituted a portion of the food of man from a very early period. The use of certain kinds is sanctioned by the Mosaic dispensation; and, 1,500 years later, we learn from the sacred volume that they were in common use as food, and were associated with the miraculous events which have given to the sea of Galilee and adjacent shores an interest so peculiarly their own. The writings of Aristotle, the great father of natural history, have given us minute description of species which may be still recognised in the Ægean sea, and which continue to be sought for as nutritive and delicious food. If we turn from mammiferous animals to birds, and regard them, at present, merely as food for man, the range of subject, even when thus limited, embraces every country on the globe and every isle that gems the ocean. The picture of the feathered creation, commenced by Milton, may be enlarged and completed by the reader:—

> The eagle and the stork
> On clifts and cedar-tops their eyries build;
> Part loosely wing the region, part, more wise,
> In common, ranged in figure, range their way,
> Intelligent of seasons; and set forth
> Their airy caravan, high over seas
> Flying, and over lands, with mutual wing,
> Easing their flight.

—*Extract from "The Uses of Animals to Man."*

FOOD.—There is an article under this head in "Good Words," by the late Archbishop Whately, in which that learned theologian informs the numerous readers of the periodical to which he contributed, that, amongst the Aborigines of Australia, a mother eats her baby, under the idea that she has merely deferred its birth, and that the next child she bore would be merely a reappearance of the eaten one. We cannot think where Dr. Whately obtained the information on which he put forth such a statement; but we can assure the reader that, although the aboriginal inhabitants are not very particular, either in their food or *cuisine*, such a curious plea for devouring their offspring is quite as imaginary as the fact of their doing so.

GARIBALDIAN FRUGALITY.—The general for months has denied himself and his household the luxury of meat. Beans, kidney beans, and salads, along with rye bread and sheep's milk, form their staple diet. This simple fare is adopted for the purpose of saving some money for the Polish fund, as the general says he cannot be luxurious while "three millions of his brethren are sunk in misery." Fish is plentiful; but Bosso, who undertakes to dress it, is not a famous cook. Garibaldi, who is the soul of hospitality, sometimes gives him lessons on the art of frying sardines and a small fish caught in the Straits of Maddelina; but the master is not so skilful as the man, although he is under the delusion that he has of late achieved some gastronomic triumphs.—*Late News from Caprera.*

CXIII.—DRINKS.

BRANDY.— "Brandy for heroes!" Burke could once exclaim;
No doubt a liquid path to epic fame.
The Island; or, Christian and his Comrades.

It appears to be Dr. Johnson who thus gave honour to cognac:—"He was persuaded to take one glass of claret. He shook his head and said, 'Poor stuff! No, sir; claret is the liquor for boys, port for men, but he who aspires to be a hero (smiling) must drink brandy.'"—*Boswell.*

Sherbet: a Persian cooling drink, prepared with the juices of fruit and water, variously sweetened and flavoured. Tavernier says that the sherbet the Turks most approve of, and which the Grand Signor himself uses, is made of violets and sugar.

The beverage was various sherbets, composed of the juice of boiled raisins, oranges, and pomegranates, squeezed through the rind.—*Tully's "Tripoli."*

Negus: wine and water, with sugar and nutmeg, named after Francis Negus, Esq., in the drinking days of George I.

Mr. Negus was present at a drinking party of Whigs and Tories, and he recommended them to dilute their wine with water, as he did. Hence wine and water came to be designated *negus*; but Lever, in one of his works, makes a heroine (Miss Macan), when taken bad, call for that nondescript drink, whisky-negus.

Sangaree, or Sangurorum.—The same liquor so called in our Eastern Empire.

Mug: equal quantities of claret and soda-water.

Sarsaparilla: a cooling drink now much in vogue, made from aerated water and a small quantity of sarsaparilla, bottled, or drank with soda-water. According to Dr. Pereira, there are two kinds, the mealy, and the non-mealy. We have the authority of Brande and Cooley, that it is a wholesome drink, and is recommended as a mild but efficacious alterative, diaphoretic, and tonic. It is the root of the *similax sarsaparilla*, and several varieties are imported from South America, but the best is the Jamaica or red kind.

Glasgow Punch.—This beverage is made from cold water, the best Jamaica rum, loaf-sugar, and lemons; and to give the proportionate quantity of each is quite an impossibility, for it all depends on the softness of the water, the strength of the rum, and the acidity of the lemons, sugar being sweet all the world over. We have in our mind's eye a Scotch friend, who was *au fait* at compounding this liquor, but he would not be hurried, and after a time, with many tastings, he managed to produce a bowl, in which the flavour of no one ingredient predominated; and it certainly was very pretty and insidious tipple. This is one of the most healthy of drinks, for it has a bracing effect on the stomach, and the acid operates as a diuretic. Its daily use is a certain specific for the gout and rheumatism, more so than any quack medicine. The reason that the followers of Moses and the prophets are not troubled with these latter ailments, is solely owing to the quantity of lemon acid which they take with their food.

Apicius. I am afraid you beat us in wines, not to mention your cider, perry, and beer, of all which I have heard great fame from some English with whom I have talked; and their report has been confirmed by the testimony of their neighbours who have travelled in England. Wonderful things have been also said to me of a liquor called Punch.—*Dialogues of the Dead.*

Regent's Punch.—This favourite beverage of the late King George IV. is made from three bottles of champagne, one bottle of hock, one bottle of curaçoa, a quart of brandy, a pint of rum, two bottles of Madeira, two bottles of seltzer-water, four pounds of bloom raisins, stoned, Seville oranges, lemons, white sugar-candy, and, instead of water, green tea. The whole to be iced in summer and warmed in winter.

Oxford Punch (*by a Christchurch man*).—Rub the rind of three fresh lemons with loaf sugar, so as to extract the oil; peel finely two lemons more, and two Seville oranges. Use the juice of ten lemons and four Seville oranges; add six glasses of calf's foot jelly; put it into a large jug and stir the whole. Pour in four quarts of boiling water, and set the jug on the hob for twenty minutes. Strain the liquor into a large bowl, pour in a bottle of capillaire, half a pint of sherry, a pint of brandy, a pint of old rum, and a quart of orange shrub. Stir it well as you pour in the spirits.

Jelly Posset.—Take eight eggs, leave out the whites of four, and beat the remainder well together in a basin; then add half a pint of white wine, a little strong ale, and sugar; put it into a saucepan, and set it over a slow fire, stirring it all the time. Boil a pint of milk with a little nutmeg and cinnamon, just enough to flavour it, and when the eggs and wine are hot, add the boiling milk to it. Remove it from the fire, pour into a punch-bowl, and serve. Lemon, orange, and wine possets are made in a similar way.

Quick. Go; and we'll have a posset for't soon as night, in faith, at the latter end of a sea-coal fire.—*Merry Wives of Windsor.*

Buttered Toddy.—Mix a glass of rum-grog pretty strong and hot, sweeten to taste with honey, flavour with nutmeg and lemon-juice, add a piece of fresh butter about the size of half a walnut. Simple toddy is the name of spirits and water in the East Indies.

Toddy, the term for a mixture of spirits and water, appears to be taken from the Indian word *tari* or *tadi*, pronounced *toddy* by Europeans, the sap or wine of a palm.—*Crauford.*

Ale Posset.—Boil a pint of new milk, with a slice of toasted bread sweeten a quart of ale, and pour it into a basin with nutmeg and ginger. Add the boiling milk to it, and when the head rises, serve.

Oxford Night Cap.—Take half a tumbler of tea, made as usual with sugar and milk; add a slice of lemon, a wine-glass of new milk, and the same of rum or brandy. Beat up a new-laid egg, and add to the mixture.

Milk Punch.—Pare six oranges and lemons as thin as you can; grate them over with sugar to get the flavour. Steep the peels in a bottle of rum or brandy for twenty-four hours. Squeeze the fruit on two pounds of sugar, add to it four quarts of water, and one of new milk boiling hot. Add the rum. Run it through a jelly-bag, bottle and cork.

<small>Wines we have of grapes, and drinks of other juice, of fruits, of grains, and of roots; and of mixtures with honey, sugar, manna, and fruits dried and decocted; also of the tears or wounding of trees, and of the pulp of canes. And these drinks are of several ages, some to the age or last of forty years. We have drinks also brewed with several herbs and roots and spices.—*New Atalantis.*</small>

Mulled Ale.—Boil a pint of good sound ale, with a little nutmeg and sugar; beat up three eggs, and mix them with a little cold ale; then add the hot ale to it gradually, and pour backwards and forwards from one vessel to another, to prevent its curdling; warm and stir till it thickens; then add a table-spoonful of brandy, and serve hot, with toast.

Athol Brose.—Add two wine-glassfuls of Scotch whisky to a wine-glassful of heather-honey; mix well, and stir in a well-beaten egg.

<small>Dr. Kitchener informs us that toast-and-water is a refreshing summer drink, and that a roll of fresh lemon, or dried orange-peel, or apples sliced or roasted, are grateful additions to such beverage. This would be excellent drink for teetotalers, or for persons who cannot restrain themselves; and if any one is unable to master his appetites, it is a wise and prudent course for him to become a complete abstainer, although it is somewhat opposed to Scriptural authority:—" Drink no longer water, but use a little wine for thy stomach's sake, and thine often infirmities."—1 Tim. v. 23.

That most learned of all learned works, Burton's "Anatomy of Melancholy," tells us that " Temperance is a bridle of gold; and he that can use it aright is liker a god than a man; for, as it will transform a beast to a man again, so will it make a man a god." The great moralist has informed us that he " could *abstain*, but he could not trust himself to be *temperate*." Yet it appears that in warm climates stimulants are necessary. At the last meeting of the British Association at Newcastle, Dr. Hunt maintained that in India a certain amount of stimulant was required. To advocate a water, teetotal system was, he thought, entirely objectionable, as the troops certainly required some amount of stimulant for that climate. Paley says:—" There is a difference, no doubt, between convivial intemperance and that solitary sottishness which waits for neither company nor invitation. But the one, I am afraid, commonly ends in the other; and this last is the basest degradation to which the faculties and powers of human nature can be rendered." Although propounding many recipes, we desire to advocate the principles of *temperance* in both eating and drinking, for whoever cannot moderate himself in both enjoyments descends to the level of the lower creation, to which a certain Port Phillipian was once rather coarsely compared, in the Melbourne *Punch:*—</small>

> " The beasts that roam over the plain
> My form with indifference see;
> In truth, we are so much the same,
> And our habits entirely agree."

Bang.—Take a pint of cider, and add to a pint of warm ale; sweeten with sugar; grate in some nutmeg and ginger, and add a wine-glass of whisky.

King Cup.—Take the rind and juice of a lemon, a lump of sugar, a small piece of bruised ginger, and pour on them about a pint and a half of boiling water. When cold strain, and add a wine-glass of sherry.

Lemonade.—Take sixteen lemons, pare them, cut in halves, squeeze well, and throw them into a pan; add a pound and a half of white sugar, a gallon of boiling water, and a wine-glass of sherry wine. Mix, strain, and cool.

A very wholesome and excellent cooling drink in hot weather; none more healthful.

Appleade.—Cut apples in slices—the more juicy the better—and pour on them boiling water; strain and sweeten. To be cooled with ice. Apricots, peaches, and raspberries may be similarly treated, and they make a pleasant summer beverage.

Pine-appleade, strawberryade, currantade, and, in fact, any description of fruit may be made into a summer drink, partaking of the flavour of the ingredients used, and they may either be cooled or iced.

Hippocras.—Add half a drachm of mace, ginger, cloves, and nutmegs to three quarts of Lisbon wine; also cinnamon. Let it stand for a few days, when strain, and add twenty ounces of white sugar to the liquor. This is an old and favourite drink, and invariably given at weddings.

Sack, hippocras now, and burnt brandy,
Are drinks as warm and good as can be.
Poor Robin's Almanac, 1696.

Imperial Pop.—Take three ounces of cream of tartar, an ounce of bruised ginger, a pound and a half of white sugar, an ounce of lemon-juice; pour a gallon and a half of boiling water on them, and, when cool, add two table-spoons of yeast; strain and bottle.

Lait Sucré.—Boil a pint of milk, sweeten with white sugar, and flavour with lemon.

Mountain Dew: Whisky Glenlevit, clandestinely distilled in the Highlands of Scotland, and potteen spirit, made in a similar manner in Ireland, both having a peculiar smoky taste, which no lawful distillery can give.

FERINTOSH WHISKY. — The word Ferintosh signifies thanes' land, it having been part of the thanedom of Cawdor (Macbeth's), or Calder. The barony of Ferintosh belonged to the Forbeses of Culloden, and contained about 1,800 acres of arable land. All barley produced on this estate was privileged to be converted into whisky duty free, the natural consequence of which was that more whisky was distilled in Ferintosh than in all the rest of Scotland. In 1784 Government made a sort of compulsory purchase of this privilege from the Culloden family, after they had enjoyed it a complete century. The sum paid was £21,500.—*Things Not Generally Known.*

Ginger-beer.—One gallon of boiling water, one pound of loaf sugar, one ounce of best ginger, bruised, one ounce of cream of tartar, or a sliced lemon. Stir them until the sugar is dissolved. Let it remain until it cools to the heat of milk, then add a table-spoonful of good yeast. Cover and let it stand for twenty-four hours. Bottle it, not filling the bottles. Cork well and tie down, and it will be ready for use in two days. Cost, a halfpenny per bottle and the trouble of making.

Ginger-beer (*Family Recipe*).—Best white sugar, five pounds; lemon-juice, a quarter of a pint; bruised ginger, five ounces; honey, a quarter of a pound; water, four gallons and a half. Boil the ginger in three quarts of the water for half an hour, then add the sugar, lemon-juice, and honey, with the remainder of the water, and strain through a cloth or strainer. When cold add the white of an egg, and a small quantity of essence of lemon—a dozen drops. Let the whole stand four days, and then bottle.—*Dr. Pereira on Diet.*

This is an excellent recipe for beer for family use. It is not so violent in its action when opened as fermented beer, but it is very pleasant, mellow, and good flavoured, and will keep for months.

Ginger-beer (*Ure's Dictionary*). — Barbadoes ginger, twelve ounces; tartaric acid, three ounces; white sugar, eight pounds; gum arabic, eight ounces; essence of lemon, two drachms; water, nine gallons. The ginger-root, bruised, to be boiled for an hour; then, the liquor being strained, the tartaric acid and sugar added, boiled, and the same renewed. The gum arabic, dissolved in a separate portion of water, added with the essence of lemons. When the whole has cooled to about 130° Fahr. some fresh yeast is to be added, and the beer carefully fermented. Then bottle for use.

Orangeade.—Squeeze the juice of an orange, pour boiling water on some of the peel, and cover it close. Boil water and sugar to a thin syrup and skim it. When all are cold, mix the juice, the infusion, and the syrup with as much water as will make a rich drink. Strain through a jelly-bag, and ice.

Pineapple Rum: sliced pineapples, put into rum, and hence the name. The rum should be of a brown transparent colour, smooth, oily taste, strong body and consistence, and good age. Jamaica is the very best spirit of this kind.

Girambing (*a French drink*).—Boil four ounces and a half of powdered ginger in fourteen quarts of water, wine measure. Then beat up the whites of four eggs to a froth, and mix them together, with nine pounds of white sugar; add to the preceding water and ginger. Then take nine lemons, and add the juice and the rind. Put the whole in a barrel, with a little yeast. In a few days bottle it off, and it will be soon fit for drinking. It improves by keeping.

Sorbet.—The sweet-scented violet is one of the plants most esteemed in the East, particularly for its great use in sorbet, which they make of violet sugar.—*Hasselquist.*

Dog's Nose.—Warm half a pint of ale, and add a wine-glassful of gin to it; then add half a pint of cold ale, and serve with toast.

"Welcome, thrice welcome, thou man of Galway," cried out Power, as he pointed to a seat, and pushed a wine-glass towards me. "Just in time to pronounce on a new brewery: taste that; a little more of the lemon you would say, perhaps? Well, I agree with you. Rum and brandy, Glenlevit and guava jelly, limes, green tea, and a slight suspicion of preserved ginger—nothing else, upon honour, and the most simple mixture for the cure, the radical cure, of the blue devils, and debt, I know of; eh, doctor? You advise it yourself to be taken before bedtime; nothing inflammatory in it—nothing pugnacious; a mere circulation of the better juices and more genial spirits of the marly clay, without arousing any of the baser passions: whisky is the devil for that."

"I canna say that I dinna like whisky toddy," said the doctor. "In the cauld nights it's nae so bad."—*Charles O'Malley.*

Rum Shrub: bitter almonds, cloves, cassia, and the peel of oranges, infused in the best rum, with the addition of a thread of ambergris and vanilla. Good shrub is very delicious, and were it fashionable it would obtain rank as a liqueur.

Sack Posset.—

From fam'd Barbadoes on the western main
Fetch sugar ounces four; fetch sack from Spain
A pint; and from the Eastern Indian coast
Nutmeg, the glory of our northern toast.
O'er flaming coals let them together heat,
Till the all-conquering sack dissolves the sweet;
O'er such another fire put eggs ten,
New born, from tread of cock and rump of hen.
Stir them with steady hand and conscience pricking
To see the untimely fate of ten fine chicken;
From shining shelf take down the brazen skillet,
A quart of milk from gentle cow will fill it.
When boiled and cold, put milk and sack to eggs,
Unite then firmly like the triple league,
And on the fire let them together dwell
Till Miss sing twice, "You must not kiss and tell."
Each lad and lass take up a silver spoon,
And fall on fiercely like a starved dragoon.
—*Sir Fleetwood Shepherd.*

Posset was a drink composed of hot milk, curdled by strong infusion, which was much in favour by our ancestors, both as a luxury and medicine. All the guards that attended the King in *Macbeth* seem to have had their possets; for Macbeth says, "I have drugged their possets." In Fletcher's "Scornful Lady" two of the characters take a posset on the stage before they retire to rest. The sack posset was a treat usually prepared for a bridegroom.

In came the bridemaids with the posset
The bridegroom eat in spight.—*Suckling.*

Dryden mentions a "pepper posset;" Dr. John Floyer, a posset in which *althea* (marshmallow) roots are boiled; and Dr. Arbuthnot orders gruel and posset drinks to increase the milk. Our nearest approach to the old posset is whey—or milk curdled with wine or acid—and treacle posset.—*Things Not Generally Known.*

To improve British brandy, put eight French plums into every pint of spirits. Steep ten days, then strain, and it will have much of the flavour of French brandy.

Orgeat.—Orgeat is a drink made from almonds as follows:—Take a pound and a quarter of bitter almonds, and half a pound of sweet almonds, which have been blanched, nine pounds of loaf sugar, six pints of water, and the rinds of three lemons. Pound the almonds in a mortar with the sugar, and add the water a little by degrees; then put the mixture on the fire with the lemon-peel. After a boil pour off the syrup and press the almonds, to extract the milk; add this to the syrup, and strain the whole through a sieve. When cold add a little orange-flower water, and bottle the mixture. The orgeat is used as a summer drink, mixed with water, according to taste.

Mead, or Metheglin.—This ancient and, for a long time, favourite drink of the northern nations, is manufactured from honey and water. In England, makers of mead must take out an annual licence. One part of honey is dissolved in three parts of boiling water; it is flavoured with spices, and a portion of ground malt is added to a piece of toast dipped in yeast, to allow the malt to ferment. The Scandinavian mead is flavoured with rose-blossoms. It is frequently mentioned in Ossian.

West India Punch.—He made his appearance with a respectably-sized bowl, an enormous jug of boiling water, and a large paper-bag filled with sugar. Our punchmaker then commenced operations, and having extracted from his secret store a bottle of his matchless *rum*, his limes, and a small pot of guava jelly, he brewed about a pint of green tea (two ounces); and, the infusion finished, two-thirds of the sugar was dissolved in it. After the tea-leaves had been thrown aside, the remainder of the sugar was rubbed on the rind of the limes, Mr. Hamilton observing that the essential oil which conveyed the requisite flavour was thus more strongly diffused throughout the compound than when the skin was peeled; then the delicious acid of the fruit was added to the already impregnated sugar, and as soon as the several lumps had imbibed the proportion required, the guava jelly (and without this confection no punch can be pronounced perfect) was dissolved in a pint or so of boiling water. This done, the tea, the sweets, and acids were commingled, and the foundation or sherbet tasted by the experienced palate of the grand compounder; six glasses of cognac, two of Madeira, and the bottle of old rum were added, and over all about a quart more of boiling water, and, as a finishing touch, the slightest possible sprinkling of nutmeg. Here was punch! it out-nectared nectar! I have, in the West Indies, since the period I am recording, drank some very luscious and fascinating mixtures nearly resembling it; but I never knew it surpassed, if equalled, even in the tropical regions —*Tolpey's* "*Sportsman in Canada.*"

HARD DRINKING.—That hard drinking was introduced from Flanders and Holland, and other northern countries, seems probable from the derivation of many of the expressions used in carousing. The phrase of being "half seas over," as applied to a state of drunkenness, originated from *op see*, which is Dutch, meaning *over sea*; and Gifford informs us that it was a name given to a stupefying beer introduced into England from the Low Countries, and called *op see*. An inebriating draught was also called an *up see freese*, from the strong Friesland beer. The word "carouse," according to Gifford and Blount, is derived from the name of a large glass, called by the Danes *rouse*, or from the German words *gar*, all, and *aus*; hence drink *all out.—Things Not Generally Known.*

Mint Julep.—This is a compound of brandy-and-water, sweetened with white sugar, in which are stuck leaves of fresh-gathered mint. Wenham Lake ice is put into the tumbler, and the drink is taken through the medium of a straw or glass tube. At the American bars, the brandy-and-water is first put into a large silver or glass goblet, then the broken ice; powdered white sugar is then dashed over; the whole is then violently shaken, or tossed from one goblet to another. The American bar-keepers are very expert at this manipulation.

I must descant a little upon the mint julep, as it is, with the thermometer at 100°, one of the most delightful and insinuating of potations that ever was invented, and may be drunk with equal satisfaction when the thermometer is as low as 70°. There are many varieties, such as those composed of claret, Madeira, &c., but the ingredients of the real mint julep are as follows. I learned how to make them, and succeeded pretty well:—Put into a tumbler about a dozen sprigs of the tender shoots of mint, upon them put a spoonful of white sugar, and equal proportions of peach and common brandy, so as to fill up one-third, or perhaps a little less. Then take rasped or pounded ice, and fill up the tumbler. Epicures rub the lips of the tumbler with a piece of fresh pine-apple, and the tumbler itself is often encrusted outside with stalactites of ice. As the ice melts you drink. I once heard two ladies talking in the next room to me, and one of them said, "Well, if I have a weakness for anything, it is for a mint julep." A very amiable weakness, and proving her good sense and good taste. They are, in fact, like the American ladies—irresistible.—*Marryatt*.

FASHIONABLE DRINKS AT WASHINGTON.—The following is a list of refreshments, among others, to be obtained at one of the most celebrated bars of Washington, where the *élite* of society, as well as the brave soldiery, rush for liquid consolations after a reverse, or to toast the hero of a tall *skedaddle*:—Hammock's Special List of Drinks.—Sea Brook Dash, Spirituous Consolations, Ladies' Blush, Hop Up, Get Back, Brandy Hash, Brandy Sour, Old Julep, Morning Glory, Catawba Cobbler, Hen Fruit Cobbler, Dry Smash, Ethereal (old and dry), Tippecanoe Sangaree, De Poscaffee, Cocktail Dipped, Old Sow Cocktail, Shamporough, Annisette Blush, Black Hock Sangaree, Champagne Frappee, Wedding Night, Rum Croak, Stomacher, Legal Lush, Strawberry Smash, Island of Cuba (for ladies), Railroad Smash, Take Her Off, Spiced Rum, Cocktail Soured, Apple Toddy, Claret Smash, Twelve o'Clock (very sweet), Old Sally, Curaçoa Sangaree.—*The News of the World.*

Sherry Cobbler: made in a similar way to mint julep, *sans* lemon-peel or mint, sherry being substituted for brandy, and nutmeg grated on the liquor. Sometimes strawberries are used.

Sherry Cobbler (*another recipe*).—Take a lump of ice; fix it at the edge of a board; rasp it with the proper tool; collect the fine raspings in a capacious tumbler; pour thereon two glasses of cool sherry, and a spoonful of white sugar, with a few small pieces of lemon. Stir with a macerator, and drink through a tube of macaroni.

Claret for boys, port for men, and brandy for heroes.—*Dr. Johnson.*

Stonewall is an admixture of cider, wine, brandy, &c., served with ice and a straw.

The name of this liquor will remind the reader of the *sobriquet* bestowed on the celebrated Confederate general, whose untimely fate must be lamented, for he was the personification of the chivalrous people of the South, who are working out the poet's axiom—

"Who would be free themselves must strike the blow.
By their right arm the conquest must be wrought."

The last words of this great, good, and lamented man (General Jackson), just before his death, were, "Bury me at Lexington, in the valley of Virginia;" and, in accordance with his sacred command, all that is mortal of the most renowned and successful military genius that the war, or probably modern ages, has produced, now lies interred within the walls of the Presbyterian cemetery, located in the south-western suburbs of this delightful village. Nothing marks the spot where his mortal remains lie to distinguish his grave from that of others, save a diminutive Confederate flag, not larger than a lady's handkerchief. This tiny emblem is fastened to a staff not more than two feet long, and placed at the head of the grave; and there waves, as if to illustrate the modest pretensions of the great hero of the valley of Virginia.—*New York Express.*

Stone Fence: the same as the above.

Gin Sling: a similar liquor, made with gin, prepared in the same way as mint julep.

Mississippi Punch.—One glass of Outard brandy, half ditto of Jamaica rum, a table-spoonful of arrack, a quarter of a lemon, and a table-spoonful of white sugar; fill the tumbler with water and ice. Let it be thoroughly mixed, and serve with a straw.

> Fill the goblet again! for I never before
> Felt the glow which now gladdens my heart to its core:
> Let us drink!—who would not?—since through life's varied round,
> In the goblet alone no deception is found.—*Byron.*

Badminton.—Peel half a moderate-sized cucumber, and put it into a mug, silver or crockery; with four ounces of powdered sugar, a little nutmeg, and a bottle of claret. When the sugar is dissolved, add a bottle of soda-water, and it is then fit for use.

Supreme Nectar.—Put into a nine-gallon cask six pounds of moist sugar, five ounces of bruised ginger, four ounces of cream of tartar, four lemons, and seven gallons of boiling water. When cool, add half a pint of yeast. Let it work a couple of days; then strain, and add a pint of brandy. In a few days bottle and wire down.

> Here sparkles the nectar, that, hallow'd by love,
>   Could draw the angels of old from their sphere;
> Who for wine of this earth left the fountains above,
>   And forgot heav'n stars for the eyes we have here.
> *Lalla Rookh.*

Common Nectar.—Put half a pound of loaf sugar into a large jug; add one pint of cold water; stir the sugar till dissolved; pour over it a bottle of hock and one bottle of Madeira. Mix them well together, and grate in half a nutmeg, with a drop or two of essence of lemon. Set the jug in a bucket of ice for an hour.

Welsh Nectar.—Cut the peel of four lemons thin, pour on it two gallons of boiling water; when cold, add the strained juice of the lemons, and a pound of raisins, stoned and chopped fine. Let it stand a few days, and then strain it and bottle for use. A small addition of brandy is an improvement.

Tamarind Drink.—A very wholesome summer drink can be made from an ounce and a half of tamarinds, three ounces of currants, and two ounces of stoned raisins, boiled in three pints of water. Strain, and add a little lemon-peel.

Spanish Drinks.—First and foremost, peerless and revivifying, was *agraz*—a pearl of drinks, pressed from the pulp of the unripe grape, tempered with water of icy coldness, mixed with the chamomile wine of Southern Spain—the manzanella; next comes *orchata de cheifas*—white, creamy, nutty liquor; then we drink orangeade and lemonade, only to be made in Spain; and last, *leche lilada*, rendered more palatable with sugar and beaten snow.—"*Tales of Spanish Life*," *in Bentley's Miscellany.*

There has been, in all governments, a great deal of absurd canting about the consumption of spirits. We believe the best plan is to let people drink what they like, and wear what they like; to make no sumptuary laws either for the belly or the back. In the first place, laws against rum and rum-and-water are made by men who can change a wet coat for a dry one whenever they choose, and who do not work up to their knees in mud and water; and, in the next place, if this stimulus did all the mischief it is thought to do by the wise men of claret, its cheapness and plenty would rather lessen than increase the avidity with which it is at present sought for.—*Sydney Smith.*

Orange Brandy.—Take the rind of three or four lemons and of eight Seville oranges, peeled thin, and three pounds of sugar-candy, powdered. Steep the whole in a gallon of brandy for four or five days, stirring it frequently, and afterwards run it through a filterer to clear it.

Drink Divine.—Mix a bottle of cider, half a bottle of perry, and the same of sherry, with half a gill of brandy; then add a sliced lemon, the rind pared thin, and a toasted biscuit. Drink, iced or cooled.

DRINKING.—Three cups of wine a prudent man may take.
The first of these for constitution's sake;
The second to the girl he loves the best;
The third and last to lull him to his rest;
Then home to bed! But if a fourth he pours,
That is the cup of folly, and not ours.
Loud, noisy talking on the fifth attends;
The sixth breeds feuds and falling-out of friends;
Seven beget blows and faces stain'd with gore;
Eight, and the watch-patrol breaks ope the door;
Mad with the ninth, another cup goes round,
And the swill'd sot drops senseless to the ground.
"*Eubulus.*" *Poetical fragment quoted by Athenæus, turned into English verse by Cumberland.*

Drink Superb.—Put a wine-glass of brandy into a tumbler; add more than half lemonade, and fill up with green lime shrub. A very lovable tipple.

Soda-water.— Get very drunk, and when
You wake with headache, you shall see what then:
Ring for your valet, bid him quickly bring
Some hock and soda-water, then you'll know
A pleasure worthy of Xerxes the great king:
For not the best sherbet sublimed with snow,
Nor the first sparkle of the desert spring,
Nor Burgundy in all its sunset glow,
After long travel, *ennui,* love, or slaughter,
Vie with that draught of hock and soda-water.—*Byron.*

Soda-water ought to contain about twenty grains of bicarbonate of soda to the half pint, and is strongly impregnated with carbonic acid gas, but much is made without soda. When used as a drink the omission is unimportant, but not so when it is required as an œnta acid. As a drink in febrile disorders, soda-water is often beneficial and grateful, but it should not be drunk in quantities.

Cambridge Drink.—This is merely a mixture of equal quantities of ale and soda-water; it is highly refreshing and of a very agreeable flavour. When made, there must be in the liquor a sprig of borage. Some parties use lemon and a little sugar.

Soda-water and brandy is called in India *peg,* so writes Sidney Laman Blanchard.

Spruce Beer.—Put four gallons of cold water into a nine-gallon keg; then add four more gallons, boiling, and six pounds of molasses, with eight table-spoonfuls of the essence of spruce, and on its cooling put to it about half a pint of yeast. Let it work, and just before it has done working bottle in stone bottles. Ure's recipe is somewhat different:—Essence of spruce, half a pint; pimento and ginger, bruised, each, four ounces; hops, from four to five ounces; water, three gallons. Boil for ten minutes; then strain, and add eleven gallons of warm water, a pint of yeast, and six pints of molasses. Mix, and allow it to ferment for twenty hours.

Lemonade au Lait.—Take half a pint of lemon-juice, the same quantity of white wine, three-quarters of a pound of white sugar, and a quart of boiling water; mix, and when cold add a pint of boiling milk. Let it stand twelve hours; then pour through a jelly-bag. This will make two quarts.

Pomona wine is made in America by adding one gallon of brandy to six of cider, after it is racked off.

Raspberry Vinegar.—Put a pound of fruit into a bowl, pour upon it a quart of the best white wine vinegar; next day strain the juice on a pound of fresh raspberries, and the following day do the same. Bottle and cork well.

Apricot Drink.—Take a pint of apricot juice, and add half a pound of sugar, then add an ounce of tartaric acid. Bottle and cork for use. Use it with water and a small quantity of carbonate of soda. Peaches and any ripe fruit may be used in a similar way.

Gin Punch.—Pour half a pint of gin on the outer peel of a lemon, then a little lemon-juice, sugar, a glass of maraschino, about a pint and a quarter of water, and two bottles of iced soda-water. The result will be three pints of punch.

"The Art of Dining" says that the gin punch made on the above principle at the Garrick Club was one of the best things known, and that it was a favourite beverage of the late Theodore Hook; while Basil Hall has it that good whisky punch is the most insinuating and the most loving of tipples. If another authority is wanted, Burke, on one occasion, *spiritually* exclaimed, "*I for one stand up for gin.*"

Lamb's Wool.—In days of yore this was a favourite liquor with common people, and was composed of roasted apples and ale; the pulp of the apples worked up with the ale till the mixture formed a smooth beverage, with the addition of sugar and spice.

> Now crown the bowle
> With gentle lamb's-wooll;
> Add sugar, and nutmegs, and ginger.—*Herrick.*

Cool Tankard.—Put to a quart of mild ale a wine-glassful of white wine, the same of brandy and capillaire, the juice of a lemon, and some of the rind. Add a sprig of balm or borage, some toasted bread, and nutmeg grated on the top. Borage is said to impart coolness to this drink.

Borage is one of the four cordial flowers. "It comforts the heart, cheers melancholy, and revives the fainting spirits," says Salmon, in his "Household Companion," 1710.

Brande writes that liquor in which borage itself is plunged, when fresh, becomes cooled, and hence the *borage officinalis* is the principal ingredient in a cool tankard.

Capillaire, according to Brande, is a simple syrup, or a concentrated solution of sugar in water, flavoured with orange-flower water and some similar aromatic. The name is derived 'from the mucilaginous syrup formerly directed to be made of the Canadian maidenhair (*Adiantum capillus veneris*). It is diluted with ice-water for use.

Spider: brandy and lemonade, or brandy and ginger-beer.

Cocktail: brandy, aniseed-water, and sugar.

SUMMER DRINKS (From the *Field: the Country Gentleman's Newspaper*).—Amongst the numerous prescriptions for summer drinks in the *Field*, I have never observed one which, as a beverage to work upon, is entitled to a prominent place, i. e., cold tea, flavoured with sliced lemon and dashed with cognac. The tea should be properly made, not allowed to stand until it becomes rank, but boiling water should be poured on the leaves, allowed to stand five minutes, then poured into a jug with slices of lemon at the bottom. A wine-glass of good brandy added when cool, sugar to taste (of course), no milk.—*H.* Some one in the *Field*, a week or two since, asked for recipes for cider cup, &c. Several were sent for other things, but not for cider cup, so I send him one I had from a certain college some years since, no less famed for learning than good living:—Mix together two quarts of best bottled cider—old, if possible—sweeten to taste, taking care that the sugar is perfectly melted. Add half a nutmeg grated, a glass of brandy, a glass of noyeau, cut a lemon in moderately thin slices, and let them remain there. Make it two hours before wanted, and stand it in some ice. There is no better recipe than the above.—*A Taker in of the "Field."*

Recipes for Wine Cup.—*Moselle Cup:* No. 1. To each bottle of still or sparkling Moselle add one bottle of soda-water, a glass of sherry or brandy, four or five thin slices of pineapple, the peel of half a lemon cut very thin, and powdered sugar according to taste; let the whole stand about an hour, and before serving add some lumps of clear ice. No. 2 as No. 1, except the pineapple, for which substitute a pint of fresh strawberries, or three or four peaches or nectarines. No. 3 as No. 1, but add instead of fruit some sprigs of woodruffe; woodruffe is an herb much used on the Rhine for making "May Trank," its peculiar flavour being most powerful in May; it is to be found in forests in many parts of England also. No. 4. When neither fruit nor woodruffe can be obtained, add instead of sherry or brandy a glass or two of milk punch or essence of punch, and a little more of the lemon-peel.—*Rhenish Cup:* No. 1. "May Trank" is the most popular beverage on the Rhine. Take with each bottle of light hock about a dozen sprigs of woodruffe, a quarter of an orange cut in small slices, and about two ounces of powdered sugar. The herbs are to be removed after having been in the wine half an hour or longer, according to taste. A bottle of sparkling wine added to four or five bottles of still hock, is a great improvement. A little ice is recommended. No. 2. Instead of woodruffe and orange, take to each bottle of hock about half a pint of highly-flavoured strawberries. Sugar as above. The fruit is to be taken with the wine after having been in it about a nhour. No. 3. Take some thin slices of pineapple instead of the strawberries. No. 4. Take to each bottle of hock two highly-flavoured peaches peeled and cut in slices. Sugar as above.—*Claret Cup:* No. 1. To each bottle of ordinary claret add a bottle of soda-water, a glass of sherry or curaçoa, the peel of a lemon cut very thin, powdered sugar according to taste. Let the whole remain an hour or two before serving, and then add some lumps of clear ice. No. 2. To the above add a few slices of cucumber, or some sprigs of borage instead of the cucumber. No. 3. As No. 1, except the lemon-peel, for which substitute, when in season, a pint of ripe raspberries or four or five peaches or nectarines cut in slices. This is a most delicious beverage.—*Frederick Johnson* (Wath-upon-Dearne, Rotherham).

Brandy Smash: a nip of brandy, a table-spoonful of port wine, a table-spoonful of ice; sugar and water to taste, with a sprig of mint.

John Collins is a composition of gin, sugar, syrup, and soda-water.

Shandy Gaff: equal proportions of ale and ginger-beer.

Bishop.—Take three best oranges, and grill them to a pale brown colour over a clear fire. Place them in a small punch-bowl, and pour over them half a pint of claret, in which a pound and a quarter of loaf sugar is dissolved, and cover it. When served, cut the oranges into pieces, and place in a jug containing the remainder of the bottle of claret, made hot. Some use Lisbon wine instead of claret.

> Fine oranges
> Well roasted with sugar, and wine in a cup,
> They'll a sweet bishop make when gentlefolks sup.—*Swift*.

Cardinal.—This compound is made the same way as bishop, only old wine of the Rhine is used.

Pope: made in a similar manner to cardinal, only using tokay, vermuth, or malmsey.

Cocoa-nut toddy is much in demand in the neighbourhood of villages, especially where European troops are stationed. When it is drunk before sunrise it is a cool, delicious, and particularly wholesome beverage; but by eight or nine o'clock fermentation has made some progress, and it is then highly intoxicating.—*Marshall's "History of the Cocoa-nut Tree."*

Arrack: a spirituous liquor from the East Indies. This term, or its corruption, *rack*, is applied to any spirituous liquor in the East. The true arrack is said to be distilled from *toddy*, the fermented juice of the cocoa-nut tree. It is, however, frequently distilled from rice and sugar, fermented with the cocoa-nut juice.—*Ure*.

Crambambull.—Take two bottles of porter or ale and boil them; then add half a pint of rum, and from half a pound to a pound of white sugar. After this has boiled remove it from the fire, and put into the mixture the whites and yolks of six eggs previously well whisked. Stir it for a minute, and serve in a punch-bowl.

Devilled Ale.—Cut a slice of bread about an inch thick, toast and butter it; then sprinkle it with cayenne pepper and ginger, and place in the bottom of a jug; add a pint of warm ale, and sugar to taste.

LIQUEUR DE QUATRE FRUIT.—Take strawberries, raspberries, currants, and morella cherries; extract the juice from them separately, and add to it a small proportion of white sugar, so as to make it sweet and rich, but not a thick syrup; strain it off as clear as possible. When you have the juices of the four fruits ready, mix them together, observing to put in a smaller proportion of currant and raspberry juice than of the cherry and strawberry. To a pint of juice add a gill of brandy, and then bottle it. The addition of some cherry and apricot kernels will be found an improvement.—*French Recipe.*

Egg Wine.—Beat up an egg, and mix it with a table-spoonful of water. Put a wine-glass of wine, half a glass of water, and sugar and nutmeg to taste, into a small saucepan, and place over a slow fire, and when it boils add it gradually to the egg, stirring well; then return the whole to the saucepan, and place over the fire again, and stir for a minute; remove, and serve with toast. If it boils a second time, it will curdle.

Falstaff. Go, brew me a pottle of sack finely.
Bardolph. With eggs, sir?—*Merry Wives of Windsor.*

Hot Purl.—Put a quart of mild ale into a saucepan, add a table-spoonful of grated nutmeg, and place it over a slow fire until it nearly boils. Mix a little cold ale, with sugar to taste, and, gradually, two eggs well beaten; then add the hot ale, stirring one way to prevent curdling, and a quarter of a pint of whisky. Warm the whole again, and pour it from one vessel into another until it becomes smooth.

Dibdin has immortalised rum-flip as the favourite beverage of sailors, although they seldom use it. It is made by adding a quartern of rum to the beer. The essential in all "flips" is to produce smoothness in the drink by repeated mixtures, and beating the eggs well up; the sweetening and spice according to taste.

Hydromel.—Boil eight pints of water and one of good honey till reduced half, then add a glass of brandy. This hydromel will keep ten or twelve years.

Shuv'-in-the-Mouth.—This drink is simply cold brandy-and-water, with the addition of a little sugar.

During the passage of the Stamp Act, in the Tasmanian House of Assembly, the hon. member for Selby remarked that a publican waited on his solicitor to ask what was the amount of the stamp duty on a *verbal* agreement. The hon. member for Morven replied, that the answer was a "shuv'-in-the-mouth."—*Hobart Town Advertiser.*

Jingle.—Roast a few apples, grate some nutmeg on them, and sugar to taste, and place them in a jug, with some slices of toasted bread, heat some ale, and fill the jug.

Dr. Kitchener writes, Before our readers make any remarks on this composition, we beg of them to taste it; if the materials are good, and their palate vibrates in unison with our own, they will find it one of the pleasantest beverages they ever put to their lips; and Lord Ruthven says, "This is right gossips' cup, that far exceeds all the ale that ever Mother Bunch made in her lifetime." See his lordship's "Experiments on Cookery," 1654.

Tewahdiddle.—A pint of small beer, a table-spoon of brandy, and a tea-spoonful of brown sugar, a little grated nutmeg, and a roll of thin lemon-peel.

Blow my Skull.—This was a colonial beverage in use in the earlier days of Tasmania, and was named and drank by an eccentric governor, who had a stronger head than most of his subordinates. A wattle hut used to be improvised within a few miles of the capital, and temporary chairs and a strong table being fixed, the governor would take the seat of honour, having in front of him a barbecued pig, and on his honour's right hand, a cask of "blow my skull"—sufficient for all comers—no special invitation being necessary. A challenge to liquor from the representative of majesty in a roomy pannikin, could not well be declined, although the ceremonial observed in the bush was not over strict. "No heeltaps!" called out the governor in a voice of authority, and the unfortunate stranger was at once *hors de combat;* while the governor having an impenetrable cranium, and an iron frame, could take several goblets of the alcoholic fluid, and walk away as lithe and happy as possible, attended by an orderly who could scarcely preserve his equilibrium. Now for the component parts. "Blow my skull," as its name imports, was a remarkably powerful drink, and it was made in the following proportions:—Two pints of boiling water, with *quantum sufficit* of loaf sugar, and lime or lemon-juice, one pint of ale or porter, one pint of rum, and half a pint of brandy.

How few of the "old hands" there are in Hobart Town, who recollect the flavour of this celebrated liquor, or the days of Colonel Davey; and we believe that there are none living at Sydney who remember the time when an invitation "at dinner," to Government House, was accompanied by the polite request to bring your own bread, owing to its scarcity.

Claret Cup.—Sherry, six table-spoonfuls; brandy, two ditto; sugar, an ounce and a half; two or three shreds of lemon-peel; the above to be added to one bottle of claret, and a bottle of soda-water. They should be kept in a cool place, a refrigerator for instance, and only opened before drinking. A lump of ice and a little borage are improvements.—*Crack in the "Field; or, the Country Gentleman's Newspaper."*

The Loving Cup.—The loving cup is a splendid feature of the hall-feasts of the City and Inns of Court. The cup is of silver or silver gilt, and is filled with spiced wine, immemoriably termed "sack." Immediately after the dinner and grace, the master and wardens drink to their visitors a hearty welcome; the cup is then handed round the table, and each guest, after he has drunk, applies his napkin to the mouth of the cup before he passes it to his neighbour. The more formal practice is, for the person who pledges with the loving cup to stand up and bow to his neighbour, who, also standing, removes the cover with his right hand, and holds it while the other drinks: a custom said to have originated in the precaution to keep the right, or dagger hand employed, that the person who drinks may be assured of no treachery, like that practised by Elfrida on the unsuspecting King Edward the Martyr, at Corfe Castle, who was slain while drinking. This was why the loving cup possessed a cover.—*F. W. Fairholt, F.S.A.*

The components of the above loving cup are—half a tea-cupful of capillaire, sugar, a few drops of orange-flower water, a pint of brown sherry, one bottle of ale, and just before placing it on the table, a bottle of soda-water must be added, with some grated nutmeg on the top of the liquor, and a piece of toast put in it. A napkin is placed on the handle of the cup, to be used as described by Mr. Fairholt.

A very agreeable beverage is made by mixing seltzer-water with Bordeaux wine, a little lemon-juice, and sugar.

Brandy.—The spirituous liquor, obtained by the distillation of wine; when pure it is perfectly colourless, and only acquires a pale brown or yellow tint from the cask. The deep colour of common brandy, intended to imitate that which it acquires from great age in the cask, is generally given by the addition of burnt sugar. The average proportion of alcohol in brandy varies from forty-eight to fifty-four per cent. The best brandy is made in France, the preference being given to that shipped from Cognac. The imports of brandy for home consumption amount to about 1,400,000 gallons a-year; but there can be no doubt that the quantity would be much larger, were it not for the oppressive duty of 15s. per gallon, reduced by Sir R. Peel from 22s. 6d., with which it is charged.—*Brande's "Dictionary of Science."*

Rum.—A spirituous liquor distilled from the fermented juice of the sugar-cane, or from molasses. Its flavour is due to the presence of a peculiar volatile oil; its average proportion of alcohol fluctuates between fifty and fifty-six per cent. The rum consumed in the United Kingdom is entirely the produce of the West Indies, and to a great extent of Jamaica; and for this preference it is indebted partly to its superior quality, and partly to its being protected against rum of East India produce, by a differential duty of 6s. per gallon, that on East India rum being 15s. per gallon. The quantity entered for home consumption for the year 1839-40, averaged 2,670,515 gallons; the duty on it for the three years 1837-39, averaged £1,372,540; and in 1840, the gross amount was £1,154,544. The consumption of rum in this country has long been gradually declining.—*Ibid.*

Gin (*Fr. Genièvre, Juniper*).—Ardent spirit flavoured by the essential oil of juniper. It was originally made by the Dutch, and is hence distinguished in this country by the name of Hollands. The liquor bearing the above name in this country is of British manufacture, and rendered biting on the palate by caustic potash. In Holland the finest gin bears the name of Schiedam, the principal place of its manufacture, and where there are many distilleries. Owing to the excessive duty (15s. per gallon), gin is one of the principal articles of clandestine importation.—*Ibid.* McCulloch writes that English gin is said to be one of the most wholesome spirits.

Whisky.—A spirit obtained by distillation from corn, sugar, or molasses, though generally from the former. It is extensively used and manufactured in Scotland and Ireland.—*Ure.*

Geneva.—A grain spirit flavoured with juniper-berries, manufactured exclusively in Holland; hence it is frequently called Hollands. Gin is manufactured in London and other places, and flavoured generally with juniper-berries; it is a corn spirit, and is rendered sweet and cordial-like by the use of several injurious substances. Plymouth gin, as manufactured by Coates and Co., is a far purer spirit. The rectifiers employ a pure grain spirit, and flavour with the wash of the whisky distilleries.—*Ibid.*

A WHET.—In Turkey nothing is more common than for the Mussulmans to take several glasses of strong spirits by way of appetisers. I have seen them take as many as six of raki before dinner, and swear that they dined the better for it. I tried the experiment, but fared like the Scotchman, who, having heard that the birds called kittiwakes were admirable whets, ate six of them, and complained that "he was no hungrier than when he began."—*Note to "Don Juan," Murray's Edition.*

Aleberry.—A beverage made by boiling ale with spice, sugar, and toasted bread. A domestic remedy for a cold.

To Mull Wine (*French recipe*).—Boil in a wine-glass and a half of water a quarter of an ounce of spice (cinnamon, bruised ginger, and cloves) with three ounces of fine sugar, until they form a thick syrup, which must not on any account be allowed to burn; pour in a pint of port wine, and stir it gently until it is on the point of boiling only: it should be served immediately. In France, light clarets take the place of port wine, in making it, and the better kinds of *vins du pays* are very palatable, when thus prepared: water, one and a half wine-glassfuls; spice, quarter of an ounce; port wine or claret, one pint; orange-rind, if used, to be boiled with the spice; sherry, or fine raisin, or ginger wine, as above, stirred hot to the yolks of four fresh eggs, will be found excellent.—*Hints for the Table.*

INTEMPERANCE.—The best way of weaning the poor man from intemperance is by counter-agents, by education, by good food, and by good cookery, by good ventilation, by the establishment of well-regulated clubs and institutions, to be conducted by the working men themselves, by free access to parks and public places, by exhibitions and museums, by good available libraries, and by entertainments and rational diversions in the widest as well as the best sense of the word.—*Lord Neaves, at the last Social Science Congress.*

ANCIENT WINES.—The names of the drinks and drinking-cups of the ancients, according to Athenæus, translated by Yonge, are as follows:—*Drinks*—Abates, Acanthus, Adrian, Alban, Ambrosia, Amphis, Ancona, Autocratic, Babylon, Barbine, Bibline, Buxentine, Cæcuban, Calenian, Capua, Caucine, Chalydonian, Chian, Cnidian, Coan, Coptos, Corcyrean, Corinthian, Erbulian, Eubœan, Falernian, Formian, Fundan, Gauran, Halicarnassus, Hermes, Icarian, Italian, Labican, Lesbian, Mamertine, Mareotic, Marseilles, Marsic, Mitylenæan. Myndian, Myrtile, or Myrrhine, Nectar, Nomentum, Passum, Peparethian, Phoenician, Pollian, Præneste, Pramnian, Privernium, Psithian, Rhegian, Rhodian, Sabine, Samagorian, Scented, Sciathus, Setine, Signine, Spoletum, Surrentine, Tæniotic, Tarentine, Thasian, Thebais, Tibur, Trebellian, Trifoline, Ulban, Veliternian, Venafrum, and Zacynthian. The names of the drinking-cups are more numerous than the drinks:—Acatia, Acicis, Aleison, Amalthea, Ancyla, Aotus, Aracis, Argyris, Aroclum, Aryballus, Arystichus, Batiacium, Baucalis, Bessa, Bicus, Bombylius, Bromias, Calpinum, Cantharus, Carchesium, Capua, Celebe, Chonni, Chutrides, Ciborium, Cissybium, Cononius, Cothon, Cotylisca, Crounea, Culix, Cupellum, Cyathis, Cymbium, Dactylotos, Deinias, Depas, Depastron, Dinus, Ephebus, Ethanion, Gyala, Hedypotides, Hemitomus, Herculeum, Holmus, Hystiacum, Iphicratis, Labionius, Lacena, Lepaste, Lesbian, Luterium, Manes, Mastus, Mathalides, Mele, Nidos, Oinisteria, Ollix, Oon, Ooscyphia, Oxybaphum, Panathenaicum, Pelica, Pella, Pelleter, Pentaploa, Petachnum, Phiale, Philotesia, Phthoïs, Plemochoe, Pristis, Proaron, Prochytes, Psygeus, Rheonta, Rhodias, Rysis, Scallium, Scaphinum, Scyphus, Seleucis, Tabaitas, Thermopotis, and Tragelaphus.

The bard of Ceos says:—
"'Tis not enough to mix your wine with taste,
Unless sweet converse seasons the repast;
And Bacchus' gifts well such regard deserve,
That we should e'en the stones of grapes preserve."

FERMENTED LIQUORS.—Volumes have been written to prove that spirit in every form, is not only unnecessary to those that are in health, but that it has been the prolific source of the most painful and fatal diseases to which man is subject; in short, that Epimetheus himself did not, by opening the box of Pandora, commit a greater act of hostility against our nature, than the discoverer of fermented liquors. Every apartment, it is said, devoted to the circulation of the glass, may be regarded as a temple set apart for the performance of human sacrifice; and that they ought to be fitted up like the ancient temples of Egypt, in a manner to show the real atrocity of the superstition that is carried on within their walls. This is mere rant and nonsense; a striking specimen of the fallacy of reasoning against the *use* of a custom from its abuse. There exists no evidence to prove that a temperate use of good wine, when taken at seasonable hours, has ever proved injurious to healthy adults. In youth, and still more in infancy, the stimulus it imparts to the stomach is undoubtedly injurious; but there are exceptions even to this general rule. The occasional use of *diluted* wine has improved the health of a child, by imparting vigour to a torpid stomach; we ought, however, to consider it rather as a medicine than a luxury.—*Paris on Diet.*

CXIV.—THE LAST DINNER.

"The small and great are there; and the servant is free from his master."—*Job* iii. 19.

We have extracted from Professor Newman's "System of Rhetoric" an admired example of descriptive writing, which we have given at the end of this work, as it is a meal that we ought often to be reminded we must all, sooner or later, partake of:—

"THE FIRST AND LAST DINNER.—Twelve friends, much about the same age, and fixed by their pursuits, their family connections, and other local interests, as permanent inhabitants of the metropolis, agreed one day, when they were drinking wine at the Star and Garter, at Richmond, to institute an annual dinner among themselves, under the following regulations:—That they should dine alternately at each other's houses on the *first* and *last* day of the year; and the *first* bottle of wine uncorked at the *first* dinner should be re-corked and put away, to be drunk by him who should be the *last* of their number; that they should never admit a new member; that, when one died, eleven should meet, and when another died, ten should meet, and so on; and when only one remained, he should, on these two days, dine by himself, and sit the usual hours at his solitary table; but the first time he had so dined—lest it should be the only one—he should then uncork the *first* bottle, and, in the *first* glass, drink to the memory of all who were gone.

"Some thirty years had now glided away, and only ten remained; but the stealing hand of time had written sundry changes in most legible characters. Raven locks had become grizzled; two or three heads had not as many locks as may be reckoned in a walk of half a mile along the Regent's Canal; one was actually covered with a brown wig; the crows' feet were visible in the corner of the eye; good old port and warm

Madeira carried it against hock, claret, Burgundy, and champagne; stews, hashes, and ragouts grew into favour; crusts were rarely called for to relish the cheese after dinner; conversation was less boisterous, and it turned chiefly upon politics and the state of the funds, or the value of landed property; apologies were made for coming in thick shoes and warm stockings; the doors and windows were more carefully provided with list and sand-bags; the fire is in more request; and a quiet game of whist filled up the hours that were wont to be devoted to drinking and riotous merriment. Two rubbers, a cup of coffee, and at home by eleven o'clock, was the usual cry, when the fifth or sixth glass had gone round after the removal of the cloth. At parting, too, there was now a long ceremony in the hall—buttoning up great coats, tying on woollen comforters, fixing silk handkerchiefs over the mouth and up to the ears, and grasping sturdy walking-canes, to support unsteady feet.

"Their fiftieth anniversary came, and death had, indeed, been busy. Four little old men, of withered appearance and decrepid walk, with cracked voices, and dim, rayless eyes, sat down, by the mercy of Heaven (as they tremulously declared), to celebrate, for the fiftieth time, the first day of the year—to observe the frolic compact which, half a century before, they had entered into at the Star and Garter, at Richmond. Eight were in their graves! the four that remained stood upon its confines! Yet they chirped cheerily over their glass, though they could scarcely carry it to their lips if more than half full; and cracked their jokes, though they articulated their words with difficulty, and heard each other with still greater difficulty. They mumbled, they chattered, they laughed (if a sort of strangled wheezing might be called a laugh); and, as the wine sent their icy blood in warmer pulses through their veins, they talked of their past as if it were but a yesterday that had slipped by them, and of their future as if it were a busy century that lay before them.

"At length came the *last* dinner; and the survivor of the twelve, upon whose head fourscore and ten winters had showered their snow, ate his solitary meal. It so chanced that it was in his house and at his table they celebrated the first; in his cellar, too, had remained, for more than fifty years, the bottle they had then uncorked, re-corked, and which he was that day to uncork again. It stood beside him. With a feeble and reluctant grasp he took the 'frail memorial' of a youthful vow, and, for a moment, memory was faithful to her office. She threw open the long vista of buried years, and his heart travelled through them all. Their lusty and blithesome spring, their bright and fervid summer, their ripe and temperate autumn, their chill, but not too frozen winter. He saw, as in a mirror, one by one the laughing companions of that merry hour at Richmond, had dropped into eternity. He felt the loneliness of his condition, for he had eschewed marriage, and in the veins of no living creature ran a drop of blood whose source was in his own; and as he drained the glass which he had filled, 'to the memory of those who were gone,' the tears slowly trickled down the deep furrows of his aged face.

"He had thus fulfilled one part of his vow, and he prepared himself to discharge the other, by sitting the usual number of hours at his desolate table. With a heavy heart he resigned himself to the gloom of his own thoughts. A lethargic sleep stole over him; his head fell upon his bosom; confused images crowded into his mind; he babbled to himself; was silent; and when his servant entered the room, alarmed by a noise which he heard, he found his master stretched upon the carpet at the foot of the easy chair, out of which he had slipped in an apoplectic fit. He never spoke again, nor once opened his eyes, though the vital spark was not extinct till the following day. And this was the LAST DINNER."

INNS.—All the comforts of life in a tavern are known,
 'Tis his home who possesses not one of his own;
' And to him who has rather too much of that one,
 'Tis the house of a friend, where you're welcome to run.
 The instant you enter my door you're my lord,
 With whose taste and whose pleasure I'm proud to accord;
 And the louder you call, and the longer you stay,
 The more I am happy to serve and obey.

To the house of a friend, if you're pleased to retire,
You must all things admit, you must all things admire;
You must pay, with observance, the price of your treat;
You must eat what is praised, and praise what you eat.
But here you may come, and no tax we require;
You may loudly condemn what you greatly admire;
You may growl at our wishes and pains to excel,
And may snarl at the rascals who please you so well.—*Crabbe.*

CXV.—CONCLUSION

Now good digestion wait on appetite,
And health on both.—*Macbeth.*

We now bring our aristological labours to an end, and it is necessary that we should state that we have not, as a general rule, given the periods when game or fish are in season, nor have we fixed the time that dishes would take to have them ready for the palate. To do so is impossible, for it depends entirely on the radiation of heat to which they are subject. The economy of heat is not well understood by many cooks; some will waste more fuel than others could make an excellent fire of. The celebrated Count Rumford, who was well up in this subject, once dined a thousand persons at Munich, and the cost of the fuel was fourpence halfpenny; so writes Sir Richard Phillips. Francis of Austria once declared that, in his opinion, it required as much talent to warm a room as to govern a kingdom. The emperor might have said more, according to his judgment, as he was not well versed in the rationale of government. *A fortiori*, if it requires ability to warm a room, it needs *nous* to keep up the same continuous degree of heat in the range, as well as to govern men, unless, according to the dictum of the celebrated Chancellor Oxenstiern, that little wisdom was required to rule the nations of the world; the truth of which axiom is partially exemplified by such a number of stupid people being found in the ministries at home, and in the colonies—so many Lord Fitzboobies, as D'Israeli designates them in one of his novels. Were we to prescribe time, or give seasons for either meat or vegetables, we fancy we should think the *artiste* an automaton, instead of having a head, which he or she should possess, as much as a general, perhaps even more so. We have refrained from introducing the feeding of cattle, sheep, or poultry, or the management of the dairy; nor have we overloaded our work with recipes, either household or medical, but have confined it to cookery, and matter incidental to eating. Indeed, we have gone a little beyond this course of conduct, in detailing the mode of making hams and bacon; but this latter is a subject in which we fancy we are more than an amateur. A work consisting solely of instructions and recipes must always be dull and monotonous, except as a reference; so we have introduced and dispersed in the foregoing pages numerous appropriate quotations and easy extracts, all bearing on the subject matter of the *cuisine*, which we hope will be found piquant, and interesting, as a kind of literary garnish to the culinary fare we have served up.

We have shown the MS. to a critic of discernment, who is hopeful, and possibly the lines of Campbell may be applicable to his judgment:—

"'Tis the sunset of life gives me mystical lore,
And coming events cast their shadows before."

If the work is patronised, it can be improved in many ways, as well as enlarged, keeping down the price, as we live in cheap times. We desire that it may be remunerative, being of Ensign O'Doherty's opinion, as given by Professor Wilson, in *Blackwood*:—that every unpaid writer is, *ex vi termini*, an ass. Should it not be in request, it can be consigned to the Capulets' tomb, or, more appropriately speaking, to the trunk-maker's. We now take leave of the indulgent reader, and of any one who may have used these pages as a reference (especially if he, she, or they have partaken of any of the viands hereinbefore propounded), in the language of a great writer, whom we have previously quoted, by wishing

"To all and each a fair good night,
With rosy dreams and slumbers light."

COOKERY BOOK.—M. Alexandre Dumas, *père*, has been offered by a Paris publisher the moderate sum of 60,000f. down, and 10,000f. a-year, if he will write a cookery book. The author of "Les Trois Mousquetaires," however, hesitates, fearing that his work would not be above the average intellect of the kitchen, and so would be useless. In his apology for refusing to emulate Mrs. Glasse (Dr. Hill), M. Dumas quotes the following dictum of a cuisinier at Marseilles:—"I consider a cook who invents a dish a much greater man than an astronomer who discovers a star; for, as far as stars are concerned, there are as many as we shall ever consume, but a new dish is a new pleasure for every man who knows how to dine." Dr. Kitchener wrote a similar observation years ago. M. Dumas assures us that he is a very good cook.—*Late Letter from Paris*. Dr. Kitchener informs us that the best books on cookery have been written by physicians:—Sir Kenelm Digby, Sir Theodore Mayene, Professor Beasley, Dr. Hill, Dr. Le Cointe, Dr. Hunter, &c.

FINIS.

_{*} In the event of a second edition being called for, the compiler would feel thankful to receive any additional practical recipes from the ladies of Australia and others, pertaining to the subject, so as to make the book, as a reference, as useful as possible.

INDEX TO AUTHORS AND BOOKS, ETC., QUOTED.

Abernethy, 65
Adam's Roman Antiquities, 242
Albert, Prince, 126
Albury Advertiser, 178
All the Year Round, 98
Almanach des Gourmands, 12
Art of Dining, 277
Athenæus, by Yonge, 34, 55, 89, 102
  ,,   Eubulus, 276
Austral, in Once a Week, 25

Baglivi, 4
Baker's Chronicle, 47
Beau Villiers, 246
Bendigo Advertiser, 177
Bennett, Dr., Gatherings, 85
Bentley's Miscellany, 136, 275
Blackwood's Magazine, 264
Blessington, Lady, 102
Bostock's Pharmacologia, 39
Brande, 69, 73, 80, 87, 103, 109, 135, 173, 199, 282
British Rural Sports, 128
Brummel, Beau, 160
Buchanan on Fuel, 15
Builder, 127
Burke, Edmund, Pref. v.
Burns, 168
Burton on Melancholy, 41, 102
Butler's Canterbury, 76
  ,,   Hudibras, 123, 198
Byron, Pref. vi., 130, 233, 275, 276
Byron's Don Juan, 52

Cadogan, Dr., 121
Californian Farmer, 199
Campbell, Thomas, 287
Caprera, News from, 266
Cassell's Paper, 52
Chambers' Journal, 23
Charles O'Malley, 209, 272
Chaucer, 219

Child's, Mrs., Frugal Housewife, 242
Christian Witness, 126
Christison on Poisons, 209
Chronicles of Clovernook, 111
Cicero, 8
Cobbett, 38, 55, 77, 207
Cogan's Haven of Health, 200
Coke upon Littleton, 20
Cooley's Practical Receipts, 14, 38, 92, 128, 142, 156, 168
Coombe, 17
Cornhill Magazine, 186
Correspondent of Domestic Economy, 13
     ,,   Pastoral Times, 118
Count D'Orsay, 112
Court Journal, 127
Cowper, 135
Crabbe, 172, 286
Crawford, 84, 268
Cuisine at the Hop-pole, 93
Curiosities of London, 185

Daily Telegraph, 37
Davy, Sir Humphry, 48, 94
Deipnosophists, 11, 29, 178
Derby, Lord, 131
Descartes, Life of, 209
Deuteronomy xiv. 2, 3, 4, 248
Dialogues of the Dead, 268
  ,,   sur la Gastronomie, 184
Dictionary of Daily Wants, 91
Digby's Closet of Cookery, 141
Disraeli's Coningsby, Pref. viii., 201
  ,,   Tancred, 125
Donovan's Domestic Economy, 262
Dryden, 32, 217
Dublin Royal Society's Report, 14

Eden on the Poor, 76
Edinburgh Cyclopædia, 116
Epicurean, The, 77

INDEX TO AUTHORS AND BOOKS, ETC., QUOTED.

Esquiros, 162
Exodus xii., 15, 149

Fairholt, F. W., 281
Field, The, 129, 130, 278
,, Correspondent of, 145
Fleming's Phil. of Zoology, 97
Ford's Spain, 66
Fortune's China, 137
Fosbroke, 150
Fraser's Magazine, 176, 200
French Culinary Adage, 245
,, Recipe, 280
Fudge Family, 140

Galen on Health, 18
Galignani, 122
Gardeners' Chronicle, 155
Gay, 22
Genesis ix. 20, 171
Gil Blas, 248
Gleig's Wellington, 50
Goldsmith, 29, 81
Good-for-Nothing, in Fraser, 79
Gore, Mrs., 140
Goulburn Chronicle, 84
Gower's Domestic Life, 57
Graham on Indigestion, 216
,, Mrs., 81
Grant's Flood and Field, 220
Grote's Greece, 113
Gryll Grange, in Fraser, 4

Hack, Dr., 48
Hall, Dr. E. S., 70
Hassall, Dr., in the Times, 122
Hasselquist, 271
Hector, Dr., 85
Henderson, 173
Herrick, 277
Hints for the Table, 37, 50, 54, 95, 130, 207, 214, 242, 283
,, on Etiquette, 134
Hobart Town Advertiser, 145, 280
Home News, 7, 98, 127
Hone's Every Day Book, 76
Hook, Theodore, 72, 264
Hopkins' Sandwich Islands, 118
Hull, 84
Hunt's Merchants' Magazine, 143

Illustrated London News, 70
,, Melbourne Post, 178
Ingenious Gentlewoman, 161
Instructions for Bread Making, 78
Irish Newspapers, 115
Irving, Washington, 87

Jameson, Mrs., 202
Jerrold, D., 219
Jewish Manual, 228
Job iii. 19, 284; vi. 6, 195
Johnson, Dr., 91, 207, 274
,, Frederick, 279
Johnston, J. F. W., 81, 169
Johnston's Chemistry of Common Life, 10, 159
,, Physical Atlas, 69
Journal des Connoissances Usuelles, 193

King, 119
Kitchener, Dr., 3, 6, 7, 32, 50, 51, 211, 269, 280
Koran, chap. lxxxiii., 178

La Cuisinière Bourgeoise, 33
Lamb, Charles, 11, 16, 89
Lancet, 136, 213
,, Correspondent of, 45
Landon, Miss, 130
L'Art de Cuisinier, 17
Lavater, J. C., 73
Le Manual des Amphitryons, 203
Leslie's Confectioner, 169
Leviticus ii. 7, 258
Liebig, Pref. ix., 5
Littleton, 20
Liverpool Albion, 180
Lloyd's Tasmania, 86
London Salter's Company's Books in the Reign of Richard II., 43
London Saturday Journal, 264
Longfellow, 175
Lytton, Sir E. B., 191; Pelham, 220; Last Days of Pompeii, 239

Macaulay, 262
Mackay, Charles, 67
Macnish, 174
M'Culloch's Commercial Dictionary, 76, 175, 247
Magazine of Domestic Economy, 80, 93
Maitland Mercury, 178
Markham's English Housewife, 186
Mark Lane Express, 191
Marryatt, 274
Marsden, 81
Marshall's Cocoa Nut Tree, 279
Martineau, Harriet, 37, 134
May's Accomplished Cook, 63
Mayo, 18, 52, 67, 81, 204
Medical Circular, 164

INDEX TO AUTHORS AND BOOKS, ETC., QUOTED. 291

Melbourne Argus, 178
  ,,   Yeoman, 233
Melville's Australia, 84
Mercier's Tableau de Paris, 202
Meredith, Mrs., 62, 86, 121
Milton, Pref. vi.
Moore, T., 109, 127, 180
Moore's Diary, 264; Lalla Rookh, 275
More, Hannah, 198
Morgan, Lady, Pref. viii.
Morning Chronicle, 96
  ,,   Star, 37
Morris, Captain, 186
Moseley, 183
Mowbray, 48

Nares' Glossary, 79, 158
Neaves, Lord, 283
New Atalantis, 269
  ,, Crusade, The, 94
  ,, York Express, 274
Newman's, Professor, System of Rhetoric, 284
News of the World, 274
Newspaper Paragraph, 132, 156, 160, 192
  ,,   Scrap, 35
Nimrod, 185
Noctes Ambrosianæ, 238
North British Review, 171
Northcote, Sir S., Pref. xii.
Notes and Queries, 48, 69

Old Magazine, 148
  ,, Saying, 155, 246
Osborne, Mr., Debate in the House of Commons, 123

Pakeha Maori History of the War in New Zealand, 11
Paper on Charity Soups, 211
Paris, Dr., 9, 62, 78, 95, 117, 118, 141, 165, 183, 245, 284
Parmentier, Vegetables, 118; Code Pharmaceutique, 262
Pearson, Dr., 169
Pegge, 36
Pelham, 104
Peregrine Pickle, 171
Pereira, 26, 98, 271
Pharmaceutical Journal, 184
Philip, Dr., 124
Piscator, 93, 99
Poor Richard, 226
  ,, Robin's Almanack, 270

Pope, 97, 99, 182, 203, 236
Practical Housewife, 262
Praed, W. M., Australasia, Ded., p. iv.
Prior, 123
Proctor's Life of Kean, 19
Proverbs xxxi. 27, 28, Pref. vi.
Punch's Almanack, 119
Punch, Melbourne, 269

Quarterly Review, Pref. ix., xi., 13, 54, 70, 90, 138, 161, 216, 239
Queensland Newspaper, 233
Quetelet, 29, 46

Raffald's, Mrs., Cookery, 64
Raspail's Organic Chemistry, 74
Razor Grinder, The, 71
Revels of Rokesby, 226
Robinson, 181
Ross, Sir James, 245

St. John, J. A., 201
Salmon's Household Companion, 277
Salomons, D., 259
Scheibler, 96, 108
Schulz Schulzenstein, 140
Scientific American, 133
Scotsman, The, 162
Scott, Sir Walter, Pref. xii., 147
Scottish Farmer, 116, 193
Scrap, 243
Shakespeare's—Comedy of Errors, 9, 16, 45, 128, 138, 200; Cymbeline, 50, 64, 104; Henry IV., Part II., 59, 81; Lear, 67; Macbeth, 171, 191, 286; Merry Wives, 112, 216, 268, 280; Much Ado About Nothing, 19, 134; Richard II., 144; Timon of Athens, Apemantus' Grace, 201; Titus Andronicus, 34; Troilus, 74, 111; Twelfth Night, 147
Shepherd, Sir Fleetwood, 272
Sir John Barleycorn's Ballad, 9
Smith, Dr. S., 103
  ,, Sydney, 65, 276
Society of Arts' Journal, 215, 246
Spectator, The, 209
Spenser, 161
Stonehenge, 128
Suckling, 272
Swift, Dean, 10, 279
Swift's Letters, 68
Sydney Morning Herald, 170

Sylvester on Domestic Economy, 146
Symington's Pen and Pencil, 95
Szemere on Hungarian Wines, 178

Table Anecdotes, 209, 210.
Tatler, The, 9
Tavernier, 73
Temple on Health, 39
,, Sir W., 233
Tennyson, 217
Thackeray, W. M., 12, 119
The Island, 267
Therry, R., New South Wales, Pref. xi., 177
Thiers' Consulate, Pref. xii., 201
Thomson's New Zealand, 214, 227
,, Researches on Food, 179
Timb's Things Not Generally Known, 27, 53, 75, 104, 119, 140, 153, 201, 270, 273
Times, The London, 15, 196, 201, 205
Tite, W., 45
Topley's Sportsman in Canada, 273
Tully's Tripoli, 267
Tusser's Good and Bad Huswifery, 159
Two Foscari, 59

Ude, 44, 96, 124, 141, 215,
Uncle Tom's Cabin, 43, 72
Ure, 41, 63, 64, 72, 76, 78, 142, 143, 158, 184, 191, 192, 193, 200, 206, 210, 215, 243, 248. 271, 279, 282, 283
Uses of Animals, 266

Walch's Literary Intelligencer, 231
Walker, the Original, 100, 114, 124, 186, 259
Walsh's Constantinople, 1
Washington Evening Star, 81
Waterhouse, 34
Wellington, Duke of, 208
Wentworth's Australasia, Ded., p. iii.
,, New South Wales, 86
Wilberforce's Munich, 166
Winslow, Dr., 114

Yarrell, 92
Yass Courier, 232
Yeoman, The, 11
Youl, J. A., 225
Young's Epicure, 92

BORWICK'S BAKING POWDER

Is used by thousands of Families for raising Bread, with half the trouble and in a quarter the time required with Yeast, and for rendering Puddings and Pastry light and wholesome.

Dr. HASSALL remarks: "The ingredients of which it is composed are pure and good, and none of them are in the least degree injurious."

The Queen's Private Baker says, "It is a most useful invention."

Captain ALLEN YOUNG, of the Arctic Yacht "Fox," states, that "It keeps well, and answers admirably."

E. HAMILTON, Esq., M.D., F.S.A., observes, that "It is much better for raising Bread than Yeast, and much more wholesome."

Sold by all Chemists, Grocers, and Corn Chandlers in the United Kingdom, in 2s. 6d., 4s. 9d., and 9s. Bottles. Wholesale by G. BORWICK, London.

THE PATENT OZONIZED COD LIVER OIL

Conveys artificially to the lungs of the delicate and consumptive, OZONE, the vital principle in oxygen, without the effort of inhalation, and has the wonderful effect of reducing the pulse to its proper standard, while it strengthens and invigorates the system—restoring the consumptive to health, unless in the last stage. The highest medical authorities pronounce it the nearest approach to a specific for that most dreadful of all maladies yet discovered—in fact, it will restore to health when all other remedies fail. See *Lancet*, March 9, 1861.

Sold by all Chemists, in 2s. 6d., 4s. 9d., and 9s. Bottles. Wholesale by G. BORWICK, Sole Licensee, 21, Little Moorfields, London.

NO MORE PILLS OR ANY OTHER MEDICINE.

Perfect digestion, strong nerves, sound lungs, healthy liver, refreshing sleep, functional regularity, and energy, restored to the most disordered or enfeebled —removing speedily and effectually indigestion (dyspepsia), cough, asthma, consumption, habitual constipation, diarrhœa, all gastric derangements, hæmorrhoids, liver complaints, flatulency, nervousness, biliousness, fevers, sore throats, diphtheria, catarrhs, colds, influenza, noises in the head and ears, rheumatism, gout, impurities, eruptions, hysteria, neuralgia, irritability, sleeplessness, acidity, palpitation, heartburn, headache, debility, dropsy, cramps, spasms, nausea and sickness even in pregnancy or at sea, sinking fits, bronchitis, scrofula, tightness of the chest, pains at the pit of the stomach and between the shoulders, &c.—by

Du Barry's Delicious Health-Restoring Revalenta Arabica Food.

EXTRACT FROM 60,000 CURES.—Cure No. 58,216, of the Marchioness de Brehan, Paris, of a fearful liver complaint, wasting away, with a nervous palpitation all over, bad digestion, constant sleeplessness, low spirits, and the most intolerable nervous agitation, which prevented even her sitting down for hours together, and which for seven years had resisted the careful treatment of the best French and English medical men. Cure No. 1,771: Lord Stuart de Decies, Lord-Lieutenant of the County of Waterford, of many years' dyspepsia. Cure No, 49,842: "Fifty years' indescribable agony from dyspepsia, nervousness, asthma, cough, constipation, flatulency, spasms, sickness, and vomiting.— Maria Joly." Cure No. 47,121: Miss Elizabeth Jacobs, Nazing Vicarage, Waltham Cross, Herts, of extreme nervousness, indigestion, gatherings, low spirits, and nervous fancies. Cure No. 54,816: The Rev. James T. Campbell, Fakenham, Norfolk, of indigestion and torpidity of the liver, which had resisted all medical treatment. Cure No. 54,812: Miss Virginia Zeguers, of consumption. In Tins, 1lb., 2s. 9d.; 2lb., 4s. 6d.; 12lb., 22s.

Barry Du Barry and Co., 77, Regent Street, London; 26, Place Vendôme, Paris; 12, Rue de l'Empereur, Brussels; and 2, Via Oporto, Turin.

ADVERTISEMENTS.

THE BEST REMEDY FOR INDIGESTION.
NORTON'S CAMOMILE PILLS

Are confidently recommended as a simple but certain remedy for Indigestion, which is the cause of nearly all the diseases to which we are subject, being a medicine so uniformly grateful and beneficial, that it is with justice called the "Natural Strengthener of the Human Stomach." NORTON'S PILLS act as a powerful tonic and gentle aperient; are mild in their operation; safe under any circumstances; and thousands of persons can now bear testimony to the benefits to be derived from their use. Sold in Bottles at 1s. 1½d., 2s. 9d., and 11s. each, in every town in the kingdom.

CAUTION!—Be sure to ask for "NORTON'S PILLS," and do not be persuaded to purchase the various imitations.

A CLEAR COMPLEXION!!!
GODFREY'S EXTRACT OF ELDER FLOWERS

Is strongly recommended for Softening, Improving, Beautifying, and Preserving the SKIN, and giving it a blooming and charming appearance. It will completely remove Tan, Sunburn, Redness, &c., and, by its Balsamic and Healing qualities, render the skin soft, pliable, and free from dryness, &c., clear it from every humour, pimple, or eruption, and by continuing its use only a short time, the skin will become and continue soft and smooth, and the complexion perfectly clear and beautiful. Sold in bottles, price 2s. 9d., by all Medicine Vendors and Perfumers.

FOR GOUT, RHEUMATISM, AND RHEUMATIC GOUT.
SIMCO'S
GOUT AND RHEUMATIC PILLS

Are a certain and safe remedy. They restore tranquillity to the nerves, give tone to the stomach, and strength to the whole system. No other medicine can be compared to these excellent Pills, as they prevent the disorder from attacking the stomach or head, and have restored thousands from pain and misery to health and comfort.

Sold by all Medicine Venders, at 1s. 1½d., or 2s. 9d. per box.

INFLUENZA, COUGHS, AND COLDS.
SIMCO'S ESSENCE OF LINSEED

Is the most efficacious remedy ever discovered for the relief of persons suffering from Influenza; the first two doses generally arrest the progress of this distressing complaint, and a little perseverance completely removes it. Children's Coughs, as well as recent ones in Adults, will be removed by a few doses (frequently by the first); and Asthmatic persons, who previously had not been able to lie down in bed, have received the utmost benefit from the use of SIMCO'S ESSENCE OF LINSEED.

Sold by all Medicine Venders, in Bottles, at 1s. 1½d. and 2s. 9d. each.

BROWN & POLSON'S
PATENT CORN FLOUR,

GUARANTEED PERFECTLY PURE.

———o———

To obtain the full and delicate flavour of BROWN & POLSON'S Corn Flour, it should be boiled from seven to ten minutes.

Some of the following Recipes are upon each Package :—

BAKED PUDDING, CUSTARDS, BLANC-MANGE, ARROWROOT, FRUIT PIE, CAKES, TEA-CUP PUDDING, INFANT'S FOOD, CORN-FLOUR, CREAM THICK MILK.

BROWN & POLSON trust that the superior quality of their Corn Flour will still secure that preference which it has hitherto maintained, and also protect them from the substitution of other kinds which are sometimes urged upon families to obtain extra profit by the sale. Inferior qualities that are supplied at little more than half-price are made to counterfeit BROWN & POLSON's in appearance of package.

KEEN'S
GENUINE MUSTARD,

FIRST MANUFACTURED A.D. 1742,

OR MORE THAN

ONE HUNDRED AND TWENTY YEARS.

This well-known brand of Mustard has been sold by the trade of Great Britain for more than a Century, and is held in high estimation for

ITS PURITY AND PUNGENCY OF FLAVOUR.

The qualities that are recommended for family use are the Double Superfine and the Genuine, both of which can be

Obtained from most Family Grocers, in Canisters of One Pound and Half-Pound each.

KEEN, ROBINSON, BELLVILLE, & CO., LONDON.

IMPERIAL FIRE INSURANCE COMPANY
OF LONDON.
ESTABLISHED 1803.
SUBSCRIBED AND INVESTED CAPITAL, £1,600,000.

General Manager in Melbourne—A. J. WRIGHT.
Agent in Launceston—R. W. BUTLER.
Agents in Hobart Town—JUSTIN BROWNE & Co.
Solicitor, Hobart Town—S. W. WESTBROOK.

THIS Office undertakes the Insurance of Buildings and all other Property in all parts of Tasmania at the current reduced rates of premium, and offers to Insurers the following advantages :—

UNDOUBTED SECURITY guaranteed by a large Invested Capital and a wealthy English Proprietary, with the addition of an ample Reserve Fund to meet any unforeseen loss.

MODERATE PREMIUMS, carefully adapted to each particular risk.

PROMPT AND LIBERAL SETTLEMENT immediately upon proof of loss, no reference home being required.

JUSTIN BROWNE & Co.
27, New Wharf, Hobart Town, Jan. 1, 1863.

SHIP HOTEL, HOBART TOWN,
TASMANIA.

W. BUTLER begs to acquaint the inhabitants of Victoria, South Australia, and New South Wales, and the public generally, that this well-known and long-established house having been re-decorated and newly furnished throughout, offers the best accommodation to the public, and particularly to visitors from the adjoining Colonies.

To Gentlemen travelling for health or pleasure, the climate of Tasmania offers attractions unsurpassed by any colony in the Australian group.

Families can be accommodated with Private Sitting-rooms and separate Bed-rooms, combining the comfort and privacy of a home, with all the conveniences and attendance of a first-class Hotel.

The Ship Hotel occupies a central position; convenient proximity to the Post-office, Wharves, Exchange Rooms, Public Library, and Government Offices. Coaches and conveyances to all parts of the island daily.

BATHS AND BILLIARDS.

Ship Hotel, July 16, 1863.   WALTER BUTLER, Proprietor.

WILLIAM WIGGINS,
"DUTCHESS OF KENT,"
MURRAY STREET, HOBART TOWN.

☞ PRIVATE ENTRANCE.   FIRST-RATE ALES, ENGLISH & COLONIAL.

R. BALLANTYNE,
WINE AND SPIRIT MERCHANT,
98, COLLINS STREET, HOBART TOWN.

CHARLES PLATTS, BOOKSELLER AND STATIONER, ADELAIDE.

ADVERTISEMENTS.

ADVERTISEMENTS.

SAMPSON LOW, SON, & MARSTON,
ENGLISH, AMERICAN, & COLONIAL
BOOKSELLERS AND PUBLISHERS,
14, LUDGATE HILL, LONDON,

Execute Commissions in Books, Stationery, and all matters connected therewith, for shipment to any part of the world.

MAGAZINE PARCELS forwarded by the speediest routes, and indents for Books, Stationery, and General Merchandise attended to with promptitude and care.

WORKS PUBLISHED BY SAMPSON LOW, SON, AND MARSTON,
14, LUDGATE HILL.

The Colony of Victoria: its History, Commerce, and Gold Mining; its Social and Political Institutions, down to the end of 1863. By WILLIAM WESTGARTH. One vol., demy 8vo, pp. 520, cloth, 16s.

"The author has produced a book of first-rate excellence."—*Australian and New Zealand Gazette.*

A History of the Discovery and Exploration of Australia; or, an Account of the Progress of Geographical Discovery in that Continent, from the Earliest Period to the Present Day. By the Rev. JULIAN EDMUND WOODS, F.G.S., Author of "Geological Observations on South Australia." In two thick vols., demy 8vo, of about 900 pp. [*In the press—preparing for publication.*]

Tracks of McKinlay and Party across Australia. By JOHN DAVIS, one of the Expedition. Edited from the MS. Journal of Mr. Davis, with an Introductory View of the recent Explorations of Stuart, Burke, Wills, Landsborough, and others. By WILLIAM WESTGARTH. With numerous Illustrations in chromo-lithography, and Map. 8vo, cloth, 16s.

WORKS IN GENERAL LITERATURE SUITED FOR COLONIAL READING.

A Walk from London to John O'Groat's. With Notes by the Way, with Photographs. By ELIHU BURRITT. Post 8vo, cloth, price 12s. [*This day.*]

"Mr. Burritt has written a book which, though addressed principally to his own countrymen, will not fail of readers on this side of the Atlantic."—*Athenæum.*

"Admirably calculated for wiling away the tedium of a few dull hours."—*London Review.*

"Both pleasant to the eyes and good to read."—*Illustrated News.*

"Heartily welcome are any of Elihu Burritt's cheerful, pleasant words. 'The learned blacksmith' is as much at home in England as in the country of which he is a native."—*The Patriot.*

"We cannot reproduce any of these beautiful musings without curtailing them, and that would be to spoil them."—*Nonconformist.*

N.B.—*A new and cheap edition of this work will be ready for publication in September, price 6s.*

Her Majesty's Mails: an Historical and Descriptive Account of the British Post Office. By WILLIAM LEWINS, Esq. Post 8vo, cloth, price 7s. 6d. [*This day.*]

"As a history of the postal system, and a description of its present condition, Mr. Lewins's book leaves little to desire."—*The Athenæum*, May 7th.

"It should be put into the hands of every young Englishman and foreigner desiring to know how our institutions grow."—*The Reader*, May 14th.

"It would be difficult to mention another book of the same size where an equal amount of information and entertainment could be obtained."—*Illustrated News*, May 14.

"The author has exhausted his subject, and all who wish for an able and carefully written history of the Post-office should peruse 'Her Majesty's Mails.'"—*The Press.*

"The publication ought to contest the palm of popularity with Mr. Dickens or Mr. Trollope."—*The Home News.*

ADVERTISEMENTS. ix

BOOKS FOR PRESENTS AND PRIZES.

This day, New and Cheaper Edition, choicely printed in Elzevir, on toned paper, bevelled boards, 6s.

The Gentle Life: Essays in aid of the Formation of Character of Gentlemen and Gentlewomen.

"Full of truth and persuasiveness, the book is a valuable composition, and one to which the reader will often turn for companionship."—*Morning Post.*

"A compendium of cheerful philosophy."—*Daily News.*

"The writing is beautiful and truthful."—*London Review.*

"The volume will make many anxious to listen further to the teaching of this gentle 'Parson in a tie-wig.'"—*Nonconformist.*

"The delicate perception and scholarly treatment of his subjects constantly remind one of Leigh Hunt in his happiest moments . . . deserves to be printed in letters of gold, and circulated in every house."—*Chambers' Journal.*

"The most charming essays of modern times."—*The Photographic News.*

About in the World. By the Author of "The Gentle Life." Fcp. 8vo., uniform with previous work, price 6s.

"'Tis pleasant from the loopholes of retreat
To peep at such a world, and see the stir
Of the huge Babel, and not feel the crowd."—COWPER.

LONDON: SAMPSON LOW, SON, AND MARSTON.

"EXCELSIOR" FAMILY
SEWING & EMBROIDERING MACHINE,

Sews from the ordinary Reels, requires no re-winding, finishes its work where it stops, and the seam, if cut at every inch, will not rip.

The style of the Machine is Ornamental, and is so easily managed that a child can work it with facility. It will HEM, FELL, STITCH, GATHER, QUILT, BRAID, and EMBROIDER in a very superior manner, and with the most wonderful rapidity. It is eminently adapted for FAMILY SEWING; no Mantle Maker, Dress Maker, Tailor, or Trimming Manufacturer should be without it.

Price complete, from SIX GUINEAS.

Also first-class new and improved DOUBLE-ACTION ARM MACHINES, at greatly reduced prices, specially for manufacturing purposes.

WHIGHT AND MANN,
143, Holborn Hill, London.

MANUFACTORY:
GIPPING WORKS, IPSWICH.

CASSELL'S POPULAR HAND-BOOKS.
12mo, cloth, 1s. each.

Amusing and Instructive Experiments; containing an endless variety of Winter Evening Amusements for Youth. "Will be an acceptable present to an ingenious boy."—*Spectator.*

Book-keeping, by Single and Double Entry. Ruled Acount Books to ditto, extra, 1s. 6d. each set. "A very handy little work."—*Brighton Gazette.*

Business; a Dictionary of the Terms and Technicalities used in Commerce, and Tables of Foreign Moneys, Weights and Measures. "Exceedingly useful to every one desirous of knowing exactly what the various terms employed in business represent."—*News and Bankers' Journal.*

Chess and Draughts; containing a clear exposition of the Games, Laws of Chess, Technical Terms, Advice to Young Players, &c.; with an account of the different Openings and Endings of Games, &c. "A most useful little manual."—*Edinburgh News.*

Civil Service; being a complete Guide to the Examinations for the Appointments to the various Departments in the Civil Service.

How to Colour a Photograph in Oil or Water. It contains all the information necessary to acquire proficiency in the art of Colouring Photographs in Oil or Water, on Paper or Glass, together with a list of the pigments used, their method of preparation, &c. &c.

Investments; a Complete Account of the Public Securities, Railway Shares, Foreign Stocks, and other means of Investment, Explanatory and Statistical, with Information to the latest date.

Letter Writing; with Hints on Composition and Style, and Fac-similes of Handwriting, including models of the Style required in the Civil Service.

Natural Philosophy; being a Popular Guide to Physical and Experimental Philosophy, from the simplest Elements to the Phenomena of Electricity and Magnetism. With Eighty Wood Engravings.

Domestic Recipes; including Cookery, and a variety of valuable and interesting information.

Elocution and Oratory; being a systematic Compendium of the necessary Rules for attaining proficiency in Reading and Speaking.

Emergencies; containing Hints and Cautions to those engaged in Dangerous Occupations, and to Sufferers by the common Casualties of Life.

Etiquette; being a complete Guide to the Usages of Polite Society.

Gardening. By George Glenny. A Guide to the Cultivation of Fruits, Vegetables, and Flowers. Especially adapted for Amateurs.

Health and Physiology. Containing the Best Rules for the Preservation of Health, with a Popular Description of the various functions of the Human Body as affecting its General Health.

Our Domestic Pets; containing Descriptive Notices of favourite Birds and other Animals, the Mode of Preserving them in Health, &c.

Photography. Will be found invaluable; containing a complete system of instruction in the art of taking pictures by means of light, including descriptions of all the various processes in use, the best method of performing, the causes of failure, &c.

Railway Situations; including the complete System of Railway Accounts and Returns, to which are added valuable Hints on Commercial Employments generally.

LONDON: CASSELL, PETTER, AND GALPIN, LA BELLE SAUVAGE YARD, LUDGATE HILL, E.C.
AUSTRALIA: MESSRS. ROBERTSON & CO., MELBOURNE.
TASMANIA: MESSRS. WALSH & CO., HOBART TOWN & LAUNCESTON.

CASSELL'S ATLASES AND MAPS.

Cassell's Complete Folio Atlas, containing 260 coloured Maps, engraved in the first style of art, and presenting one of the fullest and most perfect delineations of the Surface of the Globe ever published. Price, in paper boards, 42s. Bound in half-roan, 50s.; in half-morocco, 63s.

Cassell's British Atlas, of 122 Maps. Half-bound, in paper boards, 21s. Strongly half-bound, 28s.

Cassell's Folio General Atlas, consisting of 60 Maps of the Countries of the World, with all their Geographical Boundaries, Rivers, Navigable Canals, Roads, Railways, &c., forming one of the most complete Atlases of Modern Geography extant. Price, in paper boards, 10s. 6d. Strongly half-bound, 18s.

Cassell's Folio County Atlas, containing 50 Maps of the Counties of England and Wales, with all Roads and Railways fully and accurately laid down. Price, in paper boards, 10s. 6d. Strongly half-bound, 18s.

Cassell's Railway Atlas, consisting of 20 Folio Maps (four being double) of the principal English Railway Routes. Price 5s.

Cassell's Oriental Atlas, of 36 Folio Maps. Price, in paper boards, 8s. Strongly half-bound, 15s.

Cassell's Colonial Atlas, of 30 Folio Maps. Price, in paper boards, 8s. Strongly half-bound, 15s.

Cassell's Indian Atlas, consisting of 15 Folio Divi-sional Maps of India. Price, in a Wrapper, 3s. 6d.

Cassell's Emigrant's Atlas, of 14 Folio Maps of Colonies and Places of especial Interest to the Emigrant. Price, in a Wrapper, 2s. 6d.

Cassell's Great Map of London, in Nine Double Sheets, and on a scale of nine inches to the mile. In a Wrapper. Price 5s. Mounted on Canvas, with rollers, coloured and varnished, 12s. Mounted on Canvas, and folded in a Cloth Case, 12s. Coloured and varnished, and mounted on Canvas, with patent spring rack, and mahogany head-box, gold lettered, 25s.

—— **The same, with Two Additional Maps of** Old London. Price 6s.

Cassell's Map of the Environs of London, in Eight Sheets; in a Wrapper. Price 2s. 6d. Mounted on Canvas, with rollers, and varnished, 7s. 6d. Mounted on Canvas, and folded in Cloth Case, 9s. Coloured and varnished, and mounted on Canvas, with patent spring rack, and mahogany head-box, gold lettered, 15s.

Cassell's Separate Maps. Various prices.

Cassell's County and Home Maps, folded in a neat Wrapper for the pocket, 4d. each. These Maps are wrought out with such laborious fulness and exactitude, that they present the most complete delineation of the British Isles ever published; so full and detailed, indeed, that scarcely a hamlet, and in many instances scarcely a farm, is omitted.

Foreign Maps, in sheets, 3d. each.

LONDON: CASSELL, PETTER, AND GALPIN, LA BELLE SAUVAGE YARD, LUDGATE HILL, E.C.
AUSTRALIA: MESSRS. G. ROBERTSON & CO., MELBOURNE.
TASMANIA: MESSRS. WALSH & CO., HOBART TOWN & LAUNCESTON.

ADVERTISEMENTS.

THE
WHEELER AND WILSON
SEWING MACHINE,

WITH EVERY RECENT IMPROVEMENT AND ADDITION, AS

CRYSTAL CLOTH PRESSER, BINDER, CORDER, HEMMER, TRIMMER, &c.,

Has obtained the first Prize at every Exhibition and Fair at which it has been exhibited, and performs with ease all descriptions of Household and Manufacturing Work, making with great speed the only firm work—

THE WHEELER & WILSON LOCK STITCH.

This stitch is the same on both sides of the fabric, is very permanent, will not ravel, or break up with the smoothing iron, as is the case with the Chain or Tambour Stitch; executes neat, strong work, with a speed equal to ten experienced seamstresses; and is so easy that a child of ten years of age can work it.

It is a pleasant and healthful exercise, and an ornament in the drawing-room.

Fells or Hems any width, turning own Hem as it its Stitches.

Gathers any kind of material with any quantity of fullness.

Gathers and sews on a band at the same time without basting.

Embroiders in beautiful designs, with Cord, Braid, or Silk.

Sews in Cord without basting.

Hems, enclosing a Cord at the same time, without basting.

Binds any material, without basting.

Marks any width of tucks and stitches them without basting.

Trims skirts with braid, velvet, or ribbon, without basting.

Quilts any material in any design with silk or cotton.

Illustrated and descriptive Pamphlet, with Testimonials, free by post on application. Instruction gratis to every purchaser.

OFFICE & SALE ROOMS, 139, REGENT STREET, LONDON.

HEALTH FRESH AIR PURE WATER
AND
CONDY'S PATENT DISENFECTING FLUID
BOTTLES 1s. 2s. & 4s. GALLON BOTTLES 5s. & 10s. SOLD EVERYWHERE.

www.ingramcontent.com/pod-product-compliance
Lightning Source LLC
Chambersburg PA
CBHW052052110526
44591CB00013B/2183